BRITISH LITERATURE IN TRANSITION, 1940–1960: POSTWAR

'Postwar' is both a period and a state of mind, a sensibility comprised of hope, fear and fatigue in which British society and its writers paradoxically yearned both for political transformation and a nostalgic reinstatement of past securities. From the Labour landslide victory of 1945 to the emergence of the Cold War and the humiliation of Suez in 1956, this was a period of radical political transformation in Britain and beyond, but these changes resisted literary assimilation. Arguing that writing and history do not map straightforwardly one onto the other, and that the postwar cannot easily be fitted into the explanatory paradigms of modernism or postmodernism, this book offers a more nuanced recognition of what was written and read in the period. From wartime radio writing to 1950s travellers, Cold War poetry to radical theatre, magazine cultures to popular fiction, this volume examines important debates that animated postwar Britain.

GILL PLAIN is Professor of English at the University of St Andrews. She has research interests in British literature and culture of the 1940s, war writing, crime fiction, British cinema, feminist theory and gender studies. Her publications include *Women's Fiction of the Second World War* (1996), *Twentieth-Century Crime Fiction* (2001), *John Mills and British Cinema: Masculinity, Identity and Nation* (2006) and *Literature of the 1940s: War, Postwar and 'Peace'* (2013). She has also edited a number of volumes including *A History of Feminist Literary Criticism* (co-edited with Susan Sellers, 2007) and *Scotland and the First World War: Myth, Memory and the Legacy of Bannockburn* (2017). She is General Editor of the *British Literature in Transition* series.

BRITISH LITERATURE IN TRANSITION SERIES

Editor

Gill Plain, *University of St Andrews*

British Literature in Transition maps a century of change. It also seeks to change the way we think about British literary history by reconsidering the canonical certainties and critical norms that shape our understanding of twentieth-century writing. Breaking down the century into twenty-year blocks, each substantial volume surveys, interrogates and challenges prevailing assumptions of critical memory to create a vibrant picture of literary culture in its time. Importantly, this revisionary series both recognises the contingency of the 'experimental' and argues that long-established canons do not do justice to the many and various forms that innovation took across the breadth of the twentieth century. As a result, Transition reinstates lost complexities and reanimates neglected debates, its authoritative new essays setting familiar figures alongside forgotten voices to generate a rich and provocative picture of a transformative century. Exploring transitions in writing, performance, publication and readership from the *fin-de-siècle* to the new millennium, the series offers new routes to an understanding of how British literature arrived in the twenty-first century and what made the nation's writing what it is today.

Books in the series

British Literature in Transition, 1900–1920: A New Age? edited by JAMES PURDON

British Literature in Transition, 1920–1940: Futility and Anarchy edited by CHARLES FERRALL AND DOUGAL MCNEILL

British Literature in Transition, 1940–1960: Postwar edited by GILL PLAIN

British Literature in Transition, 1960–1980: Flower Power edited by KATE MCLOUGHLIN

British Literature in Transition, 1980–2000: Accelerated Times edited by EILEEN POLLARD AND BERTHOLD SCHOENE

BRITISH LITERATURE IN TRANSITION, 1940–1960: POSTWAR

EDITED BY
GILL PLAIN
University of St Andrews

CAMBRIDGE
UNIVERSITY PRESS

CAMBRIDGE
UNIVERSITY PRESS

University Printing House, Cambridge CB2 8BS, United Kingdom

One Liberty Plaza, 20th Floor, New York, NY 10006, USA

477 Williamstown Road, Port Melbourne, VIC 3207, Australia

314–321, 3rd Floor, Plot 3, Splendor Forum, Jasola District Centre,
New Delhi – 110025, India

79 Anson Road, #06–04/06, Singapore 079906

Cambridge University Press is part of the University of Cambridge.

It furthers the University's mission by disseminating knowledge in the pursuit of education, learning, and research at the highest international levels of excellence.

www.cambridge.org
Information on this title: www.cambridge.org/9781107119017
DOI: 10.1017/9781316340530

© Cambridge University Press 2019

This publication is in copyright. Subject to statutory exception and to the provisions of relevant collective licensing agreements, no reproduction of any part may take place without the written permission of Cambridge University Press.

First published 2019

Printed and bound in Great Britain by Clays Ltd, Elcograph S.p.A.

A catalogue record for this publication is available from the British Library.

Library of Congress Cataloging-in-Publication Data
NAMES: Plain, Gill, editor.
TITLE: British literature in transition, 1940–1960 : postwar / edited by Gill Plain, University of St Andrews.
DESCRIPTION: Cambridge ; New York, NY : Cambridge University Press, 2018. | Includes bibliographical references and index.
IDENTIFIERS: LCCN 2018042046 | ISBN 9781107119017 (hardback)
SUBJECTS: LCSH: English literature – 20th century – History and criticism. | Literature and society – Great Britain – History – 20th century.
CLASSIFICATION: LCC PR478.S57 B775 2018 | DDC 820.9/0091–dc23
LC record available at https://lccn.loc.gov/2018042046

ISBN 978-1-107-11901-7 Hardback

Cambridge University Press has no responsibility for the persistence or accuracy of URLs for external or third-party internet websites referred to in this publication and does not guarantee that any content on such websites is, or will remain, accurate or appropriate.

Contents

List of Contributors	*page* viii
General Editor's Preface	xiii
Acknowledgements	xvi

	Introduction *Gill Plain*	1
PART I: AFTERMATH: THE BEGINNING OR THE END?		31
1	Slender Means: The Novel in the Age of Austerity *Marina MacKay*	37
2	Impossible Elegies: Poetry in Transition 1940–1960 *Nigel Alderman*	52
3	Democracy, Decentralisation and Diversity: The Renaissance of British Theatre *Rebecca D'Monté*	68
4	National Transitions: Wales, Scotland and Northern Ireland *Katie Gramich*	85
5	Heroes of Austerity: Genre in Transition *Gill Plain*	101
6	Wireless Writing, the Second World War and the West Indian Literary Imagination *James Procter*	117
PART II: THE POLITICS OF TRANSITION		137
7	Narrating Transitions to Peace: Fiction and Film after War *Mark Rawlinson*	143

Contents

8 Poetry, the Early Cold War and the Idea of Europe 161
   Adam Piette

9 *Horizon, Encounter* and Mid-Century Geopolitics 176
   Thomas S. Davis

10 Public Intellectuals and the Politics of Literature: The Causes and Collaborations of J. B. Priestley and Jacquetta Hawkes Priestley 192
   Ina Habermann

11 Prizing the Nation: Postwar Children's Fiction 209
   Lucy Pearson

12 Artists of Their Time: The Postwar Battle for Realism in Literature and Painting 225
   Alice Ferrebe

PART III: RECONFIGURATIONS 243

13 Demob: The Postwar Origins of the New Nature Writing 249
   Leo Mellor

14 Old Haunts: Childhood and Home in Postwar Fiction 267
   Victoria Stewart

15 New Uses of Literacy: The Blank Page and Writing in the Aftermath of War 282
   Tracy Hargreaves

16 The Pursuit of Love: Writing Postwar Desire 297
   Charlotte Charteris

17 Creating Vital Theatre: New Voices in a Time of Transition 313
   Claire Cochrane

PART IV: NO DIRECTIONS 331

18 Covert Legacies in Postwar British Fiction 337
   James Smith

19 'The Sights are Worse than the Journeys': Travel Writing at the Mid-Century 353
   Petra Rau

20	The Future and the End: Imagining Catastrophe in Mid-Century British Fiction *Allan Hepburn*	369
21	Exhausted Literature: The Postwar Novel in Repose *Kate McLoughlin*	385

Index 400

Contributors

NIGEL ALDERMAN is Associate Professor of English at Mount Holyoke College. He has published on British poetry from John Milton to the present. Most recently he has co-written with Michael Thurston, *Reading Postwar British and Irish Poetry* (2014).

CHARLOTTE CHARTERIS is a former Leverhulme Early Career Fellow in English and By-Fellow of Churchill College, Cambridge, specialising in literature of the *fin-de-siècle*, modernist and mid-twentieth-century periods, with a particular interest in queer studies and the aesthetics of transgression. She has published on a range of authors, including Edward Upward, Julian Maclaren-Ross, Patrick Hamilton and Graham Greene.

CLAIRE COCHRANE is Professor of Theatre Studies at Worcester University. She has published widely on twentieth- and twenty-first-century British theatre, with particular interests in regional building-based theatre and Black British and British Asian theatre and audiences. Her monograph *Twentieth Century British Theatre: Industry, Art and Empire* was published in 2011. Most recently she has co-edited with Jo Robinson a collection of essays in *Theatre History and Historiography: Ethics, Evidence and Truth* (2016).

THOMAS S. DAVIS is Associate Professor of English at The Ohio State University. He is the author of *The Extinct Scene: Late Modernism and Everyday Life* (2015). His work on twentieth- and twenty-first-century literature and culture has appeared in edited collections and journals such as *Textual Practice, Literature Compass, Twentieth Century Literature* and *English Language Notes*. He is currently working on a book about the aesthetics, politics and cultural life of climate change.

REBECCA D'MONTÉ is Senior Lecturer in Drama at the University of the West of England. She specialises in the work of women writers and twentieth-century British drama and is the author of *British Theatre and Performance 1900–1950* (2015). She is currently working on a book about British theatre in the Second World War.

ALICE FERREBE is Subject Leader for English at Liverpool John Moores University. Her publications include *Masculinity in Male-Authored Fiction, 1950–2000* (2005) and *Literature of the 1950s: Good, Brave Causes* (2012). She is currently working on the intersections between visual art and literature in 1950s British culture.

KATIE GRAMICH is Professor of English Literature at Cardiff University. Her research interests are in the literatures of Wales, women's writing, modern poetry and translation. She has published a history of twentieth-century Welsh women's writing and a monograph on Kate Roberts, and is currently working on a translation of the work of the fifteenth-century Welsh female poet, Gwerful Mechain.

INA HABERMANN is Professor of English at the University of Basel and Director of the Centre of Competence Cultural Topographies. Her fields of research include early modern literature and drama with a focus on Shakespeare, 1930s and 1940s literature and film, including middlebrow studies, cultural history and theory and spatial studies. She is the author of *Staging Slander and Gender in Early Modern England* (2003) and *Myth, Memory and the Middlebrow: Priestley, du Maurier and the Symbolic Form of Englishness* (2010).

TRACY HARGREAVES is Senior Lecturer in Modern and Contemporary Literature in the School of English, University of Leeds. Her most recent publications include a co-edited edition of literature of the 1950s and 1960s with Alice Ferrebe and essays on Doris Lessing and film censorship in the 1960s. She is currently working on a critical study of 'Intimacy and the English Imagination: 1945–1968'.

ALLAN HEPBURN is James McGill Professor of Twentieth-Century Literature at McGill University. In addition to writing *Intrigue: Espionage and Culture* (2005) and *Enchanted Objects: Visual Art in Contemporary Literature* (2010), he has edited four volumes dedicated to the short stories, essays, broadcasts and book reviews of Elizabeth Bowen. He also edited *Troubled Legacies: Narrative and Inheritance* (2007) and *Around 1945: Literature, Citizenship, Human Rights* (2016). His next book is a monograph about religious faith in British culture at mid-century.

MARINA MACKAY is Associate Professor of English and Tutorial Fellow of St Peter's College, University of Oxford. Her books include *Modernism and World War II* (2007) and *The Cambridge Companion to the Literature of World War II* (2009), and her articles on mid-century fiction have appeared in journals such as *PMLA*, *Representations*, *ELH* and *Modern Fiction Studies*.

KATE MCLOUGHLIN is Professor of English Literature at the University of Oxford and Fellow and Tutor in English at Harris Manchester College. She is the author of *Authoring War: Literary Representation of War from the Iliad to Iraq* (2011) and *Veteran Poetics: British Literature in the Age of Mass Warfare, 1790–2015* (2018), and is the editor of *British Literature in Transition 1960–1980: Flower Power*, the fourth volume in this series.

LEO MELLOR is the Roma Gill Fellow in English at Murray Edwards College, University of Cambridge. His first book was *Reading the Ruins: Bombsites, Modernism and British Culture* (2011), and he has subsequently written about war journalism, Welsh literature in English and contemporary poetry. With Glyn Salton-Cox, he co-edited a special issue of *Critical Quarterly* on 'The long 1930s' (2015).

LUCY PEARSON is Lecturer in Children's Literature at Newcastle University. She is the author of *The Making of Modern Children's Literature: British Children's Publishing in the 1960s and 1970s* (2013) and editor of *Jacqueline Wilson: A New Casebook* (2015). She is currently working on a major new history of the Carnegie Medal and its role in shaping British children's literature.

ADAM PIETTE is a Professor of Modern Literature at the University of Sheffield, and currently Head of the School of English. He is the author of *Remembering and the Sound of Words: Mallarmé, Proust, Joyce, Beckett* (1996), *Imagination at War: British Fiction and Poetry, 1939–1945* (1995) and *The Literary Cold War, 1945 to Vietnam* (2009). He co-edited with Mark Rawlinson *The Edinburgh Companion to Twentieth-Century British and American War Literature* (2012) and is co-editor with Alex Houen of the poetry journal *Blackbox Manifold*.

GILL PLAIN is Professor of English Literature and Popular Culture at the University of St Andrews. She is the author of *Women's Fiction of the Second World War* (1996), *Twentieth-Century Crime Fiction* (2001), *John Mills and British Cinema: Masculinity, Identity and Nation* (2006) and *Literature of the 1940s: War, Postwar and 'Peace'* (2013). Her edited work includes *A History of Feminist Literary Criticism* (with Susan Sellers, 2007) and *Scotland and the First World War* (2016).

JAMES PROCTER is Professor of Modern and Contemporary Literature at Newcastle University. He is the author of *Dwelling Places* (2003), *Stuart Hall* (2004) and (with Bethan Benwell) *Reading across Worlds* (2014), and the editor of *Writing Black Britain* (2000) and (with Jackie Kay and Gemma Robinson) *Out of Bounds* (2012). He is currently completing a monograph as part of the Leverhulme-funded *Scripting Empire* project on West Indian and West African radio writing at the BBC between the 1930s and 1960s.

PETRA RAU is Senior Lecturer in Modern Literature at the University of East Anglia. She is the author of *Our Nazis: Representations of Fascism in Contemporary Literature and Film* (2013) and the editor of *Long Shadows: The Second World War in Contemporary British Fiction and Film* (2016). She is currently working on a book on postwar expulsion and on a family memoir.

MARK RAWLINSON is Reader in English Literature at the University of Leicester. He wrote *British Writing of the Second World War* (2000) and, with Adam Piette, edited *The Edinburgh Companion to Twentieth-Century British and American War Literature* (2012).

JAMES SMITH is Reader in English and Director of the Centre for Modern Conflicts and Cultures at Durham University. He is the author of *Terry Eagleton* (2008) and *British Writers and MI5 Surveillance, 1930–1960* (2013). He is currently editing *The Cambridge Companion to British Literature of the 1930s*.

VICTORIA STEWART is Reader in Modern and Contemporary Literature at the University of Leicester. She is the author of *Women's Autobiography: War and Trauma* (2003), *Narratives of Memory: British Writing of the 1940s* (2006), *The Second World War in Contemporary British Fiction: Secret Histories* (2011) and *Crime Writing in Interwar Britain: Fact and Fiction in the Golden Age* (2017).

General Editor's Preface

British Literature in Transition maps a century of change. It is a project of revision and reappraisal that aims, through innovative juxtaposition and ambitious realignments, to reconsider the habitual practices and critical norms that shape our understanding of twentieth-century writing.

Each volume is distinctively the work of its editors and contributors: there has been no attempt to impose theoretical or methodological conformity. Rather, the aim has been to create a space of possibility for the reimagining and reconfiguring of twentieth-century literature. The century has been broken down into twenty-year blocks, with a view to disrupting habits of periodisation (most obviously, the decade). Twenty-year blocks are no less arbitrary or problematic, but, by moving to this model, British Literature in Transition is able to ask new questions of the boundaries, books and narratives, the critical perspectives and the canons, through which the century has come to be known. Crucially, the volumes seek to build a picture of literature *in its time*. This historical focus gives new impetus to old questions, while also requiring us to interrogate the selective picture of the century that survives in publishers' catalogues and the reading lists of academia. The multiple volumes of the British Literature in Transition series ask, then, questions as diverse as: What is the modern and whose writing exemplifies it? Does the First World War represent a break in the development of literary practice? Why, habitually, have we come to see the literature of the 1920s and the 1930s as radically different? Why has the writing of the first age of austerity seemingly disappeared without a trace? What were the effects on literature of decolonisation and mass immigration? What did the Cold War do to British literary culture, and how did one woman – Margaret Thatcher – come to have such a profound influence on the writing of a generation?

As these questions suggest, this series pays close attention to the dynamic relationship between literature and history, asking questions not just about the canon that has survived, but also about the writing that has been unjustly forgotten or excluded. The series examines both the prestigious and the popular and aims to understand literature's role in mediating the developments of the past hundred years. British Literature in Transition argues for the importance of both politics and aesthetics and it seeks to understand the constraints and generative possibilities of challenging cultural contexts. An acknowledgement that the outside world shapes literary creativity, or that literature engages in a process of 'world-making', is hardly new, but the seeming onset of an age of historical amnesia suggests it is acquiring fresh significance. What, we might ask, in the aftermath of the 2016 'Brexit' vote, will *British* literature come to mean in the next decades of the twenty-first century? The evidence of the vote suggests that a significant proportion of the nation had forgotten why a European Union was once so urgently needed and desired. It also suggests the instability of narratives of progress, tolerance and integration, exposing the fears of a world that – at the end of the twentieth century – seemed to be becoming inescapably global. At the time of writing, the political and economic consequences of the Brexit decision remain mired in uncertainty, but statistics already reveal its profound social impact. The rhetorical register of the campaign, suffused with a misplaced nostalgia for the 1940s, has given new legitimacy to the violent expression of prejudice. Reasserting a firmly bounded concept of the island nation has equally reinstated discredited discourses of xenophobia, racism and homophobia.

The 'contemporary' thus tells us that transition itself is unstable, unpredictable and even – disturbingly – cyclical. Its manifestations across the twentieth century are far from uniform, and there is no necessary correlation between historical event and literary transition. The years 1940 to 1960, for example, a time of almost unimaginable geopolitical change and social upheaval, emerge as a period of relative stasis – full of radical innovations, but uncertain in direction and beset by more or less readily acknowledged nostalgia. It is hard here to detect a paradigm shift in *literary* form. Quite the opposite might be argued of 1920 to 1940, where 1922 stands out as a defining year in the literary understanding of the modern. But is 1922 an end or a beginning? Should the game-changing literary outputs of that year – *The Waste Land, Ulysses, Jacob's Room* – be taken as the zenith of a modernity evolving since the nineteenth century, or do they represent a year zero, the moment that literature took a decisive turn – a transition – that criticism would herald, and thus enshrine, as an aesthetic watershed? The answer, of course, is both, and more. Consequently, as each volume in the series approaches its subjects, it does so with multiple concepts of transition in mind. Transition might mean movement – some notion of progress, transit or return – or it might mean flux, indeterminacy and the liminal. Transition is equally a change of state, a recognition of the unsettled and the refusal to occupy a fixed or determined place. In literary terms, this means that the innovative and the experimental might take radically different forms – and, to expose this, the Transitions series changes both the *dramatis personae* of literary history and the company they keep. The usual suspects of the twentieth-century canon are here, but they appear in different contexts and in dialogue with unexpected others. These realignments are not the product of editorial whim, but rather an attempt to reconstruct a historical context that recognises the worlds in which these writers wrote, and in which their work was received. The five volumes of the Transitions series thus seek to reinstate the often complex and disingenuous relationship between literature and its contexts. Previous critical work is scrutinised and debated, and fossilised canons are cracked apart and enlarged, to provide readers at all levels, from undergraduate to research professional, with a richer picture of the possibilities of a transformative century.

I began by suggesting that British Literature in Transition was a mapping project, but no map is ever definitive. Cartographers revise their work in the light of emergent knowledge, fresh technologies and new ways of seeing; they fill in blank spaces and reveal occluded paths. To function effectively, critical maps must also periodically be redrawn, and this is one such re-plotting that forges new routes through territory we have, perhaps erroneously, long thought familiar.

University of St Andrews GILL PLAIN

Acknowledgements

Like most transitions, this one didn't happen overnight, and over the years of its gestation and development, many debts have accrued. First and foremost, I owe immense thanks to the *Postwar* contributors. Their enthusiasm for the project was inspiring and their thoughtful, innovative and provocative essays have been a pleasure, and an education, to edit. I'm also enormously grateful to Ray Ryan at Cambridge University Press for his help both with *Postwar* and the whole *British Literature in Transition* series: undertaking a project of revision and reappraisal on this scale simply would not have happened without his support – or the invaluable insights of the many anonymous readers who have helped shape the *Transitions* volumes. Bringing the series together would also not have been possible without the wholehearted commitment of the other volume editors: James Purdon, Dougal McNeill, Charles Ferrall, Kate McLoughlin, Berthold Schoene and Eileen Pollard. Their imaginative responses to the 'transitions' brief have been a delight to encounter, and I'm grateful to them all for their professionalism and good humour in the face of the hitches, glitches and catastrophes that inevitably beset large-scale, multi-author projects.

For the making of *Postwar*, and the maintenance of editorial sanity in the process, particular thanks are due to the many people who have provided feedback, insight, advice and moral support over the past few years. I am fortunate to work in a kind and collegial environment and the School of English at St Andrews has enabled me to keep chipping away at this book through difficult times, assisted by research funds and the invisible support that comes from a team of exemplary administrators. Friends, colleagues and collaborators – at St Andrews and elsewhere – have also helped to bring this book to completion. Sam Haddow, Leo Mellor, Susan Sellers and Emma Sutton generously read, responded and advised; Lisa Griffin produced the epic index; Andy Murphy and Lorna Hutson made welcome reassuring noises while comparing notes on editing; Rhiannon Purdie, Gordon McMullan and Ben Winsworth offered wine. I'm particularly grateful to Marina MacKay,

Kate McLoughlin and Petra Rau for the knowledge they have so generously shared, the practical support they've given and the number of times they've made me laugh. Thank you for sending emails I actually enjoy opening.

James McKinna has, as ever, had to put up with a great deal of book-related anti-social behaviour, not least of which was *Postwar*'s habit of coming on holiday with us. In the circumstances, the least I can do is dedicate the book to him, with love and thanks.

University of St Andrews　　　　　　　　　　　　　　　　　　GILL PLAIN

Introduction

Gill Plain

> Sophia Garfield had a clear mental picture of what the outbreak of war was going to be like. There would be a loud bang, succeeded by inky darkness and a cold wind. Stumbling over heaps of rubble and dead bodies, Sophia would search with industry, but without hope, for her husband, her lover, and her dog. It was in her mind like the End of the World, or the Last Days of Pompeii, and for more than two years now she had been steeling herself to bear with fortitude the hardships, both mental and physical, which must accompany this cataclysm.[1]

Transition – in life and literature – is seldom as clear cut as Sophia Garfield's imagination might suggest, even in the case of something as politically, culturally and ethically cataclysmic as the Second World War. Sophia, the hapless heroine of Nancy Mitford's 1940 comic novel *Pigeon Pie*, manifests here the apocalyptic traces of the interwar literary imagination, her attempt to articulate her fears conditioned not by the shape of things to come, but by impressionistic reports of the Spanish Civil War. *Pigeon Pie* was composed during the so-called 'phoney war', and by the time the book was published, Mitford felt the need to preface it with an apology. It was, she said, 'an early and unimportant casualty of the real war which was then beginning'.[2] But Sophia's vision, while absurd in its hyperbolic self-dramatisation, is also disturbingly accurate: there would be rubble, there would be bodies and, in the desecration of the camps, there would be something very like the 'End of the World'. Mitford's mistimed comedy thus tells us that writing and history do not map tidily one on to the other, the one offering a record of the other's stately progression: rather literature erupts into history – and vice versa – subverting, applauding, anticipating, avoiding, resisting, recording and sometimes misreading the often overwhelming stimuli of a rapidly changing world. Transition gets

---

[1] Nancy Mitford, *Pigeon Pie* (Harmondsworth: Penguin, 1961 [1940]), p. 7. [2] Ibid., n. p.

ahead of itself, and it lags behind – and it struggles to be noticed in a period persistently mediated through the shadow of 1945.

With the annihilating qualities of 1945 in mind, this volume of the *Transitions* series prioritises the aftermath rather than the act of war. It looks at cultural, critical and imaginative transformations that are part of a continuity of literary development, as well as those brought about by the rupture of war. That it is able, at least in part, to avert its gaze from the mesmeric power of Britain's 'finest hour' is the result of a revival of critical interest in the literature of 1939 to 1945. Since the turn of the millennium, there has been an explosion of new writing on the Second World War: Mark Rawlinson's *British Writing of the Second World War* (2000), Marina MacKay's *Modernism and World War II* (2007) and her *Cambridge Companion to the Literature of World War II* (2009), Lyndsey Stonebridge's *The Writing of Anxiety* (2007), Patrick Deer's *Culture in Camouflage* (2009), Sara Wasson's *Urban Gothic of the Second World War* (2010) and Leo Mellor's *Reading the Ruins* (2011), to name but a few.[3] The recognition that the conflict had a literature of its own is long overdue, but while this 'curious gap in the knowledge of many readers'[4] is now being plugged, the same cannot be said for what came after. Indeed, between the technical end of hostilities and the emergence of the angry young man, the student of British literature might be forgiven for thinking – in Cyril Connolly's redolent terms – that it was 'closing time in the gardens of the West'.[5] So who wrote in the postwar? And what did they write? Did British culture react through nostalgic re-entrenchment, or did it find expression in subversive spaces and unexpected forms? Was it exhausted or reinvigorated, at an end or a beginning, or – as Sophia's vision suggests – both? This introduction, and the twenty-one chapters that follow, explores these questions, mapping some of the literary reconfigurations that took poetry from T. S. Eliot to Thom Gunn, the theatre from Noel Coward to Shelagh Delaney, and the novel from the bedsits of Patrick Hamilton to the

---

[3] There has also been a growing interest in the resonances and rewritings of the war across the full breadth of the twentieth century. See Victoria Stewart, *The Second World War in Contemporary British Fiction: Secret Histories* (Edinburgh University Press, 2011); Danielle Hipkins and Gill Plain (eds), *War-Torn Tales: Literature, Film and Gender in the Aftermath of World War II* (Oxford: Peter Lang, 2007); Petra Rau, *Long Shadows: The Second World War in British Fiction and Film* (Northwestern University Press, 2016).

[4] Patrick Deer, *Culture in Camouflage: War, Empire, and Modern British Literature* (Oxford University Press, 2009), p. ix.

[5] *Horizon*, vol. XX, nos 120–1, December 1949–January 1950, p. 362. The phrase was adopted by Malcolm Bradbury to argue that the postwar arts in Britain were characterised by 'minimalism and muteness'. Malcolm Bradbury, '"Closing Time in the Gardens" or, What Happened to Writing in the 1940s' in *No, Not Bloomsbury* (London: Andre Deutsch, 1987), p. 71.

bunkers of Ian Fleming. Yet the volume also, crucially, resists the stability of 'transition' and its metaphors, exploring writers – such as Elizabeth Bowen, Agatha Christie, Graham Greene and Stephen Spender – who persisted and, more or less, mutated, in the face of unprecedented cultural change.

'Postwar' as concept and *Postwar* as title are consequently designed to draw attention to the missing link between two mythical moments of British historical becoming. The selective habits of cultural memory have ensured that 1940 to 1960 is a period more powerfully marked in its opening (the shock of war) and its closure (the shock of Suez), than in its substantial middle. Yet these middle years are of fundamental importance to understanding both what went before and what came after: in these lost years we find the impact of total war and the challenges of reconstructing cultural life in a world on the brink of a new – and frequently terrifying – modernity. As with the other volumes in this series, *Postwar* displaces the conceptual category of the decade in favour of a twenty-year period. A twenty-year block is, of course, no less arbitrary than a ten-year one, and this categorisation should not be seen as anything other than a provisional necessity – a spatio-temporal holding cell – which enables us usefully to interrogate the movements, displacements, transformations and transitions of mid-century Britain. Not surprisingly, as the chapters of this volume reveal, interrogation also exposes the contradictions, reversals, denials and recantations of a period in which, for many, 'transition' must have seemed a double-edged sword. Yet in the particular case of the postwar, changing the shape of the holding cell has considerable critical value. It uncouples the glib distinction between war and after, insisting that wars neither begin nor end with formal declarations, and it enables close attention to the forgotten middle years, 1945 to 1955, a 'decade' that in literary terms has been both misread and overlooked. In so doing, the volume is part of, and a showcase for, new literary critical work that examines continuity as well as change, and which seeks to trouble conventional categories and canons of mid-century British culture.[6] Crucially, though, 'postwar' constitutes not only a temporal space, but also a cultural sensibility, reaching back into the war and forward into the second half of

---

[6] The bulwark between the 1930s and the 1940s, while seemingly held in this volume, is equally insecure, as the lines of influence and affiliation that survived the war reveal. See volume 2 in the *Transitions* series, Charles Ferrall and Dougal McNeill (eds), *British Literature in Transition 1920–1940: Futility and Anarchy?* (Cambridge University Press, 2018), and the concept of the 'long 1930s' posited by Leo Mellor and Glynn Salton Cox, 'The Long 1930s' *Critical Quarterly* (2015) 57(3) pp. 1–9.

the twentieth century; it is a political condition and a state of mind, a mode of being that oscillates between a violent impetus for change, and a desperate longing for the security of the known and familiar. In the section that follows, I explore this sensibility and the contexts from which it emerged.

Interrogating the Postwar Sensibility: Hope, Fear and Fatigue

I suggested above that 1940 to 1960 might be thought of as a 'holding cell', a potentially disturbing image of confinement and interrogation designed to suggest transience, instability and uncertain outcomes. These are all terms singularly applicable to the situation in which the country and its writers found themselves in September 1939. The outbreak of war, shocking yet long anticipated, rendered previously articulate commentators, such as Stephen Spender, temporarily speechless (a state of affairs announced in his eloquent 'September Journal'). Others by contrast were keen to document new experiences and participate in the emergent propaganda war. This war of words would be integral to the conflict and its aftermath, and it is hard to overestimate the impact of mass mobilisation on the national psyche. To win the war for democracy, the British Government assumed unprecedented control over its citizens' lives, subjecting them to rationing, conscription, evacuation and a 'white noise' of rhetoric that – while undoubtedly effective – had a crushing impact on what Adam Piette terms the 'private imagination'.[7]

There was, then, much to write about and very little opportunity to write it, and the conditions of the conflict had an inevitable impact on the possibilities of publication and performance. London theatres, for example, were initially closed for the duration, but when the expected cataclysm proved slow to arrive, activities resumed – and continued throughout the blackout and the bombs. Yet, as Rebecca D'Monté's chapter demonstrates, this was just the beginning of a radical transition in the infrastructure and practice of theatre across the nation. The novel faced different problems, not least, as the conflict progressed, a shortage of paper, but Elizabeth Bowen was not the only writer to find the conditions of total war inimical

---

[7] Adam Piette, *Imagination at War: British Fiction and Poetry, 1939–1945* (London: Papermac, 1995), p. 2. For participation, see Phyllis Lassner, *British Women Writers of World War II: Battlegrounds of Their Own* (Basingstoke: Macmillan, 1997) and Jenny Hartley, *Millions Like Us: British Women's Fiction of the Second World War* (London: Virago, 1997). For speechlessness, see Gill Plain, *Women's Fiction of the Second World War: Gender, Power and Resistance* (Edinburgh University Press, 1996) and *Literature of the 1940s: War, Postwar and 'Peace'* (Edinburgh University Press, 2013), pp. 39–44.

to the writing of long fiction.[8] In its place, however, other forms flourished, with the chief literary beneficiary being the short story, which alongside diaries, reportage and documentary observations of wartime life found itself well suited to composition under fragmentary and disruptive conditions.[9] The short story was also well suited to radio, and broadcast media became a vital conduit for the consumption and production of literature in the war years, as is evident from James Procter's study of West Indian writing at the BBC in Chapter 6.[10] The benefits of bite-sized literary forms were felt by readers as well as writers, and a feature of the conflict was the proliferation and success of literary magazines such as *Horizon*, *Penguin New Writing*, *The Welsh Review* and *Poetry London*. These magazines published new writing, but they also provided a forum for critical self-reflection. Indeed, as Thomas Davis demonstrates in Chapter 9, *Horizon* under its charismatic editor, Cyril Connolly, argued itself almost to exhaustion debating what, exactly, should be the role of the writer in wartime.

The holding cell image also reminds us that in historical as well as literary terms, the boundaries dividing war from postwar are porous; the concept is not tethered to treaties and the term acquires its cultural validity long before the cessation of hostilities. Indeed, almost from the outbreak of war, British culture was imagining and writing towards a future postwar world – most famously in *Picture Post*'s January 1941 'Plan for Britain' issue. This early emergence of the postwar would become particularly marked after 1942's decisive victories in North Africa: the point at which – for those on the home front – the war became less of a threat and more of a regime to be endured. Without imminent danger to make sense of sacrifice, the war increasingly became a site of crippling lethargy and imaginative exhaustion, a state of mind evoked at the time in the documentary fiction of Inez Holden, and effectively reconstructed by Patrick Hamilton in the magnificent *Slaves of Solitude* (1947).[11] People no longer wanted to read about the war, nor to watch it on screen, and cinemas filled instead with audiences

---

[8] For the concrete impact of war on book production and consumption, see Angus Calder, *The People's War* (London: Pimlico, 1992 [1969]), pp. 511–13.
[9] Stories themselves differed radically in style: from the uncanny snapshots of Elizabeth Bowen, to the overtly symbolic modernism of William Sansom, the surrealism of Anna Kavan and the pared-back, deceptive simplicity of Elizabeth Berridge.
[10] For a full exploration of the diverse roles played by radio in generating and disseminating a literature of war, see Ian Whittington, *Writing the Radio War: Literature, Politics and the BBC, 1939–1945*, (Edinburgh University Press, 2018).
[11] Documentary writing was a significant aesthetic feature of the war, and Holden's 'docudramas', including *Night Shift* (1941) and *There's No Story There* (1944), provide particularly good examples of the form. For the world evoked by Hamilton, see Marina MacKay's chapter in this volume.

desperate to escape a deeply dreary contemporaneity through the good offices of James Mason's man in grey and Margaret Lockwood's wicked lady.[12]

Yet the emergent features of a postwar sensibility were not confined to a desire for imaginative liberation. In a war in which the boundaries between home front and frontline, civilian and combatant had become increasingly indistinct, both men and women lived in a state of suspended reaction, and the postwar would be marked by the gradual emergence of grief and post-traumatic symptoms. Returning soldiers and POWs were confronted by a world changed out of all recognition, while women, variously liberated or coerced into radical new subjectivities, were confronted by men they scarcely recognised, and who were all too frequently traumatised by experiences they could neither express nor understand.[13] Indeed, it was largely through fiction – from Henry Green's *Back* (1945) to Nigel Balchin's *A Sort of Traitors* (1949) to Elizabeth Taylor's *A Wreath of Roses* (1949) – that the psychological impact of war found expression in the postwar period. Publicly, men were told to 'move on', while women were urged to go back, resuming conventionally gendered domestic roles in an attempt to reconstruct an illusory pre-war ideal. And integral to public pronouncements on postwar reconstruction was the resumption of heteronormativity: the family was to be reconstituted, relocated and encouraged to reproduce.[14] The tensions, anxieties and pressures consequent upon such reassembly make themselves felt throughout the period and throughout this volume. They are present in Marina MacKay's survey of the novel, in Nigel Alderman's analysis of transitions in poetic language, in Charlotte Charteris's chapter on postwar desire, and in my own examination of the re-gendering of postwar genre fiction. Repression, understood as a keynote of 'Britishness', cannot be underestimated as a force determining the limits of articulation in this period and its literature.

The term 'postwar' also, deliberately, speaks to a signifying absence: peace. Global conflict persisted in spite, or because, of the treaties of 1945, while for a Britain struggling to reconstitute itself in the aftermath of an

---

[12] Both actors starred in *The Man in Grey* (1943) and *The Wicked Lady* (1945). The box office success of these early Gainsborough Studio melodramas was matched only by the degree of middle-class critical opprobrium they attracted. See Sue Harper, *Picturing the Past: The Rise and Fall of the British Costume Film* (London: BFI, 1994).

[13] For an insightful account of demobilisation and its repercussions, see Alan Allport, *Demobbed: Coming Home after the Second World War* (New Haven, CT: Yale University Press, 2009).

[14] On the challenges of finding a home, see Michael Sissons and Philip French (eds), *Age of Austerity* (Oxford University Press, 1963); on pro-natalism and the restoration of 'home', see David Kynaston, *Austerity Britain, 1945–51* (London: Bloomsbury, 2007), pp. 98–104.

economically devastating conflict, American cultural hegemony caused almost as much disquiet as the threat of Communism. However, for many it was technology that most profoundly symbolised the end of security. What peace was possible after the invention of a weapon that could annihilate a city and carry on killing with invisible power? John Hershey's *Hiroshima*, first published in Britain by Penguin in 1946, and broadcast by the BBC, brought home to many the immense implications of the atomic age, and ensured that when Mass Observation surveyed public attitudes regarding 'peace' in 1947, respondents voiced feelings of ambivalence and despair. The fears generated by American cultural and technological hegemony are addressed in Ina Habermann's chapter on J. B. Priestley and Jaquetta Hawkes Priestley, whose postwar work, both individual and collaborative, sought tirelessly to resist the culture of 'admass' and the prospect of nuclear annihilation. Both became active supporters of the Campaign for Nuclear Disarmament, founded in 1958. More mediated fears of technology are also integral to Allan Hepburn's analysis of catastrophe fiction – a significant genre of the 1950s that addressed, in a range of pessimistic, dystopian contexts, fears of unchecked scientific ambition and its consequences.

Yet postwar exhaustion co-existed with a powerful will-to-change: a desire to build a better Britain. The Labour landslide victory of 1945 emerged from a widespread desire *not* to return to pre-war poverty and unemployment, and this vote symbolises the contrary, and hard-won, strand of regenerative hope that runs through the period. The general election was a political turning point, as – in terms of the resurgence of cultural debate – was the British Council's decision to sponsor a controversial exhibition of wartime work by Matisse and Picasso at the V&A. In 1946, the wartime Council for the Encouragement of Music and the Arts (CEMA) emerged in the new plumage of the Arts Council, and 1947 saw the foundation of the Edinburgh International and Fringe Festivals. There was even, in 1948, an Olympic games. Optimism's zenith was reached, however, with the belated arrival of the 1951 Festival of Britain, a much-postponed outburst of social, artistic and scientific self-celebration imagined as a 'tonic to the nation'. The festival aimed both to entertain and to 'set the broad parameters of a social democratic agenda for modern Britain',[15] it also – by accident rather than design – ushered in

---

[15] Becky Conekin, '"Here is the Modern World Itself": The Festival of Britain's Representations of the Future' in Becky E. Conekin Frank Mort and Chris Waters (eds), *Moments of Modernity: Reconstructing Britain 1945–1964* (London: Rivers Oram Press, 1999), p. 228. Conekin argues that the festival 'betrayed surprisingly little nostalgia', but was rather a vision of technologically mediated

a series of 'national' achievements that similarly seemed to symbolise the birth of a newly modern nation. A symbol of Britain's technical prowess, the de Havilland Comet became the first commercial jetliner, entering service with the British Overseas Airways Corporation (BOAC) in May 1952, while 'national' character was showcased in the Conquest of Everest in May 1953. The achievement of the New Zealander Edmund Hillary and the Nepalese Sherpa Tenzing Norgay, as part of a massive 400-strong British expedition, seemed to close the book on narratives of courage in adversity and heroic failure, and the coronation of Queen Elizabeth II in June 1953 was perceived as the beginning of a 'New Elizabethan' era.[16]

However, before Britain could celebrate anything it had to rebuild, and in 1945 the task ahead of the newly elected government was monumental. Tony Judt puts the challenge into perspective: 'Britain was insolvent ... The cost of World War Two to Britain was twice that of World War One; the country lost one quarter of its national wealth.'[17] Judt goes on to observe that perhaps this would not have mattered quite so much had Britain not also been responsible for a global empire. As it was, the only solution was austerity, a programme of ongoing rationing and restrictions in which pretty much everything was unavailable. And it was this quotidian deprivation, an all-pervasive grey chill, which more than anything made its mark on the culture of the immediate postwar years, as Marina MacKay demonstrates in her analysis of the austerity novel. How writers responded to the constraints of victory was, she suggests, largely a matter of political alignments: J. B. Priestley saw the potential for a new beginning, Barbara Pym made light comedy out of cultural disorientation and Angela Thirkell gave voice to a deeply conservative middle-class nostalgia for a semi-mythical pre-war in which boundaries were respected and places known. Britain was building anew, but behind the builders there still remained an intellectual infrastructure permeated with the products of conventional public school and Oxbridge educations.[18]

---

modernity that could enrich the lives of all. Nonetheless, Conekin doubts its effectiveness, wryly concluding that: 'For whatever reason, it seems that many found in the Coronation Day celebrations two years later a more reassuring balance of the modern and the quintessentially British' (p. 246).

[16] See Philip Gibbs, *The New Elizabethans* (London: Hutchinson, 1953) for a representation of this brave new Britain.

[17] Tony Judt, *Postwar: A History of Europe Since 1945* (London: Pimlico, 2007), p. 161.

[18] Ross McKibbin, *Classes and Cultures: England 1918–1951* (Oxford University Press, 1998), p. v. See also Sissons and French, *Age of Austerity* and Kenneth O. Morgan, *The People's Peace: British History 1945–1990* (Oxford University Press, 1992) for the tensions of reconstruction, including the controversies attending the birth of the National Health Service.

Introduction

A similar paradox emerges in examining Britain's relations to the wider world of its empire. Indian independence, enacted through partition and the creation of Pakistan in 1947, might have seemed to symbolise a radical transformation in British colonial attitudes, but the empire had been fundamental to the wartime survival of the nation and politicians left and right were agreed in their belief that the remaining colonies were essential to the reassertion of Britain's status as a world power. Consequently, considerable effort was made to strengthen the ties between the mother country and her dependencies. In spite of a desperate shortage of manpower, 'new blood' was dispatched to administrate the colonies, while the 1948 British Nationality Act extended citizenship to all Commonwealth countries. For the many West Indians who answered the mother country's demand for labour, however, the welcome was cold. Making a journey now metonymically linked to the arrival of the *Empire Windrush* in 1948, the emigrants rapidly discovered that some citizens were more equal than others, and in the late 1940s and throughout the 1950s, the issue of who belonged to Britain became a complicating factor in a postwar landscape already fraught with industrial unrest, anti-Semitic riots and dire prognostications of juvenile delinquency.[19]

That one of the most influential literary transitions of the postwar period would be the emergence of black British voices and a postcolonial aesthetic is, in consequence, something that would have surprised the bulk of the nation in 1945. As David Kynaston's poetic snapshot suggests, austerity Britain was literally as well as metaphorically monotone:

> Britain in 1945. No supermarkets, no motorways, no teabags, no sliced bread, no frozen food, no flavoured crisps, no lager, no microwaves, no dishwashers, no Formica, no vinyl, no CDs, no computers, no mobiles, no duvets, no Pill . . . Four Indian restaurants. Shops on every corner, pubs on every corner, cinemas in every high street, red telephone boxes, Lyons Corner Houses . . . Central heating rare, coke boilers, water geysers, the coal fire, the hearth, the home, chilblains common. Abortion illegal, homosexual relationships illegal, suicide illegal, capital punishment legal. White faces everywhere.[20]

In such a context it is, as Gail Low has observed, remarkable that much of what is now considered the canon of postcolonial Anglophone West

---

[19] Kathleen Paul, *Whitewashing Britain: Race and Citizenship in the Postwar Era* (Ithaca, NY: Cornell University Press, 1997); Tony Kushner, 'Anti-Semitism and Austerity: The August 1947 Riots in Britain' in Panikos Panayi (ed.), *Racial Violence in Britain in the Nineteenth and Twentieth Centuries* (London: Leicester University Press, 1996); Kynaston, *Austerity Britain*, pp. 364–9.
[20] Kynaston, *Austerity Britain*, p. 19.

African and Caribbean writing was first published in London in the 1950s. Low opens her study of postcolonial publishing with a list that includes Amos Tutuola's *The Palm-Wine Drinkard* (1952), George Lamming's *The Emigrants* (1954), Sam Selvon's *The Lonely Londoners* (1956), V. S. Naipaul's *The Mystic Masseur* (1957) and Chinua Achebe's *Things Fall Apart* (1958). This is an impressive list, but also one that could be longer. Low's concern is solely with African and West Indian contexts, but mainstream British publishers in this period also published – to give a contrasting example of literary exchange – popular Indian women writers such as Attia Hosain and Kamala Markandaya. Hosain's *Phoenix Fled and Other Stories* appeared in 1953, Markandaya's bestseller *Nectar in a Sieve* followed in 1954.[21]

Publishing tells a fascinating story about the relationship between metropole and periphery in the 1950s, but the literary success of the so-called 'Windrush Generation' and, indeed, the influence of an earlier generation of South Asian writers, including such notable figures as Mulk Raj Anand and M. J. Tambimuttu, give a deceptive sheen to the wider reception of colonial immigrants.[22] Alan Sinfield observes that 'racial discrimination was ubiquitous and continuous', and 'Liberal optimism about the tolerance (let alone fairness) of English society was rudely undercut by outbreaks of violence against Blacks in Nottingham and then Notting Hill (London) in August and September 1958'.[23] Sinfield indicts the dangerously prejudicial newspaper reporting of these events, but it was not only race that generated postwar press hysteria. The virulence of mass media attacks on minority communities and cultural outsiders is replicated in debates about sex and sexuality in the 1950s. Here too we find anxiety about the emergence of a police state and the abuse of institutional power. *Against the Law*, Peter Wildeblood's 1955 memoir of his arrest and imprisonment for homosexual offences as part of the 'Montagu Case', is a remarkable document, both admirable in its delineation of prejudice,

---

[21] Gail Low, *Publishing the Postcolonial: Anglophone West African and Caribbean Writing in the UK 1948–1968* (London: Routledge, 2011). For Markandaya and Hosain, see Maroula Joannou, *Women's Writing, Englishness and National and Cultural Identity: The Mobile Woman and the Migrant Voice 1938–1962* (London: Palgrave, 2012), pp. 134–60; and Ruvani Ranasinha, *South Asian Writers in Twentieth-Century Britain, Culture in Translation* (Oxford: Clarendon Press, 2007). For the preoccupations shaping early black British writing, see James Procter, *Dwelling Places: Postwar Black British Writing* (Manchester University Press, 2003).

[22] See Ranasinha, *South Asian Writers*, for discussion of the writing, reception and influence of writers in the 1930s and 1940s, including Anand, Tambimuttu, R. K. Narayan and Raja Rao. Anand is also discussed in Kristen Bluemel, *George Orwell and the Radical Eccentrics: Intermodernism in Literary London* (Basingstoke: Palgrave, 2004).

[23] Alan Sinfield, *Literature, Politics and Culture in Postwar Britain* (Oxford: Blackwell, 1989), p. 126.

legal abuse and the appalling conditions in British prisons, and disturbing in its prejudice against a feminine 'other'. Wildeblood's strategy of seeking cultural acceptance by setting a subdued and stoical 'masculine' homosexuality against the 'obvious' vain, affected homosexual with his 'ceaseless chatter' is an understandable response to vitriolic attacks, but as Chris Waters observes, the 'portrait of the homosexual who could not be recognised as such ... served the tabloids' agenda of encouraging both the fears and voyeuristic fascination of their readers'.[24]

Wildeblood's book also reveals the resilience of class structures in the postwar period. Depicting the 'homosexual world' as something of a classless utopia, Wildeblood argues that the 'real crime of Lord Montagu ... was that he became acquainted – on no matter what basis – with a man who (to quote the prosecuting counsel) was "infinitely his social inferior"'.[25] Yet *Against the Law* also testifies to a paradox. As the law and the press became increasingly obsessed with the definition, persecution and punishment of homosexual desire, often with devastating consequences, writing transgressive pleasures became more possible in the 1950s. As the chapters of Charlotte Charteris and Victoria Stewart suggest, queer plots and queer possibilities proliferated in the fiction of writers as diverse as Rodney Garland, Mary Renault and Angus Wilson, and – significantly – the outcomes of such illicit relations were no longer necessarily fated to disaster. Mary Renault's charioteers might, like Radclyffe Hall's Stephen Gordon, only have enjoyed a discreetly veiled night together, but in the cautious optimism of the novel's ending emerges the possibility and the vindication of 'virtuous homosexuality'.[26] Wildeblood, meanwhile, would go on to give evidence to the Departmental Committee on Homosexual Offences and Prostitution, chaired by Sir John Wolfenden, whose Report, published in 1957, would recommend the decriminalisation of homosexuality.

Anxieties about unknowable others were not confined to sexual deviance and immigration. Indeed, fuelled by perceptions of the so-called 'decline of deference', arguably the most destabilising cultural panic of the 1950s was the fear of youth. Mapping transitions in working-class culture, Richard

---

[24] Peter Wildeblood, *Against the Law* (Harmondsworth: Penguin, 1957 [1955]), p. 29. Chris Waters, 'Disorders of the Mind, Disorders of the Body Social: Peter Wildeblood and the Making of the Modern Homosexual' in Conekin, Mort and Waters, *Moments of Modernity*, pp. 138–9.
[25] Wildeblood, *Against the Law*, pp. 31–2.
[26] Mary Renault, *The Charioteer* (London: Longmans, Green & Co., 1953). For a nuanced account of postwar moral panic and the intersection of class and sexuality, see Matt Houlbrook, *Queer London: Perils and Pleasures in the Sexual Metropolis, 1918–1957* (University of Chicago Press, 2005).

Hoggart suggests a movement from pre-war tolerance to a post-war fetishisation of 'freedom':

> The tolerant phrases have been joined by others in similar dress; the new depreciate the old, and together they become the ritual uniforms of a shared unwillingness to admit that freedom can have its punishments. Anything goes and there is no scale.[27]

Hoggart's analysis of the 'dangerous comforts of unreason' fomented by an aggressively anti-intellectual press still resonates today,[28] but at the time of writing his concerns focused on the 'juke-box boys' in thrall to a debased American culture, and the dangers of National Service, which detaches young men from community, bores them and addicts them to 'fragmentary and sensational' reading.[29] Hoggart's accusations of 'spiritual dry-rot amid the odour of boiled milk' speak, paradoxically, to both continuity and change. There was undoubtedly genuine fear in postwar Britain about the impact of total war on a generation of children who had witnessed unprecedented destruction and been variously uprooted, traumatised and bereaved, and this concern underpins the chapters by Lucy Pearson and Victoria Stewart in this collection.[30]

Yet Hoggart's anxieties speak also to a very different, and more familiar, threat: American popular culture. In the interwar years, as the cinema emerged as a powerful medium of mass entertainment, critics such as Q. D. Leavis articulated a belief that technologically mediated pleasures would numb and deform the minds of the masses. In the 1950s, Hoggart would say much the same of music and magazines. British cinema, by contrast, entered the decade enjoying new levels of cultural legitimacy, having experienced a golden age of critical approval in the 1940s. However, the 'documentary realism' applauded by middle-class critics and audiences would not hold sway in the 1950s. Rather, the decade became a 'period of transition for the British Film Industry', in which financial crisis and the power of the American studio system made genre films one of the few possible sources of profit.[31] Before the radical upheaval represented by the

---

[27] Richard Hoggart, *The Uses of Literacy* (Harmondsworth: Pelican, 1958 [1957]), p. 178.
[28] Ibid., pp. 182–9.   [29] Ibid., pp. 247–9.
[30] See Michal Shapira, *The War Inside: Psychoanalysis, Total War and the Making of the Democratic Self in Postwar Britain* (Cambridge University Press, 2013). Damaged and dangerous children may be found in fiction such as Noel Streatfeild's *Saplings* (1945) and, more famously, William Golding's *Lord of the Flies* (1954).
[31] Sue Harper and Vincent Porter, *British Cinema of the 1950s: The Decline of Deference* (Oxford University press, 2003), p. 1. See also Christine Geraghty, *British Cinema in the Fifties: Gender, Genre and the 'New Look'* (London: Routledge, 2000), pp. 1–20 for a valuable summary of the transitions in cinema-going in this period.

Introduction 13

British 'New Wave', crime, comedy and war films dominated the box office, alongside a significant strand of 'social problem' narratives, many of which focused on the anxieties outlined above: changing patterns of desire, racial tensions and the emergence of the teenager.

It was not only financial constraints, though, that contributed to the cinema's gradual decline in this period. After its wartime shut down, television resumed broadcasting in 1946, although – with only around 20,000 sets in the country – Kynaston notes that nobody, especially the BBC, was yet inclined to 'take the new medium seriously as a force for the future'.[32] By the mid-1950s, however, things were looking very different. The broadcast adaptation of George Orwell's *Nineteen Eighty-Four* (1954) set a new benchmark for what the medium could achieve, shocking the public and prompting MPs to outrage: television was fast becoming the means through which cutting-edge drama could be transmitted to a far wider audience than had ever previously been the case.[33] By the time that independent commercial television began broadcasting in 1955, over 4 million British homes boasted sets, offering viewers such diverse delights as *The Quatermass Experiment* (1953), *Dixon of Dock Green* (1955–76), *Sunday Night at the London Palladium* (1955–74), *What's My Line?* (1951–64) and, in due course, such early youth programming as the BBC music show *Six Five Special* (1957–8). By the end of the decade, the TV was becoming a focal point and the core of a greater 'home-centredness'.[34] The implications of such a transition are debatable, but the image of the family, gathered around its TV set, undoubtedly represents a degree of technologically mediated cultural atomisation that would have been unimaginable in the communal environments of the Second World War.[35]

This survey of social, political and generational transitions evokes a radically changing world, but what impact did these changes have on aesthetic practice and the textures of writing? In the section that follows, I consider literature's role in – and resistance to – the mediation of these transformations, focusing in particular on the representational challenges of war and decolonisation that bookend this period.

---

[32] Kynaston, *Austerity Britain*, p. 117.
[33] A good example is provided by Ted Willis's race relations drama *Hot Summer Night*, which premiered on stage in 1958 and appeared in ITV's prestige *Armchair Theatre* slot in 1959.
[34] David Kynaston, *Family Britain, 1951–57* (London: Bloomsbury, 2009), pp. 463–4, 671.
[35] Hoggart speculates that 'undiscriminating looking-in' at the TV might generate the sense that 'you are one in the big group watching the world (the world of events and personages) unroll before you', but his ambivalence about the medium is evident in his description of spectators' shared passivity. They are, he suggests, 'dead from the eyes downwards' (*The Uses of Literacy*, p. 189).

Writing the Postwar: Transition, Continuity and Conflict

As Mark Rawlinson argues in his chapter on narrating the postwar, writers struggled to register the 'demands of the times'. In the negotiation of guilt, complicity and grief, writing remained persistently 'at war', and a teleological narrative of transition is almost impossible to plot – a problem perhaps nowhere more clearly encapsulated than in the work of Stevie Smith. For Smith, there is no perceptible change between the condition of war and what comes after: the two are interchangeable, and it is from her plangent, yet pragmatic, cry of 'shall we win the post-war' that this volume takes inspiration.[36] Smith's third novel, *The Holiday*, was written during the war but – perhaps unsurprisingly given the extent of the characters' despair – it took her some years to find a publisher. The book that eventually appeared in 1949 was a curious assemblage of short stories, poems, dialogues and political comment, underpinned by moments of comedy and a dark melancholic yearning for death. In formal terms, the book's collage construction looked backwards to a literary war shaped by fragmentary reading practices and magazine publishing, but it was at the same time rendered bizarrely topical through Smith's addition of 'post' to every war reference. The audacity of the strategy is undeniable and the end product is not as absurd as might have been expected. Indeed, Smith's translation exposes exactly that continuity which this volume seeks to explore: 'It cannot be said that it is war, it cannot be said that it is peace, it can be said that it is post-war; this will probably go on for ten years.'[37]

'Postwar', then, is a liminal concept: neither war nor peace, it speaks to what might be termed the 'long Second World War', a conflict anticipated well in advance of 1939 and experienced long after 1945. Yet postwar is also displacement – a space of writing postponed – of emotion recollected, not so much in tranquillity as in the cold, bleak aftermath of immediate danger. Kate McLoughlin has argued that one of the dominant tropes of war writing is 'adynaton': a rhetorical displacement device that insists upon the impossibility of describing events.[38] And this is fundamental to the writing of the Second World War, as writers found themselves

---

[36] Stevie Smith, *The Holiday* (London: Virago, 1979 [1949]), p. 90.
[37] Smith, *The Holiday*, p. 13. Although recognised as challenging by publishers and critics, the book sold well, perhaps for the reasons identified by P. H. Newby, who concluded that 'I know of no novel which has caught so much of our post-war confusion of mind.' Quoted in Jack Barbera and William McBrien, *Stevie: A Biography of Stevie Smith* (London: William Heinemann, 1985), p. 170. For further discussion of the novel, see Plain, *Literature of the 1940s*.
[38] Kate McLoughlin, *Authoring War: The Literary Representation of War from the* Iliad *to* Iraq (Cambridge University Press, 2011), pp. 152–4.

overwhelmed by the political, cultural and geographical scale of the conflict. Elizabeth Bowen succinctly summarises the experience:

> The outsize world war news was stupefying: headlines and broadcasts came down and down on us in hammer-like chops, with great impact but oddly little reverberation. The simple way to put it was: 'One cannot take things in.' What was happening was out of all proportion to our faculties for knowing, thinking and checking up.[39]

Total war is an inhibiting force. It silences writers, exhausts them or – at best – generates 'saving' hallucinations, fantasies and compensatory dreamscapes,[40] displacements that enable survival but refuse engagement both with the fear of death and with the numbing boredom of existing in a warfare state.[41] Writing happens in wartime, but it happens in fragments of immediacy – impressions, perceptions, observations – what Bowen terms 'snapshots taken from close up, too close up'.[42] Making sense of these fragments requires distance and time.

Yet postwar begs a further question, and offers a further, transitional, resonance. In terms of understanding the extent to which war shaped writing in the period 1940 to 1960, one could and should ask, which war? In the early 1940s, it was the memory of the First World War as much as the actuality of the Second that shaped the creative imagination of Britain. The poets of 1914 to 1918 had generated the belief that poetry was an appropriate accompaniment to war, but in 1939 expectation was confounded by the 'failure' of writers to find appropriate words for battle.[43] Those who did attempt a response found that the legacy of the soldier poets proved almost as inhibiting as war itself, an anxiety of influence memorably encapsulated in Keith Douglas's frustrated apostrophising: 'Rosenberg I only repeat what you were saying'.[44] The Second World War does not supersede or overwrite the First, rather it co-exists with the potent cultural shaping force of the earlier conflict – not least because the events of 1914 to

---

[39] Elizabeth Bowen, 'The Demon Lover [Preface to the American Edition]' in *Collected Impressions* (London: Longmans Green & Co., 1950), p. 49.
[40] Ibid.
[41] The term 'warfare' state, designed to echo and contrast the more familiar 'welfare' state, is David Edgerton's. In *Warfare State: Britain 1920–1970* (Cambridge University Press, 2006), Edgerton argues against dominant discourses of decline by exploring Britain's status as a military-industrial power in the mid-century period.
[42] Bowen, 'Preface to the Demon Lover', p. 52.
[43] Calder, The People's War, pp. 517–18. See also Martin Francis, 'Attending to Ghosts: Some Reflections on the Disavowals of British Great War Historiography' *Twentieth Century British History* (2014) 25(3) pp. 347–67.
[44] Keith Douglas, 'Desert Flowers' in Desmond Graham (ed.), *The Complete Poems* (London: Faber & Faber, 2000 [1978]), p. 108.

1918 stood as a benchmark of atrocity, the worst that could be conceived. Imagined futures are inevitably limited by known worlds and, as Mitford's Sophia Garfield so ably demonstrates, we can only ever understand war through existing paradigms. This perhaps makes sense of the cry, 'where are the war poets?' that echoed around the first months of the war. 'Where are the documentary makers, essayists, broadcasters and short-story writers?' not only lacks the same succinct resonance, it is – at war's opening – literally unimaginable. The Second World War would find its own voice, and its representative media, but the First World War would continue to permeate the conflict in texts as diverse as Vera Brittain's ghost-ridden morale booster *England's Hour* (1941) and Evelyn Waugh's nostalgic panegyric *Brideshead Revisited* (1945).

Waugh's novel, one of the most famous texts to emerge from the 1940s, provides a test case for the concept of 'war writing' – as does another well-known fiction of the period, Virginia Woolf's *Between the Acts* (1941). Both novels expose the limits of a concept determined by the experience of combat, and force us to ask where the boundary falls between war writing and writing in wartime? In the case of *Between the Acts*, the familiar intimacies of modernist interiority disguise both unexpected patriotic sentiment and a pervasive violence, manifest through historical allusion and textual rupture. Time and again, pastoral timelessness is invaded by the symbols of a deadly contemporaneity.[45] This is a mode of writing about war that understands conflict as an all-pervasive condition that inescapably shapes texts, something that Elizabeth Bowen, describing her own short stories, would term 'war-climate'.[46] Writing which is more obviously about the experience of war-as-combat, by contrast, is often an act of memorialising: an ordering of a past that was at the time unassimilable. This has long been a truism in studies of First World War literature: lyric poetry was an immediate visceral response; fiction and memoirs were only possible some ten years later.[47] But the distinction is not always so obvious, and if not attended to, risks oversimplifying the process of writing war. The work of Evelyn Waugh is a case in point. Waugh's *Sword of Honour* trilogy, on first appearance, seems a key text of the Second World War. But its three volumes were published in 1952, 1955 and 1961. While the 1950s can arguably be understood, at least imaginatively, still to be war years, *Sword*

---

[45] For patriotic sentiment, see Marina MacKay, *Modernism and World War II* (Cambridge University Press, 2007); for violence, see Daniel Ferrer, *Virginia Woolf and the Madness of Language* (London: Routledge, 1990).
[46] Bowen, 'Preface to the Demon Lover', p. 48.
[47] For analysis of this conventional assumption, see *Transitions*, vol. 2.

of Honour nonetheless represents Waugh's considered, and comical, *post hoc* organisation of experience. When we look at what he actually wrote during the war itself, we find *Brideshead*: a book in which the Second World War is displaced to the margins through a frame narrative, and whose profoundly nostalgic central *bildungsroman* is haunted by the spectre of the First World War. It is also a novel that gives voice to Waugh's deep-rooted terror of social change, as manifest in women and the lower classes, and these forces come together in Lady Marchmain's emasculating fetishisation of her three brothers killed in the trenches. No men, least of all her husband or sons, could match up to the memory of these 'garlanded victims' whose pictures haunt both the survivors and the succeeding generation.[48]

Waugh, then, spent the Second World War worrying about the sociocultural impact of the First, a process that by the time of completing *Brideshead* had stewed itself into a paranoid fear of mass mediocrity and the rise of the common man. It illustrates how the pressures of conflict might be displaced, and how difficult it is to unpick the boundaries dividing the two wars – at least in terms of affect, memory and cultural anxiety. Nancy Mitford bears quoting again – this time from *The Pursuit of Love*, published almost simultaneously with *Brideshead* in 1945:

> 'It's rather sad,' [Linda] said one day, 'to belong, as we do, to a lost generation. I'm sure in history the two wars will count as one war and that we shall be squashed out of it altogether, and people will forget that we ever existed. We might just as well never have lived at all, I do think it's a shame.'[49]

Mitford's version of the 'lost generation' conveys a powerful sense of the persistence of war and its chronological instability. Cinema too speaks to continuity as much as change. Early films of the Second World War, such as the propaganda family comedy *Old Bill and Son* (1940), looked remarkably like representations of the first war, while a more complex film product of the 1940s, Michael Powell and Emeric Pressburger's *The Life and Death of Colonel Blimp* (1943), suggests that an even earlier war, the Boer War, was still shaping at least part of the cultural imaginary. This should not surprise us. As Michael Paris has argued, 1914 to 1918 'seemingly had little effect on the pleasure culture of war', and the imaginations of interwar schoolboys continued to be shaped by violent fictions of empire

---

[48] Evelyn Waugh, *Brideshead Revisited* (Harmondsworth: Penguin, 1962 [1945]), p. 134. In between these contrasting mediations of war, Waugh returned to his pre-war satirical habits in *The Loved One* (1948), a blackly comic assault on American cultural values.
[49] Nancy Mitford, *The Pursuit of Love* (Harmondsworth: Penguin, 1986 [1945]), p. 147.

and adventure.[50] But those schoolboys were equally products of an interwar cultural climate of stoicism and restraint, and they grew up with the dead of the First World War. Small wonder, then, that the generation who fought and wrote about the Second World War did so with a curious mixture of detachment, deference, curiosity and guilty pleasure. For all the 'lessons' of the soldier poets, the majority of British boys were still being taught that war was a 'must have' experience for men, an opportunity to prove oneself to the ghosts of an earlier generation. Young women, by contrast, were left to negotiate a hybrid identity, combining a residual and powerfully symbolic domesticity with an emergent modernity that made them newly minted citizens and a previously untapped labour force for the warfare state. Trousers may have been 'selling like hot cakes', as Monica Dickens recalled, but 'beauty' was still very much regarded as women's primary duty.[51]

If these examples speak to the continuum that connects the literary imagination of the First and Second World Wars, what of the boundary between conventional warfare and the nebulous, evasive, yet all-pervasive innovation of the Cold War? The transition from 'old war' to 'cold war' has a pleasing symmetry, but is too reductive to encompass a period in which American cultural hegemony seemed almost as threatening as Soviet ideology, and reinvestment in empire seemed a more promising prospect to a British Labour Government than emergent models of European cooperation.[52] The fault-lines that would shape the politics of the next forty years took time fully to concretise, and while they did, the world did not lack for crises and conflicts, in Palestine, India, Kenya and Korea – to name but a few. British culture's capacity to confront such crises and encounter a changing world is addressed here in Petra Rau's chapter on

---

[50] Michael Paris, *Warrior Nation: Images of War in British Popular Culture, 1850–2000* (London: Reaktion Books, 2000), p. 184.

[51] Monica Dickens, *One Pair of Feet* (Harmondsworth: Penguin, 1956 [1942]), p 7. The slogan 'beauty is your duty' was deployed by women's magazines to emphasise the temporary nature of women's wartime transformation. For wartime gender double standards, see Sonya Rose in *Which People's War? National Identity and Citizenship in Wartime Britain, 1939–1945* (Oxford University Press, 2003), and Plain, *Literature of the 1940s*, pp. 77–90.

[52] Although Britain sent delegates to the inaugural meeting of the 'Council of Europe' in May 1949, they declined to participate in the European Coal and Steel Community founded by the Paris Treaty of 1951. Tony Judt suggests that the British saw the scheme as 'the thin edge of a continental wedge in British affairs, whose implications were the more dangerous for being unclear'. It was also seen as something that would disrupt Britain's relationship to the Commonwealth, a 'World-wide Anglophone imperial community' that remained both integral to British national identity and a valuable source of raw materials. Judt, *Postwar*, pp. 159, 160. On the anxiety provoked by American 'mass' culture, see Genevieve Abravanel, *Americanizing Britain: The Rise of Modernism in the Age of the Entertainment Empire* (Oxford University Press, 2012).

Introduction

postwar travel writing, in the final section of this collection. That this section is entitled 'No Directions' speaks to the uncertainty with which writers resume the business, and pleasure, of travel – as a once confident colonial command of territory is replaced by more provisional modes of encounter.

While it is difficult, politically or culturally, to determine the exact start of Cold War hostilities, the shaping force of this ideological conflict nonetheless rapidly became a fact of life for British writers, a source of anxiety that would have a profound influence on literary practice and possibilities.[53] The Cold War's shadowy presence, and its perverse entanglement in the concrete war that preceded it, can be felt throughout *Postwar*, from the residual fears of fascism traced by Adam Piette in the poetry of Auden and Spender, to Thomas Davis's exploration of *Encounter*'s cultural cold war, to James Smith's analysis of the literary legacy of wartime covert practices. Surveillance, as fact or trope, serious threat or black comedy, would become a staple in the writing of those, like Muriel Spark and Graham Greene, who had themselves been engaged in so-called 'black' operations. Yet Cold War paranoia was not the only nebulous political force shaping literary practice. The loss of overseas territory – a subject surprisingly little debated in the politics of the early 1950s – nonetheless registered profoundly in the stories that Britain told about itself in popular film and fiction.[54] John Darwin attributes the relative absence of political debate about Empire to the 'indispensable painkiller' of the Commonwealth,[55] but while politicians avoided the subject, or asserted a belief in Britain's ongoing global relevance, literature was less reluctant to face up to the facts of imperial decline. Anthony Burgess's *Malayan Trilogy* (1956, 1958, 1959) provides a rich example. What begins as a relatively benign alcohol-infused exercise in absurdity, a comedy steeped in a tradition of ineffectual Englishmen abroad, gradually mutates into a nihilistic registration of British redundancy in the face of 'professional' American colonialism and the potent multiculturalism of the new Malaya. Burgess, the writer, relishes the linguistic multiplicity of his ungovernable, yet pragmatic,

---

[53] Sinfield, *Literature, Politics and Culture*, p. 94.
[54] See Wendy Webster, *Englishness and Empire 1939–1965* (Oxford University Press, 2005) for discussion of the regeneration of conquest, heroism and adventure ideals.
[55] John Darwin, quoted in Dan Rebellato, 'Look Back at Empire: British Theatre and Imperial Decline' in Stuart Ward (ed.), *British Culture and the End of Empire* (Manchester University Press, 2001).

Malay states: Victor Crabbe, his numb imperial protagonist, seems happier to drown.[56]

Burgess is an eloquent commentator on British decline, but has less to say about the racial policies that so long underpinned the imperial ideal and formed perhaps its most toxic legacy. It was left to writers from Britain's current and former colonies to articulate the direct and diffuse consequences of racist thought, government and infrastructure. From Sam Selvon's acute observation of the fear behind the façade of cold British politeness to Chinua Achebe's clinical dissection of white culture's missionary obliteration of cultural otherness, late colonial and postcolonial writers generated potent new 'ways of seeing' and understanding political belonging.[57] *The Leopard* (1958), by West Indian writer V. S. Reid, provides a powerful example. The novel is set in Kenya and focalised through the half-Kikuyu, half-Masai hunter Nebu, who has both worked for a British planter and participated in the Mau Mau rebellion. The narrative point of view and Reid's deceptively simple poetic prose combine to defamiliarise the customary colonial narrative of a threatening black other. Instead, the reader is given a different way of seeing in which the knowable world, both rational and beautiful, is that of Nebu, and the violence of the Mau Mau rebellion – subject 'at home' to selective reporting that ignored atrocities committed by the British[58] – is figured as a reactive response. Yet by far the most disturbing aspect of the book is its depiction of the 'grey' biracial child whose white 'father', Bwana Gibson, is killed by Nebu for his gun.[59] This child, product of an earlier encounter between Nebu and Gibson's wife, is crippled both literally and metaphorically, taught the language of a master race to which he cannot belong. He is sadistic, his vulnerable exterior hiding an inner 'murderer' that would rather destroy Nebu than ensure his own safety.[60] Meanwhile, Nebu, wounded by the gun he had so

---

[56] 'Crabbe had never noticed very much': which perhaps accounts for the resilience of his well-meaning but naive intellectual paternalism. His ultimate defeat, however, emerges not from the clash of ideas, but the bathos of the personal, and his final journey into the jungle suggests nothing so much as *Heart of Darkness* re-enacted as farce. Bitten by a scorpion, the semi-delirious Crabbe becomes a cut-price Kurtz: 'A book is a kind of lavatory. We've got to throw up the past, otherwise we can't live in the present. The past has got to be killed.' Unlike Conrad's novel, the jungle and its inhabitants do not trouble to register his passing. Anthony Burgess, *The Malayan Trilogy* (London: Vintage, 2000), pp. 207, 538.

[57] See Thomas S. Davis, *The Extinct Scene: Late Modernism and Everyday Life* (New York: Columbia University Press, 2016), pp. 191–5. Drawing on George Lamming's *The Pleasures of Exile* (1960), Davis argues that '[t]ransformation at the level of language transforms a way of seeing' (p. 192) and in so doing exposes the determining force of colonialism.

[58] See Webster, *Englishness and Empire*, pp. 119–20.

[59] V. S. Reid, *The Leopard* (London: Heinemann, 1958), p. 42. [60] Ibid., p. 131.

desired, attempts to take the boy back to secure British territory. In the journey that ensues, he is tormented by the boy, while both are stalked by the leopard. It is a claustrophobic microcosm of empire that exposes the myth of mutual benefit, and only occasionally does Reid step outside his African focaliser to explain the motivations at play:

> Now it is a fact that Nebu was hurrying towards a murder, but it did not appear that way to him at all. To him, he was stalking a dangerous man-animal. An animal you could never get upwind of, for he had no upwind or downwind. He was a gun: he hid a mile away behind a tree and slew you. And you were able to hate him as you could never hate a lion, for a lion never ignored your customs, nor laughed at them.[61]

The inversion of conventional racial paradigms is striking, as is the metaphor that translates all of white power into the inhumanity of the gun. Discussing the novel some thirty years later, Reid emphasised his desire to make the book into a form of 'pure poetry', an effect achieved through extreme economy, rapid pace and the avoidance of polysyllaby.[62] The result might be termed modernist, but if so, it is an explicitly political modernism. As such, it forces a consideration of transition less in temporal or aesthetic than in spatial terms: a writing not of, from or about Britain, but rather an investigation of a legacy of Britishness most appropriately figured as postcolonial.

The search for points of transition, from war to peace, from old war to Cold War, from Empire to decolonisation, fixes on dates that then become what Fran Brearton has termed 'magic numbers': numerical configurations that acquire almost poetic resonance and in so doing distort our reading of the past.[63] 1939 and 1945 function in this way, as, in the context of postcolonial literary studies, does 1948. But while 1945 is the date most commonly used to divide and manage understandings of the century, in terms of literary transition the most potent of the magic numbers in this period is 1956. Described by Robert Hewison as a retrospective '*annus mirabilis*',[64] this is the year in which the emergence of the 'angry young man' seems miraculously to coincide with both the Hungarian Revolution and the national humiliation of the Suez crisis. From the first performance of John Osborne's *Look Back in Anger*, to the

---

[61] Ibid., p. 27.
[62] 'The Writer and His Work: V. S. Reid' *Journal of West Indian Literature* (1987) 2(1) p. 6.
[63] Fran Brearton, 'Missing Dates and Magic Numbers: Reflections on 1914' in Gill Plain (ed.), *Scotland and the First World War: Myth, Memory and the Legacy of Bannockburn* (Lewisburg, PA: Bucknell University Press, 2016).
[64] Robert Hewison, *In Anger: Culture in the Cold War 1945–60* (London: Methuen, 1988 [1981]), p. 148.

publication of the new vernacular voices of Sam Selvon's *The Lonely Londoners* and the arrival of *The Outsider* – Colin Wilson's handbook of existential alienation – it seemed a corner had been turned beyond which lay a new generation and a new relationship to class, belonging, community, social mobility, education and aspiration.[65] 1956 has also, retrospectively, been consecrated as a transitional year for poetry through the publication of Robert Conquest's *New Lines* anthology. Conquest, like Osborne on the stage, is deliberately confrontational, opening his polemical introduction with an attack on the 'bad principles' of the excessively metaphorical, sentimental and indulgent poetry of the 1940s. Perhaps unfortunately, his method of attack is itself through metaphor – an opening image so absolutist in judgment as to inadvertently evoke the style of *1066 and All That*:

> In the 1940s the mistake was made of giving the Id, a sound player on the percussion side under a strict conductor, too much of a say in the doings of the orchestra as a whole. As it turned out, it could only manage the simpler part of melody and rhythm, and was completely out of its depth with harmony and orchestration. This led to a rapid collapse of public taste, from which we have not yet recovered.[66]

Under Conquest's firm leadership, the Roundheads ('*Right but Repulsive*') confront their Cavalier predecessors ('*Wrong but Wromantic*') with the belief that poetry should be 'empirical in its attitude to all that comes'.[67] A line had been drawn that would shape the landscape of poetry criticism for decades, yet while Conquest undoubtedly had an eye for talent – *New Lines* included the work of Elizabeth Jennings, Philip Larkin, Thom Gunn, Donald Davie and John Wain – his arguments for the value of this work rest as much on tradition as innovation. These poets are, he suggests, primarily indebted to Yeats, a claim that consigns the symbolism of the Apocalypse and the new Romanticism, dominant voices of the war years,

---

[65] See Alice Ferrebe, *Literature of the 1950s: Good, Brave Causes* (Edinburgh University Press, 2012), pp. 163–82 for a persuasive account of the transitions at play in the work of writers such as Alan Sillitoe, John Braine and Arnold Wesker. Ferrebe also explores the interventions of Raymond Williams and Richard Hoggart, whose influential studies *Culture and Society* (1958) and *The Uses of Literacy* (1957) not only capture postwar transitions in working-class experience, but also represent paradigm shifts in the relationship between literature, autobiography and sociology. For Selvon's innovative vernacular and his remapping of the metropolis, see James Procter, *Dwelling Places: Postwar Black British Writing* (Manchester University Press, 2003), p. 50 and Davis, *The Extinct Scene*, pp. 211–12.

[66] Robert Conquest (ed.), *New Lines: An Anthology* (London: Macmillan, 1956), p. xi.

[67] W. C. Sellar and R. J. Yeatman, *1066 and All That* (London: Methuen, 1930), p. 63; Conquest, *New Lines*, p. xv.

to the status of a temporary aberration, and asserts the poets of the Movement as agents of restoration rather than revolution.[68]

In both poetry and prose, then, new voices were emerging, but so too were old songs, and in this context 'transition' appears a provisional and insecure term. What was most innovative in these years was not necessarily best recognised, and in some cases – for example, the development of Black British writing – the impact would not fully be felt until the final decades of the century.[69] Also complicating the picture of transition in the period is the hindsight of literary critical practice, and the final section of this introduction considers the retrospective constructions of period and canon that have shaped – and in some cases limited – our understanding of 1940 to 1960.

Framing the Mid-Century: Conceptual Transitions

As the example of 1956 suggests, critical habits form around apparently decisive breaks – and most surveys of the century choose 1945 for this definitive moment. Here, critics have sought and found a transition from modernism to postmodernism, locating in the traumatic impact of Hiroshima and the Holocaust an irrevocable loss of innocence. For Paul Crosthwaite, however, attempts to determine the origin of postmodernism are fundamentally 'misconceived', and run counter to the characteristics of a sensibility that distrusts the claims of grand narratives.[70] Rather, in a project that speaks to continuities and transitions that move beyond the end point of this volume, he argues that the novels of 'postmodern' writers such as Thomas Pynchon and J. G. Ballard are 'every bit as much "World War II" novels ... as those produced during or immediately after the conflict'.[71] This is a useful reminder of the extent to which the literature of the entire twentieth century has been shaped by war, but it also highlights the interpretative limits arising from conventional categories of analysis. Indeed, it is thinking through the *post-hoc* organising paradigms of 'modernism' and 'postmodernism', and the hierarchies of value they

---

[68] For a more detailed history of literary developments in the period, see Plain, *Literature of the 1940s* and Ferrebe, *Literature of the 1950s*.
[69] This impact is mapped across the chapters of Berthold Schoene and Eileen Pollard (eds), *British Literature in Transition 1980–2000: Accelerated Times* (Cambridge University Press, 2018).
[70] Paul Crosthwaite, *Trauma, Postmodernism and the Aftermath of World War II* (Basingstoke: Palgrave, 2009), p. 8.
[71] Ibid., p. 3.

impose, that has consigned to oblivion some of the most important writing of the 1940s and 1950s.

Narratives of periodicity and canon formation, in particular the story of modernism's rise and fall, have presented a problem for the literary history of the mid-century. The Second World War and its aftermath were, put simply, judged inadequately innovative, and key works of the period failed the gate-keeping tests of a field of study premised on difficulty, experimentalism and a lack of mass appeal. A narrow – or, as critics such as Paul Saint-Amour would term it, 'strong' – theory of 'Modernism' limits the modernities available for study, and in the case of the postwar, this has meant a critical practice ill-equipped to absorb aesthetic developments as diverse as the period's potent documentary aesthetic and its rich vein of fantasy and science fiction.[72] Criticism has also, historically, struggled with the resurgence of a realist aesthetic, often marginalising as 'middlebrow' fictions that powerfully engage with what Alice Ferrebe has called the 'increasingly complicated politics of difference: age, class, gender, racial, sexual, regional and national' that mark the 1950s.[73] Writing in this volume, Ferrebe emphasises not only the importance of realism in the period, but also the extent to which 'realism' itself was contested territory. In a literary battleground, a new wave of writers and critics championed a realist aesthetic that could negotiate a changed world and its priorities, while condemning modernism as contaminated by association with a pre-war order. Yet even as they did so, new fault lines appeared and Ferrebe also, valuably, demonstrates the multiplicity of realisms at play in this new aesthetic – and their fundamental imbrication in the project of the modernism they supposedly superseded.

As Ferrebe's findings suggest, for all the contemporary claims of realism and the critical desire to usher in the dawn of the postmodern, what might be termed traditional modernist writing still mattered in the postwar. However, a more radical development than the recognition of residual forms of modernist writing is the emergence of a new critical practice that has radically altered the parameters of the category itself. Saint-Amour describes the revolution: 'once a capitalised singular noun with a bounded referent, modernism in the hands of contemporary literary scholars has

---

[72] Another example of writing that seems to have resisted analysis or simply been forgotten, in spite of palpable difficulty, is verse drama. Produced by writers as diverse as Ronald Duncan, Anne Ridler, Dorothy L. Sayers and T. S. Eliot, this was a vital and innovative dimension of the war and postwar years. See Irene Morra, *Verse Drama in England 1900–2015: Art, Modernity and the National Stage* (London: Bloomsbury, 2016).
[73] Ferrebe, *Literature of the 1950s*, p. 2.

been pluralized, adjectivalised, decoupled from high culture, and rethought as a transnational and transhistorical phenomenon'. Or, more succinctly, it has 'stopped playing bouncer and started playing host'.[74] 'Modernism' has lost its capital letter, becoming variously late, long and twinned with an infinite variety of supplementary terms, but while this expansion has rejuvenated the field of study, its extreme elasticity might also give cause for concern. Indeed, for Leo Mellor and Glynn Salton-Cox, modernism risks turning into a colonising force, exhibiting a 'manic inclusivity' that threatens to hoover up 'pretty much all of the twentieth-century'.[75] For critics seeking to dismantle the canon, or to diversify understandings of how literature was received at the time of publication, the expansion of modernism is a double-edged sword. To claim a text for modernism affords it legitimacy, but discourses of innovation and experimentation do not always best explain popular or critical appeal – nor can they necessarily account for why a book or play succeeded, or why we should read it today.

These are debates that this introduction cannot resolve, but at its best, new modernist criticism has revolutionised our understanding of postwar literary cultures, not least by exposing previously occluded lines of affiliation and influence. Peter J. Kalliney's *Commonwealth of Letters* exemplifies the benefits of the approach in its exploration of the astonishing persistence – and unexpected repurposing – of Eliotic concepts of aesthetic autonomy in the work of late colonial and early postcolonial writers. Kalliney argues that concepts of impersonality, reconfigured as the idea that 'a work of art could be judged solely by its imaginative merits [and] not by reference to the racial status of its creator', offered a valuable – and, ironically, political – tool for the subversion of racial barriers and the furtherance of an anti-imperial agenda.[76] For the modernist establishment,

---

[74] Paul K. Saint-Amour, *Tense Future: Modernism, Total War, Encyclopedic Form* (Oxford University Press, 2015), pp. 41, 42. Explaining the transition, Saint-Amour argues: 'Modernist studies has become a strong field – populous, varied, generative, self-reflexive – in proportion as its immanent theory of modernism has weakened and become less axiomatic, more conjectural, more conjunctural' (p. 41). Perhaps the most striking instance of this conceptual expansion is Susan Stanford Friedman, *Planetary Modernisms: Provocations on Modernity across Time* (New York: Columbia University Press, 2017). For the influence of modernism beyond conventionally accepted boundaries, see David James, *Modernist Futures: Innovation and Inheritance in the Contemporary Novel* (Cambridge University Press, 2012).

[75] Leo Mellor and Glynn Salton-Cox, 'Introduction' to the 'Long 1930s' issue of *Critical Quarterly*, vol. 57, no. 3 (2015), p. 4.

[76] Peter J. Kalliney, *Commonwealth of Letters: British Literary Culture and the Emergence of Postcolonial Aesthetics* (Oxford University Press, 2013), p. 6. Kalliney's case studies include the BBC's *Caribbean Voices*, the common ground shared by F. R. Leavis and Kamu Braithwaite in their valorisation of vernacular speech, and Faber & Faber's curiously unmediated publication of *The Palm-Wine*

faced by attacks from 'angry' playwrights and Movement poets, forging new networks of collaboration with non-metropolitan, postcolonial intellectuals offered hope of both ideological continuity – the preservation of the 'aesthetic temper of interwar literature' – and the prospect of vast new audiences in a newly expanding literary world.[77]

Kalliney's work draws on diverse archival resources to reanimate a vital cultural milieu, and in the process points us towards another critical development that has revolutionised understandings of postwar literature: the study of broadcasting. The BBC was integral to the networks of intergenerational influence at play in the 1950s, and – through the commissioning and dissemination of new work by the famous and the unknown alike – had a transformative impact on literary practice and consumption.[78] And its output permeated the nation. According to David Kynaston, in austerity Britain reading 'played second fiddle to the wireless in most homes', and although the majority of listeners were tuned in to the popular comforts of the Home Service or the Light Programme, the Corporation believed they could be educated into a taste for higher things. The launch of the 'Third Programme' in September 1946 was a statement of highbrow intent. Broadcasting talks, readings, music and drama, the station would go on to critical success, commissioning such influential works as Dylan Thomas's *Under Milk Wood* (1954) and Samuel Beckett's *All That Fall* (1956).[79] Listening figures, by contrast, suggest that – particularly for working-class audiences – the Third's cultural mission made little impact. What really united British listeners in this period was comedy: from *ITMA* in the 1940s to *The Goon Show* and the astonishingly influential *Hancock's Half Hour*, first broadcast in 1954.[80]

BBC radio enjoyed a global reach, but its home was London, and a final critical commonplace that begs consideration is the metropolitan bias of cultural memory. Although wartime necessity and postwar Arts Council funding saw the reinvigoration of regional theatre across the nation – as

---

Drinkard. This final example is particularly effective in exposing the tensions between aesthetic autonomy, the anthropology of primitivism and the high stakes of a developing nationalist agenda. See also Low, *Publishing the Postcolonial*, pp. 1–25.

[77] Kalliney, *Commonwealth*, p. 4.
[78] See Debra Rae Cohen, Michael Coyle and Jane Lewty (eds), *Broadcasting Modernism* (Gainsville, FL: University Press of Florida, 2009); Matthew Feldman, Erik Tonning and Henry Mead (eds), *Broadcasting in the Modernist Era* (London: Bloomsbury, 2014); and Ian Whittington, *Writing the Radio War: Literature, Politics and the BBC, 1939–1945* (Edinburgh University Press, 2018).
[79] Kynaston, *Austerity Britain*, pp. 211, 176–7. See also Kalliney, *Commonwealth*, p. 120.
[80] Kynaston, *Family Britain*, pp. 434–5.

Introduction

discussed in this volume by Rebecca D'Monté and Claire Cochrane – it is literary London that has been immortalised as the hub of creative possibility in this period. Undoubtedly, the capital exerted a centripetal force, pulling writers from across the United Kingdom and the Empire into its orbit (and, in the case of a significant cadre of Fitzrovian writers, its pubs).[81] But while this generated connections – such as those between old modernists and new Caribbean writers – that would have a lasting impact on the nation's literary culture, a wider-angled lens is necessary to understand the full picture of *British* literature in transition.

The relationship between centre and periphery, metropolitan and regional, rural and urban is not constant across the century, and in consequence, the five volumes in the *Transitions* series take different approaches to exploring literature beyond the metropole. *British Literature in Transition 1900–1920: A New Age?* recognises from the outset that 'British' was a site of contestation, and the early years of the century were marked by complex negotiations of the relationship between nation and empire. By contrast, the second volume – *Futility and Anarchy* – registers in the period 1920 to 1940 the centrifugal pressures at play in the 'First break up of Britain'. Further realignments characterise the later decades of the century: *Flower Power*, covering 1960 to 1980, offers a series of case studies exploring the proliferation of the regional, while the final volume, *Accelerated Times*, negotiates both devolution and the drive towards globalisation and an information technology revolution. The Second World War, however, significantly interrupts these national trajectories and the 1940s in particular saw, perhaps for the last time, writers from across England, Northern Ireland, Scotland and Wales committing to the development and propagation of a largely consensual 'Britishness'. This is not to suggest there were not significant tensions, not least over the frequent slippage in broadcast and print media between England and Britain, but conscious efforts were made on radio and in the cinema to emphasise the multinational make-up of the country and its war effort. The success of such efforts was variable. The wartime group hero of films such as *Millions Like Us* (1943) and *The Foreman Went to France* (1942) of necessity included national, regional and class diversity, but English paternalism and the whiff of imperialism (in particular the conscription of young Welsh and Scottish women) continued to generate resentment. Sonya Rose quotes from a 1944

---

[81] Andrew Sinclair, *War Like A Wasp: The Lost Decade of the Forties* (London: Hamish Hamilton, 1989); Robert Hewison, *Under Siege: Literary Life in London 1939–45* (London: Methuen, 1988 [1977]), pp. 61–85.

broadcast by the Welsh playwright Emlyn Williams, whose rhetoric effectively encapsulates a not altogether happy 'union':

> We Welsh are not, as I had thought, flesh and bone relations of our English neighbours ... we are rather betrothed to the English in friendly bondage in the same way as a dutiful but philosophical wife is tied to a successful but slightly overpowering husband.[82]

Much the same could be said of the rather more acrimonious bond uniting England and Scotland. How these marriages came to collapse – and the role played by literature in the divorce – while hinted at in Katie Gramich's overview of 'national' literatures in transition, will only become clear in later volumes.[83] What will also only later become clear is the legacy of Empire in relation to how we define British literature. Writers came from the colonies in 1948, and throughout the 1950s, in the belief that they were British citizens. Their writing introduced new voices and brought about a new mapping of the metropolis, but by the end of the decade the assumption of a British literary identity had become increasingly troubled, generating a parting of the ways as a range of African, Caribbean and Indian writers concerned themselves less with integration than with the forging of new national literatures. It is perhaps this transition – the emergence of postcolonial literatures in English, divorced and distanced from British preoccupations – that most clearly marks the end of the nebulous 'postwar' sensibility this volume has attempted to map.[84]

It is tempting, in introducing a collection which aims, among other things, to restore complexity to an all-too-often overlooked period of literary history, to list all those writers who might have featured in the volume but for whom there was not space. Or, indeed, to imagine and construct the contents of shadow volumes, parallel universes of critical possibility boasting chapters on London literature, landscape poetry, verse drama, the 'middlebrow', the university, the short story, existentialism, the Catholic novel, radio drama, family sagas, queer cultures, sub-cultures, exile, psychoanalysis and the kitchen sink. Some of these subjects will

---

[82] Rose, *Which People's War?*, p. 236.
[83] The power of consensus in crisis – and the inevitable return of more complex historical and cultural divisions – was recognised at the time, perhaps most strikingly in Bridget Boland's *Cockpit* (1948). Boland's drama, set in a Displaced Person's camp, focuses on the challenge of European reconciliation, but it functions as an effective allegory for the multiple social and political divisions papered over by wartime necessity.
[84] The full impact of these devolutionary and postcolonial transformations on British literature would not be felt for decades, but their impact is undoubted. See Schoene and Pollard, *British Literature in Transition 1980–2000*.

appear in other *Transitions* volumes, as will writers – such as Ted Hughes, Harold Pinter and Iris Murdoch – whose careers were just beginning as the 1950s drew to a close. But it has not been the intention of this volume, nor of the series, to rehearse the familiar stories of canonical twentieth-century writing. The chapters that follow range widely across the works of writers both known and forgotten, innovative and conventional, popular and critically acclaimed. They seek, in so doing, to forge new critical connections and to bring about a fresh understanding of literature and its readerships in a period of devastating political change.

Postwar's account of how British writing slowly, and sometimes painfully, got to grips with a post-traumatic, post-atomic and post-imperial world is organised in four parts, two of which might be considered pragmatic, and two conceptual. Part I, 'Aftermath: The Beginning or the End?' offers a series of wide-ranging chapters that explore what happened to fiction, poetry and drama in this period, and begin the work of undoing easy assumptions of development or transformation. Part II, 'The Politics of Transition', asks the question, 'what was at stake?' Here, readers will find emergent and residual anxieties surrounding the politics of a new era and the possibility of formulating an aesthetic response to an uncertain new world. Part III, 'Reconfigurations', might be paraphrased as 'how did it feel?' The chapters here recognise the return of the personal to a world dishabituated from the expression of emotion and consider the emergence of new voices articulating unprecedented feelings and opinions. The final part, somewhat pessimistically, is entitled 'No Directions', after James Hanley's 1943 novel of the same name. *No Directions* offers an utterly disorientating modernist evocation of the Blitz, featuring a drunken sailor, an impotent artist and a vision of a white horse galloping through the burning city. Perhaps nothing more need be said, but the section seeks to demonstrate that insofar as transition was possible, literature did not know where it was going, and was deeply anxious about what it might find when it got there. It was also, as Kate McLoughlin's concluding chapter suggests, distinctly weary. This is a poetic ending, an intimate examination of rhetorical tropes and faint traces of regenerative possibility and it leaves *Postwar* balanced – like the late 1950s themselves – on the edge of the new and chaotic proliferation of voices that is *British Literature in Transition 1960–1980: Flower Power*.

PART I

Aftermath: The Beginning or the End?

Introduction

The opening chapters of this section survey the territory of the postwar across the genres of fiction, poetry and drama, setting up questions, debates and lines of discussion that will resonate throughout the volume. In the case of Marina MacKay's examination of the austerity novel, they also create a vivid depiction of a newly denuded and disorientating world, in which 'pre-war material pleasures' emerge as a 'kind of phantom limb for the novel'. The end of war was not the end of wartime constraint, and in a world where words were perhaps the only unrationed commodity, MacKay reveals an unexpected refusal of verbal excess. Poetry mapped a different trajectory. As Nigel Alderman demonstrates, the Apocalyptic poets who rose to prominence in the early war years held nothing back, as if words alone – the power of symbol, metaphor, allegory and allusion – could save the self, if not the nation. Unlike the novelists explored by MacKay, however, they seldom manifested much in the way of a light comic touch. Yet these poets' concern with the organic, the rural and the sacred spoke to deep-rooted anxieties about modernity and the 'machine', a concern that – as Katie Gramich's later chapter confirms – often assumed a national dimension. Repeatedly, Celtic landscapes were figured as sites of resistance against the corruption of a fallen technocratic imperial England.

Yet this devolutionary trajectory is not the whole story and Alderman also exposes a poetry of retrospection evident in the realignments of established poets such as Eliot and Auden. The legacy of war also prompted, he notes, a crisis in elegiac conventions, a religious turn, an empirical turn and the first signs of fractures in poetic voice – the movement from impersonality to identity – that would find full expression in the 1960s. Here too is existentialism, a profound influence on a cadre of writers in the period, the echoes of which will resonate in later sections of this book. The translation of Sartre and Camus in the 1940s, and a potent Francophilia fed by magazines such as *Horizon*, speaks to the porous borders dividing British literature from its European and American others – and nowhere is this more evident than in the theatre. Here, as Rebecca D'Monté confirms, what changed the dramatic landscape was less the angry young man than a whole host of wartime initiatives and the long-term impact of such influential European theatre practitioners as Bertolt Brecht. D'Monté also explores transitions in theatrical subject matter, in particular a series of gradual transitions in what it was possible to express on the stage. The war had disrupted social and sexual practices, it had opened literal and metaphorical doors, and however powerful the postwar rhetoric of normativity might have been, transgressive desire could not easily be unlearned. These incremental transitions and the literature they generated will resonate throughout the diverse chapters comprising *Postwar*.

The strong vein of internationalism shaping poetry and drama also emerges in Chapter 4. Examining transitions in the writing of poets and novelists from Wales, Scotland and Northern Ireland, Katie Gramich exposes, on the one hand, a movement away from wartime British coalition towards a resurgent sense of national particularity, and on the other, a generational shift that would give rise to radical counter-cultural creativity. These new voices were often the product of exile, as a new generation turned away from the same 'national' traditions that had formed potent sites of resistance to colonial Englishness. Internationalism took different form, however, in popular writing. Here, Europe, rather than being a site of literary influence, became a backdrop for the adventures of the thriller hero and a space within which wartime risk could profitably be extended and enjoyed. This was a significant transition from the predominantly domestic conventions of interwar British crime fiction, and Chapter 5 explores what was at stake in the reinvention of the popular genre hero. Crime fiction had been the pre-eminent genre of the interwar years but, by the end of the 1950s, amateur detectives had been replaced by alienated veteran tough guys, policemen and spies. As these transitions in the construction of heroism demonstrate, remaking a generation of men 'damaged' by war was a major preoccupation of the period, but whether this was best achieved through the continuation of wartime homosocial structures (as in the police), or through the restoration of heteronormativity (the love of a good woman), was debatable. However, given the success of Ian Fleming's James Bond, who made his debut in 1953, returning women to an appropriately subordinate place would seem to have been a popular strategy for the reconstitution of the vulnerable male ego.

The final chapter of this section examines radio, a crucial technology of the war years that opened up new possibilities for literary practice – and for the broadcasting of previously unheard voices from the British nation and its empire. James Procter's chapter is included in this opening section, however, not for its chronological scope, but for its chronological disruptions. The main introduction discusses the 'magic numbers' that shape our understandings of literary periodisation, and just as the chapters of Alderman and D'Monté challenge the assumptions surrounding 1956, so Procter complicates the foundation myths of 1948. This is not to dispute the undoubted significance for British history of the arrival, in June 1948 at Tilbury Docks, of the *Empire Windrush*. Nearly 500 Jamaicans travelled to Britain on the ship, eager to capitalise on the British Nationality Act, which had extended citizenship to all members of the British Empire. Their arrival and consequent disillusionment with the limited conception of citizenship extended to them by the motherland is a now familiar story, seen to underpin the writing of the so-called 'Windrush generation'. Yet once again, a seemingly 'obvious' moment of transition is less stable than it seems, and Procter's essay, based on new research in the archives of the BBC, exposes the extent to which a West Indian literary culture invested in Britain, and its war, from the early 1940s.

As this introduction suggests, beginnings and endings were complexly imbricated in the poetry, prose and theatre emerging from Britain in the aftermath of war. Old voices sought new words, and new voices brought transformative possibilities to British culture and its literature. Aftermath, then, even when tinged with nostalgia, was far more of a beginning than an end.

CHAPTER I

Slender Means: The Novel in the Age of Austerity

Marina MacKay

Meat rationed, butter rationed, lard rationed, margarine rationed, sugar rationed, tea rationed, cheese rationed, jam rationed, eggs rationed, sweets rationed, soap rationed, clothes rationed. Make do and mend.
David Kynaston on 'Britain in 1945'[1]

Set between the surrender of Germany and the end of the war in the Far East, Muriel Spark's *The Girls of Slender Means* (1963) opens by announcing that '[l]ong ago in 1945 all the nice people in England were poor, allowing for exceptions'.[2] These economic conditions explain why the novel's climactic event is the theft of a gorgeous taffeta dress that stands in the minds of Spark's upper-middle-class 'girls' for a pre-war affluence wistfully remembered in a period of austerity with no end in sight. While her fatter friends await their deaths by fire in their burning hostel, slender Selina slips back in and out through a tiny window in order to salvage the famous dress – or to 'liberate' it, in that needy decade's eloquent euphemism for theft. This chapter argues that the British novel in this period when 'the nice people in England were poor' represents a highly distinctive body of fiction whose characteristic mood Spark captures in *The Girls of Slender Means* not only in her concern with middle-class material deprivation – ironically in the era of rationing, these girls are habitual dieters, with telling consequences for a novel about the survival of the thinnest – but also in her attention to linguistic excess. Surplus wordage proves as troublesome as superfluous physical flesh.

Spark might seem a special case given both her real-life interest in dieting and the insistence with which all her retrospective fiction about the austerity period links material and verbal bulk.[3] *A Far Cry from*

---

[1] David Kynaston, *Austerity Britain, 1945–1951* (London: Bloomsbury, 2008), p. 19.
[2] Muriel Spark, *The Girls of Slender Means* (London: Penguin, 1966 [1963]), p. 7.
[3] Spark wrote that hallucinations generated by the appetite-suppressant Dexedrine helped to create her first novel, *The Comforters* (1954). Muriel Spark, *Curriculum Vitae: A Volume of Autobiography* (London: Penguin, 1993), pp. 200–8.

Kensington (1988) is narrated by a formerly large woman whose nemesis is a hack writer she devastatingly nicknames the *'Pisseur de copie'* ('it means that he urinates frightful prose'): 'His writings writhed and ached with twists and turns and tergiversations, inept words, fanciful repetitions, far-fetched verbosity'.[4] The discipline with which this word-conscious publisher's assistant sheds half her weight by eating exactly half of every meal is virtually an allegory of the economical slenderness of Spark's prose. Fleur, in *Loitering with Intent* (1981), also set in the mid-century world of sugar-hoarding and petrol-snooping, notes 'how little one needs, in the art of writing, to convey the lot, and how a lot of words, on the other hand, can convey so little'.[5] Still, this is not the purely Sparkian obsession it might appear. The periphrastic excretions of the *pisseur de copie* are no far cry, as Spark would say, from the abundances mourned and feared in the period in which she began her career. One symptomatic text here is Elizabeth Taylor's first novel, *At Mrs Lippincote's* (1945), in which married couple Julia and Roddy become wartime tenants of a sickeningly over-furnished house, with a claustrophobic excess of drawers stuffed with another family's documentary memorabilia: 'We shall never make a home of this'.[6]

Yet in this period we would expect people to be irritated not by superfluity, but by a sense of need. Rationing had been introduced early in 1940, limiting access to butter, bacon and sugar in January and then meat soon afterwards. Such scarcity had been anticipated from the war's outset among those old enough to remember the home-front privations of the First World War. Within twenty-four hours of the war's outbreak, for example, middle-aged Mass-Observation diarist Nella Last ('Housewife, 49') describes her intention to divide her lawn into henhouses and potato plots, thinking back to the scarcities of the prior war.[7] Such self-sufficiency would prove essential not only for the six-year duration of hostilities, but also, dismayingly, for nine years afterwards. As late as 1950, rationing still applied to a range of staple foods including sugar and fats, and not until the summer of 1954, when restrictions were lifted on meat, could it be said that rationing was finally over. What was perhaps most depressing about the early postwar period was not that it felt so much like wartime, but that conditions were sometimes even worse. According to

---

[4] Muriel Spark, *A Far Cry from Kensington* (London: Penguin, 1989, [1988]), pp. 109, 46.
[5] Muriel Spark, *Loitering with Intent* (London: Virago, 2012), p. 60.
[6] Elizabeth Taylor, *At Mrs Lippincote's* (London: Virago, 2012), p. 13.
[7] Nella Last, *Nella Last's War: The Second World War Diaries of Housewife, 49*, Richard Broad and Suzie Fleming (eds) (London: Profile, 2006), p. 3. This diary entry is dated 4 September 1939, and on 13 May 1941, she recalls being 'dreadfully short in the last war – not only money but food' (p. 145).

Susan Cooper, writing in Michael Sissons's and Peter French's classic *Age of Austerity*, rations dropped 'well below the wartime average' by 1948, and even the loathed war-ersatz of powdered egg was mourned now that it was no longer easily obtained.[8] Necessities that had gone unrationed through the war's hungriest years became subject to restrictions, with bread rationed for the first time only in 1946, followed by potatoes, Britain's other indispensable starch, which were controlled in 1947. But, as evidenced by the endless governmental advice on making do with little, what wartime and afterwards always produced in abundance was text: directives, propaganda, posters and all the related verbal apparatus of conflict.[9] The 1940s state was nothing if not a *pisseur de copie*.

None of the decade's novelists wrote better than Patrick Hamilton about this historical juxtaposition of material absences with verbal excesses. Set in a boarding house in the winter of 1943 to 1944, *The Slaves of Solitude* (1947) catalogues the war's appropriations of what was once taken for granted:

> The war, while packing the public places tighter and tighter, was slowly, cleverly, month by month, week by week, day by day, emptying the shelves of the shops – sneaking cigarettes from the tobacconists, sweets from the confectioners, paper, pens, and envelopes from the stationers, fittings from the hardware stores, wool from the drapers, glycerine from the chemists, spirits and beer from the public-houses – while at the same time gradually removing crockery from the refreshment bars, railings from familiar places, means of transport from the streets, accommodation from the hotels, and sitting or even standing room from the trains. . . . The war, which had begun by making dramatic and drastic demands, which had held up the public in style like a highwayman, had now developed into a petty pilferer, incessantly pilfering.[10]

Even though it had always robbed its participants, in Hamilton's uncompromising metaphor, the war was initially experienced as a dramatic, even romantic affair as it 'held up the public in style, like a highwayman'; now it is a seedy kleptomaniac who pinches your things whenever your back is turned. The war infiltrates all corners of life, and nationwide governmental

---

[8] Susan Cooper, 'Snoek Piquante' in Michael Sissons and Philip French (eds), *Age of Austerity* (Oxford University Press, 1986), p. 25.

[9] Allison Carruth implies a parallel between political verbiage and literary economy in the US context when she notes that 'the most prolific printing presses and radio tickers in the United States during the 1940s were those funded by the Office of War Information' (p. 770), shortly after quoting Lorine Niedecker's 'What would they say if they knew / I sit for two months on six lines / of poetry?' (p. 769). Allison Carruth, 'War Rations and the Food Politics of Late Modernism' *Modernism/Modernity* (2009) 16(4) pp. 767–95.

[10] Patrick Hamilton, *The Slaves of Solitude* (New York: NYRB Classics, 2007), p. 101.

intrusions are mimicked domestically in the novel's boarding house by the heroine's overbearing German housemate Vicki Kugelmann (the virtuous protagonist Miss Roach agonises over the temptation to conflate Vicki's nastiness and her nationality).

But worse even than Vicki's thoughtlessly invasive habits of lolling uninvited on Miss Roach's bed and using her hairbrush without permission is her vacuous language; Vicki, like Miss Roach's other boarding-house enemy Mr Thwaites, speaks in a perversely irritating idiolect. Her dated verbiage drives almost literally insane the heroine, who is, like Spark's economy-minded Mrs Hawkins, a publisher's assistant who works with words for a living. Vicki's obsolete 1920s slang ("*Sporty*"! "*Sporty play*"! "*Sporty shot*"! "*Wizard shot*"!), along with bullying Mr Thwaites's pseudo-medievalisms ("And dost thou go forth this bonny morn ... into the highways and byways, to pay thy due respects to Good King Sol?"), are merely verbal tics and clichés, but the fastidiously articulate Miss Roach experiences them almost as physical injuries.[11] They, like Vicki's incursions upon her personal space, have their public counterpart in the verbose 'snubbing and nagging' of governmental directives:

> She was not to waste bread, she was not to use unnecessary fuel, she was not to leave litter about, she was not to telephone otherwise than briefly, she was not to take the journey she was taking unless it was really necessary, she was not to keep the money she earned through taking such journeys where she could spend it, but to put it into savings, and to keep on putting it into savings. She was not even to talk carelessly, lest she endangered the lives of others.[12]

Wartime poster slogans have been internalised so fully that they can be recited as if through free indirect discourse; they constitute a list of prohibitions so comprehensive that there is no longer inviolable space for people like Miss Roach, 'an ardent lover and pursuer of privacy'.[13] As Adam Piette has argued, fears about 'the destruction of privacy' are an important undercurrent in the literature of the Second World War, despite that public memory of the war rehearses instead the period's propagandistic emphasis on communality and solidarity.[14]

Perhaps it goes without saying that mid-century fiction's preoccupation with material scarcity often points to rather rarefied class perspectives, as

---

[11] Ibid., pp. 128, 65. [12] Ibid., p. 100. [13] Ibid., p. 91.
[14] Adam Piette, *Imagination at War: British Fiction and Poetry 1939–1945* (London: Papermac, 1995), p. 2.

Slender Means: The Novel in the Age of Austerity 41

with the faintly snobbish connotations of Miss Roach's characterisation of the war as a 'petty pilferer'. Nonetheless, there were also major mid-century novels about actual rather than relative poverty – poverty as a lived experience, that is, as distinct from the high-minded but occasionally touristic attention to socioeconomic deprivation in some literature of the 1930s – alongside a comic exasperation at the bureaucratisation of ordinary life in the era of the Welfare State. Moses Aloetta, the protagonist of Sam Selvon's *The Lonely Londoners* (1956), is a Trinidadian immigrant of a decade's standing who is perpetually recruited to help newer arrivals with their acculturation: 'Big City always confuse when he have forms to full up, and in the old Brit'n it have bags of that to do'.[15] *The Lonely Londoners* is set in the mid-1950s, but food is still always referred to in the novel as 'rations' and food cupboards are always kept locked; one of Moses's mordantly funny anecdotes records his friends eating urban pigeons and seagulls. The connection between poverty and racism is underlined when Moses's friend Galahad asks 'What it is we want that the white people and them find it so hard to give? A little work, a little food, a little place to sleep. We not asking for the sun, or the moon'.[16] Even so, Selvon also emphasises what West Indian immigrants have in common with their white working-class neighbours, the only other Londoners who, as Moses puts it, know all 'about hustling two pound of brussel sprout and half-pound potato, or queuing up for fish and chips in the smog'.[17]

Still, it has often been noted that working-class living conditions were materially improved in the 1940s, and that rationing had raised dietary standards well above the interwar norm. Historian Lizzie Collingham points to a closing gap between the working class and the well-to-do when she cites a wartime regional food officer who noted that 'while the poor had always had to struggle to come by food, the wealthy were, often for the first time in their lives, faced with the fact that they could not buy all the food that they wanted'.[18] At the other metropolitan social extreme from Selvon, and in keeping with the novel's concern with what it calls 'habitat', Elizabeth Bowen's *The Heat of the Day* (1949) is sharply attentive to the class implications of different styles of eating.[19] Protagonist Stella Rodney only ever eats in restaurants: in fact, no less than lobster mayonnaise is consumed at her dinner with the counterspy Robert Harrison.

---

[15] Sam Selvon, *The Lonely Londoners* (New York: Longman, 2007), p. 95.   [16] Ibid., p. 88.
[17] Ibid., p. 74.
[18] Lizzie Collingham, *The Taste of War: World War Two and the Battle for Food* (London: Penguin, 2012), p. 393.
[19] Elizabeth Bowen, *The Heat of the Day* (London: Vintage, 1998), p. 90.

And so it is not gentry like Stella who experience the war as deprivation, since her 'footloose habits of living, in and out of restaurants, had kept from her many of the realities of the home front', but women of several social degrees lower.[20] Attending the funeral of Francis, her ex-husband's cousin, Stella leaves London and sees for the first time the emptiness of the shops where 'the housewives had swarmed':

> A scale or two adhered to the fishmonger's marble slab; the pastrycook's glass shelves showed a range of interesting crumbs; the fruiterer filled a longstanding void with fans of cardboard bananas and a 'Dig for Victory' placard; the greengrocer's crates had been emptied of all but earth by those who had somehow failed to dig hard enough. The butcher flaunted unknown joints of purplish meat in the confidence that these could not be bought; the dairy restricted itself to a china cow; the grocer, with costless courage, kept intact his stocks of dummy cartons and tins. In the confectioner's windows the ribbons bleached on dummy boxes of chocolate among flyblown cut-outs of pre-war blondes. Newsagents without newspapers gave out in angry red chalk that they had no matches either.[21]

Underlining how her metropolitan 'habitat' with her lover Robert Kelway has become an ominously enclosed world it is only – but always – when Stella leaves London that she encounters wartime scarcities. Unwittingly, for example, she burns through the winter's stock of candles at Mount Morris, the 'Big House' her son has inherited from Francis, not realising that Ireland is also suffering from shortages. Most significantly for the spy plot, when Stella leaves London a third time to visit Kelway's family home, she discovers middle-class people who take pride in their disciplined performance under scarcity conditions. Robert's formidable, sinister mother proves to be a silent but scandalised judge of Stella's failure to bring her own butter ration to tea, and of her admission to drinking tea off the ration at work. Patrician Stella finds something suspect about this middle-class readiness to 'do' the war with such self-admiring civilian rectitude. (Just to damn them conclusively, such apparently patriotic virtues are ironically associated with the perverted development of the Nazi traitor Robert.)

Some novelists were attuned enough to the outraged social entitlement underpinning their complaints to find there the possibility of dark class comedy. In Henry Green's late modernist *Nothing* (1950) – an austerity title if ever there was one – the bright young things who populated Green's and his friend Evelyn Waugh's interwar fiction are now, in 1948, aging in

---

[20] Ibid., p. 111.   [21] Ibid., pp. 72–3.

an economic climate that they refuse to allow to change their habits. Thus, they continue to throw lavish 'twenty-firsters' for their children, even if hosting a party means flogging another heirloom from their depleted stock: 'So what is one to do?' asks the derelict beauty Jane Weatherby: 'Just go on in the old way until there's nothing left?'[22] Austerity is this novel's subject and also its main formal principle: *Nothing* takes the pared-down form of a series of dialogues among three couples whose members merely part and recombine in the course of the novel. Meanwhile, their old friend Arthur Morris is dying in the background, or, more precisely, dying by increments as a gangrenous toe becomes a gangrenous foot, which becomes a gangrenous leg and kills him, in a macabre comic symbol of both the lethal stagnancy of his once-privileged group and the process of attrition that they associate with the material depletions of the late 1940s.

Although his characters typically live at a lower social altitude than those of the aristocratic Conservative Green, his admirer Angus Wilson, beginning his career in the late 1940s, also reveals a sharp awareness of the class dynamics underpinning complaints against early postwar conditions. In 'The Wrong Set' (1949), the title story of Wilson's first collection, complaining about austerity is a way for insecure Vi, a working-class Tory of only marginal respectability, to claim higher social status by rehearsing standard middle-class laments about the Attlee administration:

> 'With this government you have to be grateful for the air you breathe. Look at the things we can't have – food, clothes, foreign travel'.
>
> 'Ah, yes, foreign travel', said Mrs Lippiatt, though she knew damn well Vi had never been abroad.[23]

The story hinges on the irony of what it means to be in 'the wrong set' because Vi uses the phrase about a student nephew succumbing to the influence of left-wing academics – 'the wrong set'. Meanwhile, Vi herself is very much in the wrong set: a nightclub hostess cohabiting with her squalid, scrounging lover, Trevor, for whom 'Jews and foreigners, the Labour Government and the Ballet' are collectively 'the ruin of England'.[24] If this story offers rather an oblique instance of how social class and austerity-whining intersect in the late 1940s – working-class Vi thinks that she will sound middle class if she complains about largely fabricated deprivations, while the story's authentic middle class cheerfully vote Labour off-stage, just like Wilson himself – other stories in the same collection are more straightforward. For example, the

---

[22] Henry Green, *Nothing; Doting; Blindness* (London: Penguin, 1993), p. 147.
[23] Angus Wilson, 'The Wrong Set' in *Collected Stories* (London: Penguin, 1992), p. 64.   [24] Ibid.

whimsically named Flopsy, a dependant of the insufferable, self-proclaimed 'crazy' Cockshott family in 'Crazy Crowd' (it is in keeping with the period's linguistic fastidiousness that such verbal self-definitions elicit Wilson's squeamish distaste), 'suspected that to get decent food it would soon be necessary to descend the [coal] mines, where she had no doubt that caviare and foie gras were being consumed hourly'.[25] Complaining about austerity has become a ready form of social bonding among the privileged: even in Rose Macaulay's *The World My Wilderness* (1949), a tortured drama of war-traumatised children and marital crisis, there is no middle-class social situation so awkward that unspoken antipathies cannot be surmounted by polite, neutral talk 'of the new government, of food difficulties, of the black market' among people who otherwise despise each other.[26]

Given the traditionally gendered nature of domestic economy, it is not surprising that austerity conditions appear in the work of the period's women novelists, but these writers are typically interested less in realist documentation of contemporary circumstances than in the symbolic meanings of 'doing without'. While Elizabeth Taylor's *A Wreath of Roses* (1949) is more about emotional rather than material deprivation, its setting during the period responsible for what the novel terms 'this evened-out England' allows it to reflect explicitly on how shortages have exacerbated class tensions.[27] Taylor's heroine Camilla contemplates how the equalising tendency of austerity has paradoxically created class antagonisms whereby a seemingly stoical but privately complaining middle class blame 'those who have less, that they themselves have not more'.[28] Also set in mid-century Middle England, Barbara Pym's comic novels also contemplate the 'social revolution in England ... the dynamics of culture change', as a character puts it in *Less than Angels* (1955): 'Of course one *does* want things to be shared more equally ... Provided one gets the larger share oneself'.[29]

Like the novels Spark set during those years, Pym's mid-century comedies capitalise wittily on the symbolic properties of austerity. Her famous 'excellent women' are undernourished in all sorts of ways, with their dreary string bags of 'something not very interesting for my supper', to quote a characteristically reticent aside from Mildred Lathbury in *Excellent Women* (1952), and their tendency to subordinate their needs to those of largely undeserving men.[30] When Mildred is believed in a later novel to

---

[25] Angus Wilson, 'Crazy Crowd' in *Collected Stories*, p. 82.
[26] Rose Macaulay, *The World My Wilderness* (London: The Book Club, 1949), p. 153.
[27] Elizabeth Taylor, *A Wreath of Roses* (Harmondsworth: Penguin, 1967), p. 87.   [28] Ibid., p. 88.
[29] Barbara Pym, *Less than Angels* (London: Virago, 2014), p. 79 (emphasis in the original).
[30] Barbara Pym, *Excellent Women* (London: Virago, 2013 [1952]), p. 147.

have married an 'anthropophagist' – she has married the wonderfully named anthropologist Everard Bone – the malapropism epitomises how Pym's undernourished women get served up to others.[31] Pursuing this equivalence of male entitlement and cannibalism, the promiscuous narcissist Fabian Driver in *Jane and Prudence* (1953) enjoys a lunch of 'a casserole of hearts', thanks to his enterprising woman cook – 'I believe he eats the hearts of his victims *en casserole*', writes Jane.[32] An empty larder sends Jane and her clergyman husband into the village for lunch:

> [The café owner] Mrs Crampton put in front of Jane a plate containing an egg, a rasher of bacon and some fried potatoes cut in fancy shapes, and in front of Nicholas a plate with *two* eggs and rather more potatoes.
>
> Nicholas exclaimed with pleasure.
> 'Oh, a man needs eggs!' said Mrs Crampton, also looking pleased.
>
> This insistence on a man's needs amused Jane. Men needed meat and eggs – well, yes, that might be allowed; but surely not more than women did?[33]

It helps to explain Pym's interest in the cultural meanings of consumption that she worked among the anthropologists of London's International Africa Institute, but her austerity-era characters are all simply longing for any remotely appealing food. One character regrets that Spam is no longer available as it was during the war; hot breakfasts are merely a remembered feature of 'novels about Edwardian country house parties'; and the pleasure of Prudence's restaurant date with handsome Fabian is diminished rather than enhanced by the need to pay attention to her consort as well as her food ('[t]he chicken will have that wonderful sauce with it, thought Prudence, looking into Fabian's eyes').[34] In *Excellent Women*, characters have forgotten the taste of real as opposed to 'mock' cream ('might be like the top of the milk?'[35]), a single woman can make a tin of baked beans last two dinners, and the Corner House restaurant offers only scrambled eggs (powdered) and whale curry. Small wonder, then, that vicar's daughter Mildred consoles herself nightly with 'the most comforting bed-side reading': not devotional works, but cookbooks.[36]

---

[31] Barbara Pym, *Jane and Prudence* (London: Virago, 2013 [1953]), p. 134. [32] Ibid., pp. 30, 44.
[33] Ibid., p. 49.   [34] Ibid., pp. 147, 93, 106.
[35] Pym, *Excellent Women*, p. 43. Collingham reports that 'mock cream' could be made by mixing a little fresh milk with margarine, sugar, and dried milk powder, but '[i]t would probably have been better just to do without cream' (Collingham, *The Taste of War*, p. 392).
[36] Ibid., p. 19.

Not all comic novelists of the period shared Pym's lightness of touch in exploiting austerity as a way to investigate social relations. Probably because of her 'enormous postwar vogue', in David Pryce-Jones's words, Angela Thirkell makes appearances in the major histories of austerity, although David Kynaston's otherwise equable survey of the period coins the telling verb 'shrilling on' to describe her fiction.[37] Thirkell's *Love among the Ruins* (1948) is set shortly after the war, and the gentry who populate her novels are now 'the underfed shivering people of England'.[38] In this representative passage, Mrs Belton lies awake dreading the following day's packed schedule of the Women's Institute, the Deanery and Lady Fielding:

> In which she was only behaving like most other people who had taken six years of war with uncomplaining courage and were now being starved, regimented, and generally ground down by their present rulers, besides the deep hidden shame of feeling that England's name had been lowered in the eyes of all lesser breeds.
>
> This condition was so widespread in England that people had to recognize it and to try rather unsuccessfully to laugh themselves into a happier state of mind; but it was not easy to keep it up. Sleep that did not refresh, the endless struggle to get food and clothes, and the nastiness of the food and the clothes when you got them, the gradual disappearance from the shops of everything except horrible fancy articles made of plastics, the surging crowds of foreigners everywhere, the endless waits at the Food Office and the Fuel Office; the overcrowded buses and trains, the daily humiliation of one's country and oneself, the gradual decay of houses and gardens for want of labour and materials, the increasing difficulty of finding anywhere to live when the Government stopped building plans, the increasing inquisitioned prying of officials into private affairs, were all bringing people into a state of dull resentful apathy with no hope of relief.[39]

If it is initially tempting to seek irony in the discourse of national humiliation and Britain's diminished prestige 'in the eyes of all lesser breeds', the pursuit is cut short by the narrator's readiness to generalise the perspective of Mrs Belton into a 'widespread' one; indeed, not just a widespread perspective, but a widespread *condition*. Thirkell's inventory of ways in which the country has gone to the dogs (all those foreigners!) suggests that Mrs Belton's view is perfectly reasonable. A dispirited 1940s audience is asked to sympathise with Mrs Belton, and, although it is easy to imagine

---

[37] David Pryce-Jones, 'Towards the Cocktail Party: The Conservation of Post-War Writing', in Sissons and French, *Age of Austerity*, p. 202; Kynaston, *Austerity Britain*, p. 121.
[38] Angela Thirkell, *Love among the Ruins* (Wakefield, RI: Moyer Bell, 1997 [1948]), p. 41.
[39] Ibid., pp. 155–6.

the toll taken by drab, exasperating years of makeshift, Thirkell solicits that identification through a degree of rhetorical inflation that rather strains the later reader's sympathies.

Although writing from an even more privileged perspective, her fellow comic novelist Nancy Mitford captured more engagingly the same elegiac appetite for luxury in her early postwar fiction. James Lees-Milne's memoir attributes to Mitford a wartime joke at the expense of both her aristocratic friend Henry Green and the hungry reading public when she affected to lament that he had written about ordinary working people in his Blitz novel, *Caught* (1943), because 'if only Henry had spelt the title *Court* and written about royalty and the aristocracy instead of firemen the novel would, in those days of austerity when everyone pounced upon books recalling glamour and glitter, have sold like hot cakes'.[40] Seen in this light, it is noteworthy that the austerity years produced the semi-autobiographical aristocratic fiction for which she is best known, the superlatively funny *The Pursuit of Love* (1945) and *Love in a Cold Climate* (1949); but it is more noteworthy still that these novels should refuse to attribute to the pre-war British past the luxury so conspicuously absent from its present. Indeed, the memorable interwar scene in which the Radlett sisters come out at their makeshift debutante ball sees the girls shivering by the stinking gas heaters in their dowdy and inept home-made gowns; to the extent that there is wishful excess, it comes in the camp and fantastical form of the painted pigeons and bejewelled whippets of the Radletts's eccentric gay neighbour Lord Merlin or the fairy-tale transformation of Linda, two disastrous marriages later, at the hands of a French aristocrat.

The obvious contrast with Mitford's alternately deflationary and outlandish treatment of pre-war affluence is her friend Waugh's *Brideshead Revisited* (1945), which, along with George Orwell's *Nineteen Eighty-Four* (1949), is a rare instance of an unquestionably canonical 1940s British novel. Famously, the wartime gluttony Waugh later identified in the novel's lavish descriptions of food and wine is mimicked by a superfluity on the level of the prose, in a marked departure from the pared-down narration of Waugh's interwar fiction. The novel supports eloquently Paul Fussell's argument in his study of the Second World War that linguistic luxury served as orally fixated 'compensation' for the period's culinary drabness: 'the rich sauces of Churchill's oratory and the over-ripe poems of Edith Sitwell and Dylan Thomas, the toothsome luxury of Osbert Sitwell's

---

[40] James Lees-Milne, *Fourteen Friends* (London: John Murray, 1996), p. 123.

sinuous sentences'.[41] Waugh himself made a similar (and self-mocking) point in the *Sword of Honour* trilogy (1952–61), in which a character writes a 'very gorgeous, almost gaudy' novel called *The Death Wish*:

> But it was not an old-fashioned book. Had he known it, half a dozen English writers, averting themselves sickly from privations of war and apprehensions of the social consequences of the peace, were even then … composing or preparing to compose books which would turn from the drab alleys of the thirties into the odorous gardens of a recent past transformed and illuminated by disordered memory and imagination.[42]

This is *Brideshead Revisited* to the life, but only half the story of the early postwar period. *Nineteen Eighty-Four*, that other classic of the decade, could hardly be more different, with Orwell's bare, functional prose enacting at the level of style a depleted world of crumbling flats and gut-rot Victory gin. As described in passages that could come from many austerity-set novels, something is always lacking: 'Sometimes it was buttons; sometimes it was darning wool, sometimes it was shoelaces; at present it was razor blades'; and it is difficult to remember that life was ever different: 'there had never been quite enough to eat, one had never had socks or underclothes that were not full of holes, furniture had always been battered and rickety, rooms underheated, Tube trains crowded, houses falling to pieces, bread dark-coloured, tea a rarity, coffee filthy-tasting, cigarettes insufficient'.[43] Writing in the 1950s, Irving Howe defended Orwell's prose from accusations that it was 'drab or uninspired', on the grounds that its 'gritty and hammering factuality' is inherent to the novel's argument about a world in which 'delicacies of phrasing or displays of rhetoric come to seem frivolous'.[44] Orwell offers an obvious contrast to *Brideshead Revisited*'s famously plush prose. But what both novels symptomatically share is their sense that the body retains a wordless memory of what is now missing: 'the mute protest in your own bones, the instinctive feeling that the conditions you lived in were intolerable and that at some other time they must have been different'.[45]

In keeping with the idea that pre-war material pleasures have become a kind of phantom limb for the 1940s novel, Green's *Back* (1946), casts the

---

[41] Paul Fussell, *Wartime: Understanding and Behavior in the Second World War* (New York: Oxford University Press, 1989), p. 209.
[42] Evelyn Waugh, *Sword of Honour* (New York: Knopf, 1994), pp. 658–9. The trilogy comprises *Men at Arms* (1952), *Officers and Gentlemen* (1955), and – the novel in which this nostalgic fiction appears – *Unconditional Surrender* (1961).
[43] George Orwell, *Nineteen Eighty-Four* (New York: Signet, 1977), pp. 49, 59–60.
[44] Irving Howe, *Politics and the Novel* (New York: Horizon, 1957), p. 237. [45] Ibid., p. 73.

difference between pre-war and postwar as a literal amputation. Just as Arthur Morris's gangrenous foot in *Nothing* speaks to the atrophying of his *rentier* class, shell-shocked Charley Summers in *Back* has been repatriated from a German prison camp with an artificial leg and cannot understand the England through which he limps bewildered. This is the incomprehensible austerity world of clothing coupons as well as food rationing, and it is through the metaphor of dress that Green renders Charley's predicament as a displaced veteran, for Charley has no civilian clothes other than a suit he had paid for before the war and which his tailor laid aside for him when he was taken prisoner. Symbolically, the reclaimed suit fits oddly upon his return, and makes conspicuous rather than conceals his prosthetic leg. However, Charley's increasingly animated pursuit of clothing coupons in the course of the novel suggests the possibility of change. Like the pre-war suit in the tailor's storeroom, Charley has been suspended in a form of limbo, and jettisoning these old clothes may imply that he is ready to give up his pathological efforts to re-inhabit a former life that ended with the war.

Given that clothes rationing continued until 1949, it is not altogether surprising that the decade's fiction is so preoccupied by dress, the preoccupation Spark recalls by putting a hand-me-down frock at the centre of *The Girls of Slender Means*. Perhaps we might see some parable of austerity's democratising tendency in King George VI's plea that Attlee raise the clothing allowance, for 'We must *all* have new clothes – my family is down to the lowest ebb'.[46] What is most surprising, though, is how emphatically new clothes get associated with positive transformation, even with social optimism. That the demobilisation suit could symbolise a new way of life is explicit in the very title of J. B. Priestley's *Three Men in New Suits* (1945). Three men from completely different classes go through the war together and have their perspectives profoundly changed by the experience, most consequentially in the case of upper-class Alan Strete, who reaches the view that the miserable social inequality of the interwar period must not survive the war. Here, the men's identical demobilisation suits visibly dramatise Britain's democratic aspirations. Old clothes, in contrast, are among Pym's comic staples. A jumble sale scrum in *Excellent Women* means that Mildred's second-hand clothes stall swiftly sells out, leaving only the shabby relics of bygone luxury: an 'old velvet coat trimmed with

---

[46] Anthony Howard, '"We Are the Masters Now": The General Election of July 5th, 1945' in Sissons and French, *Age of Austerity*, p. 13 (emphasis in the original).

moth-eaten white rabbit, a soiled pink georgette evening dress of the nineteen-twenties trimmed with bead embroidery, a mangy fur with mad staring eyes priced at sixpence – these things were "regulars" and nobody ever bought them'.[47] When the excellent women tackle the wardrobe of Fabian Driver's deceased wife in *Jane and Prudence*, the lady companion Miss Morrow silently eyes up a few pre-war items for herself, even though she and the others are supposed to be dividing Mrs Driver's clothes for charitable purposes. In a question that could only ever be asked in a Pym novel, a character wonders: 'On what principle are we to sort out these things? Distressed gentlewomen and jumble? Or should there be more and subtler distinctions?'[48]

Spark's fiction refers often to (literally) no-frills 'Utility' clothes: characters in *The Girls of Slender Means* remove 'the utility stamp, two half-moons facing the same way' from the inside of their dresses, while Fleur from *Loitering with Intent* recalls that even people who could afford to buy grander clothes with coupons still spend theirs on 'the People's garment ... Utility, bestowing upon it, I noticed, the inevitable phrase, "perfectly alright"'.[49] 'I have always been on the listen-in for those sort of phrases', Fleur explains, with all her period's acuity about linguistic cliché, and 'perfectly alright' returns in the novel to describe the government-issued clothes that marked soldiers' return into civilian life: 'Wally described in detail the range and styles of demob suits. He himself had taken a tweed coat and flannel trousers. "Perfectly all right", said Wally'.[50]

If British food was terrible and the national outlook bleak, at least the demobilisation suit was 'perfectly all right'. The Second World War trilogy within Anthony Powell's *A Dance to the Music of Time* (1951–75) concludes with the narrator Nick Jenkins meeting in an army demob store his old friend Archie Gilbert, formerly famous as '"spare man" par excellence' for interwar hostesses and, even in those elegant days, an object of universal admiration for his perfect comportment and flawless evening dress.[51] While it is reductive to cast *A Dance to the Music of Time* purely as a work about the socially elite, it is fair to say that the general approval there of the demob wardrobe is both surprising and funny. In the closing words of the final war novel, Archie and Nick agree that they will take 'everything ...

---

[47] Pym, *Excellent Women*, p. 68.   [48] Pym, *Jane and Prudence*, p. 113.
[49] Spark, *The Girls of Slender Means*, p. 96; Spark, *Loitering with Intent*, p. 6.
[50] Spark, *Loitering with Intent*, p. 150.
[51] Anthony Powell, *The Military Philosophers, A Dance to the Music of Time, Third Movement* (University of Chicago Press, 1995), p. 243. The war trilogy or 'movement' consists of *The Valley of Bones* (1964), *The Soldier's Art* (1966) and *The Military Philosophers* (1968).

except the underclothes'.[52] Perhaps Powell's upper-class sangfroid reflects the retrospective assurance that the British class order was robust enough to absorb the social shocks of 1945, but, more generally, one of the most likeable aspects of Powell's sequence is precisely this kind of comic equanimity. In Powell's broad and humane perspective, it is hardly a tragedy that war reduces immaculate Archie Gilbert to rummaging happily for ties in a demob warehouse, and Powell refuses to treat it as anything other than one of the amusing contingencies of the age.

From the literary point of view, then, austerity had its generative side. This was especially true for writers with comic and ironic sensibilities, which may explain why Spark kept returning to this period for decades. Indeed, perhaps Philip Larkin's famous witticism that 'deprivation is for me what daffodils were for Wordsworth' might be extended to cover the literature of the early postwar period more generally.[53] Appropriately, Larkin's own two novels emerged in the age of austerity: in *Jill* (1946), a lonely undergraduate in wartime Oxford fantasises into life a soulmate to soothe his feelings of class displacement; in *A Girl in Winter* (1947), a friendless foreign refugee comes to embrace her isolation by abandoning an illusory love for a man whom she realises she barely knew to start with. In both novels, 'doing without' in the 1940s serves as a material correlative to the less tangible problem of recognising and renouncing unmet emotional needs. Such austere interests would outlive Larkin's brief career as a novelist. Written in the year in which rationing finally ended in Britain, the poem 'Continuing to Live' (1954) summed life up with characteristically deflationary economy as a 'habit formed to get necessaries'.[54] Continuing to live is, Larkin concludes, 'nearly always losing, or going without. / It varies'.[55]

---

[52] Ibid., p. 244.
[53] Philip Larkin, 'An Interview with the *Observer*' in *Required Writing: Miscellaneous Pieces, 1955–1982* (London: Faber, 1983), p. 47.
[54] Philip Larkin, 'Continuing to Live' in Anthony Thwaite (ed.), *Collected Poems* (New York: Farrar, Straus & Giroux and The Marvell Press, 1989), p. 94.
[55] Ibid.

CHAPTER 2

Impossible Elegies: Poetry in Transition 1940–1960
Nigel Alderman

The dominant literary history of the poetry of the immediate postwar period begins with the publication of Robert Conquest's *New Lines* in 1956 and the corresponding emergence of Philip Larkin as the paradigmatic voice of postwar England, alongside the naming and consolidation of the Movement. As critics – most influentially Andrew Crozier – have noted, this has led to the dominance of a particular poetics based upon 'the enunciation ... of an empirical subject' in which figurative language is generally used to emphasise the empirical reality of the everyday world and to ironise attempts to transcend, question or subvert such a world.[1] Indeed, the dominance of this poetics has been such that it has often been termed the 'mainstream', from which all other poetics deviate.[2] In such literary histories the poetry of the 1940s and early 1950s has not only been subsumed under the term 'New Romantics' or 'New Apocalyptics', for which the poetry of Dylan Thomas has stood as exemplary, but has also been discredited using, in John Goodby's words, the same 'Movement stereotypes of a dire decade dominated by drunken Fitzrovian draft-dodgers and third-rate hysterical versifiers'.[3] Indeed, in such histories, the poetry written in the immediate aftermath of the Second World War has been virtually removed from belonging to the term 'postwar.' Although the more recent reassessment by critics such as Goodby, James Keery, and Tony Lopez of this period's non-Movement poetry has been persuasive, it has a tendency to be as polemical as the dominant literary history it seeks to overturn; more often than not it reverses and

---

[1] Andrew Crozier, 'Resting on Laurels' in Alistair Davies and Alan Sinfield (eds), *British Culture of the Postwar: An Introduction to Literature and Society, 1945–1999* (London: Routledge, 2000), p. 193. See also Stephen Burt, 'The Movement and the Mainstream' in Nigel Alderman and C. D. Blanton (eds), *Concise Companion to Postwar British and Irish Poetry* (Oxford: Wiley-Blackwell, 2009), pp. 32–50; and Neil Corcoran, *English Poetry since 1940* (London: Longman, 1993), pp. 82–3.
[2] Burt, 'The Movement and the Mainstream', pp. 46–9.
[3] John Goodby, 'Dylan Thomas and the Poetry of the 1940s' in Michael O'Neill (ed.), *The Cambridge History of English Poetry* (Cambridge University Press, 2010), p. 860.

Impossible Elegies: Poetry in Transition 1940–1960

transvalues the same terms.[4] If Movement poetics values the centered self, denotation, and figurative language that gives preference to the referential, then this poetics values the decentered self, connotation, and figurative language that gives preference to figuration itself.

In *A Singular Modernity*, Fredric Jameson assesses the historical moment between the emergence of the high moderns in the first two decades of the twentieth-century and their institutionalisation in the Anglo-American Academy in the 1950s and 1960s, and, in so doing, argues that periodisation is a necessary foundational move for understanding itself ('we cannot not periodize'), and yet at the same time, as he shows with the concept of modernity, the point at which periodisation begins and ends provides different meanings to the same events and objects.[5] Is Dylan Thomas, for example, best seen as the continuation and development of a modernist and surrealist poetics that turns from a transnational and metropolitan focus to a regional and pastoral one, or is he best seen as a revival and extension of romantic poetics with its emphasis on the quest romance and on the exploration of the sacred in a post-Christian world? Similarly, *New Lines* provides a persuasive beginning because it appears in the same year as *Look Back in Anger*, the Suez crisis and the Soviet invasion of Hungary. The fact of 1956, in other words, over-determines the question of poetry's relationship not only to other artistic and media forms, but also to larger historic contexts.

The dates of 1940 to 1960 highlight the difficulty of a larger historical periodisation and, perhaps, emphasise that these twenty years were a time of transition or, more specifically, a moment where, in Raymond Williams's terms, the lines between dominant, residual and emergent cultures became less clear-cut.[6] In social, economic and political terms, it is the period where what Alan Sinfield calls 'welfare-capitalism' becomes dominant, with Keynesian economic policies replacing classical liberal ones, and with an expansion of the state into all areas of public and private life.[7] It is also the period where the European empires are mostly dismantled and global economic and political ascendancy is primarily contested between the United States and the Soviet Union. It is the time that

---

[4] Ibid., pp. 858–78; James Keery, 'The Burning Baby and the Bathwater' *PN Review 150* (2003) 29(4) pp. 58–62; and Tony Lopez, *The Poetry of W. S. Graham* (Edinburgh University Press, 1989), pp. 1–25.
[5] Fredric Jameson, *A Singular Modernity: Essay on the Ontology of the Present* (London: Verso, 2002), p. 29.
[6] Raymond Williams, *Marxism and Literature* (Oxford University Press, 1977), pp. 121–7.
[7] Alan Sinfield, *Literature, Politics and Culture in Postwar Britain* (Berkeley and Los Angeles, CA: University of California Press, 2004), pp. 16–18.

not only heralds the dominance of a consumer culture with a massive expansion of commodities and purchasing power, but also signals the exponential increase in white-collar occupations and the service economy. Finally, it heralds the beginning of increasing postwar immigration from the former colonies, signalled by the arrival of the *Empire Windrush* in 1948. The words 'emergent', 'becomes dominant', 'heralds' and 'signals' are crucial here, indicating a world in the process of developing, but not yet fully formed. Rationing, for example, does not end until 1954 and there are only strong intimations of a fully blown youth culture. Revealingly, David Kynaston's chronological division of his magisterial history of postwar Britain distinguishes 1945–51 (*Austerity Britain*), 1951–57 (*Family Britain*) and 1957–62 (*Modernity Britain*).

Aside from the difficulty of connecting the poetry of 1940 to 1960 to this larger, transitional socio-historical context, the era resists the usual methods of literary historical periodisation. In contrast to the 1930s, the 1950s or the 1960s, the 1940s do not fall easily into the structure of a decade, perhaps because the first half is taken up by the Second World War. There also remains the question of how to interpret poets in relation to their own individual careers: how do we calibrate the writing during the period of older poets such as W. H. Auden, T. S. Eliot, David Jones, Ezra Pound and Stevie Smith in relation to their earlier work and the writing of younger poets such as W. S. Graham, Thom Gunn, Ted Hughes, Elizabeth Jennings and Philip Larkin in relation to their later work? In addition, there is a gap in time between the writing of a poem, its initial publication, its serial publications (in a magazine, a slim volume, an anthology and so on) and its dissemination into the wider currency of the literary world. Thom Gunn, for example, was published in *New Lines*, but became closely associated with Ted Hughes and the poetry of the 1960s because Faber published a joint selected edition that sold well.[8] In a similar disruption of conventional categorisation, it is worth noting that Ted Hughes's first two books, *Hawk in the Rain* (1957) and *Lupercal* (1960), were also written in the 1950s.

Indeed, poets and poems always have a complex relationship with the poetry of the past, the poetry of the immediate past and the poetry of the present – all of which is mediated through an overdetermined multiplicity of contexts (familial, psychological, educational, social, historical, literary and so on). Philip Larkin himself highlights an aspect of this in his 1966 'Introduction' to the republication of his slim 1945 volume, *The North Ship*:

---

[8] Burt, 'The Movement and the Mainstream', p. 42.

> Looking back, I find in the poems not one abandoned self but several – the ex-schoolboy, for whom Auden was the only alternative to 'old-fashioned' poetry; the undergraduate, whose work a friend affably characterized as 'Dylan Thomas, but you've a sentimentality that's all your own'; and the immediate post-Oxford Self, isolated in Shropshire with a complete Yeats stolen from the local girls' school. The search for a style was merely one aspect of a general immaturity.[9]

Auden, Thomas and Yeats are not here simply part of Larkin's context or horizon, but make their marks within the style of his poems themselves. Also, characteristically of Movement criticism, Larkin locates his previously discarded styles as signs of immaturity and effeminacy – Auden the ex-schoolboy, Thomas the sentimentalist, Yeats the poet of schoolgirls – in favour of a putatively, mature, plain-speaking, heterosexual masculinity.[10] Revealingly, at the end of the 'Introduction', he folds this into national allegory as he concludes the 'Celtic fever abated'.[11]

Equally typical of the period, and not just of Larkin or the Movement, is Larkin's historicising and periodising. Obviously, the war itself provides a dominant way of thinking about a break with the past. The previous decades become the interwar period – often seen as a brief, failed parenthesis between two wars – and the period's poets often look back at their immediate predecessors to take stock of their attainments and failures. Eliot himself in the *Four Quartets* (1943) measures and judges his generation's poetic and cultural projects, most notably in the second part of *Little Gidding* (1942) where, in the aftermath of a bombing raid, he encounters in the London streets 'a familiar compound ghost' made up of not only Eliot's younger self, but also Yeats and Pound.[12] In the Dante-esque dialogue that ensues, Eliot and his interlocutor confront their various failures, in particular their attempt 'to purify the dialect of the tribe'. As the ghost departs, he leaves Eliot with 'the rending pain of re-enactment':

> Of all that you have done, and been; the shame
> Of motives late revealed, and the awareness
> Of things ill done and done to others' harm
> Which once you took for exercise of virtue.[13]

---

[9] Philip Larkin, *The North Ship*, rev. edn (London: Faber & Faber, 1966), p. 8.
[10] See Praseeda Gopinath, '"One of Those Old-Type Natural Fouled-Up Guys": The Belated Englishman in Philip Larkin's poetry' *Textual Practice* (2009) 23(3) pp. 373–96.
[11] Larkin, *The North Ship*, p. 10.
[12] For the allusion, see T. S. Eliot, *The Poems of T. S. Eliot*, in Christopher Ricks and Jim McCue (eds) (Baltimore, MD: Johns Hopkins University Press, 2016), vol. 1, p. 1012.
[13] Eliot, *The Poems of T. S. Eliot*, vol. 1, p. 205.

Eliot's poem, then, rejects both his own, earlier larger cultural projects and those of his modernist contemporaries and ends with a retrenchment to a moment prior to the English Civil War, but after the English Reformation, a moment when the international ideology of Christianity had transformed into a national myth of an English Church with the monarch as its head. This moment, in turn, envelopes and collapses the particular moment of the poem's writing (after the fall of France, but before the attack on Pearl Harbour) into a single, immanent present: 'So, while the light fails / On a winter's afternoon, in a secluded chapel / History is now and England.'[14]

Crucially, *Little Gidding* ends gesturing towards the elegy and the elegiac mode, claiming, 'every poem and every sentence is an end and a beginning, / Every poem an epitaph'.[15] Auden, similarly, turns to the elegy in his own weighing of his poetic and historical past, most notably in his 'In Memory of W. B. Yeats' (1939). If Eliot excuses his and his contemporaries' words and actions by emphasising their failure, then Auden forgives Yeats by firstly locating his work within the realm of individual psychology: 'Mad Ireland', he claims, 'hurt you into poetry'.[16] In the poem, Yeats's primary political and historical context and provocation – Ireland itself – becomes personified and Yeats's poetry is seen not as a response to outside public matters, but rather as emerging from an inner psychological wound. Secondly, Auden pardons Yeats by removing Yeats's poetry (and indeed poetry itself) from any social or political action, claiming, 'poetry makes nothing happen'.[17] Both Eliot with his assertion of failure and Auden with his claim of inefficacy are symptomatic of a process in which numerous writers sought to negotiate the increasingly troubling relationship between modernist poetics and totalitarian, especially fascist, politics. Indeed, in 1952, Donald Davie famously asserted that 'the development from imagism in poetry to fascism in politics is clear and unbroken'.[18] The idea of the autonomy of art that both Eliot and Auden reach for in these poems becomes increasingly commonplace in the immediate postwar period, especially with the influence of New Criticism, and helps elide the disquieting cultural projects of writers such as Yeats, Pound, Lawrence and Eliot himself.

---

[14] Eliot, *The Poems of T. S. Eliot*, vol. 1, p. 208. Eliot sent these lines in what he calls the 'first draft for consideration' of 'Little Gidding' to John Hayward on 7 July 1941. For the details of the various drafts, see Helen Gardner, *The Composition of the Four Quartets* (New York: Oxford University Press, 1978), pp. 154–224; and Eliot, *The Poems of T. S. Eliot*, vol. 1, pp. 883–90.
[15] Eliot, *The Poems of T. S. Eliot*, vol. 1, p. 208.
[16] W. H. Auden, *Collected Poems*, ed. Edward Mendelson (New York: Vintage Books, 1991), p. 246.
[17] Auden, *Collected Poems*, p. 246.
[18] Donald Davie, *Purity of Diction in English Verse* (London: Chatto & Windus, 1952), p. 99.

Both Eliot and Auden use the elegy or the elegiac to revise the literary past and indeed the poetry of 1940 to 1960 is littered with elegies, many of which reveal what Jahan Ramazani argues distinguishes modern elegy: a refusal of mourning and a confrontation with anonymous death, mass death or the death of a seemingly socially unimportant person.[19] Obviously, the brute fact of the Second World War, with its military killing fields, its mass civilian bombing and its genocidal exterminations, has an impact upon the content of poetry in both the war and the war's aftermath. The traditional recuperative move of the conventional elegy, in which the poem culminates by offering itself as some form of compensatory mechanism by which, and through which, successful mourning can be achieved, no longer seems available, indeed seems perhaps specious to many poets. In his still-astonishing 1946 slim volume, *Deaths and Entrances*, Dylan Thomas writes a number of what Goodby calls 'Blitz elegies' in which he explores the desire for some greater ceremonial meaning to individual death when it disappears into mass fatalities.[20] In poems such as 'A Refusal to Mourn the Death, by Fire, of a Child in London', 'Deaths and Entrances' and 'Ceremony after a Fire Raid', Thomas's language uneasily generates a polysemy that, as Steve Vine observes, 'compounds irony with affirmation'.[21] In other words, Thomas's use of ambiguity in both individual words and syntax often generates an interpretive impasse since, on the one hand, the poems seem to proclaim the impossibility, indeed the meretriciousness, of finding some form of greater, regenerative meaning – poetic or sacred – in individual deaths, while on the other, they conclude by gesturing towards a cyclical, fertile and organic plenitude. As Goodby argues, 'a myth of organic community is raised, but qualified by the possible failure of symbolic reparation – of language itself – in the face of Total War'.[22]

'Ceremony after a Fire Raid', for example, finishes by alluding to the older sexual pun of 'die' in order to figure sexuality as the reproductive action of the 'masses of the infant-bearing sea' that ends with them 'utter-[ing] for ever / Glory glory glory / The sundering ultimate kingdom of genesis' thunder'.[23] At one level, Thomas's language reuses Christianity to

---

[19] Jahan Ramazani, *Poetry of Mourning: The Modern Elegy from Hardy to Heaney* (University of Chicago Press, 1994), pp. 1–22.
[20] Goodby, 'Dylan Thomas and the Poetry of the 1940s', pp. 864–6.
[21] Steve Vine, '"Shot from the Locks": Poetry, Mourning, Deaths and Entrances' in John Goodby and Chris Wigginton (eds), *Dylan Thomas: New Casebooks* (London: Palgrave, 2001), p. 140.
[22] Goodby, 'Dylan Thomas and the poetry of the 1940s', p. 866.
[23] Dylan Thomas, *The Collected Poems of Dylan Thomas: The New Centenary Edition*, ed. John Goodby (London: Weidenfeld & Nicolson, 2014), p. 144. For the classic formulation on the sexual pun on

assert an organic and sexual eschatology of regeneration. On another level, the language subverts this assertion because this moment of seemingly fertile reproduction and regeneration takes the form not only of speech ('utter') rather than action, but also of speech that instead of heralding the everlasting nature of procreation, in fact reveals its endless 'sundering'. The difficulty of such elegiac occasions is explicitly thematised in 'A Refusal to Mourn the Death, by Fire, of a Child in London', where Thomas declares he will neither 'murder' nor 'blaspheme' the child's death by writing 'any further / Elegy of innocence and youth'. Despite this disavowal in the first three stanzas, the fourth and final stanza motions towards some form of reparation when the child is first called 'London's daughter' and then emerges 'robed in ... / ... the dark veins of her mother'. As such, she moves from being particular and singular, to being representative and symbolic. The poem ends, however, by returning to its initial renunciation by revealing that the child's representative and symbolic nature arises precisely because her death is particular and singular: 'After the first death, there is no other.'[24] All the elegy can do then is emphasise the singularity of individual death and renounce the possibility of regeneration.

If Thomas's poems seem emblematic of the immediate challenge to poetry presented by the events of the Second World War, Geoffrey Hill's first collection, *For the Unfallen* (1959), reveals a later, more measured, but equally conflicted confrontation with the impossibility of elegy and displays a similarly ornate rhetoric. *For the Unfallen* announces many of the concerns that preoccupied Hill throughout his career. The poems investigate the ethical position of the poet/observer who seeks to address unethical acts, the relationship between historical violence (in particular the Holocaust) and the representation of such violence, and the continuing power of the sacred, especially Christianity, as past tradition and as present possibility. They also introduce what becomes Hill's distinctive use of etymology, allusion, polysemy and ambiguity as markers of his thematic concerns. *For the Unfallen* contains numerous elegies or elegiac poems. Notably, 'The Distant Fury of Battle' begins by specifically taking to task the pastoral elegy's recuperative and compensatory claim that the renewal of the natural world can signify the fact, or at least the figurative possibility, of rebirth: 'Grass resurrects to mask, to strangle, / Words glossed on stone,

---

'die', see Cleanth Brooks in *The Well-Wrought Urn* (New York: Harcourt, Brace, Jovanovich, 1957), p. 16.
[24] Thomas, *The Collected Poems of Dylan Thomas*, pp. 172–3.

lopped stone-angel.'[25] In the conventions of pastoral elegy, organic growth becomes symbolically connected to the dead and to the words of the poet, words that metaphorically spring forth to create the poem itself. Here, however, the grass's resurrection destroys the representations both of the dead and for the dead. The long lyric sequence, 'Of Commerce and Society', elegises, in turn, the idea and ideals of Europe (including those of elegy itself) that the poem's investigation reveals not only have been destroyed by the history of the twentieth century, but also have been complicit in their own destruction: a destruction and complicity at the heart of which stands, as the central, fourth section of the sequence declares, 'Auschwitz' and 'its furnace chambers and lime pits'.[26] Indeed, this section indicts 'artistic men' who 'prod dead men' and whose elegiac impulse is not only called an 'obsession', but is also so aestheticising that it produces 'the connoisseur of blood'.[27]

'Two Formal Elegies' is explicitly subtitled 'For the Jews in Europe' and its two dense sonnets continue to explore this difficulty of elegising the dead when their deaths are so recent, so numerous and, because of the sheer scale of the killing, almost anonymous. The poem focuses on what it means to be a witness of such events as Hill teases out the similarities and dissimilarities between the concept of judgement in secular and religious terms and, by so doing, reveals the inadequacy of both paradigms to provide explanation or recompense. The second sonnet avers that 'We have enough / Witnesses' and the ambiguous referent of 'witnesses' brings together both the Jews who were witnesses and victims of the Holocaust and the Jews who were witnesses and survivors of it (some of whom became witnesses at the various war-crime trials), as well as those Germans and others who were not Jewish but witnessed the crimes (either directly or indirectly), and everyone else after the war who became aware of the death camps, primarily through newsreels.[28] There are 'enough witnesses' both in the sense of proving guilt beyond doubt, and in the sense of there being too many to take all the guilty actions into consideration. All the poem can do is end with a parenthetical question that cannot be answered: '(At whose door does the sacrifice stand or start?)'[29] For Hill, an ethical elegy can offer neither identification (one sort of witness is not like another) nor recompense and, as such, he uses the rigid form of the sonnet to create the empty shell of impossible elegy (hence the title, 'Two Formal Elegies', not 'Two Elegies').

---

[25] Geoffrey Hill, *For the Unfallen: Poems 1952–1958* (London: Andre Deutsch, 1959), p. 27.
[26] Ibid., p. 51. [27] Ibid. [28] Ibid., pp. 31–2. [29] Ibid., p. 32.

This crisis in elegiac conventions signals another crucial crisis in the period, that of modernity itself alongside corresponding questions of secularisation, the place of religion and the sacred. Movement poetics famously sets itself against all forms of metaphysics and idealisms and, as Blake Morrison observes, Movement poems tend to mock grand designs and ironically subvert various idealisms by emphasising the empiricism of everyday objects.[30] Larkin's 'Church Going', from his 1955 volume *The Less Deceived*, quickly turned into a set-piece poem that came to represent not just this empirical turn, but also the decline of Christianity in postwar Britain. In the title's Empsonian ambiguity, Larkin is going to church as a tourist, not as a believer, and the church itself is going as an institution and as a faith. Larkin presents himself in the figure of a bemused, middle-class masculinity with his 'cycle-clips' and half-remembered higher educational background.[31] Symptomatic of this type of empirical and secular poetics, Larkin removes from the present moment the historical past; that is to say, traditions and memories no longer connect or explain the present. Similarly in 'I Remember, I Remember', Larkin undermines any attempt to explain his present self from childhood events, mocking romantic clichés about the growth of a child's imagination. Looking out of the window when the train unexpectedly stops, Larkin says, 'Coventry, why I was born here', but the poem then proceeds to empty the name of any personal or public history and it concludes by him saying of his place of birth, 'Nothing, like something, happens anywhere'.[32] (Larkin here revises Auden's famous line – rather than poetry making nothing happen, nothing makes poetry happen.) However, as Adam Piette emphasises, the extraordinary and deliberate act of forgetfulness that occurs in the poem is not Larkin's childhood, but rather the place where Larkin's childhood occurred.[33] In 1955, for any reader of the poem, Coventry would at some level have signified the catastrophic devastation of the city by aerial bombardment in 1940. This reduction of public memory to the immediate present of the self and of the object world it inhabits characterises the secular empiricism that frames and energises poetry such as Larkin's as poets strive to represent a newly emerging welfare-capitalist world where the increasing richness of the consumer lifestyle vies with an increasing

---

[30] Blake Morrison, *The Movement: English Poetry and Fiction of the 1950s* (Oxford University Press, 1980), pp. 145–91.
[31] Philip Larkin, *Collected Poems*, ed. Anthony Thwaite (London: Faber & Faber, 1988), pp. 58–9.
[32] Ibid., pp. 168–9.
[33] Adam Piette, 'Childhood Wiped Out: Larkin, His Father, and the Bombing of Coventry' *English* (2013) 62(238) pp. 230–47.

sense of bureaucratic standardisation. Indeed, Coventry would also have signified one of the centrepieces of postwar planning and redevelopment, celebrated in the 1945 government-sponsored film, *A City Reborn* (with words by Dylan Thomas).[34]

The dialectical other of this empirical and secular poetics, Romana Huk argues, appears in the emergence during the period of a preoccupation not only with Christian belief and the institution of Christianity, but also with the sacred more generally.[35] Writers such as Auden, Eliot, Jones and Kathleen Raine wrote explicitly Christian poetry and prose, while the New Apocalyptic and New Romantic anthologies are full of references to various sacred myths, including Christian. Poets of this so-called religious turn often critique secular modernity by attempting to imagine or locate the survival of mythic rites whose performance unites the individual and the collective, and for which the writing and reading of the poem itself stands as an attenuated, archetypal ritual. The poem becomes an object that resists empirical atomisation through an intense self-referentiality. For example, Jones structures his long, late-modernist poem, *The Anathemata* (1952), in the form of a religious quest-romance whose explicit goal is the 'thing' from which the poem seeks to materialise a cultural whole out of dispersed historical fragments. Pointing out in his 'Preface' the etymological origin of 'thing' as meaning a 'public assembly' in Anglo-Saxon, Jones traces the word's development from a precise term for a particular matter, action or object under consideration to its contemporary use as a universal abstraction.[36] For Jones, the rediscovery and recuperation of the 'thing' reveals the incarnate sign of God not only in human form, but also in the material craft of human sign-making in opposition to the empty, mechanical universality of bureaucratic writing.

Like many writers of the period, and indeed the twentieth century as a whole, Jones locates an epochal change, what he terms 'The Break', when 'Western Man moved across a rubicon' and the sacred disappeared from the world.[37] For Jones, this break follows many of the usual thematics of standard narratives of the fall into modernity: it is a fall from plenitude to privation, from the full sign to the empty signifier, from orality to literacy,

---

[34] See Dylan Thomas, *The Complete Screenplays*, ed. John Ackerman (New York: Applause Books, 1995), pp. 82–95.
[35] Romana Huk, 'Poetry and Religion' in Nigel Alderman and C. D. Blanton (eds), *Concise Companion to Postwar British and Irish Poetry* (Oxford: Wiley-Blackwell, 2009), pp. 221–42.
[36] David Jones, *The Anathemata: Fragments of an Attempted Writing* (London: Faber & Faber, 1952) pp. 10–11.
[37] Ibid., p. 15.

from the collective to the individual, from unalienated to alienated labour, from use-value to exchange value and so on. More specifically, Jones symptomatically folds this narrative of modernity under the figure of technology itself and he turns to the notion of the landscape as a site of resistance to the machine. Landscape, for Jones, becomes a complex site that contains both the abstraction of human history and what he sees as the materiality of the organic. For him, the combination of these things produces what he considers to be the archetypal sign: that is to say, the very name given to a specific place, a name that the poet, in turn, uncovers.

This notion of a hermeneutical poetics that reveals the fundamental depth behind the surface world links the period's explicitly Christian poets with those poets who sought the sacred elsewhere. At the heart of the anthologies of the New Apocalyptic or New Romantic poets lies some notion of the organic as a site of vitality. In his introduction to the 1942 anthology *The White Horseman*, G. S. Fraser stresses the link between the organic world and human subjectivity. Emphasising the dual importance of the 'discoveries of Freud' and the 'work of the Surrealists',[38] he argues for something akin to the Jungian unconscious in which poets' exploration of their subjectivity through language goes beyond the surface and contingent accidents of their individual present and enters into the depth and universal substance of some form of collective 'life movement'.[39] For poets such as George Barker, Thomas, and Henry Treece, this connection between the subjective voice, the unconscious, and a vitalist, organic sex-drive usually becomes figured in explicitly masculine and heterosexual terms – a connection whose most influential and explicit poetic allegory is made in Robert Graves's *The White Goddess* (1948), where he argues that a poem originates in a male poet's visitation by a female muse whose antecedent is some notion of an ancient Celtic Matriarchal Goddess.

Graves's and Jones's turn to a historical moment long before the conception of the United Kingdom also typifies the hermeneutical drive of this religious turn and places much of its poetry in opposition not only to conceptions of modernity, but also to the idea of England and Englishness as a marker of this modernity. Revealingly, in the third and final anthology of the New Apocalypse, entitled *A New Romantic Anthology*, the contents are divided into four sections: 'English Poetry', 'Irish Poetry', 'Scottish Poetry' and 'Welsh Poetry', and each begins with a short prose

---

[38] G. S. Fraser, 'Apocalypse in Poetry' in J. F. Hendry and Henry Treece (eds), *The White Horseman* (London: Routledge, 1941), p. 29.
[39] Ibid., p. 3.

introduction, entitled 'Romanticism and [English/Irish/Scottish/Welsh] Poetry', respectively.[40] Repeatedly, the poets locate historical deposits in the so-called peripheral nations and regions of the British archipelago and use them to construct alternative national and regional counter-narratives to the hegemonic narrative of their status as tributaries to an ever-widening, Anglo-centric, imperial universe. What C. D. Blanton calls a devolutionary poetics symptomatic of the postwar period has a complex provenance;[41] it is related not only to the rise of nationalism in the nineteenth century, in particular Irish nationalism leading to the establishment of the Irish Free State in 1922, but also to the postwar decline and dismantling of the British Empire, most spectacularly manifest in the Partition of India and the creation of Pakistan in 1947.[42] Often, as in Larkin's quotation from his preface to *The North Ship*, such poetry was simply labelled 'Celtic' – either in terms of praise or dismissal. In such poetry of a newly resurgent Welsh and Scottish identity (or what was then called the Celtic fringe), the historical and etymological deposits revealed in the landscape stand in opposition to a secular modernity seen as hostile to the poetry's newly defined national identity, bringing as it does not only technology and machinery, but also the English language and a homogenising Englishness.

R. S. Thomas's poetry of the 1940s and 1950s often makes this narrative his theme, in particular with his portrayals of Welsh farmers, agricultural labourers and peasants. Repeatedly in the poems of his first three volumes, *The Stones of the Field* (1946), *An Acre of Land* (1952) and *Song at the Year's Turning* (1955), he deliberately revises the English pastoral tradition of William Wordsworth and Thomas Hardy; in contrast to them, he no longer elegises the last remnants of a pre-industrial world, but instead emphasises the inhabitants' endurance in order to recognise the continuation of a national identity that survives in the people who work the land – as 'A Peasant' ends: 'Remember him, then, for he, too, is a winner of wars, / Enduring like a tree under the curious stars.'[43] Edwin

---

[40] Stefan Schimanski and Henry Treece (eds), *A New Romantic Anthology* (London: Grey Walls Press, 1949).

[41] C. D. Blanton, 'Nominal Devolutions: Poetic Substance and the Critique of Political Economy' in Nigel Alderman and C. D. Blanton (eds), *Pocket Epics: British Poetry after Modernism, Yale Journal of Criticism* (special issue), (2000) 13(1), pp. 129–52.

[42] Outside the archipelago, instead of this devolutionary poetics, a various and varied post-colonial and decolonising Anglophone poetics emerges that unravels the national and racial centring of poetry written in English. See Jahan Ramazani, *The Hybrid Muse: Postcolonial Poetry in English* (University of Chicago Press, 2001).

[43] R. S. Thomas, *Collected Poems, 1945–1990* (London: J. M. Dent, 1993), p. 4.

Muir's poetry of the Orkney Islands, especially his 1956 volume, *One Foot in Eden*, similarly traces the survival of a separate and particular identity in a landscape that has been bent to human shape through centuries of labour. In 'The Difficult Land', for example, he explicitly declares:

> We are a people; race and speech support us,
> Ancestral rite and custom, roof and tree,
> Our songs that tell of our triumphs and disasters
> (Fleeting alike), continuance of fold and hearth,
> Our names and callings, work and rest and sleep,
> And something that, defeated, still endures –
> These things sustain us.[44]

The conventional nationalist unification of blood, soil and culture is, however, not portrayed as expansionist in aim, but characteristically is instead depicted as endurance, an endurance moreover of defeat. This is perhaps a consequence of Welsh and Scottish nationalism in this period needing to negotiate a path between an English colonialism of which they were a victim and a British Imperialism of which they were a part.

Indeed, the critically dominant Movement might better be seen as a reaction to these various counter-narratives, asserting a distinctive Englishness in opposition both to these revitalised forms of nationalism in the archipelago and to the decolonisation of the British Empire. In contrast to these other emerging postwar nationalisms, Englishness is always predicated upon its decline since it arises at the precise moment when it can no longer centre Britain, let alone an empire.[45] Indeed, in further contrast, as Blanton argues, the postwar devolutionary poetics of English poetry leads not to some form of imagined community (as it tends to in Welsh or Scottish poetry), but instead further unravels England into its own separate regional identities, whether these be Basil Bunting's Northumbria, Roy Fisher's Midlands, Ted Hughes's Yorkshire or Norman Nicholson's Cumbria.[46]

Anchored in a critique of modernity and the historical fact of decolonisation, this devolutionary poetics connects to a central philosophical context of the period – French existentialism. Jean-Paul Sartre and Albert

---

[44] Edwin Muir, *Collected Poems* (London: Faber & Faber, 1984), p. 239.
[45] See Nigel Alderman, '"The Life with a Hole in It": Philip Larkin and the Condition of England' *Textual Practice* (1994) 8(2) p. 282.
[46] Blanton, 'Nominal Devolutions', pp. 132–4. A. T. Tolley's *The Poetry of the Forties* (Manchester University Press, 1985) points out this emergent regionalism in the poetry of the 1940s, especially in his chapter 'Regional and Traditional', pp. 149–83.

Camus were translated and published in Britain throughout the period, beginning with a special issue of *Horizon* in 1945, and their writings set up many of the crucial debates concerning the role of the writer and intellectual in the postwar world.[47] Existentialism's popularity has been seen as responding to a world in which various grand narratives appear to have collapsed in the face of the horrors of the Second World War and the new possibility of atomic war. Indeed, the influence of *Waiting for Godot* after its first London performance in 1955 and the extraordinary popular success of Colin Wilson's *The Outsider* (1956) show existentialism as one of the most important intellectual horizons of the period. However, Jameson has recently relocated postwar existentialism away from Europe's own borders and into its imperial space:

> ... we must link ... modern existentialism within demography rather than with modern warfare and must identify its fundamental moment of truth not so much in the slaughter of world wars as in the moment of decolonization that followed them and suddenly released an explosion of otherness unparalleled in human history.[48]

Taking his provocation from Sartre's famous declaration that 'Not so long ago, the earth numbered two thousand million inhabitants; five hundred million men, and one thousand five hundred million natives',[49] Jameson argues that existentialism can be seen as primarily a defence reaction, insisting upon the authenticity of individual existence in the face of 'the multiplicity of other people'.[50] Jameson's emphasis upon the emergence of new subjects of history, of innumerable others demanding recognition, enables a reading of the insistent masculinity of much of the poetry of the period as a powerful counter-reaction to the exposure of the unmarked universal subject as white, bourgeois, European, male and complicit with oppression.

Although its literary genealogy can be traced to Dostoevsky's novels, Albert Camus's *The Stranger* (1942) can be seen as the most important foundation for existentialism's post-1945 incarnations. The narrative is organised around the successive overthrowing of conventions and social codes as the main character refuses to sit through the wake of his mother, then murders a man and, in so doing, constructs a meaningful narrative for

---

[47] See Sinfield, *Literature, Politics and Culture in Postwar Britain*, pp. 86–115.
[48] Fredric Jameson, 'The End of Temporality' in *Ideologies of Theory* (London: Verso, 2008), p. 648.
[49] Jean-Paul Sartre, 'Preface' to Frantz Fanon, *The Wretched of the Earth* (New York: Grove Press, 1965) p. 7.
[50] Jameson, 'The End of Temporality', p. 648.

himself through his personal (and chosen) world of morality, punishment and execution. Succeeding versions of this narrative organisation often became structured around a self/other and/or master/slave binary in which the central character(s) fight for recognition in opposition to an Other. Consequently, human relationships tend to be seen as necessarily antagonistic. This helps explain why many works in this tradition usually now read as both disturbing and problematic, since the Other is often a woman who becomes stereotyped and a focus for often hateful misogyny. Mothers and wives, in particular, are attacked since they are made to exemplify the middle-class world the male character wishes to escape.[51] Also, revealingly, the 'someone' Camus's Algerian Frenchman murders is an Algerian Arab and, equally revealingly, criticism for the first twenty or so years often failed to mention this fact (as I deliberately failed to do above). If it was mentioned, it was usually regarded as unimportant to interpreting the novel. Symptomatically, writing indebted to existentialism with protagonists who are women, people of colour or queer tends to destabilise the form since the final moment of individual freedom usually leads to a realisation of group consciousness or identity.[52]

In poetic terms, Thom Gunn's work highlights this dynamic starkly. From its first publication, the existentialist contours of his male protagonists have been complicated by Gunn's portrayal of sexuality, as the implication of male same-sex desire became increasingly explicit. In his famous 'The Unsettled Motorcyclist's Vision of His Death', Gunn revises Yeats's earlier, classic existential lyric, 'An Irish Airman Foresees His Death'. Whereas in Yeats's poem, the Airman-speaker sheds all the structures of the social world and flies above it 'in balance with this life, this death', inhabiting an exemplary freedom,[53] in Gunn's poem the Motorcyclist-speaker is driven by a search for pleasure and seeks to defeat the organic through powerful physical movement.[54] In this poem and many others in his first two collections, *Fighting Terms* (1954) and *The Sense of Movement* (1957), such figures who, as Burt suggests, 'exempl[ify] self-control' are made into 'symbols for individuating heroic – and

---

[51] This is perhaps most obvious in the drama and films of the period; see for example, John Osborne's 1956 play, *Look Back in Anger* (London: Penguin, 1982) and the 1960 film adaption of Alan Sillitoe's 1958 novel, *Saturday Night, Sunday Morning* (London: W. H. Allen, 1958).
[52] The major examples of this are in the novel form, most notably Ralph Ellison's *Invisible Man* (New York: Random House, 1952), James Baldwin's *Giovanni's Room* (New York: Dial Press, 1956) and Doris Lessing's *The Golden Notebook* (London: Michael Joseph, 1962).
[53] W. B. Yeats, *The Collected Works of W.B. Yeats,* vol. I: *The Poems* (Revised Second Edition), ed. Richard J. Finneran (New York: Simon & Schuster, 1989), p. 135.
[54] Thom Gunn, *Collected Poems* (New York: Farrar, Straus and Giroux, 1995), pp. 54–5.

homoerotic – strength'.[55] In Gunn's 'Elvis Presley', for example, Presley 'turns revolt into style' and the poem's final stanza teasingly places interpretation between an essentialist and a performative self:

> Whether he poses or is real, no cat
> Bothers to say: the pose held is a stance,
> Which, generation of the very chance
> It wars on, may be posture for combat.[56]

Whether it is a pose or not, the pose itself becomes the meaning of this braced, eroticised masculine figure. At this moment, situated after the allegorical codes of Auden's homoerotic love poetry, Gunn destabilises the existentialism of his poems with the physical surplus of his male speakers and heralds what would be the more explicit representations of his poetry written and published in the 1960s and beyond. As such, he foreshadows the breaking up of the unmarked lyric subject that would exemplify poetry after 1960, as new successive previously marginalised and excluded groups began to occupy the poetic marketplace.

[55] Burt, 'The Movement and the Mainstream', p. 41.   [56] Gunn, *Collected Poems*, p. 57.

CHAPTER 3

Democracy, Decentralisation and Diversity: The Renaissance of British Theatre

Rebecca D'Monté

The conventional view of the immediate postwar British theatre used to be that it was in the doldrums, composed mainly of imports, revivals and facile domestic comedies. Deemed conservative in both political and theatrical terms, the critic Kenneth Tynan famously asserted: 'Never believe that there is a shortage of playwrights; there are more than we have ever known, but they are all writing the same play.'[1] It was, Tynan judged, the appearance of John Osborne's *Look Back in Anger* in 1956 that brought about the rebirth of drama with its kitchen-sink realism and abrasive anti-hero, Jimmy Porter.[2] However, it can be argued that prior to this event, the war years had already instigated a number of changes to the theatrical landscape that would have a significant effect on the postwar period, including the reconsideration of theatrical space and a dismantling of the matrices of power. This was augmented by a growing transnationalism, more prominent at this time than in any previous decade. The influence of the work of Erwin Piscator, Bertolt Brecht, Eugène Ionesco and Jean-Paul Sartre, as well as – later – Samuel Beckett, all had a profound effect on British dramatic technique.

The material conditions of the war – bombings, blackouts, mobile audiences – helped to reconfigure perceptions of what theatre might be and where it might be located, and led to a conceptual democratisation in terms of access and accessibility. Damage to Victorian and Edwardian playhouses, as well as increased use of touring companies, enabled greater freedom in the use of theatrical space: schools, churches, village halls and factories were pressed into service by professionals and amateurs, on tour and in situ. Even in more traditional venues, productions started earlier

---

[1] Kenneth Tynan, *Curtains: Selections from the Drama Criticism and Related Writings* (London: Longman, 1961), p. 86.
[2] See Dan Rebellato's reassessment in *1956 and All That: The Making of Modern British Drama* (London: Routledge, 1999), pp. 1–9.

because of the blackout, enabling audiences to come straight from work. Beverley Baxter believed that 'the abolishing of that waiting period created a flow, a continuity, which made the theatre a part of the normal life of the day'.[3] Audiences were also more transient because the majority of the population – both male and female – was involved in some kind of war work, and they could consist of regular theatre attenders or those who had never previously seen a play.

During this time, the regions became as important as London, historically the theatrical centre of Britain, thus dismantling preconceived notions of cultural access.

This was helped by a number of government initiatives, including the Council (later Committee) for the Encouragement of Music and the Arts (CEMA), set up in 1940 to strengthen common values, provide support for the entertainment industry and bring culture to all parts of the country.[4] For the first time, state funding was given to theatres – most notably Bristol's Theatre Royal (later known as the Bristol Old Vic) – and, as the first chairman of the Scottish committee of CEMA, James Bridie boosted theatre in his country through the founding of the Citizens' Theatre, Glasgow, in 1943, 'with a guarantee against loss from CEMA'.[5] Funding was also given to smaller touring companies such as the Pilgrim Players, and all of this done 'in such a way as to emphasize "good drama" as a right of the nation, not just the metropolis'.[6]

Another government initiative was the Army Bureau of Current Affairs (ABCA). This was in operation from 1941 to 1946 and designed to boost the morale of the troops through both educational events and drama. Its Play Unit had to avoid party politics, but much of their work had a socialist intent and Andrew Davies argues that 'in the radical context of the war years their plays chimed with the undercurrents which resulted in the substantial Labour Party victory at the 1945 election'.[7] This is also true of the work done by the Glasgow Unity Theatre.[8] Founded in 1940, its

---

[3] Beverley Baxter, *First Nights and Noises Off: A Selection of Dramatic Criticisms* (London: Hutchinson, 1949), p. 143.
[4] CEMA would develop into the Arts Council after the war.
[5] Euan McArthur, *Scotland, CEMA and the Arts Council, 1919–1967* (Aldershot: Ashgate, 2013), p. 61.
[6] Olivia Turnbull, *Bringing Down the House: The Crisis in Britain's Regional Theatres* (Bristol: Intellect, 2008), p. 23.
[7] Andrew Davies, 'The War Years' in Michael Balfour (ed.), *Theatre and War 1933–1945: Performance in Extremis* (New York: Berghahn, 2001), pp. 54–64, p. 61.
[8] The Unity Theatre movement started in London in the previous decade, formed out of amateur workers' drama groups, and then spread across the country. Glasgow Unity would turn professional after the war in 1945.

members were 'drawn from the ranks of ordinary working people, whose background and everyday life is identical with the masses who form its audience'.[9] Foreshadowing kitchen-sink realism, they championed both local Scottish and socialist playwrights, including Robert McLeish, Ena Lamont Stewart and Sean O'Casey.

Touring companies, such as the Adelphi Players, Pilgrim Players and Compass Players, were also often composed of radical thinkers in terms of socialism, pacifism and religion, and did much to fuel the postwar interest in community theatre and theatre-in-education (TIE).

While Brian Way's Theatre Centre in 1950 was the first properly to launch TIE, nascent forms had existed before. School audiences were targeted by theatre companies during and immediately after the war, with Nancy Hewins's Osiris Players touring with all-female Shakespeare productions and John Ridley's Century Theatre offering a mixture that included commercial, avant-garde and set texts. The 1944 Education Act and local councils helped to promote widening participation with notable figures such as J. B. Priestley and James Agate starting to view drama as worthy of both academic and practical study in schools, colleges and universities. Significantly, the first University Drama Department was opened by Glynne Wickham just three years later. This was in Bristol, meaning that the city now housed 'a famous "triangle" of Theatre school, Repertory Company and University Drama Department, promising a three-sided perspective of vocational training, professional production and theoretical study'.[10]

From these seeds – greater egalitarianism, the growth of small companies and regional theatre, an awareness of theatre's civic and educative function – postwar drama would develop. As I have suggested elsewhere, 'the more democratic, egalitarian, younger and theatrically innovative experiments of the war gradually filtered through to find presence in the development of the working-class drama of the 1950s and the fringe theatre from that decade onwards'.[11] Indeed, such figures as Joan Littlewood, Ewan MacColl and Bridget Boland helped a generation to realise that theatre was not just the perquisite of the rich or the intellectual, with Littlewood famously stating that she wished to create a 'Fun Palace'.[12]

---

[9] Quoted in David Hutchison, *The Modern Scottish Theatre* (Glasgow: Molendinar Press, 1977), p. 106.
[10] Shirley Brown, *Bristol Old Vic Theatre School: The First 50 Years 1946–1996* (Bristol: BOVTS Productions, 1996), p. 25.
[11] Rebecca D'Monté, *British Theatre and Performance 1900–1950* (London: Bloomsbury, 2015), p. 198.
[12] See Nadine Holdsworth, *Joan Littlewood's Theatre* (Cambridge University Press, 2011), ch. 6.

Significantly, the style and subject matter of these theatre practitioners fused both populist and modernist forms, a key component of European staging techniques. British dramatists and directors had grown more cognisant of foreign theatre in the interwar period, as demonstrated via the politicised Unity Theatres and companies headed by Ewan MacColl and Joan Littlewood.[13] These stylistic transitions were given impetus by the wartime influx of refugees whose productions foreshadowed the appearance in Britain of works by Bertolt Brecht and Samuel Beckett (whose *Waiting for Godot* would cause controversy when it was produced in 1955 at the Arts Theatre, London).[14] Approximately 60,000 had fled Nazism by the start of the war, but they were classified as aliens rather than political refugees and their German-speaking activities closely monitored by the authorities. Nevertheless, German and Austrian exiles opened theatres in London, introducing British people to the work of continental playwrights.[15] Performances were attended by several influential figures in the theatre, including J. B. Priestley, whose dramatic output became determinedly experimental during the war years, evidenced by *They Came to a City* and *Desert Highway* (both 1944).

By 1945, there was a new socio-political landscape, charted by both middlebrow and radical playwrights who dealt with fissures that were appearing in terms of gender, sexuality and class. Women, for example, were being cajoled back into the domestic sphere having experienced many of the freedoms of mobility and economic independence accorded by the war. 'If this scenario does not assure a public articulation of feminine discontent', Andrew Wyllie argues, 'it does suggest a domestic atmosphere in which men began to feel that their former privileges were under threat'.[16] Nicholas de Jongh goes further, arguing that the Second World War 'precipitated the erosion of the symbolic barriers dividing one class from another' and began the dissipation of

---

[13] MacColl and Littlewood founded several political companies in the 1930s and 1940s: Red Megaphones (1931), Theatre of Action (1934), Theatre Union (1936) and Theatre Workshop (1945). Their work fused British working-class drama with techniques drawn from European and Russian practitioners such as Piscator, Brecht, Yevgeny Vakhtangov and Vsevolod Meyerhold.

[14] This was first completed in French as *En Attendant Godot* (1949) and rewritten in English as *Waiting for Godot* (1953). The production of *Godot* was followed by *Endgame* at the Royal Court in 1958. See the chapter by Claire Cochrane in this volume for the censorship problems surrounding Beckett's work.

[15] See Clare George, 'The Opening of the First Austrian Exile Theatre in London', https://norbert miller.wordpress.com/2012/12/10/60 (2015).

[16] Andrew Wyllie, *Sex on Stage: Gender and Sexuality in Post-War British Theatre* (Bristol: Intellect, 2009), p. 80.

automatic deference to authority – law, military, religious.[17] The fear felt by some was that the old certainties of the pre-war years had fragmented to the detriment of society; the hope for others was that this would herald a fairer world based on personal freedoms rather than adherence to rigid rules.[18] Middle-class drawing rooms and country houses were symbolically replaced by more transient places, where people of different backgrounds and ages were thrown together in a way that was rare before 1939, except in terms of a master/servant relationship. Thus, the settings of widely disparate plays such as Bridget Boland's *Cockpit* (1948), Ewan MacColl's *The Travellers*, Rodney Ackland's *The Pink Room*, Terence Rattigan's *The Deep Blue Sea* (all 1952) and Osborne's *Look Back in Anger* suggest a postwar society unmoored from previous class surety.[19] This increased interest in stage depictions of 'minority' experience – women, the working classes, the younger generation – rather than those of the 'establishment', as well as a growing dissatisfaction with an outdated morality enshrined in theatre censorship, signalled a move towards a more liberal society, which would come to fruition in the 1960s.

Democratisation, Decentralisation and Dramatic Staging

As indicated above, London had, historically, been the centre of the theatre industry in this country, with regional theatre viewed as the metropolis's 'poorer cousin'. The Second World War destabilised this belief and, for the first time, the regions started to be seen as just as important as the capital, leading the critic W. A. Darlington to observe that in 'stage terms, London had become a "touring date"'.[20]

This transition is exemplified by the Old Vic Theatre, based in London and at the time considered the nearest Britain had to a national theatre.[21]

---

[17] Nicholas De Jongh, *Politics, Prudery and Perversions: The Censoring of the English Stage 1901–1968* (London: Methuen, 2000), p. 169.

[18] See David Pattie, *Modern British Playwriting: The 1950s: Voices, Documents, New Interpretations* (London: Methuen Drama, 2012).

[19] *The Pink Room* was written in 1945, but not staged until 1952; it was rewritten as *Absolute Hell* in 1987. As with *The Deep Blue Sea*, Harold Pinter's *The Birthday Party* (1958) is described as taking place in a boarding house, but in fact only one room is rented and, as with everything in this play, there is ambiguity about its status.

[20] W. A. Darlington, *The Actor and His Audience* (London: Phoenix House, 1949), p. 170.

[21] This view was based on the Old Vic's acclaimed repertoire of classical works. Lilian Baylis described it as 'The Home of Shakespeare and Opera in English' and imagined a 'natural growth of a National Theatre from the Old Vic': Elizabeth Schafer, *Lilian Baylis: A Biography* (University of Hertfordshire Press, 2006), p. 167.

However, in 1941, its artistic director Tyrone Guthrie moved the theatre to Burnley in Lancashire for the duration of the war, a decision that, as Olivia Turnbull points out, emphasised '"good" drama as a right of the nation, not just the metropolis'.[22] A second Old Vic company took up residence at Liverpool Playhouse and several touring companies formed to take a repertoire of Shakespeare, George Bernard Shaw, Eugene O'Neill and Greek tragedy to Wales and the north. London critics were aghast that such fare was being presented to those who had, in the main, never before visited a theatre. In fact, audiences responded openly to the material, which led many to develop a lifelong love of the theatre or to embark on careers in the industry.[23]

It is understandable, therefore, that when the Edinburgh International Festival of Music and Dance (EIF) started in 1947, audiences were primed to respond to the work that took place on its 'fringes'. This second festival had started spontaneously in the inaugural year as an alternative to the main event, and gradually grew in size to overshadow it.[24] Each initially had its own agenda. The International Festival, Angela Bartie tells us, 'encapsulated many of the new values given to culture in the immediate postwar world: a means of spiritual refreshment, a way of reasserting moral values, of rebuilding relationships between nations, of shoring up European civilisation and of providing "welfare" in its broadest sense'.[25] By contrast, the Festival fringe wanted to bring to the fore home-grown talent, much of which was Scottish, working class and left-wing in its politics. Glasgow Unity, whose aim was to harness the language of the people in both domestic drama and the adaptation of international writing, put on their successful production of Maxim Gorki's *The Lower Depths*, which had already been enthusiastically received in Glasgow and London.[26] They also staged Robert McLellan's *The Laird o' Torwatletie* (1947), and had intended to present Ena Lamont Stewart's *Starched Aprons*, but the Arts Council withdrew its support and Unity's appearance was only

---

[22] Turnbull, *Bringing Down the House*, p. 23.
[23] Charles Landstone, *Offstage: A Personal Record of the First Twelve Years of State Sponsored Drama in Great Britain* (London: Elek, 1953), p. 54.
[24] From the 1950s onwards, university theatre companies, including those of Oxford, Cambridge, London and Edinburgh, saw the fringe as a way to get a toehold in the industry or to espouse their non-Establishment beliefs.
[25] Angela Bartie, *The Edinburgh Festivals: Culture and Society in Post-War Britain* (Edinburgh University Press, 2013), p. 2.
[26] Bill Findlay (ed.), *Scottish People's Theatre: Plays by Glasgow Unity Writers* (Glasgow: ASLS, 2008). See also Bill Findlay, '"By Policy a Native Theatre": Glasgow Unity Theatre and the Significance of Robert Mitchell's Scottish Adaptation of *The Lower Depths*' *International Journal of Scottish Theatre*, (2001) 2(1) http://journals.qmu.ac.uk/index.php/IJoST/article/view/74/html

possible with the help of a private donation. As a result, argues David Hutchison, Unity 'could claim to have founded the Edinburgh Festival Fringe since it performed [those shows ...] without official support'.[27]

The war's diversification of theatrical spaces was instrumental in moving theatre away from the proscenium arch of stage realism.[28] This was exemplified by the ABCA's Play Unit. Their documentary-style plays were reminiscent of the Federal Theatre's Living Newspapers of the 1930s, which in turn were a development of Russia's revolutionary theatre.[29] Faced with non-traditional spaces and non-traditional audiences, the Unit developed a style that blurred cinematic practices, such as speedy scene changes, with live action, including staged fights in the auditorium.[30]

Bridget Boland honed her playwriting skills during her time with the ABCA, her later work becoming a forerunner of Environmental – or Site-Specific – Theatre. Popular in the 1960s, this eliminated the space between actors and audience to intensify the emotional impact of the drama. Thus, while *Cockpit* may have been staged in a traditional space – the Playhouse in London – its treatment was anything but traditional. The auditorium and front-of-house was transformed into a German Assembly Point for Displaced Persons and the unsuspecting audience were given a sense of the refugees' bewilderment when faced with signs in foreign languages and an incomprehensible argument onstage between two Polish characters. This provided a striking symbol of the human suffering caused by displacement in a Europe ripped apart by war. London spectators were horrified because it did not conform to conventional standards, but as Mary F. Brewer observes, working-class audiences in Wales and the northeast understood 'the play as a historical document, a political critique of life in postwar Europe and Britain's role therein'.[31]

Boland's meshing of style and subject matter had much in common with other British dramatists who found a mutual synergy with European, and sometimes American, staging techniques. This European influence would continue to impact upon postwar British drama, especially through the

---

[27] Quoted in ibid.
[28] The connection between space and style was already a key component of earlier political drama, including the Actresses' Franchise League, the Workers' Theatre Group and Unity Theatre. See D'Monté, *British Theatre and Performance*.
[29] Living newspapers were first used in Russia by the Blue Blouse groups (1923–8), named after the colour of workers' shirts, before being taken up by Erwin Piscator and Brecht in Germany.
[30] Estimates suggested that the majority of the army audience had previously seldom or never visited the theatre. See Davies, 'The War Years', p. 60.
[31] Mary F. Brewer, *Staging Whiteness* (Middletown, CT: Wesleyan University Press, 2015), p. 46.

figure of Beckett. The dramatist's stripped-down action, rich allusiveness and territorial power struggles were greatly admired by Harold Pinter, and influenced the writing of his early plays: *The Room, The Birthday Party* (both 1957), *A Slight Ache* (1959) and *The Caretaker* (1960).[32] As with Beckett, these plays were considered obscure, but gradually accrued critical acclaim: Pinter progressed from being savaged by a critic who derided his characters for speaking 'in non sequiturs, half-gibberish and lunatic ravings' to being awarded the Nobel Prize in 2005.[33] In particular, *The Birthday Party*, which nearly ended his career even as it began, demonstrates Ronald Knowles's observation that 'Pinter came to maturity in the postwar world of bomb-scarred London, the world of cold war peace. How could people reconcile the reality of peace – the resumption of the pedestrian, everyday world – with the reality of war and the Holocaust'?[34] This is suggested in *The Birthday Party* through its fusion of the everyday (a seaside boarding house location, children's toys and games) with comedy of menace (the dismantling of language, the oppressive power of 'the list' held by Goldberg and McCann).[35] Martin Esslin famously categorised such drama as Theatre of the Absurd, along with that by Beckett, Luigi Pirandello and Eugène Ionesco.[36] With the exception of Pinter, this was not a long-lasting genre in this country, but there was a wider, more general legacy which was to familiarise audiences with new kinds of drama, thereby changing expectations of what might be seen in the theatre.

The same could be said for the work of Brecht. This was little known in this country until 1955, when Joan Littlewood directed and took the central role in *Mother Courage and Her Children* (1939) at the Devon Festival in Barnstaple.[37] This innovation was followed by the appearance of the Berliner Ensemble at the Royal Court a year later. These events introduced Brecht's Epic Theatre and *Verfremsdungeffekt* (also known as the alienation or estrangement technique) to the British public, where the focus upon the constructed nature of theatre was designed to lead the spectator away from empathetic bourgeois realism towards Marxist debate. This chimed with

---

[32] Harold Pinter, *Plays 1* (London: Faber & Faber, 1996); *Plays 2* (London: Faber & Faber, 1996).
[33] M. W. W., *Manchester Guardian*, 21 May 1958. Quoted in John Elsom (ed.), *Postwar British Theatre and Its Criticism* (London: Routledge & Kegan Paul, 1981), p. 83.
[34] Ronald Knowles, *Understanding Harold Pinter* (Columbia, SC: University of South Carolina Press, 1995), p. 3.
[35] Irving Wardle was the first to label Pinter's work as 'comedy of menace' in a review of *The Birthday Party, Encore*, vol. 5 (July–August 1958), pp. 39–40.
[36] Martin Esslin, *The Theatre of the Absurd* (New York: Doubleday, 1961).
[37] Howard Goorney, *The Theatre Workshop Story* (London: Methuen, 1981), p. 102.

Littlewood's own political views and that of her first husband, the playwright Ewan MacColl. Theatre Workshop, founded immediately after the war, aimed to provide entertainment for the working-class East End of London, and although local audiences were not as forthcoming as expected, the company was integral to the development of fringe theatre from the 1950s onwards.[38] Littlewood's creation was the opposite of typical middle-class theatre: there was no proscenium arch, no curtain, no fussy sets, and the mechanics of theatre were exposed. The importance of 'teamwork' and collaboration drew upon Constantin Stanislavski and Rudolf Laban, with improvisation and research at the heart of her methods. Brecht's work was the greatest influence, however, and this was evident in Littlewood's direction of *A Taste of Honey* (1958).[39] Imposing Brechtian techniques upon the raw youthfulness of Delaney's drama, Littlewood turned Helen and Jo into a comic duo whose banter replicates that of traditional music-hall routines, while characters directly addressed the audience, and were played on and off stage with their own signature tunes.[40] This approach, devised during the rehearsal process, and undoubtedly innovative, nonetheless cut uncomfortably across the Northern, working-class realism suggested by Shelagh Delaney's play text.

It is interesting to compare Littlewood's East End theatre with the Royal Court in Sloane Square, as both saw themselves in ideological opposition to mainstream theatre and as centres of new styles of writing and direction. George Devine, who worked at the Old Vic, and went on to create its Theatre School and the Young Vic, claimed that 'the urgent need of our time is to discover a truly contemporary style wherein dramatic action, dialogue, acting and method of presentation are all combined to make a modern theatre spectacle'.[41] Aided by Ronald Duncan and Tony Richardson, Devine established a new theatre company, the English Stage Company (ESC), whose first season opened at the Royal Court in 1956. He was an advocate of the Theatre of the Absurd, directing Beckett's work himself, but Devine realised that the prospect of commercial and critical success for the ESC lay elsewhere, and 'the press releases of the Court proclaimed "we are not avant garde, or highbrow, or a coterie set.

---

[38] See Richard Eyre and Nicholas Wright, *Changing Stages: A View of British Theatre in the Twentieth Century* (London: Bloomsbury, 2000), p. 269.
[39] Shelagh Delaney, *A Taste of Honey* (London: Methuen Drama, 1982).
[40] This is in contrast to the later *Oh, What a Lovely War!* (1963), where the music-hall format is woven seamlessly into the depiction of the First World War.
[41] George Devine, 'The Royal Court Theatre Scheme', quoted in Philip Roberts (ed.), *The Royal Court Theatre and the Modern Stage* (Cambridge University Press, 1999), p. 26.

We want to build a vital, living, popular theatre"'.[42] It is not surprising, therefore, that the first three productions were American or British in style: Arthur Miller's *The Crucible* (1953), Angus Wilson's *The Mulberry Bush* (1955) and John Osborne's *Look Back in Anger* (1956).

Osborne's play formed part of the British New Wave, or 'Kitchen Sink' realism. Encompassing theatre, literature and cinema from the mid-1950s to the early 1960s, such works focused mainly on the lives of young, alienated working-class northerners. *Look Back in Anger* supposedly represented a break with the past through its setting in a bleak bedsit, where previously hidden domestic labour and sexual activity are displayed through the visual symbols of an ironing board and a double bed, and its aggressive language (Jimmy persistently baits the other characters, his main targets being the stultifying class system, the lack of 'any good brave causes' to fight and women).[43] This was applauded, not just by Kenneth Tynan, but by four young members of the Royal Court audience: 'It seems to us the first time that our home-grown brand of mixed up kid has been presented on any stage ... [we] can only applaud the complete truthfulness and alarming realism of the whole production'.[44]

Nevertheless, while Osborne's play was touted as the future of British theatre, it can also be seen as curiously backward-looking, mainly due to its emphasis upon stage realism. Even the dramatist himself recognised this, calling it 'a formal, rather old-fashioned play' with its formulaic content, over-reliance on plot devices and well-timed entrances and exits.[45] Comparisons can be made with Terence Rattigan's *The Deep Blue Sea*, generally viewed as a less radical play. In both there are repetitions (the positioning of Alison/Helena at an ironing board; Hester at the gas fire), the use of a stock device to heighten emotional impact (the loss of a child; an attempted suicide) and gloomy boarding houses to represent a fragmented postwar society. Rattigan's representation of quietly desperate lives had made him 'the leading British playwright' of the period.[46] However, his suggestion, in the preface to his *Collected Plays* (1953), that audience expectations could be understood through the figure of 'Aunt Edna' – a 'respectable, middle-class, middle-aged, maiden lady' – was

---

[42] David Ian Rabey, *English Drama Since 1940* (London: Longman, 2003), p. 31.
[43] John Osborne, *Look Back in Anger* (London: Faber & Faber, 1996), p. 89.
[44] Quoted in Philip Roberts, *The Royal Court Theatre and the Modern Stage* (Cambridge University Press, 1999), p. 48.
[45] Quoted in John Heilpern, *John Osborne: A Patriot for Us* (London: Viking, 2007), p. 184.
[46] Dan Rebellato, 'Introduction' in Terence Rattigan, *After the Dance* (London: Nick Hern Books, 2014), p. xii. Rebellato defends Rattigan, observing that he believed the writer should 'engage in a gentle tug-of-war with the audience's expectations', p. xii.

misunderstood, and Rattigan was accused of pandering to a banal conservative anti-modernism. This, combined with the success of *Look Back in Anger*, led quickly to the assumption that his plays were dated.[47] Ironically, in the context of Beckett and Brecht's meta-theatrical and minimalist challenge to British realism, the same could be said of Osborne, although it would take a considerable while for his work to be reappraised in this light.[48]

Refiguring Class, Gender and Sexuality

Osborne's play may not have been radical in terms of its staging, but it certainly defined a number of distinctively postwar social experiences – disillusionment, anger, betrayal, confusion – all of which came to the fore in the 1950s. Significantly, it evinces problematic and contradictory views on class, gender and sexuality, inevitable in a period of rapid social change. For example, on the surface, Jimmy seems to despise everything that Alison and her family stand for: her brother is a 'chinless wonder from Sandhurst' and her parents are 'Militant, arrogant and full of malice'. Yet Jimmy has a sneaking regard for the security of the past represented by her father, Colonel Redfern: 'I hate to admit it, but I think I can understand how her Daddy must have felt when he came back from India, after all those years away. The old Edwardian brigade do make their brief little world look pretty tempting.' He sees how it has been mythologised, but believes it is preferable to live in the time of the British Empire than 'in the American Age'.[49] In this way, Osborne's play represents the twin modes of thought that existed in the immediate postwar period. The first was that the war had provided an opportunity to rethink society; the second looked back with nostalgia to the past and saw the war as a disruption to normality: both views were encapsulated in the 1951 Festival of Britain, which was designed to echo the Victorian Great Exhibition a hundred years earlier, while also heralding a bright, technological future.

Enid Bagnold's *The Chalk Garden* (1956), which appeared a month before Osborne's play, also deals with the changing class system, but from the perspective of the upper middle classes. Mrs St Maugham, a widow who is a descendant of a Governor in India, is unable or unwilling to control her 16-year-old granddaughter, Laurel, who – referencing the

---

[47] Quoted in Christopher Innes, *Modern British Drama 1890–1990* (Cambridge University Press, 1992), p. 90.
[48] One of the best of these reappraisals is Rebellato, *1956 and All That*.
[49] Osborne, *Look Back in Anger*, pp. 14, 11.

title – cannot flourish in her surroundings. It is only Miss Madrigal, the new governess, who feels comfortable, coming as she does from the confines of a prison cell. The characters are ensnared within a troubled household run by the mysterious, yet unseen, butler Pinkbell. Clinging to past decorums, which have no meaning in the new world, this character epitomises the dangers of looking to the past rather than the future, of putting custom above emotion. Eventually, Pinkbell's destructive patriarchal rule is overturned, symbolised by his death and Laurel's growing maturity. If Pinkbell represents the emptiness of social habit, so Mrs St Maugham's friend, the Judge, represents the heavy weight of law and tradition. The language he uses to describe his ritualistic entrance into the courtroom underlines the dead emptiness of what he stands for: 'Learned and crumpled like a rose leaf of knowledge I snuffle and mumble. I sham deaf. I move into the red glory of a dried saint carried in festival.'[50] Eventually, he comes to realise that his adherence to the rules is not as important as human compassion as he finally realises his part in Madrigal's unjust imprisonment.

The importance of justice and reparation also stands at the heart of J. B. Priestley's best-known play, *An Inspector Calls* (1946). Again, it draws upon the past, not as a form of nostalgia, but rather as a way of arguing for social change. The plot centres on an investigation into the suicide of an unmarried, pregnant woman in 1912. Inspector Goole arrives at the house of the wealthy Birlings whose actions are gradually revealed to be responsible for Eva Smith's death. Sexual and social double standards are laid bare as the working-class Eva is punished while the well-to-do Birlings seemingly escape censure, in spite of their complicity in her death. Goole is both real and representative of a higher court of justice, and his role as narrator/observer makes the point that a reassessment of society is urgently required. His final speech echoes Priestley's socialist views on the exploitative nature of capitalism, and its devastating consequences for the powerless: 'We don't live alone. We are members of one body. We are responsible for each other.'[51]

If the war had destabilised the class hierarchy, the perceived breakdown of conventional morality also ignited a debate about censorship. Both established writers and the new generation dealt increasingly openly with what were regarded as unsavoury topics: prostitution, incest, homosexuality, and the rejection of marriage and motherhood. An early example of

---

[50] Enid Bagnold, *The Chalk Garden* (London: William Heinemann, 1956), p. 57.
[51] J. B. Priestley, *An Inspector Calls* (London: Heinemann, 1992), p. 56.

this was *Pick-up Girl* by Elsa Shelley, which opened in America in 1944 and was produced in Britain two years later.[52] The play provides an early mention of the term 'juvenile delinquency' which encapsulated for some commentators many of the problems in postwar society: disrespect for social conventions, intergenerational conflict and lax morality. The play revolves around the trial of Lizzie Collins, a 15-year-old girl who is accused of leading a life of prostitution: 'a problem about which something must be done'.[53] Left in charge of her younger siblings while her father's war work takes him away and her mother goes into service, the teenager is seduced by a supposedly better life. She is found in bed with an older man, having already had an abortion and contracted venereal disease. Lord Clarendon in the Lord Chamberlain's Office, responsible at this time for stage censorship, made minor cuts, but although he thought 'the story was sordid, it was also sincere and stressed the vital importance of parental responsibility'.[54]

It was rare for novels to be prosecuted for obscenity (the 1960 trial of *Lady Chatterley's Lover* was unusual), but between 1942 and 1955 alone, forty-two plays were refused licences by the Lord Chamberlain's Office. Mainly this was for sexual reasons, and cuts were made to plays which attempted to tackle prostitution and the breakdown of the family, such as *Women of Twilight* (1957), Sylvia Rayman's tale of single mothers who fall foul of a baby-farming operation. The greatest problem for the theatre, however, was homosexuality. Concerns about this subject had increased in the postwar period, fuelled by the 1948 publication in America of *The Kinsey Report* which suggested that its prevalence was far greater than previously thought. In this country, the Home Secretary, Sir David Maxwell Fyfe, was determined to prosecute men for gross indecency in order to re-establish what he saw as the moral standards of the 1930s, and there were several high-profile cases, including those of Sir John Gielgud and Alan Turing. The Report of the Departmental Committee on Homosexual Offences and Prostitution, better known as the Wolfenden report, was published in 1957, and recommended that homosexual activity between men over 21 should no longer be considered illegal, but a law was not passed to this effect until ten years later; stage censorship, meanwhile, was finally abolished in 1968. Andrew Wyllie charts this growing tolerance in the theatre, suggesting that 'male homosexuality moved from

---

[52] Elsa Shelley, *Pick-up Girl* (London: Transworld, 1959).
[53] Bill Riley, *Pick-up Girl, The Billboard* (6 May 1944), p. 30.
[54] Anthony Aldgate and James Crighton Robertson, *Censorship in the Theatre and Cinema* (Edinburgh University Press, 2003), p. 24.

a sympathetic but covert treatment in Terence Rattigan's *Separate Tables* ... through a neutral but overt representation in Shelagh Delaney's *A Taste of Honey*, to a sympathetic *and* overt characterization in the 1960s'.[55]

Yet while postwar theatre struggled with sexual desire, it was remarkably explicit in its representation of men physically or emotionally emasculated by the war. This emasculation is also linked to the fragmentation of the family and a radical questioning of the role of wife and mother, which ran counter to society's attempts to entice women back into the home. This can be seen in Daphne du Maurier's *The Years Between* (1944). Just pre-dating the end of the war, as well as Labour's landslide election victory, it foreshadows the problems of peacetime reconstruction. Taking over her absent husband's position as MP, Diana negotiates a successful career and life as a single mother. When the wounded Michael unexpectedly returns from the war, he is unable to recognise the timid, submissive wife he left behind, seeing her now as 'one of those managing, restless women'.[56] Given that women were supposed to slot into male roles 'only for the duration', and that he was a war hero, audiences sided with Michael, but du Maurier presents him as being the one out of step in seeking a return to a past that no longer exists. In contrast, Diana sees her work as part of a continuum of change, and argues that, in the rebuilding of postwar Britain, equality should become the key, rather than blind service to duty. This awareness of the need for a break with the past would gradually permeate all levels of society and, for women, lead to the seismic transformations brought about by second-wave feminism.

Terence Rattigan's *The Deep Blue Sea* presents another aimless postwar figure. Freddie Page may have once commanded a squadron in the Battle of Britain, but now his life is empty. Missing the challenges and homo-sociality of the war, he squanders his time playing golf and uses alcohol as an emotional crutch. His lover Hester chooses passion over duty by leaving her childless marriage to a judge for him. Untrained for work and no longer shielded by her privileged class position, she is forced to live vicariously through Freddie and his abandonment leads her to consider suicide. Unlike earlier depictions of the 'fallen woman' whose 'sin' required her to be punished, Rattigan presents two alternatives: returning to an empty marriage or continuing to live alone, supported by an unpromising artistic

---

[55] Wyllie, *Sex on Stage*, p. 15 (emphasis in the original).
[56] Daphne du Maurier, 'The Years Between' in Fidelis Morgan (ed.), *The Years Between: Plays by Women on the London Stage 1900–1950* (London: Virago, 1994), p. 373.

career.[57] These options may be bleak, but there is at least the suggestion that a woman might choose independence.

A different generation from Freddie Page, Jimmy Porter has not fought in the war, but the loss of his father in the Spanish Civil War has left him with a complex sense of disempowerment. Feeling that he has no sociopolitical agency, he directs his anger towards family and friends. His heartfelt cry that 'There aren't any good, brave causes left' is wrapped up in a verbal onslaught against women, violently directed towards Alison, his wife: 'If only something – something would happen to you, and wake you out of your beauty sleep! . . . If you could have a child, and it would die.'[58] For Michelene Wandor, there are 'few plays which show masculinity/ manhood in crisis with such honesty and violence', but the gender trouble at the heart of the play finds echoes across the canon of 1950s theatre.[59]

In Arnold Wesker's *Chicken Soup with Barley* (1956), for example, the matriarch is controlling but vibrant, in contrast to her husband's physical and mental incapacity; Tony Bolton in Doris Lessing's *Each His Own Wilderness* (1958) retreats into child-like behaviour and rejects his militant mother's stance; most potently, Stanley in Pinter's *The Birthday Party* is caught between the archetypes of woman as mother/whore, as exemplified by Meg and Lulu, and the paternal/patriarchal father figures of Goldberg and McCann. Andrew Wyllie suggests that Stanley's failure to deal with his 'quasi-Oedipal relationship with Meg' leads to his humiliation and final appearance in a pre-linguistic state: a regression indicative of the uncertainty surrounding gender roles in the period.[60]

While Pinter's work suggests a fear of, or retreat from, the mother, Ann Jellicoe's *The Sport of My Mad Mother* (1958) offers a symbolic exploration of the figure through the juxtaposition of ancient beliefs and modern psychoanalysis.[61] Highly experimental in its mixture of dance, music and ritual, and unapologetically challenging for those schooled in the English stage tradition, the play follows a power struggle between teenage gangs in London's East End. Greta's 'primitive, violent and maternal rule' challenges that of Dean, with 'his sense of rational, moral responsibility'.[62] Her

---

[57] For the Victorian and Edwardian 'fallen woman', see Sos Eltis, *Acts of Desire: Women and Sex on Stage, 1800–1930* (Oxford University Press, 2013).
[58] Osborne, *Look Back in Anger*, pp. 89, 36.
[59] Michelene Wandor, *British Drama: Looking Back in Gender* (London: Routledge, 2001), p. 43.
[60] Wyllie, *Sex on Stage*, p. 73.
[61] Ann Jellicoe, *The Sport of My Mad Mother* (London: Faber & Faber, 1985).
[62] Lib Taylor, 'Early Stages: Women Dramatists 1958–68' in Trevor R. Griffiths and Margaret Llewellyn-Jones (eds), *British and Irish Women Dramatists since 1958: A Critical Handbook* (Buckingham: Open University Press, 1993), pp. 9-25, p. 22.

behaviour identifies her with the Hindu goddess Kali (as the title suggests, all 'creation is the sport of my mad mother, Kali'), a figure who destroys and creates, nurtures and disciplines. A number of interpretations are possible: Greta, the mother figure, threatens male dominance through female creative power; the subject of motherhood, key to later feminist drama, is brought to the fore and celebrated; yet Greta's behaviour is even more horrific than that of her predecessors – the Bacchae – and her all-consuming maternity can be seen to reduce women to their bodies.[63] This essentialist conception of the female body is also challenged, and yet arguably reinforced by Delaney's *A Taste of Honey*. Both Helen and Jo resist functioning as traditional homemakers. Although they express some vague understanding of what is expected of a 'proper' mother, neither can conform to this ideal. Helen's chaotic lifestyle as a 'semi whore' stands in opposition to maternal responsibilities, and the rejection of the maternal is replicated by her daughter Jo, who says of her unborn child that she wants to 'bash its brains out'.[64] Delaney seems to question two deeply rooted conceptions: that motherhood automatically denotes fulfilment for a woman and that it remains the exclusive province of the female; instead, Jo's homosexual partner, Geof, seems the more maternal of the two. However, Lib Taylor questions whether Delaney's play challenges gender stereotypes: 'motherhood is defined as "natural" for women and, although it fails to satisfy, neither Helen nor Jo are given alternative aspirations'.[65] Ultimately, though, this is as much an issue of class as gender, with the women experiencing only a 'taste of honey' as they fight to survive in a society that gives few opportunities to working-class women.

***

The freeing up of theatre during the Second World War had massive ramifications in terms of how drama was conceived, funded and consumed in this country. Far from being a period of conservative timidity within the theatre, the war years saw instead a degree of experimentation that both reached into the past and presaged postwar changes. A number of theatre practitioners saw the unique wartime conditions as a means to devise, develop and enact their individual agenda, and the various types of theatre seen during the conflict enfranchised a new generation – and a new demographic – of theatregoers. In many ways, the use of unusual spaces, the fusion of amateur and professional, and the expansion of geographical

---

[63] See Jozefina Komparaly, *British Women Playwrights: 1956 to the Present* (Basingstoke: Palgrave Macmillan, 2006), p. 12.
[64] Delaney, *A Taste of Honey*, pp. 7, 75.   [65] Taylor, 'Early Stages', p. 19.

access all led to an increase in theatre going, in whatever form. To this we can also add a whole range of theatre-based initiatives: from the first Drama Department at the University of Bristol, the foundation of the Society of Theatre Research, and a series of new theatres built during the 1950s in cities such as Coventry, Ipswich, Derby and Kidderminster.

While London and realism still ruled the theatre industry, there was a much greater awareness of the importance of diversity engendered during the war years. Britain had long had a mutually enriching relationship with foreign practitioners, and this continued with the emergence of Brecht and Beckett, who helped provide a new stage language for the representation of a post-Holocaust world. This, in turn, influenced Pinter's absurdist studies of territory and power. Further debate about the civic function of drama meant greater opportunities for study, scholarship and training, and this helped to reinforce the perception that theatre's purpose was to educate, entertain and enlighten. Postwar Britain was shaken by the impact of two world wars within twenty years, the nuclear threat, the Cold War and an increasingly imperilled empire. It was struggling with intergenerational tensions and the erosion of old convictions about class, gender and sexuality. Increasingly, it was in the theatre that these socio-political anxieties found voice, leading eventually to the further development of feminist, gay and working-class drama in the 1960s and 1970s.

CHAPTER 4

National Transitions: Wales, Scotland and Northern Ireland

Katie Gramich

The 1930s had been a period of literary and cultural reawakening in Scotland and Wales, despite economic hardship and the advent of war at the end of the decade. Led by iconoclastic *enfants terribles* like Hugh MacDiarmid and Dylan Thomas, the two nations witnessed a flowering of poetry and fiction in English, Welsh, Gaelic and Scots. Northern Ireland, however, was still in the throes of defining its own identity after partition, although John Hewitt was already beginning not only to articulate a distinct Northern Irish voice in poetry, but also to uncover a native tradition of Ulster poets. Many writers from Wales, Scotland and Northern Ireland were actively engaged in the war, doing so willingly or reluctantly as *British* subjects. Very quickly, though, in the aftermath of war, the cohesive British identity that was part of the experience and propaganda of wartime began to disintegrate, and writers from each of these three distinct territories register this disintegration in differing ways. Nevertheless, this postwar writing was by no means simply a belated reflection of the decline of empire, but rather a celebration of new, distinctive identities and energies.

From 1941 until the end of the war, Dylan Thomas was employed as a documentary scriptwriter for Strand Films in London; this he called, only half-jocularly, his 'war work'.[1] Thomas wrote and produced many films over these years, including the acclaimed *Our Country* (1945) and *Wales – Green Mountain, Black Mountain* (1943). The focus of these beautiful and poetic works is on a shared British identity and on the united efforts of all to fight for freedom. Nevertheless, Thomas's scripts were not quite British enough for the British Council, which rejected *Wales – Green Mountain, Black Mountain* as 'unsuitable for overseas audiences' because of its pointed criticism of unemployment in Wales

---

[1] John Ackerman (ed.), *Dylan Thomas: The Filmscripts* (London: Dent, 1995), p. xii.

during the Depression.[2] Indeed, the script tips over into poetry to make this political commentary:

> Remember the procession of the old-young men
> From dole queue to corner and back again,
> From the pinched, back streets to the peak of slag
> In the bite of the winters with shovel and bag . . .
> Nothing in their pockets, nothing home to eat . . .
> Remember the procession of old-young men.
> It shall never happen again.[3]

Both the rhyming couplets and the overt political protest are unusual for Thomas and strike a somewhat dissonant note in a film intended to celebrate togetherness. Thomas's later film, *Our Country*, is less overtly political and written in a surprisingly Modernist poetic idiom that Thomas defended in a letter to his producer, Donald Taylor: 'written down, the verse looks a little chaotic . . . and "modern". Heard spoken to a beautiful picture, the words gain a sense & authority which the printed word denies them'.[4] The film takes us on an impressionistic travelogue through the British Isles, accompanying a sailor home on leave. At Dover, Thomas eschews any patriotic rhetoric about 'Albion' and evokes instead the following somewhat surreal image: 'from this island end white faced over the shifting sea- / dyes / a man may hear his country's body talking / and be caught in the weathers of her eyes . . .'.[5] In the north of Scotland, though, the scene and the words become ominous, as a landscape of trees is felled: 'walk deep through the forbidding timber temples / count the Samson pillars fall / the thwacks of the wood-and-wind-splintering axe / crack of the trunk-shorn boughs / shuffle of leaves / the suddenly homeless birds' tree-call'.[6] If Thomas's films are not on the surface dissimilar to the films of the English documentary-maker, Humphrey Jennings, there are significant hints within them of a different, and distinctly less patriotic, view of the nation in wartime.

After the war, Jennings's *Family Portrait*, made for the 1951 Festival of Britain, designed as a 'united act of national reassessment, and a . . . reaffirmation of faith in the nation's future', emphasised the unity of the people of these islands and our 'family history' of achievement in literature, art, technology and science.[7] It has a poignant postwar atmosphere created

---

[2] Ibid., p. 27. [3] Dylan Thomas, *Wales – Green Mountain, Black Mountain* in ibid., p. 31.
[4] Ackerman, *Dylan Thomas: The Filmscripts*, p. 65. [5] Thomas, *Our Country*, in ibid., p. 69.
[6] Ibid., p. 73.
[7] Ian Cox, *The South Bank Exhibition: A Guide to the Story It Tells* (London: HMSO, 1951).

partly by a photograph in a family album showing people standing beside a bombed and ruined building; this shot appears at the beginning and end of the film. It was certainly an image designed to unite people in London, Swansea, Belfast and Glasgow, and everywhere in between. Jennings's artistic vision and his erudition makes this a compelling and persuasive film, but he himself was well aware of internal differences in Britain which the Central Office of Information may have been eager to conceal. Eight years earlier, he had made *The Silent Village* (1943), which pays tribute to the people massacred by the Nazis in the Czech mining village of Lidice in the previous year by reimagining the story in the setting of a small Welsh mining valley. Jennings filmed the work in the village of Cwmgïedd, near Ystradgynlais in the Tawe valley, and he commented on his experience there:

> Down here I'm working on a reconstruction of the Lidice story in a mining community – but more important than that really is being close to the community itself and living and working inside it, for what it is everyday. I really never thought to live and see the honest Christian and Communist principles acted on as a matter of course by a large number of British – I won't say English – people living together.[8]

For Jennings, here, 'British' is an inclusive term containing internal differences; for many of his Welsh, Scottish and Irish contemporaries, though, the sheltering British umbrella was becoming a little moth-eaten.

After the war, Jennings's 'British family' was seen by some as beginning to fall apart; this is suggested by the tenor of Dylan Thomas's broadcast on 'The Festival Exhibition' in the summer of 1951. It is humorous, whimsical and emphasises differences, not unity. The broadcast becomes a list of the eccentric people who walk around the Exhibition and their differing reactions to it, in one long, adjective- and image-stuffed sentence. Thomas relishes the event – at least it's not a 'shoddily cajoling Emporium of tasteless Empire wares'[9] – but when 'The Lion and the Unicorn' tent is said to celebrate 'the British character', it is hard not to hear a hint of irony in his voice.[10] Yet this scepticism about a unifying British character had been present under the surface from the pre-war period; indeed, one aspect of the cultural renaissance of the 1930s in Wales and Scotland, at least, could be said to derive from a sense of shared Celtic,

---

[8] Quoted in Kevin Jackson, *Humphrey Jennings* (London: Picador, 2004), p. 272.
[9] Dylan Thomas, 'The Festival Exhibition' in *Dylan Thomas: The Broadcasts*, ed. Ralph Maud (London: Dent) p. 248.
[10] Ibid., p. 249.

rural ideals set against an England figured as urban, modern and machine-driven. Of course, the fact that parts of both Wales and Scotland were themselves highly industrialised and urbanised, while many parts of England remained rural and undeveloped, contradicts the stereotype, but it nonetheless shows that writers and artists continually seek to create their own ideal homelands; as R. S. Thomas puts it, in the postwar world he was in search of 'the true Wales of [his] imagination'.[11]

The urge to create artistic homelands and to imagine a Celtic ideal was evident from the mid-1930s, when, for example, the Welsh painter and writer, Brenda Chamberlain, set up home in remote Llanllechid in Snowdonia with her English fellow-artist, John Petts. They had met at art college in London, but moved to rural Wales as a gesture of rebellion against commercialism and modern technology. Chamberlain wrote, 'Under the influence of D. H. Lawrence, we hated the machine'.[12] The two artists established the Caseg Press in their cottage in Snowdonia and set about living the life of 'primitive' craftspeople. In November 1939, Chamberlain and Petts published an evocative travel essay with wood engravings about their wanderings in the Scottish Highlands: 'From Other Hills'.[13] The Highlands, like Snowdonia, embodied their ideal of an unspoilt, ancient wilderness, a place where 'the roots of the ancient Highland forest lie in the black peat like bleached bones'.[14] Throughout the essay, links are made between Scotland and Wales: Chamberlain is surprised to see 'a Welsh coracle used here for fishing in the high lochans' and at the end of their travels they return to reconnect with a 'place [no] less lovely than here ... the white house under Moel Faban'.[15] Even here, though, the outside world intervened. The Second World War broke out and Petts registered as a conscientious objector, but later was separated from Chamberlain and worked as an agricultural labourer in southern England. Chamberlain stayed on in the Welsh mountains, but could not escape the consciousness of war, as she memorably expresses in her poem 'Dead Ponies'.[16] The plangent voice laments 'There is death enough in Europe without these / Dead ponies on the mountain', while the final image of the ponies' bodies stripped clean – 'soft entrails have gone to make

---

[11] R. S. Thomas, 'Y Llwybrau Gynt/The Paths Gone By (1972)', translated and reprinted in Sandra Anstey (ed.), *R. S. Thomas: Selected Prose* (Bridgend: Poetry Wales Press, 1986), p. 138.
[12] Brenda Chamberlain, *Alun Lewis and the Making of the Caseg Broadsheets* (London: Enitharmon Press, 1970), p. 1.
[13] Brenda Chamberlain and John Petts, 'From Other Hills' *The Welsh Review* II(4) (1939), pp. 197–205.
[14] Ibid., 197.   [15] Ibid., 205.
[16] Brenda Chamberlain, 'Dead Ponies' in *The Green Heart: Poems* (London: Oxford University Press, 1958), p. 31.

the hawk arrogant' – is a chilling reminder of the carnage going on elsewhere.

Yet in the midst of the war, Chamberlain received a letter from a stranger encouraging her to produce poetic broadsheets for 'the People'; this stranger turned out to be the poet, Alun Lewis, who, though reluctantly a soldier in the British Army, shared Chamberlain and Petts's ideals about art and life. Between 1941 and 1942, Chamberlain and Petts, aided by Lewis, produced six 'Caseg Broadsheets', featuring woodcuts and poems by ancient and contemporary Welsh writers, including Lewis, Chamberlain and Dylan Thomas.[17] But the series ground to a halt owing to the pressures of the war; and – since 'caseg' is the Welsh word for mare – perhaps the 'dead ponies' of Chamberlain's wartime poem can also be seen to commemorate the demise of the Press itself.[18] Another Welsh-identified poet, David Jones, was ruminating on similar ideas in this period: he wrote about the inimical nature of the modern, machine-driven world which alienated human beings and prevented them from fulfilling their roles as artist-makers. According to Jones: 'In our present megalopolitan technocracy the artist must still remain a "rememberer" (part of the official bardic function in earlier phases of society) ... of things which tend to be impoverished, or misconceived, or altogether lost or wilfully set aside in the preoccupations of our present intense technological phase.'[19] These Welsh artists saw technology, industry, consumerism and urbanism threatening Welsh landscapes, and responded by retreating to artist-havens in the remotest parts of Wales.

R. S. Thomas, who published his first volume of poetry in 1946, belongs very much to the same generation of Welsh writers and artists; his opposition to the reign of the Machine and his desire to retreat to the remotest parts of an idealised rural Wales 'of the imagination' soon became manifest in his work. Even in the ostensibly humorous poem 'Cynddylan on a Tractor' (1952), there is an unmistakably elegiac tone to the description of the Welsh farmer astride his new tractor: 'he's a new man now, part of the machine, / His nerves of metal and his blood oil', for this new creature is deaf to 'all the birds ... singing, bills wide in vain'.[20] In this way,

---

[17] See Chamberlain, *Alun Lewis*; Alan Vaughan Jones, 'The Caseg Broadsheets: Self, Wales, War' (1)', *International Journal of Welsh Writing in English* (2013), pp. 94–121 and 'The Caseg Broadsheets: Self, Wales, War (2)' *International Journal of Welsh Writing in English* (2014), pp. 168–94.

[18] Chamberlain recalls that 'We named it the Caseg Press, partly for our pony mare, partly for the Caseg river which drained the wild valley high above the village', *Alun Lewis*, p. 2.

[19] David Jones, 'Note to the Bollingen Foundation (1959)' in *The Dying Gaul* (London: Faber, 1978), p. 11.

[20] R. S. Thomas, 'Cynddylan on a Tractor', originally published in *An Acre of Land* (1952); reprinted in *Collected Poems 1945–1990* (London: Dent, 1993), p. 30.

Thomas's poems seem to begin by being rooted in rural Wales and end with an all-encompassing – and bleak – vision of an encroaching and corrupting modernity. And yet that trajectory is misleading, for Thomas never ceases to be a specifically Welsh and a self-consciously un-British poet. In his polemical pamphlet, *Cymru or Wales?* (1992), he makes this very clear when he states: 'Britishness is a mask. Beneath it there is only one nation, England.'[21]

In Scotland, scepticism about the inclusiveness of the 'British family' was expressed as forthrightly, and earlier, by Hugh MacDiarmid, whose hostility towards England had begun at least as far back as the First World War. His antagonism was triggered by the Easter Rising in Ireland in 1916, when he was a soldier in the British Army stationed in Sheffield. In a 1977 interview, he remembered the shock of that news, stating: 'If it had been possible at all I would have deserted at that time from the British Army and joined the Irish.'[22] Later, he expressed solidarity also with Welsh nationalists, seeking to expose the 'Little Englander' attitudes of literary London; as he puts it in his 1943 autobiography, *Lucky Poet*, 'London is rotten through and through . . . Dylan Thomas alone is worth a dozen Audens or Spenders or Day Lewises any day, and *Wales* was a far more wholesome and promising affair than all the organs of the London Literary Left together'.[23]

Yet both R. S. Thomas and MacDiarmid could be as scathing about their own people as about the English. A poem like 'Glasgow' (1943) is as bitter and contemptuous as Thomas's denunciation of the Welsh in the infamous last lines of the 1952 poem 'Welsh Landscape', which pour contempt on 'an impotent people, / Sick with inbreeding / Worrying the carcase of an old song':[24] 'Glasgow, *arida nutrix* of hundreds of thousands of callous Scots, / Incapable of any process of spiritual growth and conquest, / Destitute of all rich and lively experience . . .'.[25] This vigorous

---

[21] R. S. Thomas, *Cymru or Wales?* (Llandysul: Gomer, 1992), p. 5.
[22] Hugh MacDiarmid interviewed on BBC Radio 4, 15 September 1977, quoted in Alan Bold (ed.), *The Thistle Rises: An Anthology of Poetry and Prose by Hugh MacDiarmid* (London: Hamish Hamilton, 1984), p. 289. See also Scott Lyall, *Hugh MacDiarmid's Poetry and Politics of Place* (Edinburgh University Press, 2006), p. 32ff.
[23] Hugh MacDiarmid, *Lucky Poet: A Self-Study in Literature and Political Ideas* (London: Methuen, 1943), p. 173. *Wales* was the literary magazine edited by Keidrych Rhys, which ran initially from 1937 to 1949, and published the work of writers such as Dylan Thomas, Saunders Lewis, Lynette Roberts, Glyn Jones and Idris Davies.
[24] R. S. Thomas, 'Welsh Landscape' in *Collected Poems*, p. 37, lines 27–9.
[25] Hugh MacDiarmid, 'Glasgow', originally published in *Lucky Poet* (1943), reprinted in Michael Grieve and W. R. Aitken (eds), *Complete Poems 1920–76* (London: Martin, Brian & O'Keefe, 1978), vol. I, p. 648.

jeremiad is, almost in spite of itself, a symptom of the new energy infusing Scottish writing of the time, partly from MacDiarmid's own pen, partly from the work of very different, and gentler, writers, such as Sorley MacLean and Nan Shepherd.

In both Scotland and Wales, literature in the vernacular languages – Scottish Gaelic, Scots and Welsh – was in the midst of a resurgence which also had its beginnings before the war. That difference which Humphrey Jennings was struck by in Cwmgïedd in the mid-1940s was frequently expressed as a difference of language and cultural memory. One of the most memorable expressions of these differences was the work of Sorley MacLean. From the island of Raasay, off the coast of Skye, MacLean showed that poetry coming from a place which cartographers might designate 'peripheral' could nevertheless express widely shared feelings of loss, dispossession and despair at the ways in which wars ravaged both lands and people. MacLean's lyrical voice translates into English versions of his poems, often printed in parallel-text volumes, and in so doing mediates between Gaelic difference, specificity, and the shared language and history of these islands. A poem such as 'Hallaig', first published in 1954, with its memorable epigraph, '*Time, the deer, is in the wood of Hallaig*', is about the historical clearances of one of the settlements on Raasay, but it is a Coleridge-like 'vision' which presents the landscape still haunted by its past inhabitants: 'They are still in Hallaig, / MacLeans and MacLeods, / All who were there in the time of Mac Gille Chaluim: / The dead have been seen alive.'[26] By the close of the poem, Time, the deer, is threatened by 'a vehement bullet from the gun of Love', which will freeze time, arrest the past and conserve this moment of love and liveliness forever – everything suddenly stops, like the blood of the deer; everything is preserved by and in this one poem.

For a Welsh reader, 'Hallaig' inevitably calls to mind the 1951 poem 'Rhydcymerau' by the Welsh-language poet D. Gwenallt Jones (1899–1968). Like 'Hallaig', it takes its name from a rural area of the country which has family and cultural memories for the poet. The poem begins with an image of trees and war, like Hallaig and the Scottish scene in Dylan Thomas's *Our Country*: 'Plannwyd egin coed y trydydd rhyfel / Ar dir Esgeir-ceir a meysydd Tir-bach / Ger Rhydcymerau.'[27] [Tree saplings for the third war have been planted / on the land of Esgeir-ceir and the meadows

---

[26] Sorley MacLean, 'Hallaig' in Tom Scott (ed.), *Four Points of a Saltire: The Poetry of Sorley MacLean, George Campbell Hay, William Neill, Stuart MacGregor* (Edinburgh: Reprographia, 1970), p. 148.
[27] D. Gwenallt Jones, 'Rhydcymerau' in *Eples* (Llandysul: Gomer, 1951), p. 20. My translation.

of Tir-bach / in Rhydcymerau]. The poem continues as an elegy for Gwenallt's grandparents, who once lived on this farmland which has now been taken over by the 'English Minotaur' who lurks among the labyrinthine plantations. The tone of the poem is both sad and angry, animated as it is by a sense of outrage evident in the concluding macabre vision of the unburied bodies of the ancestors hanging from the branches of the coniferous trees: 'ar golfenni, fel ar groesau, / Ysgerbydau beirdd, blaenoriaid, gweinidogion ac athrawon Ysgol Sul / Yn gwynnu yn yr haul, / Ac yn cael eu golchi gan y glaw a'u sychu gan y gwynt'[28] [on the branches, as on crosses / hang the bodies of poets, deacons, ministers, and Sunday School teachers, / bleached by the sun, washed by the rain, desiccated by the wind]. Although the poetry of Gwenallt and R. S. Thomas speaks of loss and dispossession, it is written with an extraordinary command of voice which suggests not the end of a tradition, but a Welsh poetic renaissance, in both languages.

The resurgence of Scottish Gaelic poetry in the hands of MacLean and others was also recognised and celebrated by Hugh MacDiarmid in 'The Gaelic Muse', where his speaker imagines seeing 'her again / In our long-lifeless glen, / Eidolon of our fallen race, / Shining in full renascent grace'.[29] MacDiarmid's *Lucky Poet* is full of robust advice to young poets, impassioned rejections of the British Empire and, above all, ruminations on Scottishness and Scotland. In 'The Kind of Scot I Want', MacDiarmid ends with a succinct image of where the poet stands: 'A plover requires a ploughed field to set his flight off. / It is a flight that needs a good staging. / So the Scottish spirit must be seen / In relation to Scotland'.[30] This image shows how MacDiarmid draws on traditional imagery of the poet as bird and of the flight of the poetic imagination, and at the same time adapts that imagery to a specific nationalist purpose and sense of place. The nightingale of the English poetic tradition becomes a plover, the bird of the high moorland with its plaintive call, and yet that very moorland is now ploughed, furrowed, ready to receive the seeds of cultural and national rebirth. The scene is typical of the rural mythologising of poets of this period, and yet it retains a solid particularity which protects it from any hint of the sentimental. If Scotland was always 'centre-stage' for MacDiarmid, who resolutely rejected the British Empire and the English

---

[28] Ibid., p. 21. For insightful discussion of the use of forests and water as images in modern Anglophone Welsh poetry, see: Matthew Jarvis, *Welsh Environments in Contemporary Poetry* (Cardiff: University of Wales Press, 2008); and Kirsti Bohata, *Postcolonialism Revisited* (Cardiff: University of Wales Press, 2004).
[29] Hugh MacDiarmid, 'The Gaelic Muse' from *Lucky Poet* (1943), reprinted in *Complete Poems*, p. 657.
[30] Hugh MacDiarmid, 'The Kind of Scot I Want' from *Lucky Poet*, p. 630.

(but not the Cornish), he is nonetheless positive in his remarks about the Welsh and the Irish, who are consistently portrayed as fellow Celts in his work. In the poem 'On Reading Professor Ifor Williams's "Canu Aneurin" in Difficult Days', for instance, the sixth-century Welsh epic poem, the *Gododdin*, a lament for the death of the tribe, is seen as a clear parallel for the present: '[It] is still the same war the Britons fought in at Catraeth / And Aneirin sings. The Britons were massacred then. Only one / Escaped alive. His blood flows in my veins to-day'.[31]

The cultural links between Scotland, Ireland and Wales were well established, then, but the 'Irish connection' did not necessarily acknowledge the distinction between the Republic of Ireland and Northern Ireland, separated by partition since 1922. Many Welsh and Scottish writers of the time published their work in the vibrant Irish literary journals, such as the *Dublin Magazine* and *The Bell*.[32] *Rann: An Ulster Quarterly of Poetry*, which was published between 1948 and 1953, also carried a number of contributions from Welsh and Scottish writers.[33] But Northern Ireland saw itself as a place apart. 'Britishness' itself was, in one sense, its *raison d'être*, and yet its Irishness was, and is, incontrovertible. The historical Protestant links with Scotland were strong. In the 1940s, there was an effort to create a distinctive 'regionalist' literature in Northern Ireland partly through a re-evaluation of an Ulster Scots poetic heritage, embodied by the early nineteenth-century weaver poets of Antrim and Down, rediscovered by the poet John Hewitt.[34] As Hewitt later put it, 'I became a regionalist in my thinking during the war years ... we were different and I thought this emphasised our difference and identity ... but I was wrong. Ulster is not one region, it's several regions ... My concept of regionalism was trying to bring together incompatible pieces'.[35] Even if, in retrospect, Hewitt saw his attempt to cultivate a distinct regional consciousness in the North as a failure, it nonetheless shaped his own poetry of the 1940s and 1950s. Although the 1950s were seen by some Northern Irish

---

[31] Hugh MacDiarmid, 'On Reading Professor Ifor Williams's "Canu Aneurin" in Difficult Days' from *A Kist of Whistles* (1947), reprinted in *Complete Poems*, p. 690.

[32] R. S. Thomas published no fewer than twenty poems in *The Dublin Magazine* between 1939 and 1955. In 1947, *The Bell* carried a review of R. S. Thomas's obscure first published volume, *The Stones of the Field*, by the Northern Irish poet, Valentin Iremonger; the latter also reviewed Dylan Thomas's *Deaths and Entrances* in the same journal in 1946.

[33] For example, an article by Glyn Jones in 1953, along with reviews of work by Dylan Thomas and David Jones.

[34] John Hewitt, *Rhyming Weavers and Other Country Poets of Antrim and Down* (1974), a work based on his postgraduate research undertaken in the 1940s and early 1950s.

[35] Interview with Ketzel Levine, *Fortnight*, no. 213 (4–17 February 1985), p. 17.

poets as a period of cultural stagnation, the stirrings were already present of the remarkable flowering of poetry which came to be known as the 'Northern Renaissance', led by such internationally recognised figures as Seamus Heaney, Michael Longley and Derek Mahon. In 1960, John Montague's poem 'Like Dolmens Round My Childhood, the Old People' won a literary prize in Belfast, revealing to the young Derek Mahon that the North was not the 'cultural desert' that he had assumed it to be.[36] John Montague, who spent his youth in Counties Tyrone and Armagh, was acutely aware of his anomalous position as a poet of the North living and publishing in the Republic, and yet expressing what for him was a uniquely Northern sensibility and experience. His way out of the impasse was to cultivate a self-conscious internationalism, an exilic way out not unknown to other writers from Ireland and Scotland both before and after.

To look at Montague's 'Like Dolmens Round My Childhood' and Hewitt's 'The Colony' (1953) side by side is to see clearly the similarities and differences between these two voices of the North. Ambiguity and ambivalence about identity is clearly marked in both poets' work; neither is able to offer an unalloyed celebration of their own cultural and ethnic inheritances. Montague's naming and fond evocation of the characters of the people in his childhood ends with an abrupt break in the final stanza, where the speaker stems the flow of his own reminiscence with the sardonic exclamation 'Ancient Ireland, indeed! I was reared by her bedside'.[37] And yet the irony is tempered by the enduring image of the 'ancient forms' of the protective, encircling dolmens, their shape and name so redolent of a Celtic inheritance.[38] Nevertheless, these structures are, after all, Neolithic tombs, and they unavoidably carry an air of death. This is not a vibrant, living regional culture, but the remains of what once was. The memorable plangency of Montague's lyric is matched by the bold allegorical sweep of Hewitt's 'The Colony'. In blank verse, it tells of the founding of a colony; the voice is in the first person plural, and its talk of 'Caesar', 'legions' and 'barbarians' ostensibly points to a story of the Roman Empire, and yet we are unmistakably invited to read 'the colony' as Northern Ireland. The voice's reference to 'plant[ing] little towns to garrison / the heaving

---

[36] Quoted in Fran Brearton, 'The Poetry of the 1960s' in Matthew Campbell (ed.), *The Cambridge Companion to Contemporary Irish Poetry* (Cambridge University Press, 2003), p. 98.

[37] John Montague, 'Like Dolmens Round My Childhood, the Old People' in Patrick Crotty (ed.), *Modern Irish Poetry: An Anthology* (Belfast: Blackstaff, 1995), p. 180.

[38] The etymology of 'dolmen' is disputed, but it certainly derives from one of the Celtic languages, perhaps Cornish 'tolmên' (hole of stone), cognate with similar words in Breton and Welsh.

country' and 'smoking out the nests / of the barbarian tribesmen, clan by clan' brings to mind the early modern history of the North.[39] But the voice is no historical persona. It is unmistakably inflected with a modern sensibility, a modern sense of guilt: 'We took the kindlier soils. It had been theirs / ... We took it from them. / We laboured hard and stubborn, draining, planting, / till half the country took its shape from us'.[40] Religious difference is acknowledged and at the same time distanced: 'They worship Heaven strangely, having rites / we snigger at, are known as superstitious ...'.[41] Yet the speaker seeks reconciliation, acceptance through 'small friendly gestures', attempting to assert a right to belong, to be recognised if not as 'kin', at least as 'co-inhabitants', for 'this is our country also, nowhere else'.[42] There is a poignancy in Hewitt's voice here, too, but a different one from Montague's; Hewitt's dignified blank verse tells a collective story and seeks, in vain, for the healing of a cultural wound which would, all too soon, be torn apart once more with the advent of the Troubles.

At first glance, Hewitt and Montague provide a more nuanced, insider's view of Northern Ireland than does their contemporary, Louis MacNeice. Like Dylan Thomas, during the war MacNcice wrote pieces intended to bridge the gaps among the different peoples of these islands, so that we see him in an essay such as 'Northern Ireland and Her People' (c. 1941–4) pandering to some of the stereotypes of the 'dour' Ulsterman and skimming over the political and sectarian differences of the North.[43] Yet in both *Autumn Journal* and 'Western Landscape', MacNeice captures the '*odi atque amo*' of the relationship with Northern Ireland hinted at in the work of Hewitt and Montague. MacNeice's voice is simultaneously impassioned and cynical when he conjures up 'The land of scholars and saints: / Scholars and saints my eye, the land of ambush, / Purblind manifestoes, never-ending complaints, / The born martyr and the gallant ninny'.[44]

Impressive as *Autumn Journal* is, though, the peculiar repressive atmosphere of Northern Ireland in the 1950s is more unambiguously captured by the novelists than the poets. The Belfast-born Brian Moore, in his astonishing novel *The Lonely Passion of Judith Hearne* (1955), conjures up such a bleak and death-dealing portrait of his native city that it is no

---

[39] John Hewitt, 'The Colony' (1953) in Crotty (ed.) *Modern Irish Poetry*, pp. 69–72, 69.
[40] Ibid., p. 70. [41] Ibid., p. 71. [42] Ibid., p. 72.
[43] Louis MacNeice, 'Northern Ireland and Her People' in Alan Heuser (ed.), *Selected Prose of Louis MacNeice* (Oxford: Clarendon Press, 1990). See also Peter MacDonald, *Mistaken Identities: Poetry and Northern Ireland* (Oxford: Clarendon, 1997), ch. 2.
[44] Louis MacNeice, *Autumn Journal* in Crotty (ed.), *Modern Irish Poetry*, p. 81.

surprise to find that Moore actually wrote it in Canada, to where he had escaped seven years earlier. Moore's debut novel provides a particularly negative vision of Belfast: the spinster Judith Hearne has led a self-sacrificing, lonely life and now, in middle-age, is a secret alcoholic. Miss Hearne's snobbish propriety and social respectability form a veneer over her long-repressed passions. Her 'beloved' aunt, who raised her when she was left an orphan, is revealed to have been a selfish tyrant; meanwhile, James Madden, a fellow tenant in the lodging house, has returned to his hometown from America, having failed to make good, and now feels unsettled and embittered. There is a moment in the plot when the two lonely people may come together, but that easy happy ending is brutally dismissed by an author hell-bent on showing how this stagnant religious society destroys any hint of love or fulfilment.

The air-raids of 1941 are still vivid in Miss Hearne's memory, acting as ironic manifestations of life, a source of remembered excitement, but in the present there is nothing: there is 'the dead Ulster Sunday', 'the staring white ugliness of City Hall' and, in the institution where she ends up – after visiting the priest 'stocious drunk' and, addressing herself to God, announcing 'I hate you' loudly – whispering nuns with 'voices like the sound of mice behind the walls of an old house'.[45] The novel is a particularly devastating exposé of the vulnerable and desperate position of women in this hidebound society: the maid, Mary, is raped by Madden, but she is silenced when he tells her, authoritatively, 'Nothing happened'.[46] Women cannot escape from this impasse because the borders are patrolled by other women, like Judith Hearne's aunt and the nuns in the institution. The deft use of free indirect style, reminiscent of the work of Jean Rhys, and the unsettling attribution of agency and speech to inanimate objects, makes the novel particularly haunting: 'The bottle said: I am almost empty ... It stood on the floor, near the bed, a small black accusing smoke-stack. Empty, it said, your fault'.[47]

If John Hewitt can be seen as offering a Protestant counterpoint to John Montague, the Protestant novelist Janet McNeill can similarly be compared with her Catholic contemporary, Brian Moore. Her novels, such as *Tea at Four O'Clock* (1956), also conjure up a vision of a Belfast steeped in outmoded traditions and rituals, repressed by religious dogma and riven by sectarian differences. Laura Percival, the spinster at the centre of *Tea at*

---

[45] Brian Moore, *The Lonely Passion of Judith Hearne* (Boston: Backbay Books, 1983 [1955]), pp. 67, 90, 205, 209, 190.
[46] Ibid., p. 103.   [47] Ibid., pp. 186–7.

Four O'Clock, is not dissimilar to Moore's Judith Hearne; her life, too, has been one of sacrifice and disappointment. The Percival family, though, which made its fortune in the linen trade, is in decline, and their great house is now encroached upon by the Belfast suburbs. Laura appears to be the last of the line and, chillingly, at the end of the novel she reverts to the ritual 'tea at four o'clock' which has kept her 'in prison' all her life. Others escape – she watches an emigrant train bound for Cork, where the passengers would set sail for America – but she herself remains behind, perhaps in an echo of 'Eveline' in Joyce's *Dubliners*. Laura knows that the exiled Irish, of whatever religious persuasion, will grow 'shamrocks of impossible size and vigour', but she herself will grow nothing, for 'the poison is [still] living in us now'.[48]

Yet the emigrants' train in McNeill's novel is indicative of what would be a new, internationalist trend in writing from Northern Ireland, Scotland and Wales from the 1960s onwards. Of course there had been internationalist elements in the work of individual writers before this period, notably Hugh MacDiarmid, but the transition became more general and was accompanied by a difference in the angle of vision. There was, increasingly, a probing look towards the future rather than a backward search for consolation and authenticity in the past.[49] In effect, then, the 1950s laid the foundations for the new work of the 1960s, which moved definitively beyond the shadow of the war in all three territories: the 'Northern Renaissance' in Northern Ireland, the Second Flowering in Wales and, especially in Scottish fiction, a new *avant gardisme*.

By the early 1960s, Scotland was becoming aware of a new generation of *enfants terribles* who were challenging the passionate nationalism of MacDiarmid. In a famous 1962 public debate, the Glasgow-born novelist Alexander Trocchi clashed with MacDiarmid, putting forward a new aesthetics based on 'sodomy', while MacDiarmid hit back, denouncing Trocchi as 'cosmopolitan scum'.[50] Trocchi had lived a bohemian, drug-addicted life

---

[48] Janet McNeill, *Tea at Four O'Clock* (London: Virago, 1988 [1956]), pp. 80, 97, 178.
[49] R. S. Thomas's vision of the Welsh 'warming our hands at the red past' may be seen as an early critique of this tendency, to which he himself was susceptible, as the poem 'Welsh History' acknowledges. The poem was originally published in *An Acre of Land* (1952); reprinted in *Collected Poems*, p. 36.
[50] Quoted on the back cover of Alexander Trocchi, *Young Adam* (Edinburgh: Rebel Inc., 1996). A number of contemporary Scottish writers have noted how important Trocchi was to them precisely because of his difference from MacDiarmid. Irvine Welsh, for example, said in an interview: '*Young Adam* ... was a breath of fresh air after all those horrible, sickly celebrations of Scottishness which some Scottish writers feel obliged to do ... Trocchi was ... the antithesis of Hugh MacDiarmid.' Quoted in Allan Campbell and Tim Neil, *A Life in Pieces: Reflections of Alexander Trocchi* (Edinburgh: Rebel Inc., 1997), pp. 17–18.

in Paris, making a living by writing pornography, and there was a serious and challenging new aesthetic at work in his early novels, such as *Young Adam*, first published in 1954.[51] The novel is self-conscious and morally dubious; its protagonist, Joe, an anti-heroic first-person narrator, is gradually revealed as a murderer who is unperturbed by his crime and who escapes punishment for it. Joe works on a canal barge transporting anthracite from Glasgow to Leith, but the focus is not on Scottish individuality, but rather on movement and instability ('not tied up in one place').[52] Joe is utterly self-absorbed and cold: 'I dislike the way most other people expect me to share their attitudes'.[53] The novel itself is also self-aware and self-referential: 'I don't have a plot. I don't have characters. I'm not interested in all the usual paraphernalia. Don't you understand? That's literature, false.'[54] Another man is sentenced to death for the murder; Joe thinks about confessing, but then simply walks away. Although this is an experimental book showing traces of French philosophical influences, it conjures up a vivid sense of Glasgow in the 1950s and, again, like Brian Moore's novel, there is a strong suggestion that this stagnant patriarchal society is a very dangerous place for women.[55]

Women writers themselves were, nevertheless, beginning the emergence from obscurity which would make the 1970s, particularly, a fruitful time for new literary work by women across the British Isles. In the late 1950s, alongside the work of Janet McNeill in Northern Ireland, and writers such as Brenda Chamberlain and Menna Gallie in Wales, a distinctive new voice was heard in the first books of the Edinburgh-born novelist, Muriel Spark. Like Trocchi's *Young Adam*, Spark's first novel, *The Comforters* (1957), was self-consciously experimental and set out to challenge the reader's moral and aesthetic preconceptions. Caroline, the writer-protagonist, is experiencing a crisis which takes the form of hearing noises and voices; these turn out to be the sound of the typewriter being used to type this novel and the voices are the voices of the text itself: 'At this point in the narrative, it might be as well to state that the characters in this novel are all fictitious, and do not refer to any living persons whatsoever. *Tap-tappity-tap. At this point in the narrative* . . .'.[56] In retrospect, the surprising thing about this novel is

---

[51] Alexander Trocchi, *Young Adam*. First published in what Trocchi called a 'sexed up' version by Olympia Press in 1954, reissued in a revised edition by Heinemann in 1961.
[52] Ibid., pp. 6, 30.   [53] Ibid., p. 83.   [54] Ibid., p. 125.
[55] Joe and the bargee, Leslie, scan the newspaper for news of the 'stiff' they have fished out of the water, but find nothing: 'An old woman's had her head bashed in in Paisley, but there's nothing about our one', says Leslie (p. 59).
[56] Muriel Spark, *The Comforters* (Harmondsworth: Penguin, 1963 [1957]), p. 69.

that it remains engaging almost in spite of the author's determination to be *avant garde*. It also reveals a writer of great comic and stylistic gifts, and one unafraid to transgress taboos: *The Comforters* addresses disability, homosexuality, diabolism and madness, among other things, while, in a manner very different from her Welsh contemporary, R. S. Thomas, Spark asks probing questions about the possibility of religion in a secular age. Four years later, Spark would abandon the *nouveau roman* and return to her Scottish roots with *The Prime of Miss Jean Brodie*, an anatomisation of spinsterhood far removed from Brian Moore's Belfast tragedy, although both novels offer astute visions of loneliness and sexual repression in a sectarian, stagnant society.

Sex and sodomy were also, surprisingly, coming into their own in Welsh writing. Dylan Thomas had already forged the way with works that made his strait-laced editors distinctly uncomfortable, while novelists such as Gwyn Thomas and Emyr Humphreys began to open up the psycho-sexual dramas of Welsh society. Texts like Gwyn Thomas's 'Oscar' and 'Simeon' in *The Dark Philosophers* (1946) reveal sexual exploitation and obsession, religious mania and incest under the surface of chapel respectability, while Emyr Humphreys's *A Toy Epic* (1958) makes a novel of three interwoven voices, a story of three boys growing up, struggling with religion, sex and politics, and creating a powerful, composite picture of a nation in flux.

This transitional period in the cultural life of the three territories can be seen, then, as one of literary reawakening. Led by iconoclastic figures such as Hugh MacDiarmid and Dylan Thomas, Wales and Scotland witnessed a flowering of poetry and fiction in English, Welsh, Gaelic and Scots which continued throughout the 1940s and 1950s. Northern Ireland, meanwhile, though still in the throes of defining its own identity after partition, was already producing work that anticipated the extraordinary flowering of the 1960s. These were, then, transformative years, and although Scotland, Wales and Northern Ireland had each experienced the Second World War as constituent parts of the United Kingdom of Great Britain and Northern Ireland, and many writers had, as we have seen, participated to some degree in the construction of a united British wartime identity, a concern with the particularity of nation and place remained. There were always those who refused and sought escape from a cohesive Britishness, through their ways of life and through their works of art, and the aftermath of war saw their voices strengthen and their number swell.

Nevertheless, these nations' cities – notably Belfast, Swansea and Glasgow – suffered extensive bombing by the Luftwaffe, and the aftermath of war also produced a literature with a sombre, bleak and sometimes elegiac tone. Elegies were written not only for the dead of the recent war: the work of writers as diverse as R. S. Thomas, Brenda Chamberlain, Sorley MacLean and John Hewitt shares an often anguished note of regret at the loss (or imminent loss) of a native language, culture or way of life. Yet in Wales and Scotland at least, if less so in Northern Ireland, those native languages were proving themselves to be resilient and pliable in the modern world, as evidenced in the distinctively modern idiom and sensibility of the poetry of Sorley MacLean and Gwenallt. Others, though, looked not to their own vernacular languages and cultures for inspiration, but elsewhere: MacDiarmid, Dylan Thomas and John Montague, among others, brought fresh draughts of the European *avant garde* into their native literary traditions. Many – such as Alexander Trocchi, Brian Moore and Muriel Spark – uprooted themselves from home and established themselves in the Joycean tradition as writers in exile who nevertheless were capable of bringing a candid gaze to bear on life back home. By the end of the 1950s, these writers, in their different ways, were beginning to explore new modes of liberation from traditional ways of life, exploring counter-cultural strategies and ideologies ranging from drug-taking to feminist rebellion and atheism – preoccupations that were already heralding the more widespread cultural revolutions of the 1960s. The literature that emerged from these two decades in the three territories, then, is both transitional and unfairly neglected, for it is stimulatingly engaged with all three distinctive cultural traditions, while at the same time looking outwards for inspiration from more international trends and influences.

CHAPTER 5

Heroes of Austerity: Genre in Transition
Gill Plain

The Second World War changed many things, not least of which was the dominant configuration of heroic male agency. Surveying the period, historians and cultural critics have noted the rise of the 'temperate' hero, a figure characteristically quotidian, meritocratic and understated, but nonetheless reliant upon uniform for his cultural authority.[1] Studies of the aftermath of war, meanwhile, have revealed intense anxiety surrounding the process of demobilisation and the return to a domestic context of men distorted and disorientated by their exposure to exactly that uniformed subjectivity which had so recently been the cultural norm.[2] These rapid transitions had a profound impact on the preoccupations of popular fiction and the conventions of genre. My primary concern in this chapter is the impact of the Second World War on crime fiction, the most popular generic form of the interwar period, which underwent a radical transformation in the years 1940 to 1960. Indeed, if – as Alison Light has so persuasively hypothesised – the aftermath of the First World War saw a 'feminisation' of middle-class cultures in general and the detective hero in particular, it might similarly be suggested that the aftermath of the Second World War produced an equal and opposite process of remasculinisation, albeit one riven with self-doubt and anxiety.

In her ground-breaking work on the 'conservative modernity' of Agatha Christie, Light argues that the 1920s and 1930s witnessed a 'move away from formerly heroic and officially masculine public rhetorics of national destiny ... to an Englishness at once less imperial and more inward-

---

[1] Sonya Rose argues that the hegemonic masculinity of wartime combined 'two contradictory masculinities – one exemplified by the soldier-hero, and the other generated from the anti-heroic mood of the inter-war period and fashioned in opposition to the hyper-masculine German other. But to perform it successfully men had to be in uniform'. Sonya O. Rose, *Which People's War? National Identity and Citizenship in Wartime Britain, 1939–1945* (Oxford University Press, 2003), p. 195.
[2] Alan Allport, *Demobbed: Coming Home after the Second World War* (New Haven, CT: Yale University Press, 2009).

looking, more domestic and more private'.[3] This reconfiguration of the 'national temperament' produced, variously, a celebration of civilian virtues and a refusal of seriousness that turned the heroes of popular fiction from masculine archetypes into Belgian refugees, watchful spinsters and aristocrats hiding psychological wounds under a veneer of superficial frivolity. The reaction of austerity, by contrast, seeks not to ridicule, but to reconstruct a masculine ideal. The emergent postwar genre hero is a figure marked by cynicism, frequently bearing the scars of personal betrayal or wartime trauma, who fights to construct a viable peacetime masculinity through the agency of investigation and the business of work. His emergence can be traced across a range of generic transformations. While the clue-puzzle mystery – exemplified by such writers as Agatha Christie, Dorothy L. Sayers and Margery Allingham – did not die in the war, in the conflict's aftermath its cultural centrality was challenged, complicated and reconfigured by the resurgence of the thriller, the emergence of the police procedural and the new hegemony of the spy.

This chapter, then, will trace the postwar reconfiguration of the hero and the literary forms within which he finds himself. I use 'himself' advisedly. With the notable exception of Miss Marple, who grew in popularity throughout the period, the protagonist's role remains stubbornly male – and indeed, even the 'feminised' figures of Marple and Poirot often find themselves investigating the legacy of war as manifest in a range of damaged young men.[4] That Christie's novels should trouble to make such investigations is noteworthy. Christie was a writer of astonishing adaptability, remaining a bestseller even when the form at which she excelled was becoming residual, and she achieved this in part through her alertness to the emergent anxieties of postwar Britain. Nowhere is this more evident than in *Taken at the Flood* (1948), in which she adapts the trope of damaged masculinity to produce a novel featuring a demobbed woman struggling to adjust to life with her non-combatant fiancée. *Taken at the Flood* weaves a fascinating study of veteran dislocation around the familiar structures of golden-age plotting: a dubious will, a stolen identity and a jealous family in pressing financial need. Although notionally a Poirot novel, much of the narrative is focalised through returning

---

[3] Alison Light, *Forever England: Femininity, Literature and Conservatism between the Wars* (London: Routledge, 1991), p. 8.
[4] While crime fiction in this period provides relatively few opportunities for female agents, it is worth noting the popularity of Mary Stewart's novels. These hybrid romance adventures usually obliged their plucky heroines to exhibit considerable self-sufficiency en route to the satisfactions of desire and the security of marriage.

WREN, Lynn Marchmont. Her inability to reintegrate into family or village life is exacerbated by her attraction to the seductive and dangerous ex-commando David Hunter, a figure who activates the community's latent anxieties surrounding returning combatants. The book also explores the psychological damage done to non-combatants by the war: Lynn's fiancée, a farmer in a reserved occupation, feels emasculated by his enforced non-involvement, and – being a typically inarticulate British man – can only express his suffering through the medium of violence. Yet although it draws on a familiar readjustment narrative, *Taken at the Flood* remains atypically gendered: it was damaged men who dominated heroic roles in the popular fiction of this period. In the sections that follow, I consider three case studies that demonstrate different strategies for representing and resolving the problem of wounded masculinity. In the thrillers of Hammond Innes, male damage is evident in the explicit disorientation of demobilisation: it is in turn repaired through a combination of violence, work and heterosexual desire. Work again is crucial to the innovative police procedurals of John Creasey: here, though, the damage done by war appears as a crisis of inheritance, and the novels are preoccupied with the importance of nurturing 'cadet' masculinities and finding healthy new structures of homosocial community. Finally, male damage can be seen to underpin the epic story arc of Ian Fleming's spy thrillers. Although this dimension has been lost in the series' translation into a global film franchise, the novels make clear that the rejuvenated individual agency represented by James Bond is built upon a legacy of damage, both national and personal. Significantly, it is also the case that Bond, in alignment with Innes's engineers and Creasey's policemen, demonstrates the emergence of a postwar professional meritocracy, and my diverse examples of the transitions in popular fiction are linked by a series of technocratic tropes designed to re-energise both masculinity and nation.

Risk and Responsibility: The Postwar Thriller

The spy thriller was not an unfamiliar form in the interwar years. As practised by writers such as Eric Ambler, it presented a more or less naive Englishman abroad, confronted by the complexity of European politics and forced to navigate unfamiliar situations with the aid of inscrutable, and unreliable, foreign guides. There is something of the picaresque about a novel like *Journey into Fear* (1940), as the hero staggers from one ill-judged encounter to another, without ever fully grasping the extent of the intrigue or achieving control over his circumstances. Arguably, such a narrative framework made perfect sense for the bewildering years leading up to the Second World War, but as the 1940s progressed, a rather different mode of thriller emerged.[5] Criticism to date has mainly identified this transition in the cinema, exploring the films of the so-called 'spiv cycle'.[6] However, the preoccupations of these domestic noir films – personal and cultural malaise, black market criminality, loss of purpose and disorientation – were equally the subject of the postwar 'demob thrillers' of Hammond Innes.

Innes, whose work grew in popularity across the late 1940s and 1950s, offered a version of the genre in which a disaffected, displaced or even criminal hero struggles to find a role in a hostile postwar world. Within this formula, the protagonist's journey usually involves confrontation with a significant adversary – sometimes civilian and sometimes, like the hero, ex-military – and these villains are configured as mesmeric, even Satanic, types who seduce the hero with the promise of risk and the reward of a strangely perverted version of wartime homosociality. Such promises come at a cost, which is usually revealed to be the hero's 'soul', if soul can be equated with social integration and the reconstruction of heteronormative bonds. In other words, the demob thriller demands that the hero abandon inappropriate wartime loyalties and (violent) habits, defeat both a powerful enemy and a hostile environment, and claim the loyalty of a good woman – a process that will reinstate him as a citizen within a society from which he feels excluded and disenfranchised.[7]

This characteristic narrative pattern is repeated with variations in Innes's work of the immediate postwar. *The Lonely Skier* (1947) features an unemployed demobbed soldier enticed by a charismatic former army colleague into making an action film in the Dolomites; *The Killer Mine* (1947) presents the hero as a misunderstood deserter, deceived by a corrupt old acquaintance and left to battle both smugglers and the ghosts of his past

---

[5] Ambler continued to produce this style of thriller as a response to the equally opaque intrigues of the Cold War, for example in *Judgement on Deltchev* (1951).

[6] The cycle is usually considered to start with *Waterloo Road* (1945), which features a soldier going AWOL to deal with the threat posed to his wife by an amorous spiv. Although lighter in tone than later examples such as *They Made Me a Fugitive* (1947) and *Night and the City* (1950), the film was nonetheless radical for its portrayal of working-class disobedience and the seductions of a black-market subculture (seductions helped by the casting of Stewart Granger as the spiv). See Robert Murphy, *Realism and Tinsel: Cinema and Society in Britain, 1939–1948* (London: Routledge, 1989); Andrew Spicer, *Typical Men: The Representation of Masculinity in Popular British Cinema* (London: I. B. Tauris, 2001); and Gill Plain, *John Mills and British Cinema: Masculinity, Identity and Nation* (Edinburgh University Press, 2006).

[7] The problems of postwar reintegration are widespread and find diverse textual form, as demonstrated by Leo Mellor's and Mark Rawlinson's chapters later in this volume.

in a Cornish tin mine; *Air Bridge* (1951) has another hero on the run and in conflict with a particularly mesmeric adversary, whose manipulations threaten to pervert national as well as homosocial values.[8] In all these novels, the heroes find redemption through female support and their non-military workplace skills. Yet it is in *Campbell's Kingdom* (1952), a novel less concerned with the perversion of old allegiances than with the forging of new ones, that the restoration of damaged masculinity receives its most thorough-going treatment. In this novel, the love of a good woman, healthy fresh air and a strong sense of purpose prove capable not just of repair, but of resurrection.

Campbell's Kingdom begins with an explicit assertion of the failure of readjustment, as the narrator Bruce Weatheral compares his military past to the 'lonely, wasted' postwar years: 'for me the army had been the big chance. Once out of it I had drifted without the drive of an objective, without the competitive urge of a close-knit masculine world'.[9] Weatheral begins the novel as a spectral figure: diagnosed with cancer, he is a sick man in a dead-end job, his borderline hysteria only legitimised by reference to a respectable war record. The process of rehabilitation begins when a lawyer informs him he has inherited a defunct oilfield – Campbell's Kingdom – from his disgraced grandfather. Greedy developers, the powerful antagonists of the novel, want to flood the land for a dam, and Bruce sets off on a mission to redeem his grandfather's reputation, defeat human venality and conquer a harsh natural environment reluctant to give up its reserves of black gold. Knowledge of death proves strangely liberating, and the wounded hero is reborn: 'I was no longer afraid, no longer alone. I had a purpose and an urgency'.[10] Although physically weak, Bruce is equipped with a powerful command of language and a natural aptitude for leading men. Building a team of outsiders and like-minded individuals, he forges allegiances and outwits his adversaries, while acquiring the support of a strong, independent woman. Jean Lucas, herself a displaced and unhappy war veteran, believes in Bruce and thus becomes the necessary mirror reflecting wholeness back upon the fragmented form of postwar masculinity.[11] Jean's support will give Bruce the self-belief to endure in the face of overwhelming odds and endless disappointments. The book,

---

[8] Innes diagnoses the cultural work of his own fiction in the early pages of *The Lonely Skier*: 'There's a colossal market waiting for a fast-moving ski picture. Plenty of spills and thrills. The world has gone crazy about sport – artificial excitement to replace the excitement of war.' Hammond Innes, *The Lonely Skier* (London: Fontana, 1974 [1947]), p. 18.

[9] Hammond Innes, *Campbell's Kingdom* (London: Vintage, 2013 [1952]), p. 3.   [10] Ibid., p. 15.

[11] Ibid., pp. 71, 236.

then, offers two distinct modes of resurrection. Bruce's fight against powerful vested interests resuscitates the classic underdog narrative of Second World War propaganda, as inspiration triumphs over organisation and the individual defeats the machine.[12] And it is also a potent fantasy of personal rebirth. Fresh Canadian air and the love of a good woman can, it would seem, cure cancer.

Campbell's Kingdom ends with Bruce and Jean celebrating their new power to make plans, repeating over and over that the 'great thing is to have a future'.[13] In this, the book is more explicitly optimistic and redemptive than some of Innes's earlier works, which end with the hero frankly just grateful to be alive and still with much to do to complete the journey into a viable future.[14] It is possible that Weatheral's remarkable restoration is in part enabled by the novel's setting in a new world, uncontaminated by European war. As with Nevil Shute's 1950 bestseller, *A Town Like Alice*, geographical relocation enables the trauma of the past to be displaced and the hero to forge a new society in a land free from the disillusionments of peace. The battle-scarred veterans of European war, then, are ideal new colonialists, displaced from a 'home' that has no use for them. The lessons of war make them frontier leaders, building a commonwealth through their resourceful resilience.

The discomfort with 'home' that permeates Innes's novels is in marked contrast to my next example. While the thriller hero's victory is seldom translated into the restoration of a wider community, the concept of community – its welfare and trust – is central to the ideology of the newly emergent police procedural form.

Citizens in Uniform: The Police Procedural

While Hammond Innes's battered, bruised and misunderstood heroes found themselves divorced from community and betrayed by (the perversion of) wartime male bonds, in other modes of crime fiction the homosocial remained a viable space for the development of male agency. Indeed, in the police procedural, the male group was reconfigured as a mode of postwar rehabilitation. The British procedural – like the police force itself – was built upon the potent ideological construct of the 'citizen in uniform': an ideal of policing based upon a belief in consensus and the fundamental stability of British society. The citizen in uniform

---

[12] Ibid., p. 187. [13] Ibid., p. 301.
[14] In *The Killer Mine*, for example, the hero remains a fugitive, forced into exile.

extended 'people's war' ideology into the postwar, sustaining a myth of unity and shared purpose while ensuring that for the duration of the 1950s, the policeman could be seen as 'one of us'. Writing in 1951, sociologist Anthony Martienssen argued that the policeman 'must live among, and be a member of the community he serves', a concept of social embedding and public service that would ensure that he could act against 'possible excesses of state authority'.[15] The policeman was to be, then, a hero of modernity in his capacity to guard against totalitarian tendencies. This community ideal, which re-imagines the constable as the conscript soldier defending freedom, is evident in the film that set the agenda for popular cultural representations of the police, *The Blue Lamp* (1950).[16] Here, paternal PC George Dixon takes rookie Andy Mitchell under his wing and into his home, welcoming him into both a domestic and a police family. These units, like the broader community within which they are embedded, are imagined as fundamentally homogeneous. Even the criminal fraternity is part of this balanced ecosystem, offering a parallel, well-ordered counter-culture. Yet this sense of social order is under threat in the film from a disturbing new force: the juvenile delinquent. This free radical that respects neither the rule of law nor the conventions of criminality makes Dixon's 'adoption' of Andy Mitchell essential. Not only does Mitchell become a surrogate for the son the Dixons have lost in the war, he also becomes a symbol of healthy 'cadet' masculinity to set against the disordered and directionless young men looking for purpose in the atomised aftermath of war.[17]

The police procedural, then, offers the demobbed soldier the security of a new uniform as well as the comforting promise of ongoing danger against which a peacetime masculinity can be forged. And the threat is a substantial one. In John Creasey's *Gideon's Day* (1955), for example, policemen fight a 'never-ending war' demanding constant vigilance, not least because every citizen is a potential criminal: 'many law abiding people would readily become law-breakers if they had a good chance and believed that they would not be found out'.[18] The war on crime is both anxiety and opportunity: it confirms the realisation of a newly threatening modernity, but it also reassures that there is work for men to do, and structures

---

[15] Anthony Martienssen, *Crime and the Police* (Harmondsworth: Penguin, 1953 [1951]), pp. 15, 252.
[16] *The Blue Lamp*, dir. Basil Dearden, Ealing Studios, UK 1950.
[17] The term 'cadet' masculinity is Raymond Durgnat's: see *A Mirror for England: British Movies from Austerity to Affluence* (London: BFI Palgrave, 2011 [1970]), p. 176.
[18] John Creasey, *Gideon's Day* (London: Hodder & Stoughton, 1964 [1955]), p. 19. The image is repeated across the series, for example, in *Gideon's Staff* (London: Coronet, 1965 [1959]), p. 18.

through which they might profitably do it. This perhaps is why the form captured the imagination of the 1950s public: police heroes emerged in the cinema, on radio and on the fledgling form of television. Indeed, it was here that PC George Dixon, murdered in *The Blue Lamp*, would make a remarkable recovery to star in his own series. *Dixon of Dock Green* made its BBC debut in 1955, following in the tracks of drama documentaries such as *Fabian of the Yard* (1954).[19] But it was not simply on screen that the policeman was enjoying new prominence: the figure was also undergoing a simultaneous and significant fictional transformation.

Across the first half of the twentieth century, the dominant forms of crime fiction had figured the detective as outsider. In the predominantly American hard-boiled mode, the private investigator was a working man, set at odds with a world of wealth and corruption, within which the police were as likely as anyone to be on the take. In British classical crime narrative of the interwar years, by contrast, the police appeared as sidekicks, assistants, bureaucrats, impediments and occasionally friends, but seldom more than walk-on parts in the investigations of inspired amateurs. In a process requiring imagination and critical distance, the police were, habitually, found lacking.[20] By the postwar period, this was changing, even within conventional clue-puzzle fictions. Miss Marple was greatly assisted by the astute Inspector Craddock, while in Margery Allingham's *The Tiger in the Smoke* (1954), the amateur detective Albert Campion is overshadowed both by the anarchic villainy of Jack Havoc and his gang of demobbed soldiers, and the vital energy of DDCI Charlie Luke. Yet none of these novels represents the police force as an organisation and as a body of men working together to combat not the single mystery of a puzzling corpse, but the full range of criminal activity threatening the stability of society. Policing the postwar presented new challenges and new representations of the police evolved to meet them.

John Creasey, already the author of a number of crime series featuring assorted amateur and professional heroes, was among the first to turn his hand to the procedural form, and his series featuring Superintendent, later Commander, George Gideon CID was both popular and influential.[21]

---

[19] Sue Turnbull, *The TV Crime Drama* (Edinburgh University Press, 2014), pp. 35–41.

[20] Mapping trends in genre fiction inevitably obscures exceptions. Interwar detective fiction did produce intelligent police figures, most notably Ngaio Marsh's Roger Alleyn, but they tended to function more as individual agents than as representatives of an organisation.

[21] In a writing career that began in the 1930s, Creasey published over 500 books. The Gideon series, originally written under the pseudonym J. J. Marric, comprises twenty-one novels published between 1955 and 1976. After Creasey's death in 1973, a further five novels were written by

From the outset, the shift in representation is evident. The first novel, *Gideon's Day*, presents the police as dedicated, professional, largely intelligent and engaged in a process of criminal investigation that requires not thoughtful inspiration, but massive multi-tasking. The novels' other major innovation was the balance they struck between group and individual heroism. The individual hero is Gideon; the group hero is the composite body of citizens in uniform who work under his leadership and – for the most part – worship the ground on which he treads. Gideon is a constant, other serial characters move in and out of focus and each novel includes plot-specific subaltern characters introduced largely for the purpose of heroic sacrifice. Although the characterisation is sketchy, the novels are persuasively structured to give a relatively realistic representation of police business, weaving multiple story lines together to demonstrate that policing the city requires not only panoptical vigilance and the rigorous processing of information, but also a fair proportion of accident and chance. In this sense, the novels are closer to hardboiled than to classical form, not least in their suggestion that crime is endemic. Their proximity to hardboiled modes is also evident in the depiction of violence: the cases under investigation are marked by a mundane and disturbing brutality. In *Gideon's Day* alone, the police must deal with armed robbery, assault and battery, child murder, corruption, gang violence and paedophilia.

The quotidian brutality that runs through the series gives substance to the repeated claims that the police are engaged in a 'constant bitter war'.[22] How this war is fought, and how heroic agency is imagined in relation to it, though, marks a significant shift in the terms of hegemonic masculinity – in what a man might *do* to be heroic. *Gideon's Staff* (1959), like the previous four novels in the series, makes use of multifocal third-person narration. However, there is no doubt that Gideon remains the protagonist, leading his troops in a relentless battle. Configured as a man of the people – of 'obscure' family, he left school at the age of 14 and now lives in the suburbs with his wife and six children, doing DIY in his spare time – he has reaped the rewards of meritocracy to rise through the ranks. But this assumption of authority inevitably removes him from 'combat' agency, and *Gideon's Staff* is obliged to compensate by rendering bureaucracy heroic. In the high-level boardroom battle for police resources, Gideon emerges as the only man brave enough to speak his mind, and his reward is to be allowed

---

William Vivian Butler. See Gill Plain, 'Structures of Authority: Postwar Masculinity and the British Police' *Itinéraires*, (2015) 2014–3 Le polar en Europe: réécritures du genre.
[22] John Creasey, *Gideon's Staff* (London: Coronet, 1959), p. 44.

to make his case on paper. The transition from action to advocacy speaks to the postwar re-inscription of masculine norms, both through the bureaucratisation of agency and through the identification of a paradigm shift in risk. In arguing that the 'Armed Services aren't fighting a war ... we are',[23] Gideon re-inscribes himself as a battlefield commander. War has been domesticated, and the police are now frontline troops.

The perception of a never-ending war against crime is not the only cultural anxiety shaping the Gideon novels. They also evidence a belief that the war has disrupted and damaged patriarchal structures. Unlike George Dixon, Gideon struggles to find a suitable cadet to nurture. He struggles, indeed, even to find a decent subordinate, eventually coming to rely not on a younger man, but on the calm, competent, but very much older Joe Bell.[24] Time and again, promoted men are given responsibility and found wanting, with the result that Gideon seems often to be carrying the burden of policing London – and symbolising a viable postwar masculine authority – on his own. And this perhaps explains the anomalous condition of his character's visibility. While, in theory, the CID officer requires a degree of anonymity to enable his detection, Gideon is the antithesis of this bland neutrality. Rather, he is instantly recognisable to every police officer, journalist and criminal in London. It is a curious feature of a set of novels otherwise carefully concerned with the delineation of procedure, the collation of information and the business of mass organisation, that they should also have at their centre a heroic figure of almost epic proportions. This characterisation suggests a fundamental need for reassurance: Gideon may be carrying the weight of the world, but the novels reassure us that he, like London, can 'take it'.

That such reassurance might be needed brings me to my final example. Although radically different in their international preoccupations, Ian Fleming's James Bond novels prove surprisingly similar in their attempt to render postwar bureaucracy spectacularly heroic.

Civil Service: Bond and the Embodiment of National Defence

James Bond, by far the most successful popular hero to emerge from the 1950s, might seem very far removed from the prosaic group heroism, mindless violence and quotidian crime of Creasey's Gideon novels. However, just as each of the procedurals signifies that crime is a never-

---

[23] Ibid., p. 18.
[24] Perhaps as an index of further cultural change, Bell is blown up at the end of *Gideon's March* (1962).

ending internal threat which it takes constant vigilance to repel, so SMERSH and its tentacles represent an external threat demanding a thoroughly professional, panoptical vigilance if the nation is to be secure. Similarly, Bond, like Gideon, is an outstanding professional, someone who is recognised and singled out for his hyperbolic competence. And, like Gideon, he is symbol more than man, an ideal through which the uncertain, displaced masculinities of the postwar can triangulate and take their reference. Indeed, it is perhaps in this 'spectacular visibility' that Bond most closely approximates Gideon: Gideon the detective and Bond the spy are both seen where they should be unseen, achieving their impact as much through reputation as action. Bond is not a spy to be killed, but a point of reference to be measured against, which perhaps explains the creativity Bond-villains put into imagining complex deaths for the hero to evade.[25] In their study of Bond as a 'popular hero', Tony Bennett and Janet Woollacott analyse 'Bond' as simultaneously providing solace for a damaged national ego and a displacement strategy for the anxieties generated by this damage. He is a figure who enables larger world problems to be reduced to individual conflict, and a crisis of national agency to be resolved through the comforts of gender dominance.[26] 'Women were for recreation', notes Bond in *Casino Royale* (1953),[27] and while this approach to the 'problem' of women's role in the postwar world looks superficially very different from the well-ordered domesticity favoured by Gideon, the two men also share an unquestioned adherence to a gender normativity that ensures men's public agency and women's private submission.

With women safely returned to the domestic and decorative spheres, the workplace can once again function as the space of male agency and genre can once again function as a mode of rehabilitation. And this is necessary. Scarcely a character in the early Fleming novels does not bear the mark of war: in *Casino Royale*, the French landlord of Bond and Vesper's rehabilitation hideaway has lost an arm in combat; in *Live and Let Die* (1954), Strangways, chief agent for the Caribbean, is a one-eyed Navy veteran, and Bond's Monday morning trip to the office in *Moonraker* includes the following brief encounter: 'The liftman could smell the cordite on him. They always smelled like that when they came up from the shooting

---

[25] This is perhaps most evident in *From Russia with Love* (1957). See Michael Denning, 'Licensed to Look: James Bond and the Heroism of Consumption' in Christoph Lindner (ed.), *The James Bond Phenomenon: A Critical Reader* (Manchester University Press, 2003), p. 59.
[26] Tony Bennett and Janet Woollacott, *Bond and Beyond: The Political Career of a Popular Hero* (Basingstoke: Macmillan, 1987), p. 29.
[27] Ian Fleming, *Casino Royale* (London: Coronet, 1988 [1953]), p. 33.

gallery. He liked it. It reminded him of the Army. He pressed the button for the eighth and rested the stump of his left arm against the control handle.'[28] The minutiae of character and *mise-en-scène* are permeated by the war and its aftermath, and within this landscape Bond functions both to valorise past sacrifice and to enable the transition to a complex modernity. He will be an avatar reminding men of a potent past and enabling the fantasy of future agency, but this process is more mundane than the later mythologisation of the series suggests.

For the purposes of this chapter, it is perhaps the third Bond novel, *Moonraker* (1955), which offers the clearest demonstration of Fleming's engagement with the processes of bureaucratic remasculinisation. *Moonraker* is unusual in being set wholly in Britain. Bond finds himself seconded to Special Branch and temporarily licensed to 'work' on home soil in order to investigate the enigma that is Sir Hugo Drax, a multimillionaire who cheats at cards. Drax combines elements of the already emergent Bond-villain type – larger than life, physically grotesque, charismatic and monumentally organised – with a more unusual trait. He is also the archetypal 'people's war' hero. 'Drax' was, effectively, born in the war: given the identity of a Liverpool dock worker after the explosion that destroyed half his face and left him amnesiac. This origin story renders him classless, an ideal figure for popular fantasy, and indeed, his narrative becomes a fairy tale as he miraculously turns into a jet age pioneer. Drax makes his millions in rare metals and returns to Britain as the ultimate anti-austerity fantasy, spending money with reckless, pleasurable abandon: '. . . the people simply loved it. It was the Arabian nights. If a wounded soldier from Liverpool could get there in five years, why shouldn't they or their son?'.[29] In addition to single-handedly revitalising the postwar economy, Drax has made the nation the gift of security – an atomic rocket, the 'Moonraker' – which will give Britain an independent nuclear deterrent and, it is implied, the third power status the country so desperately desires.[30]

Drax's appeal is thus both forward-looking and nostalgic, and the same can be said of the threat he poses. Drax is in many respects a 'retro-villain', a classical Nazi *Übermensch* whose ability to inspire unthinking loyalty in both his fanatical German supporters and the British nation speaks to ongoing desires for a mode of wartime unity, purpose and leadership.

---

[28] Ian Fleming, *Moonraker* (London: Vintage, 2012 [1955]), p. 6.   [29] Ibid., p. 26.
[30] Ibid., p. 114. For an analysis of Anglo-American relations and nuclear policy, see Adam Piette, *The Literary Cold War: 1945 to Vietnam* (Edinburgh University Press, 2009), pp. 36–44.

However, his comfortable familiarity is married to a very modern threat, nuclear annihilation, and the new anxieties of the Cold War remain disturbingly present in the shadows. Indeed, Drax acts as a particularly potent fantasy for the nuclear age, in that he is a known entity that can be defeated, unlike the amorphous mass of the USSR, its allies, dependents, ideologies and organisations. Ironically, then, under the aegis of Drax – the familiar overweening Nazi brought down by hubris – the nuclear threat becomes more manageable, an enemy that can and will be defeated.

A wartime retro-villain needs, at least superficially, a 'temperate' hero, and *Moonraker* places unusual emphasis on Bond's status as an everyday meritocratic professional.[31] Considerable time is taken to establish Bond as an office worker: he is a civil servant with an unpredictable boss and an unusual skill set; an organisation man who admires his secretary, takes his car to the garage and makes shopping lists on the office stationery.[32] In what might be seen as a nostalgic reinstatement of wartime homosocial structures of authority, and a counterpoint to the mythos of intense individualism that supposedly characterises the fiction, the Bond of *Moonraker* is intensely loyal to M and worries about his colleagues (008 is laid up after a close shave, while 0011 is missing in action). He verges on the brink of cadet masculinity, and in what is undoubtedly a recognition of the technocracy emerging in the aftermath of war, his exceptional skills are repeatedly demonstrated to be not so much the gift of inspiration (or of interwar amateur genius) as the result of practice, training and professional standards. All that sets this quotidian Bond aside from the postwar masses, then, is the red telephone on his desk. This prosaic object has the potency of the superhero's space of transformation: it has the power to take him 'out of one world and set him down in another'.[33]

Yet the transformation effected by the red telephone is far from super-human. Indeed, it speaks to the exploits of men who barely more than a decade previously had been conscripted into unimaginable new roles. Bond is a well-trained man with a strong work ethic: it is simply the tools of his trade that differentiate him from the scientist or engineer. *Moonraker* opens with Bond practising at the firing range. When M asks whether Drax

---

[31] For discussion of gentlemanliness and professionalism in the Bond canon, see Praseeda Gopinath, *Scarecrows of Chivalry: English Masculinity after Empire* (Charlottesville, VA: University of Virginia Press, 2013).

[32] Fleming, *Moonraker*, p. 106. The organisational dimension of *Moonraker* is also noted by Edward P. Comintale in his analysis of 'corporate' Bond. See Edward P. Comentale, Stephen Watt and Skip Willman, *Ian Fleming and James Bond: The Cultural Politics of 007* (Bloomington, IN: Indiana University Press, 2005), p. 3.

[33] Fleming, *Moonraker*, p. 15.

is cheating, Bond goes home and researches the answer,[34] and then rigorously practises the card-sharping skills he had earlier acquired on a training course. Bond knows his skills, he knows his specialism and he is a creature of habit, as is demonstrated when five minutes in the Special Branch waiting room proves enough to plunge him into depression: 'He was getting tangled up with strange departments. He would be out of touch with his own people and his own Service routines. Already, in this waiting-room, he felt out of his element.'[35]

Bennett and Woollacott suggest that *Moonraker* is characterised by 'a set of disequilibrating/equilibrating tendencies which centre specifically on England and the ideology of Englishness', and indeed, Bond's key task within the text is to undertake a reading of national characteristics – to make sense of the misalignment in Englishness represented by Drax's cheating.[36] That he fails in this task – not seeing the evidence of 'Germanness' under his nose – is perhaps less surprising than it might at first seem. Indeed, back in 1941, Agatha Christie made comedy out of the interchangeability of German and English national characteristics in her spy thriller *N or M?*. Nonetheless, Sir Hugo's legion of regimented scientists might have given pause for thought to a man not distracted by the twin beauties of technological modernity and English womanhood. Again, then, the book is Janus-faced, simultaneously nostalgic and modern in its construction of desire. Bond is in awe of Drax's rocket, 'dazzled by the terrible beauty of the greatest weapon on earth'[37] and rendered speechless by this 'pencil of glistening chromium'.[38] Such an awe-inspiring vision of the atomic sublime needs the picturesque to counter it: faced by the pastoral ideal of the English coastline, Drax's miracle of modernity becomes an 'ugly concrete world'.[39] But it is not only the English landscape that does vital symbolic work in the novel: this role is also fulfilled by Gala Brand, whose initials alone mark her out as idealised English maidenhood personified. Indeed, the initials are not enough: she turns out to have been named after a Royal Navy cruiser.

Brand is an undercover policewoman, and it is perhaps the novel's return to wartime tropes of national defence that prompt Fleming to gift her far greater agency than either of her predecessors. While *Casino Royale*'s hapless spy Vesper Lynd is undone by her desires and some pretty shoddy spy-craft, and *Live and Let Die*'s Solitaire acts only by calling Bond for help, Gala is a calm, proficient, professional agent. She has successfully

[34] Ibid., p. 35. [35] Ibid., p. 117. [36] Bennett, *Bond and Beyond*, p. 101.
[37] Fleming, *Moonraker*, p. 140. [38] Ibid., p. 141. [39] Ibid., p. 188.

operated undercover as Drax's secretary and she proves utterly resilient in the face of sexual assault and physical danger. She also works out exactly what Drax is going to do – bomb London – and shows initiative in planning to stop him.[40] That Bond nonetheless feels the need to protect her is more the product of his self-confessed sentimentality than her role within the narrative.[41] Bond remorselessly sexualises Brand, scarcely able to concentrate in the face of such a beautiful English female body on a beautiful English summer's day, and up until the point at which a cliff is collapsed on top of them, the beach walk chapter assumes an almost prelapsarian quality.[42]

The equation of Brand with Englishness has implications for her function within the novel. Bennett and Woollacott are among many critics to have argued that Bond's role in relation to women is to reposition misaligned femininity.[43] They also note, as does Praseeda Gopinath, that Gala Brand is in an anomalous position as she needs neither ideological nor sexual repositioning: indeed, there is a disjunction between the narrative presentation of Brand as equal agent, and Bond's patriarchal focalisation. Yet, in spite of her unusual agency, Brand's textual position could not be described as comfortable. Her very association with Englishness makes her unable to respond directly to Bond's desire: in the sexual politics of virtuous womanhood, he cannot have her without violating the nation, and she cannot have him without betraying the nation. Her virtue resides in her withholding, and the reader, unlike Bond, is given insight into this through occasional focalisation from Gala's point of view (reassuring us that she finds Bond appropriately desirable) and through Fleming's psycho-sexual analysis of another beautiful professional woman. Bond's secretary, Loelia Ponsonby, exists in a state of 'perpetual concubinage to … King and Country',[44] her workplace authority in constant tension with maternal anxiety for the agents she serves. Fleming reiterates a series of conventional assumptions: that a woman must choose between career and marriage, that women should be chaste and men experienced, and that a desiring woman represents a security risk. However, what is of particular interest here is the association of Lil's subjectivity with wartime: her desires are circumscribed by national need. I suggested earlier that *Moonraker* was Janus-faced, simultaneously looking backwards to the war and forwards to

---

[40] Ibid., p. 290.
[41] Ibid., pp. 217, 295, 322. This sentimentality is evident across the Bond canon. In *Dr No* (1958), for example, the wounded Bond attempts to rescue Honeychile Ryder, only to discover she has calmly and competently rescued herself.
[42] Fleming, *Moonraker*, pp. 198–9.   [43] Bennett, *Bond and Beyond*, p. 116.
[44] Fleming, *Moonraker*, p. 9.

modernity. And so profoundly nostalgic is one facet of *Moonraker* that Fleming will even resuscitate *female* wartime agency as part of his fantastical rewriting of Britain's finest hour. Yet the book is characteristically postwar in its ultimate assertion of heteronormativity. Gala does not succumb to Bond at the end – except for a kiss in the legitimate erotic space of danger – but she does succumb to marriage. A Detective Inspector is waiting for her: she has been always already contained throughout the novel.

Perhaps unsurprisingly, then, Bond is denied the organic English beauty of Gala Brand at the book's end, as – in the absence of a big, shiny nuclear rocket – the nation needs a suitably technocratic, professional male protector. It needs Bond to 'play the role which she expected of him ... The tough man of the world. The Secret Agent. The man who was only a silhouette'.[45] Bond must be symbol rather than man, and as such becomes the archetypal embodiment of the thriller genre's capacity to remasculinise. In *Moonraker*, rather than realigning femininity, Bond replaces masculinity, and he is rewarded not with the satisfaction of physical desire, but with the newly phallic power of displacing the 'pencil of glistening chromium' and embodying national defence.

The patterns and preoccupations outlined here will not remain stable throughout the Bond canon. Even by the time of *Goldfinger* (1959), a novel that reworks many of the tropes at play in *Moonraker*, Bond is a more cynical, arguably more 'sixties' figure. Relying on chance and inspiration as much as training, he approaches his assignment with the fatalistic observation that 'it was no good practising himself'.[46] The transition evident in *Goldfinger* is instructive, not least in its demonstration of the complex interrelationship between cultural and generic change. Bond is a hero of austerity who will become a hero of affluence and, beyond that, a sixties icon. In so doing, he – like the other masculine 'agents' examined here – reveals the vital role played by popular heroism in mediating culturally acceptable modes of masculinity and enabling at least imaginative repair to the damage wrought by war.

---

[45] Ibid., p. 325. [46] Ian Fleming, *Goldfinger* (London: Vintage, 2012 [1959]), p. 119.

CHAPTER 6

Wireless Writing, the Second World War and the West Indian Literary Imagination

James Procter

The 1940s mark a 'caesura' in histories of both British and black British writing, where the end of the Second World War (1945) and the arrival of the *Empire Windrush* (1948) typically divide the decade around inaugural moments of absolute beginning.[1] These two posts (postwar/post-Windrush) have in turn become estranged from each other. It is now well established that the *Windrush*, a German troopship commandeered following Allied victory, brought nearly 500 West Indians to Britain, heralding a postwar boom in Commonwealth immigration.[2] Yet the specifically *literary* crossovers between a nation-bound wartime home front on the one hand, and late colonial migration to the metropole on the other, are rarely considered holistically as part of the same narrative. In other words, as discrete symbolic moments, '1945' and '1948' tend to separate out British and black Atlantic literary production at the mid-century, where at best the latter comes after, as part of a staggered, supplementary visitation from the outside; an external and belated West Indian artistic presence which is essentially *postwar* in character.

The example of the wartime BBC, already by this point a behemoth of British national culture, invites us to reconsider this period as part of a synchronic rather than a staggered history.[3] With the outbreak of the Second World War, the BBC brought not just British writers like Louis MacNeice, Dylan Thomas, Rebecca West and J. B. Priestley to the airwaves (including to its Overseas Service), but budding South Asian, West Indian and West African authors from across the

---

[1] Jay Winter, *Sites of Memory, Sites of Mourning* (Cambridge University Press, 1998), p. 228. See also Gill Plain, *Literature of the 1940s* (Edinburgh University Press, 2013).
[2] For critiques of this received history, see, e.g., James Procter, *Writing Black Britain* (Manchester University Press, 2000), pp. 1–12 and 78–82; and Matthew Mead, '*Empire Windrush*: The Cultural Memory of an Imaginary Arrival' *Journal of Postcolonial Writing* (2009) 45(2) pp. 137–49.
[3] The author and editor are grateful to the BBC Written Archives Centre, Caversham Park, Reading for the right to reproduce materials from its holdings.

Commonwealth.[4] Further research is needed into the cross-cultural literary encounters and networks forged through the corporation during this period. For example, the Welsh poet Dylan Thomas, perhaps most famous for his 1954 radio play, *Under Milk Wood*, influenced or endorsed a number of late colonial radio artists during his BBC years. The Barbadian George Lamming read Thomas's poetry on *Calling the West Indies*, while critics have identified echoes of the Welsh poet in the work of the Jamaican novelist Roger Mais and the early poetry of the Saint Lucian poet, Derek Walcott. Thomas who famously praised the West African Amos Tutuola's *The Palm-Wine Drinkard* (1952) as a 'thronged, grisly and bewitched story' was also, along with Louis MacNeice and E. M. Forster, a mutual friend of Mulk Raj Anand, the Indian author of *Untouchable* (1935). Elsewhere, on the BBC's Eastern Service, Anand worked closely with George Orwell, who was a Talks Producer appointed by the Indian Section in 1941.[5] In the same year, the corporation appointed the Jamaican poet Una Marson to head up the West Indian Service. Orwell, Anand and Marson all appeared together with T. S. Eliot and William Empson on the BBC's literary magazine programme 'Voice' in the following year.

Focusing on radio literature broadcast from London to the Caribbean during and just after the Second World War, this chapter works across the striated 1940s to reveal a body of West Indian literary activity that joins up the cultural production across that decade. Where available scholarship has focused on isolated accounts of the BBC's 'Caribbean Voices' programme, as it was produced by Henry Swanzy (1946–1954) after the war, this chapter returns to the neglected archive of wartime wireless writing which precedes and intersects with that now famous literary magazine series.[6] Radio is a peculiarly apposite medium for rethinking the relations between nation and West Indian migration in the 1940s, not only because of its endurance

---

[4] See Emily C. Bloom, *The Wireless Past: Anglo-Irish Writers and the BBC, 1931–1968* (Oxford University Press, 2016), Melissa Dinsman, *Modernism at the Microphone: Radio, Propaganda, and Literary Aesthetics during World War II* (London: Bloomsbury, 2015) and Ian Whittington, *Writing the Radio War: Literature, Politics and the BBC, 1939–1945* (Edinburgh University Press, 2018) for recent monographs covering these and other wartime British writers at the BBC.
[5] These and many other South Asian connections within and beyond the BBC's Eastern Service can be explored on the 'Making Britain' database: www.open.ac.uk/researchprojects/makingbritain/
[6] Key accounts include Phillip Nanton, 'What Does Mr. Swanzy Want? Shaping or Reflecting? An Assessment of Henry Swanzy's Contribution to the Development of Caribbean Literature' *Kunapipi* (1998) 20(1) pp. 11–20; Glyne Griffith, 'Deconstructing Nationalisms: Henry Swanzy, Caribbean Voices, and the Development of West Indian Literature' *Small Axe* (2001) 10 pp. 1–20; and Peter Kalliney, *Commonwealth of Letters: British Literary Culture and the Emergence of Postcolonial Aesthetics* (Oxford University Press, 2013), pp. 116–45.

across both the wartime and postwar years, but because its airborne transmissions were unbound by national frontiers. Many of the major West Indian writers now indexed through the early metropolitan novels of the 1950s were first broadcast by the BBC before they even set sail for England, their fiction travelling to London by ship and plane before being transmitted back to the British West Indies. Edgar Mittelholzer, Roger Mais, George Lamming, V. S. Naipaul and Sam Selvon had in this sense all 'arrived' in London before they physically moved there. The first novels by these and other pioneering male writers (sometimes collectively labelled the 'Windrush Generation') capture the Caribbean as a wartime space in ways that stretch the imaginative frontiers of Britain's finest hour. The events of Naipaul's *Miguel Street* (1959) and Selvon's *A Brighter Sun* (1952) unfold against the backdrop of the American military presence in Trinidad. For G, the childhood narrator of George Lamming's *In the Castle of my Skin* (1953), radio broadcasts by Lord Haw Haw turn the war into an immediate reality in Barbados: 'This wasn't history. It was real, and we walked out every morning ... saying farewell to the class room. We expected to hear the bomb fall.'[7] A few paragraphs on, a merchant ship is torpedoed in the island's harbour. John Hearne's *Voices under the Window* (1955) frames scenes of political unrest and violence in urban Jamaica, with flashbacks centred on the protagonist's RAF sorties in England. Some of these writers served in the war, along with hundreds of other unlettered West Indian men and women. Other artists positioned themselves against the prevailing wartime narrative of loyalty to the mother country. The Jamaican nationalist Roger Mais was imprisoned for sedition following the publication of his essay 'Now We Know' (1944), a tirade against Winston Churchill's imperialist stance during the war. But what connected all these writers was BBC air space and the London studios from which they broadcast to the Caribbean during and shortly after the Second World War.

The war profoundly captured the West Indian literary imagination not just during, but also after the years 1939 to 1945. This emphatic return, in mid-century West Indian literature, to the milieu of war may suggest an unlikely flirtation, in a literature on the cusp of 'independence', with narratives of loyalty and patriotism to the mother country. But these writings can equally be seen as attempts to wrestle over the meanings, memories and provenance of a victory in which West Indians were also active participants.[8] Increasingly, during the 1940s, West Indian writing on

---

[7] George Lamming, *In the Castle of My Skin* (Essex: Longman, 1987 [1953]), p. 214.
[8] See, e.g., Wendy Webster, *Englishness and Empire, 1939–1965*, (Oxford University Press, 2005).

air used 1945 to register a transitional moment in late colonial relations – the dawn of a new world. Yet, as this chapter will demonstrate, one of the most prevalent narratives in the archive rehearses 1945 as a threshold, beyond which narrators and characters struggle to move. Here, 1945 marks neither an absolute beginning, nor end, but a sticking point, and something closer to what Jed Esty describes, within the context of a very different literary form (*Bildungsroman* as opposed to broadcasting) as a narrative of non-development.

Wartime broadcasts brimmed with first-hand accounts of West Indian participation; acts of heroism; aerial sorties, landings in France, munitions factory work, or stories of escape and endurance by West Indian prisoners of war. Calypsos like 'Hitler Beware' and 'Slide Mongoose' offered listeners rousing lyrics:

> Hitler come with him bluff an shouting,
> Say brown boys don't worth corn meal dumplin'
> But we all gwine show him sometin'
> Slide Hitler.[9]

On 31 August 1943, the Jamaican Sergeant Flight Engineer, Vivian Hazell, delivered a message to his mother in Kingston that included an impromptu performance of 'After the Raid', a poem he composed following his return from the major bombing raids over Berlin:

> We saw them burst, like winged hells,
> The Hun's resentful ack-ack shells:
> We saw them burst, yet in we went –
> Into it all – with grim intent.
> Now it is past – oh, hours ago!
> And here are English towns below!
> And there, by distance dimly seen,
> Soft rivers parting England's green.[10]

Hazell's 'Hun', like his return to a bucolic village landscape, reproduces symbolically potent images of wartime Englishness that apparently compromise the slightly later story of West Indian cultural nationalism associated with postwar 'Caribbean Voices'. Yet the enthusiastic 'CHEERS' that Hazell's performance generates from the live West Indian studio audience perhaps signals more than spontaneous affection and loyalty for the mother country. Like the 'Slide Mongoose' calypso, this poem is

---

[9] BBC Written Archives Centre (WAC) (microfilm), 'Greetings to Jamaica', 26 September 1940. 'Slide Mongoose' is also known as 'Sly Mongoose'.
[10] BBC WAC *Calling the West Indies*, 'Message Party', 31 September 1943.

a heroic celebration of West Indians as an active wartime presence: not just eye-witness observers ('we saw'), but participants ('in we went') shaping world historical events. Expressions of West Indian loyalty within the wartime radio archive amount to more than so many expressions of colonial mimicry and blank patriotism. Rather, I argue narratives of loyalty and 'service' also seeded proto-nationalist declarations of West Indian agency and autonomy during the early 1940s, before the emergence of a more assertively independent and coherent nationalism in the postwar years.

The victory broadcast to the West Indies in August 1945 captured the general spirit of these transmissions when it declared: 'We all know that without the full backing of the Commonwealth and Empire, Britain alone could not have achieved this seemingly impossible task. So let's take you back over the years and recall to mind the part the West Indies have played in restoring peace to the world.'[11] War temporarily suspended, even inverted, narratives of dependence and independence as West Indians were called upon to step up and take responsibilities previously unavailable to them. It put into circulation narratives of democratisation, welfare and development, mobilising not just personnel, but associations of modernity, youthful optimism and prospects of genuine political change. It was in this context that the first producer of *Calling the West Indies*, Una Marson, introduced a 'girl-about-town' series to BBC wartime programming in order to highlight the contribution of women: 'I am convinced that the future progress of the West Indies is largely in the hands of women', she said. 'Women will be women in spite of Hitler.'[12]

Despite her metropolitan isolation from the West Indian literary scene, and George Orwell's observation to her in a radio interview that writing had 'gone into cold storage' for the war's duration, Marson remained convinced that literature was a core 'bond' linking Britain and the West Indies.[13] Poetry provided what she called on a Home Service talk in July 1940, 'A common language, a common tradition',[14] something exemplified in 'Just for Today', a programme of 'quiet music and poetry' launched in January 1945. Taking its name from Sister Mary Xavier's poem rejoicing in faith for today over fears for the future, the programme's selections included Francis Thompson's 'The Hound of Heaven', a long

---

[11] BBC WAC *Calling the West Indies*, 'West Indian Victory Party', 21 August 1945.
[12] BBC WAC *Calling the West Indies*, 6 April 1943; 20 June 1944.
[13] BBC WAC *Calling the West Indies*, 7 May 1942.
[14] BBC WAC (microfilm) Home Service 'Talking It Over', 11 July 1940.

mystical poem about delivery from evil, and Arthur Hugh Clough's 'Say Not the Struggle Naught Availeth', probably chosen in the light of Churchill's use of the final two stanzas in his 1941 radio appeal to America. Later editions focused on elegy, mortality and death, and included Tennyson's 'Crossing the Bar' and Gray's 'Elegy Written in a Country Churchyard'. Longfellow's famous anti-war poem, 'The Arsenal at Springfield' (which resonates with both the American Revolution and antislavery), and Kipling's 'If' (an expression of stoicism in the face of adversity often linked to the Boer War in South Africa) appear to earn their place not just for their parallels with the ongoing war in Europe, but for their echoes with empire.

While it tends to be assumed that literary contributions on *Calling the West Indies* were singularly Caribbean in content, programming throughout the 1940s and 1950s accommodated both British and (to a lesser extent) American authors. Anancy folk stories were broadcast in creole alongside rousing recitals of Shakespeare or, following the death of the American wartime president Franklin Roosevelt in April 1945, Walt Whitman.[15] English Romantic poetry appeared beside African American and West Indian writing. Wordsworth's 'Tintern Abbey' was preceded by a recording of 'the great coloured composer' Samuel Coleridge-Taylor. Among Marson's early suggestions for content were both representatives of the nineteenth-century English literary canon, and the precursors and protagonists of the Harlem Renaissance such as Claude McKay, Paul Laurence Dunbar and James Weldon Johnson. These seemingly unlikely combinations spoke both to the BBC's wider appeal to ideas of imperial unity and togetherness during the war, *and* to a black transatlantic imaginary connecting Europe and the Americas.

Marson was especially interested in literature's capacity to heal the divisions of war; its therapeutic potential to soothe and suture. A volunteer shelter warden during her BBC years, she survived several near misses during the Blitz, while one of her earliest radio guests, the Guianese dancer Ken 'Snake Hips' Johnson, was killed when German bombs hit the Café de Paris on 8 March 1941.[16] In July 1944, Marson broadcast a series of five poems on *Calling West Africa*, the sister programme of *Calling the West Indies*. 'The Warning' ('an admonition to the death-dealing aeroplane'), 'The Dolls', 'In the Darkness', 'The Poet' and

---

[15] Anancy is a mythical spider figure who appears in multiple guises within the West African and West Indian folk traditions.
[16] For a more detailed account of Marson's years at the corporation, see James Procter, 'Una Marson at the BBC', *Small Axe*, (2015) 19/3 (48), pp. 1–28.

'Wishing' evoke her experiences of the blitzkrieg of 1940 to 1941.[17] Their shared focus is aerial bombardment and expressions of biblical faith in the face of both the spiritual darkness of Nazi Germany and the physical darkness of the blackout.

'The Dolls' describes the poet transfixed by the sight of childhood toys among the debris of a bombed home; arms outstretched in vain, 'awaiting their little mistress'. The poem reworks Blakean images of innocence and experience, counterpointing the grubby clothes of the dolls and the 'golden hair' of their absent owner; the former gaiety of the child and the figure of the weeping mother; the violent 'fury' of the bomb's blast and the tender 'little hands' of the girl. Images of love and loss, the animate and inanimate, the embodied and dismembered are combined in the twinned images of the child with her once 'live limbs', 'bright' eyes, 'rippling laughter' and the 'unseeing', unfeeling immobility of the dolls.

In 'The Poet', Marson dwells more reflexively on the appropriateness of poetry and rhyme during wartime:

> When bombs and shot and shell
> So eloquently tell
> Of that deep barbarism
> Upsprung from hell.

Aerial tropes, and related images of dismemberment jostle, not just with a biblical firmament, but with the very medium through which Marson transmits her verse. If, in 'The Poet', rhyme is found wanting beside war's 'eloquence', then Marson also sees, in the airborne medium of radio, connectivity and solidarity, a horizon-less space beyond the worldly divisions of war. In 'Wishing', the final poem of her 1944 broadcast, Marson's declared wish is to 'write a poem addressed to all men ... That Peace must reign in the world for all time'. Of this poem, she says:

> I would send it by wireless over the world
> That the banner of peace might be unfurled

Poetry on air carried for Marson the prospect of planetary peace, and a temporary escape from what she called the 'nervous and fretful' conditions of a world which 'for the moment lies battered and bleeding'.[18]

As a radio producer and editor, Marson's earliest West Indian selections were largely limited to the small circle of Jamaican poets with whom she was already familiar, including Clare MacFarlane, Vivian Virtue and

---

[17] BBC WAC *Calling West Africa*, no date, circa July 1944.
[18] BBC WAC *Calling the West Indies*, 11 July 1940; 'Carry on West Indies', 28 October 1940.

Constance Hollar. For example, on 18 May 1944, a typical broadcast included an excerpt from MacFarlane's epic poem 'Daphne', set in the 'dew-moist' hills of St Andrew, Jamaica; sonnets of the Caribbean as a site of idyllic or exotic escape by Vivian Virtue and Tom Redcam's 'O Little Green Island Over the Sea'.[19] Much of this work had been previously published locally in the West Indies, and was already part of an established tradition of verse in the islands celebrating romanticised pastoral visions of West Indian landscapes. However, in Marson's hands, these texts were redefined on air as expressions of escape from the primary scene of urban destruction, and what she called 'the ~~rigours~~ drabness of an English winter'.[20] Understood within the Second World War's wider symbolic investment in rural England as a loaded site of national identification, these reorientations towards bucolic *tropical* landscapes would have suggested alternative sites of patriotic identification and desire beyond Britain for the Caribbean listener.

Introducing Macfarlane's 'Daphne', Marson was quick to flag how such work spoke to the recent history of West Indian participation and presence in European struggles (the British West India regiment in the First World War), and selected extracts accordingly:

> One full year,
> With fascinated eyes and beating hearts,
> We watch'd the mighty tragedy unroll
> Upon the stage of Europe; then at last,
> E'en like an actor who has heard his cue,
> Our Island's manhood rose and claim'd a part
> In the dread drama.[21] (15,716)

For all its archaic diction and old-fashioned heroic sentiment, the lines capture something of the refashioning of the West Indies during the Second World War from the point of view of the participant rather than the passive onlooker. If Europe remains the stage on which the action unfolds, the Caribbean islands are not simply a peripheral audience, but actors with parts to play in the drama.

Other emerging West Indian poets drew on established repertoires of wartime destruction in Britain's urban centres to address Europe in more dismissive terms. In 'Nostalgia', Mrs E. Laurie Stone 'of Jamaica and England' states:

---

[19] BBC WAC, *Calling the West Indies*, 18 May 1944.
[20] Strikethrough and emphasis in the original. [21] Ibid.

> You may keep
> Your monstrous cities of iron and soot
> Give me
> The print of a slim, brown foot
> In the rich, red dust of a mountain road,
> A mincing donkey with panniered load,
> And the plaintive song of a coloured girl.[22]

In 'War Planes', the Grenadian-born poet and medical student Calvin Lambert records the 'lethal instruments of war / that lay historic cities into dust', while making 'litter of the blithesome youth' in order to ask: 'What will remain to speak of Europe's Art? / Who will survive the page of time?'[23] Lambert answers his rhetorical questions in another of his broadcast poems, 'A Requiem for the West'. Its dedication to a dying Europe, an expression of *carpe diem* as much as requiem, is also a stirring call for West Indians to intervene and bring harmony to 'world' disorder through poetry:

> Awake, O brothers of the Western Isles!
> Let us awake and give the world our share
> Of literature to mould the destiny
> Of the tempestuous age in which we live[24]

As the war drew to a close and allied victory seemed increasingly certain, there were growing opportunities for literary programmes at the BBC. During the spring and summer of 1944, Marson regularly urged West Indian listeners to submit writing for broadcasting, and in October 'Caribbean Voices' began. Arthur Calder-Marshall, a prominent English critic appearing on the programme, spoke in 1948 of his future hopes for West Indian writing residing in a fuller understanding of the region's past. He elaborated by comparing the situation to a wounded soldier: 'you know how a war veteran may live on, with a bullet in his body or a bit of shrapnel . . .'.[25] War remained an enduring theme of 'Caribbean Voices' for much of its lifetime (1944–1958), but it was oriented to the future as much as the past.

This is evident in 'Oh Europe, Europe', in which the Jamaican nationalist poet H. D. Carberry uses the war to locate a future beyond the confines of that continent. Starting as an apparent lament for Europe ('Truly you are dying'), the poem turns into something closer to

---

[22] BBC WAC, *Calling the West Indies*, 25 May 1944.
[23] BBC WAC, *Calling the West Indies*, 14 June 1942.   [24] Ibid.
[25] BBC WAC, *Calling the West Indies*, 'Caribbean Voices', 1 February 1948.

a provocation, as Carberry envisions postwar as a successional moment marking the provincialisation of a dying culture ('your own small courtyard'), and the phoenix-like rise of 'new growth', a 'new ideal' in the new world beyond British shores:

> I felt – as the world's youth feel –
> That out of so much suffering
> Must come new growth,
> As out of the ruins of the bombed out houses in the cities
> New strange, and unfamiliar flowers
> Raise their heads amid the debris in the courtyard.
> I felt that out of the ashes
> Of this burned out land
> Must rise some new ideal, ...[26]

Images of awakening and future destiny appeared with increasing regularity on *Calling the West Indies* programmes during the final stages of the war. The West Indian 'Victory Party Programme' of August 1945 proclaimed the arrival of a 'new era': 'Our way stretches now straight before us, if we choose it.'[27] The broadcast closed with the Trinidadian singer and actor Edric Connor performing 'Song of the Dawn'. Similarly, on 18 March 1945, 'Caribbean Voices' closed with the Jamaican Ruth Horner's poem, 'The Hour'. Although first published in 1940, its remediation on radio in 1945 resonated with the wider anticipation of peacetime which characterises broadcasts in the final months of the war. As the announcer notes, Horner's poem 'seems particularly suitable at this time':

> Come, Peace.
> Mellow the morning.
> Hallow the day.
> Sanctify the sorrow
> Of the hour's tragedy
> That Hate may not again steal forth
> To build tomorrow's Peace.[28]

'1945': Narratives of Non-Development

If the end of war promised a new dawn for some poets, the wider archive of radio literature reveals a fixation with that momentous mid-century event,

---

[26] BBC WAC, *Calling the West Indies*, 'Caribbean Voices', 9 November 1947.
[27] BBC WAC, *Calling the West Indies*, 'Victory Party Programme', 21 August 1945.
[28] BBC WAC, *Calling the West Indies*, 'Caribbean Voices', 18 March 1945.

and a certain reluctance to leave it behind. In the immediate aftermath of the Second World War, many West Indian writers remembered or celebrated a victory that was also theirs. Louise Bennett's occasional poem, 'The Victory Parade', captured Commonwealth soldiers marching through the streets of London on VE-Day. Taking her 'seat' on the Victoria Memorial, Bennett's bird's-eye view playfully occludes that of the imperial monarch as the people's empire is rendered in Jamaican vernacular:

> Everyting wat help fe win de war
> Wat do dem lickle bit
> Every soul who gi dem lickle chenks
> A help was eena it[29]

Bennett draws upon the euphoric energies of victory to register a patriotic pride in the West Indian contribution. A few months earlier, Bennett's skit on the formation of the United Nations comically claimed, with faux naivety, that 'war is dun / we got atom boamb / An Peace pon de lan ...'.[30] But the war was not done, in the sense that it remained an enduring legacy in the literary imagination of West Indian radio writing, not just in hopeful visions of a youthful postwar dawn, but in narratives lingering on the elegiac and traumatic subjects of loss, grief and mourning. A Sunday night talk by Rev Douglas Wilson in 1945 included commemorative verse by a West Indian soldier whose friend fell 'Somewhere in Western Europe', his grave apparently unmarked, but his spirit 'A shining star where all the freemen go'.[31] Edric Connor's autobiographical talk, 'Bus ride in Paris – Cattle Truck to Calais', describes wandering through a military cemetery and breaking down in tears 'when I remembered and spoke slowly to myself a poem written by my friend Una Marson: "... If I, in one corner, See so much sorrow / That is to-day / And will be tomorrow- / God of the broken-hearted, Dost thou see? Or are thine eyes / Too dimmed with tears?"'[32] West Indian poetry became in such contexts an important monument to late colonial courage and loss.

As with earlier literary broadcasts, 'Caribbean Voices' accommodated European alongside West Indian literary selections. British literature from both the First and Second World Wars was particularly conspicuous during 1944 to 1945. Programmes included 'Requiem' by Glen Dresbach, 'A Soldier – His Prayer' by Gerald Kersh and work by the holocaust poet

---

[29] BBC WAC, *Calling the West Indies*, 11 June 1946.
[30] BBC WAC, *Calling the West Indies*, 5 March 1946.
[31] BBC WAC, *Calling the West Indies*, 10 September 1944.
[32] BBC WAC, *Calling the West Indies*, 17 August 1947.

Ada Jackson, famous at the time for her early poetic rendering of Jewish suffering, *Behold the Jew* (1944). H. E. Bates, identified on the script by his wartime alias 'Flying Officer X', was represented by 'Something in the Air'; Siegfried Sassoon by 'The Colonel's Cup' and 'Fox Hunting Man'; John Pudney by 'When Bullets Prove'. Stella Mead, to whom Marson dedicated her last published poetry collection *Towards the Stars* (1945), contributed a poignant piece of literary journalism on France as a monument to postwar ruin: 'Normandy'.

These European wartime narratives were increasingly eclipsed after 1945, with broadcasts by West Indians seeking to make sense of their own place in relation to the war. In Lennox de Paiva's 'The Spy and the Informers' (1950), the arrival of a camera-carrying stranger raises suspicion that a member of the Nazi Secret Service has infiltrated the remote Trinidadian village of Blanchisusse. L. A. M. Bridge's 'Jamaican Interlude' (1947) is set in mid-November 1944, as an RAF officer returns home on temporary leave to Jamaica. In Ian Williams's 'Cassie' (1947), the wartime military presence looms large, but Cassie is still forced to look for work to support her sick child because her no good husband, Heribert, reckons himself a conscientious objector: 'I ain goin' fo no sojer ... I ain' killin' no fellas I ain' got no quarrel wid, see. It's govinments what starts wars an' far's I concern' its govinments what kin finish dem'.[33] The protagonist of R. B. R. Brathwaite's 'The Backslider' slips back into his old habits when the American troops arrive in wartime Trinidad.

Many of these narratives take possession of the war, not so much to fix and monumentalise the recent past, as to mobilise its events so that they are forced to coincide with the Caribbean. The stories are less in thrall to a dominant national narrative of victory in Europe, than concerned with an exposure of history to a more inclusive cross-cultural vision. These were not openly interventionist works of counter-memory, but implicitly or explicitly they present a refusal to forget or be forgotten. Perhaps the most striking example of this was broadcast on 'Caribbean Voices' in June 1946, when the Trinidadian Fernando Henriques stitched together two seemingly discrete if not radically incommensurate events into a single contribution entitled 'Earthquake and Bombs' (1946). The script cuts between the natural disaster that raised Port Royal (the former mercantile centre of Jamaica) to the ground in 1692 and the Blitz of Britain in 1940:

---

[33] BBC WAC, *Calling the West Indies*, 'Caribbean Voices', 29 March 1947.

> I doubt but you have heard of the dreadful calamity that hath befallen this island, by a terrible earthquake ... which hath thrown down almost all the houses, churches, sugar works, mills and bridges of the island ... in the space of 3 minutes, the fairest town of all the English plantations ... was shaken and shattered to pieces ...[34]

This eyewitness account from 1692 is placed beside that of a fireman in 1940 as Coventry is razed to the ground by the Luftwaffe bombings:

> The last resistance of bricks and mortar at the pivot point cracked off like automatic gun-fire. The violent sound both deafened us and brought us to our senses. We dropped the hoses and crouched ... There was an incredible noise – a thunder-clap condensed into the space of an eardrum – and then the bricks and mortar came tearing and burning into the flesh of my face[35]

The occasion for the broadcast is premised on what Benedict Anderson might call the 'calendrical coincidence' of June as the month of the earthquake, the beginning of the bombing and of the radio broadcast itself.[36] Drawing on the dramatic immediacy of eye-witness accounts, there is no framing metacommentary to rationalise the historical relations between the two catastrophes. Rather, listeners are left to associatively counterpoint the urban destruction, human suffering and tragic death caused by these natural and man-made disasters otherwise distant in time and place, as a converging, collective trauma that makes a sort of common sense.

Other contributors staked out more direct claims to the war. In addition to his first novel, *A Brighter Sun* (1952), Sam Selvon produced a number of pieces of literary journalism and short fiction dealing with the war.[37] He had served as a wireless operator in the Royal Navy Reserve (1940–1945) and one of his adopted pen names was Ack Ack, a reference to the anti-aircraft regiments of the war. One of his earliest radio broadcasts, 'We Also Served' (1948), is on one level a testimony to Trinidadians in the making of modern world history. We are told of the regular blackout practices on the island, a submarine torpedoed in the harbour and mine-sweeping to protect the transatlantic shipping channels. Broadcast directly after a piece on the folklore of Jamaica, the script is billed as a departure from stories of buccaneers and Captain Morgan; a look at 'modern West Indians in a modern war'.[38] As well as the daily duties of serving Trinidadians, the

---

[34] BBC WAC, 'Caribbean Voices', 9 June 1946. [35] Ibid.
[36] Benedict Anderson, *Imagined Communities* (London: Verso, 1983), p. 33.
[37] Journalism included 'We Join the Navy' (1946), 'The Last Outpost' (1947) and 'A Man I Remember' (1948). See also his short story, 'Wartime Activities' in *Ways of Sunlight* (Essex: Longman, 1957).
[38] BBC WAC, 'Caribbean Voices', 29 August 1948.

text records the racism of Canadian commanders and the provincial ignorance of English superiors. The public history of Trinidad's 'peripheral' wartime role is, suggests Selvon, unreliable, and the piece closes: 'when heroes and war-scarred men gather in drawing rooms and clubs and discuss exploits, we West Indians, too, will have memories to recount, and we are happy that we were part of it all, that we also served'.[39] Like so many of the broadcasts considered above, 'We Also Served' is partly an insistence on West Indian wartime participation and presence.

Yet if Selvon's account, like Bennett's earlier, suggests that a more progressive, inclusive and accurate picture of victory emerges when official history is exposed to local, perspectival memory, other contributors appeared altogether less confident of the meaning of 1945. M. G. Smith, a young Jamaican poet who served with distinction in the RAF, captures that year in his broadcast poem '1945', not through the clean dividing lines of day and night, darkness and light, but through the haze, myopic indeterminacy and indirection suggested by a London fog:

> Here is not form nor motion
> Day nor light
> Stillness nor music
> Touch of ice nor flame
> But the bridge trembles and its iron pain
> Echoes like thunder the tramp of marching feet.
> Here is not will nor guidance
> Faith nor doubt
> End nor beginning
> Birth nor death nor life
> Only the river remembers under all
> Unseen, unheard remembers the lost dream[40]

1945 is neither beginning nor end in this poem, but loss and negation. The forward march of history suggested by tramping feet is pre-emptively halted by the absence of 'motion', 'guidance' and 'light', and in the suspended, liminal image of the trembling bridge. '1945' seems to evade human memory, slipping away silently and imperceptibly like the river beneath.

The progress of history is similarly retarded in John Mansfield's 'Celebration' (1947), a short story set in Montego Bay on the eve of VE Day, 1945.[41] While most islanders are preparing to take a holiday and

---

[39] Ibid. [40] BBC WAC, 'Caribbean Voices', 30 May 1948.
[41] BBC WAC, 'Caribbean Voices', 19 October 1947.

join in the celebrations, protagonist and wharf man Arthur Williams knows he'll be at work, loading the Florida-bound *SS Persister* with bananas: a perishable commodity that will not stand on ceremony. Arthur is to be paid double for his troubles and decides to mark the occasion with his friend Sylvester ('higgler, ice-vendor, and newsmonger') at the Five Star Bar. The story's title thus apparently refers to a double celebration. At the Five Star, the VE-Day festivities are already underway as couples 'jitterbug' around the room, while a three-piece band performs with 'inebriated gusto':

> Missa Hitla, you gwine fe dead!
> Missa Hitla, you lose your head!
> When Jamaica bomber fly over you,
> Berlin will mash like banana fou-fou![42]

But for Arthur and his crowd, joining in the festivities appears not so much a patriotic occasion as an opportunity to party, and when the characters speak of drinking to the 'celebrations', the word is placed in scare quotes. In this context, the VE festivities abruptly give way to the unfolding personal drama and petty jealousies of Arthur and Walter as they fight for the affections of the bar woman, Uraline. The evening ends with Arthur leaving the bar defeated, heading 'back to his little room on Swine Lane he paid no attention to the listless flags which stood out here and there along the streets in the reflected lights of street lamps'.[43] If the limp flags of victory echo Arthur's personal impotence, the sounds of revelry, song and rum shop laughter that assail his ears only reinforce his personal isolation. The next day is VE Day, but the remaining narrative makes no reference to the festivities. Rather, the focus is on Arthur and his fellow labourers loading the boat with bananas: a 'human chain' that together forms a regular rhythmical conveyor belt of movement, 'like black automata'. Bodily repetition displaces the historical narrative of progression associated with VE-day. The story closes in melodrama as Arthur learns that Walter, his rival at the Five Star, has killed Uraline with a machete and has been sent to prison. Among the questions left over by 'Celebration' is the significance of its title. How, other than through irony, is the story marking VE Day and the formal end of war in Europe? What is it that connects heroic victory and misogynistic violence, wartime liberation and individual incarceration; epochal 'world' celebration and the transnational shipment of perishable commodities from periphery to centre?

[42] Ibid. [43] Ibid.

War, and its symbolic representation, also forms a barrier to meaning and progression in the Jamaican F. D. Weller's short story, 'There is a Tavern in the Town' (1956). A music teacher walks slowly home following an aborted piano lesson. He is reluctant to return to his empty house, and beyond that to make his planned passage to England in search of financial security. The story is haunted by music, sound and hearing: by the piano's keys, by the sound of overseas radio 'coming from thousands of miles away' (presumably the BBC), by whispering 'reproachful voices', but most of all by the sound of a trumpet, which stops the teacher in his tracks. Like a scratched record, a trumpeter repeatedly plays 'There is a Tavern in the Town' into a silent but increasingly stormy evening.[44] The sound casts a 'quiet spell' over the teacher who instantly recognises its tune: 'it reminded him of an old film he had seen during the war, when he was a boy, about an English spy who was parachuted into Germany, and that song was a sort of password, and for a long time afterwards he had remembered the hero whistling "There is a Tavern in the Town" as he plodded along a dark country road somewhere in Germany'. The allusion (unidentified in the story) is to the 1941 anti-Nazi thriller, *Pimpernel Smith*. To the teacher the tune is both oddly captivating and a melancholic premonition of his journey to Europe. The song's associations with death reverberate in the protagonist's mind, heightening within him a sense of loneliness and wistful regret. Entranced, he seems to lose his earlier sense of purpose and mission, of 'making a clean and decisive break with everything'. Arrested by the trumpet's 'web of sound', consumed – possessed even – by the tune, the teacher returns to memories of his Jamaican past. The story closes with the teacher suspended at a threshold; yearning for the wartime music to take him back, while both fearful and faintly hopeful about the future. Like Arthur in 'Celebration', the teacher's stasis suggests parallels between the public memory of war and personal alienation. The trumpet's tune both forges an aural imagined community – 'Although he couldn't see them, he knew that people all over must be listening and humming the tune' – while all the time highlighting the teacher's sense of isolation and loneliness. The titular war song is not so much an unqualified site of identification as an uncanny experience of the familiar as foreign.

The same is true of Basil MacFarlane's 'The Heroes' (1955), a fictional exploration of demobilisation and homecoming following the war. The story focuses on John and Jennings as they journey from Tilbury to

---

[44] BBC WAC, 'Caribbean Voices', 9 April 1956.

Jamaica by troopship. The main body of the narrative is preoccupied with this sea crossing, and its suggestion 'of suspended existence in an element free of the exactness of the landbound world'.[45] The two men pore over photographs of their English girlfriends, and both appear uncertain in this context as to where their future destiny lies: in England or Jamaica. The proliferation of wartime memories and flashbacks to London cut across the forward trajectory of the ship as it moves closer to the Caribbean. As John and Jennings dock in Jamaica in the final paragraph, the style of the narrative (which until this point is firmly grounded in the generic conventions of realism and literary journalism) abruptly shifts, adopting the symbolic and mythical repertoires of modernism and Joycean exile. John imagines Jennings as Ulysses, and his waiting father as Telemachus, as they peer from the deck of the ship in a 'blinding noon':

> The quayside buildings seemed unnaturally squat and disheveled. Not even the mountains, nearer and more lofty than at morning, assumed any of the grandeur I remembered. From the deck we looked down upon a sea of perspiring, human faces and on the brass band who, in their gaudily coloured uniforms, made me think of Clytemnestra.[46]

The classical allusion to Clytemnestra, the final word of the story, reveals the title of 'The Heroes', like 'Celebration' and '1945', to be ironic. The scene of patriotic pageantry and victorious homecoming is punctured in another story of emasculation that alludes to the symbolic death of the archetypal hero. The withering, shrunken landscape of Jamaica, where mountains are 'wreathed' in mist, and where the city beneath is 'fetid' and 'rank', suggests John and Jennings's destiny lies in the land they've just left. Yet the 'great grey city' of London was also described earlier as 'wreathed in mists' and the cabin dialogues between John and Jennings make it clear they are unwelcome among the English families to whom their girlfriends belong. As with the earlier pieces, memories of the war are associated with blockage. 1945 is not so much a 'post' or passageway as a barrier. In different ways, the contributions by Smith, Mansfield, Weller and MacFarlane capture war's end, less as a transitional moment, than as what Jed Esty calls an impasse.[47]

Esty's focus is upon novelistic discourse and extended narratives of individual and national growth. The condensed forms of radio writing considered in this chapter carry none of the expository expectations of the

---

[45] BBC WAC, 'Caribbean Voices', 26 June 1955. [46] Ibid.
[47] Jed Esty, *Unseasonable Youth: Modernism, Colonialism, and the Fiction of Development* (Oxford University Press, 2012), p. 35.

Bildungsroman, nor is the short story or poetry associated with subject development. Yet precisely because it tends to repudiate plotted historical progress in favour of implication and impressionistic moments of time, the short broadcast form shares a certain affinity with the modes of arrested development Esty also identifies with wartime and postwar novels of the early- to mid-twentieth century. If, as Esty suggests, the emergent novel of antidevelopment needs to be read alongside the decline of the European nation-state, imperial decline and the emergence of anti-colonial nationalism, then the stories of postwar stasis considered above point, on a smaller scale, to a wider crisis of narrative representation surrounding 1945.

This chapter began by questioning the developmental historical narrative of linear chronological time that takes us from a moment of national victory (1945) to the story of postwar mass immigration (1948), and which preserves the integrity of the first moment as an internally unfolding story of Europe. By dwelling on the wartime literary imagination of West Indians on air, it is possible to negotiate the staggered history of these otherwise seemingly discrete epochal moments in time, revealing diaspora narratives that occupy an inside-out position in relation to the accepted historiographical accounts of postwar. At stake in these recurring narratives of arrested movement and development is more than a pitting of historical evolution against the twists, turns, absences and aporia of experimental fiction. In addition to a series of lost literary materials, the archive at the BBC reveals absences in the historical record of the *Windrush* itself.

We have already seen that 'The Heroes' begins with West Indian troops departing from Tilbury, the famous dock at which the *Windrush* passengers disembarked in 1948. As it has been handed down through history, the *Windrush* is an emblem of arrival rather than departure, a metonym for the unprecedented large-scale influx and settlement of West Indians in the mother country. However, the BBC archive reveals that this now generally accepted narrative is at best a truncated story of the *Windrush*'s journey, which actually involved not just a voyage in, but a voyage out. What follows is an excerpt from the script of the weekly *Calling the West Indies* programme, 'West Indian Diary'. On Saturday 24 April 1948, two months before the *Windrush* famously 'arrived' at Tilbury, the following news item was broadcast from London to the Caribbean:

> The Colonial Office have announced that the last big draft of airmen for repatriation will sail from Tilbury on May 8th on the Empire Windrush. This draft which is about five hundred strong will consist of ordinary

airmen who are anxious to be repatriated ... more than half will be from Jamaica, fifty from British Guiana, twenty from Trinidad, fifteen from Barbados, three from British Honduras and two from Antigua. The Officers-in-Charge will be Flight Lieutenant Johnny Smythe, a West African who still carries around several bits of shrapnel in his lungs and side from his war service and Flight Lieutenant J. J. Blair of Jamaica who won the D.F.C.[48]

This now forgotten narrative from the radio archive, of the boat's prior journey to return West Indian war veterans from motherland to homeland, casts a very different light on the history of the *Windrush*: a story of West Indian arrival in 1948 was one of departure in 1945. We might ask in this context why historical accounts of the *Windrush* begin belatedly. What is at stake in our collective amnesia around that earlier moment? On one level, it is a form of forgetting that keeps intact the staggered history with which this chapter began. What is today understood as a story of postwar *influx* was once a story of exodus that points to the West Indian wartime *presence* and active participation of the wider Commonwealth. In other words, this slightly earlier Windrush narrative at the BBC complicates the inside/outside, before/after binaries that fall either side of 1945, not just pushing back, but reframing 'postwar' as a diasporic as well as domestic narrative.

[48] BBC WAC, *Calling the West Indies*, 'West Indian Diary', 24 April 1948.

PART II

The Politics of Transition

Introduction

As its title suggests, ideological battles are integral to this part of the book. Each chapter explores an aspect of belief, fear or cultural anxiety that helped to shape the aesthetics of the postwar period. From covert agendas to 'Admass', political changes distorted the cultural landscape, presenting new challenges to writers struggling to make sense of the postwar world. This was no easy task, and the chapters repeatedly return to the complexity, and difficulty, of negotiating what Mark Rawlinson calls 'worlds in the making'. For Rawlinson, transition – the long-awaited 'progression' from war to peace – is not just unstable, it is unattainable: something that can scarcely be imagined, let alone coherently inscribed, in a world dedicated to the *enforcement* of peace. Rawlinson's chapter crucially stresses the intermediality of 1940s imaginative culture, drawing on a wide range of film and fiction, including Marghanita Laski, Alex Comfort, Humphrey Jennings, Colin McInnes and Graham Greene, to interrogate the underlying question of how, exactly, the story of the Second World War would be organised. The answer he offers is one that makes explicit the mutual contamination of politics, war and writing: namely, Winston Churchill's *The Second World War*, a six-volume history that would garner the 1953 Nobel prize for literature.

Rawlinson's concern with worlds in the making is followed by Adam Piette's analysis of European ideological reconstruction, which finds Stephen Spender and W. H. Auden struggling to imagine, in the latter's words, any 'workable world'. The two poets, who had taken diametrically opposed routes to the confrontation of conflict (Spender opting for proximity, Auden for distance), now both found themselves in Europe, contemplating the devastation of bombed cities which, like the Holocaust and the atomic bomb, seemed almost to defy description. Piette traces lines of continuity linking the literary responses to two world wars, and he also observes the extent to which the existential philosophies of the interwar years permeate and complicate the postwar. What emerges is a poetry of traces, glimpses and deep anxiety: as much about the persistence of fascism as any new Cold War threat. While Piette reads the tensions of geopolitics in his close attention to poetic textures, Thomas Davis turns to the politics of publishing, exploring two exemplary journals through which the cultural value of literature was put to the test. *Horizon*, which ran under Cyril Connolly's editorship from 1940 to 1950, was dedicated to the promotion and preservation of literary culture in wartime and deeply invested in Connolly's belief that art could transcend the limitations of history. The Cold War newcomer *Encounter*, by contrast, was more concerned with shaping history. Recognising that literature could be a potent ideological weapon, the magazine presented itself as a beacon of artistic liberty. That it pursued this mission with funding from the CIA is now well known – but Davis's nuanced exploration looks beyond the money to the ethical anxieties at play in the 'mobilisation' of culture.

The covert agendas of *Encounter* and the allusive poetics of anxiety were not for J. B. Priestley, one of the most prominent public intellectuals of the postwar era. Rather, in his popular novels, plays and broadcasts, he argued for a postwar settlement that would fulfil the socialist promise of the wartime years. In this mission, he was joined by his second wife, Jaquetta Hawkes, archaeologist and author of perhaps the most unlikely bestseller of the postwar years, her 'biography' of Britain, *A Land* (1951). The Priestleys represent an important and under-recognised dimension of the postwar cultural landscape: that attracted not to concepts of fragmentation, alienation and decline, but to a belief in common humanity, spiritual values and a holistic conception of an equal society. Both pragmatic and visionary, the Priestleys' Jungian philosophy and their belief in social responsibility made them ardent campaigners, most significantly in the fight for nuclear disarmament. Far removed from Philip Larkin's avowed desire for 'infinite recession in the face of the world' (discussed by Tracy Hargreaves in Part III), Ina Habermann's case study of the Priestleys exposes energetic debates about the function of literature and the responsibility of the writer.

Concern for the future, and a belief in social responsibility, are equally central to Chapter 11, which examines the politics of writing for children. The Carnegie Medal was awarded annually to the best book published for children, and Lucy Pearson's exploration of the values endorsed by the winners exposes a significant preoccupation with history which, like the mythic past favoured by the Priestleys, was politicised in service of a series of wartime and postwar agendas. Embedded in this fictional recourse to the past, though, is deep anxiety about the future. What has war done to children? What has been its psychological impact? What sort of world awaits the generation born out of traumatic global conflict? This question underpins a final preoccupation explored by Pearson: the representation of work. From the various adventures in and celebrations of a national landscape enriched by history emerges a persistent figuration of the child as a vital and active participant in the rebuilding of the postwar world.

Part II concludes with a return to conceptual challenges. Postwar reconstruction not only demanded a new understanding of citizenship, it also required – in the commitment to cultural regeneration – a realignment of literary values. The result was an intense debate, extending across the period, about the ethics and aesthetics of representation. Alice Ferrebe's analysis of the ekphrastic novels of Joyce Cary and Elizabeth Taylor complicates the transition from modernism to postmodernism by reminding us of the 'battle' for realism. Drawing on vibrant 1950s debates in the visual arts, Ferrebe explores the anxieties underpinning the resurgence of realist forms, and the 'disaffected scrutiny' to which they were subject. In the fault-lines dividing David Sylvester's subjective individualist realism from John Berger's 'kitchen sink' painting, Ferrebe exposes both the challenge of 'direct' representation and the remarkable persistence, in the most unlikely of places, of a residual modernist aesthetic.

CHAPTER 7

Narrating Transitions to Peace: Fiction and Film after War

Mark Rawlinson

What do we know about how wars end, and what might we mean by a transition to peace? The idea of transition acknowledges that war, unlike a sporting contest, doesn't end with a final whistle, but what kind of euphemism is this gradualist model – for instance, it might imply the restoration of circumstances labelled peace, but going back to the way things were is the last thing possible in the wake of the demographic, political, economic and technological upheavals of global, total war. So, is postwar (an apparently more neutral term) a new set of legal, political and existential conditions (a peace settlement symbolised by a treaty document) or is it simply succession? To Sir Walter Moberly, reviewing the prospects of British universities at the end of the 1940s, postwar didn't redeem war, it threatened, in a Clausewitzian vein, to exceed it: 'Two world-wars have culminated in the threat to civilization of the atom-bomb [and] the presumed will to use it.'[1] This is the world in which Orwell took his boy to the fastness of Jura, 'the only hope is to have a home with a few animals in some place not worth a bomb'.[2] The political scientist Johan Galtung recognised that the term 'peace' was an instrument of 'verbal consensus', and that using this word was propaganda, a way to avoid mirroring 'semantically a basically un-harmonious world'.[3] *Stunde nul* – Zero hour – as some Germans referred to 1945 in 1945, was just such a fantasy of reconstruction, of beginning again.[4] Most Germans in 1945 still lived in a violent world, and there was no 'wiping of the slate', although by the 1960s the Baader-Meinhof generation instigated its own violence because the *Wirtschaftswunder* – the West German 'economic miracle' –

---
[1] Sir Walter Moberly, *The Crisis in the University* (London: SCM Press, 1949), p. 15.
[2] George Orwell, *Collected Essays, Journalism and Letters*, vol. 4 (Harmondsworth: Penguin, 1968), p. 387.
[3] Johan Galtung, 'Violence, Peace, and Peace Research' *Journal of Peace Research* (1969) 6(3) pp. 167–91.
[4] Keith Lowe, 'Introduction' in *Savage Continent: Europe in the Aftermath of World War II* (Harmondsworth: Penguin, 2013), para. 6.

appeared to have been bought at the price of forgetting. Writing of the very different circumstances in Britain after 1945, Anthony Barnett refers to 'a wartime peace ... that was austere, rationed, shared and run from above'.[5] This apparent oxymoron captures the paradoxical character of these years which is not registered in a merely legalistic or constitutional frame of reference. So, not only were the most important structural circumstances of the Home Front (not the blackout, say, but limits on civil liberties) sustained after 1945, but they could be valued as major social and political achievements of the war against Nazism.[6] The way we name what occurred in 1945 (not the dropping of the atom bomb and the violence of the war, but what was symbolised by VE and VJ day) is clearly not very helpful in describing, let alone understanding, what these occurrences meant. '[T]he War was over, and the peace had not yet set hard'.[7]

Let's take a self-conscious example of the subjunctive as well as contradictory character of this so-called transition to peace. Tom Harrisson is now best known as the anthropologist who teamed up with the poet Charles Madge in the 1930s to create Mass-Observation, a project joining social science and the literary imagination. By the early 1940s, M-O had become an unofficial branch of the Coalition Government's growing intelligence and publicity machine for imagining the postwar world, and by then Harrisson had been recruited to the Foreign Office's Political Warfare Executive, to stir up anti-colonial feeling against the Japanese, another ambiguous project of postwar projection. Retrospective distance contributes to the ironic poise of Harrisson's memoir of his wartime service in Borneo, and in particular the handling of the manifold valences of ends of war and transitions to postwar:

> By the latter half of 1944 the Japanese had been in occupation of all Borneo – and South-East Asia – for three years. By 1944 the first glow of a new order had faded; the signs that this new mastery was only temporary began to multiply rapidly. By the end of 1944 the 'Greater Co-prosperity' regime was visibly foundering. Before the end of the following year it had been overthrown by force of arms and atoms. It was the singular fortune of the present writer to be the first visible sign, and in some ways symbol, of this transition, reversion or progression, in one of the remotest and until then least known parts of tropical Asia.[8]

---

[5] Anthony Barnet, *The Lure of Greatness: England's Brexit* (London: Unbound, 2017), ch. 21, para. 3.
[6] Ken Loach's 2013 documentary film, *Spirit of '45*, re-commemorates these social and socialist victories seventy years on, and thirty years into the Thatcherite, neo-liberal campaign to overturn them.
[7] Patrick White, *The Riders in the Chariot* (Harmondsworth: Penguin, 1964 [1961]), p. 7.
[8] Tom Harrisson, *World Within: A Borneo Story* (London: Cresset Press, 1959), p. 3.

The refusal to pre-empt the experience of the natives in that apparently quibbling 'transition, reversion or progression' – which eschews the triumphalism of the war for democracy while hinting at the equivalence of all imperialisms – is amplified by *the* mid-century symbol of the ambivalence of progress, 'arms and atoms'. The author's status as 'visible sign, and in some ways symbol' reminds us that whatever came after the end of hostilities was achieved, it had to be made and in some cases enforced: it was not the restoration of a world outside and prior to violence which the word peace, with its half-forgotten religious over-determinations, seems to imply. And anti-colonial feeling was not a weapon of warfare that could be sheathed at the legal cessation of hostilities. Peace had to be performed, and peace understood as the restoration of European imperial power would, by 1975 and the US evacuation of Saigon, be revealed as a thirty-year war of imperial retreat under a Cold War rubric.

In another context, the question of what 'transition' signifies in aesthetic terms is begged by the very idea of literary history, notably by the teleological forms it has taken in modern literary education, a tendency reinforced by a tenacious narrative undercurrent in historiography. There is good sense in Franco Moretti's judgement, in *Signs Taken for Wonders*, that 1939 to 1945 'does not seem to have much usefulness for literary periodization or interpretation'. This is not because the Second World War lacks salience, but rather due to the absence of 'a system of concepts which are both historiographic and rhetorical' on which scholars might ground an intuition about an aesthetic discontinuity. Such a discontinuity may be already overdetermined as a compulsion to repeat the claim that 1914 to 1918 was a cultural watershed or 'deluge'.[9] In a recent history of institutional literary criticism, an activity that is inaugurated in the era of the world wars, Joseph North proposes that a bi-epochal conception of the twentieth century – 'with a crucial break occurring somewhere around its centre: a break between pre- and post-1945, for example; or a break between "modernism" and "postmodernism,"' has 'nowadays' given way to a tripartite construction. This 'new clarity about the history of the twentieth century' is conditioned by newly salient concepts of a first era bounded and troubled by the world wars, a second characterised by 'welfare-statist compromise' and a 'third, neoliberal period'.[10] The

---

[9] Franco Moretti, *Signs Taken for Wonders: Essays in the Sociology of Literary Forms*, rev. edn (London: Verso, 1988), pp. 20, 9; the title of Arthur Marwick's social history of the Great War, published in 1965.

[10] Joseph North, *Literary Criticism: A Concise Political History* (Cambridge, MA: Harvard University Press, 2017), pp. 12–13.

admixture of professional scruple (those inverted commas) and 'strategic' signalling (welfare, neoliberal) in this historical claim about historical self-consciousness is congruent with the recognisable yet elusive qualities of any number of sub- or intra-periodisations; this is narrative by a kind of principled bricolage, ranging between recognisable formations in the past and present compulsions. The ambition of literary historians to synchronise the joints in several narratives (literary-historical and historical) – led by the promise of ever-better hindsight – throws light on the situation of writers in the 1940s attempting to make sense out of what would become for those same historians a nodal conjunction in and around 1945. What was the function of narrative in interpreting or symbolising a moment or era which might be perceived or construed as transitional, 'passing ... from one condition ... to another'?[11] How did those writing in this transition, which is also a node in history and perhaps literary history, emplot their awareness of this?

This approach reminds us of the problem of identifying the beginning of the condition of peace or the 'postwar': while peace may lag experientially behind the official cessation of hostilities (as testified by the figures 1914–1919 on many war memorials), preparations for after war must be made in war's midst. Hence the initially common-sense appeal, and then paradoxical resonance, of a theoretical statement from the early 1940s and the emergent field of group psychology (developed to meet growing demand for therapies to return 'exhausted' servicemen to the field):

> Following the principle that the 'outbreak' of any war occurs some considerable time before the actual declaration, it is reasonable to assume that the 'outbreak' of peace occurs shortly after the war has reached it major climax; in other words, about the time when it is at its bloodiest.[12]

The primary concern of this chapter remains, however, to identify and analyse some of the literary registrations of the demands of the times, which are often also the demands of the legal, psychological, economic and symbolic structures of war.

Crowds celebrating in London on 8 May 1945 are fixed by photographic images in the memories of those born long after in a supreme social fiction of the unified nation and the violence-redeeming and heteronormative embrace of, commonly, uniformed men and women in civvies (also the iconic costume of the liberation of occupied European cities, but not of

---

[11] *Oxford English Dictionary*, n 1.a.
[12] Edward Glover, *War, Sadism and Pacifism: Further Essays on Group Psychology and War* (London: George Allen & Unwin, 1947), p. 243.

European camps). A day of celebration was and is a boundary drawn between six years of violence and the future. But for thousands of British servicemen in other theatres of war, the slow process of demobilisation would extend into 1946 and 1947, when bread would be rationed at home for the first time (conscription itself lasted for nearly twenty-five years, and the last National Servicemen would be discharged in 1963). The Labour Government started out as a wartime administration, and it would pass its own National Service Act in 1949, ten years after Chamberlain's government had passed the original Act in a single day, 3 September 1939.[13]

On VJ Day, the Argentinian-born, Welsh-resident modernist poet Lynette Roberts, author of the visionary poem of war 'Gods with Stainless Ears: A Heroic Poem' (1951), made a journal entry which anticipated William Golding's 1950s fables of the inner Nazi – *Lord of the Flies* (1954) and *Pincher Martin* (1956). Her image of occupied Europe is extraordinary because in the representational repertoire of modern warfare, from Belgium in 1914 to ISIS in 2015, rape marks off the behaviour of the enemy:

> ... who are we, that create atomic bombs to sneer and condemn the flying rocket. Who are we, who allow our men ten days after the surrender of Germany to turn our enemies into the future mothers of our race. Today statistics show that 4000 German girls are pregnant by our soldiers and many of them to become their wives. Where then the enemy ... the true enemy ... but within ourselves.[14]

The implausibility of the idea of the cessation of struggle – the real battles are still to be fought in this heterodox vision – is a symptom of how much cultural work was required to make the peace. Europe was a continent without institutions; UK institutions were intact but conditioned by a command economy and military direction. Across Europe, hundreds of millions had been mobilised or worked in war economies and had been targets of strategically endorsed violence.[15]

In fact nowhere did the ramifications of the war end in 1945. West German and Japanese sovereignty was restored in 1952, but occupation military forces of the Allies remained long after that date; in the case of Soviet formations in the DDR, until 1994, after German reunification. War criminals were still being indicted, and war crimes legislation was

---

[13] See B. S. Johnson (ed.), *All Bull: The National Servicemen* (London: Allison & Busby, 1973); and Richard Vinen, *National Service: Conscription in Britain 1945–1963* (London: Allen Lane, 2014), ch. 3.
[14] Lynette Roberts, 'A Carmarthenshire Village', TS, HRC Austin, Texas, box 1 files 8–9, pp. 117–18.
[15] See Keith Lowe, *Savage Continent: Europe in the Aftermath of World War II* (Harmondsworth: Penguin, 2013).

being instituted, at the end of the century (the British War Crimes Act passed into law in 1991). States occupied by the Nazis set about dissolving the stain of collaboration in acts of institutional amnesia as their populations struggled to rebuild lives shadowed by indelible memories of terror, betrayal and loss. Ho Chi Minh planned the overthrow of his country's imperialist liberators from the Japanese, a campaign which would culminate in the American war in the 1960s and 1970s. In China, within a year of the defeat of the Japanese, who had controlled the eastern third of the country from Manchuria to Canton, Chiang Kai-shek's Guomindang were at war with Mao Zedong's communists, a civil conflict which would only appear to end with the former's retreat to offshore Taiwan in 1949. The transfer of power in India, a major creditor of impoverished Britain, was accelerated by Mountbatten towards a violent partition, with up to 1 million dead and 17 million refugees.[16]

Even where the fantasy of a punctual military victory was most insistent, there were reasons to contest the as-yet empty signifier of 'peace'. On the left, the end of war could be interpreted as the end of wartime planning, and therefore as the threat of a reversion to distributive *in*justice. John Mills – who had acted in the uniforms of all three services in *In Which We Serve* (1941), *Waterloo Road* (1945) and *The Way to the Stars* (1945) – steps out of the audience in Paul Rotha's dialectical and dialogic documentary on housing policy, *Land of Promise* (1946), and insists that Britain is an occupied territory awaiting liberation by the experts of welfarism:

> It's not enough to end one war, we've got to end them all ... they're waiting for us down there in those occupied territories, they're waiting for D Day and the armies of liberation. Come on then you leaders, come on, where are you? Architects, doctors, planners, engineers, social workers, step out into the light. It's you who have to plan this invasion ... a thousand years we've been waiting.[17]

There is an argument here for extending the disciplines of war into 'the piping time of peace': Dalton, as Chancellor of the Exchequer, called his civil servants 'post-warriors'.[18]

If the prolongation of war conditions – economic and other controls – could be represented as the vice of privation or the virtue of planning, a threat to the individual or a boon to the collective, in another respect the

---

[16] Judith M. Brown and Wm. Roger Louis (eds), *The Oxford History of the British Empire* (Oxford University Press, 1999), p. 27; David Reynolds, *One World Divisible: A Global History Since 1945* (Harmondsworth: Penguin, 2001), pp. 69–70.
[17] *Land of Promise: The British Documentary Movement 1930–1950* (Dir. Various), UK: BFI.
[18] David Edgerton, *Warfare State: Britain 1920–1970* (Cambridge University Press, 2005), p. 89.

last year of the war was marked in Britain by 'regime-change', an electoral manifestation of a will to transform values and power relations. The imaginative challenge of Labour's summer 1945 victory over their Conservative senior partners in coalition is now the most striking element in the 1940s fiction of Jewish writer and later broadcaster Marghanita Laski. Her novel *Love on the Supertax* imagines a political salvation for the wealthy in the form of an anti-egalitarian leader seeking a 'really reactionary peace whereby the German Army is firmly established as a bulkwark (sic) against Russian Imperialist expansion'. This programme may anticipate Cold War realignments (the *Bundeswehr* was created in 1955), but at the time of writing it represented a crude restoration of ruling socio-economic interests, and an acknowledgment of the strength of Churchillian, as well as Bevinite, anti-communism.[19] Of the convergence of the interests of workers and employers which was 'apparently institutionalized in 1945', Jeremy Seabrook notes, with studied irony, that it was as if the impact of war reduced 'the rancour of centuries ... to murmurings', which would have been peace indeed on the domestic, economic front of the class war. Our apperception of 'postwar consensus', as rhetorical a signifier as wartime 'reconstruction', is now modified by the reinvention of (meritocratic) inequality in the twenty-first century which has reversed the postwar symbolic relationship of the British Welfare and Warfare States.[20] It may be lost to us now, but in the early 1960s, *Age of Austerity* was a title offered as a periodisation of 1945 to 1951, rather than post-2008, and Laski's narratives make fun of the presumption of a transition to distributive justice.[21] *Tory Heaven*, for example, opens by disrupting the already-received narrative of 1945:

> It is difficult after the passage of years to recall the precise emotions with which the population of England switched on their radio-sets one summer evening in 1945 and prepared to hear that the Tories had won the General Election.[22]

This is a 'Conservative Utopia', a dream-vision of a *coup d'état*, in which a general revulsion against 'egalitarian rule' is seized upon as a 'popular mandate' for a 'perfect flowering of the class system' in a strictly graded social order.[23]

---

[19] Marghanita Laski, *Love on the Supertax* (London: Cresset Press, 1944), p. 121.
[20] Jeremy Seabrook, *Pauperland: Poverty and the Poor in Britain* (London: Hurst, 2013), p. 23.
[21] Michael Sissons and Philip French (eds), *Age of Austerity, 1945–51* (London: Hodder & Stoughton, 1963).
[22] Marghanita Laski, *Tory Heaven, or Thunder on the Right* (London: Cresset Press, 1948), p. 5.
[23] Ibid., pp. 16, 26, 48, 52.

Laski's approach would be used later by Michael Young in *The Rise of the Meritocracy 1870–2033: An Essay on Education and Equality* (1958), a satire on the adaptation of inherited privilege to new times which was traduced by the adoption of its title as camouflage for the neoliberalism of the Blair era and after. In making an ideologically heterodox comedy out of resistance to both war-socialism and postwar socialism, Laski nevertheless can on occasion achieve an Orwellian amplitude: 'It has been an article of British faith that Fascism is a nasty foreign notion, whereas the anti-egalitarianism I am describing seems to be totally and basically English.'[24] The economic logic which is articulated in the dystopic allusion to a Huxleyan alphabetic-hierarchy – A.B. restaurants, which serve to make Bs feel posh, for no A would ever be seen in one, have replaced A.B.C.s – is prescient of the neo-liberal reconcentration of wealth in our era:

> 'You remember how people used to point out that if you took Lord Rothschild's money and divided it among everyone, they'd only get about a farthing each? Well, we found that quite a different situation arose when we took the money from the workers and divided it among *us*.'[25]

To Bed with Grand Music (1946) is similarly troubling to the idea that the spirit of 1945 will achieve permanent monuments to a more equal society, and might be read against Humphrey Jennings's celebrated collaboration with E. M. Forster in *A Diary for Timothy* (1945). The film bids to manage the transition from war to peace symbolically: the events of the sixth year of the war are articulated alongside the first months in the rural, bourgeois existence of a fatherless-for-the-duration baby. It is a charmingly pedagogic or propagandistic displacement of political contradictions. Laski's heroine, by contrast, is written so as to bring tensions to the surface. Unlike the mother in Jennings's documentary, she refuses to 'stay here and rot till the war's over' with *her* son Timothy. Her chosen war work is producing sexual solace for wartime separations. In the wake of the first Victory celebrations, a former employer with official 'pull' offers to demobilise her husband quickly in exchange for sex, or indeed keep him out of England if she prefers that. Laski's previous satires had terminated rather artlessly; in this case, the heroine's assumption of the role of pedagogue of the *demi monde* to a girl whose husband is sent East to fight against Japan creates a cyclical pattern in which the uncertainty of the meaning of war's end resonates plangently.

---

[24] Ibid., p. 48. [25] Ibid., p. 86 (emphasis in the original).

The labile and indeterminate quality of the 'event' of war's cessation contradicted its theoretical and performative decisiveness. Jennings's film *A Defeated People* (1946) opens, like Elizabeth Bowen's short story 'Summer Night', by impersonating public dissent about the significance and outcomes of the war: 'They asked for it / You can't let them starve/ ... good thing if some of them did die.'[26] A contemporary review of the film confirms that its task was perceived as a delicate one: 'There is no attempt to work up pity for the Germans, only a desire that we should realise what the war they started has brought back to them on recoil.'[27] If, as is suggested here, the British public were expected to recoil at pity for the enemy, why is it that they need to be taught that the Germans 'asked for it' and indeed got it? The historian Richard Overy writes of a 'German lesson to be taught to the Germans' when he analyses the arguments made by the Air Staff in 1941 for a Bomber Command strategic campaign against the working-class districts of German cities (in imitation of German tactics of 'area' concentration in the London Blitz). Overy notes, too, both the Air Ministry's preference for not publicising its new policy so that it might be inferred that it had 'scruples', and American incredulity at an argument about the morale of bombed civilians that overlooked the globally broadcast 'valorous experience' of the British during the 1940 raids.[28] Was the cinematic lesson for the British the result of scepticism about the efficacy of that 'German lesson', the supposed wartime demoralisation of the civilian population killed, hurt or unhoused by the RAF? In the film, an air raid siren marking curfew 'reminds them that they lost a war of their own making', but it also connects the German experience with the cinematic and auditory representation of the London Blitz, most famously in Jennings's own *Fires Were Started* (1943). In Jennings's postwar film, the demonstration that the enemy was defeated consists in assertions in the commentary of the Germans' own knowledge of that defeat. But privately, Jennings confessed that he could achieve no 'reliable picture' of occupied Germany, 'the contradictions were too many'.[29]

---

[26] Humphrey Jennings (dir.), *A Defeated People* (Crown Film Unit, 1946) in *The Complete Humphrey Jennings*, vol. 3: *A Diary for Timothy* (BFI, 2013).
[27] British Film Institute, *Monthly Film Bulletin*, vol. 13, issue 147 (March 1946), p. 41.
[28] Richard Overy, *The Bombing War: Europe 1939–1945* (Harmondsworth: Penguin, 2013), pp. 264–5.
[29] Undated letter to Cicely Jennings [1945], Kevin Jackson (ed.), *Humphrey Jennings Film Reader* (Manchester: Carcanet, 2004), p. 101. In the anthology of writings on industrialisation which Jennings started to collect during the war, he was systematically drawing attention to another category of 'new problems of description and comparison', those confronted by the natural philosophers of the seventeenth century. See *Pandaemonium 1660–1886: The Coming of the Machine Age as Seen by Contemporary Observers* (London: Pan, 1987), p. 20. In another example

Lindsay Anderson's 1954 *Sight and Sound* appreciation of Jennings, who died in 1950, is curiously Churchillian in its imagining the importance of the director's legacy, as if heroic virtues of wartime had not yet been grown out of: Jennings's 'films stand alone ... They will speak for us to posterity, saying: "This is what it was like. This is what we were like – the best of us."'[30] Yet Jennings's answer to the question posed by the end of the war – what were the Germans like? – was the antithesis of Anderson's invocation of a wartime version of an Arnoldian 'best self'. Writing of getting nearer to the problem of German character, he told his wife in September 1945 about the 'rabbit-eyed' 'near-zombies' he encountered, using the waiters who served the British personnel of MILGOV (Military Government), UNRRA (United Nations Relief and Rehabilitation Agency) and the Belsen trials to personify the Germans: '"the dwarfs" we call them – scurrying like Black Beetles' and later 'Dusseldwarfs'.[31] But Jennings's anxiety about the passivity of the Germans reflects a pedagogic paradox which threatened the denazification and state-building policies of the British occupation of Germany: the teachers' authority appears at once to contradict the spirit of the lesson (here the importance of democratic self-determination) and to be vulnerable to the counter-constructions of the pupils, who may resist, or indeed act out, in a grudging excess, their own objectification as the worst of humanity by their occupiers.[32] As we shall see, the moral price of peace-as-occupation was a high one.

It was in these terms that writer, physician and pacifist Alex Comfort complained in 1946 in the pages of the *British Medical Journal* that the British Zone of occupation was characterised by 'actions as stupid and as reminiscent of Hitler' as imprisoning a German doctor for not standing for the British National Anthem.[33] For Comfort, the problem of the era after 1945 would be the aftermath of the thorough 'militarisation' of humanity: 'Few people can remember what it was like to be sane, to live in a world where one could not earn a decoration for butchering a few thousand civilians, where a good many national heroes would have qualified for the

---

of the irony of the inescapable re-contextualisation generated by historical consciousness, *Pandaemonium* – reinterpreted as history from below – was Danny Boyle's declared primary source for the pageant opening the 2012 Olympic Games.

[30] Quoted in Brian Winston, *"Fires Were Started – "* (London: BFI, 1999), p. 8.
[31] *Jennings Film Reader*, pp. 103–4.
[32] See Michael Bell, *Open Secrets: Literature, Education and Authority from J.-J. Rousseau to J.M. Coetzee* (Oxford University Press, 2007), pp. 1–3.
[33] Alex Comfort, letter to the editor, *British Medical Journal* (1946) 2(4463) p. 104.

gallows.'³⁴ From his anarchist perspective, warlike behaviour and warlike morals weren't put away in 1945. The very prospect of the extension of an expedient wartime collectivism required, in his view, that the individual 'learn the lesson of the resistance, evasion, disappearance' and carry on an undercover war as 'the Maquis of the peace'. Not only Comfort's analysis but his vocabulary attests to the persistence of militarised values (throughout France, as in Italy, there really was a 'Maquis of the peace', but these were camouflaging their collaboration behind the screen of a fictitious involvement in the resistance).³⁵ In *The Novel and Our Time* (1948), Comfort noted that literature is threatened by this collective tendency too: 'the novel remains socially and commercially tolerated' as a form of negation because its patron is the individual, not the state.³⁶ But for the moment, the novel's capacity for the 'literary interpretation of events is as much out of control as events themselves', and the technical problem of introducing a 'viewpoint-character into every event' is less compelling than the fact that 'the real literature of events is tending to pass out of fiction ... into individuals who are themselves walking fiction'.³⁷ Comfort's own declared preference for 'concentration on the fixed points' sounds like a literary Maginot line, a prescription for an imaginative defensiveness in the concrete – 'the soldier in his pillbox watching Hitler's body burn'. This was an optimistic image of the future of Fuhrer iconography: the young soldier Hugh Trevor Roper was about to make his reputation with *The Last Days of Hitler* (1947), based on his own counter-intelligence work, a reputation diminished by his role in the Hitler Diaries affair of the 1980s.³⁸

The protagonist of Jack Aistrop's novel *Pretend I Am a Stranger* (1949) could be one of Comfort's 'walking fictions': discharged from psychiatric treatment, he publishes a novel under the name of Connor to bury his previous identity, 'the corpse of Maclaren'.³⁹ The protagonist's traumatic and narrative stratagems are rooted in a conviction that he has betrayed his unit under interrogation. Jack Aistrop had promoted creative writing from the Forces in the wartime anthology *Bugle Blast* (1943 and 1944), the title perhaps representing an accommodation between duty and Vorticist iconoclasm, echoing Wyndham Lewis's *Blast* (1914 and 1915) to suggest a militarist modernism. His novel explored the idea that there might be aspects of Britain's war that it would not do to remember – in the story, the

---

[34] Alex Comfort, *Art and Social Responsibility* (London: Falcon Press, 1946), p. 79.
[35] Ibid., pp. 83, 88.
[36] Alex Comfort, *The Novel and Our Time* (London: Phoenix House, 1948), p. 27.
[37] Ibid., pp. 75, 68, 75.   [38] Ibid., p. 76.
[39] Jack Aistrop, *Pretend I Am a Stranger* (London: Dennis Dobson, 1949), p. 138.

trial of an SS officer redeems Maclaren from his guilty imaginings. Nigel Balchin, novelist and industrial psychologist, probed similar issues of demobilisation as boundary formation in *Mine Own Executioner* (1945), containing the troubling return of violence to the Home Front in the frame of institutional satire. Adam Lucian, pilot and repatriated prisoner of the Japanese, confesses for a second time to a therapist, and having confronted the fact that he gave up information under torture, thinks he can exit therapy, only to kill himself at the end of the novel after he's produced the 'symptom' of violence against his wife. *Pretend I Am a Stranger* is more akin to Henry Green's *Back* (1946) in its optimism, narrating a qualified romantic after-war resolution to unheroic wartime crises of identity ('choking' or 'puzzling' events), but Aistrop's novel is more insistent than Green's on an evidential unravelling of its puzzles, as if peace promised an explicit settling of accounts. Contemporary reviewers were unconvinced by another walking fiction, Michael Redgrave's 'phoney' Czech veteran, surviving the war in a POW camp in Basil Dearden's film *The Captive Heart* (1946) under the assumed identity of a British officer killed in action. They preferred the documentary qualities of the reconstruction of British POW life on location 'in an actual prisoner-of-war camp' as the *Daily Film Renter* reported in July 1945: A. L. Kennedy would use the same reflexive *mise-en-scène* – the cinematic re-staging of POW life – in her novel of war, *Day* (2008).[40] Aistrop's earlier narrative *Backstage with Joe* (1946) is formally more disjunct than *Pretend I Am a Stranger*, representing a bonfire of decorum – 'I do not believe there is any prescribed form for anything and there never will be again' – with the device of breaking up the text with boldface titles every fifteen to thirty lines, like the 'Aeolus' chapter of *Ulysses*.[41] This form also enacts a preoccupation which is residually present in *Pretend*, the contingency of self on its relations to others: the book was ostensibly written over twenty-one nights after duty, 'each completed page the common property of a unit, the mounting pile of pages public reading'.[42] This collective literary production is quite distinct then, from T. E. Lawrence's secret composition of his RAF memoir, *The Mint*, 'putting down these notes on our Depot life, often writing in bed from roll-call till lights out, using any scrap of paper. So I seemed only to be writing letters'.[43] Where Lawrence saw in the regimentation of the service the

---

[40] Alan Burton and Tim O'Sullivan, *The Cinema of Basil Dearden and Michael Relph* (Edinburgh University Press, 2009), p. 77. POW films can be seen as one of the earliest British attempts to colonise the memory of the war in Europe with familiar narrative conventions (the school novel).
[41] Jack Aistrop, *Backstage with Joe* (London: Dennis Dobson, 1946), p. 5.   [42] Ibid.
[43] T. E. Lawrence, *The Mint* (London: Jonathan Cape, 1955), p. 67.

production of 'generations of standard airmen', Aistrop declares, echoing Wyndham Lewis's 1914 *Blast*, that the war is '[the] crowd's war'.[44]

The apotheosis of the people at war translated to liberated but not to occupied territories. The endpapers of Aistrop's novel of the occupation of Germany, *The Lights Are Low* (1946), were adapted from a late sixteenth-century compendium of bird's-eye views of European towns, *Civitates orbis terrarium*, a holistic vision of urban order which provides an ironic contrast to the indifferent ruins of the continent in 1945: the opening of Aistrop's narrative describes a single surviving white arrow pointing at the cellar entrance to an air-raid shelter: 'It was as if it had been left purposely – a reminder of days and nights they wanted to forget'.[45] As with John Bayley's novel *In Another Country* (1955) and Colin MacInnes's earlier *To the Victors the Spoils* (1950), liberation is an act which carries with it a surprising burden of responsibility, as if war guilt were somehow transferred to the victors (anticipating revisionist themes in 1970s theatre and end-of-century fiction). In Bayley's novel, that guilt is the antithesis of the innocence of the occupier, a young man for whom Germany represents an interval of 'pastoral calm' before a resumption of the competitiveness of civilian life. This naivety is contrasted with the resentment of the occupied, chaffing at their 'pastoralisation' by Allied occupation and re-education policy.[46] McInnes's occupiers, on the contrary, lose any claim to moral authority as they dispense justice and simultaneously imitate the pillaging of their Reichswehr predecessors: 'when you've behaved as we've often done, the only thing that entitles you to blame the enemy is your pistol'.[47]

After 1945, 1930s tropes of borders and border-crossing – ways of escape from normative identities and destinies – are superseded in some writing by the complexities of zones of occupation. Within the zone of occupation, the identification of adversaries as fellow subjects of war, which had powered the writing of Siegfried Sassoon and Wilfred Owen, and fed the pacific-fascism of Henry Williamson and David Jones, turns to recognitions of shared guilt. These zones of political contradiction seep into the domestic spaces of the supposedly unified home front too. Fascistic bullying usurps the social rituals of the Rosamund Tea Rooms in Patrick Hamilton's *Slaves of Solitude* (1947) and in Bowen's *The Heat of the Day* (1948), Louie's one salvation and discipline, the newspapers, are a channel

---

[44] Ibid., III, 18, *Backstage*, p. 118.
[45] Jack Aistrop, *The Lights Are Low* (London: Dennis Dobson, 1946), p. 9.
[46] John Bayley, *In Another Country* (Oxford University Press, 1986 [1955]), p. 223.
[47] Colin MacInnes, *To the Victors the Spoils* (Harmondsworth: Penguin, 1966 [1950]), p. 376.

for the tyrannical urgings of 'the Russians keeping going on [nagging] at us to do something'.[48]

Graham Greene's 1940s and early 1950s fictions, set against an ideological and topographical background in which borders are reinstalled in zones of occupation, are also genre-crossings, narratives that preceded screenplays. Alex Comfort claimed that both readers and writers in this era had had their powers enlarged by cinema:

> The film has developed the power of audiences to react to direct visual presentation in narrative, and it has also given a far wider insight to the writer into the nature of techniques which he uses, largely by extending his experience.[49]

But there is a sense in which *The Third Man* (1949), *No Man's Land* (commissioned by Carol Reed in 1950) and *The Stranger's Hand* (which began with Greene's 1949 entry for a *New Statesman* competition for a Greene parody) are between media, as if the literary is about to be displaced by the cinematic, culturally as well as economically. In *The Third Man* narrative, the figure of the writer is deprecated in the form of the pulp-novelist duped into a job writing propaganda for a black-marketeer and, in the evolution of this treatment to the screenplay, storytelling is itself demoted and supplanted, the frame narrator first substituted with an animation, and then restored as the 'commentator'.[50] Something similar, in terms of authority, is going on in *No Man's Land*, Greene's attempt to exploit the success of the film *The Third Man* with a story of the Cold War, which was displacing occupation and liberation as the frame of war and militarism's persistence beyond 1945. The frame narrator of this treatment, which was not filmed, is a member of the 'Boundary Inspection', a bureaucrat of the new global frontiers carving up Europe, even before Churchill's Iron Curtain had concretised into the Berlin Wall.[51] The story's protagonist, Brown, whose indifferent, 'neutral' name makes him redolent of Julian Maclaren-Ross's khakied conscripts of the early 1940s, 'brown jobs', is a Cold warrior going under the guise of the writer. His most profound alienation is the absence of a uniform, of rules: 'there was no

---

[48] Elizabeth Bowen, *The Heat of the Day*, holograph draft and typescript, HRC, box 5, folder 3, ch. 8, p. 10.
[49] Alex Comfort, *The Novel and Our Time* (London: Phoenix House, 1948), pp. 37–8.
[50] Graham Greene, 'The Third Man' TS drafts and Release Script, HRC, Austin, Texas, Container 34.4–6. Reed's film was released in the United Kingdom in 1949 and in the United States in 1950. Greene's narrative appeared in *The Third Man and the Fallen Idol* (London: Heinemann, 1950).
[51] The 'Iron Curtain' was, Greene observed, a 'stupid phrase' because 'you can easily get lost in the folds'. Graham Greene, *No Man's Land*, (ed.) James Sexton (London: Hesperus, 2005), p. 4.

limit, just as there was no war', the condition of Clausewitzian total war – no limit – spilling outside the traditional markers of conflict.[52]

The question of how far the represented and unconscious psychodynamics of war and peace in the 1940s are an internalisation of geopolitical forces is one that the writings of Adam Piette have focused in troubling ways.[53] In an undated proposal for a TV programme on the 'Forties' (subtitled 'The Shadow of Cain'), Jocelyn Brooke suggested that the crusade against Hitler itself had unconscious motives: 'This refusal to face defeat was quite irrational: a kind of psychological defence-mechanism.' The end of the war had been 'as unimaginable [as] the Day of Judgement', in part because, he claimed in the retrospect of the age of the Atom, the 'elation of victory … was soured with guilt'.[54] In a long poem 'Something about a War', Brooke wrote of the uncertainty of the hinge between war and peace:

> Living between two worlds
> I cannot solve the equation:
> Hoping for the war's ending
> But fearing the peace-time future –
> The summer-term protracted,
> The holidays uncertain,
> Shadowed by a strange climate.[55]

The war, because of its longueurs, was in some ways the making of Jocelyn Brooke the writer, but it also held the man captive, his postwar narrations a series of circlings back to imitate, rewrite or reconfigure his own published fictions of military conscription and occupation. *The Image of a Drawn Sword* (1950) is a text which bridges the uncanniness of the 1930s figure of the enemy as the fascist within – from Upward's 'Mortmere' to Auden's '1 September 1939' – with the paranoia of the unravelling of emergency alliances, both domestic and international, which sutured divisions of class and ideology. *Image* could equally be described in less parochial literary-historical terms: it translates *The Trial* into postwar Kent, generating distinctly Anglo-inflected versions of two influential formal components of Kafka's fiction, the protagonist interpellated by obscure

---

[52] Ibid., pp. 3, 22. Julian Maclaren-Ross, *The Stuff to Give the Troops* (London: Jonathan Cape, 1944).
[53] See Adam Piette, *Imagination at War: British Fiction and Poetry 1939–45* (London: Macmillan, 1995) and *The Literary Cold War, 1945-Vietnam* (Edinburgh University Press, 2009).
[54] Jocelyn Brooke, 'The nineteen-forties', Jocelyn Brooke Papers, HRC, Austin, Texas, Container 5.2, pp. 6, 9, 11.
[55] Jocelyn Brooke, 'Something about a War', Jocelyn Brooke Papers, HRC, Austin, Texas, Container 7.8, p. 49.

compulsions, and an occluded, para-state organisation. These helped make *The Trial* a master-narrative for imagining aspects of life under totalitarianism, Rex Warner's *The Aerodrome* (1941) being a familiar example. In Brooke's hands, the psychic dimension is manifested as a sexualised conscription, the organisational dimension as a militia conspiring not at civil war so much as civil occupation. Brooke returns to the topographical and libidinal territory of *Image*, and those Kafkaesque narrative forms in his unpublished 'Crothers' novel, drafted in the mid-1950s, but what was an intradiegetic inference in the earlier fiction is now made explicit in the context of superpower relations – 'a military <u>coup</u>' and a 'policy of open warfare (as opposed to the present "cold" war)'.[56] The protagonist's subjection to cinematic pornography as military-psychiatric treatment for what is alternatively diagnosed as his 'defeatism' and his desire to be 'forcibly enrolled ... in an insurgent force' anticipates the fantasies of mind control in Anthony Burgess's *A Clockwork Orange* and Len Deighton's *Ipcress File*, both published in 1962.[57] But Brooke's punning on well-camouflaged defence forces and repressed defence mechanisms – 'a phantasy system to cover one's tracks' – as well as the cinematic framing of the central drama of guilty love, reaches back to the concerns of Greene's occupation writing.[58] Brooke's rewriting of the transition from war as a serial fantasy of the resumption of war, as if peace represented a critical loss of energy, reminds us of the occulted militarism in English culture, all too clearly apparent in his namesake's 1914 Sonnets.

The victory of Labour in 1945 did much to determine how the story of the Second World War would be organised. Indirectly, defeat in the General Election caused Churchill to capitalise on his unprecedented access to Cabinet papers: he had ordered the monthly printing of his 'Personal Minutes' (official directives) and 'Personal Telegrams'.[59] These source materials are one of the reasons that his 'six volume history *The Second World War*, was generally accepted as a definitive interpretation'.[60] He was Nobel Literature laureate, cited for his oratory as well as his historiography, in 1953, five years after T. S. Eliot. Churchill was unique as a war leader in writing the war, and *The Second World War* had a clear

---

[56] Jocelyn Brooke, [Untitled novel re. Crothers], Jocelyn Brooke Papers, HRC, Austin, Texas, Container 1.8, pp. 172–3 (emphasis in the original).
[57] Ibid., p. 245.   [58] Ibid., p. 268.
[59] David Reynolds, *In Command of History: Churchill Fighting and Writing the Second World War* (Harmondsworth: Penguin, 2005), p. 28.
[60] Paul Addison, 'The Three Careers of Winston Churchill' *Transactions of the Royal Historical Society*, Sixth Series, (2001) 11 pp. 1183–99, 183.

field, in contrast to the situation after 1918 when a 'battle of the memoirs' was waged over the conduct of the Great War and its political legacies. Then, Churchill had contributed the six volumes of *The World Crisis* (1923–31), which were notably traduced by Balfour as autobiography disguised as a history of the universe.[61] But in the late 1940s, when the 'public history of the Second World War had still not set firm', the historiographical fruits of Churchill's marshalling of the documentation and his transatlantic successes in securing serialisations were highly significant in giving recent history authoritative narrative form, both in terms of nodes of crisis, action and decision (the Battle of Britain, El Alamein, inter-Allied Conferences) and periods of strategic and logistical endurance or preparation (the Battle of the Atlantic, the Second Front).[62]

In contrast to the uncertainties, hesitations and evasions which characterise the fictional and cinematic writing examined so far, Churchill's was a didactic text. The 'Moral of the Work' was '*In War*: Resolution / *In Defeat*: Defiance / *In Victory*: Magnanimity / *In Peace*: Goodwill', and its narrative structure was retrospective irony. The origins of the 'unnecessary war', a consequence of 'HOW THE ENGLISH-SPEAKING PEOPLES / THROUGH THEIR UNWISDOM / CARELESSNESS AND GOOD NATURE / ALLOWED THE WICKED / TO REARM', occupied the bulk of the first volume, *The Gathering Storm* (1948).[63] The second, *Their Finest Hour* (1949), narrated Britain's war 'ALONE' from Churchill's accession and the fall of France. The narrative was concluded in 1953 by *Triumph and Tragedy*, like the other five volumes a diptych, which balanced 'The Tide of Victory' (from D Day) with 'Iron Curtain', citing his own March 1946 speech in Fulton, Missouri, and tempering the familiar suspense of the eve of (successful) battle with the prolepsis of frightening atom-era superpower rivalries.[64]

So although the war had its story, it did not have an end. Elizabeth Bowen, having resumed her wartime start on *The Heat of the Day*, as Churchill organised his research team, situated her fiction both inside and beyond the conflict:

> This is a story set, outwardly, in a particular phase of the Second World War, but it is not a war novel, being perennial in subject ... For each of [the

---

[61] Reynolds, *In Command of History*, p. 23. [62] Ibid., p. xxi.
[63] Winston Churchill, *History of the Second World War* (London: Cassell, 1948), vol. 1, p. xiv.
[64] Patrick Wright, *Iron Curtain: From Stage to Cold War* (Oxford University Press, 2009).

protagonists], the war is an exteriorization of an internal conflict – such wars do not finish, only shift their ground.[65]

Patterns of publication in the wake of the Great War, notably the war books boom of the late 1920s, centred on the sales of Erich Maria Remarque's *All Quiet on the Western Front*, have tempted critics to formulate psycho-historical narratives of the literary representation of war. John W. Aldridge, surveying modern American war writing at mid-century in *After the Lost Generation*, did just that, arguing 'the general public fully accepted the new war literature' only in 1948 with Mailer's *The Naked and the Dead*: 'the war was far enough away for people to remember it with some detachment and to begin to speculate on its larger meaning'.[66] But this separation of event and representation is implausible. Symbols and narratives of transition are an important dimension of political, legal and social processes of demobilisation, displacement and occupation, and literary texts are bound up with those discourses, not remote from them. And just as the idea of the punctual end of war is an existential falsehood, so too does the notion of a transition to peace misrepresent the work, imaginative and practical, of worlds in the making. With so much sense-making going on, it should not surprise us that writers worked the interstices of ruined and reconstructed systems of meaning, rather than constructing myths of their own.

---

[65] Elizabeth Bowen, author's 'blurb' for *The Heat of the Day*, HRC Austin, Texas box 5, folder 5.
[66] Quoted in Leah Garrett, *Young Lions: How Jewish Authors Reinvented the American War Novel* (Evanston, IL: Northwestern University Press, 2015), p. 31.

CHAPTER 8

Poetry, the Early Cold War and the Idea of Europe
Adam Piette

The postwar years 1945 to 1949 acted as a rediscovery, traumatic for the most part, of Europe as a space of broken cities, as a potential new political arena split into East and West, but haunted by wartime horrors. Military morale organisations such as the US Bombing Survey, but also cultural institutions like the BBC and British Council, as well as shadier information propaganda units like the Information Research Department and the wartime Cultural Relations Department, were all involved in measuring the tasks needed for European ideological reconstruction under the new Cold War circumstances. There were many poets who made the journey into the heart of a devastated Europe stunned into rubble-strewn submission to the new order, and under the compulsions of the vast bureaucracies and forcefields generated by the emergent Cold War stand-off. Among them were Stephen Spender and W. H. Auden, and the covert side to their exploration of the war-traumatised cityscapes of Germany has been the subject of much debate, particularly with James Smith's important book, *British Writers and MI5 Surveillance, 1930–1960*.[1] This chapter seeks to explore, through politically informed close readings, the poems and prose works they wrote in the period 1945 to 1950.

In April 1945, W. H. Auden joined the Morale Division of the US Strategic Bombing Survey, travelling to Germany to inspect the ruins caused by the area bombing campaigns, and to register the psychological consequences of the devastation on the German people. What he saw shocked him into silence. He had planned to write a book about his experiences of war-destroyed Germany with James Stern; but returning back to the States after the war he quietly withdrew, leaving Stern to write *The Hidden Damage*. Stern himself acknowledged the unspeakable nature of what the Survey witnessed, visually in terms of the bombed-out cities;

---

[1] A new essay by Smith on the legacies of covert practices in postwar literature is included in this volume.

culturally with the interviews of those who had undergone the bombing; and also of the concentration camp victims:

> I tried to rehearse an imaginary conversation about the continent of Europe with my wife and friends, but I didn't know how to begin ... for I realized as never before that between those who have seen and those who haven't, there is a gulf fixed which the spoken word cannot bridge.[2]

Cornelia Pearsall has argued that the vision of wrecked cities, the ghastly horrors experienced by the people he interviewed, function as an active blank in Auden's postwar poetry, signifying as a destructive barbed wire trope running through the poems.[3] The image occurs most clearly in 'Memorial for the City', the 1949 poem that reflects on the time in Germany:

> Across the square,
> Between the burnt-out Law Courts and Police Headquarters,
> Past the Cathedral far too damaged to repair,
> Around the Grand Hotel patched up to hold reporters,
> Near huts of some Emergency Committee,
> The barbed-wire runs through the abolished City.[4]

Reflecting on the uncanny efficacy of the barbed wire as marker of border, an imprisoning, excluding, ensnaring force, Pearsall writes:

> Barbed wire does not protect the city, but functions instead perpetually to divide it from itself, rendering arbitrary and vicious the line between the permissible and the prohibited, between who has the right to enter, and who the inability to leave. All are detained, entangled in its snares, and not only in their attempts to navigate the criss-crossed, abolished city.[5]

This is well put, for it acknowledges the implications of Auden's exploration of the new Europe of the Cold War: where divided cities like Vienna and Berlin intimate a future as Iron Curtained division of superpower spoils, with all citizens targeted as hostile. Barbed wire had haunted the interwar as a frontline nightmare of Great War memory; played with fitfully in Auden's 1937 'The biscuits are hard and the beef is high', uneasily

---

[2] James Stern, *The Hidden Damage (1947)* (London: Chelsea Press, 1990), p. 372.
[3] Cornelia Pearsall, 'The Poet and the Postwar City' *Raritan* (1997) 17(2) pp. 104–21. Cf. also Vincent Giroud, *Nicolas Nabokov: A Life in Freedom and Music* (Oxford University Press, 2015), for Auden's views on the Survey as communicated to Nabokov: 'Morale with an e at the end is psycho-sociological nonsense. What they *want* to say, but *don't* say, is how many people we killed and how many buildings we destroyed by that wicked bombing' (p. 184, emphasis in the original).
[4] W. H. Auden, 'Memorial for the City' in *Collected Poems* (London: Faber & Faber, 1994), pp. 591–96, 594.
[5] Pearsall, 'The Poet and the Postwar City', p. 113.

bright, dark with undertone: 'The subaltern's heart was full of fire, / Now he hangs on the old barbed wire / All blown up like a motor-tyre.'[6] The plight of concentration camp victims had also been there in Auden's work as far back as the late 1920s. In *Paid on Both Sides* (1928), a prisoner-of-war man-woman behind barbed wire tells his/her story and is shot by the spy. Interwar intimations of totalitarianism, issuing from the anti-fascist movement, had understood the resemblances between the Great War's violent division of landscape and Nazi destructive enclosure of the racial and sexual Other within concentration camps. That understanding is, then, in 'Memorial for the City', *recalled* through the barbed wire trope, so that the Cold War division of Europe into Soviet and French/American/British zones within a divided Germany (and in 1949 Austria) is felt to be fulfilling at the level of a continental geopolitical schism the interwar prognostications of a totalitarian future that divides in order the better to annihilate. Division as border-zone and enclosure enables the erasure and destruction of imprisoned populations, a lethal liminality that contains and incarcerates.

'Memorial for the City' expresses, then, an idea of Europe structured according to fascist war-logistics and spatiality, inaugurating the Cold War machine as analysed by Deleuze and Guattari. Fascism, according to their view, had launched the 'worldwide war machine', with war as an endless movement with no other aim than itself; but fascism's version is only a rough sketch – its real manifestation is in the Cold War's technologies of global destruction: the 'post-fascist figure is that of a war machine that takes peace as its object directly, as the peace of Terror or Survival. The war machine reforms a smooth space which now claims to control, to surround the entire earth.'[7] That control of space in terms of containment and divisive enclosure is effectively captured in Auden's barbed wire image; for Reviel Netz, barbed wire 'encapsulates violence in a static defensive manner', the violence being a 'prevention of motion'.[8] The icy stillness of the imaginary associated with the Cold War, the barbed and armed border zones symbolising Cold War containment within the zoned cities: we might read the Cold War machine as a barbed wire technology running

---

[6] Edward Mendelson (ed.), *The English Auden: Poems, Essays and Dramatic Writings, 1927–1939* (London: Faber & Faber, 1977), p. 289.
[7] Gilles Deleuze and Félix Guattari, *A Thousand Plateaus: Capitalism and Schizophrenia*, transl. Brian Massumi (Minneapolis, MN: University of Minnesota Press, 1987), 421.
[8] Reviel Netz, *Barbed Wire: An Ecology of Modernity* (Middletown, CT: Wesleyan University Press, 2004), pp. 102, 233. Cf. also Alan Krell, *Devil's Rope: A Cultural History of Barbed Wire* (London: Reaktion, 2002).

through all cities. The captive cities at the borders of East and West were also under nuclear threat – especially after the explosion of the Soviet Union's bomb in September 1949. There is here a sense of being psychically abolished that speaks to the fears and anxieties of European citizens under the compulsions of a nuclear culture that made everybody feel targeted by potentially hostile weapons. What was enclosing all citizens, as barbed wire had enclosed the victims of the camps during the war, was this armed apprehension of city-destructive death.

Auden's investment in the analysis of the new chilling geopolitics spawned by the world wars is semi-censored; there is a paucity of poems written directly about his time among the ruins. 'Memorial for the City' gives a measure of the simultaneous urge to bear witness, ironised down to the cool, heartless gaze of '[t]he eyes of the crow and the eye of the camera', and the need to withdraw into another supernatural realm of the self-redeemed, the 'Image' of the religious subject, 'Adam waiting for his City': together the two needs coalesce to abstract the cities Auden saw in Germany into the 'City', both a generalised global metropolis, and the holy City within the religious imagination. Some of this abstracting allegorising occurs in Auden's major early Cold War project, *The Age of Anxiety*, partly written around the period of his working in Germany. The four strangers who meet in a New York bar, and who symbolise faculties of the human mind (intuition, feeling, sensation, thought), get drunk and enter into a fantasy communion over the meaning of the Second World War, which speaks its daily horrors over the radio. Their communion is brief and fragmented, and they more often than not fall into solitary fantasies and memories, but all of them are involved in a common allegorical pursuit, a Pilgrim's Progress towards key *topoi* on a semi-collective psychic and spiritual journey. That journey includes a seven-staged section which is Jungian-geographical insofar as the four characters each experience a form of symbolic quest both dreamlike and archetypal. The seventh stage is Eliot's Waste Land, a desert space differently experienced by the four different personae; but for all four, the desert signifies something close to Auden's blitzed sense of annihilation and apocalypse. The desert is what any space might be reduced to, abolished by the war machine.[9] This waste land zone in *The Age of Anxiety* is and is not Eliotic: it has the war-zone destructive nothingness fused with the sense of a *dry* and nihilistic religious

---

[9] 'Abolished', from 'Memorial for the City', derives from Stéphane Mallarmé and Gérard de Nerval: the city, even the holy city of the redemption, might suffer radical ruination for all time, as with Nerval's 'tour abolie', or an even more oblivescent textual obliteration as in the abolition of Dawn in Mallarmé's 'Hérodiade'.

space; but equally, as so differently imagined by the four travellers, it resists the very symbolic project Auden's Jungian compositional gambit has set up.

The four come together after a time alone in separate labyrinthine ways, and stare at the vision of the waste land, as Quant sees it:

> Interdicted by desert, its dryness edged
>   By a scanty scrub
> Of Joshua trees and giant cacti;
>   Then, vacant of value,
> Incoherent and infamous sands,
>   Rainless regions
> Swarming with serpents, ancestral wastes,
>   Lands beyond love.[10]

Eliot is signalled in the enjambment ('wastes, / Lands') just as the difference is marked (these are *plural* waste lands): the Jungian collective unconscious Auden was drawn to in the late 1940s is the cause ('ancestral' implies ancient collective archetypes). Although *The Age of Anxiety* adopts the free mosaic daring of *The Waste Land* in its sequence of varying forms and free verse prosy sections, the line-specific poetic technique chosen for the whole eclogue, alliterative verse, is very alien to Eliot; and it signals what Auden felt was new to his version of the contemporary waste land – its plurality (there in the repeated lead consonants).[11] If Auden takes from Eliot the idea of a metaphysical desert which is also a war zone (Eliot's desert is the space of Biblical extremity just as it is Gallipoli where Jean Verdenal fell),[12] it is experienced in so many bewilderingly different ways by civilians and combatants around the world that its collective unconscious strikes each mind as private to themselves.

Quant, as intuition, as we have seen, registers the waste land as Eliotic and classic desert. Malin (as thought) experiences it as a cerebral *néant*, not really to be taken any more seriously than the idea of nothingness: 'Boring and bare of shade, / Devoid of souvenirs and voices, / It takes will to cross this waste'.[13] Emble, as sensation, adopts Auden's own childhood and takes us back to the desert the Pennine moors were for the boy Wystan,

---

[10] W. H. Auden, *The Age of Anxiety: A Baroque Eclogue* (1947) (Princeton University Press, 2011), p. 75.
[11] For a different line on the relations between the alliterative verse and plurality, cf. Susannah Young-ah Gottlieb, *Regions of Sorrow: Anxiety and Messianism in Hannah Arendt and W. H. Auden* (Palo Alto, CA: Stanford University Press, 2003).
[12] Verdenal was a medical student Eliot had met and fallen in love with in 1911 in Paris; Verdenal was killed in May 1915 in the Dardanelles. Eliot dedicated *Prufrock and Other Observations* to him.
[13] Auden, *The Age of Anxiety*, p. 75.

'his steps follow the stream / Past rusting apparatus / To its gloomy beginning, the original / Chasm where brambles block / The entrance to the underworld'.[14] Rosetta, as feeling, interrogates the deeper meaning of Romantic chaos, the 'landscape / Of gloom and glaciers and great storms'.[15] It is only when we have had this tour across the four landscapes that 'the world from which their journey has been one long flight rises up before them'. The contemporary world is announced by a violent storm that reads very like a bombing raid: 'Righteous wrath is raising its hands / To strike and destroy'; 'The clouds explode'; 'Violent winds / Tear us apart'.[16] And what is revealed is a world at war:

> Dull through the darkness, indifferent tongues
> From bombed buildings, from blacked-out towns,
> Camps and cockpits, from cold trenches,
> Submarines and cells, recite in unison
> A common creed, declaring their weak
> Faith in confusion. The floods are rising;
> Rain ruins on the routed fragments
> Of all the armies; indistinct
> Are friend and foe, one flux of bodies
> Miles from mother, marriage, or any
> Workable world.[17]

The common creed is merely weak faith, or, worse, faith in confusion (as in belief reduced to credence in history's violently chaotic reality). The world at war speaks in one voice only about apocalypse, an apocalypse of ruins and bombed cities. 'Rain *ruins*' on what has been ruined ('routed fragments' both referring back to 'bombed buildings' and to the defeated soldiers and civilians) – the activated verb says something about the appalling force of what Auden saw in Germany. Rain falling on the ruins summons the rain of bombs that caused them, a ghastly present tense re-enactment ('ruins *on*') as the mind tries to comprehend what the routed fragments mean. The crowd instinct that is generating and generated by these so frighteningly plural psychic apocalypses manifests as a 'flux of bodies'. The bodies seem to be secreting language, as though the ruins of the cities destroyed by the war machine were speaking. The mystery of this place, of this world, is solved if we read into these ruins the Germany Auden witnessed as part of the Bombing Survey. Stern in *The Hidden Damage* writes of the ghastly spectacle of 'Munich's ruins in pouring rain'.[18] The 'routed fragments / Of all the

---

[14] Ibid., p. 77.   [15] Ibid.   [16] Ibid., p. 78.   [17] Ibid., p. 79.
[18] Stern, *The Hidden Damage*, p. 119.

armies' summons the vision the Survey team had of the hundreds of Wehrmacht soldiers 'trudg[ing] the highways of Germany like outcasts', their filthy *feldgrau* uniforms worn like 'the stigma of defeat'.[19] The phrase 'indistinct / Are friend and foe' may relate to the way in which the Survey's questionnaire (or *Fragebogen*) needed the interviewers to distinguish their interlocutors as either 'hostile or friendly', indicating 'the shade (black, gray, or white!) of the sympathies for or against the Nazi regime'.[20] The German experience of the rootless populations, the refugees, the wandering soldiers on the roads threads its way into Auden's broader sense of the dislocating errancy of wartime subjectivity, miles from any workable world: 'In war-time', as the narrator of the prologue to *The Age of Anxiety* puts it, 'everybody is reduced to the anxious status of a shady character or a displaced person'.[21]

What is troubling in wartime subjectivity is how possessed each mind is by its enemy fascist double. When Quant tells us what he sees, he sees the ruins as haunted by the returning 'Dark Ones' who 'dwell in the statues' by the fallen wall, 'messengers from / The Nothing who nothings'.[22] Auden is quoting Heidegger's 1929 University of Freiburg inaugural lecture 'What is Metaphysics?', which notoriously argued that the Nothing nothings ('Das Nichts nichtet') – that is, that true nothingness is active, destructive, annihilates.[23] Anxiety is the mood which enables Dasein (or the human subject) to sense the active nihilative processes that are the ground of all being – but anxiety cannot fix on any object, since its object is this radical nothingness which pervades all things, all beings. Auden takes this pervasiveness of nihilating Nothing within all things and dramatises it as the Dark Ones dwelling in the statues beside a bombed-down wall, a superbly pitched theatricalising of Heidegger's metaphysics. For what it does is to politicise the staging of nothingness in the world: the Dark Ones are the ghosts of the Gestapo with their dark uniforms – they haunt the statues of the German cities as the Nazi crimes haunt the ruined *polis*. Stern saw a ruined statue in Munich, four lions toppled from the ruined Victory Arch in Leopoldstrasse: one is cast on its side, 'gazing with terrified eyes at the fury descending from the skies', seeming to unbend its elbow from a Nazi salute, clenching 'the huge hand into a fist'.[24] The lion allegorises the Nazi persona of every German citizen as a dark doppelgänger projection. If Heidegger's essay inaugurated the age of anxiety, it is an age of anxiety

---

[19] Ibid., pp. 109–10. [20] Ibid., p. 120. [21] Auden, *The Age of Anxiety*, p. 3. [22] Ibid., p. 79.
[23] Martin Heidegger, 'What Is Metaphysics' in *Existence and Being* (Chicago, IL: Henry Regnery, 1949), p. 369.
[24] Stern, *The Hidden Damage*, p. 111.

most clearly for Auden because of the fascist state and its destructive possession of Europe. By the time he composed the poem, Hannah Arendt had published her illuminating 1946 essay 'What is Existenz Philosophy?' in *Partisan Review*, where she had carefully accused Heidegger of distorting the search for existential freedom (which she finds in the communitarian existentialism of Jaspers) and opting for Dasein's self-transcendence as a solipsistic and self-divinising project obsessed with death and nothingness.[25] In a footnote she implies that this unholy mix of 'nihilist fanaticism'[26] has something to do with his flirtation with the Nazi Party as Rector at Freiburg. Talking about his 'sensational' joining of the party in 1933, his banning of Husserl 'his teacher and friend, whose lecture chair he had inherited' from campus 'because he was a Jew', Arendt says it would be a mistake to dismiss the significance of this: for her, it proves the 'complete irresponsibility' of Heidegger and his modern form of 'German Romanticism'.[27]

The inner fascist doppelgängers, the Dark Ones, inhabit the ruined German cities as Nazi revenants, obsessed with death and self-glorification (turning themselves into inanimate statues), returning as from the sick Romanticism associated with Heideggerian death-cult nihilism.[28] For Auden, contemporary anxiety is still possessed by the nothing-generating spirit of destructiveness of European fascism. The trauma of the war, its psychic wound, stages itself as the return of the Dark Ones within the ruins of the European metropolis. The trauma silenced Auden, and we only get rare glimpses of the nihilative depression triggered by the Survey experience. In a letter to his friend, the German-born Elizabeth Meyer, from Germany, he wrote: 'I keep wishing you were with us to help and then I think, perhaps not, for as I write this sentence I find myself crying.'[29] It was the Holocaust which was most devastatingly revealed to him and the Survey team: he met and tried to help a survivor of Dachau.[30] The Jewish Rosetta turns away from Emble at the end of Part Five because she fears American anti-Semitism might be triggered by the infection of the war. She intuits Emble's cowardice, and his likely silent complicity in any persecution:

---

[25] Hannah Arendt, 'What Is Existenz Philosophy?' *Partisan Review* (1946) 13(1) pp. 34–56.
[26] Ibid., p. 55.   [27] Ibid., p. 46.
[28] At Swarthmore between 1942 and 1945, Auden taught a course on 'Romantic Literature from Rousseau to Hitler' (Charles Osbourne, *W.H. Auden: The Life of a Poet* [New York: M. Evans & Co, 1979], p. 213).
[29] Quoted Alan Jacobs's 'Introduction' to *The Age of Anxiety*, p. xiii.
[30] As Alan Jacobs remarks, '*The Age of Anxiety* is among the first poems in English, perhaps the very first, to register the fact of the Nazis' genocidal murder of millions of Jews' (p. xiii).

> If you ever see
> A fuss forming in the far distance,
> Lots of police, and a little group
> In terrible trouble, don't try to help;
> They'd make you mock and you might be ashamed.[31]

This 'forget[ting] . . . / What happens' is more than cowardice – Rosetta knows Emble would confuse internal exile on the German model with social shame, an internalising of the regime's persecutory mania. The police might force him to mock the Jews or be made a mock of if he intervened and that would humiliate him: fear of social shame is at the root of the spineless liberal conscience. She also intuits a snobbery about her lowly origins in Emble which is indistinguishable from racist repulsion – 'I'm too rude a question'[32] – and his gaze on her is confused with her staggering sense of the Godhead and His gaze on the Holocaust:

> we are His Chosen,
> His ragged remnant with our ripe flesh
> And our hats on, sent out of the room
> By their dying grandees and doleful slaves,
> Kicked in corridors and cold-shouldered
> At toll-bridges, teased upon the stage,
> Snubbed at sea
> . . .
> Fly, let's face it, to defend us now
> When bruised or broiled our bodies are chucked
> Like cracked crocks onto kitchen middens
> In the time He takes. We'll trust. He'll slay
> If His Wisdom will.[33]

The 'He' is the Lord whose status as *deus absconditus* until the Second Coming abandons his people to their unspeakable fate at the hands of the Nazi 'grandees'. Note how his gaze on his chosen people, 'He'll be right there / With His eye upon me',[34] instils guilt and shame, but does not intervene to save; so parallels the awkward hypocrisy of Emble's muddle-headed compliance with the Dark Ones. The ambiguity of 'Fly, let's face it, to defend us now' is telling: Rosetta prays to God to defend the people from the Holocaust, but 'fly' means escape or run away, and 'let's face it' may just as well mean 'come on, we all should understand the ugly truth' – this god abdicates political responsibility and is guilty of the crime through the sin of omission. The syntax of the whole sentence is uneasy: is it even

---

[31] Auden, *The Age of Anxiety*, p. 99.   [32] Ibid.   [33] Ibid., p. 100.   [34] Ibid.

addressed to God, or to Emble, asleep on his sofa? And is it because God so takes His time that the Holocaust was allowed to happen, as though by default? The pronominal ambiguity of 'He'll slay / If His Wisdom will' may just as well mean 'The Nazi grandee will slay if God's Wisdom wills it' as that God will slay if he will: the confusions here speak to the ways in which Nazi power and destructive force took self-divinising as a means of totalitarian domination in the camps. The 'ragged remnant' are reduced to 'ripe flesh' for consumption by the war machine as slaying godhead; they are the superfluous; stateless, branded and broken as throwaway things on the middens of Europe.

The four characters in the Third Avenue bar are all displaced and rootless, and it is clear that Auden had sharpened his sense of wartime D.P.-subjectivity after the Survey experience of refugees, camp survivors, Wehrmacht wanderers. The Second World War haunts the postwar as an inward emptying of the subject caused by the traumatic information from occupied Europe. In other words, the self is scoured out by the horror of the information and left feeling hollowed-out by the traumatic memories of receiving that information: the information is so terrible it occupies everything, yet as traumatic material cannot be faced, so the effect is of a painful emptiness inside. That emptying generates anxiety, but it is an anxiety which is focused only on death-saturated nothingness, the annihilating nothingness Heidegger had announced in 1929: an anxiety which infiltrates the ego making it lapse away, become as nothing too. The Europe Auden witnessed in Germany in 1946, subject to emergent superpower ideological pressure from Soviet and American forces, was infected by fascist nihilist fanaticism making the whole world a world of displaced persons. It is only by a communion of D.P.s, through acceptance of the plurality of the differences as much as acknowledgement of commonalities, that the anxiety can be assuaged: all this Auden drew from Germany, and disguised within *The Age of Anxiety*.

Stephen Spender was also in Germany, working for the Allied Control Commission to enquire, as he put in his book about his experiences, *European Witness*, into 'the lives and ideas of German intellectuals', and to report on the condition of libraries.[35] He had wangled the job expressly to be able to visit and interview his mentor, Ernst Robert Curtius, but it became a journey into the ruins of Europe that set in motion Spender's transformation from a fireman and poet during the war into a major player in the cultural Cold War. James Stern had used a language of negativity

---

[35] Stephen Spender, *European Witness* (London: Hamish Hamilton, 1946).

rhetorically to capture, by deliberate failure, the enormity of the ruined state of Germany: the destruction of Darmstadt is 'hard to absorb';[36] Darmstadt's nightmare 'cannot be imagined';[37] the imagination baulks at the enormity, so witnesses avoid even wondering what 'the ruins mean to the ruined'.[38] Spender, similarly, adopts the rhetoric of negative impotence, but the prose is stunned into strange, awkward metaphor: the 'internal ruin' of the inhabitants of Cologne turn them into 'parasites sucking at a dead carcass';[39] they are like a 'tribe of wanderers who have discovered a ruined city in a desert and who are camping there, living in the cellars and hunting among the ruins for the booty, relics of a dead civilization'.[40] The city is dead, the people are ghosts, but ghost vermin, 'rats in the cellars', like 'insects in the crannies of walls'.[41] The rhetoric Spender is drawn to here is low Gothic, appropriate in a way since it is the nihilism of Gothic which Auden identified as possessing the Nazi regime and its existential nothingy core (the dark Gestapo ghosts of Nazi sick Romanticism). 'The sermons in the stones of Germany,' writes Spender, 'preach nihilism'.[42] They also reveal Spender's own shocked repulsion, a defence mechanism against the enemy victims, a strange replay of Germany's racist ideology.

The poems he wrote about air-raids and bombing of cities, fruit of his experience as a fireman in blitzed London, accompany *European Witness*'s return again and again to the ethical problem raised by German guilt and the darkness of the area bombing campaign. 'Responsibility: The Pilots Who Destroyed Germany, Spring 1945' recalls his fire-watching time on the roofs of London: he watches the bombers fly over in the daytime, and he likens their serried ranks to a cage, both a cage created by their droning engines and the idea of their destructive power, and the cage of the bomb bays. The cage carries its terrible load, but it signifies, to the observing poet, a concentrated objective correlative to his own will to violence: 'they carried my will'. That will is described as 'Exalted expanding singing' in an 'aerial cage'. Spender repeats the phrase 'they carried my will' and tells us they dropped the 'will' on a town in Germany: 'My will exploded. Tall buildings fell down.'[43] A political principle (institutions like the army in democracies represent the will of the people) is rendered uncanny and insane by the Blakean deranged childishness of the lines, and the deliberate designed absurdity of the metaphorical chain from will to songbird to

---

[36] Stern, *The Hidden Damage*, p. 83.   [37] Ibid., p. 94.   [38] Ibid., p. 95.
[39] Spender, *European Witness*, p. 22.   [40] Ibid.   [41] Ibid., p. 24.   [42] Ibid.
[43] Stephen Spender, 'Responsibility: The Pilots Who Destroyed Germany, Spring 1945' in *New Collected Poems* (London: Faber & Faber, 2004), pp. 247–8, 247.

bomb. What holds this together is the enactment of guilt at the war crime of area bombing, that guilt including the guilt of writing poems about the war – the songbird in the bomb-bay cage is the war poem as falsely innocent lyric. Spender sings of the propagandised jingoist emotions of revenge for the Blitz: 'Exalted expanding singing' is a fine sequence that captures the quasi-fascist war-exaltation. Like Auden, Spender is sensing, too, a line running from Romanticism through German philosophy to Second World War culture.

Having seen the bombers fly over, the trip to Germany forced him to bear witness to what that will to destructive power inflicted. The bombs fall like red ribbons on the cities, but are only visible from England as the illusory ribbons of a sunset on the horizon (the days of the war are imagined as melting into 'satin ribbons / Falling over heaven's terraces near the sun'). Once in Germany, and another April, those ribbons become something else, markers of war guilt; they are tied around 'the most hidden image in my lines', an image which makes him '[assume] their guilt'. The most hidden image in the poem must be the fact that the red ribbons signify not a day melting into a Romantic sunset, but the red blood spilt by the falling bombs: it is the blood of the bomb victims which is the real trauma demanding payment. The incessant anxiety at the death *of others* turns the poet into the bomber, invites him to take on the pilots' guilt – a different kind of identification to the Blitz spirit and hawkish will to revenge fostered by wartime propaganda.

European Witness is a curious amalgam: it aims to explore German guilt, and does so thoroughly and exactingly, through the quality of the interviews with German intellectuals, and the compassion felt for the range of strange broken minds of the people he met, including a half-Jewish, half-German boy who enacted the persecution of the Jews within his own psyche. Such civil war within the mind is enacted too at the level of national debates: the Germans are all convinced that the Soviets will take over Germany, and that the zones will become power-play territories during the Third World War – an attitude Spender rightly associates with the Machiavellian brain-washing fostered by the Nazi regime. The exploration of war guilt, a form of de-Nazification- and Nuremberg-effect,[44] is accompanied by reflections on the potential for cultural regeneration after the war years – and here Spender is not optimistic, seeing the poison of Nazi ideology everywhere, infecting even the best minds.

---

[44] The Nuremberg trials were the most visible attempt by the Allies to de-Nazify Germany by putting on trial twenty-two Nazi war criminals at tribunals in November 1945.

The third move is a charting of the potential for a regeneration of Europe itself on liberal principles – and it is this ambition which gives strange structure to the book: for though ostensibly about Germany, there is a long forty-seven-page interlude (a fifth of the book) on his experience returning to Paris. The rationale for this is that Europe will be regenerated only if Germany, France and England can work together to revitalise the postwar culture of Europe. For Spender in the apocalyptic days of the war and immediate postwar, Europeans were faced with a stark and radical choice, 'between creation and destruction'.[45] The 'social automatism of conflict', in the mass movements of Darwinian social energies in culture, he argues, has developed in mid-century the 'means of destroying itself in internecine conflict' which only world government animated by '*human* interest', not power and wealth, can resist and redeem.[46]

The Cold War postwar was for Spender, then, a time of absolute critical choice, a choice only the experience of the 'cries of the fallen and of the wandering herds of the less fortunate in Europe' makes stark enough:

> All those old prophecies of burning cities, transcendent powers and of a final choice between good and evil seemed to be fulfilled in us: those prophecies which point with equal clarity to two worlds: a world destroyed by fire and a world created by the human spirit.[47]

If this sounds like a new form of propaganda, this time for world government by the West and its democratic values, then that would not be too far from the truth. James Smith notes that Spender ceased to be a target for surveillance once he had contact with the secret state when he worked for the Political Warfare Executive (PWE) at Bush House in 1944. It looks now almost certain that the Control Commission work was a cover for other plans and projects, for his journal notes meetings with Richard Crossman, director of PWE in Germany, and with Sefton Delmer, the PWE's radio expert (who was Muriel Spark's boss with the black propaganda radio operations during the war).[48] His German journal also notes association with Nicholas Nabokov, very deeply involved as Director of the Congress for Cultural Freedom (CCF): they first met at a party thrown to welcome Auden back from Germany.[49] What those projects were almost certainly enabled Spender to become a powerful player in postwar Europe, through his work with the British Council and UNESCO, and of course as

---

[45] Spender, *European Witness*, p. 92. [46] Ibid., p. 93 (emphasis in the original). [47] Ibid., p. 95.
[48] James Smith, *British Writers and MI5 Surveillance, 1930–1960* (Cambridge University Press, 2012), p. 78.
[49] Stephen Spender, *Journals, 1939–1983*, (ed.) John Goldsmith (London: Faber & Faber, 1985), p. 59.

co-editor of *Encounter*. Spender collaborated with Crossman on the anticommunist *The God That Failed*, which fact was used by MI5 'as evidence of his break with a communist past'.[50] He also provided copy to the Information Research Department's *Why I Oppose Communism* in 1956, as well as being a very prominent figure in the British Society for Cultural Freedom, the CCF's British wing. What this all points to is Spender's willing adoption of a role as cultural Cold Warrior within the European and American scene, in order to foster the anti-communist liberal policies that were do-or-die for him in the years of the early Cold War. The starkness of the choice facing Europe was partly due to the fact that the ruined countries were 'nearer to the reality of our time' and that that reality had to do with a radical reinvention of the geopolitical world, the necessity of '[thinking] out a new world from the beginning – from ... zero'.[51] But it was also because the ruins of the European cities provided a clear vision of what nuclear war would reduce any city in the world to: the US Bombing Survey's most celebrated work was in the cities of Hiroshima and Nagasaki. 'They might be us and we might be them' was the lesson his European act of witness had revealed.[52]

A fourth project animated Spender's mind during his months in Germany: this was to understand fascism so as to explain what happened, but also to track the fascist spirit into the postwar. He reads Goebbels's dreadful novel *Michael* (1929), and Ernst Jünger's First World War memoir *Feuer und Blut* (1929). In both, Spender tracks a mad Romanticism: in the case of *Michael*, 'with its roots in the nineteenth century', 'one can sum up the impulse behind it as the desire of the individual to become a self-consuming and perhaps world-consuming flame in the modern world'.[53] The Jünger text, described as 'one of the best war books I have read, and also one of the most deeply repulsive',[54] gives Spender an insight into the militarist cult of the right-wing in Germany, where war technology (as 'matériel', rendered as 'material' by Spender) triggers transcendence:

> War is the occasion on which man most fully exploits and enters into the struggle of material, and it is also the occasion in which he discovers that margin of his own courage, his own isolation, his own existence, which is not dependent on material.[55]

Putting Jünger and Goebbels together, Spender arrives at his own sense of the fascist totalitarian drive: it summons a de-creative destructive sublime

---

[50] Smith, *British Writers and MI5 Surveillance, 1930–1960*, p. 157.
[51] Spender, *European Witness*, p. 96.   [52] Ibid.   [53] Ibid., p. 189.   [54] Ibid., p. 198.
[55] Ibid., p. 199.

based on corrupt forms of German Romanticism, an aesthetic of nihilist abandonment to wild warrior energies generated by the struggle to transcend war technology. This was a demoniac possession, a possession explicitly espoused by Goebbels and praised by Jünger: 'we are possessed, possessed by an over-powering will'.[56] The war drive and the anarchic celebration of destruction and mass hysteria raises the demon within the elite fascist warrior leaders: and Spender notes how assured Nazi propaganda was in not only hypnotising the masses into an espousal of 'hysterical tensions',[57] but also in appealing, through deliberate revelation of its rabble-rousing techniques and lies, to the private intelligence of the Nazi citizenry: 'sometimes [the masses] liked as it were to be treated confidentially and separately, and to take the side of Hitler in despising the "masses"'.[58]

And it is this that might make one pause. Spender and Auden witnessed in Germany the final throes of an insane, self-divinising, blindly violent warrior cult of death and nihilative nothingness that had its roots in nineteenth-century Romanticism. The ruins of Germany spoke to the nightmare of a future where totalitarian concentrationary warrior logic might inform the new super-powerful nuclear arrangements of Cold War history. At a time of barely reconstructable apocalyptic fears and mind-destroying scenes and eye-witness accounts, which the Bombing Survey and Allied Control Commission interviews were gathering, is it any wonder both poets felt drawn to the cause of the liberal, cultural Cold War? It is useful to remember that the two poets, as they turned into ideologues of cultural freedom, were at least as animated by their fear of a continuation of European fascism as they were by the spectre of a Stalinist postwar Europe.

---

[56] Quoted in ibid., p. 202.   [57] Ibid., p. 177.   [58] Ibid.

CHAPTER 9

Horizon, Encounter *and Mid-Century Geopolitics*

Thomas S. Davis[*]

Mid-century is typically viewed as a momentous period of transition by historians, literary and cultural critics, and students of geopolitics. In the two decades covered by this volume, British life experienced a series of profound transitions; its population and cities weathered aerial attacks and endured the lingering austerity that accompanied its transformation from a war state into a welfare state; its sprawling empire contracted and the nation struggled to accommodate both new migrants from former colonies and an insurgent youth culture. These national transitions are all nested within a broader geopolitical transition that would force British power into a smaller corner on the world stage, one largely playing host to the United States and the Soviet Union's Cold War. The literary and cultural sphere did not develop autonomously from this vast range of transitions. How we understand the relationship between aesthetics and geopolitics greatly informs, if not determines, what we read from an ideologically and aesthetically diverse mid-century literature, how we read it and what value we attribute to it. This chapter examines the way in which aesthetic and geopolitical transition is imagined and managed in the pages of two signature mid-century magazines: Cyril Connolly's *Horizon* (1940–9) and Stephen Spender's *Encounter* (1953–90). The former's reputation stands on its wartime work and the efforts it made to promote literary culture in the most dire of circumstances; the latter is remembered largely for being a CIA-funded weapon in what Frances Stonor Saunders has called the cultural Cold War.[1] These magazines not only curated some of the best writing from mid-century; they also served as venues for conceptualising the role of literature during the

---

[*] The archival work for this essay was funded by the Mershon Center of International Security Studies. Many thanks to Julie Cyzewski for research assistance.
[1] Frances Stonor Saunders, *The Cultural Cold War: The CIA and the World of Arts and Letters* (New York: The New Press, 2013).

geopolitical upheaval that relocated the base of the world-system from Britain to America.[2]

Although *Horizon*'s wartime and immediate postwar world is quite a different place from *Encounter*'s Cold War one, the magazines share editorial staff, a roster of highly regarded authors and aesthetic affinities. Stephen Spender served as Connolly's uncredited co-editor in the early days of *Horizon* and, along with Irving Kristol and, later, Dwight MacDonald and Mel Lasky, he was the driving force behind *Encounter* until the magazine's ties to CIA funding were made public in 1967. Both *Horizon* and *Encounter* would advance some version of a modernist aesthetic.[3] Connolly believed modernist art from the 1910s and 1920s modelled how culture could thrive despite the choking effects of war; Spender and his cohort at *Encounter* advanced similar ideas of intellectual and aesthetic autonomy, but these were ideas that survived, they claimed, only in the non-Soviet world. These similarities ensured that many of the most significant writers who published in *Horizon* would also appear in *Encounter*, including W. H. Auden, Christopher Isherwood, Louis MacNeice, Arthur Koestler, Geoffrey Grigson, Olivia Manning, Nancy Mitford, Dylan Thomas, Leonard Woolf, Virginia Woolf (posthumously) and, of course, Connolly and Spender. Perhaps unsurprisingly, *Horizon*'s success served as a model when Spender, Kristol and the CIA-backed Congress for Cultural Freedom (CCF) conjured up *Encounter*.

Horizon and *Encounter* both understood their charge as reimagining the work of culture during periods of geopolitical distress. *Horizon*'s mission, at least initially, was to increase the prominence of culture in the 1940s and safeguard it from the corrosive effects of war and political commitment. For Connolly, art was crucial to the survival of civilisation, but art would not survive if it concerned itself with the war or submitted itself to political ends. For *Encounter*, the situation was a little more complicated due to its ties to the CCF. The CCF promoted ideas of freedom and liberty through the cultural sphere – ideas, they hoped, would lure the European left away from any affiliation with the Soviet Union and bind them more tightly to the West. In this conception, culture became yet another front in the

---

[2] My periodisation of world systems comes from Giovanni Arrighi's *The Long Twentieth Century: Money, Power, and the Origins of Our Times* (New York: Verso, 1994) and John Darwin's *The Empire Project: The Rise and Fall of the British World System, 1830–1970* (Cambridge University Press, 2011).

[3] Hugh Wilford likens *Encounter*'s aesthetic to a belated Bloomsbury modernism, while Greg Barnhisel plots it within a broader world of Cold War modernism. See Hugh Wilford, *The CIA, the British Left and the Cold War: Calling the Tune?* (London: Frank Cass, 2003); and Greg Barnhisel, *Cold War Modernists: Art, Literature, and American Cultural Diplomacy* (New York: Columbia University Press, 2015).

expanding Cold War. In what follows, I examine how both magazines attempted to make culture a vital component of what John Agnew calls 'the modern geopolitical imagination', or the way in which world space is conceptually divided into zones of affiliation and enmity.[4] Over its near decade of existence, *Horizon* constantly assesses the relationship between Britain's waning global power and its cultural life, but ultimately, Connolly and *Horizon*'s theories of art and culture would lose pace with the transition to the Cold War. *Encounter*, on the other hand, took up those same concerns and tied artistic and intellectual liberty to the West's larger Cold War objectives.

Horizon (1940–1949) is remembered as one of England's few cultural bright spots during the blacked-out days of the war. Despite the hardships that led notable magazines such as T. S. Eliot's *Criterion* and Geoffrey Grigson's *New Verse* to close at the end of the 1930s, Connolly, Stephen Spender, and the wealthy art patron and future co-founder of the Institute of Contemporary Arts (ICA), Peter Watson, launched *Horizon*; moreover, the magazine grew and joined Tambimuttu's *Poetry London* and John Lehmann's *Penguin New Writing* as a premiere venue for fine writing during the war. In each edition, Connolly's 'Comments' joined several other essays that engaged literary and cultural questions as well as contemporary debates over wartime policy and postwar reconstruction. Above all, though, Connolly hoped to carve out a cultural sphere that could operate semi-autonomously from the politics of the day. Because he was sharply attuned to the shifting historical conditions of the 1940s, his 'Comments' often exhibit wildly different views on the social role of art. These editorials range in tone from the dreamily utopian to the bleakly apocalyptic. In one moment Connolly will declare his suspicion of the state's involvement with artists and at the next he will demand that it subsidise all forms of cultural activity. And while Connolly would present himself as a champion of literature that ignored the war, he was sensitive to the pressures placed on writers as England endured the Blitz, struggled through the tighter controls on everyday life and entered the dark days of postwar austerity. Despite his vacillations in tone and content, then, Connolly and *Horizon* try to imagine a place for art in the changing geopolitical landscape that would not reduce it to the demands of the state or any political ideology.

The preoccupation with wartime art and politics that surface in so many of Connolly's 'Comments' appears first in his essay 'The Ivory Shelter',

[4] John Agnew, *Geopolitics: Re-visioning World Politics* (New York: Routledge, 2003), p. 6.

a short essay published on 7 October 1939 in *The New Statesman and Nation*. That publishing date is significant. Michael Shelden writes that Connolly convinced Peter Watson to help launch his magazine at one of Elizabeth Bowen's parties at the end of September.[5] The proper birthdate of *Horizon*, Shelden writes, is 18 October 1939, the day Watson signed a publishing contract.[6] Nestled between these dates in late September and mid-October, Connolly's essay reads like a condemnation of the politicised literature of the 1930s and a demand for something new to assume its place. In other words, this essay serves as an argument for *Horizon*'s existence and it previews how Connolly will understand the relationship of art and politics in the coming decade.

For Connolly, the high level of political engagement in the 1930s by writers such as W. H. Auden and Christopher Isherwood had, in the end, accomplished very little. 'The writers with the deepest sense of humanity have expended and often wasted that sense in the hopeless struggle for Manchurians, Abyssinians, Austrians, Spaniards, Chinese and Czechs.'[7] The decade's committed literature, then, was at once an aesthetic and political failure. With war approaching British shores, Connolly advises writers to 'keep off the war'[8] and become like James Joyce, Virginia Woolf and André Gide, 'the escapists [who] carried on a literary renaissance during the last war'.[9] The high modernists serve as a model for aesthetic innovation during times of political distress. Thus, Connolly concludes that 'the best modern war literature is pacifist and escapist, and either ignores the war, or condemns it, with the lapse of time'.[10] Connolly himself would find that ignoring the war was not so easy.

It should be of little surprise to find Connolly declare 'our standards are aesthetic, and our politics are in abeyance'[11] in his inaugural 'Comment'. And yet Connolly swiftly qualifies this very principle. 'This will not always be the case, because as events take shape the policy of artists and intellectuals will become clearer, the policy which leads them to economic security, to the atmosphere in which they can create, and to the audience by whom they will be appreciated.'[12] While there is little doubt that Connolly yearned for something like aesthetic autonomy, he is aware that these standards are at best aspirational. And it would not take very long for

---

[5] Michael Shelden, *Friends of Promise: Cyril Connolly and the World of Horizon* (New York: Harper & Row Publishers, 1989), p. 30.
[6] Ibid., p. 4.
[7] Cyril Connolly, 'The Ivory Shelter', *New Statesman and Nation* (7 October 1939), p. 482.
[8] Ibid.   [9] Ibid.   [10] Ibid.   [11] Cyril Connolly, 'Comment', *Horizon* (January 1940), p. 5.
[12] Ibid.

Connolly's 'escapist' aesthetics to be directly challenged. Perhaps the most forceful criticism comes by way of a letter from the Welsh writer, academic, future *Encounter* contributor, and friend of Connolly, Goronwy Rees. Rees volunteered for military service prior to the outbreak of war and was serving in the Royal Welch Fusiliers. He took issue with Connolly's claim in the May 1940 'Comment' that 'war is the enemy of creative activity',[13] astutely observing that 'each month, while urging writers to ignore the war, you cannot avoid the subject yourself'.[14] Rees insists that 'the hour of an event' should amplify a writer's relationship to his world, not lead to a retreat into Connolly's Ivory Shelter. Rees maintains that such responsibility would not restrict formal experimentation or require political commitment; this responsibility, as it turned out, was not the antithesis of Connolly's own aesthetic ideology, but perhaps its fullest expression: 'the content of the artist's imagination', Rees writes, 'should be the reality of his time, so that, if an artist followed your direction to explore "the deeper level of emotion", it would be precisely that reality which he would explore'.[15] It is hard not to see Rees's idea as a more sophisticated and thoughtful articulation of art and politics than anything Connolly published during the war. Connolly tacitly acknowledged as much by putting Rees's letter at the front of the issue and locating his own 'Comment' near the end (the only time we would ever find Connolly's 'Comment' at the end of an issue). Connolly admitted that *Horizon* could no longer 'afford the airy detachment of earlier numbers'.[16] Still, somewhat impossibly in the face of Rees's letter, he continued to maintain that war was the enemy of creative activity.

Ana Mitric rightly asserts that Rees's letter engenders a 'noticeable shift in the magazine's tone'.[17] 'The contents of *Horizon*', she argues, 'became decidedly more engaged with "reality"'.[18] Connolly, for example, begins calling for state support of writers and artists whose activity should be seen as national service. But this is not to say that Connolly's understanding of art, or *Horizon's* role in shaping wartime aesthetics, changed in dramatic fashion. Even the inaugural 'Comment' demonstrates Connolly's awareness that the cultural sphere is never securely cordoned off from politics and economics. Material realities – money and patronage, an audience

---

[13] Cyril Connolly, 'Comment', *Horizon* (July 1940), p. 467.   [14] Ibid.
[15] Goronwy Rees, 'Letter from a Soldier', *Horizon* (July 1940), p. 469.
[16] Cyril Connolly, 'Comment', *Horizon* (July 1940), p. 533.
[17] Ana Mitric, 'Turning Points: *Atonement, Horizon*, and Late Modernism' *Modernism/Modernity* (2014) 21(3) p. 725.
[18] Ibid.

willing to spend money, publishing venues, paper rations – mould artistic production and its very possibility at every turn. Yet, four years after Rees's letter, Connolly collected the charges against *Horizon*'s literariness and gleefully wore those criticisms as badges of honour: 'Accused of "aestheticism", "escapism", "ivory-towerism", "bourgeois formalism", "frivolity", and "preferring art to life" it pleads on all these counts "guilty and proud of it"'.[19] Connolly's aestheticism, if it can even be so called, makes a distinction between political engagement, or a knowledge of political theories, realities and emerging situations, and political commitment, or an ideological position that uses art to advance a position or a cause. It is, I believe, the latter that moulds his suspicions about art and politics, a suspicion that changes gradually from postwar optimism into the exhaustion and disappointment that would lead to *Horizon*'s end in 1949.

Connolly enthusiastically greeted the new postwar Labour Government and he had high hopes that this form of socialism would give writers and artists the support they needed. That enthusiasm would not hold for very long. By the autumn of 1946, Connolly's hopes for state patronage are tempered by fears of state interference. His October 1946 'Comment' frames the Soviet Union's intervention in the cultural sphere as a warning for all artists and intellectuals (like himself) who seek greater support from Britain's new socialist regime. The Soviet state, he argues, establishes aesthetic doctrine and supplants the reading public by purchasing books that reflect that doctrine. These conditions, Connolly predicts, virtually ensure that 'literature will die out in Russia'.[20] They also reframe the artist's relationship to the Soviet state, something that forecasts the ideology of artistic liberty that will become *Encounter*'s calling card: 'The artist who cares truly for individual freedom, aesthetic merit or intellectual truth must be prepared to go once more into the breach against the Soviet view with all the patience, fervour and lucidity with which, ten years ago, he went into action against the nascent totalitarianism of the Nazis.'[21] These admonitory remarks consume the majority of his editorial, but he does point to the BBC's *Third Programme*, which he sees as 'so admirably free from such doctrinaire rantings',[22] indicating, for the moment anyway, that other models exist and all hope is not lost.

As austerity wore on, Connolly's disenchantment with the Labour Government reached a critical point. The shortages and cuts hit rather close to home when *Horizon*, which had managed to endure paper

[19] Cyril Connolly, 'Comment', *Horizon* (December 1944), p. 367.
[20] Cyril Connolly, 'Comment', *Horizon* (October 1946), p. 214.   [21] Ibid.   [22] Ibid.

shortages during the war, fell victim to fuel cuts; for that reason, there was no March issue in 1947. In the April issue, Connolly swaps out the possible futures offered by a socialist government for a rather ludicrous and desperate plea for the empire's quasi-rebirth: 'What we are really witnessing is the collapse of the Industrial Revolution, of that British Empire which was founded on geographical position, business daring, foreign investments, cheap labour, food and goods, wise administration, coal, iron, and seapower. We are decadent only if we fail to replace it by another.'[23] His imperial reboot calls for the full exploitation of Britain's remaining colonies and possessions to avoid further decline into a 'minor power' status akin to Sweden, Holland and Switzerland. With state support for the arts not materialising, Connolly cannot imagine any place for artistic activity in a weakened Britain. His editorial turns from his panicked calls for a new empire to the worrisome state of contemporary literary culture. He laments that twenty years ago the modernists were producing their first novels, but 'no new crop of novelists has arisen commensurate with them'.[24] Against the distinguished cast of Hemingway, Faulkner, Bowen and others, the literary icons of 1947 'resemble a galaxy of impotent prima donnas, while round them rotate tired business men, publishers, broadcasters, and civil servants who once were poets, novelists and revolutionary thinkers'.[25] In a wry editorial gesture, Connolly follows his meditation on imperial and literary decline with W. H. Auden's 'The Fall of Rome,' which bears the dedication 'To C. C.'.

In July 1947, Connolly finally buried the idea that socialism would stimulate a new era of literary innovation; 'the honeymoon between literature and action, once so promising, is over'.[26] By the end of 1947, he states rather baldly that the Labour Government 'bears no relation to the kind of Socialism which many of us envisaged'.[27] His 'Comments' become less frequent over the next few years and in November 1949 he announces that *Horizon* will close (although he speculates that it could reappear within a year). Connolly uses this penultimate 'Comment' not only to bemoan once again the tired, barren world of British culture, but also to make a rather counterintuitive case for *Horizon*'s importance and historical legacy. Aware that *Horizon*'s popularity and prestige resides mostly on its status as a wartime publication, Connolly argues that the magazine's best years were actually post-1945. 'It is fashionable to exclaim

---

[23] Cyril Connolly, 'Comment', *Horizon* (April 1947), p. 151. [24] Ibid., p. 154. [25] Ibid.
[26] Cyril Connolly, 'Comment', *Horizon* (July 1947), p. 1.
[27] Cyril Conolly, 'Comment', *Horizon* (December 1947), p. 300.

that *Horizon* was much better in the war "when it really stood for something", and that it has gone off since. In fact the opposite is true.'[28] To Connolly's credit, he rightly perceived the contemporary and future regard for his magazine. Michael Shelden's assessment of *Horizon* essentially reaches the conclusion that Connolly feared: 'During the war *Horizon*'s purpose had been clear … *Horizon*'s historical moment had come and gone.'[29] Shelden may be right about *Horizon*'s purpose, but Connolly may also be right about the quality and achievement of postwar *Horizon*. Connolly was the first to publish any part of Jean-Paul Sartre's 'Engaged Literature' as well as the first to introduce copies of *Huis Clos* beyond France's borders; the October 1947 issue featured for the first time anywhere selections from Ralph Ellison's *Invisible Man*; Dylan Thomas's most beloved and anthologised poems appeared after the war in *Horizon*, as did the first short story in England by Truman Capote; Lucien Freud and Francis Bacon were both featured in *Horizon* in 1947 just as they were catching fire in the art world; George Orwell's 'Politics and the English Language' appeared in the April 1946 issue. If *Horizon* had lost its *raison d'être*, its contents had certainly not suffered.

Connolly maintained that art was an end in itself; at times, he would go so far as to say that art was the highest end of life. He so desperately wanted to believe that art's power and value could transcend its historical moment, however propitious or unpromising that moment may be for aesthetic innovation. His November 1949 assessment of *Horizon* bears out that belief. Connolly pushes against much of his own analysis of the cultural effects of austerity, an apathetic socialist government and imperial decline. In this reckoning, some of the most important work to appear in the pages of *Horizon* does so despite those crippling historical conditions. And yet, as mercurial as ever, Connolly famously ends *Horizon* with a withering criticism of the 1940s and this stark premonition: 'For it is closing time in the gardens of the West and from now on an artist will be judged only by the resonance of his solitude or the quality of his despair.'[30] So how do we reconcile the claim that *Horizon* has played host to some of its best work since 1945 with these melancholic notions that few prospects remain for literary value and cultural life? We might say that Connolly could no longer imagine where culture would fit in the emerging Cold War world.

---

[28] Cyril Conolly, 'Comment', *Horizon* (November 1949), p. 285.
[29] Shelden, *Friends of Promise*, p. 220.
[30] Cyril Connolly, 'Comment', *Horizon* (December 1949), p. 362.

By contrast, the brains trust behind *Encounter* could not have envisioned a more auspicious time to launch a literary and cultural magazine. *Encounter*'s lifespan (1953–90) roughly follows that of the Cold War. The story of *Encounter* has been meticulously reconstructed by Frances Stonor Saunders and Hugh Wilford, and Greg Barnhisel has explored the magazine's early days and its interest in promoting a Cold War modernism. The full details do not need to be rehearsed here, but it is worth recounting some of the magazine's early history in order to clarify how it saw the cultural sphere in relation to the early Cold War and the onset of decolonisation. *Encounter* was one of several magazines, seminars and cultural events funded by the Congress for Cultural Freedom. From its earliest days, the CCF presented itself as an autonomous group of writers, artists, scientists and intellectuals invested in the free exchange of ideas. The promotion of intellectual and artistic liberty was inextricably tied to their independence from state support. Melvin Lasky, founder of *Der Monat* and an editor at *Encounter* from 1958 until it closed shop, rather bluntly acknowledged in a report on the CCF's inaugural meeting that had their events 'been organized, sponsored, officially backed or conspicuously supported by a government participating or leading in the Cold War, there would have been immediate distrust against motives and aims of the Congress'.[31] Lasky knew the CIA was bankrolling the Congress and, thus, knew that such support needed to remain secret.

The CCF launched *Encounter* to influence the non-communist Left and to draw them away from sympathy with the Soviet Union. In the years after the Second World War, American and British intelligence officials were working separately on launching a publication that would appeal to such an audience. In 1951, Frank Wisner, a CIA agent, met with British intelligence and the two groups decided to collaborate. Crucially, this meeting determined that the publication should appear independent and its funding sources remain meticulously hidden. In the spring of 1952, Lawrence de Neufville, Michael Josselson and Monty Woodhouse 'outlined their plan for the launch and covert sponsorship of a new highbrow magazine'.[32] Josselson's plan was to funnel CIA funds to the nominally independent CCF through the sham charitable organisation the Farfield Foundation. The magazine would be identified with the CCF, but the CCF would always declare its absolute autonomy from any state. Two co-

---

[31] Melvin Lasky, 'Proceedings: The Congress for Cultural Freedom', 5 July 1950, Box 390, Folder 2, IACF Papers.
[32] Saunders, *The Cultural Cold War*, p. 141.

editors were quickly identified: Irving Kristol and Stephen Spender. Kristol would bring the political and intellectual heft from the New York Intellectuals and Spender, who had so often bemoaned Connolly's preference for aesthetics over politics, was selected because of his standing in the British literary world.

Encounter's early success was also measured against *Horizon*.[33] Although *Encounter*'s wide-reaching ambitions were evident in its impressive first-issue print run of 10,000, Josselson nonetheless felt the need to argue, in a letter to Spender, that 'we need a magazine with a wider appeal than *Horizon*'.[34] There was concern that the perception of *Encounter* as a highbrow magazine would limit its appeal and, ultimately, the political work it was created to do. Josselson thought the first number was too literary, but his push to change this was strongly rebutted by Kristol: 'The best thing about this issue is that it is so literary, that it has poems by Edith Sitwell and C. Day Lewis. This is our *billet d'entré* (or is it *carte d'entrée?*) into British – and Asian – cultural circles.'[35] The wide appeal of *Encounter*, Kristol believed, hinged on its curation of admired literary figures, not its political posturing. Kristol pleaded for Josselson to give him and Spender more time; in due course they could make *Encounter* 'the idol of the intelligentsia, East and West'.[36] Surely Josselson did not anticipate these sorts of arguments from Kristol, but Kristol was indeed right that turning the magazine into a political forum would spell doom. The magazine already had to quell concerns that it was a covert pro-American outlet. T. S. Eliot, for one, expressed scepticism about a journal 'published under American auspices'.[37] Kristol quotes other letters from E. M. Forster and Czesław Miłosz to emphasise that the magazine could:

> ... easily exhaust the goodwill which supports us at the moment if we make any serious blunders in the political line ... If we could publish a magazine which was excellent on the creative side, excellent on the arts and unchallengably disinterested in politics, we could promote a tremendous feeling of gratitude for the American support which had made such a magazine possible.[38]

---

[33] Irving Kristol and Stephen Spender to International Executive Committee, CCF, 6 November 1953, Box 129, Folder 7, IACF Papers. Spender and Kristol's report stated that the print run for *Encounter*'s first issue exceeded the 'highest circulation ever achieved by *Horizon*'.
[34] Josselson quoted in Saunders, *The Cultural Cold War*, p. 146.
[35] Irving Kristol to Michael Josselson, 16 September 1953, Box 129, Folder 7, IACF Papers.
[36] Ibid.   [37] Ibid.   [38] Ibid.

To be clear, Kristol's defence of the literary is not an argument against politics as such. If *Encounter* could achieve the status of an independent venue for literary, cultural and intellectual discussion, its apparent autonomy would be its greatest political asset. Achieving goodwill for the Americans would require a continued display of their commitment not to any political line as such, but to the general principle of intellectual and artistic liberty. *Encounter*'s brand of cultural diplomacy could best advance American interests by declaring ideological independence.

This debate between Josselson and Kristol suggests that there was little need for direct influence from the CIA on *Encounter* or many of the CCF's other projects. As Barnhisel documents, and as my reading of the *Encounter* correspondence suggests, the intellectuals making the calls at *Encounter* – Spender, Kristol, Josselson – needed little coercion to make the magazine turn intellectual and artistic liberty into its first principle. Their ideological orientations, however different their personalities, were, in Barnhisel's words, 'largely of one mind'.[39] This shared orientation would appear in public statements attesting to their commitment to free expression, individual liberty and open debate. In remarks prepared for the BBC's Eastern European Service (1960), Spender looked back on *Encounter*'s eight-year history and defined its work as the cultivation of free expression. He acknowledges that the founders initially targeted the Soviet Union as 'the chief threat to intellectual freedom', but, in its spirit of democratic openness, Spender did not consider the magazine, or at least himself, as 'anti-anything'.[40] In that sense, *Encounter* lived up to its name: 'it should not only be a meeting place of talents, and of discussion of general ideas and the arts ... it should also, in a very real sense, be a debate between, or express the attitudes of, those with very different viewpoints'.[41] This openness, he assured listeners, would find its limits at 'the line where people start using freedom to take away freedom'.[42] *Encounter* featured communists, socialists and conservatives, even when such viewpoints diverged from those of the editors. At the same time, *Encounter*'s commitment to free expression across the globe meant that it would actively seek out writers and artists in the Soviet sphere of influence 'who are prepared to take the risks of writing and painting freely'.[43]

Encounter's professed democratic openness had more limits than Spender acknowledged. Behind the scenes, the editors were expressly

---

[39] Barnhisel, *Cold War Modernists*, p. 157.
[40] Stephen Spender on BBC Eastern European Service, 20 October 1960, Box 297, Folder 4, IACF Papers.
[41] Ibid. [42] Ibid. [43] Ibid.

concerned with how they would support and manage writers, artists and publications, especially those from contested zones in Eastern Europe and the decolonising world. After the Hungarian Revolution of 1956, Josselson and Kristol discussed with some urgency the need to publish a profile of Georg Lukács, Hungary's famous heterodox Marxist who helped inspire the revolt against the Soviet-aligned government. Lukács had been on the CCF's radar from the very beginning; in 1950, the CCF considered launching a radio broadcasting project and they specifically mention reaching out to him,[44] but a full profile would not appear until Spender wrote of his visit to Lukács in Budapest in the December 1964 issue of *Encounter*.[45] Nonetheless, the magazine kept tabs on Lukács's fate after the failed revolution and relayed how swiftly he had been disowned by his students and subjected to abuse in the Hungarian press. Lukács's participation in Imre Nagy's short-lived revolutionary government and his subsequent exile exemplified *Encounter*'s argument that intellectual and artistic freedom could not exist in communist states.

The editors at *Encounter* also closely observed the movements in the decolonising world. Josselson was particularly eager for *Encounter* to review George Padmore's *Pan-Africanism or Communism*: 'I think it is quite important that this book be reviewed in Encounter by one of "our" people, possibly Rita Hinden or otherwise by an anti-Marxist African scholar.'[46] Padmore had been a very visible and vocal figure in the Comintern until he was derided as a 'black nationalist'; his association with the Communist Party ended in 1934. His break with the Soviets and party orthodoxy did not lead to a retreat from Leftist, or even explicitly Marxist, politics. Padmore remained fervently committed to anti-imperialism, democratic socialism for African nations and Pan-Africanism. He organised a Pan-African Congress in Manchester in 1945 with Kwame Nkrumah, who would go on to become the first Prime Minister of a newly independent Ghana. What was most worrisome for Josselson and the CCF, especially in the period directly after the Bandung Conference,[47] was Padmore's ability to stake out a non-aligned anti-imperial position, one that was as suspicious of Soviet influence as it was of Western interests. In his 'Author's

---

[44] Melvin Lasky, 'Proceedings: The Congress for Cultural Freedom', 5 July 1950, Box 390, Folder 2, IACF Papers.
[45] Stephen Spender, 'With Lukacs in Budapest', *Encounter* (December 1964), pp. 53–7.
[46] Michael Josselson to Irving Kristol, 9 August 1956, Box 130, Folder 8, IACF Papers.
[47] The Bandung Conference was held in Bandung, Indonesia, 18–24 April 1955. The twenty-nine participating countries were all from Asia and Africa. The conference is remembered primarily for advancing a neutral position in the Cold War and advancing the Non-Aligned Movement.

Note' to *Pan-Africanism or Communism*, Padmore explicitly targeted Western intellectuals, especially those affiliated with the Labour Party, who argued that anti-colonial movements were clandestine communist plots. African resistance was the 'spontaneous expression of the hopes and desires of the Africans';[48] yet, the continued presence of imperial powers in Africa, he warned, might drive Africans into the arms of the communists. Padmore's criticism of Labour and his advocacy for African socialism likely made Josselson and the CCF feel that his views needed to be carefully framed, and mostly negated, for their non-Soviet Leftist readership.

Josselson got his wish. Hinden's review appeared in the December 1956 issue of *Encounter*. Hinden had the necessary credentials to critique Padmore's anti-colonial arguments from the Left. She had joined the Fabian Society and the Labour Party in 1939 and was prized for her thinking on colonial affairs. She also served as an assistant to Leonard Woolf and articulated the Fabian Society's colonial policies in *Plan for Africa* (1942). Her demonstrated expertise and growing body of publications led to appointments in the Colonial Office's Economic and Development Council. Her position as editor at *Socialist Commentary* only increased her value to the CCF; Wilford notes that 'the Congress undertook subscription drives on behalf of the magazine in Asia and Africa in order to show that (as Irving Kristol put it) "there's another kind of socialism possible, aside from the *New Statesman's*"'.[49] In other words, Kristol saw Hinden's socialism, and her support for development policies in the Third World, as compatible with Western political objectives.

In many ways, Hinden's review masterfully dances between blistering criticism and a sober acknowledgment that Padmore's 'frustrating book'[50] represents a powerful trend in anti-colonial thought. Her opening lines treat Padmore as merely one of many writers whose minds are incapable of grappling with the rapidly changing events in the colonial world:

> No sooner is the printer's ink dry on their careful description of a new constitution, or political movement, or an event or conference which seemed momentous at the time, than the constitution is scrapped, the political movement supplanted by another, the conference forgotten, the

---

[48] George Padmore, *Pan-Africanism or Communism* (Garden City, NY: Doubleday & Company, 1971 [1953]), p. xv.
[49] Wilford, *The CIA, the British Left and the Cold War*, pp. 198–9. Padmore's argument for a socialism independent of Soviet influence and Western imperial powers potentially offered another direction through which Leftist intellectuals and cultural figures might align themselves politically. Because *Encounter* and the CCF targeted non-aligned Leftists, it is highly likely the group around *Encounter* felt the need to discredit Padmore and, in effect, to eliminate competing alternatives.
[50] Rita Hinden, 'White Man's Pride', *Encounter* (December 1956), p. 85.

event submerged beneath a dozen new events. This, certainly, is the unhappy fate of much of George Padmore's book, which already bears a curiously archaic stamp. Who now remembers the Pan-African conference held in Manchester in 1945, of which Padmore was one of the organisers and to which he attributes such tremendous implications?[51]

Padmore's status as an intellectual is simultaneously announced and undercut. His greatest fault, it seems, is his own failure to liberate himself entirely from 'Communist ideology',[52] which here is synonymous with any anti-imperial critique that perceives the West as solely interested in the exploitation of the colonial world. Hinden argues that the orientation of the West to the colonial world has changed, but anti-colonial thinkers like Padmore, still shackled to communist ideas and ideological jargon, have not evolved intellectually or politically. This, she argues, is precisely why Padmore's book is worth reviewing; it emblematises a widespread, yet antiquated form of thinking which poses incredible challenges for any positive change in the West's relationship with the decolonising world. As imperial rule transforms into more cooperative relationships comprised of regional federations and independent nation-states, the greatest threat to this emerging international community, Hinden argues, resides in the intellectual torpor of African and Asian intellectuals. Padmore's greatest crime is to have cast his argument in 'so antagonising an idiom'.[53] To be sure, Hinden's reading of *Pan-Africanism or Communism* is highly selective and fails to treat Padmore's advocacy for a non-aligned African socialism with the nuance and patience it deserves. Yet the purpose of the review is to suggest that Padmore's title offers a false choice: there is no distinction between Pan-Africanism and communism. The only real option is for further collaboration with the West and the capitalist world.

The interest in promoting collaboration between the decolonising world and the capitalist West seems to underwrite Josselson's interest in other areas, including the Caribbean, which was not otherwise a primary target of *Encounter*'s cultural diplomacy. In a letter to Spender on 14 May 1957, Josselson urges him to look over A. J. Seymour's revised *Anthology of West Indian Poetry*, which had recently appeared as a special number of *Kyk-Over-Al*, the Guyana-based literary magazine. 'We have helped him modestly with this and he, in turn, has devoted the back page to advertising *Encounter*.'[54] Seymour not only advertised *Encounter* to his Caribbean readership; he made a strong case for its literary value and intellectual

---

[51] Ibid. [52] Ibid. [53] Ibid., p. 86.
[54] Michael Josselson to Stephen Spender, 14 May 1957, Box 297, Folder 2, IACF Papers.

heft (while also misspelling Spender's name as 'Spencer'). Under the heading 'The most discussed magazine in Britain',[55] Seymour characterises *Encounter* as 'humming with ideas'[56] in the form of poetry and fiction by notable luminaries – Auden, Connolly, Faulkner and Koestler are among those mentioned – but also essays that will appeal to a non-British, more internationalist audience. To this effect, he references Dwight MacDonald's 'In Search of Asian History' and John Strachey's 'The Indian Alternative'. Curiously, Seymour also lists his personal address for subscriptions.

Seymour's revised anthology itself included writers such as George Lamming, Una Marson and Derek Walcott, who had already begun making a name for themselves at the BBC.[57] Additionally, Seymour's 'Preface' establishes a specific relationship between West Indian poetry, colonialism and a sense of cultural community within the British Caribbean. Although Seymour provides only the slightest of updates to the 1952 'Preface', his statements are important: 'The voices are surer and I have changed some of the songs; the Federation is a reality and nationhood is gathering rapidly.'[58] The coming Federation and the sense that collaboration and friendship were possible between the West and the Caribbean was precisely what Josselson and Hinden found to be so dangerously absent from Padmore's book.[59] It is little surprise, then, that Josselson told Spender that they needed to 'make these people feel that we take them seriously'.[60] Given *Encounter*'s approach to Padmore and Lukács, and the CCF's general political mission, it is likely that the CCF, or Josselson at least, believed that a foothold in the Anglophone Caribbean world was necessary and that, where possible, Western interests in intellectual and artistic liberty should be promoted.

The veil would be lifted from the CCF and *Encounter* in 1967 when several outlets reported the CIA's clandestine funding for these operations. *Encounter* lost much of its influential power and Spender resigned. He

---

[55] A. J. Seymour, 'The Most Discussed Magazine in Britain' *Kyk-Over-Al*, (1957) 22 back cover.
[56] Ibid.
[57] For more on Anglophone Caribbean writers and the BBC, see Peter Kalliney, *Commonwealth of Letters: British Literary Culture and the Emergence of Postcolonial Aesthetics* (New York: Oxford University Press, 2013), especially ch. 4, 'Metropolitan Modernism and Its West Indian Interlocutors'.
[58] A. J. Seymour, 'Preface to *Anthology of West Indian Poetry*' *Kyk-Over-Al* (1957) 22 p. xi.
[59] My understanding of friendship, the BBC and postwar imperial relations is indebted to Julie Cyzewski's 'Broadcasting Friendship: Decolonization, Literature, and the BBC', PhD diss. (The Ohio State University, 2015).
[60] Michael Josselson to Stephen Spender, 14 May 1957, Box 297, Folder 2, IACF Papers.

claimed to have heard rumours of CIA support, but was never privy to any firm knowledge that they were funding the magazine. Despite the revelations of CIA involvement, *Encounter* chugged along for over two more decades; the CCF, meanwhile, rechristened itself as the International Association for Cultural Freedom and severed ties with the CIA. While *Encounter* still hosted quality writing after 1967, it was no longer quite the cultural weapon it was intended to be. What is clear, though, is that the Cold Warriors behind *Encounter* saw culture as a contested zone; making Western geopolitical interests synonymous with intellectual and artistic liberty was vital. Whether or not Spender and the contributors to *Encounter* were aware of CIA support does not change the fact that their cultural and aesthetic commitments were indeed compatible with the West's geopolitical strategy.

The pairing of *Horizon* and *Encounter* reminds us that mid-century's large-scale geopolitical and aesthetic transitions were interlinked, even if in rather unexpected ways. In this regard, these two magazines, with shared editors, authors and aesthetic and cultural commitments, managed to pursue vastly different missions. We might recall Connolly's phrase from the inaugural issue of *Horizon* and recast it as the credo that both unites and distinguishes these two projects: 'our standards are aesthetic, and our politics are in abeyance'.[61] For Connolly and *Horizon*, the separation of aesthetics and politics was something to be sought and defended, even during a decade when such separation was nowhere to be found. *Encounter*'s pre-1967 status as a venue that held artistic and intellectual liberty above the fray of Cold War politics made it, ironically, a valuable political asset. If these two magazines can tell us anything about mid-century, it might be that the separation of art and politics is desired most fiercely in those moments when it is least possible.

---

[61] Cyril Connolly, 'Comment', *Horizon* (January 1940), p. 5.

CHAPTER 10

Public Intellectuals and the Politics of Literature: The Causes and Collaborations of J. B. Priestley and Jacquetta Hawkes Priestley

Ina Habermann

In John Osborne's *Look Back in Anger* (1956), the 'angry young man' Jimmy Porter singles out J. B. Priestley as an old-fashioned establishment figure: 'He's like Daddy – still casting well-fed glances back to the Edwardian twilight from his comfortable, disenfranchised wilderness.'[1] Ironically, Porter's main grievance, that people appear only half-alive, lacking enthusiasm and purpose and meekly accepting mediocrity, had already been voiced by Priestley himself in the 1920s and throughout the interwar period, and was being voiced again in the 1950s. In fact, Porter's reference to the 'disenfranchised wilderness' recalls Priestley's 'Thoughts in the Wilderness', published in September 1953 as the first of a series of articles in the *New Statesman* where Priestley takes issue with the apolitical nature of an increasingly affluent British society, stating that 'there is a wilderness atmosphere just now, with little that appears to be blossoming and fruitful',[2] and that progress is stalled by 'two vicious circles, one of frustration, rage, and violence, the other of apathy, triviality, and exhaustion'.[3] While large parts of the population may be caught in the latter, the former vicious circle describes a feeling of smouldering revolt, as expressed in the work of such 'angry' younger authors as Osborne and the contributors to the 'Movement', among them John Wain, Philip Larkin, Kingsley Amis and D. J. Enright. Judging from these writers' work, the 1950s is an incubation period, leading to an eruption which Larkin sees happen in the pivotal year 1963, as evoked in his poem 'Annus Mirabilis' (1967) – although the transition was already evident in such works as Antony Burgess's fictional exploration of juvenile delinquency,

---

[1] John Osborne, *Look Back in Anger* (1956), 1.
[2] J. B. Priestley, 'Thoughts in the Wilderness' in *Thoughts in the Wilderness* (Kingswood: The Windmill Press, 1957), pp. 1–7, 2.
[3] Ibid., pp. 6–7.

A Clockwork Orange (1962), and Doris Lessing's evocation of social fragmentation, *The Golden Notebook* (1962).[4] The mindset of the rebels is anatomised in Colin Wilson's critically acclaimed study *The Outsider* (1956), which offers the theory, as it were, to Jimmy Porter's practice. Lumping together such diverse writers and artists as Kafka, D. H. Lawrence, Van Gogh, Nietzsche and Dostoevsky, Wilson argues that psychological dislocation is intrinsic to artistic creativity in Western culture. This bold philosophical essay, seen as the 'classic study of alienation, creativity and the modern mind', made Wilson instantaneously famous.[5] In a slightly disgruntled review of both *Look Back in Anger* and *The Outsider* in the *New Statesman*, Priestley opined that 'these young Outsiders are after one bound further *In* than most of us have ever been'.[6] Casting himself as an 'Inside Outsider or an Outside Insider'[7] and accusing the rebels of self-pity, egoism and negativity, he calls for a more positive vision, characteristically quipping that '[w]e are waiting for God, not for Godot'.[8] Rewards should not be offered for stating the problem, but for presenting solutions. The problems were pressing, however, since Britain, while increasingly affluent, was losing power on a global scale and the old élites of the political establishment were slow to adapt to the modern world.[9]

Always a politically committed writer, Priestley arguably had his 'finest hour' in 1940 when he broadcast his *Postscripts* to the nation. In the late 1940s and 1950s, he had the status – and influence – of a public intellectual, a powerful voice transmitted through various media that was, simultaneously, both outmoded and urgently relevant. This is less paradoxical than it may seem, since Priestley was expressing his vision from 'within', providing both a sense of continuity between the interwar period and postwar Britain and a critical reflection of society and its institutions. As Roger Fagge observes, 'Priestley had always seen culture in political terms, and he argued forcibly that mass culture was a politically conservative force that helped destroy what was left of the vibrant wartime spirit.'[10] In Alan Sinfield's seminal study of postwar British culture, Priestley makes

---

[4] Burgess's novel is truly transitional in terms of the moral values expressed, paving the way for the more radically iconoclastic embrace of dystopian urbanism in the work of J. G. Ballard.
[5] Colin Wilson, *The Outsider* (London: Phoenix, 2001); quotation from cover.
[6] J. B. Priestley, 'The Outsider' in *Thoughts in the Wilderness*, pp. 174–80, 174 (emphasis in the original).
[7] Ibid., p. 179.   [8] Ibid., p. 180.
[9] For a detailed account of Britain in the 1950s and 1960s, see Dominic Sandbrook, *Never Had It So Good: A History of Britain from Suez to the Beatles* (London: Abacus, 2005).
[10] Roger Fagge, *The Vision of J. B. Priestley* (London: Continuum, 2012), p. 80.

a brief appearance as a 'middle-class dissident' guilty of an ultimately limiting 'Left-Culturism'.[11] Sinfield is right, I believe, to place Priestley in the same camp as Raymond Williams, a categorisation which is not contradicted by the fact that Priestley considered himself as 'at heart, an old-fashioned English 19th-century radical'.[12] There is also some truth in the image of Priestley as a wealthy member of the cultural establishment. Yet Sinfield's easy dismissal of Priestley is hardly fair, both because Priestley remained a perceptive and influential cultural critic, and because he responded to various crises with a political and philosophical vision that had an impact on British society.

Integral to Priestley's Janus-faced appeal in postwar society was his relationship with the archaeologist and writer Jacquetta Hawkes, whom he met in 1947 and married in 1953, amid the scandal of two rather public divorces. The couple worked and campaigned together, mobilising a counter-rhetoric of utopian wholeness that found widespread support, and that needs to be amplified in a representative account of the 1950s. Jimmy Porter's angry voice, the voice of the 'Outsider', should not dominate our understanding of a period where the emphasis was still more on wholeness than fragmentation. I argue that the Priestleys' work offers an excellent point of departure for an exploration of both the continuities and the disruptions of postwar culture. As an influential writing couple, they addressed, and engaged with, many pressing issues of the period, including the atomic threat and capitalist modernity. Coming together from very different backgrounds, they helped both to shape, and to anatomise, the postwar.

From Victory in Europe to the Festival of Britain (1945–1951): Working for Britain

Priestley had become an important voice in the public sphere because of his continual presence over decades, and because, at various points during his long career, he had made a significant contribution to public discourse. In 1929, his upbeat novel *The Good Companions* became a bestseller by

---

[11] Alan Sinfield, *Literature, Politics and Culture in Postwar Britain* (Oxford: Blackwell, 1985), pp. 271, 273–8.

[12] Interview broadcast on Radio 3 on the occasion of Priestley's 80th birthday and reprinted in *The Listener*, 12 September 1974, p. 338. For Priestley's politics, see also Tom Henthorne, 'Priestley's War: Social Change and the British Novel, 1939–1945' *The Midwest Quarterly* (2004) 45(2) pp. 155–67. For a vindication of Priestley as a political thinker, see Roger Fagge, 'From the Postscripts to Admass: J. B. Priestley and the Cold War World' *Media History* (2006) 12(2) pp. 103–15, expanded in his *The Vision of J. B. Priestley*.

challenging the mood of dejection following the stock market crash and the Great Depression, and in 1934, his *English Journey* presented a damning anatomy of interwar social conditions. This authority, together with Priestley's habit of choosing a 'wide channel of communication',[13] enabled him to boost British morale with his *Postscripts* in 1940 and, in his broadcasts to America, to make a powerful appeal to the United States to abandon their neutrality. In a domestic context, his most important message, memorably expressed in his pamphlet *Out of the People* (1941) and his 'Letter to a Returning Serviceman' (1944), was that people should take political action and demand a better deal for themselves after the war. Rejecting a concept of 'masses' which had always made him uncomfortable with socialism and communism, Priestley argues that individuals should forge a community to improve their quality of life and combat an exploitative capitalism cloaked in the 'fancy dress' of tradition[14] – a concern that would become even more relevant with the transition from austerity to affluence in postwar society.

In May 1945, Priestley broadcast a talk entitled 'Journey into Daylight' on the BBC Home Service which spelled out the message he wished people to draw from the war experience. Stating that 'we are ... better people than we had imagined ourselves to be',[15] he celebrates the 'community with a noble common purpose'[16] and, evoking Shakespeare's phrase that 'life was but a flower', demands, 'with all the care and compassion at our command, let us tend the flower of life'.[17] While this is the kind of upbeat message that people had come to expect from Priestley the broadcaster and journalist, his novel *Three Men in New Suits* (1945) openly expresses a concern, voiced prophetically before a more general disaffection with postwar Labour politics could take hold, that promises made during wartime might yet again be broken. The novel *Bright Day* (1946) followed with a more personal take on the same problem, presenting an autobiographical portrait of a film scriptwriter at a dead end, exhausted with war work. Both the protagonist and the century are suffering from a midlife crisis, and the optimism expressed at the end of this novel is extremely

---

[13] J. B. Priestley, 'Too Simple?' in *Delight* (London: Heinemann, 1949), quoted in *The Priestley Companion: Extracts from the Writings of J. B. Priestley Selected by Himself* (Harmondsworth: Penguin, 1951), pp. 404–6, 406. For Priestley's place in interwar debates about literary value and cultural capital, often referred to as the 'Battle of the Brows', see Ina Habermann, *Myth, Memory and the Middlebrow: Priestley, du Maurier and the Symbolic Form of Englishness* (Basingstoke: Palgrave Macmillan, 2010), pp. 31–42.
[14] J. B. Priestley, *Out of the People* (London: Collins, 1941), p. 25.
[15] J. B. Priestley, 'Journey into Daylight' in *The Listener*, 17 May 1945, pp. 543–4.   [16] Ibid., p. 543.
[17] Ibid., p. 544.

qualified, with a faint hope for recovery coming from new initiatives in art and culture. As Priestley apparently felt that the situation called for direct action, he stood (unsuccessfully) as independent candidate for Cambridge in the 1945 election, and accepted leading positions in cultural institutions such as the British Theatre Conference and the London Philharmonic Advisory Council, also acting as a UNESCO delegate. In this capacity, with his spirits considerably dampened, he met Jacquetta Hawkes.

Hawkes was born in 1910 in Cambridge, daughter to the Nobel-Prize-winning scientist Sir Frederick Gowland Hopkins. Jacquetta Hopkins was a precocious child who decided that she would become an archaeologist at the age of 9. She went on to study archaeology and anthropology at Newnham College and married the eminent archaeologist Christopher Hawkes. During the war, she did civil service work, first at the Ministry of Post-War Reconstruction and subsequently at the Ministry of Education, where she was responsible for film. One of her many projects was the educational feature film *The Beginning of History* (1946), in which she employed innovative visual techniques and wrote a lyrical script read by Cecil Day-Lewis. Her filmic celebration of Barbara Hepworth, *Figures in a Landscape*, had its premiere at the 1954 Venice Film Festival. Through a passionate relationship with the poet Walter Turner, literary editor of the *Spectator* and music critic for the *New Statesman*, she became part of a highbrow artistic coterie while continuing her work on prehistoric Britain. Increasingly estranged from her husband, she moved in a widening circle of intellectuals and artists, among other things becoming archaeological correspondent for the *Spectator*. Priestley wrote to her during the early days of their affair that they had 'a colossal gap to bridge, but I am absolutely certain that we need each other in a very special way'.[18] In his view, they each had 'a very personal vision of mankind as a whole, you through the long vista of prehistory, and I through drama and politics. We turn into poets, though of different kinds, more or less at the same moment.'[19] Extremely different in background and outlook, Priestley and Hawkes were not obvious partners, but from their respective points of origin they came to share an urgent and holistic vision of human purpose. Undertaking a sustained project of cultural archaeology, they developed what amounts to a philosophy of the 'good life'.

---

[18] Christine Finn, *A Life On Line: Jacquetta Hawkes, Archaeo-Poet (1910–1996)* (2006), available at http://humanitieslab.stanford.edu/ChristineFinn/9, ch. 6 (last accessed 12 February 2017).
[19] Ibid.

In her capacity as civil servant, Hawkes was involved in setting up the Festival Pavilion for the Festival of Britain in 1951, designing the part which dealt with the land and people of Britain. The displays also featured her remarkable biography of Britain *A Land*, which became a bestseller, and in 1952, she was awarded an OBE in recognition of her services. The success of *A Land* established Hawkes as a well-known public intellectual in the 1950s and 1960s, although she has since been largely forgotten. This obscurity is arguably due to the idiosyncratic way in which she brought together the 'two cultures' of art and science, writing lyrically and philosophically about scientific findings, and bringing a scientifically trained mind to the mysteries of art.[20] In this, as the century progressed, she was increasingly out of sync with both the literary scene and the scientific community. The intense debate about the 'two cultures' began in October 1956 with a *New Statesman* article by the novelist and scientist C. P. Snow (later expanded into his famous Rede lecture of 1959, and published the same year as *The Two Cultures and the Scientific Revolution*). Snow argued that the lack of communication between these 'two cultures' was detrimental to the development of modern society. In particular, he criticised the British educational system for a comparative neglect of scientific teaching which was bound to have negative consequences for Britain's standing in a modern concert of nations.

While Hawkes would have endorsed this analysis, she looked primarily to artists to bridge the gap. In her biography of the Priestleys, Diana Collins quotes Hawkes's article 'Art in the Crystalline Society', published in *Penguin New Writing* in 1949, as an early articulation of Hawkes's philosophy. It also presents evidence of her engagement with the emerging 'two cultures' debate. Hawkes argues that artists must 'bring imagination to science, and science to imagination where they meet in the myth'.[21] Similarly, in an article 'The Proper Study of Mankind' written for the journal *Antiquity*, she explains that the technical aspects of science must be,

---

[20] Hawkes had been thoroughly forgotten, until Christine Finn, now her official biographer, saved her papers after her death and put a biography online in 2006. See her article 'A Rare Bird. Love Her or Hate Her, Jacquetta Hawkes, with Her Intuitive, Humanistic Approach to Archaeology, Still Has Us Talking', in: *Archaeology* (January/February 2001), pp. 38–43. In recent years, interest has revived; see Ina Habermann, 'England an Island. Englishness as a Symbolic Form in Jacquetta Hawkes's A Land (1951)' in: Jürgen Kamm and Gerold Sedlmayr (eds), *Insular Mentalities: Mental Maps of Britain* (Passau: Karl Stutz, 2007), pp. 89–102. For a perceptive reading of Hawkes's contribution to the Festival of Britain, see Hayden Lorimer, 'Memoirs for the Earth: Jacquetta Hawkes's Literary Experiments in Deep Time' *Cultural Geographies* (2012) 19(1) pp. 87–106. In 2013, Rachel Cooke devoted a chapter to Hawkes in *Her Brilliant Career: Ten Extraordinary Women of the Fifties* (London: Virago, 2013), pp. 217–57.

[21] Diana Collins, *Time and the Priestleys* (Stroud: Alan Sutton Publishing, 1994), p. 166.

as Collins puts it, 'integrated into explorations of the larger meanings of life', which 'prompted much positive response from people around the world'.[22] In practice, this meant that beyond her work as an archaeological correspondent, Hawkes wrote accessible and lyrical books about cutting-edge science, supplementing this with civic engagement. For example, she joined the Council for the Preservation of Rural England, became a founding member of the Homosexual Law Reform Campaign and, most importantly, of the Campaign for Nuclear Disarmament. Taking on board her husband's social criticism, she promoted a philosophy that was intensely private, at the same time speaking to the concerns of postwar culture and forming the basis for public and political commitment. Through her influence, the alternative lifestyle that Priestley had been calling for was brought more clearly into focus. Like many intellectuals at the time, the Priestleys had a strong belief in the philosophy of C. G. Jung, conceiving the world in terms of archetypes, of binaries and polar opposites, without conceding, however, that such binaries must necessarily be hierarchical.[23] In her much later autobiography, *A Quest of Love* (1980), Hawkes reiterates her belief that 'woman and man are poles apart, but like North and South, together forming the true axis of our single humanity'.[24] Looking back, she diagnoses phenomena of the modern world, such as the atomic threat and rampant capitalism, as evidence of a preponderant 'masculine principle' that has to be balanced out.

Committed to Labour and the Welfare State, Priestley continued to promote the political ideal of community as an antidote against apathy and discontent in a manner that might well be seen as anachronistic, judging by the standards of *The Good Companions*, which was revived as a feel good film in 1957.[25] As Roger Mellor states, the film was released while Osborne's *The Entertainer*, 'with Laurence Olivier as Archie Rice, was premiered at London's Royal Court Theatre', providing 'a fascinating counterpoint to the essential optimism of *The Good Companions*'.[26] Moreover, Priestley's

---

[22] Ibid., p. 206.
[23] Early in their relationship, Priestley and Hawkes collaborated on the experimental Jungian 'platform drama' *Dragon's Mouth: A Dramatic Quartet in Two Parts* (London: Heinemann, 1952), in which four characters represented Jung's functions of sensation, emotion, intellect and intuition. Priestley also wrote an article entitled 'Jung and the Writer' for the *Times Literary Supplement* in 1954.
[24] Jacquetta Hawkes, *A Quest of Love* (London: Chatto & Windus, 1980), p. 15.
[25] The first film version of *The Good Companions* was directed by Victor Saville in 1933, starring Jessie Matthews and John Gielgud. This was remade as a musical comedy in 1957, directed by J. Lee Thompson, and starring Eric Portman and Celia Johnson.
[26] Roger Mellor, '*The Good Companions* – The Movie (1957)' *Journal of the Priestley Society* (2000) 1, pp. 34–9, 36.

drama, cutting edge in terms of theme and dramatic form before the war with plays such as *Time and the Conways* (1937), *I Have Been Here Before* (1937) and *Johnson over Jordan* (1939), looked out of date in comparison with Osborne, Beckett and the activities of the Royal Court Theatre.[27] His novel *Festival at Farbridge*, published in 1951 and intended to support the Festival of Britain, although reasonably popular with readers, received mixed reviews.[28] With hindsight, the Festival of Britain is often seen as the 'last gasp'[29] of Labour's efforts to build a satisfactory postwar society, and Priestley felt called to promote it. Planned as a 'large-scale comic novel about postwar England',[30] *Festival at Farbridge* presents a variation on the story of *The Good Companions*: in the sleepy South Midlands town of Farbridge, a mixed group of characters, led by the resourceful Commodore Horace Tribe, team up to combat the general inertia with spirited festival preparations. Although the novel was a Book Society choice for May, it was not the book significantly to capture the mood of the time. That book, *A Land*, was written by Jacquetta Hawkes.

A Land is a 'biography' and celebration of Britain, beginning with the creation of the earth, then zooming in on Britain, and fusing geography, geology, topography, climate and cultural history into one holistic vision. As Hawkes explains:

> ... the image I have sought to evoke is of an entity, the land of Britain, in which past and present, nature, man and art appear all in one piece. I see modern men enjoying a unity with trilobites of a nature more deeply significant than anything at present understood in the processes of biological evolution; I see a land as much affected by the creations of its poets and painters as by changes of climate and vegetation. The nature of this unity cannot be stated, for it remains always just beyond the threshold of intellectual comprehension.[31]

For Rachel Cooke, Hawkes's *A Land* 'hums with something akin to what we would call New Age-ism',[32] but this assessment is misleading. Hawkes

---

[27] This also applies to a certain extent to Priestley's best-known play *An Inspector Calls*, first performed in the Soviet Union in 1945 and in London in 1946. Towards the end of the twentieth century, the play was rediscovered and is now seen as a classic. Vincent Brome, *J. B. Priestley* (London: Hamish Hamilton, 1988), p. 293.

[28] Brome, *J. B. Priestley*, pp. 334–7.

[29] John Braine, *J. B. Priestley* (London: Weidenfeld & Nicolson, 1978), p. 131.

[30] J. P. Priestley, *Margin Released: A Writer's Reminiscences and Reflections* (London: Heinemann, 1962), p. 194.

[31] Jacquetta Hawkes, *A Land* (London: The Cresset Press, 1951), p. 1.

[32] Cooke, *Her Brilliant Career*, p. 222. This view appears to be shared to a certain extent by those who re-package the book as 'nature' writing. It was republished in 2012 in the Collins Nature Library; see

was an expert on prehistoric Britain, archaeology and ancient culture, and while extravagant, there is nothing bogus about her holistic view. Discussing stones and building materials in *A Land*, she states: 'Anyone who enters a Gothic cathedral must be aware that he is walking back into the primeval forest of existence, with birds, beasts, monsters and angels looking through the foliage.'[33] Hawkes considers fauna and flora of prehistoric times to be residual in sedimentary materials that have been used over centuries by artists to create a monument to religious faith, which enables contact with infinite layers of historical time. In her chapter 'Digression on Rocks, Soils, and Men', Hawkes discusses the cultural significance of building materials. Characteristically, the Victorians prefer to build with granite: 'the substance of wild moorlands was transformed into kerbstones, railway bridges, into post offices, public fountains and public houses, family fish-shops, and, above all, into banks'.[34] All these observations add up, as I have argued elsewhere, to a conception of cultural identity, and in Hawkes's case, English cultural identity, as a symbolic form which integrates the material world and the processes of perceiving and shaping it into a coherent cultural practice.[35] A visualisation of this unity is effected in the 'organic architecture' of Frank Lloyd Wright and artists promoted by Hawkes, such as Graham Sutherland, Henry Moore and Barbara Hepworth. Through this lyrical approach to science, Hawkes seeks to bridge the gap between the 'two cultures'. Hawkes felt strongly about 'the similarity between the imaginative processes of poet and scientist', as she puts it in a tribute to her father.[36] Both needed intuition, a particularly intense visual imagination and a capacity to delight in the beauties of the natural world. Properly applied, Hawkes opines, these faculties also cannot be pressed into the service of destruction, but they will by their very nature be life-enhancing.

From the Festival of Britain to Suez (1951–1956): Outsider Insiders

After their marriage in 1953, Hawkes and Priestley settled down to a joint writing life, and Hawkes, having found her voice in *A Land*, produced the second of her wide-ranging cultural archaeologies, *Man on Earth*

Robert Macfarlane's review in the *Guardian* on 11 May 2012 and his introduction to the new edition, where he sees *A Land* as a 'missing link' in the history of environmental writing.
[33] Hawkes, *A Land*, p. 141.   [34] Ibid., p. 109.
[35] Habermann, 'England an Island' and *Myth, Memory and the Middlebrow*.
[36] Jacquetta Hawkes, 'Gowland Hopkins and Scientific Imagination' in *The Listener* (2 February 1950), p. 191.

(1954). Again, there is a focus on the development and heightening of human consciousness. Hawkes's poetic approach to science leads her to dismiss the received theory of evolution as too narrow: 'One cannot see landscape through a microscope.'[37] Looking at an Argus pheasant in the Natural History Museum, she becomes convinced that there are limits to what science can explain:

> Standing in front of this prodigious fantasy of nature I found certainty had taken possession of me: the sexual selection of the hen standing primly near her mate could never even in millions of years have conjured up so wonderful a creation. Dear, demure hen pheasant, how could your natural preference for some dash and pretence in your mate produce this creation which would put Le Roi Soleil quite in the shade?[38]

In Hawkes's view, people need to transcend the limitations of Neo-Darwinism in order to form a more adequate idea of their being on earth.

The next item in Priestley and Hawkes's cultural archaeology was collaborative: in 1954, they visited the American South-West and wrote the travel(dia)logue *Journey Down a Rainbow*, which is dedicated to C. G. Jung and epitomises many of the authors' concerns with contemporary society. Their aim was to compare the ancient culture of the Pueblo Indians with the United States, which, as the most advanced urban Western civilisation, provided 'the social and cultural pattern of the mid-twentieth century',[39] thus anticipating the binary opposition that the structural anthropologist Claude Lévi-Strauss was to set up in 1959 between 'hot' and 'cold' societies, that is, societies characterised by change with a focus on history, and societies characterised by stasis, with a focus on myth.[40] Hawkes went to New Mexico to study Pueblo culture, while Priestley went to Texas, Dallas and Houston, to anatomise what he came to call 'Admass': 'the whole system of an increasing productivity, plus inflation, plus a rising standard of material living, plus high-pressure advertising and salesmanship, plus mass communications, plus cultural democracy and the creation of the mass mind, the mass man'.[41] Priestley's

---

[37] Jacquetta Hawkes, *Man on Earth* (London: The Cresset Press, 1954), p. 26.   [38] Ibid., pp. 25–6.
[39] J. B. Priestley and Jacquetta Hawkes, *Journey Down a Rainbow* (London: Heinemann-Cresset, 1957), p. viii.
[40] See the interview in G. Charbonnier (ed.), *Conversations with Claude Lévi-Strauss*, transl. by John and Doreen Weightman (London: Cape, 1969).
[41] Priestly and Hawkes, *Journey Down a Rainbow*, p. 44. The 'empire' of *Admass* includes the 'kingdoms' of *Nomadmass*, inhabited by modern nomads tied to their cars, *Hashadmass*, denoting a bogus mixture of cultural styles, French, Italian, Spanish, Chinese, in areas such as food and architecture, and *Luxad*, the realm of conspicuous spending and the performance of cultural roles, dreamt up by the copywriters (pp. 43–5, 45). The equivalent of *Admass* 'behind the Iron Curtain' (p. 44) is

cultural analysis goes beyond a reflex reaction against the modern world, even though he deliberately overstates his case in order to throw into relief the contrast with Hawkes's evocation of Pueblo culture. One powerful symbol of Admass is a 'forty-storey bank building ... sheathed in aluminium', glaring in the sun and erected at the cost of more than 25 million dollars, together with the 'gold-coloured ice-cream' offered at its monstrous 'formal dedication'.[42] Yet the fundamental alienation of capitalist over-reachers 'in oil' only gains its full significance when seen in contrast with Hawkes's private symbol for continuity, the ceremonial space of the *kiva*, 'a sacred underground chamber'.[43] Acknowledging the precarious existence of traditional societies in the modern world, Priestley and Hawkes set the phallic skyscraper, epitomising 'society entirely dominated by the masculine principle' against the womb-like *kiva*. Western alienation contrasts with the wholeness and 'universal participation' characteristic of the cultural continuity in traditional societies, performed, for example, through dances which 'express in the language of poetry the truth of man's unity with nature, the truth that science repeats to us, curing our delusions of grandeur'. These dances, they argue, 'offer us visions for which science has no eyes'.[44]

Despite their deliberate lightness of touch, the Priestleys are careful to cast themselves in the role of informed observers: Hawkes indulges in anthropological thick description, while Priestley, discussing the ills of mechanistic society, makes reference to Norbert Wiener, pioneer of cybernetics and advocate of automatisation, and to Alan Valentine's book *The Age of Conformity* (1954), thus showing his familiarity with contemporary debates about American social politics.[45] For Priestley and Hawkes, American urban society, as the epitome of masculinist Western civilisation, sins against the 'green Earth', and against women, who are bribed and bullied into submission. As Priestley observes, 'defeated woman strips and teases'.[46] Finally, *Journey Down a Rainbow* leads to the Priestleys' principal concern, shortly before the launch of CND, with 'the society of the

Propmass, dominated by direct propaganda. See also Priestley's satire on advertisement and the media *The Image Men* (London: Allison & Busby, 1984), first published as *Out of Town* and *London End* (London: Heinemann, 1968).

[42] Priestly and Hawkes, *Journey Down a Rainbow*, p. 36.   [43] Ibid., pp. 26, 46.
[44] Ibid., pp. 27, 60, 60.
[45] Ibid., p. 74. For a detailed discussion of these issues, see Robert Genter, *Late Modernism: Art, Culture, and Politics in Cold War America* (Philadelphia, PA: University of Pennsylvania Press, 2010).
[46] Priestly and Hawkes, *Journey Down a Rainbow*, pp. 224, 112.

hydrogen bomb'.[47] In his tongue-in-cheek 'Lay Sermon to Nomadmass', Priestley sketches a positive vision which revisits his earlier engagement with multi-dimensional time – a concept dramatised in his 'Time Plays'. The 'Lay Sermon' argues that in order to achieve their full potential, humans must transcend a restrictive notion of progress and linear time:

> All moments of noble living, the ecstasy of love, the compassion and understanding that enter into every genuine personal relationship, the creation and rapt appreciation of great art, the adventures of the mind among significant ideas, even an amazed wondering about ourselves, all demand this unknown dimension, this timeless being. Every greatly heightened state of consciousness involves eternity.[48]

This statement may well stand as a brief summary of the Priestleys' credo, and the philosophical basis of their political activities. Just as the Suez crisis was powerfully bringing home to the British people that their country's role as a global player had been played out, the Priestleys opened up their horizon to vast times and spaces for the heightened consciousness to roam. It is no coincidence at this point that they are looking towards the new global leader America, dangerously locked into another binary, cold on both sides, and yet prone to explode.

According to the Priestleys, conscious human beings should read nature and their environment as a cultural palimpsest and take heart from its richness, longevity and resilience. Significantly, this feeling of the richness of life is absent from Los Alamos, 'cradle of the first atomic bomb',[49] which Hawkes visits during her tour. While the laboratories are of course surrounded by high fences of barbed wire and off limits for visitors, the pleasant bungalows for employees, painted in pastel colours, are showcased as ideal homes. For Hawkes, however, they have an impermanent and fraudulent feel. Surmising that people who live in a city that has 'a destructive purpose at its very heart' would inevitably become corrupted, she registers the 'paternalism, the standardization and model planning, the virtuousness of everything that leads only to the ghastly feeling of being institutionalized for life'.[50] Looking at the menacing Black Mesa, Hawkes wishes that 'Los Alamos had been built on its summit, then we'd have the devil's stronghold without disguise'.[51] Modern evil is clean and deceptive,

---

[47] Ibid., p. 30. Priestley also briefly jibes at the Beat generation: 'Their grandparents left their homes to break the prairie: these go to break the monotony. But unless they are fairly clever, determined, courageous, they will arrive in *Nomadmass*' (p. 130).
[48] Ibid., p. 134. [49] Ibid., p. 181. [50] Ibid., pp. 184, 185. [51] Ibid., p. 182.

in tune with the duplicities of the Cold War, but it must be identified and resisted. In her activities for the Campaign for Nuclear Disarmament (CND), Hawkes acknowledges that there is only a chance of this 'if we can find the physical, mental, and above all moral courage to resist what is being done in our name. If we cannot, then we may deserve to burn.'[52]

From CND to the Nuclear Test Ban Treaty (1957–1963): Campaigning Sages

Throughout the 1950s, the Priestleys embraced political causes and committed themselves to the elaboration of a positive vision for society. This commitment proceeded from a belief, supported by Jung's psychology, in a duty that conscious human beings have on earth. Priestley famously helped to launch the Campaign for Nuclear Disarmament with his Article 'Britain and the Nuclear Bombs' in the *New Statesman* of 2 November 1957, which powerfully denounced the received 'wisdoms' of the Cold War. After overwhelming responses from readers, the editor Kingsley Martin took the initiative to combine forces with another group of prominent people, including Bertrand Russell and Canon Collins, who were protesting against nuclear weapon tests, and the Campaign was officially launched early in 1958. Hawkes took part in the Aldermaston Marches and formed a women's group, publishing the above-quoted pamphlet *Women Ask Why*, which includes a contribution by the young Iris Murdoch.[53] As Jodi Burkett argues in *Constructing Post-Imperial Britain*, middle-class radicals such as the CND founders felt a particular responsibility for action, seeking to replace Britain's waning global dominance with a claim to moral leadership after the demise of the empire.[54] Priestley withdrew when the organisation left behind its bourgeois intellectual origins and the Marxist element became stronger, although Hawkes stayed on to produce a somewhat oblique contribution to the movement,

---

[52] Jacquetta Hawkes, 'The Way Out' in *Women Ask Why. An Intelligent Woman's Guide to Nuclear Disarmament, Reproducing Three Scripts from the Meeting for Women at the Central Hall on January 15, 1962* (London: Campaign for Nuclear Disarmament, 1962), pp. 11–16, 11.

[53] Murdoch was a friend of the family and collaborated with Priestley on a dramatisation of her novel *A Severed Head*. The play was staged successfully in 1963 in Bristol and at the Criterion Theatre in London.

[54] Jodi Burkett, *Constructing Post-Imperial Britain. Britishness, 'Race' and the Radical Left in the 1960s* (Basingstoke: Palgrave, 2013). For classic accounts of CND, see Richard Taylor and Colin Pritchard, *The Protest Makers. The British Nuclear Disarmament of 1958–1965: Twenty Years On* (Oxford: Pergamon Press, 1980); and Paul Byrne, *The Campaign for Nuclear Disarmament* (London: Croom Helm, 1988). For another recent study of the impact of the end of empire on British society, see Matthew Whittle, *Post-War British Literature and the 'End of Empire'* (London: Palgrave, 2016).

the book *Man and the Sun* (1962). This comprehensive history covers the time from the sun's creation and human beings' religious relationship with it up to the scientists' disastrous attempts at imitation. Towards the end, Hawkes sharply condemns the tests which took place in 1952 in the Marshall Islands: 'Man's first artificial sun rose above the Pacific, but it was not a star of peace. The Russians watched their own sun rise within a year. So now two chosen people, each confident that they were the children of light, confronted one another across the globe with suns in their bandoliers.'[55] Despite the magnitude of the threat, Hawkes remains optimistic, concluding that future sunrises 'may awaken us to a Good Morning'.[56] She may have felt justified in her optimism when, after the hairbreadth escape of the Cuban missile crisis, the Nuclear Test Ban Treaty was passed in 1963.

In *British Fiction and the Cold War*, Andrew Hammond argues that literary criticism still tends to underestimate both the power of Cold War discourse and its ubiquity in fictional writing. Certainly, the Priestleys' emphasis on wholeness, emerging from a sophisticated notion of the 'good life', can also be seen as a paradoxical result of the magnitude of the atomic threat which cast its shadow over postwar society.[57] They believed that a philosophical and cultural reaction against the threat of annihilation could not be piecemeal; it had to be cosmic in proportion, while yet embracing a Keatsian notion of 'negative capability': the ability to exist in 'uncertainties, mysteries, doubts, without any irritable reaching after fact and reason'.[58] As Hawkes states in *Man on Earth*, a psychological balance must be found between the tragic individual life and the enjoyment of mind and the senses, embracing the ignorance that is 'one of our few certainties. No religion, no philosophical or scientific system claiming any absolute or exclusive knowledge of truth is proper to our condition as inmates of one speck in a universe the vastness and wonder of which even our trifling minds are beginning faintly to apprehend'.[59] Priestley had already dramatised such sentiments in 1939 in *Johnson over Jordan*. After

---

[55] Jacquetta Hawkes, *Man and the Sun* (London: The Cresset Press, 1962), p. 239.   [56] Ibid., p. 24.
[57] Priestley's Cold War novel is *Saturn over the Water* (London: Companion Book Club, 1961), where a sinister organisation with a global network of laboratories and business enterprises, whose sign is Saturn over the Water, is plotting to destroy all humankind with a view to creating a clean slate for a new beginning. At the end of this mysterious novel, artists and creative people are gathering to break the 'Saturnian Chain'.
[58] Keats famously argues this in a letter to his brothers on 21 December 1817. See John Keats, *The Complete Poetical Works and Letters of John Keats* (Cambridge: Houghton, Mifflin and Company, 1899), p. 277.
[59] Hawkes, *Man on Earth*, p. 246.

his death and a surreal time in limbo, the businessman Robert Johnson is fetched away by a mysterious, angelic figure. He has his moment of insight:

> I have been a foolish, greedy and ignorant man;
> Yet I have had my time beneath the sun and stars;
> I have known the returning strength and sweetness of the seasons,
> Blossom on the branch and the ripening of fruit,
> ...
> The earth is nobler than the world we have built upon it;
> The earth is long-suffering, solid, fruitful;
> The world still shifting, dark, half-evil.
> But what have I done that I should have a better world,
> Even though there is in me something that will not rest
> Until it sees Paradise . . . ?[60]

After this, Johnson walks into the Unknown, an inconclusive ending that highlights the role of literature in a context of philosophical enquiry. Literature, with its use of imagery and multiple narratives, can afford to embrace negative capability. In *Literature and Western Man* (1960), Priestley argues that the inner and outer worlds must be brought into harmony, giving voice to the belief 'that Man lives, under God, in a great mystery, which is what we found the original masters of our literature, Shakespeare and Rabelais, Cervantes and Montaigne, proclaiming at the very start of this journey of Western Man'.[61] Against the urge of Promethean transgressive ambition, then, the Priestleys set a Jungian 'intuition' that not only refuses to be undermined by insecurity about intimations of the spiritual life, but also paves the way for a New Humanism, or a 'New Existentialism', in Colin Wilson's terms. At first glance, Wilson would not be expected to have much in common with the Priestleys. However, at the end of *The Outsider*, as Priestley did not fail to note in his review, Wilson sketches a way out of the 'outsider's' dilemma, by making recourse to William Blake and the visionary tradition that had some currency in the 1950s. 'Blake has solved the Outsider's problems',[62] suggests Wilson, but while 'Blake's way' might provide a symbolism to express the visionary experience, it cannot make sense of 'a mechanical civilization with atom bombs and electronic brains'.[63]

Wilson's emphasis on the visionary experience leads him, as it led Priestley, to George Gurdjieff and P. D. Ouspensky and their teaching

---

[60] J. B. Priestley, 'Johnson over Jordan' in *The Plays of J. B. Priestley* (London: Heinemann, 1948), vol. I, pp. 335–6.
[61] J. B. Priestley, *Literature and Western Man* (London: Heinemann, 1960), p. 456.
[62] Wilson, *The Outsider*, p. 238.   [63] Ibid., p. 240.

of the 'fourth way'. This technique of meditation was seen as a focused way to achieve higher consciousness, transcending the ordinary three dimensions of human experience and opening up the fourth dimension of time past and future, as well as alternative dimensions related to the multiverse hypothesis that the American physicist Hugh Everett elaborated in 1957. In a television interview, Priestley had asked viewers to send him accounts of their experiences of strange coincidences and precognitive dreams. He discusses people's enthusiastic responses in his book *Man and Time* (1964), in which he draws heavily on the theories of Jung, J. W. Dunne and Ouspensky, stating that 'our lives are not contained within passing Time – we may not be immortal beings – I do not think we are – but we are better than creatures carried on that single-line track to the slaughter-house'.[64] Expanding consciousness on earth thus becomes a political task: 'We cannot perform this service, just as we cannot even enjoy a good life, unless our minds and personalities are free to develop in their own fashion, outside the iron moulds of totalitarian states and systems, narrow and authoritarian churches, and equally narrow and dogmatic scientific-positivist opinion.'[65] Tying these general remarks about the nature of human consciousness back to British politics, Priestley advocates a return to the visionary and creative forces represented by the 'Britain of the Unicorn'. Presenting a symbolic reading of the British coat of arms, Priestley argues that the old imperial lion has had its day, and only the 'Unicorn' qualities – creativity, magic, eccentricity and imagination – will be able to stop Britain's decline.[66]

Setting Britain in the context of the wider Cold War, the ultimate trajectory of the Priestley-Hawkes philosophy is a vision of a common humanity, united in a mystical union, to bring about a better future. That this vision emerged not from the margins, but from sober, established intellectuals, is vitally important for our understanding of postwar British society. In their commitment to peace, equality and ecology, the Priestleys anticipate opinions voiced in the civil rights and 'green' movements of the late 1960s and beyond.[67] So while there is a recognisable shift of gears in the early 1960s, 'between the end of the "Chatterley" ban / and the Beatles' first

[64] Quoted in Collins, *Time and the Priestleys*, p. 212.
[65] J. B. Priestley, *Man and Time* (London/Amsterdam: Aldus Books in association with W. H. Allen, 1964), p. 308.
[66] J. B. Priestley, 'The Unicorn' in *Thoughts in the Wilderness*, pp. 162–8.
[67] For a discussion of ecology and the Left, see James Radcliffe, 'Eco-Anarchism, the New Left and Romanticism' in John Rignall and H. Gustav Klaus (eds), *Ecology and the Literature of the British Left: The Red and the Green* (Aldershot: Ashgate, 2012), pp. 193–206. Radcliffe focuses on Theodore Roscak.

LP', as Larkin puts it in *Annus Mirabilis*, the problems had been around for some time, and so had a vision of the remedies. It is crucial not to reduce the 1950s to a sort of accident that intervened between wartime pressures and the 'Swinging 60s', but to realise that, even if it was ultimately unable to transform the fundamental shape of society, a distinctive idea of wholeness, and wholesomeness, was projected after the war whose practical side was the Welfare State. For postwar Britain, the Priestley-Hawkes philosophy combines Priestley's commitment to social critique and communalism with Hawkes's vision of a 'third culture' fusing science and art into a new spirituality. It was not, however, the only mystical and holistic vision to emerge from the centre of English culture in the 1950s, nor was it the most influential in the long run. This distinction is reserved for J. R. R. Tolkien's more fanciful as well as politically much more conservative *Lord of the Rings* (1954–5) which celebrates re-enchantment and salvation through charismatic kingship, looking back to an interwar English ruralism which leaves readers, after the great pageant of kings, orcs, elves and wizards has departed, with a vision of gardening Hobbits. When Priestley spoke after the war of tending the flower of life, this may not have been what he had in mind.

CHAPTER 11

Prizing the Nation: Postwar Children's Fiction

Lucy Pearson

At the start of Arthur Ransome's *Pigeon Post* (1936), Nancy Blackett complains that her absent adventurer uncle 'might just as well have stayed at home', asking, 'Why shouldn't he look for things here?'[1] It is fitting that this question is posed by the winner of the inaugural Carnegie Medal, for it expresses an attitude which was to characterise the first two decades of Carnegie prize-winners. These books 'look for things at home', both in seeking to promote British children's fiction and – more fundamentally – in mapping a sense of nationhood which is predicated on rediscovering history, heritage and the rural landscape. Jacqueline Rose has argued that children's fiction holds out the possibility of 'a primitive or lost state to which the child has special access', and the long association between the figure of the child and the natural world makes children's literature a potent venue for a construction of nationhood which is built around a pre-industrial past.[2] However, these books are not simply regressive or nostalgic: in employing the figure of the child, they look towards the future as well as the past, presenting change as both possible and desirable.

The years 1940 to 1960 straddle what have traditionally been seen as two distinct periods in the history of British children's literature: the 1950s, widely hailed as the beginning of a 'second golden age' of writing for children which continued throughout the 1960s and into the 1970s; and the preceding forty years, traditionally viewed as a somewhat disappointing era for British children's books.[3] A succession of commentators have characterised the children's literature of the interwar period and the years

---

[1] Arthur Ransome, *Pigeon Post* (London: Random House, 2001), p. 22.
[2] Jacqueline Rose, *The Case of Peter Pan, or, the Impossibility of Children's Fiction*, rev. edn (London: Macmillan, 1992), p. 9.
[3] The nineteenth century saw the 'first golden age', which is associated with the emergence of children's literature focusing on the amusement as well as the education of the child reader (although inevitably, this too is now a contested notion). Lewis Carroll's *Alice's Adventures in Wonderland* (1865) is perhaps the most prominent text of the 'first golden age'.

209

immediately following as 'dreary', 'derivative and stale' and lacking in vitality.[4] More recent scholarship, however, has challenged this characterisation of 1914 to 1949. Dennis Butts, for example, notes that the number of 'modern classics' written during the 1930s belies the notion that this was a period of quiescence, while Kimberley Reynolds traces a tradition of radical writing for children from the late Edwardian period to the beginning of the 'second golden age', arguing that the tendency to obscure this tradition has produced a 'hole in the cultural memory'.[5] Curiously little attention has been paid, however, to perhaps the most visible sign of continuity between the purportedly 'quiescent' interwar years and the activity of the 1950s: the Carnegie Medal. Established by the Library Association in 1936 as an award for 'the best book published for children', the Medal heralds a move towards the prizing of both children's literature and childhood itself. It is thus a key cultural site for postwar Britain: and significantly, the first two decades of Carnegie winners return again and again to themes of home, history and heritage as a means of renegotiating ideas about national identity in the postwar era.

In his discussion of the Newbery Medal (the US counterpart of the Carnegie), Kenneth Kidd notes the role of literary prize-giving in both creating and bestowing cultural capital, arguing that it 'encourages both the making and unmaking of canons, underwrites but also undercuts faith in popularity'.[6] The establishment of the Carnegie Medal was explicitly motivated by a desire to accrue cultural capital for children's books: like the Newbery, its stated aim was to raise both the standard and the profile of writing for children.[7] This concern with the standard of children's books reflects the growing concern for and about childhood itself during the first half of the twentieth century: an increasing discourse around children as

---

[4] John Rowe Townsend, *Written for Children: An Outline of English-Language Children's Literature*, 2nd rev. edn (Harmondsworth: Kestrel, 1983), p. 163; Marcus Crouch, *Treasure Seekers and Borrowers: Children's Books in Britain, 1900–1960* (London: The Library Association, 1962), p. 17; Geoffrey Trease, 'The Revolution in Children's Literature' in *The Thorny Paradise: Writers on Writing for Children*, (ed.) Edward Blishen (Harmondsworth: Kestrel, 1975), pp. 13–24, 16. See Lucy Pearson, *The Making of Modern Children's Literature in Britain: Publishing and Criticism in the 1960s and 1970s* (Farnham: Ashgate, 2013) for the discourse around the 'second golden age' of children's literature.

[5] Dennis Butts, 'The Retreatism of the 1930s: A Few Dissenters' in *Children's Literature and Social Change: Some Case Studies from Barbara Hofland to Philip Pullman* (Cambridge: The Lutterworth Press, 2010), pp.118–33; Kimberley Reynolds, *Left Out: The Forgotten Tradition of Radical Publishing for Children in Britain 1910–1949* (Oxford University Press, 2016), p. 4.

[6] Kenneth Kidd, 'Prizing Children's Literature: The Case of Newbery Gold' *Children's Literature* (2007) 35 pp. 166–90, 166.

[7] Keith Barker, 'Prize-Fighting' in Kimberley Reynolds and Nicholas Tucker (eds), *Children's Book Publishing in Britain since 1945* (Aldershot: Scolar Press, 1998), pp. 42–59.

'the future' both intensified the impulse to 'preserve' childhood and 'presented children as actually or potentially dangerous'.[8] Children's literature is a primary site for both constructing and controlling childhood: it is telling that the criteria for the Carnegie Medal included the stipulation that the tone of the winning book should be 'in keeping with the generally accepted standards of good behaviour and right thinking'.[9] Despite the inherently problematic nature of literary prizes as a barometer of either popularity or literary quality, the bestowing of the Medal in itself gave (and still gives) the winning books a particular cultural weight, and helped to ensure that they were available to (if not read by) child readers.[10] James English, in his influential study of cultural prizes *The Economy of Prestige*, suggests that the children's market is particularly responsive to awards; this is borne out by Kidd, who notes that winning the Newbery 'can keep authors and titles in print for decades'.[11] The same is true of the Carnegie: of the first twenty-four winners of the Medal, thirteen remain in print today, over fifty years after their first publication.[12] The fact that the Carnegie Medal (like the Newbery) is awarded by librarians also ensures that the books are well represented in library collections, further enhancing their contribution to canon construction; this is further augmented by histories of children's literature that typically use the Medal winners as a means of tracing trends in the development of children's books. Although in one sense a relatively arbitrary selection, the Medal therefore has a key role in curating children's books in the national imaginary, and its history intersects with those of children's publishing, librarianship and education. This chapter, however, takes a primarily textual approach.[13] Reading the

---

[8] Hugh Cunningham, *Children and Childhood in Western Society since 1500* (Harlow: Pearson Education, 2005), p. 179.
[9] See Perry Nodelman, 'The Other: Orientalism, Colonialism, and Children's Literature' *Children's Literature Association Quarterly* (1992) 17(1) pp. 29–35 on the 'colonising' qualities of children's books; W. C. Berwick, one of the founders of the Carnegie Medal, quoted in Barker, 'Prize-Fighting', p. 43.
[10] Keith Barker shows in *In the Realms of Gold: The Story of the Carnegie Medal* (London: Julia MacRae Books, 1986) that the rather haphazard administration of the Medal in its first decades almost totally excluded not only children themselves, but also specialist children's librarians.
[11] James English, *The Economy of Prestige: Prizes, Awards, and the Circulation of Cultural Value* (Cambridge, MA: Harvard University Press, 2005), p. 97; Kidd, 'Prizing Children's Literature', p. 166.
[12] The question of whether these texts also enjoy a continued readership is a more vexed one: certainly William Mayne's *A Grass Rope* (1957), which is available only as part of Faber's print-on-demand series Faber Finds, is presented as a forgotten classic rather than as a book for contemporary children.
[13] Keith Barker's two short histories *In the Realms of Gold* and 'Prize-Fighting' are the most significant scholarship on the Medal to date. Both deal primarily with the administrative history of the Medal and its position within the Library Association (Later Chartered Institute of Library and Information Professionals). This chapter represents the beginnings of a wider project on the literary and cultural significance of the Medal.

winning texts in relation to each other, it shows the continuity of themes and concerns across the period 1936 to 1960, suggesting that these too were integral to canon formation.

Much scholarship on cultural prizes has pointed to their function in relation to defining a distinctive national culture, especially – but not exclusively – in a post-colonial context.[14] The early history of the Carnegie Medal signals its connection to the shifting sense of British identity during this period. Keith Barker suggests that the establishment of the Medal was in itself 'a matter of some national pride', since the United States had launched the Newbery more than a decade previously.[15] Launching confidently as an award for 'the best book published for children in the British Empire', by 1941 it had significantly retrenched, limiting its scope to books published in England (a move which Owen Dudley Edwards characterises as 'either bigoted or parochial or both').[16] In 1944, the criteria were revised again: the Medal was to be awarded to 'an outstanding book for children by a British subject domiciled in the United Kingdom (Great Britain and Northern Ireland), published in Great Britain during the year'.[17] In the light of this uncertainty, it is striking that the first two decades of the Medal winners show a preoccupation with national identity. Whereas Kidd notes that the early Newbery medal winners typically featured 'other countries and/or indigenous North American cultures', all but seven of the Carnegie winners between 1936 and 1960 were set wholly in Britain and focus on British characters.[18] Prizing children's literature, it seems, also entails prizing the nation.

This turn towards home is evident from the inaugural winner of the Carnegie Medal, Arthur Ransome's *Pigeon Post* (1936), which establishes

---

[14] The post-colonial implications of prize culture are a key focus for James English in *The Economy of Prestige*.

[15] Barker, *In the Realms of Gold*, p. 3.

[16] Owen Dudley Edwards, *British Children's Fiction in the Second World War* (Edinburgh University Press, 2007), p. 249. Edwards notes that these criteria may have reflected the tendency during this period to use 'England' as a synecdoche for Britain rather than an intent to exclude writers from other parts of the United Kingdom. Conversely, this chapter will chiefly speak of the creation of a British identity, since although the majority of these titles are English they encompass, I argue, a range of regional identities which are not necessarily aligned with 'Englishness'.

[17] Edwards, *British Children's Fiction*, p. 249. Edwards suggests that the change was motivated by the desire to award the Medal to the Welsh-born Scottish writer Eric Linklater, one of only four non-English winners in the years up until 1960. The others are Ronald Welch (Welsh), C. S. Lewis (Irish) and Eleanor Doorly (born in Jamaica, although she moved to England at age 7).

[18] As Kidd points out, Newbery books also construct national images through their creation of an implicitly normative American identity against which other cultures are measured. It is striking, however, that early Carnegie winners largely eschew the strong adventure story tradition (which functions in the same way) in favour of narratives about home.

a deep preoccupation not simply with Britain as a nation, but with the land itself that runs through the next two decades of Carnegie winners.[19] The genre of 'camping and tramping' fiction, of which Ransome was a progenitor, reflected the 'explosion of interest in the British countryside' in the years following the First World War.[20] Alun Howkins has argued that this interest was the culmination of a cultural movement which produced 'a ruralist version of a specifically English culture'.[21] Camping and tramping fiction was important both for promoting this vision of nationhood, and for interrogating it; although it was dominated by stories set in the English countryside, these books did not universally reproduce the images of the rural south which according to Howkins underpins the ruralist ideal.[22] Ransome in particular is known for his loving representations of the Lake District, a wilder, less cultivated space than the village greens and hedgerows of the south.[23] Hazel Sheeky Bird argues that camping and tramping novels 'failed to recognise the validity of competing national identities', but they did represent specific regional identities.[24] This regional specificity allows for a construction of national identity which to some degree bypasses the problematic associations of both Englishness and Britishness by emphasising a more direct connection with the land itself.[25] *Pigeon Post*, the sixth book in the series, represents a particularly decisive turn towards the land. In earlier books in the series, Ransome's child protagonists reimagine the Lake District as a foreign space, remapping the British landscape through games which draw on their reading of adventure narratives. These games simultaneously reproduce and invert imperial conquest: instead of conferring European names

---

[19] In the first decades of the Carnegie Medal, the date of the Medal reflects the date of publication for the book. These have therefore not been separated.

[20] Hazel Sheeky Bird, *Class, Leisure and National Identity in British Children's Literature, 1918–1950* (Basingstoke: Palgrave Macmillan, 2014), p. 1.

[21] Alun Howkins, 'The Discovery of Rural England' in Robert Colls and Philip Dodds (eds), *Englishness: Politics and Culture 1880–1920* (London: Bloomsbury, 1987), pp. 85–112, 86.

[22] Howkins, 'The Discovery of Rural England', p. 86.

[23] Although only five of the twelve published books in the *Swallows and Amazons* series are set in the Lake District, it is this region with which the series is most closely associated. Peter Hunt credits Ransome with helping to create the national image of the Lake District, see *Approaching Arthur Ransome* (London: Jonathan Cape, 1992), p. 12.

[24] Bird, *Class, Leisure and National Identity in British Children's Literature*, p. 7.

[25] The complex interaction of Britishness, Englishness and regional identity deserves a more nuanced discussion than is possible here. Nevertheless, the northern setting of Ransome's Lake District novels is particularly important given that the rural ideal of Englishness often excludes the north (see Peter J. Taylor, 'Which Britain? Which England? Which North?' in David Morley and Kevin Robbins (eds), *British Cultural Studies: Geography, Nationality and Identity* (Oxford University Press, 2001), pp. 125–44).

on colonised territory, the children replace local names with foreign ones (they refer to the nearest town as Rio), investing the landscape with the allure of the unknown. By contrast, much of the action of *Pigeon Post* turns upon the desire to prove the value of the British landscape itself. Nancy Blackett's complaint at the start of the book is provoked by the absence of her uncle, who is prospecting for gold overseas. The children's desire to prove that his absence is unnecessary (and thus enable his usual role as co-conspirator in their holiday adventures) motivates them to begin prospecting for gold on the rocky, drought-stricken local fells. While their uncle's efforts overseas are a failure, 'looking for things here' proves to be much more successful and by the end of the book the children have identified a valuable seam of metal (albeit copper rather than gold). In the most vividly realised episode of the book, the children also uncover an equally precious commodity beneath the fells: a hidden spring which proves crucial to the defence of the land itself when a fell fire threatens to devastate the local landscape. This episode breaks down the boundaries between child and adult (tellingly referred to in the children's games as 'explorers' and 'natives') and between locals and visitors, as they work together to extinguish the fire before it reaches farmland. The British landscape is thus shown to hold both economic and spiritual value, and it is the recognition of this value which constitutes belonging. The children's vital role positions them as custodians of this national treasure; they will be the 'new natives' who will inherit and preserve the land.

The Carnegie winners of the years 1937 to 1939 moved away from this focus on the countryside: 1937 saw J. R. R. Tolkien's *The Hobbit*, which draws on an idealised rural England in its depiction of the Shire, passed over in favour of Eve Garnett's *The Family from One End Street*, about an urban, working-class family. In 1938, the Medal went to Noel Streatfeild's *The Circus is Coming*, another text concerned with working-class life and culture. If things had continued on this track, the first two decades of the Medal might have told a different story; however, the outbreak of war in 1939 heightened the importance both of children's books and of depictions of the land. Just three days after war was declared, Routledge and Keegan's editor T. M. Ragg wrote to Eleanor Graham: 'I do think that children's books are, if the war is continued for any time, going to become more and more important', observing that Graham's own camping and tramping novel, *The Children Who Lived in a Barn* (1938), was a good example of the kind of book which would benefit evacuated children.[26] At Penguin, the launch of Puffin Picture Books (Allen Lane's first venture for children) was similarly given impetus by the sense that 'evacuated children are going to need books more than ever, especially ... on farming and natural history'.[27] In catering for this need, children's books turned back to the land: one of the first Puffin Picture Books tackled life *On the Farm*, while the 1940 Carnegie Medal went to Kitty Barne's evacuee story *Visitors from London*. Barne's novel does not wholly embrace this enforced move towards the countryside: much of the humour of the novel rests on its depiction of the administrative challenges of evacuation and the resistance of urban evacuees to the rural environment. Nevertheless, the book is underpinned by a sense of the rural community as the source of enduring stability in a world in which you 'woke up in the morning with one set of things in front of you, you went to bed with quite another'.[28]

The turn towards the land is even more acutely present in the 1942 Carnegie winner, *The Little Grey Men* by 'B. B.' (D. J. Watkins-Pitchford), which is first and foremost a powerful celebration of the natural world – as in this description of seasonal change:

> The great tide was on the turn, to creep so slowly at first and then to rise ever higher to culminate in the glorious flood, the top of the tide, at midsummer.
> Think of it! All that power, all those millions of leaves, those extra inches to be added to bushes, trees and flowers. It was all there under the earth, though you would never have guessed it.[29]

The quasi-magical qualities which Watkins-Pitchford attributes to nature are given physical form in the little grey men of the title, gnomes who live in harmony with the natural world. The insertion of these magical creatures into a realistically described British landscape serves as an inducement to the reader to engage more closely with the world around them: as the introduction to the novel makes explicit, if you 'watch and wait by the streams and in the woods ... suddenly you will understand that the birds and wild animals *are* the little people'.[30] The sense of the natural world as magical recurs across other Carnegie-winning titles. In Elizabeth Gouge's

---

[26] T. M. Ragg to Eleanor Graham, 6 September 1936, RKP 121/2, Routledge and Keegan Archive, Reading University.
[27] Allen Lane, quoted in Ian Rogerson, *Noel Carrington and His Puffin Picture Books: An Exhibition Catalogue* (Manchester Polytechnic Library, 1992), p. xii. Eleanor Graham was shortly to join Penguin as editor of Puffin's second list for children, Puffin Story Books.
[28] Kitty Barne, *Visitors from London* (London: J. M. Dent & Sons, 1940), p. 261.
[29] 'B. B.', *The Little Grey Men* (Oxford University Press, 2012), p. 1.
[30] 'B. B.', Introduction to *The Little Grey Men*, n.p.

fantasy novel *The Little White Horse* (1946), the protagonist Maria feels apprehensive about leaving her London home to live with her uncle, but as the novel develops both her appreciation for the land and her understanding of her own magical significance within it unfold. Whereas Watkins-Pitchford focuses on wild spaces, Gouge's imaginary village of Silverydew is a perfected version of the cultivated rural south, complete with cottages 'thatched with golden straw and set in neat gardens bright with spring flowers'.[31] Howkins suggests that in the cultural construction of rural England which emerged from the 1880s onwards: 'Purity, decency, goodness, honesty, even reality itself are closely identified with the rural south.'[32] These qualities are all integral to Gouge's pre-industrial community in which 'the people looked as happy and prosperous as their homes'.[33] A defence of this space is a defence of the nation united around, and imagined through its rural heritage; an association underscored by the fact that Maria's quest to 'keep Silverydew always like this' is aided by a lion and a unicorn.[34]

Ten years later, William Mayne's *A Grass Rope* (1957) reiterates this idealised vision, and produces another unicorn. This novel, a realistic portrayal of a small community in the Yorkshire Dales, is less straightforwardly magical than Gouge's, but Mayne's prose invests the entire landscape with the numinous:

> They walked along in the dusk. The sky hung overhead in colours of new roses; and to the west lavender and marigold; to the east the green of sage, and under the cloud that rolled behind the sunset the edge of darkness came on: silver lined like a well edged with daisies.[35]

For both Mayne and Gouge, the child functions as a connection to the magical qualities of the natural world. It is Mayne's child protagonist Mary through whom the description of the dusk is focalised, and the plot turns around her belief in fairies. In *The Little White Horse*, only Maria can resolve the ancient conflicts which threaten the protected space of Silverydew. The sense of the child as what Jacqueline Rose has described as a 'pure point of origin' makes children's literature a particularly potent venue for the celebration of Britain as characterised by its natural spaces: the child is able to retrieve a connection to the land and an understanding

---

[31] Elizabeth Gouge, *The Little White Horse* (Oxford: Lion Children's, 2009), p. 50.
[32] Howkins, 'The Discovery of Rural England', p. 86.   [33] Gouge, *The Little White Horse*, p. 50.
[34] Howkins, 'The Discovery of Rural England', p. 74.
[35] William Mayne, *A Grass Rope* (London: Faber & Faber, 2010), p. 103.

of local traditions which work to build a coherent identity and heal historical rifts.[36]

These texts reflect a tradition of English nationalism which, Ian Baucom argues, 'identifies English place rather than English blood as the one thing that could preserve the nation's memory and, in preserving its memory, secure England's national identity'.[37] The link between place and history is equally important in non-fiction Carnegie winners: Agnes Allen's *The Story of Your Home* (1949) traces the development of architecture from prehistoric times, while Edward Osmond's *A Valley Grows Up* (1953) depicts the growth of a (fictional) valley. The two historical novels which won the Carnegie Medal also link place and memory, and extend the 'localist' discourse to the British Isles as a whole.[38] Ronald Welch's *Knight Crusader* (1954) is one of the few Carnegie winners of this period to be set largely outside Britain, but it retains an emphasis on a deep connection with the land. Welch's twelfth-century Norman hero Sir Philip d'Aubigny is born and bred in Syria, but when a pilgrim describes the 'grey mists [and] soft rain' of Britain, Philip is 'filled with the vision of green forests', establishing an instinctive connection with Britain.[39] The narrative deals with the fall of the Outremer states to Saladin's forces – a theme which has obvious resonance in the context of the retrenchment of Britain's imperial territories during the 1940s and 1950s – but surprisingly little emotional weight is given to the destruction of Philip d'Aubigny's own Syrian home. Instead, Philip establishes a new life by turning towards the British 'home' he has never experienced, swearing allegiance to King Richard and ultimately returning with him to Britain, where Philip travels to the Welsh marches to take up his ancestral fiefdom.[40] Paradoxically, foreign-born Philip is presented as more 'British' than the British-born noble whom he ousts from his fief, Llanstephan Castle, and he is welcomed by the Welsh men-at-arms serving in the castle. A similar connection between Britishness and an affinity for place is present in Rosemary Sutcliff's *The Lantern Bearers* (1959). The book concerns a British-born Roman soldier, Aquila, at the time of the Roman withdrawal from Britain. At the opening of the book, Aquila – returning home to his father's farm – surveys 'the farmstead under the great, bare swell of the downs: the

---

[36] Rose, *The Case of Peter Pan*, p. 9.
[37] Ian Baucom, *Out of Place: Englishness, Empire and the Locations of Identity* (Princeton University Press, 1999), p. 16.
[38] *Tom's Midnight Garden*, discussed later, is also a historical novel of a sort, but its timeslip device sets it apart from these two books.
[39] Ronald Welch, *Knight Crusader* (Oxford University Press, 2013), pp. 26–7.
[40] Ibid., pp. 18–19.

russet-roofed huddle of buildings, the orchard behind', and feels 'a sharp-edged pleasure'.[41] This deeply felt connection to the land explains and justifies his decision to go 'wilful missing' when his legion departs Britain, and his subsequent allegiance to the forces battling the invading Saxons.[42] This connection with the land is also associated with other cultural values which Sutcliff represents as part of an enduring British tradition: the forces resisting the Saxons are represented as lantern bearers against the dark of invading barbarism: 'for us to keep something burning, to carry what light we can forward into the darkness and the wind'.[43]

The connection Sutcliff makes between Aquila's affinity with the land and his role as a 'lantern bearer' of British culture reflects a more wide-ranging connection between the countryside and Britain's 'traditional' heritage. The wider cultural turn towards the rural was associated with attempts to construct a national culture by reviving traditions such as Morris dancing and folk songs.[44] This impulse is evident across many of the early Carnegie winners. B. B.'s *Little Grey Men* literalises the notion of an enduring heritage embodied in 'traditional' rural communities: they have lived on the land since 'long before Julius Caesar landed in Britain'.[45] As 'the last gnomes in Britain', they represent what Patrick Wright has termed the 'precious but imperilled traces' of an enduring British identity.[46] In *Pigeon Post*, as Peter Hunt points out, 'those who truly belong to the Lake District (by birth or in spirit) save it by traditional methods (pigeons, firebrooms, water from a well found by dowsing)'.[47] *A Grass Rope* also presents the importance of traditional knowledge and connection to the land. Its child characters work together to uncover the truth behind a local legend, and by the end of the book they have discovered part of a lost treasure; but the real value of the legend is its role in bringing the children together and creating a sense of community. In a sense, the Carnegie list shares this function: it curates and transmits a shared narrative tradition. Walter de la Mare's *Collected Stories* (1947) and Eleanor Farjeon's *The Little Bookroom* (1955) reveal the degree to which this apparently recuperative tradition was actively engaged in constructing a national heritage: both collections offer 'literary fairy tales' which draw on British traditions and settings.

---

[41] Rosemary Sutcliff, *The Lantern Bearers* (Oxford University Press, 2007), p. 1.   [42] Ibid., p. 22.
[43] Ibid., p. 305.   [44] Howkins, 'The Discovery of Rural England', p. 74.
[45] *Little Grey Men*, p. 217.
[46] Patrick Wright, *On Living in an Old Country: The National Past in Contemporary Britain* (Oxford University Press, 2009), p. 2.
[47] Hunt, *Approaching Arthur Ransome*, p. 114.

Valerie Krips identifies the turn towards 'heritage' as central to British identity construction in the postwar era, noting that '[a]fter the countryside itself ... the country house was to be one of the chief objects of postwar conservation and heritage'.[48] Changes in land ownership between the wars, and the decline of the social order which had underpinned large country estates, along with postwar taxation regimes, resulted in the decline of 'the country houses that had been historic symbols of power and influence'.[49] The ambivalent status of the country house as both an important repository of cultural heritage and a symbol of a now-defunct social order is evident in several Carnegie winners, notably Mary Norton's *The Borrowers* (1952) and Philippa Pearce's *Tom's Midnight Garden* (1958). Both books take place in formerly grand country houses: the vibrant household from which Norton's race of tiny people once 'borrowed' small odds and ends has been reduced to an elderly invalid and two servants, while the large family home in Pearce's book has been divided into 'poky flats' and 'crowded round with newer, smaller houses that beat up to its very confines in a broken sea of bay-windows and gable-ends and pinnacles'.[50] A symbolic grandfather clock is at the heart of both texts, which are deeply concerned with issues of history, change and the passage of time. In *Tom's Midnight Garden*, the clock striking thirteen signals the beginning of 'time no longer' (the quotation emblazoned on the clock's face): slipping downstairs to investigate, Tom opens the garden door to find himself back in time, before the house was divided up and the garden destroyed. In his own time, Tom (in quarantine for measles) lacks both a garden and a playmate. Stepping back in time, by contrast, he finds both. As he spends long hours in the garden with the lonely Victorian child Hatty, the urban environment of the modern era is contrasted unfavourably with the rural space of Hatty's time: looking out of her window Tom sees 'a lawn, at one end of which a giant beech-tree leaned in thought ... a lane, another hedge, a meadow, with a great elm in the middle' and decides 'I like your room better ... and I like your view much better'.[51] Pearce thus conveys a strong sense of nostalgia for a lost era. At the same time, the book suggests that it is not, in fact, entirely lost, since Tom is able to access the garden. This text is not simply concerned with passing on history to the child; the child itself becomes a point of access to history. Ultimately, Tom comes to realise that he has been able to access the garden

---

[48] Valerie Krips, *The Presence of the Past: Memory, Heritage and Culture in Postwar Britain* (New York and London: Garland Publishing, 2000), p. 3.
[49] Ibid. [50] Philippa Pearce, *Tom's Midnight Garden* (Oxford University Press, 2008), p. 4.
[51] Ibid., p. 146.

because the grown-up Hatty – now an elderly woman who has returned to live in what remains of her childhood home – has been dreaming of her own childhood:

> Yet perhaps Mrs Bartholomew was not solely responsible for the garden's being there, night after night, these last weeks. For she remarked to Tom now that never before this summer had she dreamed of the garden so often, and never before this summer had she been able to remember so vividly what it *felt* like to be the little Hatty – to be longing for someone to play with and for somewhere to play.[52]

It is Tom's own longing for 'someone to play with and somewhere to play' which has 'activated' Hatty's memories and made them into a shared space.[53] This process of sharing memories can, of course, be likened to children's literature itself. Here it is not the land which constitutes an enduring heritage, but the experience of childhood, which enables a shared re-creation of a lost era.

The Borrowers shares the motif of the grandfather clock as an enduring symbol of an earlier era, but here the time travel is symbolic rather than literal. Norton's family of Borrowers, Pod, Homily and little Arrietty, derive their surname from the grandfather clock under which they live, which has not stopped in living memory. Their home is a historical space, furnished with 'several portraits of Queen Victoria as a girl' (repurposed postage stamps) and a library of 'those miniature volumes which the Victorians loved to print'.[54] The Clock family are the last vestiges of Victorian country house society: once there was a whole race of little people living off the excess of the house, but 'the Overmantels and the Harpsichords and the Rain-Barrels and the Linen Presses' have disappeared as the human inhabitants of the house have departed and old traditions such as Afternoon Tea have been abandoned.[55] It is possible to read this shift in terms of the decline in domestic service in the postwar era: the Borrowers inhabit the 'primarily functional places and spaces in the great country houses, kitchens and servants quarters ... hidden away behind green baize doors' which Valerie Krips notes became the most-visited parts of the country house as heritage object.[56] The dependent status of the Borrowers and their practice of borrowing not only surplus items, but also names, culture and even social status from the human society on which they depend, parallels the existence of domestic servants in these spaces.

---

[52] Ibid., p. 223 (emphasis in the original).   [53] Ibid.
[54] Mary Norton, *The Borrowers* (London: Puffin, 2003), p. 19, p. 20.   [55] Ibid., p. 108.
[56] Krips, *The Presence of the Past*, p. 3.

Norton makes this explicit through her depiction of Mrs Driver, the cook, who supplements her position with some borrowing of her own, feeling that a 'drop of Madeira here, a pair of old stockings there' are 'within her rights'.[57] This link implies that the decline of the country house is potentially catastrophic for the entire household: the Boy's observation that Arrietty Clock will one day be 'the only Borrower left in the world' suggests not simply change, but the possibility of extinction.[58] Andrew O'Malley consequently sees the book as inherently conservative, arguing that Norton exhibits a 'nostalgic yearning for a world unspoiled by modernity, in which all know and keep their places'.[59] This reading encapsulates the central conflict of 'prizing the nation' in terms of history and heritage: the 'lovely things' of the past are juxtaposed against a narrative of loss and decline.

As O'Malley points out, 'Laments over [a] lost or vanishing way of life bear a great deal of resemblance to nostalgic recollections of lost childhood, and often the two impulses occupy the same ideological and textual space'.[60] This makes children's literature an effective venue for a nostalgic and conservative construction of nationhood. To read the Carnegie Medal simply in these terms, however, is to overlook the radical potential of children's literature, and indeed, the nostalgic qualities of *The Borrowers* are disrupted by the presence of the child within the text itself. Whereas Pod and Homily are fearful of change, Arrietty longs for it, complaining of being 'cooped up ... day after day ... week after week ... year after year'.[61] Like many young people in the postwar era, who benefited from the reforms enacted through the 1944 Education Act, Arrietty is more educated than her parents (Homily does not know how to read) and less respectful of traditional boundaries relating to gender and class.[62] She demands to be taught how to borrow (traditionally a male role) and when she meets the Boy, challenges the assumption that good Borrowers, like good servants, must avoid being seen. The Borrowers' expulsion from the house at the end of the book is traumatic, but from Arrietty's (focalising) perspective, it is also a longed-for opportunity.

This sense of change as both inevitable and valuable is crucial to the way in which children's literature functions as a site of national self-fashioning

---

[57] Norton, *The Borrowers*, p. 180.　[58] Ibid., p. 111.
[59] Andrew O'Malley, 'Mary Norton's "Borrowers" Series and the Myth of the Paternalist Past' *Children's Literature* (2003) 31 pp. 71–89, 72.
[60] Ibid., p. 75.　[61] Norton, *The Borrowers*, p. 64 (ellipses in the original).
[62] The 1944 Education Act extended compulsory education and established the tripartite education system, which (albeit controversially) offered more working-class children the opportunity to attend grammar schools.

in this era, for while adults may look back to childhood, children are inevitably propelled out and away from it. This is the underlying theme of *Tom's Midnight Garden*, which despite its nostalgia for the prelapsarian space of the garden, ultimately suggests that it is a space which must be left behind. Tom seeks to remain in the garden forever, but when he understands that his expulsion came about because the adult Hatty was dreaming 'of growing up, and of [her husband] Barty', he accepts it 'without bitterness'.[63] Pearce also subtly suggests that both childhood and the past are less idyllic than they appear through the filter of Tom's adventures in the garden: Hatty is an orphan dependent on the charity of an aunt who despises her and cousins who bully her. When Tom realises that he has been accessing Hatty's dreams, he understands 'why the weather in the garden had always been perfect': only in memory is the past ideal.[64]

Rosemary Sutcliff's *The Lantern Bearers* also problematises the construction of nationhood through an idealised sense of place. Although Aquila's connection with the land is presented as fundamental to his national identity, in choosing to foreground the Roman withdrawal from Britain Sutcliff brings to the surface some of the complexity and contradictions of British national identity. While the novel is focalised through Aquila, who is represented as 'belonging' to Britain in a way the invading Saxons do not, Sutcliff does not allow us to forget that despite his British birth he also represents a colonising force. The civilisation which Aquila and his fellow 'lantern bearers' are preserving against the dark is Aquila's Roman culture, not an indigenous British one, and many of the Celts Aquila encounters in the course of the novel view him as an invader rather than a fellow Briton. His marriage to a Celtish woman – contracted in order to cement allegiances between the various forces allied against the Saxons – is paralleled with his sister's marriage to one of the Saxon invaders who killed their father. Both women initially resist their husbands, but ultimately recognise that through marriage and child-bearing they have relinquished their previous cultural allegiances. The lack of agency these women have over their national identity is problematic, but their narratives also present the possibility that nationhood can be shaped by family ties as well as ties to the land.[65] Sutcliff reminds the reader that Britain has been shaped by successive waves of colonisation and immigration, and rejects the notion that Britishness is determined through race, suggesting that the assimilation of

---

[63] Pearce, *Tom's Midnight Garden*, pp. 223, 224.   [64] Ibid., p. 222.
[65] The gendering of national identity reflects contemporary debates: it was only in 1948, just a decade before the publication of *The Lantern Bearers*, that British women marrying foreign nationals were allowed to retain their British nationality.

difference is not only possible, but inevitable. In the context of the mass immigration of the 1950s, this is an inclusive message, but it is also one which destabilises the notion of national identity as fixed and immutable. Aquila's defection has implications for those living in Britain's former colonies: whereas for Ronald Welch, the collapse of Empire activates an instinctive turn towards 'home', Sutcliff suggests that it might equally prompt a re-evaluation of national loyalties.

The Little Grey Men offers a more straightforward picture of the land as part of an enduring British heritage, but even this text suggests a contested space. The chief threat to the gnomes is not simply the encroachment of human beings into wild spaces, but the gamekeeper who brutally punishes incursions onto the 'private property' of Crow Wood.[66] The gnomes' contempt for the sign warning that 'trespassers will be prosecuted' would have been met with approval by those involved in the 1931 mass trespass of Kinder Scout in the Peak District: as Hazel Sheeky Bird shows, the discourse surrounding rural spaces in interwar and wartime children's literature was radical rather than conservative, and reflected a shift towards a more egalitarian approach to land ownership and access.[67] Owen Dudley Edwards suggests that the ruthlessness of the gamekeeper's murder by the gnomes (they cause his shotgun to explode) reflects wartime sensibilities, but it equally hints at the possibility of a violent class struggle.[68]

Implicit in these narratives, then, lie concepts of progress that parallel and complicate the concern with tradition, and children here represent a force for change rather than a point of access into the past. Significantly, change is often symbolised through the transformative potential of work, and the Carnegie list shows a recurrent concern with this: Ransome's characters, for example, assert that prospecting for gold is 'serious business, with no pretence about it' (a departure from the emphasis on play in earlier Ransome titles).[69] In the prizes of the postwar period and the 1950s, this transition is increasingly evident, as is the figure of the child as worker. In *The Circus Is Coming*, Peter and Santa begin the book in the care of their Aunt Rebecca, who enforces a model of childhood belonging to both a different era and a different class by attempting to reproduce the education enjoyed by the children in the wealthy household where she was lady's maid. When their aunt dies, the children find a new home with their uncle in the circus, where they are forced out of their assumption that children will be 'just fed and looked after and then jobs found for [them] when

---

[66] *The Little Grey Men*, p. 107.   [67] Ibid., p. 88.   [68] Edwards, *British Children's Fiction*, p. 252.
[69] Ransome, *Pigeon Post*, p. 80.

they're older'.[70] The expectation in their new community is that everyone will work, and that children can assume agency by working to gain skills in a chosen profession. This is a socially progressive book: the children begin the novel with rather snobbish class assumptions which are gradually abandoned as they are absorbed into the egalitarian, hard-working community of the circus. *The Circus Is Coming* is essentially a career novel, as are both Richard Armstrong's *Sea Change* (1948) and Elfrida Vipont Foulds's *The Lark on the Wing* (1951), which in different ways are concerned with the long, slow process of developing skills. The prizing of this subgenre, which enjoyed a particular prominence in the 1950s, reflects the sense that heritage and tradition alone are insufficient. On the contrary, children become a focus for rebuilding the nation in the wake of change.

The establishment of the Carnegie Medal in 1936 can be viewed as an attempt to recapture some of Britain's former glories: the first golden age of children's literature had also been a golden age for Britain's imperial and industrial interests. In claiming cultural capital for children's books, and prizing those narratives which promoted heritage and history, the Medal worked to construct a sense of an enduring national identity. This turn to the past, however, is not simply regressive: it helps to demonstrate that change itself is integral to Britain's national character. The figure of the child – a symbol of both our nostalgia for the past and our potential future – enables the Carnegie Medal to celebrate Britain's heritage while promoting its future.

---

[70] Noel Streatfeild, *The Circus Is Coming* (Harmondsworth: Puffin, 1986), p. 232.

CHAPTER 12

Artists of Their Time: The Postwar Battle for Realism in Literature and Painting

Alice Ferrebe

From the establishment of the Committee for the Encouragement of Music and the Arts (CEMA) in 1940, cultural regeneration was anticipated as a vital part of the reconstruction of Britain. The means of achieving this rejuvenation, however, remained conflicted once the Second World War was over. Although innovation was, as ever, an artistic priority, the pull of pre-war class and aesthetic certainties was also strong: to Norman Mackenzie, postwar Britain was in a 'stalemate state, that curious interval in our social history, in which there was no way back to the world which had gutted out into war yet no clear way forward to a really new society'.[1]

Before the war began, Georg Lukács had attempted to move the debate around art's social contract beyond the presiding battle-lines. Its terms, he claimed in a 1938 essay, 'are not classics versus modernists; discussion must focus instead on the question: which are the progressive trends in the literature of today?' He added: 'It is the fate of realism that hangs in the balance.'[2] In the postwar discussions focused upon British literature, a binary (and frequently nostalgic) logic prevailed in the conceptualisation of potentially 'progressive trends'. This was predicated upon a presiding confrontation of modernism versus realism, with the latter, broadly, in cultural ascendancy. In the journal *Our Time* in 1947, E. P. Thompson cast modernism as 'the ideological defence of a dying civilization', and by 1953, C. P. Snow was ringing its knell in the *Sunday Times*, claiming modernism had now 'died from starvation because its intake of human stuff was so low'.[3] *Encounter* magazine, which began in

---

[1] Norman Mackenzie, 'After the Stalemate State' in Norman Mackenzie (ed.), *Conviction* (London: MacGibbon & Kee, 1958), p. 7.
[2] Georg Lukács, 'Realism in the Balance' in Theodore Adorno, Walter Benjamin, Ernst Bloch *et al.*, *Aesthetics and Politics (Radical Thinkers)* (London: Verso, 1980), p. 30.
[3] E. P. Thompson, 'Comments on a People's Culture', *Our Time* (October 1947), p. 38; C. P. Snow, 'New Trends in First Novels', *Sunday Times* (27 December 1953), p. 3.

1953, strove to reimagine modernism in a Cold War context, as pro-freedom, pro-individualism and pro-Western – even pro-bourgeois – and set it against an inescapably Socialist realism of communally circumscribed ambitions and dogmatic form. Even this determined project, however, was characterised by a curious resignation to modernism's contemporary death: Greg Barnhisel notes that 'a melancholy and self-aware belatedness, a wistful resignation, colors *Encounter*'s modernism'.[4] Stephen Spender's editorial to the magazine's third edition begins by summoning what he calls 'substantial ghosts, feeding life', the first of which is individualism.[5]

In other of the arts, the moribund realist/modernist binary that so dominated debates in British writing was complicated and animated. Through its various aesthetic and ethical positions around, in particular, abstraction and figuration, postwar British painting, although also engaged in what art historian James Hyman has called a 'Battle for Realism', offers a potentially more complex field of political and artistic debate than that provided by literary criticism.[6] A diverse selection of fiction writers recognised this potential, and made use of ekphrasis, the verbal representation of visual art, to explore their aesthetic and political anxieties over established modes of realism. Although still susceptible to caricature, particularly in relation to the binary politics of the Cold War, painting's philosophies and practices provide an instructive means of refracting, refiguring and reflecting upon the artistic challenges faced by postwar novelists.

Joyce Cary's novel *The Horse's Mouth*, its diegesis spanning the beginning of the Second World War, was published in 1944. Its painter protagonist Gulley Jimson is the son of an artist who met with considerable success in an earlier era ('landscape with figures. Girls in gardens') before being driven out of the Academy to make room for the pre-Raphaelites.[7] Jimson thus inherits an acute awareness of the accelerating revolutions of the cycle of artistic fashion: 'All art is bad', as he puts it jovially, 'but modern art is the worst'.[8] His own recent work draws considerable condemnation. 'Look at the awful disgusting pictures Jimson paints', he parrots his critics, 'look at that Adam and Eve – worse than Epstein or Spencer ... A shocking thing. Thank God Jimson's papa never saw it'.[9]

[4] Greg Barnhisel, 'Encounter Magazine and the Twilight of Modernism' *ELH* (2014) 81(1) p. 408.
[5] Stephen Spender, 'Editorial: Ghosts of a Renascence', *Encounter* 1.3 (December 1953), p. 2.
[6] James Hyman, *The Battle for Realism: Figurative Art in Britain During the Cold War, 1945–1960* (New Haven, CT: Yale University Press, 2001).
[7] Joyce Cary, *The Horse's Mouth* (Harmondsworth: Penguin, 1948), p. 23.   [8] Ibid., p. 24.
[9] Ibid., p. 25.

To be 'worse than Epstein', in Jimson's contrary pantheon, is an achievement indeed. Cary considered the sculptor to epitomise the original artist: 'he does something to you, and you can't overlook or forget it'.[10] For Jimson, this barrage of criticism and denigrating comparison merely evidences his engagement in the proper role of art as a constant process of repainting and renewal. Just as he cheerfully accepts that the mural he counts as his finest work lies beneath four coats of whitewash in a village hall in Devon, so he extols the virtues of classical art to season canvases for his own use: 'There's nothing like a real old Master for an undercoating.'[11] Unsurprisingly, in the light of his patrimony, Jimson recalls how the portrait of himself as an artist began, before the turn of the twentieth century, with an undercoat: 'I started as a Classic. About 1800 was my period ... I had a picture in the old Water Colour Society that year. Very classical. Early Turner. Almost Sandby.'[12] Jimson's younger self, then, aspired to be an Old Master, or at least a new classicist: Paul Sandby was the only founder member of the Royal Academy to work in water-colour, and is routinely cited as being the father of English landscape painting.

This penchant for water-colours may seem like a harmless admission of the conservatism of youth. Yet to Jimson's understanding it has more sinister associations. Talking politics at the pub, Jimson claims the Second World War has just started '[b]ecause of modern art ... Hitler never could put up with modern art. It's against his convictions. His game was water-colour in the old coloured-water style. Topographical'.[13] The affiliation between modernism, formal experimentation and fascist sympathies that lingered in literary criticism (despite *Encounter*'s best efforts) has fewer biographical precedents in relation to visual art. Instead, Kenneth Clark was to claim, 'totalitarian art must be a form of classicism: the state which is founded on order or subordination demands an art with a similar basis'.[14] Jimson's revulsion stems in part from an awareness that he is not himself immune to fascist tendencies in his personal life. When his anarchist friend Plantie commends artists for giving their lives to their art, Jimson responds ruefully, mindful of the cost of his own artistic commitments paid by the women who have loved him: 'And other people's lives ... Like Hitler.'[15]

---

[10] Joyce Cary, 'On Jacob Epstein', unpublished essay, quoted in Alan Bishop, *Gentleman Rider: A Biography of Joyce Cary* (London: Michael Joseph, 1988), p. 311.
[11] Cary, *The Horse's Mouth*, pp. 170, 142.   [12] Ibid., p. 70.   [13] Ibid., p. 357.
[14] Kenneth Clark, *The Romantic Rebellion: Romantic versus Classical Art* (London: Harper & Row, 1973), p. 32.
[15] Cary, *The Horse's Mouth*, p. 82.

Lady Beeder, wife of the 'old Lord' Beeder, Jimson's potential patron, is herself a producer of water-colours 'in the traditional style'.[16] Despite these underlying old-fashioned tastes, the 'Boorjwas' Beeders invest their money in the 'Usual modern collection'.[17] Comically catalogued by Jimson, this ranges across styles from 'Wilson Steer, water in water-colour' to 'Epstein, Leah waiting for Jacob in squawtacolour'.[18] Because of its commercially recognised value, much of this art is worthless to him. The Beeders attempt to commission one of Jimson's nudes, the only mode of his work that garners any financial value in the current market, and one he has cast off as outdated. When they go on holiday, Jimson sets about transforming their well-appointed domestic exhibition space into a combination of bohemian studio and doss-house, working on a 'raising of Lazarus' on the wall of their dining room, and sleeping on a pile of newspapers in the corner.

'Through cash to culture' is Jimson's cheerful motto, and his exuberant destruction of the Beeders' home is his demonstration of the inescapable elements of exploitation in any relationship of artistic patronage.[19] However, Jimson does make it clear that the support of artists should ultimately fall to a society's government. Asked what would happen if there were no millionaires to patronise art, Jimson invokes a culture in which:

> 'The people go on with the old stuff, and folk art and so on, until they get sick.' 'Sick of art?' 'Sick of everything. Though they don't know it. It's a kind of foot-and-mouth disease. The mouth gets very foul and the feet turn sideways, so that the patient is always going round to the pub, the same pub, of course. I'm told by experts that there's a lot of it in country districts where you only have old Masters to look at. Young chaps kind of waste away.'[20]

Predictably, Jimson is in 'the pub, the same pub' when he makes this pronouncement, but his point is a sober one. Though '[y]ou can't expect a government to know what original art is', institutional faith in (and funding for) artists potentially to produce originality is, to his mind, an investment in the nation's well-being.[21]

The health of the nation's culture took a prominent place among the panoply of national concerns in the postwar period. CEMA shared in an emerging consensual commitment to a stronger democracy of opportunity with regard to matters of education and welfare, both material and spiritual. Its chair since 1941, John Maynard Keynes, died shortly before the

---

[16] Ibid., p. 179. [17] Ibid., p. 274. [18] Ibid., p. 178. [19] Ibid., p. 180. [20] Ibid., p. 306.
[21] Ibid., p. 181.

Arts Council charter was drafted in 1946, but his political influence was crucial in securing the new organisation's relatively high levels of funding amid the competing demands of reconstruction. Culture, then, formed part of the aggregate demand of foundational Keynesian economics. As Keynes explained in a broadcast at the end of the war, CEMA (like its successor, originally at least) 'was intended to support both excellence in the arts and the widest possible access to them'.[22] The Labour Government elected in 1945 empowered local authorities to tax sixpence on the pound to fund cultural activities: a scheme Arthur Marwick has identified as 'culture as a form of social welfare'.[23] The drive towards the democratisation of art – as well as that of health and education – speaks of the postwar consensus to be mindful of what C. P. Snow called the 'human stuff' within political systems; of the individual within societal statistics.[24] Lolie, a long-suffering muse-model, puts it more viscerally in *The Horse's Mouth*: 'What is there to bite on in the abstract?'[25]

As the postwar period progresses through the 1950s, this social mission for culture has often been critically understood to manifest, in literature in particular, in dogmatic allegiance to realist practice. Yet in the case of Jimson, before and during the war, Cary works to attenuate any such straightforward links between politics and aesthetic style. His protagonist is a garrulous man, who paints with words as well as with oils: this forms a key part of the novel's ekphrastic technique. Jimson's circumlocutory, frequently contradictory, first-person narration melds visions of Blakean romanticism – 'Long flat clouds like copper angels with brass hair floating on the curls of the fire'[26] – with transfigured realist mundanities: 'the allotments were in their April state, a bit bare except for regiments of bean sticks and rows of toolhouses like drunken paupers staggering about in the mud'.[27] The most – perhaps the only – reliable tenet of Jimson's stylistic practice is that it is invariably figurative: he shares Lolie's instinctive rejection of the abstract.

In placing his faith in Blake, Jimson is anticipating postwar cultural mores. The Arts Council's exhibition of British art that formed part of the

---

[22] Randall Stephenson, *The Oxford English Literary History*, vol. 12: *1960–2000: The Last of England* (Oxford University Press, 2004), p. 33.
[23] Arthur Marwick, *Culture in Britain since 1945* (London: Blackwell, 1991), p. 70.
[24] Snow, 'New Trends in First Novels', p. 3.   [25] Cary, *The Horse's Mouth*, p. 259.
[26] Ibid., p. 304.   [27] Ibid., p. 219.

1951 Festival of Britain included 'The Tempera Paintings of William Blake', a collection the artist had gathered himself in 1809. Unusually, these works demonstrated Blake's desire to work on a scale aspired to by Jimson, and by postwar art more generally.[28] As painter John Bratby was later to claim of the period: 'The scale was important. This was an obsession. Paintings *had* to be large. It was one of those strange things that happened. A reaction against the small picture.'[29] The size of his work aside, Susan Matthews has noted the inspirational potential of Blake, as a simultaneously dissenting yet Christian cultural figure, to provide a rejuvenating postwar model for spiritual belief outside established religious structures.[30] Envisioning how to repaint the Adam of his 'Fall' painting, Jimson claims his inspiration to come 'straight from the horse': whether this is God or Blake is not revealed, and does not in effect matter.[31] Postwar, the ambiguity of faith had both religious and political associations. Peter Hennessy cautiously confirms 'the decline in active religious practice if not belief itself', noting 'the social arithmetic of belief' to be 'one of the most vexing areas' for a historian.[32] More reliable than records of churchgoing are the figures for political membership: though the Soviet response to the Hungarian uprising in 1956 proved an ideological turning point for so many, as early as 1949 Arthur Koestler was meaningfully able to pronounce Communism to be '*The God That Failed*'.[33]

Yet a faith in the regeneration of Britain had to be maintained, and this was one in which art played, as Matthews points out, a vital role. Postwar, she claims, 'art threatens to take over from religion as a means of regulating order and cultural value'.[34] Nowhere is this more apparent than in one of the iconic sites of rebuilt Britain. When his design for Coventry Cathedral was chosen in 1951, Basil Spence immediately set about securing his

---

[28] Blake planned to 'divide Westminster Hall, or the walls of any other great Building, into compartments and ornament them with Frescos' of religious scenes. Cf. Geoffrey Keynes, 'Introduction' in *The Tempera Paintings of William Blake: A Critical Catalogue with an Introduction by Geoffrey Keynes* (London: Arts Council of Great Britain, 1951), p. 5.

[29] John Bratby, 1980 conversation with J. H. Hamilton, Keeper, Sheffield City Art Galleries, quoted in Maurice Yacowar, *The Great Bratby* (London: Middlesex University Press, 2008), p. 20 (emphasis in the original).

[30] Susan Matthews, '"And *Did* Those Feet?": Blake and the Role of the Artist in Post-War Britain' in Steve Clark, Tristanne Connolly and Jason Whittaker (eds), *Blake 2.0: William Blake in Twentieth-Century Art, Music and Culture* (Houndmills: Palgrave Macmillan, 2012), p. 152.

[31] Cary, *The Horse's Mouth*, p. 28.

[32] Peter Hennessy, *Having It So Good: Britain in the Fifties* (London: Allen Lane, 2006), p. 123.

[33] Arthur Koestler (ed.), *The God That Failed: Six Studies in Communism* (New York: Harper & Brothers, 1949).

[34] Matthews, 'And *Did* Those Feet?' p. 152.

building's largest works of art. As Elain Harwood points out: 'By commissioning the artworks early, Spence ensured they could not be eliminated as budgets became squeezed.'[35] In fact, the design of the cathedral itself was recast in 1955 when it became evident that the cost of the original superstructure, in addition to the art commissions, would exceed available funds.

In the midst of the Second World War, Jimson is already sensible of the need for such triumphant national statements of public art. While negotiating the sponsorship of his next mural, he notes, 'A work this size is not suitable to a public gallery. It really needs a cathedral ... [S]uch a building, thoroughly modern in style, would really be cheaper in the long run. Lighted by daylight bulbs. Open day and night.'[36] Jimson prophesises the aesthetic of some of the most cherished postwar churches, as well as the aspirations of gallery spaces much later in the century, and his design is predicated on more than a desire for free drinks to draw in the public (although that forms an important feature). Encapsulated in an ecstatic incantation of similes and metaphors, his lengthy exposition of his vision of postwar art melds a mix of media with the growth of spiritual communities: in conclusion, a picture, he tells his acolyte Nosy, 'is like a tree or a church, you've got to let it grow into a masterpiece. Same with a poem or a new religion'.[37] Art's role in restoring a communal sense of the sacred is more important to the postwar artist than denominational concerns. This was encapsulated in Spence's response to a committee shocked at his proposal of Jacob Epstein to sculpt St Michael, Coventry Cathedral's eponymous saint: 'There was a shocked silence, at length broken by the remark, "But he is a Jew," to which I replied quietly, "So was Jesus Christ"'.[38]

Cary's attempts to figure the postwar relationship between artistic representation, politics, spirituality and morality continued to his death in 1957. The year before, he had given the Clark Lectures at Cambridge University under the title 'Art and Reality'. Here, he revealed what he considered to be the 'all-important truth in the distinction between the arts' – that it is writing which has the potential more reliably to reveal both moral (abstract, personal, religious) and ethical (communal, political) truths: 'A novelist creates a world of action and therefore he has to deal

---

[35] Elain Harwood, *England: A Guide to Post-War Listed Buildings* (London: Batsford & English Heritage, 2003), p. 148.
[36] Cary, *The Horse's Mouth*, p. 346.   [37] Ibid., p. 209.
[38] Basil Spence, *Phoenix at Coventry: The Building of a Cathedral* (London: Geoffrey Bles, 1962).

with motive, with morality. All novels are concerned from first to last with morality.'[39] Thus, Cary maintained his faith in the ekphrastic novel as a vital means of exploring the moral priorities of artistic and spiritual rejuvenation in the wake of war.

'Subject and Object and the Nature of Reality': Elizabeth Taylor's Ekphrasis

Like Cary, Elizabeth Taylor was drawn to the figure of the painter in her fiction as a means of exploring the ethical imperatives of postwar society. In the letters to Ray Russell which, for the early part of her career, provide us with the most sustained exposition of her aesthetic practice, 'the abstract thinking was about both genres'.[40] Competing allegiances to modernism and realism are given play in her most dedicatedly ekphrastic novels. Her 1947 novel *A View of the Harbour* regularly and radically invokes *To the Lighthouse*. In Woolf's novel, Lily Briscoe's incremental portrait of Mrs Ramsay ultimately becomes an object that, like the novel itself, is offered as the reconciliation of Mr Ramsay's fraught philosophical enquiry into 'subject and object and the nature of reality'.[41] Lily's painting is the material means of encapsulating her shifting subjective response to her subject and her unifying artistic vision. In *A View of the Harbour*, in Taylor's seaside town of Newby, Lily Wilson, widowed by the Second World War, seeks to defy further confrontation with that 'nature of reality' in her reading practices. Absorbed in a romance novel, 'she sank deeply as if under an anaesthetic, away from empty and makeshift reality; she went down willingly and pleasurably, relinquishing with eagerness the gritty irritations of the Harbour streets, the smell of fish, the dusty shops with their cast-off clothes and furniture'.[42] In drawing upon the aesthetics of romance, modernism and realism, Taylor uses the novel to explore their competing claims of representation, and undermines established cultural hierarchies in the process.

'Think of a kitchen table . . . when you're not there', suggests a sanguine Ramsay child as a means of summarising his father's life's work to Lily Briscoe.[43] At the kitchen table in another of Taylor's harbour cottages, Beth Cazabon, subject to the demands of maternal and marital chores, is

---

[39] Joyce Cary, *Art and Reality: The Clark Lectures 1956* (Cambridge University Press, 2013), p. 149.
[40] Nicola Beauman, *The Other Elizabeth Taylor* (London: Persephone Books, 2009), p. 201.
[41] Virginia Woolf, *To the Lighthouse* (Harmondsworth: Penguin, 1972), p. 28.
[42] Elizabeth Taylor, *A View of the Harbour* (Harmondsworth: Penguin, 1954), p. 29.
[43] Woolf, *To the Lighthouse*, p. 28.

writing yet another novel. Beth's writing is never shown to Taylor's reader, but her leading lady's name ('Allegra'), and the select glimpses afforded of the melodramatic incidents that befall her, bode precisely the kind of romantic fiction that Lily Wilson craves.[44] Beth considers objectivity to be anathema to creativity – as a result, Taylor suggests, she is unable to detect the affair between her husband and their neighbour Tory Foyle. As Tory puts it: 'Writers are ruined people. As a person, you're done for. Everywhere you go, all you see and do, you are working up into something unreal, something to go on paper.'[45]

Desperate to escape the guilt of betraying her friend, Tory agrees to marry the harbour's out-of-season visitor Bertram Hemingway. He is in Newby to paint, although in fact (Taylor notes tartly), he 'was not much of an artist, in spite of having found a very good way of painting waves with tops folding over whitely, realistically'.[46] Although produced over the few weeks of the novel's diegesis, Taylor's acerbic humour works to make Bertram's work-in-progress seem almost as attritional as Lily Briscoe's. Unlike Taylor's, the mixed nature of Bertram's stylistic allegiances is detrimental to his artistic production. He toys with the idea of gaining access to the commanding position of the lamp-room of the lighthouse to paint that eponymous view of the harbour. However, his reflex response to the tower is one of quotidian realism rather than symbolism: 'in his mind's eye, his painter's eye, he saw the two men sitting in the little building which crouched in the shadow of the tower; there they were, in shirt-sleeves, fans of greasy cards in their hands'.[47] Bertram oscillates between that realist impulse and a romantic belief in the illuminating light of artistic genius. After a long pause while she contemplates his finished painting, intended to inspire public awe in the harbour-side pub, Tory responds, '"It is very good. Very like. There is only one thing ... it is quite obvious *where* it is, but not what time of day ..." Bertram said sadly: "In fact the very thing I most hoped to do I have failed over".'[48] Oscillating between harsh daylight and the dramatic, selective beam of the lighthouse, the light in the painting is all wrong.

W. J. T. Mitchell notes an enduring cultural ambivalence about ekphrasis as a possible and desirable practice, claiming this suspicion is grounded 'in our ambivalence about other people, regarded as subjects and objects in

---

[44] Taylor, *A View of the Harbour*, p. 256. [45] Ibid., p. 63. [46] Ibid., p. 6. [47] Ibid., p. 112.
[48] Ibid., p. 247.

the field of verbal and visual representation'.[49] This might call us back to *To the Lighthouse* ('subject and object and the nature of reality'), but its focus is on the interpersonal nature of ekphrasis and the fact that it is inescapably an ideological gambit.[50] What Heffernan defined as 'the verbal representation of visual representation' is a nexus for both moral and ethical issues.[51] The politics of Taylor's work, like that of much fiction deemed middlebrow, have been overlooked. That epistolary exploration of thinking between the genres of painting and writing with Ray Russell (himself a painter) took place between two working members of the Communist Party. Postwar, Taylor, like all her comrades, had to come to terms with a creeping loss of faith in the Soviet Union as exemplar. The politics of her fiction are inarguably domestic rather than international. Yet her mixing of genres, legible as a rebellion against a cultural hierarchy that branded her work as unimportant, can also be understood to defy what David Carroll identifies as 'the totalized, organic unity of the artwork as both an aesthetic and political ideal'.[52] This is Carroll's definition of the founding principle of fascist art, but after the Hungarian Revolution of 1956, we can appreciate its uncomfortable implications for those on the Left as well.

Taylor's negotiation of ethical living and artistic creation continues in the 1957 novel *Angel*. The novel's diegesis runs from 1885 to 1947, and it is the story of a grocer's daughter, Angelica Deverell, whose fevered adolescent novel *The Lady Irania* begins a lucrative, if critically derided, career in romance writing. Her fortune made, and mindful of her civic duty as an 'artist', she donates a large work by Victorian painter George Frederick Watts to Norley Art Gallery. Her selection is made on the advice of the traditionalist Lord Norley himself, in whose circles her wealth now allows her to move. Norley introduces her to his nephew, the man who, by means of attrition rather than passion, she will marry.

Esmé Howe-Nevinson is himself a painter, in a mode that is staunchly antithetical to the genteel classicism of Watts, and contemporary to the novel's publication rather than its setting. His paintings depict '[b]armaids and jockeys, barges in the fog, back-streets in the pouring rain, slag

---

[49] W. J. T. Mitchell, 'Ekphrasis and the Other' in *Picture Theory: Essays on Verbal and Visual Representation* (University of Chicago Press, 1994), p. 163.
[50] Woolf, *To the Lighthouse*, p. 28.
[51] James A. W. Heffernan, *Museum of Words: The Poetics of Ekphrasis from Homer to Ashbery* (University of Chicago Press, 1993), p. 7.
[52] David Carroll, *French Literary Fascism: Nationalism, Anti-Semitism, the Ideology of Culture* (Princeton University Press, 1995), p. 7.

heaps … the seamy side of life'. 'Don't forget the allotments, Uncle', Esmé's sister adds spitefully, 'with all the horrid little tool-sheds and rubbish-heaps'. 'And cemeteries', Esmé adds cheerfully. 'I am particularly fond of my cemeteries.'[53] Esmé's self-esteem as an artist is founded upon a faith in the authenticity of his depictions of working-class urban landscapes and interiors: 'those subfusc bars, with their ferns and patterned glass, marble-topped tables, immense hat-stands'.[54] This sets him apart, he believes, from the fantastical nature of his wife's romance. Broken by his experience of war and his betrayal of his wife, Esmé kills himself, leaving Angel increasingly to alienate her readership as she attempts to produce realist narratives that confront conflict, rather than offering escape from it.

Just as *A View of the Harbour* reflects, rewrites and interrogates *To the Lighthouse*, so *Angel* is intertextually entwined with Woolf's 1934 essay 'Walter Sickert: A Conversation'. Sickert, who died in 1942, remained a significant influence on English culture in the later 1940s and 1950s. At the Royal College of Art, as well as other major schools, Maurice Yacowar has claimed, 'Sickert was in the air'.[55] Postwar, Sickert's art and writing were widely disseminated, along with a new biography and a critical study. There was a large Arts Council exhibition in 1949, as well as several one-man shows in commercial galleries and numerous appearances in group exhibitions. In Woolf's interwar essay, a dinner guest claims they 'once read a letter from Walter Sickert in which he said, "I have always been a literary painter, thank goodness, like all the decent painters"'.[56] Years after Esmé's death, Angel is delighted when a young academic, Clive Fennelly, visits to research an article on the painter: 'She took his essay to the window, straining her eyes to read it. "A literary painter," she said. "I like that very much. That would have pleased Esmé". It seemed to her to be praise indeed; but Clive looked away, blushing'.[57] Fennelly is embarrassed because that 'literary' is intended as derogatory: by 1962, *The Oxford English Dictionary* is able to claim of a usage in a dictionary of art that the term is 'frequently used in a pejorative sense'. Taylor uses this meeting to force the instructive reassessment of Esmé's work in relation to Angel's, in its implication that Esmé's allegedly 'realist' paintings are as much an exercise in romanticising reality as his wife's novels. Taylor's perception of the ideological nature of art is acute, and often self-coruscating. Her

---

[53] Elizabeth Taylor, *Angel* (London: Virago, 2001), p. 89.   [54] Ibid., p. 136.
[55] Yacowar, *The Great Bratby*, p. 19.
[56] Virginia Woolf, 'Walter Sickert: A Conversation' in *The Death of the Moth* (London: Hogarth, 1947 [1934]), p. 26.
[57] Taylor, *Angel*, p. 240.

allegiance to the anti-realism of interwar modernism (and her own tendency to disrupt her narratives with modernist ellipses) is offset in the novel by her celebration of the empathetic power generated by the graphic representation of Angel's return to poverty. Like Cary, Taylor upholds the need for the postwar artist constantly to critique the ethics of the aesthetics to which they pledge allegiance.

'Between Red and Blue': John Berger and Modernist Realism

In her descriptions of Esmé's work and its dilapidated urban landscapes, Taylor presents an inventory of approved subject matter for the developing movement towards social realism in 1950s art. John Berger approvingly noted in the *New Statesman* in 1951 that artists like John Bratby, Derrick Greaves and Jack Smith had a particular 'way of looking at the back garden, the railways, the wharf, the street, the herring fisheries, the deck-chairs on the pier'.[58] Yet fellow critic David Sylvester claimed in 1954 that: 'Most of the painting produced by the present vaunted revival of realism has ... been romantic painting'.[59] 'How many fictions', he went on to ask, 'are made in the name of "realism" which are simply representations of squalor treated in a highly stylized manner?'[60] Sylvester was a powerful champion of a realist art that, while still clearly figurative, is derived from a reading of late modernism and prizes allusion, emotion and phenomenological experience above illustration and narrative. In a 1951 lecture at the Royal College of Art, Sylvester defined reality as 'the series of sensations and ideas that occur in the consciousness of each individual': a notably modernist interpretation.[61] His criticism upheld Francis Bacon and Lucian Freud as exemplary exponents of this notion of realist practice.

It was Sylvester who, in 1956, identified '[o]ne of the odder intellectual conflicts of the present time', which he dubbed the 'battle for realism'. Identifying the battle as a form of 'psychological warfare, waged by propagandists', his role in this conflict was not as detached as his tone might suggest.[62] Resident critic at the anti-Stalinist *Encounter*, Sylvester's art criticism and curatorship have been uncompromisingly characterised by Juliet Steyn as attempts to sever class consciousness from realist pictorial art. In this heavily ideological gambit, she claims, art criticism produced 'a

---

[58] John Berger, 'Treasure Trove', *New Statesman*, vol. 42, no. 1069 (1 September 1951), pp. 226–7.
[59] David Sylvester, 'Round the London Galleries', *Listener* (18 February 1954), p. 304.
[60] David Sylvester, 'Response to Barlow', *Listener* (18 March 1954), p. 485.
[61] David Sylvester, *About Modern Art: Critical Essays 1948–96* (London: Chatto & Windus, 1996), p. 17.
[62] Sylvester, 'Round the London Galleries', p. 896.

version of the postwar consensus in which ideological differences, class divisions and structural inequalities were being apparently eroded'.[63] In July 1952 at the ICA in London, Sylvester co-curated the exhibition *Recent Trends in Realist Painting*. The exhibition made an eclectic grouping, including work by Bacon, Bernard Buffet, Freud, Alberto Giacommetti and Graham Sutherland. This, the introduction to its catalogue claimed, should be considered 'a cross section, inevitably arbitrary ... of what has been done in recent years by painters who have been prepared to face up to appearances'.[64] Its understanding of 'realist painting', then, inflected realism as a fundamentally individualistic, rather than communal, project, and this was borne out in its hanging of a marked preponderance of portraits and single figures.

James Hyman has called the defining style of Sylvester's championed artists 'modernist realism'.[65] Although this term jolts an exclusively literary critic, it does suggest a productive means of analysing Elizabeth Taylor's own highly ambivalent relationship with literary narrative as a means both of driving and interrupting her observation of real life. 'Neither art itself nor life itself', Woolf called the middlebrow.[66] Taylor's ultimate withdrawal of authenticity from Esmé's work by wielding the very word, 'literary', that has such value for Woolf, suggests not just an ongoing critique of her own middlebrow status, but a wider dissatisfaction with the drawing of the postwar battle lines between modernism and realism.

In September 1952, a mere two months after Sylvester's *Recent Trends in Realist Painting*, the exhibition *Looking Forward* at the Whitechapel Gallery in London offered a very different perspective on realist art. Tending towards the prosaic subject matter favoured by Esmé, its focus was upon communal and domestic settings. John Berger, its curator, and a painter and writer himself, was the critic Sylvester was to have in his sights when he later wrote of the 'propagandists' of the 'battle for realism'.[67] Berger's exhibition was engaged in framing an English realist tradition to authenticate and support the work of painters like Bratby and Smith. '[J]ust as their comparatively representational pictures imply an acceptance of revolutionary theories of the last forty years', he wrote in the *New Statesman*, 'their way of looking at the back garden ... implies a fresh intention'.[68]

---

[63] Juliet Steyn, 'Realism versus Realism in British Art of the 1950s', *Third Text: A Very Special British Issue*, vol. 22, no. 2 (2008), p. 152.
[64] Quoted in ibid., p. 152.   [65] Hyman, *The Battle for Realism*.
[66] Woolf, 'Middlebrow', *Death of the Moth*, p. 113.
[67] Sylvester, 'Round the London Galleries', p. 896.
[68] John Berger, 'Treasure Trove', *New Statesman*, vol. 42, no. 1069 (1 September 1951), pp. 226–7.

The work (and writings) of Walter Sickert formed a crucial pillar of the exhibition's ideological construction. 'The more our art is serious', Sickert had pronounced in 1910, 'the more will it tend to avoid the drawing-room and stick to the kitchen'.[69] Ironically, it was Sylvester who coined the enduring name for Berger's vaunted group of artists, in a 1954 article that denounced their aesthetic inventory (and philosophy) as he named it. Their paintings, he claimed, were full of 'every kind of food and drink, every kind of utensil and implement, the usual plain furniture, and even the baby's nappies on the line. Everything but the kitchen sink? The kitchen sink too'.[70] Berger's introduction to the catalogue of *Looking Forward* adopted what might appear as a straightforwardly anti-modernist stance: 'The aim is to show the work of painters who draw their inspiration from a comparatively objective study of the actual world ... who are concerned with the reality of that subject rather than with the "reality" of their subjective feelings about it'.[71]

Through a sequence of articles across the decade, Berger orchestrated an attack on the artist Sylvester considered to be 'the most important living painter', Francis Bacon.[72] Bacon was, Berger claimed, 'a brilliant stage manager, rather than an original visual artist', and the emotion generated by his paintings, although undeniably haunting, is 'concentratedly and desperately private'. In the nub of Berger's critique, Bacon was left 'really outside the main tradition'.[73] But that marginally exclusionary tradition is still, importantly, one of English realism. However much he may reject Bacon on the grounds of an intrusive modernist solipsism, Berger recognised him as a practising realist, albeit one at fundamental odds with Berger's own ethical conception of that practice. Back in 1936, Walter Benjamin had rejected the concept of genius in art for its potential affiliations with fascism.[74] In postwar Britain, although political principles of community and individuality rage on, their simplistic divide into realist and modernist – *in extremis*, into communist and fascist – can no longer be sustained.

Berger's own painting career had halted by the time of the 1958 publication of his first novel, *A Painter of Our Time*. Its protagonist, Hungarian

[69] W. R. Sickert, 'Idealism', *Art News* (12 May 1910), p. 217.
[70] David Sylvester, 'The Kitchen Sink', *Encounter*, vol. 3, no. 6 (December 1954), p. 62.
[71] John Berger, 'Foreword' in *Looking Forward* (London: Whitechapel Art Gallery, 1952), quoted in Hyman, *The Battle for Realism*, p. 118.
[72] David Sylvester, 'The Paintings of Francis Bacon', *Listener* (3 January 1952), p. 29.
[73] John Berger, 'Francis Bacon', *New Statesman and Nation* (5 January 1952), p. 11.
[74] Walter Benjamin, *The Work of Art in the Age of Mechanical Reproduction* (Harmondsworth: Penguin 2008), p. 2.

émigré Janos Lavin, is tormented by an era which valorises its artists as genius outsiders: 'Again I hear the sceptic's questioning encouraged by the amoral limbo in which we live, and where any attempt to connect art with social responsibility and morality is immediately ridiculed by parody.'[75] The first of Lavin's paintings described in the novel is called 'The Waves', a title shared by Virginia Woolf's most experimental (most modernist) novel. In Hungary, Laszlo, Lavin's old friend, is making speeches about Socialist Realism arousing the consciousness of the working classes: 'What would he think of my *Waves*', worries Lavin, 'moving past like clouds over mountains?'[76] The serenity – of content and of palette – is read as antithetical to Laszlo's political engagement. 'There is no red in *The Waves*,' Lavin reluctantly recognises, 'I must wait for another canvas'.[77] His subsequent paintings worry, with increasing success, at techniques that combine subject, content, colour and form to produce authentic expression. Painting an individual portrait, Lavin asserts: 'Colour and form must make the expression of the character. The expression on the face is only a sign – like a weathercock. All temperament can lie between red and blue.'[78] Traditional conceptions of political allegiance are, of course, coloured in the same contrasting way.

In 1960, in *Permanent Red: Essays in Seeing*, Berger registered the ongoing effects of the schism caused within Leftist thought by the Hungarian Uprising of 1956. As he was later to put it, with striking simplicity, 'the USSR represented ... a great part of the force of socialist challenge to capitalism. It no longer does'.[79] The cover image for the 1951 *Looking Forward* exhibition catalogue – a rural British worker, rake in hand, gazing into the future – is early evidence of the difficulty of Berger's task of distinguishing social realism from Socialist Realism as the decade progressed.

The literary form of *A Painter of Our Time* – a diary enclosed within a first-person account – is ungainly. The novel's attempt to process raw, recent history into art is obviously incomplete. Once again, this alerts us to the impossibility of representing the complex cultural and political environment of postwar Britain in a traditional realist mode (as well, of course, of the difficulty of constructing recent history as sequential literary narrative). Yet nonetheless the novel is able clearly to communicate its commitment to thinking across disciplines (writing, painting) as well as aesthetic

---

[75] John Berger, *A Painter of Our Time* (London: Verso, 2010), p. 153.   [76] Ibid., p. 50.
[77] Ibid., p. 21.   [78] Ibid., p. 101.
[79] John Berger, *Permanent Red: Essays in Seeing* (London: Writers and Readers, 1985), p. 8.

categories (realism, modernism). In its most evocative metaphor, Lavin describes the process of cross-hatching:

> You have the first series of lines, then you have the second series in opposition to the first. But out of the two you get a series of diamonds.
>
> Now, if you look at these diamonds, remembering that every one has had to be drawn, you are overwhelmed by the length and complexity of the task. The diamonds are like the future we work for. Yet, courage. The first series of lines is there. All we have to do is cross them.[80]

In part, of course, this is a representation of the theoretical foundation of Marxism, dialectical materialism. Yet the image of the diamonds – their geometric beauty as well as their natural rarity – upholds Berger's conviction that the regeneration of society can be achieved by aesthetic means. His first novel, like Lavin's painting, attempts a form that defies the constrictive, and highly politicised, categories of realism and modernism. This practice reached its height in 1972 with *G* and its multi-modal rendering of human political, psychological and sensory experience. Berger was then to recognise that 'everything I have written has been no more than a preparation for ... *G*.'[81]

After the Second World War, British culture demanded a new set of aesthetic and ethical practices. These were required to participate fully in the national aspiration towards a politics predicated upon the democratic distribution of wealth and opportunity, but they nonetheless had an increasingly fraught relationship with socialism. Art in all its forms was given an unprecedented role in the rebuilding of Britain: indeed, its communal apportioning was enshrined in the financial structure of welfare provision itself. Under established political models, traditional realist practice would seem the way forward, and the period's reputation as one dominated by dogmatic realism, in its fiction in particular, still endures. However, the turbulent politics of the Cold War, as well as the enduring influence of interwar modernism, ensured that postwar realism was under intense and disaffected scrutiny.

This chapter has examined the use of the figure of the painter in selected fiction as a means through which novelists confronted the postwar loss of faith in a range of established certainties: political, spiritual and aesthetic. Visual art, with its distinct critical vocabulary, aesthetic genealogies and politicised assumptions, has, as Cary, Taylor and Berger all recognised, the potential to destabilise ossified literary practice in potentially productive

---

[80] Berger, *A Painter of Our Time*, p. 43.
[81] James Vinson, *Contemporary Novelists* (London: St James Press, 1976), p. 129.

ways. One of these traditional forms is the traditional *Künstlerroman*, the 'artist's novel': none of the novels considered here presents a narrative of formation. Rather, their emphasis is on disintegration, as Jimson ends in committing murder, Hemingway in resigned (if comic) failure and Howe-Nevinson in suicide. Lavin simply disappears. In its juxtaposition of diverse aesthetic practices and moral effects, ekphrastic fiction allows the exploration of a range of anxieties that themselves breach existing categorisations – be these red or blue, realist or modernist. As these fictional artists prove, this process is not without its casualties.

PART III
Reconfigurations

Introduction

Writing of the debates surrounding law reform and the definition of the 'modern homosexual', Chris Waters observes that the 'project of modernity in postwar Britain cannot be fully understood without reference to the emergence of new and distinctive modes for imagining the self'.[1] The chapters in Part III reveal the challenge of determining such modes and of reconstituting subjectivity in the aftermath of war. From the damaged masculinities and displaced selves examined by Leo Mellor to the disturbing – often dangerous – child figures explored by Victoria Stewart to the alienation of a rootless social mobility mapped by Tracy Hargreaves, this section is dominated by loss and an *unheimlich* sense of dislocation. But, while the first three chapters explore personal anxieties, psychic disturbance and the difficulty of writing the self, a rather different – and frequently more pleasurable – loss of innocence figures in Chapter 16: Charlotte Charteris's anatomy of postwar desire. Finally, the section turns to the more outward-facing reconfigurations of drama. In Claire Cochrane's study of the 'vital' but increasingly disenchanted voices of late 1950s theatre, the possibility of social transition is scrutinised and shockingly enacted through confrontational dramatic forms.

The chapters in this section thus explore the long-term repercussions of the postwar, from the traumatic legacy of war to the emergent voices of a new postcolonial Britain. Leo Mellor's opening chapter is the one most directly concerned with the impact of conflict, exploring in the work of John Lodwick, Kenneth Allsop, Rose Macaulay and Gavin Maxwell the unexpectedly visceral connection between postwar dislocation and the emergence, some twenty years later, of the 'new nature writing'. For the lives, subjectivities and landscapes examined here, the trauma of *not*

---

[1] Chris Waters, 'Disorders of the Mind, Disorders of the Body Social: Peter Wildeblood and the Making of the Modern Homosexual' in Becky Conekin, Frank Mort and Chris Waters (eds), *Moments of Modernity: Reconstructing Britain 1945–1964* (London: Rivers Oram Press, 1999), p. 137.

being at war is potent and demobilisation brings not liberation, but fragmentation. In the 'war on normality' waged by the protagonists of these fictions and autobiographies, Mellor exposes the textual traces that register the long-term psychic consequences of war. Victoria Stewart's chapter pursues a related concern: the impact of war on children and on the writing of childhood in adult fiction. The child as symbol is a potent force in the postwar, as any reader of Golding's *Lord of the Flies* (1954) will confirm. However, imbricated in Stewart's examination of children in the ostensibly gentler work of L. P. Hartley, Elizabeth Taylor, Marghanita Laski and Agatha Christie is an anxiety about writing itself, and in particular the writing of development. Developing fears only implicit in Lucy Pearson's chapter on the Carnegie Medal, Stewart reveals the extent to which the postwar child was imagined as a very real and present danger.

Stewart notes the oft-repeated criticism of British fiction's postwar insularity, and this complaint is taken up and developed by Tracy Hargreaves, who observes how swiftly such accusations were levied. Already in the early 1960s, postwar British literature was facing condemnation as parochial and narrow. Yet perhaps this narrow focus is all too understandable. In a landscape shaped by ruins, concepts of family, place and self are untethered, and the writer's blank page becomes both abyss and opportunity. In exploring the fiction of Philip Larkin and John Braine alongside Doris Lessing's insightful ethnography, *In Pursuit of the English*, Hargreaves examines the challenge of writing the self, and of inhabiting the role of the writer, in a landscape of cultural displacement. In literary movements across class, and across the gulf dividing colony from metropole, the English and their habits are exposed – along with the cracks beneath the plaster of postwar reconstruction.

A rather different, but not unrelated, sense of exposing the British is central to Charlotte Charteris's encyclopaedic examination of the literature of desire. This period was, she comments, 'an era in which love, in all its forms, its objects, and its practices, was pursued as never before', and against a context of legal, scientific and media investigation, she examines the fictions that mapped – and in some cases initiated – radical changes in how the British imagined sex and sexuality. Charteris suggests that fiction offered imaginative possibilities in excess of legal and cultural constraints, but this freedom did not extend beyond the written word, and – as Claire Cochrane illustrates in the final chapter of this section – staging such social and psychic transitions presented a challenge in an age still dominated by the censor's power. Recognising this power makes the theatrical output of the late 1950s all the more remarkable, and Cochrane exposes just how robustly dramatists dealt with the ever-more apparent limits of the 'new Jerusalem'. From Arnold Wesker to John Arden and the forgotten voices of Caribbean writers such as Barry Reckord and Errol John, Cochrane explores new writing that confronted questions of class, gender, race and national identity, and considers the international influences that were integral to the radical transformation of British theatre.

Back in the 1940s, Elizabeth Bowen, with characteristic insight, observed that 'you used to know what you were like from the things you liked, and chose. Now there was not what you liked, and you did not choose.'[2] The return of choice and personal responsibility – in the wake of the overwhelmingly communal demands of total war – would facilitate emergent subjectivities and new possibilities. But it would not be unproblematic, and this section reveals the extent to which a resurgent sense of the personal remained closely imbricated with public, political discourses. The 'age of affluence', precursor of the 'swinging' sixties, was also an age that exposed the limits of choice and the ongoing power of class distinctions. It revealed censorship, prejudice and reaction. By the end of the 1950s, Bowen's longed-for choices were beginning to look more complicated, and in a rapidly decolonising world, British culture was turning away from change towards a nostalgic recollection of former 'greatness'. There were signs of recovery in 'vital' theatre, the freedoms of literary self-expression and the emergence of a new generation of writers – but these transitions were, at best, works in progress, complicated by the deep and persistent traces of wartime cultural trauma.

---

[2] Elizabeth Bowen, 'The Demon Lover [Preface to the American Edition]' in *Collected Impressions* (London: Longmans, Green & Co., 1950), p. 49.

CHAPTER 13

Demob: The Postwar Origins of the New Nature Writing

Leo Mellor

> If we are looking for wildlife we turn automatically towards the official countryside, towards the great set pieces of forest and moor. If the truth is told the needs of the natural world are more prosaic than this. A crack in the pavement is all a plant needs to put down roots.[1]

Since the mid-2000s, a hitherto fugitive strand of British prose writing has found popular acclaim: a strand that discovers nature, and the possibilities of writing about nature, in the close-at-hand rather than the remote. Its texts have explored railway sidings disappearing amid brambles, charted cracks in limestone teeming with tiny ferns and mosses or surveyed the wildlife-rich 'drosscapes' and 'edgelands' – those liminal locales Victor Hugo once termed the 'bastard countryside'.[2] For writers as disparate as Robert Macfarlane, Michael Symonds-Roberts, Kathleen Jamie and Roger Deakin, a pursuit of 'the undiscovered country of the nearby' has been vital to what has become known as 'the new nature writing'.[3] However, while this has become a recognisable genre to readers, booksellers, critics and editors,[4] such a designation has also entailed impassioned debates, including contributions from the writers themselves, about the usefulness of corralling together such a variety of literary practices and ideologies. For, in the words of one critic, these writers: 'tend to be thematically wide-ranging and stylistically digressive, combining personal reflection with natural history, cultural history, psychogeography, travel and topographical writing, folklore and prose poetry'.[5] Given such a plethora of

---

[1] Richard Mabey, *The Unofficial Countryside* (Dorset: Little Toller Books, 2010 [1973]), p. 19.
[2] Cited by T. J. Clark, *The Painting of Modern Life: Paris in the Art of Manet and His Followers* (Princeton University Press, 1999), p. 27.
[3] See Joe Moran, 'A Cultural History of the New Nature Writing' *Literature and History* (2014) 23(1) pp. 49–63.
[4] See, e.g., 'Granta 102: The New Nature Writing', *Granta* (summer 2008).
[5] Moran, 'A Cultural History', p. 49.

possibilities around how 'nature' might be represented, recent criticism has both surveyed the current scene and then looked for its roots, testing the 'new' part of the generic designation. Origins have been proposed in a strand of neo-romanticism, the growth of environmental awareness from the 1960s onwards and the particularities of American traditions of 'wild writing'.[6]

Yet I believe it is worth going back a little further to investigate the immediate postwar years as formative for the possibilities of such writing. To look anew at the late 1940s as generative may be explanatory not only for why the new nature writing inhabits such a multiplicity of forms, but also for its preoccupation with the damaged, the transient and the close-at-hand. For the landscapes and cityscapes of the late 1940s were portrayed by writers at the time through a turn to nature: from bombsite rosebay willowherb to little ringed plovers on waste-tips, and from Thames Valley woodlands to slipways for butchering sharks, writers were drawn to a damaged nature inhabited by damaged humans. Such 'edgelands', in turn, came to symbolise for their authors simultaneously the rehabilitative challenges of the postwar period *and* the continuation of trauma and the militarised imagination.

Such a critical focus requires some literary-historical archaeology, especially as the complexities of British life and culture from the mid-1940s to the early 1950s remain strangely occluded.[7] Central to the socio-cultural scene of the mid-1940s onwards was demobilisation. On VE-Day, over 5 million men and women were in the British armed forces, and the vast majority were conscripts or 'war service only'.[8] Demobilising this militarised mass back into civilian life was a process both feared and longed for: a December 1943 poll voted it the most urgent postwar challenge facing Britain.[9] Nonetheless, there initially appear few literary representations of this angst; rather the most relevant, historically contingent, genre for the years of the late 1940s was the cinema, where the 'spiv-cycle', a series of British noir films, traced the lure of crime and the instability of morality.[10] Yet the shaky transition from conflict to 'peace', reflected in the inability of individuals to revert to civilian life, is one which has long been

---

[6] For an overview, see Deborah Lilley, 'New British Nature Writing', *Oxford Research Reviews*, DOI: 10.1093/oxfordhb/9780199935338.013.155.

[7] There are few exceptions to this neglect of the period, such as Bernard Bergonzi, *Wartime and Aftermath: English Literature and Its Background, 1939–60* (Oxford University Press, 1993); and Gill Plain, *Literature of the 1940s War, Postwar and 'Peace'* (Edinburgh University Press, 2013).

[8] Allan Allport, *Demobbed: Coming Home after the Second World War* (London: Yale University Press, 2009), p. 3.

[9] Ibid., p. 4. [10] Plain, *Literature of the 1940s*, pp. 210–13.

a mainspring of literature. In the twentieth century, the classic examples appear after the First World War – Rebecca West's *The Return of the Soldier* (1918) or Woolf's *Mrs Dalloway* (1925) – and it is also in literature that more complex modes emerged to deal with the aftermath of the Second World War, complicating the dynamics typified in the 'spiv-cycle' films. Henry Green's *Back* (1946) gives an early example of what N. H. Reeve has termed the ubiquitous 'uneasy homecoming syndrome';[11] while in Elizabeth Taylor's novel *A Wreath of Roses* (1949), the fantasist anti-hero needs a return to 'things crashing against me, violence', because, he asserts, the 'quiet will kill me' – but he inevitably ends up killing someone else.[12] Yet demob narratives also took a less familiar literary form. Across so many texts of the late 1940s, both fictional and non-fictional, the return of an individual from the forces does not necessitate a return to quotidian life; rather, it presages an extensive, ambivalent, and often violent involvement with the natural world. This chapter will consider four diverse examples: John Lodwick's *Peal of Ordnance* (1947), a novel which pursues a traumatised sapper from the seas to the woods; Kenneth Allsop's *Adventure Lit Their Star* (1949), a thinly fictionalised account of birds in the scruffy reservoirs of west London; Rose Macaulay's novel of loss in the verdant bombsites, *The World My Wilderness* (1950); and finally Gavin Maxwell's *Harpoon at a Venture* (1952), an exculpatory memoir of hunting sharks. In these radically heterogeneous works, there are some common features: an urge towards danger as a way of giving value to postwar experience; and a recoil from the strictures of the armed forces, coupled nevertheless with using the training, the physical materials and, indeed, the narrative modes gifted by conflict – all in their way kinds of war surplus. Most fundamentally, perhaps, each work encodes a belief, sometimes overt and sometimes implicit, that different landscapes all encode knowledge about human selfhood. Paying attention to these texts yields a more nuanced account of writing in the late 1940s, and its relationship to both the material and literary forms provided by the war; it also offers a way of rooting 'the new nature writing' in a powerful and neglected historical context.

John Lodwick, *Peal of Ordnance* (1947)

A demobbed soldier on the run, exhausted and stricken with amnesia, gets his leg caught in the jaws of a steel man-trap and crashes unconscious to

---

[11] Cited in ibid., p. 180.   [12] Elizabeth Taylor, *A Wreath of Roses* (London: Virago, 2011), p. 71.

a woodland floor. Around him the natural world he wished to camouflage himself amongst continues regardless: '[a] dung beetle, disturbed by the sudden typhoon, measured this new obstacle to its plans, altered course, and mounted sedately amid the bristles of a softly puffing cheek'.[13] This is a key moment, a potential-filled hiatus, in the plot of *Peal of Ordnance*, a novel whose author – John Lodwick (1916–59) – has now almost vanished from literary history. After childhood and work as a journalist in Dublin (including a friendship with the novelist Francis Stuart) he enlisted in the French Foreign Legion in 1939. After escaping from Vichy France, he fought in the Aegean, and then across the Balkans with local partisans; this wartime experience was tangentially charted in his history of the Special Boat Service: *Raiders from the Sea* (1945). After the war, he then wrote fifteen novels, was praised by Anthony Burgess, Somerset Maugham and Evelyn Waugh, and his picaresque yet violent stories became bestsellers for Heinemann.[14] *Peal of Ordnance*, Lodwick's first major novel, takes its title from a stage direction at the close of Shakespeare's *Hamlet* as a canon is ordered to be shot. But it also coyly hints at Lodwick's subject matter; this is a work about the deep and irrational *appeal* of ordnance, and the pleasures of destruction.

The plot is both desultory and compelling: the anti-hero Tamplin has spent the war in the Royal Engineers, blowing things up as he fights across North Africa and through Italy up until VE-Day in May 1945. He is then, without warning, demobbed and flown home from Trieste. He takes with him, on the advice of his avuncular commanding officer, a large amount of explosives and time fuses. On arrival back in Cornwall, he seems to embrace his former life as a fisherman – until he is knocked unconscious. *Peal of Ordnance* then becomes an amnesiac thriller, a sub-genre which could be dated back to Patrick Hamilton's *Hangover Square* (1941) or Eric Ambler's *The Dark Frontier* (1936); for Tamplin, forgetting everything apart from his training in explosives, travels up to London in a fugue state, remorseless with desire to destroy. He chooses various signifiers of power as sites for destruction: the Royal Artillery Memorial, the Albert Monument and the portico of the War Office. After inspecting his handiwork in the shape of a debris-field, he telephones the BBC as 'the wrecker', and plants bombs there too at Broadcasting House (luckily killing nobody) when he is disbelieved. Escapades follow – until he returns to Cornwall, now fully conscious of who he really is, and determined to settle down to

---

[13] John Lodwick, *Peal of Ordnance* (London: Methuen, 1947), p. 123.
[14] Geoffrey Elliott, *A Forgotten Man: The Life and Death of John Lodwick* (London: I. B. Tauris, 2017).

a quiet and law-abiding life. But the wider community – including the local doctor and Tamplin's wife – have other ideas: they contend that his temperament will never be conventionally satisfied in peacetime, and persuade him to become a smuggler. He fights new battles, complete with deck-mounted machine guns, against French patrol boats and the elements. The novel ends, *in medias res*, in a bank of Channel mist – with the forces of the sea as a narrative solution. It is not quite the fog of war, but the closest he can now get.

This is therefore not a book about the peace of nature, or therapeutic immersion in the rural. It rather gives us a way of understanding landscapes – and seascapes – with values other than the conventionally aesthetic (or the pieties of interwar nature conservation). For what the novel extols at length is the importance of cover, and camouflage – and Tamplin's progress through his personal bombing campaign is one where he thinks himself into an animalistic state, the better to evade his pursuer. This is seemingly incompatible with postwar life, and under questioning from his wife, Tamplin begins to explain why being demobilised might be such a bad thing; as, actually, 'you miss the excitement'.[15] Moreover, his connoisseurship of destruction also becomes visible, such as when the Saltash Bridge into Cornwall is discussed:

> 'Well did you ever think what a pleasure it would be to blow that up; that there might be an art to it, a whole complicated art involving maths and months of training?'
>
> 'Destroying things can't be an art, Bill?'
> 'That's just where you're wrong my girl.'[16]

He does not, in the end, attack that bridge. But while Tamplin might be a monomaniacal sapper with plastic explosive in a kitbag, he is also a proponent of *Sturm und Drang* as an aesthetic choice, a believer in a form of 'beauty' combining exhilaration with fragmentation. The diagnosis of the doctor and Tamplin's wife, when it comes at the close of the novel, recasts this urgency in more pragmatic, instrumental terms: '*you did it to get a thrill*. And if you've got to have thrills you're going to have thrills you can manage'.[17] Such thrills are thus monetised in his new life as a smuggler, in a resonant symbol of postwar capitalism.[18]

---

[15] Lodwick, *Peal of Ordnance*, p. 35. [16] Ibid. [17] Ibid., p. 171 (emphasis in the original).
[18] It is interesting to note the utter lack of moral censure with which Tamplin's smuggling life is recounted. Films of the postwar period, by contrast, tended to be judgmental, notably *The Ship That Died of Shame* (1955), where an ex-Royal Navy gunboat gains some primitive form of consciousness and revolts against her postwar use for drug-running.

This trajectory is the carrier, however, for a more reflective dimension to the work; Lodwick meditates on the transition from war to peace, and on how it becomes written on bodies as well as landscapes. When Tamplin arrives back in Cornwall, he goes out in his fishing boat to chase the war-glutted mackerel. The result is a disturbing image of symbiosis: 'nor had the fish lacked variety in their food, and the crustaceans, in this year of victory, were plumper, meatier than ever before, from an unmixed diet of stinking human flesh'.[19] The observation evokes Louis MacNeice's wartime poem 'Neutrality' (1942):

> But then look eastward from your heart, there bulks
> A continent, close, dark, as archetypal sin,
> While to the west off your own shores the mackerel
> Are fat – on the flesh of your kin.[20]

For both Lodwick and MacNeice, the counterintuitive image of consumption – humans becoming food for fish – seems not so much to evoke danger, as to remind the reader of the ongoing damage of war. It is the posthumous abuse of the body which shows the legacy of battles lost amid victory rejoicing. Such questions of how the war might be interpreted also preoccupy the final chapters of *Peal of Ordnance*. After making his escape from the police in London, Tamplin attempts to go to ground in bucolic woodland, where he is caught in a man-trap set for poachers, ironically located in the grounds of a home for wounded servicemen. The disturbing sequence which follows, as he is taken in and shown the mutilated bodies in the home and their 'recuperation' through art therapy, is in a line of descent from much visceral anti-war writing of the 1930s, typified by Dalton Trumbo's *Johnny Got His Gun* (1938) with its hero – horrifically mutilated in the First World War – wishing his own body to be displayed as a warning tableau about conflict.

Tamplin is only released from the wounded servicemen's home when he is vouched for by his former comrades – and his return is celebrated by them in a mood of near-ecstatic congratulation: 'the Regiment are proud of you'.[21] For the model of demob here is not that of the collective virtues of army cooperation revisited on civilian life, as it is in, for example, J. B. Priestley's novel *Three Men in New Suits* (1945); rather, it charts the transformation of the lone veteran into an agent of righteous destruction, one who reminds the populace – and the military hierarchy – to whom

---

[19] Lodwick, *Peal of Ordnance*, p. 41.
[20] Louis MacNeice, *Collected Poems*, (ed.) E. R. Dodds (Oxford University Press, 1967), p. 202.
[21] Lodwick, *Peal of Ordnance*, p. 156.

they owe their new-found peace. Indeed, Watson (Tamplin's former commanding officer) intones: 'There's many an officer, and many a squaddie, who'd do the same if he had the nerve and thought he'd get away with it. Just to strike a blow – just to show that we're the boys who don't forget'.[22] It is not accidental that their celebration of Tamplin's return is demonstrated through a small-scale piece of conflict as performance – they fire mortar bombs into a Surrey heathland – yet such an act is not just a piece of wanton violence. Their actions are salvos in a different war, between careful communities and careless wealth; thus, a London developer wishing to build a hotel on the 'little drop of gorse and rabbit warren' where 'the local kids play' is unequivocally warned off.[23] Watson's response has been to keep firing onto the heathland: waging a new war with the technology of the last, to keep the scrub unaltered, meaning that every morning 'beyond the sham Elizabethan gables of placid Esher a cloud of phosphorous smoke arose'.[24] Many years before Edward Abbey wrote *The Monkey Wrench Gang* (1975), his influential novel of American eco-activism and fun-with-explosives, laden with heavy drinking and homo-sociability, Lodwick was mapping out a similar ideological terrain on the other side of the Atlantic; one in which a defence of the environment is both violently cathartic and yet plangently compensatory for wars gone and lost.

Kenneth Allsop, *Adventure Lit Their Star* (1949)

The demi-autobiographical figure of the pilot invalided out of the RAF – stricken with TB – and needing to find something meaningful in a postwar life animates *Adventure Lit Their Star*, a novel of nesting birds, paranoid surveillance and radical alterity (for what is it like to be a plover?). A recent biography has provided much detail about Allsop's life and shown how his involvement in Common Wealth, a progressive wartime alternative to the Labour Party, marked both his politics and his postwar career as a naturalist and broadcaster.[25] Since its first publication, *Adventure Lit Their Star* has had a continually morphing existence (with multiple revisions in 1962 and 1974), but also has gained a centrality in popular histories of both the amateur naturalist and the changing fate of nature near London. The plot covers the years 1944 to 1945 and charts attempts by little ringed plovers (*Charadrius dubius*), a species of timid wading birds, to

---

[22] Ibid., p. 156.   [23] Ibid., p. 159.   [24] Ibid., p. 160.
[25] Mark Andresen, *Field of Vision: The Broadcast Life of Kenneth Allsop* (Oxford: Trafford, 2004).

breed in Britain for the first time. The first part of the book encompasses the summer of 1944 and is told from the perspective of the birds; the second part introduces Richard Locke, pilot and birdwatcher; then the third part features the summer of 1945 and follows Locke as he attempts to protect the nest and thwart egg-collectors.

The book is a compendium of birdwatching approaches and an essay in their lineages; Locke's own tactics come from his years in RAF Coastal Command, scanning horizons and discerning meaning from silhouettes. Initially, his trips to the gravel pits of West London appear 'very tame and humdrum after the sort of birdwatching the years in the RAF had made possible ... When flying he had been surreptitiously as watchful for birds as for U-boats'.[26] Birdwatching was, of course, both training for war – and yet also an escape from it, quite extraordinarily so in the journals compiled by British POWs as they watched martins and robins through the wire.[27] The militarisation of birdwatching persists not only in the act of observation in *Adventure Lit Their Star*, but also in the behaviour of the birds themselves. For example, when plovers fly near an experimental radar station, a painful cognitive dissonance occurs and Locke uses the language of war violence to articulate the perspective of the birds:

> ... an awful sensation which pierced them like a sword. They staggered crying shrilly with confusion and terror. The noise rose and fell. Bursting their skulls with fierce intensity, riving their ear drums and destroying the co-ordination of their wings. They swerved aside and fled with the dreadful screaming raking them like machine-gun fire.[28]

The initial metaphor of terror is ahistorical, 'a sword', but as the passage develops it becomes historically specific: the sonic screaming is 'machine-gun fire'. Even a kestrel hunts with 'the whirr and velocity of a shell'[29] and then flaps off with 'a Morse code action'.[30]

But the war appears not only in the texture of the writing; it also reshapes the texture of the landscape. The humans in Locke's text simply cannot fully fathom west London's attraction for the plovers. For this is a place, as Locke notes incredulously to himself, of inherent human disturbance of the natural world: 'he re-read the part about the little ringed plovers. It seemed to him incredible that a pair of ultra-rare birds should have chosen the shabby chopped-up country around Elmford with its

---

[26] Kenneth Allsop, *Adventure Lit Their Star* (Harmondsworth: Penguin, 1972), p. 74.
[27] See Derek Niemann, *Birds in a Cage: Germany, 1941. Four POW Birdwatchers. The Unlikely Beginning of British Wildlife Conservation* (London: Short Books, 2013).
[28] Allsop, *Adventure Lit Their Star*, p. 118.   [29] Ibid., p. 43.   [30] Ibid.

arterial roads, housing estates, factory rash and airfields.'[31] This litany is reminiscent of Orwell's lyrical refraction of melancholia very near the same map coordinates in 'On a Ruined Farm Near the His Master's Voice Gramophone Factory' (1933), and Allsop revels in descriptions of mud and gravel, burnt traces and the whiff of sewage farms. One plant typifies both his botanising eye and literary method: canary grass. This weed merits a typical textual detour, for each encounter the plovers make with other aspects of flora and fauna invariably leads to a digressive narrative path. The canary grass is the product, like the entire landscape, of contingency as well as human action: 'Over a year before, an old-age pensioner had cleaned out his goldfinch's cage and thrown the dirt, rolled in a newspaper, into the dustbin.'[32] A fragile chain of coincidences follows: one seed grows, quickly flowers, is then eaten by another goldfinch (but this time a wild one), which is then caught by a hawk and eaten, a seed falls from its body by a river, this also grows, where it then provides a home for a 'tiny amber spider', who is finally eaten by the male plover: and thus a chain of events (and organic matter) is absorbed into the main narrative.

Such moments, of sheer contingency *and* the indifference of nature to human actions, also become part of an ideological aspect to this text; it shows a way of looking at the British landscape through the eyes of creatures to whom bombs and planes are apparitional pieces of strangeness and human corpses not worthy of note. *Adventure Lit Their Star* is actually the second book Allsop wrote, although it was published first. Throughout 1943 to 1944, he had composed short stories concerning the lives and deaths of British fauna in wartime: *The Sun Himself Must Die* (1949) consists of four stories, centred on a weasel, a hobby, a kingfisher and a crow. Together they chart the conditions of nature (and what it means to be wild) in wartime Britain. It is resolutely anti-sentimental, attempting not to personify creatures, but rather to imagine a world where 'death has only one meaning: it is the occurrence that transforms living matter into food. [The animal] kills to live and death is never connected in its mind with itself; therefore it holds no terror.'[33] The hawk that dashes through *Adventure Lit Their Star* is revealed as Smirril – the now-released pet of an RAF Sergeant in *The Sun Himself Must Die*. And that short story makes plain that there can be no reunion or note of lasting memory; especially in the ending as Smirril, taking wing from a shattered spar of a crashed Wellington bomber, flies with his mate:

[31] Ibid., p. 77. [32] Ibid., p. 126.
[33] Kenneth Allsop, *The Sun Himself Must Die* (London: Latimer House, 1949), p. 64.

> ... in the dimming light, they spread their slender wings and cut across the sand plains, past the groups of waders, whose wild plaintive cries filled the dusk with a pure and liquid music, past the diminished mob of gulls which still squabbled over the shapeless form, around which clung the sodden flying blouse of a Royal Air Force sergeant.[34]

The paths of human and bird may now cross again, but no great lesson can be drawn apart from cosmic indifference. In a similar way, the close of *Adventure Lit Their Star* is marked with melancholia. The upper-class egg-collector is defeated through a clever ruse, the plover's nest is saved and the summer moves on inexorably. But in the midst of such success, the efforts of Locke are weighed in the balance as he sleeps out at night by the reservoirs:

> A loneliness stole upon him, a sense of isolation which mingled with an elusive sadness, and his mind returned to scenes and faces of other years. They floated hauntingly through the night, and for the first time for many months he felt nostalgia for the war.[35]

This quintessential demob emotion, 'nostalgia' for the war, is held against the apparent sense of belonging Locke has found amid the gravel pits of West London. When the plovers eventually migrate, '[t]he knowledge gave him a strangely mixed sensation of relief and sorrow'.[36] This untethered sensation is rendered in haunted prose; it consists of having known another species and understood the alterity of their existence, especially their mode of travel – flight – something that Locke, as a demobbed pilot, will never revisit.

Rose Macaulay, *The World My Wilderness* (1950)

Recent critical attention has led to a re-appreciation of the intricate and secretive writer, Rose Macaulay; her novel *The World My Wilderness*, with its moral ambiguities amid newly verdant postwar bombsites – spaces which are rendered both as actual zones and redolent metaphors – has continued to fascinate those analysing the period.[37] Nevertheless, a nature

---

[34] Ibid., p. 40. [35] Allsop, *Adventure Lit Their Star*, p. 182. [36] Ibid., p. 187.
[37] For instance, Kate Macdonald (ed.), *Rose Macaulay, Gender, and Modernity* (Abingdon: Routledge, 2018); Beryl Pong, 'The Archaeology of Postwar Childhood in Rose Macaulay's *The World My Wilderness Journal of Modern Literature* (2014) 37(3) pp. 92–110; and Ian Whittington, 'A Rather Ungoverned Bringing Up': Postwar Resistance and Displacement in *The World My Wilderness* in Allan Hepburn (ed.), *Around 1945: Literature, Citizenship, Rights* (London: McGill-Queen's University Press, 2017), pp. 48–65. My work on Macaulay is mainly in Leo Mellor, *Reading the Ruins: Modernism, Bombsites and British Culture* (Cambridge University Press, 2011), pp. 166–202.

writing which pays attention to verdant ruins has itself a longer history in fictional and non-fictional forms, with the violence of the war making actual what had long been imagined (or even wished for). In Richard Jefferies's *After London: or, Wild England* (1885), the title itself gives the plot, and the detail of what has happened is retold with violent pleasure by the narrator: '[f]or this marvellous city, of which such legends are related, was after all only of brick, and when the ivy grew over and trees and shrubs sprang up, and, lastly, the waters underneath burst in, this huge metropolis was soon overthrown'.[38] Jefferies inspired many, including the poet Edward Thomas, whose *The South Country* (1909) included a revenge fantasy for his beloved 'Nature':

> I like to think how easily Nature will absorb London as she absorbed the mastodon, setting her spiders to spin the winding-sheet and her worms to fill in the grave, and her grass to cover it pitifully up ... I like to see the preliminaries of this toil where Nature tries her hand at mossing the factory roof, rusting the deserted railway metals, sowing grass over the deserted platforms and flowers of rose-bay on ruinous hearths and walls.[39]

Thomas was not to know that rosebay, the only species he specifically names, would become emblematic, more than thirty years later, for the re-greening of London's ruins during and after the Second World War. For this plant (*Chamaenerion angustifolium*), with its purple-pink flowers and down-coated leaves, commonly known as Rosebay Willowherb, is thick in all writings about the bombsites that littered post-Second World War London, figuring as a talismanic species in *The World My Wilderness*. Macaulay's novel is an exuberantly strange tale which re-inscribes the value of wilderness in the city – but also records the utter indifference of nature to human suffering. Set in postwar London, amid the actual, social and familial ruins, its heroine is Barbary, a 17-year-old girl who rejects convention to live amid the overgrown bombed buildings. The action of rootless individuals taking root amid ruins is ripe for symbolism, and Macaulay uses multiple strategies to layer her story – notably by answering rhetorical questions from T. S. Eliot's *The Waste Land*. The first of these occurs early on in the novel in the midst of apparent hopelessness:

---

[38] Richard Jefferies, *After London: or, Wild England* (Oxford University Press, 1980), p. 36.
[39] Edward Thomas, *The South Country* (London: Dent, 1993), pp. 75–6.

> Where are the roots that clutch, what branches grow, out of this stony rubble? ... But you can say, you can guess, that it is yourself, your own roots ... the branches of your own being that grow from this and nowhere else.[40]

A lamentation is spun into an affirmation, and the entwining sentences which follow describe the ruins in terms of resurgent growth:

> ... a few blazing days when London and its deserts burned beneath a golden sun, and the flowering weeds and green bracken hummed with insects, and the deep underground cells were cool like churches, and the long grass wilted, drooped and turned to hay; then a number of cool wet days, when the wilderness was sodden and wet and smelt of decay, and the paths ran like streams, and the ravines were deep in dripping greenery that grew high and rank, running over the ruins as the jungle runs over Mayan temples, hiding them from prying eyes.[41]

When Barbary is forced to holiday with her stepmother on a deer-stalking estate in Scotland, she finds there, ironically, a repressive order which tames nature and allows no room for anything other than class-based hierarchy – and so she escapes back to the city. For London, by contrast, has become 'a wilderness of little streets ... grown over by green and golden fennel and ragwort, coltsfoot, purple loosestrife, rosebay willow herb, bracken, brambles and tall nettles'.[42] The text becomes giddy with botanical precision turned into a litany; a floral cloak over the jagged pain of death and destruction. It has biographical as well as theoretical poignancy; Macaulay's flat had been burned to the ground in a firebomb raid during 1941, and her botanising of the wild flowers (and sending them to the Natural History Museum) was itself a form of recuperation.[43]

Barbary's elder brother, Ritchie, is the only demobilised character in the novel – all others are deserters or youths. Ritchie has a phobic dislike of the verdant bombsites, and for him Eliot emerges as both a touchstone for civilisation and the acknowledgement of barbarism. On looking towards St Pauls' amid the 'damp brown bracken, the sprawling nightshade, and the thistles', Ritchie quotes him 'with a shudder' that gives a physical index to the potency of the words: 'I think we are Rat's Alley where the dead men lost their bones'.[44] Thus, not every character in the novel wishes to celebrate the ruins or believes in the resurgent organic as recompense for

---

[40] Rose Macaulay, *The World My Wilderness* (London: Virago, 1997), p. 129.   [41] Ibid., p. 79.
[42] Ibid., p. 53.
[43] See Jane Emery, *Rose Macaulay: A Writer's Life* (London: John Murray, 1991), p. 285.
[44] Macaulay, *The World My Wilderness*, p. 253.

destruction; for – like the hawk in Allsop and the fish in Lodwick – these plants also mark the eclipse of the human (and the city as a functioning urban environment) and the unsteady status of any survivors gazing in at the new London jungle. The novel patterns an ambivalence towards this resurgent greenery covering the ruins, from the guerrilla-love of its camouflage potential shown by Barbary, through Ritchie's phobic 'shudder' and the narratorial incantations of rhapsodic lists. The plants in *The World My Wilderness* are thus wilder – and weirder – than they initially appear, not only reaching back to models from Thomas and Jefferies, but also presaging the triffids of John Wyndham and the mutant-arboreal terrors of mid-period J. G. Ballard.

Gavin Maxwell, *Harpoon at a Venture* (1952)

Not all forms of demob writing reliant on resurgent but traumatised nature, as both a war-substitute and form of conflict-amnesia, take place in lowland Britain – indeed, for some texts, the urge for continued violence is met by what initially appears a retreat to an authentic wilderness. The naturalist and writer Gavin Maxwell (1914–69) started the Second World War commanding a mobile anti-parachute column in London. His memoir *Harpoon at a Venture* begins in Limehouse, narrating how an escape from the abjection of bombed buildings and squalid air-raid shelters is imagined:

> Deep in a spirit of nursery make-believe, we spread a map of Scotland on the floor, and like children lay at full length before it, propped on our elbows... We spoke of Hyskeir, Rona, Canna, Staffa; in my mind were the high-plumed seas bursting upon Atlantic cliffs and booming thunderously into tunnelled caverns ... I had drawn an extra red ring around the Island of Soay, an island unknown to either of us, below the Cuillin of Skye. We were still playing at make-believe; Soay was my Island Valley of Avalon, and Avalon was all the world away. Presently the sirens sounded, and down the river the guns began again.[45]

This is nature as abstracted, cartographical and near-sublime in its combination of fantasy and projection. But as the war progressed, Maxwell was posted as an instructor to north-western Scotland, only a few miles from Soay; there, he trained agents who would be sent into Nazi-occupied Europe. Then as the war ended he used some of his inheritance to buy

---

[45] Gavin Maxwell, *Harpoon at a Venture* (London: Rupert Hart-Davies, 1952), p. 19.

the island; but, in 1945, having failed to secure the fishing rights, he was faced with the problem of sourcing income.

Maxwell's answer came in what the British press named 'One Man's New War'. This was his attempt, between 1945 and 1949, to hunt Basking Sharks (*Cetorhinus maximus*) for their oil-rich livers.[46] *Harpoon at a Venture* was written to try and pay off some of the debts he incurred from the failure of this ambition; it is a bloody and laboriously detailed account of how almost everything went wrong, moving between nautical descriptions of the sublime in phosphorescent water to diary-like staccato listing of the technical problems. Yet, significantly, the whole text is framed scientifically: two appendices giving biological detail about the lives of these vast fish (their name is a misnomer, they are closely related to the herring and, unlike vice versa, pose no danger to humans). What Maxwell also records is a demob-zeitgeist. As his ramshackle operation was gearing up for another stage of bloody expansion – more boats, better harpoons and quicker butchery of the huge sharks – the newspaper articles describing the business prompted multiple letters to the Isle of Soay. The letters, begging Maxwell for work, were not only excited by the prospect of employment: '[I] had attracted a growing community who had been recently discharged from the Services and were restless for adventure. They had savings, varying, usually, between five hundred and a thousand pounds, and were willing to invest it all in a project that offered release from the ennui of peace-time.'[47] Maxwell was far from alone in attracting those disillusioned with peace. There were many real-life echoes of the position Tamplin found himself in *Peal of Ordnance*. Advertisements placed in 1945 to 1946 by recently demobbed soldiers and airman specifically sought highly dangerous jobs: 'Three Australian officers ... seek any adventurous undertaking or occupation ... little regard for personal safety ...'; or in another advert: 'Ex-naval officer, intelligent, fit, able, aged 24, seeking any hazardous occupation'.[48] There is a hidden history of post-traumatic stress disorder here; for even the authorised biography of Maxwell makes clear that the shark-fishing was partly pursued as a mode of self-medication. Maxwell's army medical notes from 1944 are direct: Dr James McDougal, the SOE (Special Operations Executive) Medical Officer at Arisaig, categorised him as a 'creative psychopath'.[49]

---

[46] See, e.g., 'Shark Hunting' in *Picture Post* (21 September 1946), pp. 4–6.
[47] Maxwell, *Harpoon at a Venture*, p. 183.   [48] Allport, *Demobbed*, p. 165.
[49] Douglas Botting, *Gavin Maxwell: A Life* (London: Harper Collins, 1991), p. 57.

Demob: The Postwar Origins of the New Nature Writing 263

The transition from killing Germans to killing sharks was near-seamless, and Maxwell kept around him those who had helped to train his wartime commandos. He is happy that his mate Foxy,[50] despite demobilisation, still ostentatiously abides by military ranks – such as when offering advice on hunting a submerged shark: 'Try him with the gun, Major'.[51] Maxwell's vocabulary also remains militarised: a cyclone turns the factory into a 'bombsite'[52] and, as the shark-killing becomes efficient, 'the beaches were packed again and once more at slack tide one looked down from the hill-top upon a sea crimson with blood'.[53] Others have noted how the shoreline around Soay thus becomes an echo of the D-Day landings, which Maxwell had himself helped to plan.[54] Nature here allows for compensatory bloodbath to deal with the fact that the actual war is over, and right until the end of the narrative Maxwell seeks solutions to keep his venture alive;[55] he cannot bear that his new conflict might now, with utter finality, be lost. This fixation on the continuing hunt has a literary history stretching back to the most famous text about fixated harpoonists, *Moby Dick*. Indeed, Robert Macfarlane has perceptively characterised Maxwell as an inheritor of Herman Melville's depiction of monomania, calling *Harpoon at a Venture* 'a saga of cetacide and capital. In it Maxwell – Queequeg with an Oerlikon, Ahab with an inheritance – demonstrates an awesome lack of interspecies empathy'.[56] This emotional lacuna matters; the Maxwell of *Harpoon at a Venture* is the shadowy but bloodthirsty ghost behind all that he subsequently wrote about wildlife. The shamanistic figure who was deified after the publication of his acclaimed account of life-with-otters, *Ring of Bright Water* (1960), was the same man who had run an extractive industry with cold calculations, likening his problem – of what to do with sharks' livers while in the midst of the ocean – to that of a hunter in an African jungle who stands astride 'the mountainous carcass' of the slaughtered elephant after hacking off the tusks.[57] This violence has not gone unremarked in the writing of the 2010s; indeed, Macfarlane and others have remained interested in *Harpoon at a Venture* and other postwar texts not because they offer a template for treading lightly, but due to the fact that 'they represent – in their psychodramas and their ultraviolence – the dark side of British place-literature. To read them as hymns to tranquility is trite. To engage with their tangled understories is mesmerising.'[58]

---

[50] Maxwell, *Harpoon at a Venture*, p. 25. [51] Ibid., p. 28. [52] Ibid., p. 91. [53] Ibid., p. 210.
[54] Robert Macfarlane, 'Shark Attack: Gavin Maxwell's Harpoon at a Venture', *The Guardian* (19 July 2014).
[55] Maxwell, *Harpoon at a Venture*, p. 215. [56] Macfarlane, 'Shark Attack'.
[57] Maxwell, *Harpoon at a Venture*, p. 86. [58] Macfarlane, 'Shark Attack'.

The especially 'tangled' ending of *Harpoon at a Venture* justifies the interest, for it appears to conclude twice. The book is filled with viscera and entrails, saws and armoured gloves: the paraphernalia of whaling. Then the (apparently) climactic pages bring in another, more hideous, aspect: putrefaction. A failure to preserve slaughtered prey for sale meant '[t]he sixteen tons of shark flesh in the factory pickle-tank had turned rotten'.[59] But decay also becomes abjection: a moral judgment. When Maxwell opens the tank it assaults him:

> Ammonia, dense, suffocating and almost visible, knocked me back from that trapdoor as completely as a robot fist ... Holding my breath, I steeled myself to peer down into the dusk of that nightmare cave. To say the surface was crawling would be an understatement so gross as to defeat its own object. It was alive, heaving, seething, an obscene sea such as Brueghel might have conceived, alive as the sanctuary of Beelzebub himself, with a million million grubs, twisting turning, writhing, as though beneath that surface layer of putrescence were the struggling bodies of all the wounded but resurrected dragons that we had attacked and that had escaped us. Those million million grubs would become a million million flies; my mind's eye saw the island darkened with them as with a swarm of locusts, Avalon eclipsed by the Prince of Flies whom I had summoned up.[60]

Maxwell has brought the war – and industrial processes – to the island he dreamt of as defining purity and escape, and it is now metaphysical in its gross abjection; he is fighting locusts and dragons. Levels of self-knowledge vary in this work, and are performed in different ways; but it is in this vision of a vengeful nature that he comes closest to regret for his actions.

However, regret switches swiftly to mythologisation as Maxwell finally closes his text with quotations from Louis MacNeice's 'Life of Lord Leverhulme' (1938). The poem depicts the failure of a grandiose project to build a new herring port – Leverburgh – in the 1920s, and Maxwell's use of it historicises his own failure within a continuum of abandoned projects:

> All that remainder of Lever's plans
> Were some half built piers and some empty cans,
> And the islanders with no regrets
> Treated each other to cigarettes ...[61]

What he is also doing, by invoking transience in a *longue durée*, is converting his shark-fishing project from economics to art and showing how the aesthetic can do more with remnants and wreckage than it can from any success. His work, both physical and literary, is becoming part of the long

---

[59] Maxwell, *Harpoon at a Venture*, p. 216.   [60] Ibid., p. 217.   [61] Ibid., p. 228.

history of how nature absorbs back human structures and endeavours with remorseless incremental decay. On the isle of Soay, in a deserted cove, Maxwell's butchered sharks and plywood buildings are now themselves joining a continuum of ruins and bones, being scabbed over by moss and lost in rosebay willowherb – a plant spread far by human conflict and disturbed soil.

Coda

In 2010, Richard Mabey – doyen of British naturalists – published *Weeds*. This was a guide to the history of common weeds, and a celebration of their energy and tenacity; indeed, the subtitle offered an ideological slant as well as more descriptive detail: *How Vagabond Plants Gatecrashed Civilisation and Changed the Way We Think about Nature*.[62] The species considered by Mabey ranged from thistle to the dandelion and from knotgrass to rosebay willowherb, and he set them within multiple cultural contexts (including, in a chapter on triffids, the literary imagination). One of the talismanic moments he narrates is the lecture given on 1 May 1945, just a week before VE Day, by the director of Kew Botanical Gardens. This lecture was on the weeds of London's bombsites, and it was a mix of wonder and solemn record, covering both the biological reasons for the efflorescence of bracken and ragwort, and meditating on what Londoners thought of this new verdancy covering burnt ground and ruined buildings. Mabey chooses this lecture as important as, in his words, it stands as a formalised way of thinking taxonomically about 'a botanical invasion of their violated city'.[63] But, as Mabey acknowledges later in *Weeds*, referencing Macaulay's botanising of the bombsites, it is equally a vital example of chaos and accident. Such reaching back to moments in the botanical history of London underpins Mabey's writing, which returns again and again to the generative potential for nature in places close-at-hand, and which seem apparently marginal or hostile. Here, then, in the bombsites of London, we find the origins of a *leitmotif* shaping his oeuvre since his very first book, a compendium of a year in the margins of London, *The Unofficial Countryside* (1973).

The potency of these excursions into the edgelands has not diminished, for in the most recent edition of *The Unofficial Countryside*, Iain Sinclair's introduction shows why Mabey, being interested in 'the transitional quality of unwritten places', has been so significant for so many writers and

[62] Richard Mabey, *Weeds* (London: Profile, 2010). [63] Ibid., p. 23.

artists.[64] Indeed, Mabey is central to the genesis of 'the new nature writing' through his multiple books and the continual attention to detail they present; even if he questions the term himself. Yet the places Mabey investigates in *The Unofficial Countryside* are those of the immediate postwar years, zones not yet redeveloped, a fact he poignantly notes in the 2010 edition. Moreover, his inspirations, such as the birdwatching abilities of Allsop – to whose memory the book is dedicated – and his formative locales, come from his childhood years of the late 1940s and early 1950s; and in doing this Mabey provides both a living and textual connection. For while the 'new nature writing' may have an impact on how we conceive of our future urban environment, it is also shaped by an occluded historical moment, and by those writers who, having survived the war and demobilisation only to emerge into ennui and bewilderment, looked again at nature in the strange world of the close-at-hand.

[64] Iain Sinclair, 'Introduction' in Richard Mabey, *The Unofficial Countryside* (Toller Fratum: Little Toller, 2010), p. 7.

CHAPTER 14

Old Haunts: Childhood and Home in Postwar Fiction

Victoria Stewart

Writing in 1951, the novelist and critic P. H. Newby noted a recent propensity among fiction writers to take childhood as the subject of their narratives. He attributed this to the fact that for 'most people' who were establishing a literary reputation in the postwar years, 'experience could be divided into two halves: childhood and adolescence on the one hand and war on the other ... [O]f the two, childhood probably proved the more attractive.'[1] Although Newby had some words of praise for writing he saw as epitomising this tendency,[2] he was ultimately critical of what he saw as its implications, believing that such works were often tinged with nostalgia and underpinned by the untenable assumption 'that innocence is necessarily good and experience necessarily evil'.[3] A child's bewildered view of the world might seem to echo the bewilderment provoked by the uncertainties of postwar society, but ultimately, for Newby, these works were 'cosy ... narrow and parochial'.[4] This particular strand of postwar literature was seen by Newby, then, to illustrate the apparent inability of British writing to develop new forms and new approaches in the wake of the war.

Certainly, some of the works by the authors Newby cites recreate a child's eye view of the world and, in the process, downplay explicit engagement with social and political context in favour of the apparent timelessness of the trajectory from innocence to experience. However, if there is an evasion of historical specificity within some of these texts, they are nevertheless often powerfully inflected by the historical context from which they arise. Particularly striking is the frequency with which ideas about the domestic come into play in child-centred texts from the late 1940s and early 1950s, the period that will be my focus here. Narratives featuring children displaced from home can be read as coded engagements

---

[1] P. H. Newby, *The Novel 1945–1950* (London: Longmans, Green & Co., 1951), p. 8.
[2] He names Denton Welch, A. L. Barker, Olivia Manning and Francis King. Newby, *The Novel*, p. 8.
[3] Ibid., p. 9.   [4] Ibid., p. 10.

with the large-scale evacuations of children that characterised the war years in Britain, but, just as the anxieties provoked by returning servicemen are worked through in a variety of ways in literature of this period,[5] so the removal of children from the family and their subsequent return are seen to provoke an ambivalent response. Equally, the innocence to experience trajectory is almost inevitably far more complicated than a straightforward movement across a binary divide.

In their work on the wartime experiences of children in the home they ran in Hampstead, North London, Dorothy Burlingham and Anna Freud noted that 'normal' psychical development is made difficult in wartime not only because of the problems caused by displacement from the home and separation from parents, but also because it is hard for children to be educated away from their impulse towards aggression when the effects of violence are so prevalent in the world outside: 'Children will play joyfully on bombed sites and around bomb craters ... and throw bricks from crumbled walls at each other. But it becomes impossible to educate them towards a repression of or a reason against destruction while they are doing so.'[6] The boundaries between children's often violent fantasy life and the evidence of violence in the real world are shown to be permeable when the bomb-site becomes a playground. Ideas such as these, challenging 'the common view of the child as innocent and gentle', were, as Michal Shapira shows, increasingly influential during this period and are echoed in postwar fiction.[7] Although Francis King's novels or L. P. Hartley's *The Go-Between* (1953) focus on children from privileged backgrounds, brought up at a spatial and temporal distance from the destruction described by Burlingham and Freud, these protagonists often experience a similar puncturing of the fantasy world by the real. But these children are never completely innocent and are often seen by adults to constitute a threat because they already know too much. In this regard, narratives which attempt to recreate a child's consciousness can usefully be contrasted with those in which children are seen largely from an adult perspective, including novels as varied in approach as Agatha Christie's *Crooked House* and Marghanita Laski's *Little Boy Lost* (both published in 1949). As in these

---

[5] See Victoria Stewart, *Narratives of Memory: British Writing of the 1940s* (Basingstoke: Palgrave, 2006).
[6] Dorothy Burlingham and Anna Freud, *Young Children in War-Time in a Residential War Nursery* (London: George Allen & Unwin, 1942), p. 31. Gill Plain considers how Burlingham and Freud's ideas are engaged with in a number of novels specifically concerned with evacuation. See Gill Plain, *Literature of the 1940s: War, Postwar and 'Peace'* (Edinburgh University Press, 2013), pp. 54–61.
[7] Michal Shapira, *The War Inside: Psychoanalysis, Total War, and the Making of the Democratic Self in Postwar Britain* (Cambridge University Press, 2013), p. 72.

two examples, children can be constructed as the enemy within, or as the displaced victim, or they can vacillate between these two positions. Later in the 1950s, the anxieties expressed here are reconfigured in the context of increasing concerns about juvenile delinquency, an issue that raises questions about both the causes of criminality and, more generally, the forces at play in shaping subjectivity. Even when their action does not unfold in wartime, these novels can be read as engaging with recognisable contemporary concerns about what belonging, and, by extension, citizenship might mean in postwar Britain.[8]

Displaced Persons

Characterising twentieth-century books for children, Katie Trumpner suggests that many works 'treated the intact household as a limit to action. For the plot to begin, child protagonists needed to be orphaned, cast away, or left by negligent parents; war offered a particularly dramatic, prolonged and perilous opening to adventure and history.'[9] These comments hold true for a number of postwar novels for adults featuring child focalising narrators, but the protagonists of, for example, Francis King's novel *Never Again* (1948) and G. F. Green's *In the Making* (1952) are not the intrepid adventurers found in the works of C. S. Lewis or Arthur Ransome.[10] Instead, physical displacement from home to school is the spur for inner, psychological exploration. These novels can thus be linked to the *Bildungsroman* tradition, and each edges towards an exploration of tabooed sexuality. This is part of what makes them 'grown-up' rather than children's novels, and it complicates readings that would emphasise nostalgia, as well as the notion that growing into adulthood involves gaining a more complete sense of oneself as part of a community. King's and Green's protagonists are never under any illusion about the fact that their sexuality

---

[8] My focus here is on novels. For the treatment of childhood in wartime and postwar short fiction, see Victoria Stewart, 'Mid-Twentieth-Century Stories' in Ann-Marie Einhaus (ed.), *The Cambridge Companion to the Short Story in English* (Cambridge University Press, 2016), pp. 115–27, esp. 123–7, where I discuss stories including A. L. Barker's 'The Iconoclasts' (1947) and Angus Wilson's 'Raspberry Jam' (1949).

[9] Katie Trumpner, 'The Children's War' in Adam Piette and Mark Rawlinson (eds), *The Edinburgh Companion to Twentieth-Century British and American War Literature* (Edinburgh University Press, 2012), pp. 498–507, 499–500.

[10] Francis King (1923–2011) was a prolific and critically acclaimed novelist and short story writer whose work often dealt with the lives of gay men. *In the Making* is the only novel published by G. F. Green (1910–1977), although his small oeuvre also included short stories and essays.

must be either repressed or channelled into the acceptable forms of homosociality.

In King's novel, finding one's place is both a literal and figurative process. Hugh, a child of 7 or 8, is sent back to live with unsympathetic relatives in England after the death of his parents in India in what appears to be an arson attack. Sent on in due course to a preparatory school, he does not suffer extremes of either physical or psychological bullying and attempts to convince himself that school is, at least, better than his uncle's house. Hugh has the partial relief of his friendship with Chorley, which reaches a crucial juncture when he is invited to stay at Chorley's home for part of the holidays. Observing that 'one day' the house and grounds will belong to him, Chorley asserts that he will share his inheritance with Hugh: 'We're friends, aren't we?' Hugh does not dissent, despite having doubts:

> He knew that there would come a time when this offer would be disregarded; he had lost all confidence in the future, knowing it to be a treacherous ally, rich in promises which it never fulfilled. But it was a pleasant make-believe; he almost accepted it. Acceptance was easy, lying beside Chorley on such an afternoon.[11]

Chorley's offer to 'share' his material wealth with his friend can be read as the child's reaction to his friend's lack: Hugh would not be staying with him if he had such a home of his own. But Hugh's reaction encodes his knowledge that such 'sharing' will never be possible. He does not disabuse Chorley, but chooses to play along with his fantasy, as though silently acknowledging that he knows better than Chorley what 'sharing' could mean in an ideal world. It is significant, then, that despite the lack of historical specificity in the setting of this novel, it represents a predicament – the need for homosexual relationships to be kept secret – that is still recognisable in the postwar period.

Hugh's acknowledgment that the future is a 'treacherous ally' and his conscious decision to attempt to live in the present moment may seem a very adult rationalisation of his situation and, indeed, one specifically inflected by a wartime sensibility. There is an echo here of how G. F. Green characterises children's perceptions of time in his preface to *First View* (1950), an anthology of short stories about children that he edited. For Green, the child has 'a clarity of association' and a 'sense of timelessness'

---

[11] Francis King, *Never Again* (London: Home and Van Thal Ltd, 1948), p. 180.

that 'makes his present eternal'.[12] In this analysis, the child might be the ideal subject for a modernist narrative, one which focuses on individual perceptions and foregrounds the subjective experience of the passage of time. Parts of Green's novel *In the Making*, which, like *Never Again*, is largely set in a school, certainly echo a modernist aesthetic in their evocation of the subjectivity of the protagonist. Randal Thane is sent to boarding school after his aunt and uncle observe that he is being smothered by his over-protective mother. His aunt implies that his bedroom at home could constitute a risk to his health or even his life:

> '... Just look at the house. Look where Randal sleeps.'
> Randal looked where Aunt Grace was pointing towards his window. He had always had a great affection for his window, the kindly face of his bedroom. It was hidden high under the roof, and everything about it was especially for him; the amount it was opened, the tin on the ledge, the yellowdamp like a bear under the eaves; all these things were secrets between himself and his room concerning no one else, part of a different life.[13]

What Randal perceives as familiar and cosy is constructed by his aunt as placing him in peril; she points out that the leaning chimney could 'smash through the house like a bomb'.[14] The potential for him to be buried in the wreckage if the chimney should fall echoes the aunt's earlier assertion that his mother's affection places him in danger of 'suffocation'.[15] The comparison drawn between the chimney and a bomb reminds the reader, of course, of what possibly lies in the future, in terms of the temporal frame of the narrative, which appears to unfold in the interwar period.

Like Hugh, Randal does not have a markedly traumatic time at school: although he is, on his arrival, disorientated, lapsing into a 'fantasy of wandering through multitudinous corridors, flights of unending stairs, rooms with vast darkening windows, through a country of light and darkness, of nightmare',[16] the enduring impression is that, despite the strictures placed on pupils' movements, the school is a more pleasant environment than the crumbling attic at Randal's family home. Early on in his time at school, for example, Randal discovers the companionable pleasure of curling up on the sofa in the Green Room: 'Here he would transform as if by magic into laughter and warmth those events which had terrified him in the daytime.'[17] Transformation of a different sort is

---

[12] G. F. Green, 'Foreword' in G. F. Green (ed.), *First View: Stories of Children* (London: Faber & Faber, 1950), pp. 13–16, 15.
[13] G. F. Green, *In the Making: The Story of a Childhood* (London: Penguin, 2012), p. 20.
[14] Ibid., p. 20.   [15] Ibid., p. 19.   [16] Ibid., p. 39.   [17] Ibid., p. 42.

a keynote of a climactic scene in the novel, the Halloween fancy dress party, when, costumed as a pierrot, Randal, now aged 11 or 12, undergoes a hallucinatory sexual awakening when confronted by his schoolmate Felton, who is dressed as a harlequin:

> A world dazzled him ... It shattered on him its glittering facets, a kaleidoscope of the real and unreal ... Felton stood against the gold flames ... His slim body was pressed into the skin-tight diamonds of red and green and yellow which, without a wrinkle, barely hid his loins.[18]

For Randal, costume not only liberates the wearer, but also licenses looking, providing a pretext for his scrutiny of Felton's form. Yet this scene is also a reminder that away from this closed world, disguise and duplicity will be a necessity, given Randal's sexual preferences. Indeed, while the school may foster homosocial bonds, relations between boys are scrutinised and regulated: after Randal acts on his feelings and is discovered in bed with Felton, he is told he must leave the school at the end of term and is kept sequestered from the other pupils in the meantime.

In the Making concludes with Randal exiled from school, but, even as his train pulls out of the station, beginning to write a poem to Felton: 'He was filled with an extraordinary knowledge of himself and of the permanence of his life ... The poem and Felton possessed his mind. The two patterns of his life were achieved.'[19] Although the Halloween party scene has some of the magical qualities of the party at the lost domain that is central to Alain-Fournier's *Le Grand Meaulnes* (1913), the implication is that Randal is not doomed, as Meaulnes is, to loss. At the climax of the novel, he is literally and figuratively moving on and the *Bildungsroman* is revealed to be a *Künstlerroman*. Randal may not have found his place spatially at the end of the narrative, but the reader is not left with the feeling that he is displaced. Similarly, at the end of *Never Again*, Hugh has joined his friend Chorley, who is on a recuperative holiday in the Alps, and who regrets that Hugh must return first to school and then to his uncaring aunt and uncle. Hugh is phlegmatic: 'It won't be so bad now. I've got used to it ... Even school seems less awful ... The great thing is not to care too much. Nothing matters if one doesn't let it matter.'[20] Like Randal, Hugh seems to recognise that feeling at home in one's self is as important as feeling at one with one's surroundings. This assertion has added point given that each of these novels deals with awakening to a still socially tabooed sexuality.[21]

---

[18] Ibid., pp. 85–7.   [19] Ibid., p. 145.   [20] King, *Never Again*, pp. 213–14.
[21] Green dedicated *First View* to the memory of Denton Welch (1915–48), some of whose work also engages with these issues.

These two novels, then, contrast starkly with a much better-known text from the period which on the surface has a similar trajectory, L. P. Hartley's *The Go-Between* (1953). Like Hugh in *Never Again*, Leo, Hartley's protagonist, spends a holiday from school at a friend's home, but the difference in social status between Leo and Marcus is noted from the outset. When not at school, Leo, the son of a deceased bank manager, lives with his mother in 'an ordinary house, set a little back in the village street, behind looped chains, of which I was rather proud', and he admits that Marcus may have been misled as to his social status by the fact that this house is called Court Place.[22] Marcus's family home is Brandham Hall, described by Leo's gazetteer as 'an imposing Georgian mansion ... standing in a plot of some five hundred acres'.[23] Unlike King's and Green's novels, *The Go-Between* is narrated retrospectively, with Leo, apparently still living at Court Place, looking back to the summer of 1900 from the early 1950s. From the outset, when he describes discovering his childhood diary, dispossession and displacement are the novel's keynotes:

> had it not been for the diary, or what the diary stood for, everything would be different. I should not be sitting in this drab, flowerless room, where the curtains were not even drawn to hide the cold rain beating on the windows ... I should be sitting in another room, rainbow-hued, looking not into the past but into the future: and I should not be sitting alone.[24]

Leo admits to feeling self-pity (drawing the curtains would be easy enough, after all), but is evidently convinced that he was permanently damaged by what happened at Brandham Hall.

From the start of his visit, Leo feels socially awkward, not possessed of the right manners and unused to dealing with servants, but class-related anxiety is just one aspect of his troubles. Initially falling under the spell of Marcus's sister Marian, he is drawn into acting as go-between for her and her lover, Ted Burgess, a neighbouring farmer. The adult narrator reconstructs his childhood ignorance of the nature of Marian and Ted's relationship, while admitting that he was 'a born intriguer';[25] having a secret is as important as the nature of what is concealed. Leo is eventually confronted with an adult expression of sexuality, when Marian's mother demands that he lead her to Marian and Ted's trysting place, a half-ruined outhouse, and they see the lovers together, 'two bodies moving like one'.[26] This is only part of what traumatises Leo, however; he is made to feel guilty by Marian's mother for having facilitated the relationship, but, more importantly, he

---

[22] L. P. Hartley, *The Go-Between* (Harmondsworth: Penguin, 1958 [1953]), pp. 22–3.
[23] Ibid. pp. 32–3.   [24] Ibid., p. 8.   [25] Ibid., p. 86.   [26] Ibid., p. 262.

vacillates, throughout the novel, between constructing each of the two alluring adults as an object of desire. The sight of the lovers together belatedly provides him, in graphic form, with the knowledge that he had demanded from Ted in payment for carrying his messages to Marian, but which Ted had not supplied: 'you said you were going to tell me about spooning'.[27] Ted hedges around this issue, telling Leo that imparting this intelligence is a 'job for your dad' and feeling nonplussed at Leo's insistent demand, eventually descending into anger and sending Leo away: 'He towered above me, as hard and straight and dangerous as his gun.'[28] Whether for the child or the adult narrator, there is a promise embedded in this ostensibly threatening image.

Leo's constant movement between Ted's cottage and Brandham Hall emphasises that he truly belongs in neither place. His confrontation with Ted takes place in Ted's 'sparsely furnished kitchen, with its bare, hard, worn surfaces, its utter lack of the femininity that children of both sexes feel at home with'.[29] These unforgiving surroundings, recalled by the older Leo looking back, are echoed in the description of the room at the Hall that Leo is moved to when Marcus falls ill. He initially wonders if he will be expected to share a room, even a bed, with one of the adult guests as he has with Marcus, but is reassured, in part at least, when he opens the door: 'It was a very small room, almost a cell; and the bed so narrow it could be only meant for one person ... Whether I was more or less than I had been, I couldn't decide.'[30] This uncertainty of status is at least offset by a gain in privacy; Leo has previously retreated to the lavatory to read a letter from his mother, this being the only place in the house where he knows he will not be disturbed. The narrow bed reminds the reader that the adult Leo is alone; it is notable also that although young Leo imitates the adult male guests by walking round the breakfast room while eating his porridge,[31] the smoking room, the preserve of male sociability, is barred to him, being described as 'a room into which [he] had never penetrated'.[32] The corollary, then, of the freedom of movement that allows Leo to act as Marian and Ted's messenger is a sense of being constantly in transit, having no fixed place – socially, spatially, sexually – of his own. Leo is unable to accept or embrace this lack of rootedness because he never resolves his relationship to his adult objects of desire. Tinged with the trauma not just of confronting adult sexuality but of being at least partly responsible for the revelation of Marian and Ted's affair and Ted's

---

[27] Ibid., p. 176. [28] Ibid., p. 177. [29] Ibid., p. 115. [30] Ibid., p. 75. [31] Ibid., p. 62.
[32] Ibid., p. 121.

subsequent suicide, Leo's entry into adulthood is not characterised by the incipient adventure that seems to await King's and Green's protagonists. Visiting Brandham as an adult, Leo finds that, after most of the adult males were killed in the First World War, Ted and Marian's son was silently adopted into the family. Now, after another war, the family line seems set to die out, but this is a source of melancholy for Leo, rather than something that might finally free him from the bonds of the past.

The Enemy Within

Marian and Ted presume that Leo does not know enough to wonder what kind of relationship has been established between them. But, not unlike other child characters in works from this period, Leo is more knowing than he initially seems. Leo's childhood consciousness is of course reconstructed from his own adult perspective, meaning that he often provides for the reader a gloss on his childhood sentiments; in other novels, the child is seen from the perspective of either a first-person adult narrator or a third-person narrator, and is constructed more explicitly as a threat, an enemy within. These depictions jar with conceptions of the child as a subject in need of care, and with the assumption of nostalgia as the keynote of fictions about childhood.

Even one's own children can seem threatening. In Elizabeth Taylor's novel *A Game of Hide and Seek* (1951), Harriet, married to Charles and with a 15-year-old daughter, Betsy, meets again with Vesey, whom she loved when she was young. She has kept a stolen photograph of him, together with a note he left in her pocket after her mother's death: 'Dear Harriet, I am sorry, love Vesey.'[33] Vesey is now an actor and when Harriet and Betsy go to see him playing Laertes, Betsy is admiring of this, to her, glamorous figure. Harriet denies having any photographs of Vesey, but, hunting through her mother's dressing table, implicitly the only space in the house into which Charles would not venture, Betsy discovers a 'sealed envelope':

> What do people conceal at the bottom of jewel-boxes? she wondered. Instructions in the event of death, perhaps ... or a love-letter ... She imagined the first rather than the second ... Then, for her curiosity was too great by now to brook even a slight delay, she took a nail-file and ran it along the flap as neatly as she could.[34]

---

[33] Elizabeth Taylor, *A Game of Hide and Seek* (London: Virago, 2008 [1951]), p. 119.
[34] Ibid., p. 220.

Betsy is not completely wrong in her interpretation of the contents of the envelope, as Vesey's note is a love-letter of sorts, but her actions bring in their train a series of misunderstandings. She confesses to her much-admired teacher Miss Bell that she believes that Vesey is really her father (though whether she truly believes this, or just tells Miss Bell in order to glean her sympathy, is never spelled out). Meanwhile, discovering that the envelope has been opened and resealed, Harriet presumes that Charles is the culprit, and she also blames him when, after she begins a correspondence with Vesey, those letters are interfered with. In fact, it is Betsy again: 'When she read them, [Betsy] felt that his letters – attenuated, allusive as they were – bypassed her mother and were meant for her.'[35] Rather than feeling upset that her mother might be betraying her father, Betsy performs a double substitution, in which Vesey becomes the idealised embodiment of both a father-figure and a romantic hero.

Betsy's construction of a fantastical lineage for herself is seen in the novel to be characteristic: the reader's first encounter with her occurs when she is imagining herself accused of murder and producing 'a dramatic alibi' in court.[36] Offsetting these fantasies, and contrasting with Betsy's conventional home-life, is the alternative offered by the classics teacher Miss Bell. Notably, just prior to her discoveries in her mother's bedroom, Betsy is invited to visit Miss Bell at her 'bed-sitting-room', and imagines her 'sitting by the fire, in the blue dressing gown which hung on the door, drinking her bedtime cocoa'.[37] This is a very different version of femininity from that offered by her mother and represented by the well-stocked dressing table: the school teacher's home represents a pragmatic and self-sufficient vision of a potential future. However, when Betsy visits, she is too caught up in her fantasy world to appreciate it, and rather than showing much interest in the 'lumps of stone from Cnossos' that Miss Bell has lying around, Betsy is simply keen to 'talk about Vesey'.[38]

Betsy's snooping makes her the agent of marital discord, but a more startling expression of the 'enemy' child in the immediate postwar period emerges in Agatha Christie's *Crooked House* (1949). The narrator, Charles Hayward, the son of a senior police officer, is drawn into the investigation of the murder by poisoning of Aristide Leonides because of his attachment to Leonides's granddaughter Sophia. The Leonides household provides the limited group of suspects typical of detective fiction, but the impact of the war on this household is noted: Aristide's son Roger and his wife have

---

[35] Ibid., p. 265.   [36] Ibid., p. 152.   [37] Ibid., pp. 217–18.   [38] Ibid., p. 218.

moved into Three Gables after being bombed out.[39] The house itself strikes Charles as grotesque: 'It ... was a cottage swollen out of all proportion ... It was a Greek restaurateur's idea of something English. It was meant to be an Englishman's home – built the size of a castle.'[40] Sophia's sister Josephine appears to bear the brunt of both the hereditary and environmental influences that are gestured towards in this description. When Charles first encounters her, he sees, 'a bulging brow, combed-back hair and small, rather beady black eyes ... Josephine was, I judged, about eleven or twelve years of age. She was a fantastically ugly child with a very distinct likeness to her grandfather. It seemed to me possible that she also had his brains.'[41] Additionally, Josephine has an actress mother with a histrionic temperament who sees the murder as an ideal opportunity to generate some 'advance publicity' for the play she intends to star in about Edith Thompson, hanged for murder in 1923.[42] Over the course of his investigation, Josephine offers Charles suggestions based on her reading of detective fiction and, like Betsy, is not averse to listening at doors and reading other people's letters, but her 'assistance' proves to be a double-blind when it is revealed that she herself killed her grandfather.

Where Betsy builds for herself a romantic fantasy that has the potential to generate misunderstandings and discord, Josephine's reading of 'stock mystery stories' leads her to cause actual, bodily harm, and not only to her grandfather;[43] at one point, in order to divert suspicion away from herself, she is hospitalised with what proves to be a self-inflicted head injury. At the climax of the novel, Josephine is killed in a car crash caused deliberately by her self-sacrificing Aunt Edith, and so the question of what judicial punishment might be appropriate for a juvenile killer is bypassed. Ultimately, Charles attributes Josephine's actions to 'various factors of heredity', but this does not put him off marrying her sister Sophia; as he explains to her: 'In poor little Josephine all the worst of the family came together. In you, Sophia, I fully believe that all that is bravest and best in the Leonides family had been handed down to you [sic].'[44] But Christie also gestures towards contemporary ideas about the importance of mothering when Charles notes that the 'ruthless egotism' of Josephine's mother Magda could have been a factor in her behaviour.[45]

The encouragement of women back into the home in the immediate postwar period, a policy driven by both social and economic concerns, was underscored a little later by the popularisation of the theories of John

---

[39] Agatha Christie, *Crooked House* (Harmondsworth: Penguin, 1953 [1949]), p. 20. [40] Ibid., p. 25.
[41] Ibid., p. 71. [42] Ibid., p. 36. [43] Ibid., p. 188. [44] Ibid., pp. 189, 192. [45] Ibid., p. 189.

Bowlby. As Alice Ferrebe suggests, although Bowlby's *Child Care and the Growth of Love* (1953) was based on work with children living in institutions, 'in a society so ideologically invested in the psychological and political importance of family for postwar reconstruction, it was read as a general report on the effects of maternal deprivation'.[46] Josephine's mother, wrapped up in her acting career, stands as a warning that would have had a very particular resonance to readers in the immediate postwar period. It is illuminating, then, to compare the depiction of a postwar household in Christie's novel to George Orwell's in *Nineteen Eighty-Four*, published the same year. The children of Winston Smith's neighbours, the Parsons, appear to have been completely formed by the ideological imperatives of permanently-at-war Oceania. They harass their mother and eventually report their father to the Thought Police for uttering treason in his sleep. The organisation to which the children belong, the Spies, has echoes of both the Hitler Youth and Komsomol, the Soviet youth group, and has 'systematically turned [them] into ungovernable little savages', but has 'produced in them no tendency whatever to rebel against the discipline of the Party'.[47] Orwell indicates not only the deforming effects of totalitarian ideology on the subjectivity of the young, but also the concomitant erosion of parental responsibility and the family as a sustaining, positive force, even when children have not been physically removed from their parents' care. Reflecting on his betrayal when imprisoned, Parsons says of his daughter's actions: 'I don't bear her any grudge for it. In fact I'm proud of her. It shows I brought her up in the right spirit, anyway.'[48] Parsons may be blind to the ironies of his own position, but his predicament is the most extreme expression from this period of the child as the enemy within.

If the parents in King's, Green's and Hartley's novels have passed their responsibilities on to proxies, if Betsy's mother is distracted, Josephine's mother neglectful and the Parsons actually frightened of their offspring, one might wonder what becomes of children who lose their mothers as a consequence of the war. This scenario is evoked in Marghanita Laski's *Little Boy Lost* (1949), which is set in the chaos of postwar Europe. Hilary, an officer, is separated from his French wife Lisa during the Occupation. In Paris, and involved in Resistance work, she dies giving birth to their son Jean. After the war, Hilary is given intelligence suggesting that the child has been passed on surreptitiously to an orphanage, and goes to France in search of Jean. The narrative initially centres on whether the father, who

---

[46] Alice Ferrebe, *Literature of the 1950s: Good, Brave Causes* (Edinburgh University Press, 2012), p. 81.
[47] George Orwell, *Nineteen Eighty-Four* (Oxford: Clarendon Press, 1984), p. 177. [48] Ibid., p. 360.

has never seen the child, will recognise him as his own. Pierre, who brings the news that Jean may be alive, suggests that Hilary will simply know whether this is his son: 'I am a great believer in instinct. If this is really your son, I am sure that you will know it as soon as you set eyes on him.'[49] Initially, Pierre's inkling seems to be correct: 'The little boy came in and in the instant before [Hilary's] eyes perceived the child there was torn from his blood, his body, his very consciousness the conviction that this was his son.'[50] But this recognition, notably, comes 'in the instant before' he actually sees the boy. It concludes the second part of the novel, but the third part opens with an abrupt volte-face: 'And then he looked at the child. And told himself with a kind of horror, "How could I ever have imagined that this child was mine?"'[51] He has built his expectations on a photograph of himself as a child, an image that cannot be reconciled with the 'foreign child' before him.[52]

Any instinctual bond between parent and child seems to have been overridden in Jean's case by socio-cultural factors, particularly the bleak, unhomely, repressive regime of the convent where he has grown up. Hilary's attempts to assess whether this really is his son are hampered not only by the regulations ordering convent life, but also by the fact that Jean is, after all, a *child*, one whose various foibles are completely unknown to Hilary. Staying in a joyless pension, where he must guiltily endorse blackmarket trading in order to get a decent meal, Hilary is forced to find entertainment for Jean in the meagre surroundings of the small French town. Symbolically enough, watching trains go past proves to be as much excitement as Jean could ever hope for.

At the climax of the novel, Hilary is on the point of leaving, and leaving Jean behind; Laski contrives a situation in which Hilary has to choose between the promise of a sexual encounter in Paris with a woman he has met at the pension and the responsibilities of fatherhood. Ultimately, though, he is brought to his senses by remembering Lisa, his dead wife. His choice, then, echoes the choice that might be made in romantic fiction between the excitement of an affair and the stability of marriage. Jean represents a link to his pre-war, happy marriage, but also an investment in a cosmopolitan futurity; as Gill Plain notes, the novel points to the need for postwar European reconciliation to provide security for future citizens.[53] Whether he actually is the child of Lisa and Hilary remains an unanswered question. Hilary reflects: 'In my heart, this child is my son',

---

[49] Marghanita Laski, *Little Boy Lost* (London: Persephone, 2004 [1949]), p. 70. [50] Ibid., p. 101.
[51] Ibid., p. 105. [52] Ibid., p. 106. [53] Plain, *Literature of the 1940s*, p. 221.

a comment hardly definitive enough to counter-balance his earlier doubts.[54] The child's symbolic function as a means of honouring Lisa's memory is more important than his actual parentage. Any problems that might face Hilary and Jean in adapting to life together are side-lined for the reader in favour of relief that Jean will no longer be an orphan.

Conclusion

As the 1950s progressed, the 'problem' of children, and especially the older child, refigured as the 'teenager', became an increasingly pressing one in British culture. Ferrebe notes that William Golding's *Lord of the Flies* (1954), a novel described by Mark Rawlinson as an 'evacuation parable', and one centrally concerned with both the fears and fearfulness of children, was published the year after *The Go-Between*, a novel with which it shares many concerns.[55] Golding's novel asks in particular whether children – especially boys – are 'inherently evil or culturally corrupted'.[56] Genre fictions such as Christie's works and novels with elements of the fabular, such as *Lord of the Flies* and *Nineteen Eighty-Four*, may have approached this issue obliquely, but a final example from the later 1950s brings the issues of home, belonging and uncontrollable youth into focus in a realist idiom. Alan Sillitoe's novella 'The Loneliness of the Long Distance Runner' (1959), narrated by Smith, centres on his time in Borstal – a prison for young offenders – after he is found guilty of burglary. Smith turns to crime in part so that he can continue in the life of relative ease that has been facilitated by his mother's insurance payout following the death of his father:

> Night after night we sat in front of the telly with a ham sandwich in one hand, a bar of chocolate in the other ... while mam was with some fancy-man upstairs on the new bed she'd ordered. I've never known a family as happy as ours was in that couple of months when we'd got all the money we needed.[57]

Smith's benign neglect by his mother extends to her refusing to assist the police when they come to the house to question him. But the pleasure that Smith takes from running, despite his deliberate decision to let himself be

---

[54] Laski, *Little Boy Lost*, p. 215.
[55] Mark Rawlinson, *British Writing of the Second World War* (Oxford University Press, 2000), p. 91; Ferrebe, *Literature of the 1950s*, pp. 21–2.
[56] Ferrebe, *Literature of the 1950s*, p. 23.
[57] Alan Sillitoe, 'The Loneliness of the Long Distance Runner' in *The Loneliness of the Long Distance Runner* (London: Harper Perennial, [1959] 2007), pp. 7–54, 21.

overtaken during the race that would give his institution the All-England Cup, is an implicit acknowledgement that material comforts are not enough; his choice not to win the race indicates the limits of his ability to choose at all. The story's ending suggests that the narrator has either been caught again, or betrayed by someone he trusted:

> I'm going to give this story to a pal of mine and tell him that if I do get captured again by the coppers, he can try and get it put into a book or something, because I'd like to see the governor's face when he reads it ... And if I don't get caught the bloke I give this story to will never give me away; he's lived in our terrace for as long as I can remember, and he's my pal. That I do know.[58]

This quasi-metafictional gesture poignantly undercuts the anger of what precedes it, emphasising that the bonds of community signified by 'our terrace', as well as by Smith's semi-detached mother, may not be as strong or sustaining as Smith apparently believes. From the reader's perspective, Smith disappears into a parlous future, caught between the punitive reformatory systems of the state and the uncertain comforts of his home-life, and neither of these appears to be exempt from Sillitoe's critique.

Works including those discussed here evidence the extent to which, in the late 1940s and early 1950s, repairing family relationships broken by war was seen as key to 'democratic maturity', and that this task involved psychical as well as political work.[59] As I have shown, in novels emerging in the immediate wake of the war, the child, whether the narrating subject or the object of narration, becomes a means of expressing not so much a retreat from the present as uncertainty about the future, uncertainty that might be embraced, treated with circumspection or shied away from. In each of these cases, it is the troubling rather than comforting or nostalgic aspects of childhood that are to the fore.

---

[58] Ibid., p. 54.   [59] Shapira, *The War Inside*, p. 80.

CHAPTER 15

New Uses of Literacy: The Blank Page and Writing in the Aftermath of War

Tracy Hargreaves

The long wait for a new generation of writers as the harbingers of a distinctive postwar voice circulated (and in some cases kept circulation going) in numerous literary journals and newspapers throughout the 1950s, from *The New Statesman* to the *Observer*, the *London Magazine*, the *Times Literary Supplement* and *Encounter*. John Lehmann's symposium on 'The Future of Fiction' in his 1946 *New Writing and Daylight* anthology was one of the earliest to solicit opinions on the direction of postwar writing; he asked Arthur Koestler, L. P. Hartley, Osbert Sitwell, V. S. Pritchett, Walter Allen and Rose Macaulay for their views. Macaulay was pessimistic about the survival of the novel and about the 'incalculable effect' that the war was likely to have on the imagination of the writer, predicting: 'if he writes novels, he may evolve some new form; or, in reaction, and in search of elegance, pleasure and safety, he may turn in zest to the solid, traditional, comfortable forms of the past'.[1] Macaulay was herself left 'desolated and desperate' after she found '*everything* – destroyed'[2] when her flat was bombed in 1941 and her anticipation of 'reaction' as safe, pleasurable and traditional might seem a reasonable response, in the circumstances. But when she came to write her first postwar novel in 1950 (at which point T. C. Worsley felt there was 'still no sign of any literary revival')[3], the effect of the war remained, for her, 'incalculable'. At the end of *The World My Wilderness* (1950), one character, Richie, walks through the devastated city of London, 'sickened' by the 'squalor of ruin' while quoting T. S. Eliot ('we are in rats' alley, where the

---

[1] Rose Macaulay, 'The Future of Fiction' in John Lehmann (ed.), *New Writing and Daylight* (London: Hogarth Press, 1946), p. 73.
[2] Lara Feigel, *The Love-Charm of Bombs: Restless Lives in the Second World War* (London: Bloomsbury, 2013), p. 151 (emphasis in the original).
[3] T. C. Worsley, 'The New Statesman' in Harry Ritchie (ed.), *Success Stories: Literature and the Media in England, 1950–1959* (London: Faber & Faber, 1988), p. 2.

dead men lost their bones') as the waste land of the First World War seems to have ceded to the bleaker wilderness of the Second World War.

As the first literary-critical studies of postwar English writing emerged, 'reaction' became a derogatory keynote and English writing and writers were viewed as 'provincial or parochial', 'a little drab' or 'anti-experimental' in various turns to the picaresque and poetic traditions of the eighteenth century, to the social realism of the nineteenth century and to the poetic traditions of the early twentieth century (but never, however, matching the accomplishments of their predecessors).[4] Jed Esty has noted the tendency 'to metaphorize literary change as national decline' in critical surveys of 'the English scene' and William Van O'Connor's *The New University Wits* did precisely that: Harry Moore's introduction invited comparisons between the first and second Elizabethan eras, 'the one swelling into power and the other shrinking from the status of an empire to that of a small country'.[5] The historian David Kynaston's summation of an injured postwar society tending to its wounds in 'the instinctive retreat to familiar ways, familiar rituals, familiar relations' reaffirmed Bernard Bergonzi's view of English literature of the 1950s and 1960s as 'both backward and inward-looking'.[6] Although Kynaston readily suggests that views of 'instinctive retreat' work 'at the level of generalisation', and Malcolm Bradbury dismissed them as 'a somewhat unreliable orthodoxy',[7] these opinions nonetheless helped to shape a critical view of predominantly English mid-century writing as both 'irretrievably and disastrously minor'[8] and as a 'blank

---

[4] William Van O'Connor, *The New University Wits and the End of Modernism* (Carbondale: Southern Illinois University Press, 1963), pp. xi, 132; Rubin Rabinovitz, *The Reaction against Experiment in the English Novel, 1950–1960* (New York and London: Columbia University Press, 1967), p. viii; John Lehmann (ed.), *The Craft of Letters in England* (Boston and Cambridge: Houghton Mifflin, 1957), p. 2. See also Blake Morrison: 'To look to such poets [as Hardy and Graves] would be to restore the interrupted, temporarily discontinued, but not completely devastated tradition of 1914', *The Movement: English Poetry and Fiction of the 1950s* (Oxford University Press, 1980), p. 203. James Gindin argued that English writers were responding to the 'English tradition of Fielding and Richardson, Trollope and Hardy' in *Postwar British Fiction: New Accents and Attitudes* (Cambridge University Press, 1962), pp. 2–3. And see Rabinovitz, who argued that post-Modernist writers were influenced by the eighteenth-century novel and post-Victorian realists – Butler, Bennett, Wells, Galsworthy – in *The Reaction against Experiment in the English Novel*, p. 4.
[5] Jed Esty, *A Shrinking Island: Modernism and National Culture in England* (Princeton University Press, 2004), p. 1.
[6] David Kynaston, *Austerity Britain* (London: Bloomsbury, 2008), p. 133.
[7] Malcolm Bradbury (ed.), *The Novel Today: Contemporary Writers on Modern Fiction* (Manchester University Press, 1977), p. 17.
[8] Marina MacKay and Lyndsey Stonebridge, 'Introduction' in *British Fiction after Modernism: The Novel at the Mid-Century* (Basingstoke: Palgrave, 2007), p. 3.

space or interregnum between modernism and postmodernism, between empire and welfare state'.[9]

This chapter reappraises the early writing of Philip Larkin (*Jill*, 1946), John Braine (*Room at the Top*, 1957) and Doris Lessing (*In Pursuit of the English*, 1960) in response to Lyndsey Stonebridge and Marina MacKay's observation that 'mid-century fiction has a complex and under-thought relation to its own history'.[10] In particular, it focuses on how each of these writers navigates marginal voices (working class, colonial) in response to some of the cultural fractures wrought by the Second World War. Written and published across a fourteen-year period (1946, 1957, 1960), each of these texts returns to one of what Marina MacKay describes as war's 'nostalgia magnets': the first Blitz air raids of 1940 to 1941.[11] These returns take the form of a bombed town but intact house in Larkin's *Jill*; a bombed house but a town left intact in Braine's *Room at the Top*, and tidied bombsites and patched-up boarding houses in Lessing's *In Pursuit of the English*. There is an intriguing scene in Lessing's 'documentary' in which, as she crosses the desolation of a bomb-site shortly after her arrival in London from Southern Rhodesia in 1949, she is alerted to a noise like 'a cricket chirping with quiet persistence from sun-warmed grasses in the veld'.[12] The sound of the cricket chirping turns out to be a man typing, 'sitting on a tidy pile of rubble, the typewriter on a broken girder, clean white paper fluttering from the rim of the machine'. When Doris asks her new friend Rose who he is, she's told ('grimly') that he's '[a]n optimist ... Thinks he's going to be rebuilt'.[13] Rose's scepticism resonates with a letter, written by Larkin in 1946 to Jim Sutton, the dedicatee of *Jill*. Although Larkin excepted Henry Green from criticism (for *Caught* and *Loving*), he told Sutton that: 'When I look round on present-day writing, it's like looking at bomb damage – very bad bomb damage. There is no one who can be followed.'[14] Larkin's description of very bad bomb damage in one of the key transitional scenes in *Jill* examines relief and a momentary optimism that follow the effects of an air raid on the fictional Huddlesford; a voice advises John Kemp, the novel's hapless protagonist: 'Now there is a fresh start for you: you are no longer

[9] Jed Esty, *A Shrinking Island: p. 4.*   [10] MacKay and Stonebridge, 'Introduction', p. 2.
[11] Marina MacKay, *Modernism and World War II* (Cambridge University Press, 2007), p. 2. Dunkirk (referred to briefly in *Jill*) is the other 'magnet'.
[12] Doris Lessing, *In Pursuit of the English* (London: Panther, 1960), p. 49.   [13] Ibid.
[14] Philip Larkin to Jim Sutton 15 May 1946, in Anthony Thwaite (ed.), *Selected Letters of Philip Larkin 1940–1984* (London: Faber & Faber, 1992), p. 18.

governed by what has gone before.'[15] As the narrative moves to its denouement, the fresh start seems more carnivalesque than enduring when Kemp presides over a feast of misrule during which he destroys his embryonic writing in a sequence that unravels what the narrative has been building. That possibility of a 'fresh start' is reiterated in John Braine's best-selling *Room at the Top*. Published in 1957 but looking back to 1947, events are retrospectively narrated by Joe Lampton. Where Kemp's family home remains intact following an air raid, Lampton's is destroyed and his parents killed; his eventual move to a more affluent town allows him not only to 'live in a place without memories', but to function, initially at least, as surrogate son for a family whose own son was killed in the war: the working-class war veteran is symbolically 'born again' into a new and affluent beginning. The implications of these incidents, both textually and culturally, is what this chapter explores.

In his introduction to Faber's 1963 re-issue of *Jill*, Larkin challenged the American literary critic James Gindin's then recent appraisal of his novel as one that encouraged interest in the 'displaced working-class hero', a forerunner of that journalistic contrivance, the 'angry young man'. Larkin reserved judgement on the 'trend-spotter's comment' (he had also been tagged as a 'new University Wit' and as a 'Movement' writer) with a starched suggestion that if this was so, 'the book may hold sufficient historical interest to justify republication'.[16] He had (of course) wanted his book to be more than an historical footnote, professing in a letter to Norman Isles in 1944 that 'the creation of literature' is 'almost the only thing that interests me now'. Championing the 'aesthetical' over the 'ethical', he announced a preference for an 'increased negativeness, a kind of infinite recession in the face of the world'.[17] Early in the war, Larkin had written that he wanted 'to pretend it isn't there: that there's no war on'.[18] But as Graham Greene perceptively observed in 1948, '[public] life obtrudes through the cracks of our stories, terribly persistent like grass through cement'[19] and obtruding through Larkin's novel (whose ostensible focus is the real and imagined emotional life of a working-class scholarship boy during his first term at Oxford) are references to volunteering, rationing, the black-out, soldiers, airmen and their lorries, the declaration of war,

---

[15] Philip Larkin, *Jill* (London: Faber & Faber, 2005 [1946]), p. 202.
[16] Philip Larkin, Introduction to *Jill* (London: Faber & Faber, 1963), p. vii.
[17] Philip Larkin to Norman Isles 16 April 1944, in *Selected Letters of Philip Larkin*, p. 88.
[18] Philip Larkin to J. B. Sutton 20 November 1941, in *Selected Letters of Philip Larkin*, p. 27.
[19] Graham Greene to Elizabeth Bowen, in *Why Do I Write* (New York: Haskell House Publishers, 1975 [1948]), p. 27.

evacuation, air-raid shelter practice, the Blitz, auxiliary firemen, air-raid sirens, as well as specifically military details: news from Albania, British aid to Greece, the sinking of the *Jervis Bay* on 5 November 1940 and the bombing of Coventry, which is compared to the air raid on the fictional Huddlesford, Kemp's Lancashire home town. The raid excepted, these details occur in the hinterland of Kemp's unexceptional existence as the 'little scene' enacts itself within the 'great scene' as Virginia Woolf had described her own experience of the war.[20] Allusions to the paraphernalia of war lend weight to the narrative's historicity, but initially carry less significance than the literary creation of 'Jill', the sibling invented by Kemp to redeem his isolation and to provoke the jealous attention of his insufferable roommate, Christopher. The war is, though, repeatedly and deliberately juxtaposed with the act of writing and with coming-of-age even if it *appears* to be a relegated concern in pursuit of that 'infinite recession in the face of the world'.

The episodic structure of the narrative starts with a prelude in which Kemp, the 'mechanical' schoolboy, obediently prepares for Oxford entrance; once at Oxford, his apprenticeship as a writer is stimulated by his loneliness which leads to the creation of an epistolary correspondence with a fictive sister, 'Jill', addressing the question, as Andrew Motion puts it, of how 'to be intimate in a hostile place'.[21] The correspondence then develops into a short story and because Kemp finds that too formulaic, it shifts to diary form precisely to allow for that more intimate first-person disclosure. As his novice experimentation with form evolves, the writing reaches one of several transitional points. The first coincides with news of the sinking of the *Jervis Bay*, a tragedy which functions as tangential background to a kind of epiphany, for Kemp, about his writing:

> The sensation he had was of looking intently into the centre of a pure white light: he seemed to see the essence of Jill, around which all the secondary material things formed and reformed as he wrote them down. He thought he saw exactly what she was and how he should express it: the word was *innocent*, one he had used dozens of times in his own mind, and yet until that moment had never understood.[22]

---

[20] Virginia Woolf, *The Diary of Virginia Woolf*, vol. 5, (ed.) Anne Olivier Bell (Harmondsworth: Penguin, 1985), 8 December 1940, p. 343.
[21] Andrew Motion, *Philip Larkin: A Writer's Life* (London: Faber & Faber, 1993), p. 155.
[22] Larkin, *Jill*, p. 133.

Kemp's noumenal vision recalls the 'white light still and moving' in T. S. Eliot's 'Burnt Norton', 'surrounded / By a grace of sense', but as Kemp (or Larkin) prepares to capture (or inhabit) this late modernist vision, he is interrupted by a student inviting him to a political club to discuss postwar change. By the time he disentangles himself from the invitation (and so from any commitment to the vision of a new postwar society), Kemp's inspiration has 'gone, utterly gone' and instead of the lure of his coruscating vision 'nothing presented itself to his mind except a flat dullness, like a grey stone wall'.[23] It is a conspicuous juxtaposition, pitting social change against a preference for an insulated aesthetic and confirming the political as inimical to creativity. But the novel turns again in its description of a bombing raid where what has been destroyed and what has been preserved are both rendered significantly 'strange'.

Kemp returns to Huddlesford, following a serious bombing raid on the town, uncertain whether his parents survived it. His return has a nightmarish, uncanny quality to it as he observes 'even this most familiar spot grow strange' and is 'filled with dread'.[24] Experiencing a reversion to childhood ('[i]t was as if he had just come home from school'), he makes a wager, 'praying for his parents like a child fervently', that he will renounce adult subjectivity and be 'dependent on them for ever, if only everything was all right'.[25] It is: the family house on the resilient King Edward Street survives the raid, his parents are sitting it out in Preston, and a note, banal, reassuring, is pinned to the door to let him know. And yet, home turns out to be *unheimlich*, after all. Comparing his home to a doll's house (described elsewhere by Susan Stewart as 'the illusion of a perfectly complete and hermetic world', an ambivalent 'sanctuary ... and prison'),[26] Kemp observes that everything was 'tidy as usual'; but the coincidence of order and disorder has the effect of making both simultaneously strange.[27] In these moments, everything *and* nothing appears to have been changed by war and Larkin observes an environment that seems paralysed between, and ambivalent about, destruction and preservation. This paralysis and ambivalence is exemplified by Kemp's own position, caught as he is between two promises; one is his bargain, made in child-like prayer, that he will remain dependent on his parents; the other is raised by that ambiguously located voice: 'Now there is a fresh start for you: you are no longer governed by what went before'.[28] Kemp's first vision of a 'pure white

---

[23] Ibid., p. 135. [24] Ibid., p. 197. [25] Ibid.
[26] Susan Stewart, *On Longing: Narratives of the Miniature, the Gigantic, the Souvenir, the Collection* (Durham, NC: Duke University Press, 1993), pp. 62, 65.
[27] Larkin, *Jill*, p. 198. [28] Ibid., p. 202.

light' as he originally imagined the elusive essence of 'Jill' is now matched by a literal one as he witnesses destruction and survival through the moon 'spilling its light' on a 'wreckage [that] looked like the ruins of an age over and done with'.[29] That first 'pure white light' of creative vision was beyond Kemp's grasp when he had his near epiphany about 'Jill'. The reiteration of another light (also pure and white) in relation to a new revelation about the war signals a move that *ought* to set going that desirable 'fresh start'. No longer being governed by what went before might mean anything in a new writer's first novel about a young man who tries writing for the first time: liberation from the mores underpinning a character's formative years, or – and? – liberation from the disruptive forces that blocked the 'English tradition' as Larkin later described it: the First World War and Modernism.[30]

Kemp's return to Oxford is marked not by the recovery of his literary endeavour, though, but by a redoubled destruction as though he must re-enact the public wreckage of his town in a privately staged war and turn a scene of partial devastation to a complete one. Back at Oxford, Kemp undergoes an inebriated, dream-like odyssey which begins with the petty waste of another scholarship boy's precious rations and moves on to the destruction of his writing about Jill, a chance meeting with a down-and-out, one-eyed Dunkirk veteran and another chance meeting with a poet whose room he cannot find again. When he re-encounters Gillian, a young woman whom he regarded as the incarnation of his literary creation, he kisses (or defiles) her and sees her, significantly, as a 'false light', no longer pure or new.[31] All the parts of the novel are revisited and unravelled here, like the tearing up of a draft, from the presence of the scholarship boy and social mobility to writing and 'Jill', the debilitating consequences of the war and the emotional pull of literary and sexual desire which is sought, lost and rejected. The appeal of 'Jill' carries obvious seductions for a fledgling writer like Larkin and his creation, John Kemp. Kemp's 'Jill' is hardly the harbinger of new kind of writing; a consolatory invention in many ways, writing recuperates loneliness in

---

[29] Ibid., p. 198.
[30] Blake Morrison cites Larkin's introduction to *The Oxford Book of Twentieth Century Verse*: 'I had in mind a notion that there might have been what I'll call for want of a better phrase, an English tradition coming from the nineteenth century with people like Hardy, which was interrupted partly by the Great War, when many English poets were killed off, and partly by the really tremendous impact of Yeats, whom I think of as Celtic, and Eliot, whom I think of as American'. Blake Morrison, *The Movement: English Poetry and Fiction of the 1950* (Oxford University Press, 1980), p. 203.
[31] Larkin, *Jill*, p. 213.

the guise of a schoolgirl story and a restorative fantasy of feminine accomplishment. Kemp's 'Jill' is variously 'a perfect housewife',[32] cultured (she plays the piano) and innocent ('he liked to think of her as preoccupied only with simple, untroublesome things'[33]). She becomes, at one level, the best expression of an ideally domestic and middle-class life over the banality and disappointment of his own quotidian and clumsy existence. But Larkin's *Jill* also examines coming-of-age in a new age; she (or it) is a device that allowed him as a first-time novelist self-consciously to inhabit the conventions of narrative form, voice, formal and vernacular dialogue (both male and female, working and upper-middle class) as the narration moves in and out of Kemp's consciousness to glance at the limits of 'the aesthetical and the ethical' – the aspirational pure white light of the writer's not quite realisable vision, and the vexed issues of social and sexual mobility that flesh out the events of the narrative.

The postwar story of social and sexual mobility found one of its most paradigmatic expressions in John Braine's first novel, the best-selling *Room at the Top* (1957). Braine's cautionary tale is told through Joe Lampton's first-person narration and details his ruinous ambitions for wealth through two sexual relationships, one adulterous with Alice Aisgill and the other pre-marital with Susan Brown, daughter of a wealthy industrialist. His quest for wealth and social status proves costly when he realises, too late, that he cannot have what he most wants (Alice) and that he no longer wants (but is compelled to take) what he thought he most wanted (Susan), leaving him with an irreparable sense of sorrow and guilt. There are superficial (though by no means negligible) comparisons to be drawn between *Jill* and *Room at the Top*, including wartime and postwar guilt about class and family, anxieties about domestic disorder and displacement, and the fantasy of women's capacity for domestic repair and consolation. The perfect, desirable, tidy world of the doll's house that John Kemp desires at his most destabilised is re-imagined in Braine's novel through the comparably serene and perfected images seen in magazines and films in *Room at the Top*. But where repeated references to war anchor *Jill* to a particular sense of history, recollections of popular adverts secure *Room at the Top* to quite another, 'like the clicking-over of lantern slides with no informing pattern' as Richard Hoggart describes the ephemerality of the present.[34] References to Sulka dressing gowns purchased in Bond Street, Hamilton watches, Cannon Percale sheets, Nash Airflye Eight cars

---

[32] Ibid., p. 101. [33] Ibid., p. 117.
[34] Richard Hoggart, *The Uses of Literacy* (Harmondsworth: Penguin, 1992 [1957]), p. 191.

and Aston Martins are scattered through the narration as indices and icons of achieved and aspirational wealth. *Room at the Top* appears to close the decade between 1947 austerity and 1957 affluence by its often anachronistic references to books, plays, cars, clothes and interiors that would have been instantly recognisable to readers attuned to the cultural surfaces of late 1950s advertising, but which were as yet undreamt of in the late 1940s. Joe Lampton's narrative thus becomes a kind of palimpsest as 1957 writes over 1947 while leaving obdurate traces of the past, which also stubbornly and painfully bears the memory of a 1941 bombing raid. Braine explores the ruins of that raid as an ambivalent site of repression as well as opportunity: 'the gap where our house had stood' as Joe Lampton recalls a space that signified both familial harmony *and* total destruction.[35] Braine shapes two possible narratives out of this space: one is the story of lost structures to which the narrative wishes, impossibly and sentimentally, to return as Joe laments the destruction of domestic order upheld by his parents by indexing it to a moral and political integrity that seems to have been obliterated with them; the other narrative (and the dominant one in *Room at the Top*) offers a kind of amnesia that enables another postwar script about social mobility and new consumer affluence. Although his narration often occludes the war in a wish to compartmentalise and consign it to an irreparably broken (and at times discarded) past, he cannot entirely abandon it and Lampton, a figure who seems more symptomatic than singular, is not just marked by the trauma of war (as, say, John Kemp is): he is recreated because of it.

When he arrives in the prosperous town of Warley, he is delighted by both his new lodgings and by his new landlady, Mrs Thompson. Arrested by a photograph of her dead son (killed in the war), Lampton cannot remember who Maurice reminds him of: '[i]t seemed very important that I should recall the likeness; but the harder I tried the more anonymous his face became'.[36] Mr Thompson makes the (obvious) connection and Mrs Thompson affirms: 'He's the image of Maurice.' It is the photographic rather than the mirror image that confirms Joe's developing identity for him, as though he experiences a second entry into a new subjectivity: 'I looked at the photograph above the mantelpiece and saw my own face for the first time.' Having already considered whether or not he finds Mrs Thompson attractive (he does not, but chivalrously notes that he 'wouldn't ... have thrown her out of my bed'),[37] it seems as though the

---

[35] John Braine, *Room at the Top* (London: Arrow, 1989 [1957]), p. 91. [36] Ibid., p. 18.
[37] Ibid., p. 11.

Oedipal drama is accelerated, played out across an optic surface rather than through the subterranean unconscious, and as though the cost of acquiring identity might now be counted in shillings and pence. In the ensuing conversation, as the Thompsons discuss their dead son and Joe discusses his dead parents, a new relationship is instantaneously formed: 'the three of us were together in the best relationship possible to a young man and a middle-aged couple'.[38] This fantasy of an almost instantaneous reparation of mutual loss is sealed when Joe walks into the kitchen the next day: 'Mrs Thompson looked at me with a cool tenderness. "It's nice to have two men to look after again"'.[39] The contrived nature of this restoration of domestic order and familial restitution is emphasised by Lampton's sense that the kitchen would 'have served as a film set for any middle-class comedy'.[40] It is difficult to underestimate the significance of the fantasy of domestic order both in relation to other postwar writing (it is clearly important in *Jill*), but also in relation to how the war is made sense of in *Room at the Top*. Compare Joe's description of the Thompson's kitchen as 'film set for any middle-class comedy' with another, rather different one. When he returns to the debris of his family home just after it has been destroyed by the bomb which also kills his parents, the scene of destruction could have served (he imagines) as a Ministry of Information poster for any working-class tragedy:

> The background was ideal – the wringing-machine blown through the kitchen window, the stone sink cracked in two, a heavy grey sock, darned at the heel, lying half under a lump of plaster, and all the crockery, except one thick half-pint mug, mixed up in fragments with butter and sugar and jam and bread and sausages and golden syrup.[41]

His recollection of his mother and father highlights not just their stability in relation to the politics of class and place, but also his sense of exclusion from their mutual love ('I felt shutout, bewildered, childish'); surviving the war gives him a second chance and when the Thompsons exchange an intimate memory of their courtship, '[w]e all burst into laughter again'.[42]

David Lodge criticised *Room at the Top* for its 'thinness of texture, its lack of complexity, its simplifications, its evasions',[43] although one might argue that these are the apposite expressions of a postwar sensibility as Richard Hoggart observed it in his contemporaneous and influential cultural study *The Uses of Literacy* (1957). Part auto-ethnography, it

---

[38] Ibid., p. 22. [39] Ibid., p. 23. [40] Ibid. [41] Ibid., p. 92. [42] Ibid., p. 21.
[43] David Lodge, 'The Modern, the Contemporary and the Importance of Being Amis' *Critical Quarterly* (1963) 5(4) p. 336.

validates the rootedness of the working-class community of his childhood, and part cultural study, Hoggart's analysis (and pastiche) of contemporary newspapers, magazines, fiction, television, popular songs was an effective (if also contentious) critique of the flattening of affect in relation to the quality of literary language, where 'reading' is replaced by 'looking'[44] and 'nothing challenges, or gives joy or evokes sorrow; neither splendour or misery: only the constant trickle of tinned milk and water which staves off the pangs of a positive hunger and denies the satisfaction of a solidly-filling meal'.[45] Lampton's affect and performative identity is shaped by the flotsam of the most contemporary and impermanent elements of mass culture: the language of advertisements, magazines, pulp fictions, television are his ever-shifting points of reference, 'the worn phrase straight from the women's magazine', 'difficult to convey without using the terms of the advertising copywriter' and so on.[46] Initially beguiled by such rhetoric (if not constructed by it), he ends up trapped and voided by it: 'Whenever I make love now I feel as if I were one of the characters in a magazine advertisement.'[47] There is a limit to where this kind of regurgitation can go, though, both in the novel and as a mode of writing. Orphaned by the war, Lampton becomes a truly disinherited figure, morally and culturally adrift; as he consigns his parents to an irretrievably lost world he becomes increasingly stylised, blank and performative, an image fatally adrift from its referential source.

Jack Clayton, who directed the film version of *Room at the Top* (1959), saw something 'universal' and 'indicative' in it: 'It was about what happened to England when everybody came back from the war';[48] his film is widely regarded as inaugurating the 'new wave' in British Cinema between 1959 and 1963, intended to catch what Karel Reisz described as 'the extraordinary social changes which were in the air'.[49] The last of those films, adapted from Keith Waterhouse's novella, *Billy Liar* (1959), literally closes the door on a chapter that, told over and over by the end of the 1950s, had nowhere to go. The film adaptation, directed by John Schlesinger, catches and documents parts of England in strikingly transitional states of postwar reconstruction (the film was shot on location in Yorkshire,

---

[44] Hoggart, *The Uses of Literacy*, p. 203. [45] Ibid., p. 237. [46] Ibid., pp. 12, 28.
[47] Ibid., p. 183.
[48] Jack Clayton, 'The Way Things Are', interview with Gordon Gow in *Films and Filming* (April 1974), pp. 11–15, cited in Neil Sinyard, *Jack Clayton* (Manchester University Press, 2000).
[49] Karel Reisz, *The Cinema of Tony Richardson*, James M. Welsh and John C. Tibbetts (eds) (State University of New York Press, 1999), p. 28. The films were *Room at the Top, Look Back in Anger, Saturday Night and Sunday Morning, The Entertainer, A Taste of Honey, A Kind of Loving, The Loneliness of the Long Distance Runner, This Sporting Life* and *Billy Liar*.

Lancashire and London). As it does so, Billy's internal fantasies of military aggression are mapped by the very landscape that stifles him as the film's intra-diegetic soundtrack suggestively links the sounds of global wartime destruction to those of regional reconstruction as drills and demolition wrecking balls, artillery fire and explosions circulate. A pastiche of a Pathé News Reel ('The Rape of Ambrosia') sees Billy dressed as a wounded American General inspecting bomb damage, but this cedes to yet another impersonation, this time of his own regional voice and identity when he encounters the elderly Councillor Duxbury in the moors above the town; the cumulative effect suggests that there is little that is authentic to speak from or through. At the end of Schlesinger's film, Billy's would-be girlfriend Liz is heading for swinging London and persuades Billy to go with her. Billy buys a ticket but does not go; his gran has died, his mother says she needs him at home and he leads an imaginary troop of soldiers back to his parents' suburban semi, quietly lets himself in and closes the door, a figure back at home and at the same time, like Larkin's John Kemp and John Braine's Joe Lampton, not *quite* at home either.

I began this chapter with Doris Lessing, newly arrived in London, walking through the extant debris of the blitz with her new friend Rose, a veteran of those raids. *In Pursuit of the English* is part ethnographic study, part documentary, part fiction – or at least 'too well shaped for life', as Lessing described it in her memoirs.[50] Lessing's typing man, feasibly real, certainly symbolic, is calculatedly poised at a different moment of postwar recovery from that described by Braine, indicated by the now 'tidy rubble' and the 'clean white paper fluttering' from his typewriter. The writer's shirt-sleeves 'held neatly above the elbow' suggest a figure capable not just of imposing order from within the ruins, but also of introducing a certain capable style. Where John Kemp observes a family home 'tidy as usual' after the Huddlesford air raid or imagines Jill changing 'into a perfect housewife' in a holiday cottage[51] or Joe Lampton takes pleasure in a kitchen that would 'have served as a film set' with Mrs Thompson delighted to have two men to look after, Lessing interrogates the English domestic space with a critical eye on mid-century English writing itself. Lessing was critical of postwar writers and writing for being 'extremely provincial ... their horizons are bounded by their immediate experience of British life and its

---

[50] Doris Lessing, *Walking in the Shade: Volume Two of My Autobiography, 1949–1962* (London: Flamingo, 1998), p. 4.
[51] Larkin, *Jill*, p. 101.

standards'.[52] *Room at the Top* was one of the texts she had singled out for critique because Joe Lampton 'does not see himself in relation to any larger vision. Therefore he remains petty.'[53] Lessing's encounters with an older English generation, by contrast, read like resolute rejections of an antediluvian racism. In one house, with its 'thin bleakness', the semi-fictional 'Doris' rejects the rooms she's offered when the nurse (who presumably represents the views of the ancient, bird-like woman who owns the house) tells her 'We're not having blacks ... We don't take Jews either'.[54] Later, Doris listens to another elderly couple, evicted by legal force from the house she herself is lodging in, reiterating the prejudice: 'Justice, British justice, it's all Jews and foreigners'.[55] Louise Yelin suggests that it is Doris herself, 'the white, middle-class, colonial newcomer', who displaces the elderly couple from the home;[56] but although Doris takes wry pleasure in watching them removed from the scene, it is a group of Australian students who take the rooms once the 'War Damage' men have cleaned and repaired them, enabling the lodging house to accommodate an increasingly extended sense of family. If this makes for a lively, creative, cosmopolitan environment, it is still not thoroughly transformative. The workman who comes to repair Doris's rooms complains about 'all these blacks coming in' as he 'pasted strips of paper over the cracks'.[57] Women's lives, romanticised in Larkin and Braine, are de-idealised here: Mrs Skeffington, who has rooms below Doris, is trapped by the competing sexual demands of her husband, the anxious cries of her child and entire days spent servicing the needs of others, cooking in a café, cooking lunch for her child, cooking supper for her husband. The doll house that, as Susan Stewart suggests, might represent 'sanctuary' and 'fantasy' or 'prison' has a clear function here: '[t]his pair of prisoners', Doris calls another mother and daughter trapped in its confines.[58] But that is another story.

Lessing redirected the readers of the second volume of her memoirs back to this 'little book' as she described it for added 'depth and detail' of her experiences, almost forty years after its publication in 1960 and almost fifty years after she had arrived in London.[59] In her memoir, she returned to the

---

[52] Doris Lessing, 'The Small Personal Voice' in Tom Maschler (ed.), *Declaration* (London: MacGibbon & Kee, 1957), p. 23.
[53] Ibid., p. 23. [54] Lessing, *In Pursuit of the English*, pp. 39, 40. [55] Ibid., p. 183.
[56] Louise Yelin, *From the Margins of Empire: Christina Stead, Doris Lessing, Nadine Gordimer* (Ithaca, NY and London: Cornell University Press, 1998), p. 65.
[57] Lessing, *In Pursuit of the English*, pp. 208, 209. [58] Ibid., p. 124.
[59] Lessing, *Walking in the Shade*, p. 4.

emblem of the 'clean white paper': 'real life', hers, as she saw it, had been put on hold by the Second World War, and was about to begin as she docked in London with her small son: 'A clean slate, a new page – everything still to come.'[60] John McLeod has pointed to the optimism of that 'fresh start': 'in the confusion of London's diverse population, creativity might be possible: something as yet indefinable remains to be written'.[61] Although Doris mentions her typewriter and her writing in *In Pursuit*, she does not disclose what she was writing, but it was while living on Denbigh Road that she wrote *Martha Quest* (1952) – the first in her 'Children of Violence' sequence, a novel that drew on her own formative experiences growing up in the African veld, trying to find herself in the pages of the English literature she devoured as a young girl: she already was the writer, re-inscribing not just the clean white paper with her own experiences, but articulating, too, an urgent sense of the writer's ethical responsibility to interpret and to 'strengthen ... a vision of a good which may defeat evil'.[62] Lessing's magnificently kaleidoscopic *The Golden Notebook* (1962), published two years after *In Pursuit of the English*, shows her writer-protagonist Anna describing her lover, Michael, as 'the history of Europe'.[63] To personify 'the history of Europe' in this way, as part of a desiring, intimate relationship, is to imagine a more feeling engagement with war that reaches beyond one's immediate experience of it. But when Michael describes the murder of his family in the gas chambers, the murder of his friends by Communists, Anna, the English writer 'as usual ... failed to imagine it'.[64]

The ruined spaces of war were imaginatively reconfigured by these writers as blank pages and spaces that were both exploratory and interrogatory. If they were attentive to post-imperial, postmodern or postmodernist fractures (not that they might have imagined their writing in those terms), we see their writing as also attentive to contemporary practices of writing, from the clichés of magazines and adverts to the gesture of tearing up the drafts of writing in *Jill*, to the workman-like approach to the blank page in Lessing. Lessing had a faith in the writer as a figure capable of restoring order or meaning to chaos, but she recognised, too, 'a confusion of standards and the uncertainty of values' as a defining characteristic of the mid-century.[65] 'Innocent' is the word on which Larkin hangs Kemp's illuminating vision, but he knows that there is no return to it once it is

---

[60] Ibid., p. 3. [61] John McLeod, *Postcolonial London* (London: Routledge, 2004), p. 80.
[62] Lessing, 'The Small Personal Voice', p. 16.
[63] Doris Lessing, *The Golden Notebook* (London: Harper Perennial, 2007 [1962]), p. 297.
[64] Ibid., p. 298. [65] Lessing, 'The Small Personal Voice', p. 14.

lost: a point that he would later make emphatically in 'MCMXIV' with the repetition of the elegiac phrase 'Never such innocence again'. Larkin never returned to Coventry after it was bombed, but he recalled with gratitude that he had grown up in a house containing the works of 'Hardy, Bennett, Wilde, Butler and Shaw, and later on Lawrence, Huxley and Katherine Mansfield'.[66] Leo Mellor's invitation in *Reading the Ruins* to 'acknowledge a material basis to disorder and the possibilities for narratives of reclaiming, rebuilding and remaking' is suggestive here because there can be no 'innocent' or simple return to Hardy, Bennett, Lawrence;[67] there was, nonetheless, Larkin implies, work to be done to rebuild around what had solidly survived. It was rendered strange, too, by re-exposure in a newly denuded landscape. The destructive blank space left by bomb damage is figured as an exploratory blank page for each of these writers, opening a new perspective in which they interrogate modes of writing in relation to the continuity and discontinuity of tradition, in relation to disposable forms of mass culture and in relation to interrogative scrutiny about Englishness itself.

---

[66] Philip Larkin, 'Not the Place's Fault', *Umbrella*, vol. 1, issue 3 (summer 1959), reprinted in Anthony Thwaite (ed.), *Further Requirements: Interviews, Broadcasts, Statements and Book Reviews* (London: Faber & Faber, 2001), p. 11.
[67] Leo Mellor, *Reading the Ruins: Modernism, Bombsites and British Culture* (Cambridge University Press, 2011), p. 2.

CHAPTER 16

The Pursuit of Love: Writing Postwar Desire

Charlotte Charteris

The opening novel of Nancy Mitford's Radlett trilogy, *The Pursuit of Love* (1945), registers in the ambiguities of its title each of the revolutions in protagonist Linda Radlett's relationship with love itself. As a phrase, 'the pursuit of love' applies as accurately to Linda's tenacious if misguided pursuit of 'the facts of life' during her childhood, as to her pursuit of a husband at an age when for her 'love and marriage were synonymous'.[1] Yet it describes with equal precision both the breakdown of her first marriage – the initiation of 'proceedings for divorce'[2] representing a 'pursuit' in the legal sense of that term – and the travails of her second, to a young socialist whom she pursues first to Pimlico,[3] and then to the refugee camps of Perpignan[4] in the aftermath of the Spanish Civil War. Ultimately, in the wake of two failed marriages, the phrase comes to define the physical exertions of her 'war work in Paris'[5] – a euphemism for a love-affair that sees 'pursuit' shift in sense to 'pastime' as Linda discovers the pleasures of making love in the restive atmosphere of the phoney war. Indeed, while Linda's narrative ends during the Second World War, Mitford's own pursuit of love – her attempt to capture on paper the idiosyncrasies of desire among the upper classes – continued well into the postwar period. Despite ranging in temporal scope from the 1920s to the late 1950s, *The Pursuit of Love*, its sequels, *Love in a Cold Climate* (1949) and *Don't Tell Alfred* (1960), and its spin-off *The Blessing* (1951), all engaged with contemporary anxieties about love. Sex education, birth-control, abortion, childbirth, adultery, divorce, homosexuality, child molestation, teenage morality and interracial adoption: all are dealt with in these novels, and all can be viewed through the lens of pursuit. That this perspective was by no means an isolated one is evident from the titles of many equally unconventional 'love stories' of the period, from Elizabeth Taylor's

---

[1] Nancy Mitford, *The Pursuit of Love* (Harmondsworth: Penguin, 2010), pp. 2, 35.   [2] Ibid., p. 99.
[3] Ibid., p. 102.   [4] Ibid., p. 118.   [5] Ibid., p. 161.

characterisation of extra-marital love as *A Game of Hide and Seek* (1951) to Walter Baxter's provocative depiction of a female promiscuity contingent upon *The Image and the Search* (1953) and Mary Renault's identification of the homosexual lover with *The Charioteer* (1953).

To think, more broadly, of a postwar literature of desire characterised by pursuit is to recognise the importance of what Jeffrey Weeks terms the 'differentiated, overlapping sexual cultures' of 1940s and 1950s Britain, while remaining alert to the 'wider and dominating structures'[6] of an era in which love, in all its forms, its objects and its practices, was pursued as never before, not only by private citizens, but by scientists, statisticians and psychoanalysts, law-enforcers, legislators and judicial reformers, racketeers and journalists. A vocabulary of pursuit emerges from contemporary sources and persists today in historical accounts of postwar desire. In his introduction to the ground-breaking study *Sexual Behaviour in the Human Male* (1948), Alfred Kinsey framed the project itself as a 'pursuit' of sexual behaviour, 'a thoroughly objective, fact-finding investigation of sex'[7] undertaken in the spirit of the pioneers: 'As scientific explorers, we ... have been unlimited in our search to find out what people do sexually'.[8] Mass Observation's 1949 survey of sexual life, often referred to as Little Kinsey, echoed these terms, presenting its findings as those of a 'penetrative observational investigation into the social set-up of sex' in Britain.[9]

Accounts of prosecutions for sexual offences – particularly homosexual offences – were more emotive: if the scientists of the postwar period aimed at the exploration and investigation of love, the law and the press, according to some, sought only to harry and corner it. While evidence in fact foundered for a state-led 'witch-hunt against homosexuals'[10] such as that to which journalist Peter Wildeblood believed he and his high-profile co-defendants in the Montagu Case had fallen victim, the terminology stuck.

---

[6] Jeffrey Weeks, *The World We Have Won: The Remaking of Erotic and Intimate Life* (London: Routledge, 2007), p. 33.
[7] Alfred C. Kinsey, Wardell B. Pomeroy and Clyde E. Martin, *Sexual Behaviour in the Human Male* (Philadelphia, PA: Saunders, 1948), p. 4.
[8] Ibid., p. 51.
[9] Liz Stanley, *Sex Surveyed, 1949–1994: From Mass-Observation's 'Little Kinsey' to the National Survey and the Hite Reports* (London: Routledge, 2014), p. 70. Carried out in 1949, Little Kinsey was the first national random sample survey of sex to be undertaken in Britain, although its findings sat unpublished until 1995. The report, as Liz Stanley notes in her introduction to the rehabilitated text, 'offers an unparalleled insight into British sexual mores as these had been influenced by changes associated with, perhaps even caused by, the war, including the new expectations that women had about their lives, that young people had of what they thought was acceptable sexual behaviour, that people in general had of the relationship between marriage and sexual pleasure and between marriage and childbirth' (pp. 5–6).
[10] Peter Wildeblood, *Against the Law* (London: Weidenfeld & Nicolson, 1956), p. 47.

The Wolfenden Report, published as the 'Report of the Departmental Committee on Homosexual Offences and Prostitution' in 1957, quoted Wildeblood's account of his trial directly, arguing that despite claims 'of a nation-wide "witch-hunt" against homosexuals', it had 'found no evidence for any "drive" on a national scale'.[11] It could not, however, rule out what it termed 'deliberate drives by police'[12] at a local level, and thus tacitly confirmed that, as Weeks notes, there *were* hunters out there: 'The real reason for the rise in prosecutions was increased police zeal in hunting out miscreants, especially in key metropolitan areas such as London.'[13] Such prosecutions – by definition 'pursuits' in and of themselves – ensured in turn that, by the mid-1950s, even 'the papers had found opportunities to pursue queer stories beyond their wildest expectations'.[14] Indeed, Wildeblood himself extended the hunt metaphor to those of his own former profession in *Against the Law* (1955): 'From the peculiar vantage-point of someone who has been both hunter and hunted, I can look back on Fleet Street with amusement, but without anger.'[15]

The novels examined in this chapter span a period of fifteen years, from Henry Green's *Caught* (1943) to Michael Nelson's *A Room in Chelsea Square* (1958), and engage with a range of potentially non-normative desires, whether these be ostensibly heterosexual or homosexual, physical or emotional, adolescent or octogenarian, transient or enduring. In considering the various ways in which fiction writers of the 1940s and 1950s engaged with the theme of pursuit in their portrayals of love, connections emerge between seemingly disparate texts which fall most naturally into groups determined, I would suggest, neither by when they were published, nor by the primary modes of desire they depict. Rather, the most meaningful connections between these texts emerge when we consider them in terms of the periods that they evoke – from the seeming tranquillity of Denton Welch's and Mary Renault's interwar summers to the imagined oppressions of a new millennium in Henry Green's *Concluding* (1948) – as the attitudes and concerns of their temporal settings intersect with those of the age in which they were disseminated.

---

[11] 'Report of the Departmental Committee on Homosexual Offences and Prostitution' (London: HMSO, 1957), p. 48.
[12] Ibid.   [13] Weeks, *The World We Have Won*, p. 47.
[14] Justin Bengry, 'Queer Profits: Homosexual Scandal and the Origins of Legal Reform in Britain' in Heike Bauer and Matt Cook (eds), *Queer 1950s: Rethinking Sexuality in the Postwar Years* (Basingstoke: Palgrave, 2012), pp. 167–82, 171.
[15] Wildeblood, *Against the Law*, p. 31.

Sex Education

You'd have to buy us plimsolls and gym tunics, underclothes in a decent state and some good strong luggage. I've seen girls going off to school, they are covered with expensive things. Of course, we long for it, pashes for the prefects and rags in the dorm. School has a very sexy side you know, Sadie – why, the very word "mistress," Sadie, you know...[16]

Published in the same year as Mitford's second Radlett novel, *Love in a Cold Climate*, Dorothy Strachey's *Olivia* (1949) presented a self-conscious semi-autobiographical account of lesbian desire in the interwar schoolroom, which sought to avoid the levity enjoyed by the younger Radlett sisters. Indeed, Strachey recalled in her introduction: 'Really no one had ever heard of such a thing, except as a joke. Yes, people used to make joking allusions to "school-girl crushes." But I knew well enough that my "crush" was not a joke.'[17] Yet her heroine is in many ways not so unlike the Radlett girls, sharing their appetite – although Olivia herself is only able to recognise this with hindsight – as much for what she terms 'the sensual element' of school life as for the 'more orthodox studies' it entails.[18] While neither so resourceful as the Radletts – who, as children, glean 'far more information'[19] about sex from a book entitled *Ducks and Duck Breeding* than from anywhere else – nor nearly so direct, Olivia is, however unconsciously, pursuing sexual knowledge as surely as are the sisters.

At school, Olivia finds intimates with whom she might pursue the 'dangerous subjects' of love and marriage, their talk tending always towards the same impasse: 'that extraordinary, alluring, forbidden mystery that we sensed lying at the back of all grown-up minds, what was it? We knew dimly we should never understand anything till we understood that.' Looking back, she realises, 'how ignorant we were! How undirected, how misdirected our curiosity! How far from discovering the right track, of even suspecting its existence!'[20] Fascinated by the 'mystery' of love, Olivia-as-schoolgirl knows neither what she is searching for, nor where to search for it: she is, as the mistress for whom she later forms a passionate attachment warns, 'pursuing chimeras'.[21] Yet the urge to search, to actively explore, as 'undirected' as it may be, is instinctive and irresistible: 'I musn't [sic] rest till I found out'.[22] Olivia's ignorance, even as to her object, is, however, by no means untypical. Mass Observation's *Little Kinsey*,

---

[16] Nancy Mitford, *Love in a Cold Climate* (Harmondsworth Penguin, 2010), p. 101.
[17] Dorothy Strachey, *Olivia: A Novel* (London: Vintage, 2008), p. 9.   [18] Ibid., pp. 12, 31.
[19] Mitford, *Pursuit*, p. 14.   [20] Strachey, *Olivia*, p. 14.   [21] Ibid., p. 69.   [22] Ibid., p. 27.

choosing to 'spotlight sex education'[23] as a key component of its 1949 survey, found 'that most people – of the present adult generation, at least – have been left to stumble for themselves upon the "facts of life"'.[24] Fragmentary and disordered, the acquisition of these 'facts' did not necessarily guarantee that the stumbler walked 'the right track' when it came to assembling and interpreting them in relation to 'life' or love. For many, the survey found, 'it was literally a matter of putting two and two together on the basis of whatever information they could discover'.[25] The result arrived at was not always four, and the discrepancies, if 'no joke' to Strachey, found comic expression in novels such as Mary Renault's *The Friendly Young Ladies* and Denton Welch's *In Youth Is Pleasure* (both 1944).

Offering perhaps the most literal evocation of what Little Kinsey described as 'an unguarded stumbling upon haphazard sex facts',[26] Welch's novella explicitly frames its 15-year-old protagonist, Orvil Pym, as an explorer for whom exploration, however innocently embarked upon, inevitably exposes elements of 'the veiled but rather heavy sexuality'[27] attendant upon adolescence. Holidaying in the Surrey countryside with his father, his two elder brothers and their friends, Orvil in fact spends most of the narrative in complete solitude, opting – as he tells the London schoolmaster he meets by the river – to 'roam about, exploring' each day.[28] With little or no direction, and no clear object in mind, he is motivated solely by curiosity and a desire for peace: 'He had made no plan; he only wished to be left alone to explore for the rest of the day.'[29] Following his instincts, however, he stumbles from one 'queer' scenario to another, each in its own way 'full of sex'.[30] A glimpse of the young schoolmaster and two bare-chested boys rowing on the river – their bodies 'brown as burnt sugar'[31] – inspires Orvil to hire a canoe, from which he later watches 'hungrily' as the trio go about the chores of their riverside camp, Welch's references to appetite emphasising the instinctive nature of Orvil's pursuit. The raw homosociality of the scene overpowers him: 'his real hunger was not for the food but for the joyful life of these others. A burning pang of longing and envy shot through him while he crouched there, his face camouflaged by the long feathery blades of grass.'[32] Discovering, as he hurries agitatedly back to the hotel, a break in the railings of an abandoned garden, 'Orvil, who never could resist exploring derelict places, felt impelled to get through this hole into the garden behind. He also fiercely

---

[23] Stanley, *Sex Surveyed*, p. 74.   [24] Ibid., p. 76.   [25] Ibid.   [26] Ibid., p. 83.
[27] Denton Welch, *In Youth Is Pleasure* (London: Enitharmon, 2005), p. 74.   [28] Ibid., p. 68.
[29] Ibid., p. 30.   [30] Ibid., p. 9.   [31] Ibid., p. 30.   [32] Ibid., p. 34.

desired some very solitary place; for the frustration and excitement inside him were becoming almost unbearable.'[33] Re-emerging a few minutes later, he is dismayed to find that he has been observed masturbating by a local busybody: 'I saw you! You devil! You filthy little devil!'[34]

Seemingly undeterred, Orvil's 'love of exploring'[35] leads, in the following days, to an experiment in self-flagellation in the hotel's deserted ballroom; a trial in body painting with a shop-lifted lipstick; a kiss, forced 'juicily'[36] upon a woman figured in brass amid the memorial plaques in a local church; and a direct encounter with the schoolmaster of the riverside camp, with whom he shelters, stripped to his underclothes, during a violent storm. The knowledge of their shared seclusion sends a 'tremor, like a weak orgasm'[37] through Orvil, while it inspires the schoolmaster to a homoerotically charged lesson in knot-tying: 'Now it's your turn ... you can tie me up exactly as you like.'[38] Tempted later by what he articulates as an 'urge of restlessness' into 'going to explore'[39] the hotel grounds by night, he catches his eldest brother having sex with a married female friend, a sight which, in coalescence with disgust, fills him 'with much lust'.[40] His explorations having led him to such facts, however, Orvil is incapable of arranging them coherently in relation to his own life, telling the schoolmaster, to whom he makes one final visit, seeking 'someone of good sense and strength, someone who would offer him good advice': 'I don't understand how to live, what to do.'[41] It is a sentiment shared by Renault's Elsie Lane, whose sheltered life in a Cornwall village has 'suspended her in the most awkward stage of adolescence for quite three superfluous years'.[42] Despite having had 'the facts of life ... revealed to her behind a stand of mackintoshes in the school cloakroom',[43] Elsie is unable to reconcile these with what little she knows of love and life.

Encouraged by locum GP and budding psychoanalyst Peter Bracknell to seek out her long-absent elder sister Leonora and, in doing so, the 'queer'[44] sexual secret that led to her disappearance, Elsie stumbles blindly into Leo's London life, but fails entirely to 'pursue the subject'[45] of her sexuality to its logical conclusion. She is oblivious to the nature of Leo's relationship with her 'great friend'[46] Helen Vaughan, touching upon the truth only unconsciously as she vents her own frustrations, telling Leo: 'I'm not like you. I can't live like that, standing by myself and fighting everyone ... I'll never know how to live properly'.[47] Yet the incapacity to 'live properly' is what –

---

[33] Ibid., p. 36. [34] Ibid., p. 37. [35] Ibid., p. 47. [36] Ibid., p. 55. [37] Ibid., p. 63.
[38] Ibid., p. 71. [39] Ibid., p. 83. [40] Ibid., p. 88. [41] Ibid., pp. 116, 120.
[42] Mary Renault, *The Friendly Young Ladies* (London: Virago, 2014), p. 8. [43] Ibid., p. 7.
[44] Ibid., p. 91. [45] Ibid., p. 84. [46] Ibid., p. 109. [47] Ibid., pp. 88–9.

if only temporarily, and for very different reasons – connects the sisters, Leo telling Helen: 'There are times . . . when the facts of life strike me as so damned silly I stop believing in them.'[48] While Elsie's difficulty in reconciling the facts stems from an uneasy incomprehension, however, Leo's is the result of what Gill Plain terms a 'happy indifference to the expectations of heterosexual desire'.[49] The pursuit of an empirical knowledge of love has taught Leo that both gender and sexual desire are 'fluid and protean',[50] a possibility for which neither the inherited 'facts of life' nor the 'psychological theory' championed by Peter – which would make of non-normative sexuality 'a disorder to be cured' – leave room.[51]

A Little War Work

> We still had plenty to talk about, or rather Tom had, and it was quite amusing when the sea was right up and the spray breaking round. But it was a long time going out, and we finally got to the end of our conversation. So after a while Tom told me what a nice girl I'd grown into, and started kissing me. It was a bit of a novelty . . . and it seemed to pass the time as well as anything, so we kept it up for a bit.[52]

If the definitions of 'pursuit' can be divided roughly into two categories – those that necessarily imply movement through space and those that do not – then it is in accounts of wartime desire that the latter begin to subsume the former, love becoming a pastime, an entertainment, an antidote to restlessness and forced inactivity. As Henry Green puts it in his depiction of life in the Auxiliary Fire Service, the suggestively titled narrative *Caught* (1943): 'After the first excitement of war died down, as it soon did when there were no raids, the fun and games started.'[53] Cases have been made both for the 'new sexual opportunities'[54] afforded by the conflict and for 'the boredom of war'[55] itself, but it is with the intersection of the two that many contemporary novels are concerned, some apparently supporting John Costello's assertion that 'sexual restraint had been suspended for the duration, as the traditional licence of the battlefield invaded

---

[48] Ibid., p. 131.
[49] Gill Plain, *Literature of the 1940s: War, Postwar and 'Peace'* (Edinburgh University Press, 2013), p. 107.
[50] Ibid.   [51] Ibid., pp. 197, 317.   [52] Renault, *Ladies*, p. 93.
[53] Henry Green, *Caught* (London: Harvill, 2001), p. 45.
[54] Lesley A. Hall, *Sex, Gender and Social Change in Britain Since 1880*, 2nd edn (Basingstoke: Palgrave, 2013), p. 117.
[55] Samuel Hynes, *The Soldier's Tale: Bearing Witness to Modern War* (Harmondsworth: Penguin, 1998), p. 9.

the home front'.[56] Reading *Caught*, it is impossible to escape the sexual implications of one character's sincere belief that the 'war's been a tremendous release for most'.[57]

With 'time on their hands' and a newfound popularity with civilians, many of Green's auxiliaries see sex as a compensation for the 'anticlimax' of the phoney war.[58] Love itself becomes an almost habitual pastime, its pursuers rendering London's nightclubs 'like hotels, from double bedrooms of which the guests came, gorged with love, sleep lovewalking'.[59] Nor is this attitude restricted to male characters, Sub Officer Pye counting among his 'successes at night' a girl for whom the equation is disturbingly simple: 'War, she thought, was sex'.[60] Yet for others love proves more than an antidote to boredom. Widower Richard Roe – whose reticence leads some at the sub-station to speculate: 'Is Roe a pansy?'[61] – does initially pursue love as a pastime, a remedy for the 'restless' solitude that the wartime 'alteration in his circumstances'[62] has brought about. What he finds, however, in pursuing a physical relationship with WAFS girl Hilly, is as much a release from the tensions wrought by pre-war trauma – the premature death of his wife, the abduction of his son – as from the restlessness of war: 'The relief he experienced when their bodies met was like the crack, on a snow silent day, of a branch that breaks to fall under a weight of snow, as his hands went ... over the hills, moors, and wooded valleys, over the fat white winter of her body'.[63] For Richard, the sexual licence afforded by the war serves to heal, bringing 'contentment'[64] and meaning.

The mitigation of 'wartime licence' also served those wishing to engage with other non-normative sexualities, both Mary Renault and Walter Baxter choosing – in *The Charioteer* (1953) and *Look Down in Mercy* (1951) respectively – to historicise their accounts of male homosexual desire. The war had certainly been conducive to such desire, its upheavals greatly increasing the fluency between the two poles of what Eve Sedgwick terms 'the continuum ... extending over the erotic, social, familial, economic and political realms ... of male homosocial and homosexual bonds'.[65] For some, including Baxter's protagonist, immersion in an all-male environment combined with a heightened consciousness of danger to render the continuum between 'men loving men' and 'men promoting the interests of

---

[56] John Costello, *Love, Sex, and War: Changing Values, 1939–45* (London: Collins, 1985), p. 17.
[57] Green, *Caught*, p. 98.   [58] Ibid., pp. 28, 2.   [59] Ibid., p. 47.   [60] Ibid., pp. 47, 119.
[61] Ibid., p. 126.   [62] Ibid., p. 98.   [63] Ibid., p. 116.   [64] Ibid., p. 118.
[65] Eve Kosofsky Sedgwick, *Between Men: English Literature and Male Homosocial Desire* (New York: Columbia University Press, 1985), pp. 3–4.

men'[66] less problematic, awakening previously latent desires. For others, such as Renault's, already reconciled in some measure to their own homosexuality, wartime homosociality afforded a greater concentration of potential partners and ensured a certain invisibility. Renault's Laurie Odell, hospitalised in Hertfordshire in the aftermath of Dunkirk, sees love as an amusement. Bedridden and bored, with 'no entertainment to pass the time, except the slow procession across the ward' of a group of student doctors, he amuses himself by flirting with one of their number: 'Laurie caught his eye before he could disengage it, and gave him a deliberately dazzling smile. As he had confidently expected, the young man went crimson, and merged himself deeply in the throng.'[67]

When the pair meet again in Bridstow several weeks later, it is as old adversaries, opponents in an as yet unfinished game: 'Hanging unspoken between them, and clearly understood, were the words, "Your move"'.[68] That Laurie's inclination to play – to prolong the flirtation – is motivated by boredom rather than attraction is evident in his response. Thanking the doctor, Sandy Reid, for saving him from an evening in a public air-raid shelter, he suggests, 'I suppose if I look about this city I might find something a bit more entertaining than a hole in the ground'.[69] And, indeed, he does, the 'queer party'[70] to which Sandy invites him reuniting Laurie with his former schoolmate and boyhood idol Ralph Lanyon. The relationship that develops between the two injured men is far more than a mere pastime, despite Laurie's initial worry that he is tolerated only because Ralph 'felt bored and ... wanted someone to talk to and pass the time'.[71] If Laurie's attachment to hospital orderly Andrew Raynes brings him 'relief', his relationship with Ralph exceeds this, in bringing both 'a feeling of being looked after' and a 'feeling of fulfilment'.[72] When the pair at last engage sexually, Laurie recognises in the act Ralph's own belief in love as a restorative: 'He had offered all he had, as simply as a cigarette or a drink, for a palliative of present pain'.[73] As Ralph himself later tells him, 'you can't live without love'.[74]

This is a conclusion towards which Baxter's far more conflicted protagonist, married officer Anthony Kent, can only begin to grope his way.

---

[66] Ibid., p. 4.
[67] Mary Renault, *The Charioteer* (London: Virago, 2013), p. 45. Itself descriptive of an individual in pursuit, Renault's title is drawn from the *Phaedrus* of Plato, a dialogue on love in which Socrates figures the soul as the union of a team of winged horses – one reasonable, one reckless – and their charioteer.
[68] Ibid., p. 129.   [69] Ibid., p. 130.   [70] Ibid., p. 375.   [71] Ibid., p. 233.
[72] Ibid., pp. 65, 262, 274.   [73] Ibid., p. 349.   [74] Ibid., p. 363.

In *Look Down in Mercy* as in *The Charioteer*, love – in its most casual forms – is initially figured as a pastime, an idle habit, Kent himself making love 'perfunctorily'[75] to nurse Helen Dean aboard the troop-ship from India to Burma. Amid the horrors of open warfare, however, desire becomes at once more basic and more complex, as Kent finds himself drawn to his batman, Anson. When the pair fall asleep locked in an embrace initiated by Kent, he awakes to a 'mind chaotic with remorse and fear at what he had done, and with the pleasure and relief he felt at having done it'.[76] Yet, terrifying as it may be, love is again figured as a restorative: in all that follows, it is Anson alone who, in a seemingly godless world, is able to provide the 'refuge' and 'strength' of Baxter's epigraph.[77] Accompanying Kent to Mandalay on sick-leave solidifies Anson's dual role as nurse and lover, providing 'a comfort'[78] that no one else – not even Helen, a professional and a woman – can give the officer: 'Anson's closeness gave Kent a feeling of great tenderness for him and he fought against sleep, trying to prolong the few hours before he must leave'.[79] In an ironic volte-face, love's capacity to 'pass the time as well as anything' turns, for Kent, from its greatest attribute to its meanest.

Hunting for Witches

> They were specialists. They had not merely accepted their limitations, as Laurie was ready to accept his, loyal to his humanity if not to his sex, and bringing an extra humility to the hard study of human experience. They had identified themselves with their limitations; they were making a career of them. They had turned from all other reality, and curled up in them snugly, as in a womb.[80]

In *The Heart in Exile* (1953), Adam de Hegedus – writing as Rodney Garland – presents a homosexual protagonist who, in the aftermath of war and amid the 'social revolution'[81] of the early Welfare State, has turned life as a 'specialist' to his advantage, 'making a career' of his 'limitations' in a way quite different from that envisioned by Renault's Laurie Odell, although perhaps equally as divorced from reality. A psychoanalyst with a particular interest in the 'treatment' of homosexuality, Garland's

---

[75] Walter Baxter, *Look Down in Mercy* (London: Heinemann, 1951), p. 35.   [76] Ibid., p 137.
[77] 'O God, our refuge and our strength, look down in mercy upon Thy people who cry for Thee'. Ibid., unpaginated.
[78] Ibid., p. 189.   [79] Ibid.
[80] Renault, *Charioteer*, p. 156. Such is Laurie Odell's assessment of his fellow guests at Sandy Reid's queer party.
[81] Rodney Garland, *The Heart in Exile* (New York: Coward-McCann, 1954), p. 116.

Anthony Page numbers among those in postwar Britain pursuing love – legitimately or otherwise – as a business. As he recalls of his commitment as a medical student: 'Perhaps it was ... my desire to get on in the world. I had very little money and I wanted to make a career.'[82] As a psychoanalyst and a homosexual in 1950s London, Page occupies a position similar to that in which Peter Wildeblood would find himself, as both hunter and hunted, since, as Dorothy Strachey would complain in 1949, the psychoanalyst is a hunter by profession, 'lying in ambush, waiting and watching for the prowling beasts, the nocturnal vermin, to come creeping out of their lairs' in the subconscious.[83]

This duality is thrown into relief in *The Heart in Exile* as Page, agreeing to 'investigate' the suicide of ex-lover Julian Leclerc on behalf of his desolate but unsuspecting fiancée, begins to divide his time between his consulting-room and the queer haunts of London's 'underground society'.[84] Motivated as much by 'fear' for his own secrets as by 'curiosity' for Julian's – and uncertain of the degree to which these might still intersect – Page is acutely aware of his own status as 'the hunted criminal' as he turns 'private detective'.[85] Yet, as he begins to 'hunt and tour the pubs'[86] of his past for leads on Julian's affairs, it becomes clear that Page's capacity for pursuit derives as much from his personal as his professional life. The law has made 'hunting' the *modus operandi* of homosexual culture and every individual has his role, acquaintance Hugh Harpley reminding Page, 'you hunt. But I like to be hunted, so I have an agonising fear of growing old.'[87] If Harpley is unusual among the 'hunted' of the underground for being wealthy, his position is symptomatic of how indistinct the line between hunter and hunted – formerly divisible along class lines – has become in the age of the Welfare State. Always, at some level, a business transaction, the hunt has been exposed as such, Garland suggests, by a new generation of young, working-class homosexuals able to hone their 'selling points'[88] and even turn hunters themselves. As Page notes: 'Sometimes ... it is difficult to decide whether the other is "trade" or competition.'[89]

The more disturbing aspects of this shifting dynamic are explored in Angus Wilson's *Hemlock and After* (1952) as erstwhile-closeted homosexual protagonist Bernard Sands witnesses the arrest of a young man for 'importuning' in Leicester Square.[90] An episode one might expect to inspire solidarity, the sympathy of a fellow hunted criminal, the incident in fact

---

[82] Ibid., p. 134. [83] Strachey, *Olivia*, p. 9. [84] Garland, *The Heart in Exile*, pp. 19, 54.
[85] Ibid., pp. 109, 110, 172. [86] Ibid., p. 67. [87] Ibid., pp. 94, 125. [88] Ibid., p. 234.
[89] Ibid., p. 58. [90] Angus Wilson, *Hemlock and After* (Harmondsworth: Penguin, 1956), p. 108.

fills Bernard with excitement, his readiness 'to join the hounds in the kill' only subsiding in the realisation 'that in the detective's attitude of somewhat officious but routine duty there was no response to his own hunter's thrill'.[91] A distinguished novelist, long-standing member of London literary society, and regular guest of *salonnière* Evelyn Ramage, Bernard has spent the afternoon in pondering the altered dynamic of Evelyn's gatherings in recent years. His reaction in Leicester Square might be traced to this contemplation of the 'homosexual borderland' represented by her guests in relation to 'his present preoccupation with the nature of evil'.[92] With his 'long dark hair' and his expression of 'confident, sexy invitation', the importuner is an irritatingly palpable reminder of 'the kind of second-rateness'[93] by which Bernard believes he and 'the rest of the old order' are 'pursued' not as objects in themselves, but as a route to other more 'complicated ambitions'.[94]

For 'the golden spiv group'[95] of the postwar generation, sex has become if not a career in itself, then a career-path, in a society in which, as Alan Sinfield notes, the source of evil 'is not the working class, or the state, or a technocracy, but an amoral obsession with personal advancement'.[96] The implications of this obsession find fuller expression in the characters of Terence Lambert and Ron Wrigley. An ex-lover of Bernard's, a recent graduate of the spiv world and, by dint of this and other relationships both homo- and heterosexual, Terence – despite being described by Evelyn as a 'poor lamb' – is quite capable of bagging 'an important "catch"' from among her guests.[97] Ron, a provincial spiv who dogs Bernard's steps in and around his hometown – and the site of his planned retreat for young writers – is figured as 'at once the lone wolf and the boy who got to the top though everyone tried to kick him down'.[98] Both are, as Wilson's metaphors suggest, potential wolves in sheep's clothing, but it is the younger, ostensibly heterosexual Ron – who sees his work as middle-man for the grotesque child-procuress Vera Curry as no more than 'a bit of business'[99] – from whom, Wilson implies, society has most to fear, in part because his youth and heterosexuality render him less conspicuous and easier to dismiss.

Looking at *The Heart in Exile* and *Hemlock and After* in isolation, it is tempting to accept what Gregory Woods terms the 'standard version of the 1950s' as 'a pinched, humourless decade in which the heterosexist

---

[91] Ibid., p. 109.   [92] Ibid., p. 102.   [93] Ibid., p. 107.   [94] Ibid., p. 103.   [95] Ibid., p. 102.
[96] Alan Sinfield, *Literature, Politics, and Culture in Postwar Britain* (Berkeley, CA: University of California Press, 1989), p. 75.
[97] Wilson, *Hemlock and After*, pp. 100, 104.   [98] Ibid., p. 141.   [99] Ibid., p. 34.

institutions of state', if they could not altogether silence the 'deviant voices' of queer authors, at least ensured they spoke in harried whispers.[100] It is in contradicting this version of the 1950s that Michael Nelson's *A Room in Chelsea Square* (1958) remains so valuable. An acerbic, neo-Wildean satire on London literary life, initially published anonymously in anticipation of the wrath it might provoke in its thinly veiled models, *A Room in Chelsea Square* takes homosexuality entirely for granted, aiming neither at defence nor apology, indifferent to the legislative battles of the decade from which it was sprung. Nelson, like Garland and Wilson, is preoccupied with the commodification of sex, but his characterisation leaves little room for sympathy either with hunter or hunted. For wealthy, middle-aged Patrick, 'young men were like pictures you wanted to buy'.[101] And while it is clear that provincial journalist Nicholas Milestone is initially unaware of the true implications of Patrick's decision to 'bring him to London and launch him on a career', he is not in the dark for long, a taste of what Patrick's money can buy proving enough 'to persuade him that there were more agreeable occupations' than journalism.[102] Without a legitimate job, however, Nicholas is entirely at Patrick's mercy: the moral of the story – if there is one – is that we would do well to consider 'gold mining a dangerous pursuit'.[103]

The Ministry of Love

> 'I'm from the Ministry,' I said. We were now in the kitchen ... The Ministry; just the Ministry. It didn't matter which. This was the surest excuse in our time to obtain entry to almost any house. I was the new meaning of the word 'they' – a representative, albeit a humble one, of the State, all powerful but benevolent, rewarding the faithful, punishing the infidel.[104]

For some, the postwar pursuit of love, in its 'official' guises – by sexologists, psychoanalysts, prosecutors and government committees alike – was a worrying indicator of things to come: to undertake a survey appeared but a few short steps away from undertaking full-scale surveillance and centralised regulation of desire. Set in the grounds of a state-run institution for girls, over the course of a single summer's day at the beginning of the twenty-first century, Henry Green's sultry *Concluding* (1948) is a novel

---

[100] Gregory Woods, *A History of Gay Literature: The Male Tradition* (London: Yale University Press, 1998), p. 289.
[101] Michael Nelson, *A Room in Chelsea Square* (London: GMP, 1986), p. 89.
[102] Ibid., pp. 25, 113.   [103] Ibid., p. 65.   [104] Garland, *The Heart in Exile*, p. 243.

'drenched with love'.[105] It is a love conditioned entirely by the demands of the state, but one which, nevertheless, threatens to overrun its boundaries, taking with it the 'entire scaffolding of Reports'[106] by which the institution is constrained.

Overseen by aging spinsters Mabel Edge and Hermione Baker, while it is the explicit purpose of the institution to educate 'embryo State Servants'[107] aged between 12 and 17, implicitly – as this metaphor suggests – it serves to maintain ignorance among its charges, to infantilise and retard sexual development at the behest of the state. The object of this state-sanctioned repression is, like so much else in the novel, never explained, one mistress silently questioning:

> ... how it could ever be that the State should send these girls, who were really women, to be treated like children; she marvelled as Moira stood respectfully flaunting maturity ... that the State (which had just raised the age of consent by two whole years) should lay down how this woman was to be treated as unfunctional, like a child that could scarcely blow its own nose.[108]

The disappearance, on Founder's Day, of two of the girls – one of whom is quickly found, in a state of undress, beneath a fallen beech tree, while the other remains missing throughout the novel – serves as a catalyst for administrative and sexual dissent. Despite speculation as to possible sexual motives for the incident, the principals – apprehensive of 'laying their Institute open to the Grand Inquisition of a State Enquiry, and the horror of Reports'[109] – postpone indefinitely the required report, while the search for the remaining truant, amid preparations for the evening's ball, affords staff and students alike relative freedom in which to pursue their own romantic interests. For master Sebastian Birt, it is an opportunity to meet with Elizabeth Rock, a young woman living with her retired grandfather in the school grounds after suffering a mysterious breakdown 'from overstrain'[110] in her capacity as a state servant; for senior schoolgirl Moira, a chance to tease and flirt with Elizabeth's grandfather, her youth reminding him 'of a ripe plum, on a hot day, against green leaves'.[111] Both intrigues culminate in the uncontrolled outpourings of the ball: for Sebastian and Elizabeth, this takes the form of an 'orgiastic ... display of animalism' on the dancefloor; for Moira and the baffled octogenarian, of a sudden, fumbled kiss in the 'dead silent, underground passage' beneath it.[112]

---

[105] Henry Green, *Concluding* (London: Dalkey Archive, 2000), p. 83.   [106] Ibid., p. 109.
[107] Ibid., p. 20.   [108] Ibid., p. 40.   [109] Ibid., p. 92.   [110] Ibid., p. 5.   [111] Ibid., p. 68.
[112] Ibid., pp. 181, 188.

If *Concluding* illustrates the limitations of a system of sexual surveillance entirely dependent upon hand- or type-written reports and the discretion of individuals, the official pursuit of love reaches its logical conclusion in the surveillance techniques of George Orwell's *Nineteen Eighty-Four* (1949): 'With the development of television, and the technical advance which made it possible to receive and transmit simultaneously on the same instrument, private life came to an end.'[113] Yet it is, ironically, protagonist Winston Smith's own, hand-written documentation – a diary begun in the novel's opening chapter – which serves to corroborate the allegations of 'sexcrime' made by the state against himself and his lover Julia.[114] Orwell envisions a state able to turn any medium to its cause. United in their determination 'to kill the sex instinct, or, if it could not be killed, then to distort it and dirty it',[115] the four ministries 'between which the entire apparatus of government'[116] is divided control the production of everything – from pornographic material to domestic furnishings – concerned with the formerly 'private' life. Winston's own workplace, The Ministry of Truth, employs high-achieving members of youth movement the Junior Anti-Sex League – Julia among them – in 'Pornosec, the sub-section of the Fiction Department which turned out cheap pornography for distribution among the proles'.[117] Meanwhile, both Winston and Julia luxuriate in 'the size and springiness' of the antique bed that dominates their rented rendezvous, since one 'never saw a double bed nowadays'.[118] Technological transitions thus support environmental controls in the state's prevention of sexcrime, defined as: 'fornication, adultery, homosexuality and other perversions, and, in addition, normal intercourse practised for its own sake'.[119]

In 1957 – less than a decade after *Nineteen Eighty-Four* appeared – the Wolfenden Report would recommend that 'homosexual behaviour between consenting adults in private should no longer be a criminal offence'.[120] The committee's decision hinged, much like the plot of Orwell's novel, on the issue of privacy: 'Many heterosexual acts are not criminal if committed in private but are punishable if committed in circumstances which outrage public decency, and we should expect the same criteria to apply to homosexual acts.'[121] In collapsing the binary of public and private life, *Nineteen Eighty-Four* threw into sharp relief the double-standard which would ensure that, for the time being at least, this

---

[113] George Orwell, *Nineteen Eighty-Four* (Harmondsworth: Penguin, 2004), p. 214.
[114] Ibid., p. 319. [115] Ibid., p. 69. [116] Ibid., p. 6. [117] Ibid., p. 137. [118] Ibid., pp. 149, 150.
[119] Ibid., p. 319. [120] Wolfenden Report, p. 25. [121] Ibid.

criterion was *not* applied to homosexual behaviour – and the implication that sexual freedom should be the privilege of those provided with a private space within which to practise it. If privacy no longer existed, Orwell forecast, nor could sexual freedom, leaving normative sexuality to become the negation of sexuality itself, normative desire the negation of desire.

CHAPTER 17

Creating Vital Theatre: New Voices in a Time of Transition

Claire Cochrane

But us count? Count Mother? I wonder. Do we? Do you think we really count? You don' wanna take any notice of what them ole papers say about the workers bein' all important these days – that's all squit! 'Cos we aren't. Do you think when the really talented people in the country get to work they get to work for us? Hell if they do! Do you think they don't know we 'ont make the effort? The 'I'll wait for you in the heavens blue' writers don't write thinkin' we can understand, nor the painters don't paint expecting us to be interested – that they don't, nor don't the composers give out music thinking we can appreciate it. 'Blust,' they say, 'the masses is too stupid for us to come down to them. 'Blust,' they say, 'if they don't make no effort why should we bother?'[1]

This is Beatie Bryant. She's 22. It's 1958 and she's home from London on a visit to her family in rural Norfolk and she's just been ditched in a letter sent by her 'intellectual' socialist lover Ronnie Kahn. Reeling from the shock and humiliation made even worse by the slapped face inflicted by her mother, suddenly Beatie finds her voice pouring out her frustration and deep sense of social inequality while raging against the mental inertia which perpetuates the cultural status quo. We're very nearly at the end of the play. Her mother exasperated by her 'high-class squit' goes back to the table to eat the ample high tea laid on for the absentee, Ronnie. But Beatie is ecstatic, on her 'own two feet', able to speak and articulate her own thoughts for the first time.

The final scene of Arnold Wesker's *Roots* is one of the seminal moments within the canon of late 1950s' British drama. Wesker himself, his background, ideology and aesthetic, combined with the thematic content, narrative and characters of the play and the means of its first production

---

[1] Arnold Wesker, *Roots* (London: Bloomsbury, 2015), pp. 76–7.

in 1959, together create a complex emblem of the society and theatre of the period. The first performance was mounted at the Belgrade Theatre in Coventry in May 1959. Beatie was played by Joan Plowright relishing a role which saw her subsequently dubbed 'an angry young woman',[2] and the production was directed by John Dexter, one of the circle of young directors surrounding George Devine, the co-founder and artistic director of the English Stage Company (ESC) at the Royal Court Theatre in 1955.[3] What became known as the Wesker Trilogy, *Chicken Soup with Barley* (1958), *Roots* (1959) and *I'm Talking about Jerusalem* (1960), emerged out of the developmental environment for new writers created by Devine. All were premiered in Coventry before transferring to the Royal Court. For the Belgrade, newly opened in 1958 as the United Kingdom's first local authority-built, not-for-profit, regional producing theatre, the relationship with the Court brought a welcome element of cutting-edge excitement and metropolitan prestige. For the Court there was the immediate financial benefit gained from the additional funding on offer from the Arts Council of Great Britain (ACGB) to promote the interests of regional theatre, as well as the reputational value derived from the altruistic sharing of London-centred expertise and resources.[4]

As examples of the social realism considered most typical of the New Wave of British drama kick-started – according to the most familiar narrative of 1950s' British theatre – in 1956 by John Osborne's *Look Back in Anger*, Wesker's early plays, including *The Kitchen* written in 1957, derive much of their felt life from the raw material supplied by his own experience. Born in 1932, educated in Hackney at Upton House School following grammar school-scholarship failure,[5] his employment from 1948 until 1958 was successively as a furniture-maker's apprentice, carpenter's mate, farm labourer, seed sorter, kitchen porter and pastry cook – details of which feed into the plays.[6] What any account of Wesker as a 'working-class' playwright reveals, however, is the inadequacy and instability of this socioeconomic category and the way in which it is deployed as a generic descriptor for the emerging drama and theatre aesthetic of the period. The very specifically observed *milieux* delineated by Wesker demonstrate a

---

[2] Joan Plowright, *And That's Not All: The Memoirs of Joan Plowright* (London: Orion, 2001), pp. 43–4.
[3] For an account of the founding of the ESC, see Irving Wardle, *The Theatres of George Devine* (London: Jonathan Cape, 1978), pp. 166–89.
[4] Claire Cochrane, 'Place-Performance Relationships within the English Urban Context: Coventry and the Belgrade Theatre' *Studies in Theatre & Performance* (2013) 33(3) pp. 303–20.
[5] Sylvia Roger, 'Class Act: The Teacher Who Inspired . . . Arnold Wesker', *Telegraph* (2 August 2003), www.telegraph.co.uk/education/educationnews/3314844/Class-act.html
[6] Arnold Wesker, *The Wesker Trilogy* (Harmondsworth: Penguin, 1964), p. 1.

complex pattern of working communities at a time of increasingly blurred class boundaries and consciousness.

While not originally conceived as a unified trilogy, the three plays first staged together at the Royal Court in 1960 have an epic scope, weaving together the lives of characters first encountered in *Chicken Soup*. We first meet the London East End Jewish Kahn family (much like Wesker's) on 4 October 1936, the day of Oswald Mosley's attempt to march his British Union of Fascists through the East End. In epic style, the play jumps twice, first to 1946–7 and then 1955–6, relocating to the council flat in Hackney where the family's matriarch Sarah Kahn and her chronically work-shy and increasingly disabled husband Harry move after the Second World War with their daughter Ada and teenager Ronnie, who is clearly a version of Wesker. The mature Ronnie is an invisible, if powerfully opinionated, presence in *Roots* which is focused on the two weeks of Beatie's visit moving between her sister's and parents' homes. *Jerusalem* remains in Norfolk to chart the journey from 1946 to 1959 of Ada and her husband Dave, who try and ultimately fail to create a rural utopia through a furniture-making business grounded in a William Morris-style faith in the dignity of craft-based independence. Throughout, the other characters from the East End community enter and re-enter the story, especially Sarah and Ronnie.

As John Bull has pointed out, these are 'state-of-the-nation-plays',[7] with the Trilogy bookended by two historical events: the triumphant Cable Street collective assault on Mosley's march and, in the final scene of *Jerusalem*, the re-election to government of the Conservative Party led by Prime Minister Harold Macmillan in 1959. Threaded through is a lament for the failure of the socialist dream of class equality and the effective redistribution of opportunity and resources. The indomitable Sarah Kahn remains steadfast in her allegiance to the communist ideology which inspired her in the 1930s, even when Ronnie tries to force her to acknowledge the Soviet brutality in suppressing the 1956 Hungarian uprising.[8] Dave's retreat into rural self-sufficiency is provoked by his bleak experience of fighting both on the Republican side in the Spanish Civil War and the Second World War. Life in the Hackney flats brings a sense of isolation and battles with the inadequacies of the newly established National Health Service. Ronnie returns heart-sick after the grind of working in Paris kitchens. In *Roots*, Beatie's sister lives in a house with no electricity, gas

---

[7] John Bull, 'Arnold Wesker: The Trilogy' in David Pattie (ed.), *Modern British Playwriting: The 1950s. Voices, Documents, New Interpretations* (London: Methuen, 2012), pp. 171–97, 194.
[8] Arnold Wesker, *Chicken Soup with Barley* (London: Methuen, 2011), pp. 71–3.

or running water. As both Beatie's father and Dave Simpson discover, in Norfolk's rural economy employment rights are precarious and the arbitrary powers exercised by land owners are as patronising and callous as ever. At the end of *Jerusalem*, Ronnie, chided by his mother, stops weeping over his sense of failure. The last stage direction has him hurling a stone high into the air shouting 'We – must-be – bloody-mad-to cry!'[9]

Historians of the period routinely point out that Harold Macmillan's much-quoted 'Let's be frank about it: most of our people have never had it so good' statement, made in a 1957 speech to Tory party members, was immediately followed by anxiety about how long the feel-good factor could last. General Election victory in 1959 – won with the slogan 'Life's better with the Conservatives. Don't let Labour ruin it' – followed two years of skilful management of inflationary pressures and underlying unemployment indicators.[10] As the historian Peter Clarke has suggested, consciousness of the growing disjunction between private affluence and public squalor was raised particularly among those on the political Left by books such as *The Affluent Society*, published in 1958 by the economist J. K. Galbraith, and the Labour politician Anthony Crosland's 1956 *The Future of Socialism*.[11] In 1960, in Coventry, the Belgrade Theatre made its own comment, premiering a now little-remembered play by the South African playwright John Wiles which drew on recorded conversations among local people. *Never Had It So Good* sardonically implied that new high-rise housing, bulging wage packets from factory work and consumer goods like washing machines, televisions and cars might not necessarily bring happiness along with prosperity.[12] The uneasy critical reception given to the play, especially when staged at Joan Littlewood's Theatre Royal in Stratford East, worried that an attack was being directed at Coventry's working people rather than at the concrete fault-lines within the city's brave, new postwar vision.[13]

The extent to which drama conceived and staged in response to a particular set of cultural trends becomes embedded in a literary canon is the result of a complex process of reception, evaluation and re-evaluation. As I discuss below, the criteria for canon formation are also subject to changing priorities. Dan Rebellato's polemical *1956 and All That: The Making of Modern British Drama* (1999) offers a combative reading of the

---

[9] Wesker, *The Wesker Trilogy*, p. 218.
[10] Peter Clarke, *Hope and Glory: Britain 1900–1990* (Harmondsworth: Penguin, 1996), pp. 268–70.
[11] Ibid., p. 272.   [12] Cochrane, 'Place-Performance Relationships', pp. 310–11.
[13] For a selection of reviews, see: www.alanhoward.org.uk/never%20so%20good.htm

period which in particular challenges the impression that British theatre prior to the formation of the English Stage Company languished in some sort of dark ages.[14] Yael Zarhy-Levo's *The Making of Theatrical Reputations* (2008) shows how 'processes of mediation' together with key individuals acting as 'mediators' become significant agents in consolidating the preeminent position of particular individuals and events within the historical record.[15] By 1962, canon formation was well underway, mediated by John Russell Taylor's book *Anger and After*, which itself then became a canonical critical text as it laid claim to the precise moment when British theatre changed: 8 May 1956, the first night of *Look Back in Anger*.[16]

It is well known, however, that the success of *Look Back in Anger* was significantly enhanced by an extract televised on BBC television in October 1956 – which boosted audience attendance at the Court – followed by the transmission of the whole play by ITV in November.[17] Indeed, popular consciousness of the New Wave sensibility was subsequently largely formed through screen media. Even as cinema as mass entertainment was giving way to the effortless domestic accessibility of television, Woodfall Films – set up by George Devine's associate Tony Richardson (who directed *Look Back in Anger*) with John Osborne and the producer Harry Saltzman – offered a counter-narrative to the complacent assurances of a better life for all. Shot in black and white, the films of *Look Back in Anger* (1959), Osborne's *The Entertainer* (1960) and Shelagh Delaney's *A Taste of Honey* (1961) literally drained the colour out of the landscape of late 1950s' Britain with gritty images of dingy regional towns and cramped hand-to-mouth lives. Arguably, these early films especially reinforced the perception of social realism as the dominant mode of the theatrical avant-garde. In the case of *A Taste of Honey*, several of the original 1958 cast were replaced, as was Joan Littlewood, who had been the shaping presence behind Delaney's original script. With Richardson credited as co-author of the screenplay with Delaney, the non-naturalistic elements introduced by Littlewood were smoothed out in favour of realism.[18]

---

[14] Dan Rebellato, *1956 and All That: The Making of Modern British Drama* (London: Routledge, 1999), pp. 1–9.
[15] Yael Zarhy-Levo, *The Making of Theatrical Reputations* (Iowa City, IA: University of Iowa Press, 2008), pp. 7–14.
[16] John Russell Taylor, *Anger and After: A Guide to the New British Drama* (London: Methuen, 1969), p. 28.
[17] Zarhy-Levo, *The Making of Theatrical Reputations*, pp. 35–6.
[18] Stephen Lacey, *British Realist Theatre: The New Wave in Its Context 1956–65* (London: Routledge, 1995), pp. 163–70. See also Rebecca D'Monté, 'Democracy and Decentralisation' in this volume (Chapter 3).

Although few 'canonical' plays-as-literature emerged from Theatre Workshop in the 1950s, Littlewood must nonetheless be recognised as a key figure of the period.[19] Her dramaturgical techniques were applied through a rigorous process of company experimentation, with texts ranging from Shakespeare and his lesser-known contemporaries right through, in 1959, to *Fings Aint't Wot They Used T'Be*, an initially 'straight' play by Frank Norman featuring characters from London's disreputable underbelly speaking in Cockney rhyming slang and rogues' cant which was turned into a boisterous musical.[20] And it was Littlewood's performative methodologies and actor training techniques – the importance of which would only be fully recognised much later – that made her, along with Devine, such a significant figure in the creation of a new 'vital theatre'. Although radically different personalities, the two shared an immersion in the theory and practices of the major European theatre-makers whose ideas became more widely disseminated in the 1930s.[21] The concept of 'vital theatre' as it was consistently promoted after 1956 in the influential journal *Encore* summed up the objectives of both the ESC and Theatre Workshop and drove the educative and nurturing working environments created in both companies.[22] Devine, unambiguously dedicated to the creation of a writers' theatre, offered opportunities for promising writers to observe activity at the Royal Court, act as play readers and on occasion have their plays staged for a Sunday night 'production-without-décor' performance. In 1958, he set up the Writers' Group which, after a faltering start, consolidated itself into a weekly meeting to which writers including Ann Jellicoe, Arnold Wesker, Wole Soyinka, Edward Bond and David Cregan brought draft scenes and passages for discussion and improvisation.[23] At this time of transition for British theatre, when commercial producing interests were still dominant and before the setting-up of the Royal Shakespeare Company and the National Theatre Company in 1961 and 1962, with their access to greater public funding, the ESC and Theatre Workshop set the agenda for innovation.[24]

---

[19] Arguably, only *A Taste of Honey* and the Irish dramatist Brendan Behan's *The Quare Fellow* and *The Hostage* made their way from Theatre Workshop to the canon.

[20] Howard Goorney, *The Theatre Workshop Story* (London: Methuen, 1981), pp. 111–12.

[21] Nadine Holdsworth, *Joan Littlewood's Theatre* (Cambridge University Press, 2011), pp. 7–9.

[22] Stephen Lacey, *British Realist Theatre*, pp. 38–9. *Encore* magazine, subtitled 'The Voice of Vital Theatre', appeared every two months between 1956 and 1965, featuring contributions by most of the leading proponents of the socially concerned theatrical avant-garde, as well as cultural commentators such as Stuart Hall and Raymond Williams.

[23] Wardle, *The Theatres of George Devine*, p. 199.

[24] For a discussion of the relationship between commercial theatre interests and the newly established national companies, see Claire Cochrane, *Twentieth-Century British Theatre: Industry, Art and Empire* (Cambridge University Press, 2011), pp. 174–81.

Any survey of the new drama of the period, and that includes *Anger and After*, which for all its initial foregrounding of Osborne does cover a range of other playwrights, reveals the diversity of theme, form and genre emerging from playwrights eager to seize the opportunities on offer especially within the magic circles of influence created in the metropolis. The plays that quickly began to appear in regional producing theatre programmes were, on the whole, indicative of future durability. By 1960, *A Taste of Honey* and *Roots*, which carried the additional benefit of strong female roles, were on stages as far apart as Glasgow, Nottingham, Salisbury, Northampton and Birmingham. Nottingham Playhouse produced *Look Back in Anger* and *The Entertainer* in successive seasons in 1957 and 1958.[25] But no regional city or town could sustain more than one producing theatre even where the basic principle of municipal subsidy had been broadly accepted. Each artistic directorate had to consider the variety of local tastes and expectations and receptiveness to new, perhaps controversial, perspectives.

One playwright developed at the Royal Court who was taken up by regional houses was N. F. 'Wally' Simpson. His plays, in particular *A Resounding Tinkle* (1957) and *One Way Pendulum* (1959), represented a quirky, perhaps peculiarly British, response to the formal experimentation arriving from Europe. Described in a 2011 obituary as the leader of the British Absurdist movement,[26] the philosophical basis of Simpson's plays, while certainly not grounded in the existential bleakness of Beckett's work, manifested itself through a wildly anarchic imagination, accompanied by disquisitions on the effects of comedy and the role of the audience. John Russell Taylor drew attention to Simpson's admiration for 'the rigidly logical brand of linguistic fantasy' he found in Eugène Ionesco.[27] The surreal daftness of the elephant (inconveniently larger than the previous one) in the suburban garden of Bro and Middie Paradock in *A Resounding Tinkle*, and the weighing machines being taught to sing the Hallelujah Chorus in *One Way Pendulum*[28] also owed a lot to the wartime radio success of *ITMA*.[29] William Gaskill, who was given *A Resounding Tinkle* as

---

[25] George Rowell and Anthony Jackson, *The Repertory Movement: A History of Regional Theatre in Britain* (Cambridge University Press, 1984), pp. 198–200; John Bailey, *A Theatre for All Seasons: Nottingham Playhouse, the First Thirty Years 1948–1978* (Stroud: Alan Sutton Publishing, 1994), pp. 190–1.

[26] Richard Anthony Baker, 'Obituary: N. F. Simpson', *The Stage* (14 September 2011), www.thestage.co.uk/features/obituaries/2011/nf-simpson.

[27] Taylor, *Anger and After*, p. 11.   [28] Ibid., pp. 66–72.

[29] *ITMA* or *It's That Man Again* was a BBC radio comedy show led by the comedian Tommy Handley which ran from 1939 to 1949. *The Goon Show* was broadcast on BBC radio from 1951 to 1960. See www.comedy.co.uk/radio/itma/ and www.thegoonshow.net/beginners_guide.asp

a first directing exercise at the Royal Court, saw Simpson as a link between the postwar *Goon Show* and the subsequent 1960s' success of *Beyond the Fringe* and *Monty Python's Flying Circus*.[30] In truth, as Gaskill's recollections of audience response demonstrate, getting the laughs required a pretty high level of educated understanding.[31] With hindsight, however, Simpson's comments anticipate much later exploration of audience reception and the nature of the theatrical event: 'It is together that we must shape the experience which is the play we shall all of us have shared. The actors are as much the audience as the audience themselves, in precisely the same way that the audience are as much the actors as the actors themselves.'[32] Ultimately, Taylor damned with faint praise: 'absurdity in a much humbler form, and one which very rapidly loses its charms in a life-and-death struggle with the law of diminishing returns'.[33] Arguably, it was precisely Simpson's 'humbler form' which made his work more viable for regional theatre programmers unable to draw on the resources available in the metropolis and warier of stronger meat.

The depiction of the material realities of the lived experience of 1950s' society by ambitious theatre-makers were constrained, as they had been since the eighteenth century, by the censoring powers of the Lord Chamberlain. Every new play script and new translation of a non-English classic text had to be submitted for scrutiny and this continued until 1968. Even at the very basic level of demotic language, let alone pressing social issues, the Lord Chamberlain and his Examiners of Plays were a ubiquitous, thwarting presence. Famously, the premiere of Beckett's English translation of *Endgame*, first staged in French as *Fin de partie* by Devine in 1957, was delayed when Beckett refused the official request to cut Hamm's line about God, 'The bastard he doesn't exist'.[34] In the case of *Chicken Soup with Barley*, the censor objected to Wesker's attempt to emphasise the physical burdens of serious illness. As quoted by Steve Nicholson in his monumental history of twentieth-century theatre censorship, the Examiner of Plays, Charles Heriot, complained of 'a far too intense concentration on natural functions ... we all know that after a severe stroke some elderly people become incontinent. It is hardly necessary to remind us five times that Harry fouls his garments and his sheets.'[35] Devine, for all his ideological antipathy to establishment prejudices,

---

[30] William Gaskill, *A Sense of Direction* (London: Faber & Faber, 1988), pp. 14–16.
[31] Ibid., pp. 39–40.   [32] N. F. Simpson quoted in Taylor, *Anger and After*, p. 70.
[33] Taylor, *Anger and After*, p. 73.   [34] Wardle, *The Theatres of George Devine*, p. 205.
[35] Steve Nicholson, *The Censorship of British Drama 1900–1968, vol. 3: The Fifties* (University of Exeter Press, 2011), p. 186.

moved in the same circles and knew his enemy well. Steadily and carefully, he manoeuvred his way round the obstructions.[36]

Joan Littlewood and Theatre Workshop were another case altogether. Decried as a 'communist' in Examiners' reports and routinely accused of lying, Littlewood was a thorn in their collective flesh. The idea that a play might be a dynamic, living product capable of creative change and evolution was entirely blocked by a system which insisted that the licensed play had to remain completely fixed in performance. The prosecution brought against Theatre Workshop in 1957 for *You Won't Always Be on Top* by Henry Chapman was actioned because reports reached the police that actors were improvising dialogue in performance. Chapman, who acted in the production and was described at the time of the prosecution as a builder's labourer, had written a play which took place within the time frame of a wet Monday for a group of building site workers. Actors, taught basic bricklaying skills, literally built a wall during the course of the play and engaged in dialogue which replicated in familiar banter what Littlewood described as 'the raciness, tang and rhythm of democratic speech'.[37] There was no plot as such, but what came across – as Nadine Holdsworth puts it in her detailed account of the production – was the shared knowledge and cultural experience 'typical of their class status, revealed through conversations about the football, racing and the Saturday night fight on television'.[38] Summoned to appear at West Ham Magistrates' Court, the Theatre Royal management pleaded guilty as they were bound to do. The actor Richard Harris also pleaded guilty to imitating Winston Churchill's voice in the scene of an official opening of a public lavatory. The outcome – a fine of only £15 – will have given the Lord Chamberlain small comfort. Treated as a test case by anti-censorship campaigners, it attracted very high-profile support as well as substantial contributions to a defence fund.[39]

Stage censorship was only one example of a society still heavily controlled by authoritarian legislative structures. Homosexual relationships even between consenting adults were illegal.[40] Women lived in terror of unwanted pregnancies with no legal access to abortion, while children born outside marriage bore the stigma of illegitimacy. Suicide was illegal and

---

[36] Wardle, *The Theatres of George Devine*, p. 171.
[37] Joan Littlewood quoted in Holdsworth, *Joan Littlewood's Theatre*, p. 149.
[38] Holdsworth, *Joan Littlewood's Theatre*, pp. 145–51, 149.
[39] Nicholson, *The Censorship of British Drama*, vol. 3, pp. 141–7.
[40] For discussion of the treatment of homosexual relationships during this period, see Rebellato, *1956 and All That*, pp. 155–91.

until 1961 failed attempts could be prosecuted. National Service for all able-bodied men between the ages of 18 and 30 enforced peacetime conscription until 1963. Arnold Wesker's experience of a brutal disciplinary regime and class-based humiliation was dramatised in *Chips with Everything* (1962), which proved to be one of his most successful plays.[41] While increasingly controversial, capital punishment was still an available option for the judiciary for the most serious crimes. Behan's *The Quare Fellow*, staged in Stratford East in 1956 only two months after the House of Lords had overruled Parliament's attempt to abolish the death penalty, is set during the night of an execution in a Dublin prison. The evocation of the impact of the impending judicial killing on the collective consciousness of the enclosed prison community is rendered even more intense through the black humour of the dialogue and the grim, matter-of-fact details of the practical preparations.[42]

If the dominant mentalité was socially and culturally conservative, there were destabilising factors undermining the general complacency. Cold War tensions, combined with Britain's participation in the arms race, meant that fear of all-out nuclear war was by no means unrealistic. The creation of the Campaign for Nuclear Disarmament launched in 1958 attracted widespread support in the artistic community. While one possible reading of the dead landscape outside the walls of the room inhabited by Hamm and Clov in Beckett's *Endgame* could be the aftermath of nuclear war, in the best-known of the new British dramatic writing, allusions to the atom bomb were usually confined to passing remarks by characters: Jimmy Porter referring to the 'big bang' and Beatie Bryant on the silliness of trust in conventional weapons as protection against the hydrogen bomb both reinforce a sense of helplessness in the face of global power.[43] In Osborne's *The Entertainer*, however, the reported death of Archie Rice's son Mick fighting in the 'Middle East' aligns family tragedy with the national humiliation caused in 1956 by the bungled political and military response to the nationalisation of the Suez Canal by the Egyptian President General Nasser. The demise of the once vibrant music hall tradition, the deadness behind the eyes of Archie Rice, are symptomatic of what appears to be the lingering death of 'Great' Britain.[44]

---

[41] Bull, 'Arnold Wesker: The Trilogy', p. 172.
[42] Holdsworth, *Joan Littlewood's Theatre*, pp. 170–7.
[43] John Osborne, *Look Back in Anger* (London: Faber & Faber, 2015), p. 89; Wesker, *Roots*, p. 16.
[44] John Osborne, *The Entertainer* in *John Osborne Plays 2* (London: Faber & Faber, 1998), p. 66; Luc Gilleman, 'John Osborne: The Drama of Emotions' in Pattie, *Modern British Playwriting: The 1950s*, pp. 146–71, 158–60.

Creating Vital Theatre 323

The nation probed and prodded in John Arden's plays is challenged by a disconcerting array of characters inhabiting a morally ambiguous contemporary landscape. Arden in the late 1950s was simultaneously the most defiantly political and theatrically confusing of the Royal Court writers. Vigorously defended by George Devine who valued his intellectual and aesthetic bravura,[45] Arden's work routinely emptied the Royal Court auditorium and elicited at best contradictory reviews. That the plays have secured a place in the major dramatic canon is in part due to Devine's determined advocacy, but also, as with the other 'classic' plays of the period, the result of their publication. As Dan Rebellato points out, the publishing initiatives by Penguin and Methuen in the 1950s and early 1960s, and the commitment to retaining their lists in print, ensured a long-term future and capacity for creative reappraisal of the otherwise ephemeral performance text.[46]

The title of Arden's *The Waters of Babylon*, first staged in a Sunday night performance at the Royal Court in 1957, is taken from Psalm 137. The poet of 'By the waters of Babylon I sat down and wept' is an ancient Israelite lamenting the loss of his promised land. The core characters in Arden's play, reflective of the increasing migratory complexity of British society, are also far from home. The central character Krank (Sigismanfred Krankiewicz) is Polish and works (like Arden) in an architect's office. But he is no Wesker-esque doppelgänger. Krank sings of Nazi concentration camps he has known not, as it eventually transpires, as a Jewish victim, but as a member of the German army.[47] The other role he has in his adopted country is as the owner of a lodging house into which he has crammed some eighty assorted 'West Indians, East Indians, Cypriots'[48] – an all too familiar situation for migrant workers. Krank also controls a number of prostitutes, in particular the Barbadian Bathsheba, tasked with recruiting other newly arrived girls of assorted origin. His Irish lodger Conor Cassidy is a gents' toilet attendant for London Transport. Krank needs to acquire £500 to pay off his Polish compatriot Paul who intends to use Krank's house to mount a bomb plot on the occasion of the 1956 visit of the Soviet leaders Khruschev and Bulganin to London. Getting the money entails working with a seedy Yorkshireman Charles Butterthwaite and the West Indian Councillor Joseph Caligula on a Savings Bank and Public Lottery scheme 'in which no one can lose'.[49]

---

[45] Wardle, *The Theatres of George Devine*, p. 212.   [46] Rebellato, *1956 and All That*, pp. 121–2.
[47] John Arden, *The Waters of Babylon* in *Arden Plays: 1* (London: Methuen, 1994), p. 8.
[48] Ibid., p. 14.   [49] Ibid., p. 50.

At first glance, this only partial plot summary suggests a grim exposure of criminality. In fact, there is a gleeful quality to this parade of bizarre characters – the audience baited with every possible contemporary stereotype to test their liberal assumptions. A similar strategy is at work in *Live Like Pigs* (1958), where the disruptive, aggressive Sawney family are forced to abandon their semi-nomadic life by well-meaning housing officers who move them onto a new suburban housing estate, next door to the eminently respectable Jacksons. The final outcome – a brutal neighbourhood backlash against the Sawneys which breaks apart their family – completely reverses expectations, exposing passions and the potential for savagery lying beneath the veneer of affluent stability.

Stephen Lacey suggests that Arden inhabits the same thematic territory as social realism, but from a perspective which is 'anarchist and libertarian rather than Marxist', and in which the 'essential and reoccurring conflicts are between the instinctive anarchy of the people and the repressive order of "good" government of whatever complexion'.[50] The plays are stimulated by, but remain at a distance from, actual events: in the case of *The Waters of Babylon*, a scandal linked to the newly introduced Premium Bond scheme, and in *Live Like Pigs*, a violent episode on a northern housing estate. The origins of Arden's most famous play *Serjeant Musgrave's Dance*, premiered in 1959, lie in an incident in Cyprus, then occupied by British troops, when the shooting in the streets of a soldier's wife by terrorists led to a killing spree by soldiers. Set sometime between 1860 and 1880 in a snow-locked, strike-bound, English mining town, the play tells of four deserters led by 'Black Jack' Musgrave who, ostensibly on a recruiting campaign, are in fact carrying the skeleton of Billy Hicks, a young dead comrade from the town who was also the lover of the barmaid Annie and the father of her dead child. Musgrave's mission is to ram home the horror and futility of endlessly recurring cycles of colonial retributive violence by an exemplary act of retaliation. In the climax of the play, set in the market square, he gives a brutally graphic account of the soldier's life and demonstrates the power of modern weaponry (the Gatling gun) before hoisting Billy's scarlet-uniformed skeleton in front of the horrified crowd. The relentless logic of his intention to replicate the reprisals for Billy's death by killing an even greater number of townsfolk is shattered in a chaotic sequence of interventions by other characters. The play ends in the prison cell where Musgrave waits for death with his surviving comrade, Attercliffe, and here, as throughout the play, audiences are offered no simple direction

[50] Lacey, *British Realist Theatre*, pp. 130–1.

for their sympathies.⁵¹ Arden, describing himself as a 'timid man', reminds later readers of his play that 'complete pacifism is a very hard doctrine' and moreover 'an unwillingness to dwell upon unpleasant situations that do not immediately concern us is a general human trait, and recognition of it need imply neither cynicism nor despair'.⁵²

The deliberate exposure of audiences to complex moral problems, the use of song interspersed among the action, characters as types representing the compromises and unpredictability of human behaviour, as well as the mixture of verse and prose in the dialogue seem derived from Brecht, although Arden was resistant to that suggestion. Both men, however, were poets, and the poem which forms the Dedication to *The Waters of Babylon* uses powerful imagery to assert unequivocally the moral responsibility of the writer:

> The pen must crawl:
> The black ink fill the waiting space:
> For tortoise and child alone
> The shell is an honourable home⁵³

Arden, probably more than any of his immediate contemporaries, is preoccupied with the legacy of Empire and the consequences of colonial appropriation. As Musgrave puts it, 'we belong to a regiment is a few thousand miles from here, in a little country without much importance except from the point of view that there's a Union Jack flies over it and the people of that country can write British Subject after their names. And that makes us proud.'⁵⁴ The process of dismantling Empire and the beginning of 'colonisation in reverse'⁵⁵ after the Second World War necessitated a very significant psychological adjustment to the British population's sense of national entitlement. The terms of the 1948 Nationality Act gave any British colonial or Commonwealth citizen the right of British nationality. The result was an influx of migrants from the Caribbean, many of whom had fought in the war and who now came to the mother country in search of a better life. The disastrous consequences, in terms of violent loss of life and livelihood, of the 1947 partition of the Indian subcontinent between India and the newly created state of Pakistan also provoked a gradually accelerating stream of South Asian arrivals. The outcome for many is well

---

[51] John Arden, *Serjeant Musgrave's Dance* (London: Methuen, 2005), pp. 76–104.
[52] John Arden, 'Introduction' in *Serjeant Musgrave's Dance*, pp. 5–7, 7.
[53] John Arden, 'Dedication' in *The Waters of Babylon*, p. 1.
[54] Arden, *Serjeant Musgrave's Dance*, p. 83.
[55] Robert Winder, *Bloody Foreigners: The Story of Immigration to Britain* (London: Little, Brown, 2004), p. 257.

documented: rejection, hostility, disparagement of high levels of educational and technical attainment and municipal housing policies amounting to ghettoisation.[56] Krank's house with eighty-plus lodgers is not such an exaggeration. In the summer of 1957, within days of each other, serious race riots broke out in Nottingham and London.

I have written elsewhere about the efforts of British actors of colour to make headway in the theatre in the 1950s and 1960s especially in the face of preference given to African-American actors and the ubiquity of the blacking/browning up of white actors.[57] However, there were plays written by the 'new' British and once again it was the Royal Court management which proved, albeit very sporadically, the most hospitable. John Russell Taylor to his credit includes in *Anger and After* the work of two such playwrights: the Jamaican-born Barry Reckord, whose *Flesh to a Tiger* was directed by Tony Richardson in 1958, and the Trinidadian actor Errol John, whose *Moon on a Rainbow Shawl* reached the Court later the same year.[58] The Nigerian Wole Soyinka who was an active participant in the Court's Writers' Group is not mentioned by Taylor, although his first professional one-act play *The Invention*, a humorous but nevertheless scathing attack on apartheid South Africa, was given a Sunday night performance in 1959.[59] In addition, William Gaskill describes the Group's improvised piece *Eleven Men Dead at Hola Camp*, which was a dramatised protest about the beating to death of eleven detainees in Kenya in 1959 at the time of the Mau Mau Uprising. A diverse group of black actors was assembled on a Sunday evening for an event described as 'a strange mixture of inadequate improvisation, political passion [and] beautiful songs by Wole Soyinka'. There was, Gaskill records, a 'tremendous audience response'.[60]

As I noted above, the criteria for literary canon formation are subject to changing priorities. For the best part of four decades, the mid-century work of the black British theatre-makers of the 1940s and 1950s was rendered virtually invisible in the historical record. In recent years, however, scholarship on black theatre history has been steadily gathering

---

[56] Cochrane, *Twentieth-Century British Theatre*, pp. 141–3.   [57] Ibid., pp. 224–35.
[58] Taylor, *Anger and After*, pp. 106–8. See also Helen Thomas, 'The Social and Political Context of Black British Theatre: 1950s-80s' in Mary F. Brewer, Lynette Goddard and Deirdre Osborne (eds), *Modern and Contemporary Black British Drama* (London: Palgrave, 2015), pp. 17–31, esp. 21–2.
[59] Pushpa N. Parekh and Siga F. Jagne, 'Wole Soyinka (1934-)' in *Postcolonial African Writers: A Bio-Bibliographical Critical Sourcebook* (Westport, CT: Greenwood Publishing Group, 1998), pp. 438–54, 439.
[60] Gaskill, *A Sense of Direction*, p. 38.

momentum.[61] Now it matters that the pioneering plays are better known, open to canonical inclusion, and available for performance and analysis. The Jamaican-born actor and director Yvonne Brewster, one of the co-founders of Talawa Theatre Company in 1986, has been instrumental in the editing and publication of significant plays.[62] In the case of Cambridge University-educated Barry Reckord, whose occlusion has been so extreme as to cause chronic uncertainty about the spelling of his surname (frequently given as Reckford), Brewster collected and published three plays under the title of *For the Reckord* in 2010.

The challenge of re-establishing the original texts of plays is indicative of the marginality of the playwrights in their own time. While Yvonne Brewster recounts the contemporary difficulty of finding Reckord's scripts, new black playwrights were also confronted by difficulties specific to the period.[63] Errol John's *Moon on a Rainbow Shawl* provides a useful example. The play (written in 1953) won the 1957 *Observer* play competition – an initiative set up by the newspaper's theatre critic and influential 'mediator' Kenneth Tynan to encourage new plays.[64] Optioned by the powerful commercial management H. M. Tennent, the responsibility for directing *Rainbow Shawl* was put into the unlikely hands of West End director Frith Banbury who, while genuinely impressed by John's work, insisted on substantial rewriting and cast the three main roles with African-American actors. Poorly supported on a regional tour, it ended up on the Royal Court stage in December 1958 pretty much as an act of desperation.[65]

Linguistically, it is interesting to compare *Moon on a Rainbow Shawl* and *Flesh to a Tiger* with *Roots*. As will have been obvious in the extract quoted at the beginning of this chapter, Wesker paid considerable attention to rendering the dialect and intonation of his Norfolk characters as accurately as possible. Errol John, locating his play in the dilapidated dwellings of a Port-of-Spain backyard, uses 'nation language', eschewing standard English to evoke distinctive Trinidadian speech patterns. A similar strategy

---

[61] See, e.g.: Dimple Godiwala (ed.), *Alternatives within the Mainstream: British Black and Asian Theatres* (Newcastle: Cambridge Scholars Press, 2006); Godfrey V. Davis and Anne Fuchs (eds), *Staging New Britain: Aspects of Black and South Asian British Theatre Practice* (Brussels: PIE-Peter Lang, 2006).

[62] Yvonne Brewster, *Black Plays: One* (London: Methuen, 1987); *Black Plays: Two* (London: Methuen, 1989); *Black Plays: Three* (London: Methuen, 1995).

[63] Yvonne Brewster, 'Introduction' in *For the Reckord: A Collection of Three Plays by Barry Reckord* (London: Oberon Books, 2010), pp. 11–15.

[64] Charles Duff, *The Lost Summer: The Heyday of the West End Theatre* (London: Nick Hern, 1995), p. 217.

[65] Ibid., pp. 217–21.

is deployed by Reckord in the heightened language and Jamaican syntactical structures of the dialogue spoken by his Trench Town characters. Each of the three playwrights is working in an idiomatically specific form of English, attempting to ground the felt reality of 'other' lives in the voices heard by the audience. Both John and Reckord inhabited the in-between cultural and emotional dislocations of the migrant: fully belonging neither to the Caribbean nor to the frequently hostile environment of their adopted country, their displacement exacerbated by skin colour, the visible signifier of difference. In the 1950s, their use of nation language, described by Kamau Brathwaite as the Caribbean language 'of slaves and labourers, the servants who were brought in',[66] challenged the dominance of the white standard English voice on the British stage.

Locating their plays in vividly realised territories of the Caribbean allows each playwright to explore the different destructive effects of colonisation. 'Flesh to a Tiger' is a direct quotation from Reckord's play which makes the fate of Tata, a dying baby, the catalyst for a battle between ingrained local cultural practices, represented by Shepherd Aaron, the leader of the *obeah* (voodoo) cult, and the rational interventions of the white Doctor/White-Wolf. The potential reassurance offered by modern medicine is undermined by the sexual relationship between Della, the baby's mother, and the Doctor, which exposes the controlling, exploitative impulses of the superior white coloniser. As Miss Lal, the woman Della confides in, warns her: 'That man would batter you like a hurricane; flash his lightning against you and walk' way leave you. For black to white is flesh to a tiger. When they come cross it, they tear it.'[67] Trapped between two inimical male forces and conscious that 'a slave hide' has been drawn over her body, Della vows to 'vomit all white flesh'[68] in rejecting the Doctor, smothers her baby 'so that by death you destroy Shepherd and make White-Wolf less strong', and finally stabs Shepherd. Her personal tragedy is mitigated by an awakening to political consciousness and the hope that purging the internalised slave mentality can ultimately bring independence and self-determination.

In contrast, *Moon on a Rainbow Shawl* is set at a celebratory moment when Trinidadian troops are returning home as heroes in the aftermath of Second World War victory, symbolically a high point in the fusing

---

[66] Kamau Brathwaite, *History of the Voice: The Development of Nation Language in Anglophone Caribbean Poetry* (London: New Beacon, 1984), pp. 5–6.
[67] Barry Reckord, *Flesh to a Tiger* in Brewster, *For the Reckord*, p. 25. [68] Ibid., p. 38.

together of black and white collaborative strength in a common cause. The play is suffused with references to what these British subjects regard as theirs: pride in the Union Jack, Winston Churchill, cricket, landmark colonial buildings and the educational system. But for the central character Ephraim, the trolley bus driver, longing for 'a slice of that ole orange moon' shining on 'bigger parts of the world',[69] his job and the complicated, hand-to-mouth lives of the yard are obstacles to his fantasy of the freedom and opportunities represented by the figurative 'mother country'. 'And it ent my intention to remain here and grow a big white moustache like Ole Sam who used to drive a tramcar – and when the trolleys come they pension him off with a pittance. This Trinidad has nothin' fer me! Nothin' I want!'[70] The 'nothin' includes his pregnant girlfriend Rosa whom he abandons as he makes his escape. The irony of his likely fate when he reaches his dream destination of Liverpool will not have been lost on the play's audiences in 1958. What, given the production constraints and the interventions in John's original script, would not have been so clear, is the extent to which John wanted to stress that Trinidad was the most cosmopolitan of the Caribbean islands – the result of centuries of successive waves of colonial settlement. In his published casting instructions, John wants actors 'with the greatest variety of complexions' who visibly embody the 'racial patchwork' of the population.[71] The implications of this subliminal message for audiences gradually coming to terms with their increasingly postcolonial, patchworked society were almost certainly too subtle for 1958. However, the patchwork factor infiltrated the play's subsequent stage history in other ways. Thanks to Frith Banbury's casting decisions, it was the African-American recognition of the play which enabled John to restore the text for a New York production in 1962. In 1988, the African-American poet Maya Angelou directed a revival at the Almeida Theatre in London with a black British cast.[72] John himself directed the play at Stratford East in 1985 three years before his death.

As I hope will have become clear, the new playwrights aligned to the 1950s' campaign for a 'vital theatre' did not speak with one voice. Individually, they represented a very diverse experience of what Stephen Lacey has dubbed 'a curious and idiosyncratic decade'.[73] What they do

[69] Errol John, *Moon on a Rainbow Shawl* (London: Faber & Faber, 2012), pp. 6, 11.
[70] Ibid., p. 38.   [71] Ibid., p. xiv.   [72] See historic cast lists in ibid., pp. vii–x.
[73] Lacey, *British Realist Theatre*, p. 1.

collectively demonstrate, however, is the felt need to place before their audiences scenarios exposing the unexamined assumptions and fault-lines within British society. That they could do this, despite the constraints imposed upon them, is indicative of a growing openness to the prospect of societal change, even if such 'transition' was still at best in process.

PART IV

No Directions

Introduction

The 'third phase' of John Wyndham's 1953 science fiction disaster novel, *The Kraken Wakes*, opens with the narrator Mike and his wife Phyllis afloat in a dinghy trying to navigate their way home to Cornwall across a largely submerged home counties, the geography of which can only be guessed at from occasional roofs and landmarks. This unfortunate state of affairs is the result of an alien invasion of the seas and the consequent breakdown in civil society prompted by the play of vested interests and the refusal of anyone to listen to the desolate words of a scientific Cassandra. The invisibility of the threat renders the book as much satirical as frightening, and its extreme topicality (manifest in references to independent television, Cold War politics and the 'more regular types of atomic bomb'[1]) makes it an interesting state-of-the-nation benchmark, and one in which things certainly look grim for our heroes. However, the resourceful Phyllis – who has spent the novel ably resisting the gender prescriptions of 1950s popular fiction – is surprisingly undaunted. It might not look like Britain, or like any recognisable landscape, but there is hope: 'I think we've been here before, Mike ... And we got through last time'.[2] This level of optimism, however, proved hard to achieve in the imagination of the 1950s, and it is the image of an unreadable world without familiar landmarks, rather than the desperate assertion of hope, that resonates most strongly with the literature of the postwar. This section, therefore, concludes the book by exploring the tropes of secrecy, uncertainty, anxiety and exhaustion.

James Smith's chapter follows on from the preoccupations of Part III in its concern with the long-term impact on the national psyche of war in general, and propaganda in particular. Observing the sheer number of writers who worked in some capacity for the Ministry of Information, Smith maps the extent to which tropes of espionage and surveillance

---

[1] John Wyndham, *The Kraken Wakes* (Harmondsworth: Penguin, 1955 [1953]), p. 43.
[2] Ibid., p. 240.

infiltrated literature long after the cessation of hostilities. If war is a subject that evades direct expression, it is nonetheless an event that indelibly imprints itself upon language, reorientating and distorting expressive possibility. Smith supports these claims with close readings of George Orwell, Muriel Spark and Graham Greene, revealing the extent to which spy fiction was as much a postwar condition as a popular genre. So much for secrecy. The second trope is uncertainty, and in Petra Rau's exploration of travel writing at mid-century, it soon becomes clear that new maps are needed. This is under-explored territory and Rau's chapter acts as a valuable corrective to accounts that imagine travel stopped with the outbreak of war and did not resume until postmodernism reimagined the genre. What did change, though, between the odysseys of aimless but confident interwar travellers and the world of the postwar post-imperial self-conscious spectator, was who wrote and why. A new generation of writers turned to travel narrative to bear witness, to negotiate change, to contemplate difference and recognise it before it disappeared into a newly globalised homogeneity.

Over the course of the 1950s, seeing the world became more possible for more people, as travel was revolutionised by the advent of mass 'package' tourism. Travel became quicker and in so doing joined a whole array of cultural phenomena that seemed to suggest unprecedented and uncontrolled acceleration. As Allan Hepburn argues, the Second World War generated a state of information overload, a surfeit of experience that evaded comprehension, but which – thanks to the advent of the atomic age – was framed by a sense of impending catastrophe. The world was speeding towards disaster and the perception that time was running out is not, as Hepburn observes, conducive to literary rehabilitation. His chapter explores the temporal structure of the novel and the extent to which the dystopian fiction of writers such as Nevil Shute and John Wyndham sought to prepare for the future by imagining ends. But in the course of surveying the literature of anxiety, he pauses to observe its opposite mode, apathy. Extremes of action prompt extreme reactions, and British literary culture was, Kate McLoughlin argues, quite simply worn out.

Postwar: British Literature in Transition 1940–1960 begins and ends with the novel, but it's not clear whether even in this single genre a significant 'transition' can be traced across these twenty years. Rather, there is a continuity of preoccupation, of inwardness, of anxiety, as tropes of austerity give way to a baroque elaboration that signifies not imagination but its absence: the literature of exhaustion or – as McLoughlin carefully distinguishes – of tiredness. In McLoughlin's account, the fiction of the 1950s seems painfully self-aware, depicting the evacuation of creativity as a means of negotiating its own creative anxiety. As Tracy Hargreaves' earlier chapter indicated, instances of failed, stunted and deluded creativity symbolise a postwar malaise that a bone-tired nation could not easily shake off. Consequently, McLoughlin's analysis of the muted plotting and rhetorical habits of Elizabeth Taylor, Angus Wilson and Iris Murdoch consolidates this reading and further explains how postwar British literature came to be perceived as lifeless and insular.

Tiredness, then, is a keynote not just of this section, but of the volume as a whole. Isolated literary incidents might suggest change to come, but for all the trumpeting of 'magic numbers' such as 1956, transition in this period remains nebulous and hard to define. Yet, as McLoughlin argues, and as the counter-narratives running through the collection attest, groundwork was laid: in new voices, new forms and even in the rugged persistence of horticultural symbolism. To evoke the spirit of McLoughlin's final speculative chapter, seeds were sown in the postwar, but the flowering of radical literary possibilities would be a product of the 1960s and the subject of another volume.

CHAPTER 18

Covert Legacies in Postwar British Fiction
James Smith

In recent years, increasing scholarly attention has been given to the covert interactions between mid-century literature and the British state – that is, to how the clandestine apparatus of the British Government interacted with, influenced and, at times, employed many of the most significant writers and intellectuals of the era. Such scholarship has investigated aspects such as the roles of secrecy in later literary depictions of the Second World War, the influence of government propaganda and surveillance across literary culture, and how Cold War spy fiction acted as a site for exploring anxieties sparked by Britain's postwar geopolitical decline.[1] What unites such approaches is the sense that this era saw an unprecedented interaction between these spheres, leaving a long trace across the culture of the period. Indeed, Andrew Hammond recently argued that this was an era 'in which espionage motifs ... infiltrated genres other than the spy narrative', the extent of their use suggesting 'some national pathology finding expression in the period's fiction'.[2]

In this chapter, I want to explore in finer detail how this infiltration came about, by tracing how first-hand exposure to the propaganda and deception operations of the Second World War left its legacy in key postwar works by George Orwell, Muriel Spark and Graham Greene. Of course, the use of deception in warfare is almost as old as warfare itself, and equally, throughout history British authors have been recruited to secret government work. But such an interaction gained new urgency in the twentieth century, with the founding of Britain's professional

---

[1] For a very selective list, see Victoria Stewart, *The Second World War in Contemporary British Fiction: Secret Histories* (Edinburgh University Press, 2011); Mark Wollaeger, *Modernism, Media and Propaganda* (Princeton University Press, 2006); James Smith, *British Writers and MI5 Surveillance, 1930–1960* (Cambridge University Press, 2013); Adam Piette, *The Literary Cold War: 1945 to Vietnam* (Edinburgh University Press, 2009); and Andrew Hammond, *British Fiction and the Cold War* (Basingstoke: Palgrave Macmillan, 2013).
[2] Hammond, *British Fiction*, p. 88.

intelligence apparatus in 1909, and the growing realisation after the First World War that informational warfare was now a vital pillar of any conflict. As the classified 1942 British Government propaganda manual *The Meaning, Techniques and Methods of Political Warfare* set out, the 'importance' of propaganda and deception was 'vastly greater than ever before, both because of the changed character of war and because of the technological devices which have created new instruments for political attack'. Despite the advances in mechanised war, 'the human element' was still held to be the crux of conflict, because 'there must be the *will* to make the machines, to man the machines and to pull the trigger'. Consequently, the purpose of so-called political warfare was to engage with that 'will', whether 'to destroy the morale of the enemy' or to 'sustain the morale' of Britain and her allies.[3]

In light of this doctrine, an unprecedented number of authors were recruited into the realm of the British information agencies, whether for projects at the Ministry of Information (MOI), as employees of intelligence services or as workers in black propaganda organs. This provided such authors with access to this previously hidden sphere, and an increased appreciation for the roles intellectuals could play as potent weapons in these new battles that sought to destroy or sustain morale. But this experience also caused, in many cases, lingering unease, as authors struggled to reconcile their positions as ostensibly independent intellectuals with the secrecy, ideological constraints and deceptions demanded by such roles.

It is important to note, however, that not all authors responded to this experience with such concerns. 1953, after all, saw the release of the first James Bond novel, *Casino Royale*. Written by the former British naval intelligence officer Ian Fleming, Bond's fantastical covert exploits offered an alluring picture of glamour, luxury and martial prowess to an exhausted and diminished postwar British society.[4] What I am interested in here, though, is tracing how issues such as propaganda, conspiracy and rumour manifested across forms that ostensibly resist the label of 'spy thriller', and will suggest that what unites dystopian science fiction such as Orwell's

---

[3] Political Warfare Executive, *The Meaning, Techniques and Methods of Political Warfare*, pp. 2, 3 (emphasis in the original). This is held at the National Archives (TNA) in Kew, London at FO 898/101. In writing this chapter, I am indebted to the transcription of PWE documents provided online by Lee Richards at www.psywar.org

[4] For discussion of Bond's context and influence, see Christoph Lindner (ed.), *The James Bond Phenomenon: A Critical Reader*, 2nd edn (Manchester University Press, 2009), which brings together much of the most significant criticism.

Nineteen Eighty-Four (1949), a mysterious conspiracy such as Spark's *Memento Mori* (1959) and a satire such as Greene's *Our Man in Havana* (1958) is their shared negotiation of the legacy of the wartime British secret state.

George Orwell, the MOI and *Nineteen Eighty-Four*

During the Second World War, responsibility for Britain's domestic propaganda and media censorship fell to the newly resurrected Ministry of Information. In conducting its operations, the MOI drew upon a major proportion of the period's writers, with authors as diverse as Ruth Adam, Phyllis Bentley, John Betjeman, A. J. Cronin, Graham Greene, James Hanley, Laurie Lee, Cecil Day Lewis, Arthur Calder-Marshall, Elizabeth Jenkins and Montagu Slater (to give just a small sample) all doing stints of service for some aspect of the MOI. Many others undertook ad hoc or contract work, with Nancy Cunard working as a translator, Dylan Thomas writing scripts, Laurence Olivier convinced by the MOI to pursue the film adaptation of *Henry V* and Elizabeth Bowen writing reports to the MOI from Ireland. Indeed, given its role as censor and paper rationer, it was hard for a wartime writer *not* to be somehow concerned with its activity, and writers were only some of those used by the propaganda apparatus, with film-makers, photographers, publishers, artists and cartoonists equally in demand.[5]

The MOI was not a secret department, as its activities were openly acknowledged in a way that covert intelligence and 'black' propaganda was not: its work was conceptualised in terms of informing and persuading rather than attacking and misleading. But the unprecedented concentration of such activity in one ministry provoked suspicion and concern from across the political spectrum. Thus, in Parliament, shortly after the outbreak of war in September 1939, the Conservative Harold Macmillan demanded assurances that 'the Ministry of Information will not attempt to suppress critical examination of any aspect of Government policy', while in the same debate the socialist Aneurin Bevan sarcastically spoke about the risk that the MOI 'will bore us to death'.[6]

---

[5] For an overview of the MOI influence upon wartime literary culture, see Valerie Holman, 'Carefully Concealed Connections: The Ministry of Information and British Publishing, 1939–1946' *Book History* (2005) 8 pp. 197–226. I also discuss some of the interactions between authors and the propaganda apparatus in *British Writers and MI5 Surveillance*.

[6] Hansard, House of Commons, 21 September 1939, vol. 351 cc1058-61.

Many authors registered similar concerns about the MOI, and of these one of the most interesting cases is George Orwell – precisely because, in public imagining, few authors are as antithetical to government propaganda as the author whose work gave us Big Brother and the Thought Police. This, however, often obscures the complex relationship Orwell had with government propaganda during the Second World War and its aftermath. Across his career, Orwell's essays often dwelt on debates about art, propaganda and commitment, and his writing took equally strong views on wartime propaganda.[7] Often, Orwell bristled with dismay at official offerings. When reviewing films produced by the MOI, he would not hesitate to label them 'terrible', 'wretched', 'dreadful' and a waste 'of time and money', and when reading the MOI's best-selling book *The Battle of Britain*, he was critical of the fact that 'they did not have the sense to avoid the propagandist note altogether'.[8] But Orwell's frustration was not because he was opposed to propaganda efforts. Rather, it was because, in 'a war in which words are at least as important as guns', he believed British propaganda needed to be even more skilled and persuasive, and this was the reason that Orwell himself, at various points, agreed to be a propagandist.[9]

Orwell's major stint as an official propagandist was as a Talks Producer for the BBC from August 1941 until he resigned in September 1943.[10] Employed in the Indian Section of the Eastern Service, his role involved compiling and broadcasting talks on cultural topics, with the ambition of sustaining support from the Indian intelligentsia who typically had little love for their colonial masters. Despite an illustrious roll-call of contributors who spoke on his programmes, and his desire to maintain a degree of autonomy and political integrity, he resigned largely disillusioned with his efforts, famously describing that he felt like 'an orange that's been trodden on by a very dirty boot'.[11] And although often overlooked in the biographical records, Orwell's familiarity with wartime propaganda went beyond

---

[7] For an overview of Orwell's views on propaganda, see (to give just one example) Simon Dentith, '"The Journalists Do the Shouting": Orwell and Propaganda' in Graham Holderness, Bryan Loughrey and Nahem Yousaf (eds), *George Orwell* (Basingstoke: Macmillan, 1998), pp. 203–227.

[8] Peter Davison (ed.), *The Complete Works of George Orwell: A Patriot after All: 1940–1941* (London: Secker & Warburg, 1998), pp. 390, 467.

[9] Ibid., p. 390.

[10] These broadcasts were long thought lost until W. J. West discovered and published the scripts in *Orwell: The War Broadcasts* (London: Duckworth, 1985). West also provided a long discussion of the crucial influence of the BBC years over Orwell's career.

[11] Peter Davison (ed.), *The Complete Works of George Orwell: Two Wasted Years: 1943* (London: Secker & Warburg, 1998), p. 206.

his BBC work.[12] His wife Eileen had worked as a censor for the MOI in the early stages of the war, and there are suggestions that Orwell undertook some work for the MOI prior to his work at the BBC.[13] In addition, while employed in the BBC, Orwell gained ample opportunity to witness the operations of the MOI first hand, being a frequent (if angry) recipient of MOI policy directives, having his broadcasts subjected to MOI censorship and even at one point provoking direct complaints from the MOI to the Director General of the BBC.[14] Even after his resignation from the BBC and MOI attempts to block *Animal Farm*, he still wrote *The English People* (1947) for an MOI-instigated series, and after the war Orwell (as I will come back to) remained sympathetic to the aims of anti-Communist propaganda when approached by covert Cold War agencies.[15]

Consequently, while *Nineteen Eighty-Four* is most famous for its imagining of a totalitarian future world of near-total surveillance and governmental control, it is also a work heavily influenced by Orwell's experiences with, and concerns about, the British propaganda apparatus of the Second World War.[16] Most obviously there is the similarity between the physical locations: the Minitrue building is described as 'an enormous pyramidal structure of glittering white concrete, soaring up, terrace after terrace, three hundred metres into the air' – a building that is often held to be reminiscent of the MOI's towering Senate House home in Bloomsbury.[17] Other overlaps can be seen in the Party-mandated 'Newspeak' propagating the world of *Nineteen Eighty-Four*, which parallels the wartime advocacy of a simplified official 'Basic English' by Churchill, with a Cabinet committee going so far as to recommend 'that key works of literature should be translated into Basic, which should be promoted by the British Council,

---

[12] For example, Bernard Crick's influential biography *George Orwell: A Life* (Harmondsworth: Penguin, 1982 [1980]) only briefly mentions the MOI, mainly in the context of the publication of *Animal Farm*. W. J. West, *The Larger Evils: Nineteen Eighty-Four: The Truth Behind the Satire* (Edinburgh: Canongate, 1992) reasserts the impact of such wartime experience on Orwell, although much of its speculation needs to be treated with caution.

[13] Orwell's MI5 file records Eileen Blair's work as 'Min. of Information. Examiner A. (in charge of London Liaison Dept)' (serial 10a, *sic*), and records, on a separate 1941 BBC vetting form, that Orwell had 'Lately: Worked for Ministry of Information' (serial 4a). This file can be found at TNA, KV 2/2699.

[14] West, *Orwell*, details the MOI censorship system on pp. 279–83, and the complaint against Orwell on pp. 52–3.

[15] Holman, 'Carefully Concealed Connections', discussed the MOI series in which Orwell's book appeared (pp. 213–14).

[16] While such influence is overlooked in many accounts, it certainly has not entirely escaped notice: for example, West, in *Orwell* and *The Larger Evils*, discusses the role of the BBC and MOI as sources for many incidents in *Nineteen Eighty-Four*.

[17] George Orwell, *Nineteen Eighty-Four* (Harmondsworth: Penguin, 1989 [1949]), pp. 5–6.

the Colonial Office, the Ministry of Information, and the BBC'.[18] Similarly, the MOI's unprecedented wartime control over news and art would seem to offer an ominous precursor for Minitrue's permanent monopoly over all culture and information, where it supplied 'the citizens of Oceania with newspapers, films, textbooks, telescreen programmes, plays, novels – with every conceivable kind of information, instruction or entertainment, from a statue to a slogan, from a lyric poem to a biological treatise, and from a child's spelling book to a Newspeak dictionary'.[19]

If these are obvious sources, it is also perceivable that Orwell seems to meditate more broadly on a world where the techniques and campaigns of the MOI have become all-pervasive and banal. Take, for example, the prevalence of the word 'victory' in *Nineteen Eighty-Four*. 'Victory' is added to almost every commodity or location encountered by Winston, and newsflash announcements almost invariably trumpet some 'glorious victory'. Yet the reality hidden under the supposedly triumphant label is far from glorious: Victory Gin is 'sickly' and like 'nitric acid', his poorly constructed Victory Cigarette's 'tobacco [falls] out onto the floor', Victory Coffee is 'filthy', the 1930s Victory Mansions are 'falling to pieces', and the announcement of a 'glorious victory' in a newsflash is automatically recognised as a diversion from the 'bad news' of a ration cut.[20] The word, in this exhausted world of unrelenting propaganda, has become an empty ploy, nowhere more apparent than in the babble the now-broken Winston hears at the novel's ending: 'victory – greatest victory in human history – victory, victory, victory!'[21] Given that victory was a word equally prevalent in Second World War propaganda, perhaps most famously in the 'Dig for Victory' campaign, and that the promised victory over Germany and Japan had not resolved the austerity conditions that continued to grip a weary Britain, a reader who had just lived through the conflict could not but help find ironic resonances between Winston's world of 'victory' and their own recent experiences of official propaganda.

Amid this apparatus, Orwell particularly targets the willing acquiescence of the intelligentsia in sustaining the propaganda machine – mirroring the sense of acquiescence that the 'trodden upon' Orwell acutely struggled with as he conducted his own war work. Despite his hatred for the Party, Winston's 'greatest pleasure in life' remains 'his work' in the Ministry of

---

[18] Jonathan Rose, *The Literary Churchill: Author, Reader, Actor* (New Haven, CT: Yale University Press, 2014), p. 373. This proposal was dropped, to the relief of all concerned, by the incoming Labour Government after the war.
[19] Orwell, *Nineteen Eighty-Four*, p. 45.   [20] Ibid., pp. 7, 7, 147, 22, 28.   [21] Ibid., p. 310.

Truth, where he constructs news items that are 'delicate pieces of forgery'.[22] Not only does such work give him the relative privilege of Outer Party membership and free him from the 'heavy physical work' of the proles, it provides him with a misguided sense of importance: as he notes in his diary, 'nobody cares what the proles say'.[23] Winston, by contrast, fiercely competes to have his story on Comrade Ogilvy accepted as Big Brother's 'Order for the Day'.[24] That he might secretly produce less than optimal work here apparently never occurs to Winston; he had become a 'well-trained dog' who 'turns his somersault' to please his master without thinking – those being the words Orwell used to castigate British writers as they acquiesced to the MOI.[25]

But one of the great ironies of *Nineteen Eighty-Four* is that despite these warnings, Orwell himself was entangled in such a compromise at the outset of the Cold War. When approached by his friend Celia Kirwan in 1949 and confidentially told about the launch of the British Government's new Cold War propaganda unit, the Information Research Department (IRD), Orwell responded enthusiastically to the news, offering advice on how the department should operate and, infamously, a list of suspected crypto-Communist intellectuals. Reading the letters and comments in the IRD file on this incident, it is hard not to be struck by what Timothy Garton Ash has described as 'an almost painful eagerness': Orwell, isolated and ill in a sanatorium, suddenly flattered to have his political views courted by Kirwan and government officials, not pausing to think through how this mimics activity that he had, in others venues, attacked.[26] *Nineteen Eighty-Four* was therefore not only a warning to the world about the possibility of future tyranny; it was a document directly enacting many of the personal negotiations and doubts that Orwell faced through his engagement with the propaganda apparatus of the 1940s.

Rumour and Deception in Spark's *Memento Mori*

If the MOI represented the acknowledged face of British propaganda, it was certainly not the only organ. Across the Second World War, the British Government deployed a wide range of more secretive agencies, often

---

[22] Ibid., p. 46.   [23] Ibid., pp. 74, 11.   [24] Ibid., p. 49.
[25] Peter Davison (ed.), *The Complete Works of George Orwell: I Have Tried to Tell the Truth: 1943–1944* (London: Secker & Warburg, 1998), p. 277.
[26] Timothy Garton Ash, 'Orwell's List', *The New York Review of Books* (25 September 2003), www.nybooks.com/articles/archives/2003/sep/25/orwells-list/. The original archival documents are available at TNA FO 1110/189.

hiding under cover names, conducting deniable activity aimed at hostile countries. Of these, the most significant was the Political Warfare Executive (PWE), Britain's major 'black' propaganda organisation in the later stages of the war. The PWE coordinated the activity of the foreign language sections of the BBC aimed at enemy territories, organised subversive leaflets to be disseminated abroad, and operated 'black' broadcasts from radio stations to spread rumours and disinformation. Again, such activity required the services of talented intellectuals, and writers such as Muriel Spark, David Garnett and Stephen Spender worked at the PWE, while others (such as Arthur Koestler) undertook German-language broadcasting that was under PWE oversight.

Of these, Spark became perhaps the most prominent writer to weave such PWE experiences into later works. As detailed in her autobiography, Spark started work as a duty secretary for the PWE in 1944, apparently after a recruiter saw her with a copy of an Ivy Compton-Burnett novel in her interview. Once in the PWE's Milton Bryan compound, Spark was initiated into a clandestine world which she found 'wonderfully interesting':

> I played a very small part, but as a fly on the wall I took in a whole world of method and intrigue in the dark field of Black Propaganda or Psychological Warfare, and the successful and purposeful deceit of the enemy. ... The Foreign Office secret intelligence service was MI6, of which our department was Political Intelligence.[27]

As Spark described, her work consisted of elements such as finding and manipulating information to provide plausible context for disinformation stories about Allied bombings and sometimes acting as a sounding board for schemes Sefton Delmer (the head of the Milton Bryan section) was hatching at the next desk. Once collated, these stories would be put into the format of supposedly legitimate radio broadcasts by German dissidents and beamed across to Europe.

Although illuminating, Spark's account (whether deliberately or not) here continues many of the deceptions that surrounded the PWE. For example, her account of the 'Political Intelligence' department of the Foreign Office fails to mention that this was a cover designation for the PWE, used to obscure the fact that Britain was operating a dedicated and sophisticated black propaganda apparatus. But while this has muddied the water for some scholars following her wartime work, it is nonetheless

---

[27] Muriel Spark, *Curriculum Vitae: Autobiography* (London: Constable, 1992), pp. 147–8.

emphatic evidence of the enduring legacies of wartime secrecy, and of how such concealments and misinformation became a pervasive fact of life long after the war itself had ended.

This stint in the PWE played a formative role in Spark's literary career. Spark acknowledged that *The Hothouse by the East River* (1973) directly drew from her PWE experiences, and critics have found further influence across her works.[28] Martin McQuillan suggests that this 'experience of creating "fiction" from a "true" or empirical source' was a 'likely root for Spark's primal scene of writing and training in her craft', while Marina MacKay highlights how Spark's work with German prisoners to elicit information for PWE broadcasts feeds into the themes of treason explored in *The Prime of Miss Jean Brodie* (1961), and provides a crucial problem through much of Spark's career, with 'the illicit acquisition and deployment of information' a 'central obsession of Spark's early work'.[29]

Memento Mori (1959), for example, clearly bears the mark of this experience in black propaganda. At first glance, *Memento* appears to be a long way from the covert battles of the Second World War, concerning as it does a circle of ageing associates and their responses to the strange phone calls warning them to 'remember you must die'. Nonetheless, when Charmian utters the oft-quoted comment that 'the art of fiction is very like the practice of deception',[30] it suggests that deception is one of the novel's self-conscious themes. Through the novel we see this in action, as the 'reader's own detective work' uncovers the secret networks of blackmail, bigamy, affairs and sexual fetishes that are woven in the shadows of these ostensibly ordinary lives.[31] The novel also ironically plays with the tropes of spy and detective novels and the 'machinations of espionage', whether in Alec Warner's information-gathering research on the process of ageing, or the wider 'trade in secrets' engaged in by most of the novel's characters.[32]

---

[28] Spark, *Curriculum Vitae*, p. 159.
[29] Martin McQuillan, 'In Bed with Muriel Spark: Mourning, Metonymy and Autobiography' in Martin McQuillan (ed.), *Theorizing Muriel Spark: Gender, Race, Deconstruction* (Basingstoke: Palgrave Macmillan, 2002), pp. 78–91, 82; Marina MacKay, 'Muriel Spark and the Meaning of Treason' *Modern Fiction Studies* (2008) 54(3) pp. 505–22, 507. Adam Piette, 'Muriel Spark and the Politics of the Contemporary' in Michael Gardiner and Willy Maley (eds), *The Edinburgh Companion to Muriel Spark* (Edinburgh University Press, 2010), pp. 52–62, has also given sustained attention to the use of lies, deceptions and 'intelligence plots' across many of Spark's novels, and Stewart, *Secret Histories*, also provides detailed discussion of Spark's spy and conspiracy motifs.
[30] Muriel Spark, *Memento Mori* (London: Virago, 2010 [1959]), p. 192.
[31] Rod Mengham, 'The Cold War Way of Death: Muriel Spark's *Memento Mori*', in Marina MacKay and Lyndsey Stonebridge (eds), *British Fiction after Modernism* (Basingstoke: Palgrave Macmillan, 2007), pp. 157–165, p. 159.
[32] Ibid., pp. 163–4.

However, the pervasive influence of psychological warfare might also be detected in several other ways. Take, for example, Granny Barnacle's campaign against Sister 'Bastard' Burstead, in which she attempts to convince her fellow ward residents that the new sister is seeking to euthanise them. Barnacle is hazy about the basis for this rumour, but is adamant about the consequences: 'Anyone that's a nuisance ... they won't last long in this ward. You get pneumonia in the winter, can't help but do, and that's her chance'.[33] From these small seeds, the rumours grow and spread. The grannies begin to develop 'hostile thoughts and deadly suspicions' towards the nursing staff, becoming 'so worked up' that the rumour almost becomes self-fulfilling: Miss Taylor suspects 'it would not be surprising' if the harassed nurse did 'indeed let them die of pneumonia should she ever get the chance'.[34] Even when Sister Burstead is goaded into a breakdown, Granny Barnacle 'applied the bellows' to the rumour whenever 'the general hysteria showed signs of waning'.[35] The unrelated second stroke of Granny Trotsky is attributed to the sister, and those grannies who waver over Burstead's guilt are accused of not being 'on our side'.[36] Burstead is eventually transferred, but Granny Barnacle's agitations take another toll: Barnacle develops high blood pressure, and is so excited when the new sister arrives that she succumbs to a fever that leads to her death.

While the setting may be a geriatric ward, here in a microcosm Barnacle demonstrates one of British black propaganda's preferred methods of operating, through spreading what was known as a 'sib' (derived from the Latin for 'hiss'). These were campaigns designed to spread rumour and suspicion among the enemy in order to undermine morale from within. Spark's *Curriculum Vitae* provides examples of a few of the more benign campaigns broadcast during her time at PWE, such as attempts to demoralise German troops after D-Day by convincing them that there were no reinforcements available. However, many campaigns involved far more controversial attacks on morale, and often featured rumours designed to generate distrust in the medical profession. One particularly grotesque example consisted of attempts to convince German troops that their hospital blood-supplies were infected with venereal disease,[37] while forced euthanasia of the elderly featured as a theme of British propaganda from early in the war.[38]

---

[33] Spark, *Memento*, p. 38.   [34] Ibid., pp. 38, 41.   [35] Ibid., p. 43.   [36] Ibid., p. 46.

[37] Sefton Delmer, *Black Boomerang* (London: Secker & Warburg, 1962), p. 67. This particular rumour has been singled out for considerable attention: see discussion in Stewart, *Secret Histories*, p. 39.

[38] Lee Richards, 'Whispers of War: The British World War II Rumour Campaign' (2005), details that a rumour was spread stating 'that due to the ration situation in Germany, doctors had orders to do

If there are thus marked similarities between Barnacle's fears and those exploited by the PWE, what is significant here is Spark's deft understanding of an effective whisper campaign in action. No shot is fired or blow struck (indeed, the agitators are physically infirm), but nonetheless a single well-placed rumour has managed to destabilise and paralyse an entire institution. The nurses and patients are turned against one another, the sister is suspended and moved, the hospital management is snagged up in settling the dispute and the rumour-monger is herself unwittingly killed by the excitement that the campaign has aroused. Sefton Delmer, one could say, could not have designed it better himself.

Of course, this is only one element of the information warfare *Memento Mori* depicts, for hanging over the entire narrative are the phone calls. Unlike Barnacle's campaign, these messages are statements of fact, not malicious rumour; yet in their own way they equally present a study of how people *respond* to psychological warfare campaigns. As Spark well knew, part of the strength of British propaganda was its realisation that 'selective' truth was sometimes far more powerful than extravagant and unbelievable lies: Delmer's technique relied upon 'Detailed truth with believable lies'.[39] The same could be said for the phone calls. They offer a selective truth (of course people must die), but in providing such an uncomfortable fact without any context (how will they die? Is the call a genuine warning, an imminent threat, or a malicious hoax?), the calls provoke confusion and suspicion in many recipients. Consequently, each recipient interprets the voice in a fundamentally different way, being variously described as 'a very civil young man', 'menacing', 'strictly factual', 'sinister in the extreme' and 'gentle-spoken and respectful'. The anonymous message becomes a cypher for each individual's beliefs, fears and desires, a fact grasped by Inspector Mortimer when he states that 'I think we must all realize that the offender is, in each case, whoever we think he is ourselves'.[40]

Spark here exploits the same psychological principle that informed much of PWE's black broadcasting. Many of Delmer's stations were dedicated to broadcasts by an anonymous character (such as 'the Chief' or 'the Priest') whose supposed identity and location, while carefully

---

away with hospitalised old and permanently disabled patients'. Available online at www.psywar.org/sibs.php. Also of particular note is a May and June 1944 PWE report which records that 'Protest against inhumane treatment of the aged is a frequent theme of the German Priest [a PWE radio station]', fuelling the spread of 'stories about old people being allowed to die, [and] being refused medical aid'. See www.psywar.org/delmer/8800/1011.

[39] Spark, *Curriculum Vitae*, p. 148. *The Meaning, Techniques and Methods of Political Warfare* equally talks about 'selective' truth: see p. 13.

[40] Spark, *Memento*, p. 155.

constructed, was ultimately left for the audience to interpret, with the information provided intended to incite different listeners in different ways. Consequently, PWE's broadcasts often functioned as a similar cypher for the audience's beliefs: for example, PWE intelligence reports recorded that 'the Priest' was variously believed by listeners to be from the Vatican, England, or a German 'illegal station', and such listeners were also divided in their responses to the broadcast depending on their attitudes to religion.[41]

To be very clear, this is not an attempt to reduce Spark solely to the preoccupations of black propaganda, or to solve the mystery of *Memento Mori* by suggesting it is a satire of Delmer's techniques. But what would seem clear is the extent to which Spark's understanding of the psychology and art of rumour and deception were encouraged by her wartime exposure to the techniques of Delmer and the PWE. One might say that 'as a fly on the wall' Spark not only 'took in a whole world' of black propaganda, but learned that the hopes and fears exploited by such propaganda were still common to the world long after Delmer's units went off the air.

Double Crossings and Deceptions in Greene's *Our Man in Havana*

So far this chapter has examined the legacy of propaganda through certain key examples of post-war writing. Other authors were exposed to far more focused aspects of deception, specifically those practised by the covert intelligence services such as MI5 or MI6 (officially known as SIS) – yet these, too, found their way into the postwar literary realm.

Of these deception operations, probably the most famous now is the Double Cross system, commonly held to be one of the most remarkable intelligence successes of the Second World War. In very brief outline, the foundations of Double Cross lay in the fact that during the war, British intelligence managed to identify almost every German spy as they arrived in the United Kingdom. Crucially, rather than being executed or held incommunicado, these spies were given the opportunity to turn against their former masters. If they accepted, such double agents were provided with carefully orchestrated disinformation mixed with true but inconsequential facts, and then tasked to report back to Germany as if they had arrived safely in the United Kingdom and remained undetected. German

---

[41] These various 'Evidence of Reception' reports have been transcribed at www.psywar.org/delmer/8800/1001

intelligence, thus believing it had a successful covert network in place, unwittingly consumed information entirely controlled by their British counterparts, allowing the picture of the war, at crucial junctions, to be controlled by the Double Cross committee.

The Double Cross system became one of British intelligence's cherished but most closely guarded secrets, with the suppression of public revelations persisting into the 1970s.[42] Yet well before this, many members of the public were quite unwittingly already familiar with some of the more fantastical aspects of the Double Cross spies, through Graham Greene's ostensibly comical 'entertainment', *Our Man in Havana* (1958). Greene was one of MI6's temporary recruits during the Second World War, being posted under cover as a police officer to Freetown, Sierra Leone, before serving as a desk officer under Kim Philby in London. In his memoir he painted a largely sedate picture of his intelligence life, but acknowledged that it provided an array of experiences and incidents for his later writing.[43] Such experiences can directly be found in the characters and setting of *The Heart of the Matter* (1948), and also influence other works such as his screenplay (and novella) for the film noir *The Third Man* (1949/1950), his wartime thriller *The Ministry of Fear* (1943), his searing indictment of the CIA in *The Quiet American* (1955) and his later return to the espionage novel in *The Human Factor* (1978). Yet it is in the unlikely satirical story of a vacuum-cleaner salesman in Cold War Cuba that Greene cuts closest to the bone of British wartime intelligence, in fact drawing on source material that was still officially classified at a level above Top Secret until after the Cold War.[44]

There has been some critical debate as to Greene's source for *Our Man in Havana*, with Greene himself only providing a (probably deliberately) partial account. His biographer has established, however, that Greene's work for the Portuguese desk of SIS brought with it knowledge of the agent Juan Pujol Garcia (codenamed GARBO), who rose from being a chicken farmer to a prized double agent in the Double Cross system, and whose

---

[42] Such was the case with J. C. Masterman, the academic and wartime chairman of the committee that ran Double Cross, who was refused permission to publish his history and resorted to publication in the United States.

[43] Graham Greene, *Ways of Escape* (Toronto: Lester & Orpen Dennys, 1980), pp. 75–102.

[44] The MI5 'Summary of the GARBO case' file was classified as a Top Secret 'Y File', and can be found at TNA KV 2/41. Of course, Greene's Cuban setting for this satire was also of high political significance, given the country's role as Cold War flash point. For a detailed reading of this, see Christopher Hull, 'Prophecy and Comedy in Havana: Graham Greene's Spy Fiction and Cold War Reality' in Dermot Gilvary and Darren J. N. Middleton (eds), *Dangerous Edges of Graham Greene* (London: Continuum, 2011), pp. 149–65.

wartime career bears an obvious resemblance to the exploits of Wormold.[45] After volunteering his services and being rebuffed by British intelligence in Spain, GARBO was recruited to German intelligence. Compiling reports in Lisbon as if he was in England, GARBO sent his German handlers an extraordinary body of fictitious intelligence reports, involving bogus information culled from tourist guides but attributed to a network of sub-agents and informants. British intelligence belatedly recognised his value and brought him to the United Kingdom as part of Double Cross, where he continued his disinformation campaign, the pinnacle of which involved convincing German commanders that the D-Day landings were only a feint, consequently diverting German reinforcements away from Normandy.

Even in this outline, the similarities between Wormold and GARBO are immediately evident. Wormold, the uninspiring middle-aged vacuum cleaner salesman, is led to create his own network of agents at the prompting of the MI6 officer Hawthorne, albeit here to support the lifestyle of his daughter rather than due to any ideological commitment. Wormold, too, turns to implausible sources for his fictitious intelligence, such as country club membership lists and publicly-available government reports and local newspapers.[46] Wormold's creations reach their culmination in his sketch of vacuum-clearer components which are passed off as a scale-drawing of some giant new doomsday device being built in the Cuban wilderness, the implausibility of the drawings actually lauded by the MI6 Chief due to the 'ingenuity, the simplicity, the devilish imagination of the thing'.[47] Like GARBO, the sheer daring of Wormold's creations and reports lead them to be accepted as fact – and once reified as part of the intelligence cycle, the consequences become all too real. The anonymous opposition instigate a deadly operation against Wormold and his 'network', culminating in the murder of Wormold's friend Hasselbacker. Caught in this cycle, Wormold himself is forced to become exactly the calculating and daring secret agent previously imagined by the Chief, with Wormold manipulating Captain Segura to steal his gun before luring the enemy agent Carter to his death. And even when the absurd truth behind Wormold's creations is finally

---

[45] Greene stated in *Ways of Escape* that it was based on 'what I had learned from my work in 1943–4 of German Abwehr activity in Portugal', which neglects to mention links to any specific case or agent (pp. 204–5). Norman Sherry, *The Life of Graham Greene: Volume Three* (London: Jonathan Cape, 2004) states that Paul Fidrmuc (the German agent OSTRO) and Juan Pujol Garcia (agent GARBO) provided Greene with his sources. See p. 131. It is still unclear how much Greene knew about the Double Cross system as a whole.

[46] Graham Greene, *Our Man in Havana* (Harmondsworth: Penguin, 1971 [1958]), p. 59.

[47] Ibid., p. 79.

grasped by MI6, the vested interests involved in the intelligence process cannot permit his deception to be avowed, with Wormold instead given a training post and an OBE in order neatly to prevent any wider embarrassment.

Read in this way, *Our Man in Havana* would seem to offer a scathing critique of the intelligence establishment, following the example of Compton Mackenzie's *Water on the Brain* (1933) of using satire as an innocuous mode for evading the Official Secrets Act. Greene's merger of the GARBO case with the Cold War vacuum-cleaner salesman makes a very deliberate point. Vacuum-cleaner salesmen are famously retailers of low-repute (as perhaps most quintessentially captured in Julian Maclaren-Ross's 1947 novel *Of Love and Hunger*), relying on pushy sales tactics to earn commissions. Thus, Greene suggests the intelligence profession is similarly involved in peddling questionable items in order to keep its pay. And the image of the vacuum is of wider significance, for Wormold is soon pulled into a vacuum of his own, with the world's intelligence apparatus (whether Western or Soviet) now the machine itself, indiscriminately sucking in information to feed its void.

Yet there is a problem with adopting such a straightforward reading. If GARBO provided Greene with source material, he also probably knew that GARBO's deceptions were actually a demonstration of a British intelligence *success*; the portrayal of Hawthorne and the Chief as gullible victims ignores the fact that it was actually British intelligence who had decisively used GARBO (and others) to fool the German enemy during the war. This is further compounded by the fact that, despite his prominent literary hostility towards the logic of Cold War intelligence, in private he often remained in liaison with SIS: indeed, Norman Sherry's biography details how Greene's Cold War travels to China and Cuba involved gathering information for British intelligence.[48]

Is *Our Man in Havana* therefore really *itself* a kind of elaborate deception operation, designed to promote Greene's left-wing credentials and cover up his continued work for SIS? Sherry was clear when discussing *Our Man in Havana* that he views such deception as 'part of Greene's grand plan'.[49] The truth, I suspect, lies somewhere between these extremes: just as Orwell was scathing of much government propaganda but felt obliged to contribute to the wartime effort, so too could Greene be genuinely sceptical of the folly of many covert intelligence operations while still feeling obliged to provide information he gathered from his travels. Indeed,

---

[48] Sherry, *The Life of Graham Greene*, pp. 76–83, 135.   [49] Ibid., p. 135.

Greene's literary inversion of the Double Cross system was in itself a timely warning that all secret intelligence risked, in the long term, becoming essentially a zero-sum game, where one could never quite tell a success from a fraud – a theme that, in the decade that followed, would become the hallmark of the work of John le Carré. This timely warning is further emphasised by Greene's friendship with Kim Philby, and the possibility (as suggested by Sherry) that he suspected Philby's treachery long before it was officially unmasked – meaning that, just as Britain was deceiving the Germans, it was in turn being deceived by the Soviets.

And here we encounter a final point about the long shadow of the secret world across these works of literature. If, as I have argued, each of these works represents a significant mediation of the wartime experiences of these authors, an obvious but easily overlooked point might be made: not one of these works professes to be an account of such wartime experience, instead speaking through a satire set in Cold War Cuba, a future world in the year 1984 or a geriatric hospital ward. So often, an author's wartime propaganda or intelligence experience seems to be hidden, forgotten, evaded or repressed, with some authors going to their grave without speaking of their wartime work and the nature of many others, to this day, still only partially understood. The true legacy of wartime propaganda and deception in British literature, then, might not always lie in the obvious works it inspired, but instead in the disguises worn by these other, seemingly very different, fictions.

CHAPTER 19

'The Sights are Worse than the Journeys': Travel Writing at the Mid-Century

Petra Rau

The mid-century is a pale spot on the critical map of travel writing. This is largely the fault of Evelyn Waugh, who in 1945 predicted a long hiatus in the genre: 'There is no room for tourists in a world of "displaced persons"[:] the very young, perhaps, may set out like the Wandervogels of the Weimar period; lean, lawless, aimless couples with rucksacks, joining the great army of men and women without papers, without official existence, the refugees and deserters, who drift everywhere today between the barbed wire.'[1] Unfortunately, literary criticism has taken this statement at face value, attending either to the abundant travel corpus of the pre-war years or the postmodern versions of the genre, as if there had been literally nowhere to go and nothing to write home about in the mid-century years. Far from it. These decades are bookended by two substantial classics – Rebecca West's *Black Lamb and Grey Falcon* (1941) and Wilfred Thesiger's *Arabian Sands* (1959) – and peppered with international bestsellers in between.

Yet there is much to ponder in Waugh's statement: the myth of freedom that travel fosters; the ironic rejection of the tourist-traveller distinction; the modernist horror of the crowd; the traveller's need for a home; the impact of war on the purpose and circumstances of travel; above all, his sense of nostalgia. Aimlessness had been part of the romance of travel and the declared habitus of a whole generation of dissolute young men and women trying to escape the boundaries of predictable bourgeois lives back home, as Paul Fussell argued in *Abroad*.[2] In a world in which millions of the homeless were 'drifting' as a result of political vicissitudes, voluntary wandering seemed rather inappropriate. Hardly anyone who wrote travel books before the war continued to write them after 1945.

The war had shifted borders and the Iron Curtain erected 'barbed wire'. This radically altered itineraries. Tantalising blank spots on the map were

[1] Evelyn Waugh, *When the Going Was Good* (London: Penguin, 1990), pp. xii–xiii.
[2] Paul Fussell, *Abroad: British Literary Traveling between the Wars* (Oxford University Press, 1980).

now more likely to be military installations rather than *terra incognita*. According to Peter Fleming,

> the horizons of the British have been sharply contracted. The whole of China is out of bounds. Persia would hardly attract the casual traveller. The Indian peninsula, though still accessible, is no longer dotted with a dependable network of Government Houses and Residencies and dark bungalows, hill-stations and cantonments, between which residents and visitors formerly drifted almost without effort. French Indo-China is a battlefield.[3]

Note that tell-tale pre-war description of travelling cropping up once more: effortless drifting. Fleming's sentiment underlined the extent to which imperialism had facilitated travel, adventure and exploration, and vice versa. This 'dependable network' of convenient colonial and exotic locations was fast disappearing. No one drifted into the Malayan Emergency; no one aimlessly wandered into the Mau Mau Rebellion. The Cold War and the 'emergencies' of decolonisation radically altered the map and the very nature of travel. This raised important questions: where could one still go without becoming a package tourist?[4] Where was the British traveller still welcome? What was the purpose of travel in the modern world? The happy union between travel and politics that had produced so much writing in the 1930s seemed destined to end.[5] How could writers engage with the pressing political and historical processes of their time if they could (or would) not enter the geopolitical areas in which these changes took place? Was this one of the reasons why, according to Bill Schwartz, decolonisation could be so 'underdetermined' and 'heavily mediated' that it appeared, at home in the metropole, to be a well-managed and beneficial aspect of colonisation?[6]

---

[3] Peter Fleming, 'The Man from Rangoon' (1951) in Philip Marsden-Sedley and Jeffrey Klinke (eds), *Views from Abroad: The Spectator Book of Travel Writing* (London: Grafton, 1988), p. 7.

[4] Modern mass tourism had its humble beginning in May 1950 when Valdimir Raitz, founder of Horizon Holidays, sold the first 'package' to eleven Britons. The 'package' was the combined fixed price for transport and at least one other element, normally accommodation. Raitz's pioneering version cost £32 10s (just over £1,000 in today's money) and included a return flight in a decommissioned, unpressurised Dakota DC-3 from Gatwick via Nice to Calvi on Corsica, where the tourists spent a week in tents. Raitz would become one of Britain's biggest tour operators, quickly expanding to Spain. See 'Obituary: Vladimir Raitz', 14 September 2010, www.travelweekly.co.uk

[5] See Bernard Schweizer, *Radicals on the Road: The Politics of English Travel Writing in the 1930s* (Charlottesville, VA: University of Virginia Press, 2001).

[6] Bill Schwartz, 'Introduction' in Rachael Gilmour and Bill Schwartz (eds), *End of Empire and the English Novel since 1945* (Manchester University Press, 2015), p. 9.

'The Sights are Worse than the Journeys'

The mood that emerges from the travel books of the late 1940s and 1950s is anything but well managed. Even if we consider the hybridity of this genre – its nearly indefinable position in the interstices of memoir, reportage, picaresque fiction, adventure tale, romance quest and pastoral elegy – the overall tone was one of melancholy. Most of the travellers continued to be white, male, upper-middle class, privately educated, heterosexual and broadly sceptical of Western 'modernity', but there were noticeably more women. Many of the new voices would forge a career from travel writing and saw it as a way of escaping the bleakness of austerity Britain while retaining the excitement of wartime foreign deployment: Patrick Leigh Fermor, Wilfred Thesiger, Norman Lewis, James (later Jan) Morris, Lawrence Durrell and Eric Newby. This canon was often tacitly supplemented by non-British writers such as Alan Moorehead (from Australia), Laurens van der Post (South Africa) or Edmund Hilary (New Zealand), perhaps because their books slotted so seamlessly into the older literary tradition of heroic adventure, ethnographic enquiry and exploration. Onto the British scene 'drifted' Europeans with hyphenated existences who wrote in English and for a British audience, or who would eventually make England their home (Sybille Bedford, Arthur Koestler). Like earlier generations of travellers, these writers almost obsessively cited their predecessors in a gesture of continued belatedness, suspecting that any authentic encounter with foreign locales and people was already impossible.[7] Observing a world irrevocably changed by, and engaged in, conflict, many professed doubt over the merits of Western civilisation (one of those legitimising fictions of European expansionism). Bearing witness became as important as realising literary ambitions.[8] Even if 'the sights [were] worse than the journeys', the postwar traveller felt, on the whole, more sympathetic towards the colonial subject and concerned over the fate of indigenous tribes in spite of some 'deep-rooted imperial instinct' of racial superiority.[9] Reflecting on such instincts certainly made way for the self-irony of contemporary travel writing.

---

[7] By the mid-nineteenth century, many European travellers felt that they were too late for an 'authentic' encounter with the exotic orient and realised that their ideas of this encounter had already been mediated by earlier fiction and travel writing. See Ali Behdad, *Belated Travellers: Orientalism in the Age of Colonial Dissolution* (Durham, NC: Duke University Press, 1994).
[8] This was certainly the case for Wilfred Thesiger as Mark Cocker argues in *Loneliness and Time: The Story of British Travel Writing* (New York: Pantheon, 1992), pp. 68–81.
[9] Sybille Bedford, *The Sudden View* (London: Victor Gollancz, 1953), p. 242. (The book was later republished under the title *A Visit to Don Otavio: A Mexican Odyssey*). Jan Morris, *Sultan in Oman* (London: Eland, 2008 [1957]), p. 152.

Postwar Versions of the War Abroad

When war broke out in 1939, it put paid to even simple European transit, let alone leisure travel. Its course chased British citizens stranded on the continent from country to country. The war also created British enclaves like Cairo, where writers supported the war effort.[10] After her flight across the Mediterranean, Elizabeth David fetched up first in the cypher office in Alexandria and later in Cairo where she found work in the reference library of the Ministry of Information. She met Olivia Manning, Freya Stark, Norman Douglas, Laurence Durrell, Alan Moorehead and – equally important – her Greek and Sudanese cooks. Strictly speaking, *A Book of Mediterranean Food* (1950) is not a conventional travel book, but it is an unusually sanguine product of wartime travel and full of literary extracts by the travel writers she met in Antibes, on Syros and in Cairo. It certainly revolutionised the dismal postwar British cuisine through the introduction of such exotic vegetables as aubergines and courgettes. Others translated the experience of the foreign posting or battlefield into fiction: Alexander Baron, H. E. Bates, Nevil Shute and Evelyn Waugh all wrote novels. Olivia Manning's odyssey would provide the material for the Balkan and Levant trilogies. Much travel writing published during or shortly after the war comes from writers affiliated with British intelligence, as was the case before the war for most Arabists. Freya Stark's wartime journeys from Aden through Egypt, to the Levant and Iraq, published in 1945 as *East Is West*, are a good example of the kind of propagandistic war work a professional traveller could do to promote British interests. Sceptical of Jewish Zionism and Arab nationalism alike, she was interested in the *Effendi*, the young Westernised men of the aspiring middle classes, as the generation most likely to plough a moderate, Anglophile furrow. Her narrative comes alive when she abandons the honours list of deserving Excellencies and directly engages with local people. Then we learn how hard it is to set up girls' schools in Syria; how one could circumvent even the most intractable Iraqi customs official by appealing to his sense of chivalry; how a portable cinema opens doors to the women's quarters in the Yemen and offers surprising insights: 'there is no doubt that women boxed up in houses are much more powerful than those of us who roam about outside'.[11] Yet vignettes of female experience

---

[10] See Artemis Cooper, *Cairo in the War, 1939–1945* (London: John Murray, 2013).
[11] Freya Stark, *East Is West* (London: John Murray, 1945), p. 31.

are infrequent, as if gender should not matter, and were literally subordinated to her espousal of British paternalism.

Like many British travellers, Stark could still rely 'on that dependable network' of government houses and was hardly ever without an entourage of servants: mentioning 'my Somali driver, his two aides, my Yemeni cook and Syrian servant' tends to relativise claims about intrepid adventure.[12] Ursula Graham Bower, undertaking anthropological research and photography among the Naga tribe in a far corner of North East India, also claimed to be 'a woman alone' when war broke out, and rather close to where the Japanese would soon be dropping bombs from across the Burmese border. She, too, could employ local porters, a cook, a gardener and a general servant. District Officers, however, generally frowned on unattached females. She was ordered to abandon her 'jungle work' and run a refugee kitchen in Lumding and later a Watch and Ward scheme on the Barak River. *Naga Path* (1952), unlike so many travel books, does not include a map and this tends to disorientate the reader. It underlines how remote British outposts could be and how hidden the tribes they encompassed. It is also an important reminder of the support colonial subjects and indigenous people gave to the British at war.

It is easy to forget among the volumes of pre-war travel writing how rare any kind of foreign travel would have been for the ordinary (let alone working-class) Briton. Despite the Baedeker and Murray guides, this was not yet the age of real mass or package tourism, which really took off in the late 1950s and 1960s. Travel had remained the privilege of the (mostly male) upper-middle classes who also had the education so often implied in travel books' intended audience, and which sometimes accounts for the genre's *longeurs*: modern languages, Greek and Latin, ancient history. Those who had languages and local knowledge were more likely to be posted in the intelligence service abroad: Patrick Leigh Fermor on Crete, Freya Stark in the Near and Middle East, Norman Lewis in North Africa and Italy, and Wilfred Thesiger in the Sudan and Syria. But how did the millions of conscripted military personnel negotiate the foreign experience that war entailed, the unfamiliar climes and cultures of Burma and Malaya, Egypt and Libya, Italy and Iraq? Little preparation seems to have gone into this, as if the troop environment had to provide a sufficiently portable home. 'To have an inkling of the political situation of the country in which we found ourselves would have been useful but none was given, and we trod the hard road of trial and error', commented Norman Lewis about the

[12] Ibid., p. 29.

shoddy organisation of the Field Security Service, when he edited his notebooks in 1978 as *Naples '44*.[13] As an exemplary demonstration of the intersection of war writing and travel writing in which the immediacy of the present tense and the diary form are retained, *Naples '44* tells us – much as *Naga Path* does – that being stationed abroad involved a significant amount of contact with local civilians. Working as a military police officer, Lewis had to contend with local smugglers and military black marketeers, the Camorra's vendettas and honour killings, alongside partisan fights and rampant prostitution. His subtitle, *An Intelligence Officer in the Italian Labyrinth*, dryly summarises how bewildering the mixture of systemic local violence, wartime sexuality and Allied ignorance must have been. Yet he still finds time – as if this were a conventional travel book – to describe the eruption of Vesuvius, marvel about the local wine and remember eating eels in Amalfi. Perhaps the era's most interesting literary epiphenomenon is that travel writing's anthropological curiosity (who are these people?) informs ethical questions about war (why did they do this? Why did we do that?). Rebecca West's *Greenhouse with Cyclamens* (1946–54) and Sybille Bedford's *The Faces of Justice: A Traveller's Report* (1961) are unthinkable without this fruitful conjunction.

Foreign Office provision *was* made for part of the European theatre of war in publications that borrowed heavily from the traditional guide book. *Instructions* booklets were available for servicemen in France and Germany ahead of the Normandy invasions. (The US War Department had issued similar booklets for American Servicemen in Britain and Australia in 1942.) These booklets contained short descriptions of foreign manners and cuisine, historical précis, maps, social customs and taboos, as well as a list of stock phrases. These were of course ideological commentaries on national stereotypes aimed at bridging cultural differences for the benefit of military cooperation (France and the United States) or cementing them to avoid fraternisation or pity (Germany). Here, the private learned that the 'Germans are not good at controlling their feelings' and that French men 'may relieve nature rather openly in public'.[14] Their often patronising tone is a reminder of the sharp class distinctions that marked British society and of the cultural anxiety that surrounded wartime sexuality. The *Instructions* booklets, then, as guidebooks for encounters of military personnel with European civilians, are a testament to the British Government's

[13] Norman Lewis, *Naples '44* (London: Eland, 2002), p. 8.
[14] *Instructions for British Servicemen in Germany 1944* [abridged] (Oxford: Bodleian Library, 2005), n. p.; *Instructions for British Servicemen in France 1944* [abridged] (Oxford: Bodleian Library, 2005), n. p.

recognition that such (mass) experiences had to be managed because their scale was socially unprecedented. In this respect, France and Germany fared better than Greece and Italy, for which no *Instructions* were issued, as if all that Greek and Latin and those reams of ancient history were any use in a war that was not the *Iliad*.[15]

Sic Transit: New Ruins, New Nomads

Among those who travelled through the ruins of Central Europe are the same politically engaged writers one encounters in the 1930s: George Orwell, Storm Jameson, Steven Spender and W. H. Auden. Like Lewis in Naples, they found moral bankruptcy exacerbated by shortages of everything. So many sights and sites were unprecedented, challenging writers' ekphrastic skills and readers' imagination alike. The *loci terribiles* that became the early postwar tropes for the rupture of civilisation – the camp and the bombed city – were each so extreme that they required visual evidence to enter into the cultural imaginary. Only war correspondents and military personnel witnessed the camp liberations.[16] Their laconic accounts often send the reader back to the photographs, but are invaluable because these sites changed very rapidly, either because they were disease-ridden and had to be razed (like Belsen) or the occupation forces pragmatically requisitioned them as firewood or for housing troops, prisoners or Displaced Persons. The bombed city, however, remained ruined for sufficiently long to be turned from a site into a sight for literary writers. The sheer scale of material destruction took everyone's breath away, hence the frequent incomparability topos (a staple of travel writing) as here in James Stern's panoramic view of the medieval city of Nuremberg:

> What you saw from here you could not compare to anything you'd ever seen, not even to a dream, for dreams are too detailed, and here the sight was too vast, too overwhelming for the eye to rest on details. I have seen moving pictures of the remains of Hiroshima. Nürnberg from the Burg bore no resemblance to them, for the Japanese city appeared almost flat, and the German one was nowhere in as clean a state ... From the Burg, to the limit of vision in every direction, and that was a long way with long sight, you

---

[15] Alongside Lewis's retrospective dismissal and Waugh's sarcasm in his *Sword of Honour* trilogy, neither Edmund Wilson (*Europe without Baedeker*, 1948) nor Henry Miller (*The Colossus of Maroussi*, 1941) were impressed by the colonial habitus of British officers in Europe.

[16] The BBC's Richard Dimbleby was present at the liberation of Belsen on 15 April 1945 and his brief account for radio is available on the BBC news website: http://news.bbc.co.uk/1/hi/in_depth/444 5811.stm, accessed 29 January 2016.

saw – with the exception of the Gothic towers – an endless unbroken brickscape of jagged walls.[17]

Ruinous 'brickscapes' feature prominently in early postwar travel writing, but they are no longer picturesque or romantic even if they make for spectacular chiaroscuro settings in the films of the period.[18] Stephen Spender on visiting bombed Cologne warned his British readers: 'Everything has gone. In this the destruction of Germany is quite different from even the worst that has happened in England (though not different from Poland and from parts of Russia).'[19] The European city was not London after the Blitz; something had been irrevocably lost: 'The people who live there seem quite disassociated from Cologne. They resemble rather a tribe of wanderers who have discovered a ruined city in a desert and who are camping there, living in the cellars and hunting amongst the ruins for the booty, relics of a dead civilization.'[20] The flattened city was a paradoxical chronotope for Spender, as much an indicator of technological advances and large-scale military cooperation as a complete throwback to the neolithic state of nomads, troglodytes and hunter-gatherers: communities degenerate into 'tribes', city dwelling into makeshift 'camping' and commercial activity into 'hunting for the booty'. Violence is the common denominator across this temporal spectrum. We remember Waugh's discomfort at rubbing shoulders with Displaced Persons and refugees drifting between barbed wire. Spender's description sits uneasily between witnessing and spectatorship. This self-doubting, compromised gaze at the modern world frames postwar travel writing much more strongly than its antecedents.

The traveller's ambivalence about ruins continues for much of the mid-century. In the light of Albert Speer's monumentalism, ancient architectural ambition now looked more suspect. For Norman Lewis, the vastness of Angkor Wat pointed to the political nature of the Khmer Empire as 'nothing if not totalitarian'.[21] Similarly, Sibylle Bedford found the colossal Zapotec ruins at Mitla 'entirely successful, entirely frightening': 'If the Nazis had not been so cheap, had their taste been better and their instinct for self-dramatisation been less Wagnerian, this is the way they would have

---

[17] James Stern, *The Hidden Damage* (London: Chelsea Press, 1990 [1947]), p. 288.
[18] Ruined cities are part of the 'set' for Carol Reed's *The Third Man* (1949) and Roberto Rossellini's *Rome, Open City* (1945) and *Germany Zero Hour* (1948).
[19] Stephen Spender, *European Witness* (London: Hamish Hamilton, 1946), p. 22.   [20] Ibid., p. 24.
[21] Norman Lewis, *A Dragon Apparent: Travels in Cambodia, Laos and Vietnam*, Norman Lewis Omnibus (London: Picador, 1996 [1951]), p. 213.

built.'[22] As Rose Macaulay put it dryly in 1953: '*Ruinenlust* has come full circle: we have had our fill.' She reminded her readers that even if 'Monte Cassino put on with wreckage a new dignity', much of our cultural response to 'jagged walls' had been softened by art, poetry and the passage of time. War, revolution and conquest had ravaged earlier ages which produced their own seemingly 'staunchless grief' before we naively proclaimed the remnants picturesque.[23] Elizabeth Bowen, perambulating through Rome in 1959 and no stranger to rubble herself, reflected on the unnerving quality of a temporally vertiginous cityscape of ruins for the first, eighteenth-century British tourists:

> Rome was the archetype on which those generations had been brought up – that it fell they knew, but it had not really fallen until they saw it: the brutish actuality of a scene of violence ... they saw, of course, very much more of a mess than we see now – indiscriminate, tottery, overgrown ... blotchy façades, weed-grown *piazze*, foetid alleys. The palaces in which they were entertained (if they had introductions) were dark as catafalques inside, cobwebby, musty ... Much of antiquity could not be got at – carved doorways, capitals, columns, scraps of inscription, portions of arches had got themselves embedded into the Ghetto, amid flapping black rags and a stinking fishmarket. *Sic transit.*[24]

Bowen shows that the difference between remnants and ruins, rubble and relics lies in the eye of the beholder as much as in artifice. Augustan Romans' scant veneration of antiquity had not yet promoted the excavation, preservation and presentation of the past as cultural capital for the tourist gaze. The synchronic architectural 'mess' of the eighteenth-century city underlined the perturbing fact that all empires fall precisely when Britain's was ascending and expanding.

When Bowen and Macaulay reflected on the transition from rubble to ruin, the British Empire was indeed in sharp decline. Lawrence Durrell's *Bitter Lemons of Cyprus* (1958) is one of the few books to engage with independence movements. Less a travel book than one of foreign residence in the years of Cypriot *enosis* (the island's independence movement from 1953 to 1956), it deplores the British administration's shortcomings. The pejoratively abbreviated 'Cyps' of colonial parlance did not even enjoy 'the amplitude of our own civic and cultural resources' – universities, swimming pools, rail networks, cricket grounds, libraries – leading Durrell

---

[22] Bedford, *The Sudden View*, p. 231.
[23] Rose Macaulay, *The Pleasure of Ruins* (London: Weidenfeld & Nicholson, 1953), p. 454.
[24] Elizabeth Bowen, *A Time in Rome* (Harmondsworth: Penguin, 1989 [1959]), p. 104.

to join a number of mid-century travellers who cast doubt over the cultural life promulgated by Fleming's 'dependable network'.[25] Durrell was exasperated by the British colony that 'lived a life of blameless monotony, rolling about in small cars, drinking at the yacht club, sailing a bit, going to church, and suffering agonies of apprehension at the thought of not being invited to Government House on the Queen's Birthday.'[26] For the same reason, Leigh Fermor slated Barbados as 'parochial and grey and fiercely Anglo-English'.[27] Blameless monotony in colonial outposts also drove Elizabeth David and Diana Shipton to distraction; the realisation that Kashgari women smoked like chimneys among themselves is the social climax in *An Antique Land* (1950). Wilfred Thesiger was so frustrated about his isolation from local life in the Sudan that he resigned. Even after Burmese independence, when colonisers had become expatriates, Norman Lewis saw how the racial seating order on his steamer on the Irrawaddy was strictly maintained. In this 'enclave of diehard Englishry', everyone would 'boastfully display their ignorance, their contempt and distaste for everything about the country'.[28] In contrast, Durrell's vignettes about his neighbours, in the village where he was building a house, were replete with sozzled anecdotes and vibrant characters whom he portrayed with unfaltering affection. For Stark, who visited Durrell on Cyprus, it took *enosis* to reflect on the premise and durée of imperialism: sailing along the Turkish Coast tracing Alexander's journey (and describing ruin after ruin), she wondered: 'the only way to establish lasting empire anywhere was and is to bring to a nation a pattern of civilization whose intrinsic merits it can feel to be better than its own'.[29] What were those merits now? What would remain?

Nostalgia, Anti-Modernity and the Perma-War

If imperial decline and the crisis in Western civilisation produced a more consistently elegiac mood, travel writers' nostalgia was tempered by a quest for authenticity and a quasi-curatorial need for witnessing people, customs and ways of life that were about to vanish. Some titles of the era – *The Last Grain Race, The Lost World of the Kalahari, Tristes Tropiques* – captured their chagrin. Other indicators of exhaustion were anthologies of pre-war

---

[25] Lawrence Durrell, *Bitter Lemons of Cyprus* (London: Faber & Faber, 1958), p. 132.
[26] Ibid., p. 29.
[27] Patrick Leigh Fermor, *The Traveller's Tree* (London: Penguin, 1994 [1950]), p. 154.
[28] *Golden Earth* [1952], *Norman Lewis Omnibus*, pp. 330, 360.
[29] Freya Stark, *The Lycian Shore* (London: John Murray, 1956), pp. 84f, 145.

travel writing such as Alec Waugh's *The Sugar Islands* (1949) or Evelyn Waugh's *When the Going Was Good*.[30] However, some of the best-selling travel books were picaresque narratives of failure: Sybille Bedford's *The Sudden View: A Mexican Journey* (1953) and Eric Newby's *A Short Walk in the Hindu Kush* (1958). Enduring bumpy detours, eating horrifically indigestible food, being marooned on awful trains in torrential rain or stuck below the summit after weeks of struggle and dismissed as a 'couple of pansies',[31] are all exasperating experiences chivalrously endured. Yet, as critics have observed, the role of the antiquated lady or gentleman traveller comically battling obstreperous 'natives', incomprehensible customs and adverse circumstances often masks a 'residual feeling of moral superiority' concomitant with the imperial instinct.[32]

Exploration used to have an aim; postwar travel seemed like a faintly absurd quest for melancholic nomads – a quest complicated by the forces of globalisation and modernisation made more palpable by the habits of consumption and by the machine. The most modern form of transport, the aeroplane, held virtually no narrative potential and was seen as a particularly faceless agent of violence. Flying over Indo-China in 1950 (a region that would be engulfed in war for three decades), Norman Lewis observed smoke billowing from the villages and mused, 'what an aid to untroubled killing the bombing plane must be'.[33] The more humble motorcar also featured as an unreliable, even hazardous mode of getting about, often accompanied by the soft sibilants of deflating tires or the screams of people being run over. In fact, the failing automobile was the objective correlative for humankind's ongoing battle with nature or natives. Freya Stark required locals to mend her overheating engine and flat tyres in the Persian desert. Mexican topography was so challenging, and roads so poor, that the broken-down car is virtually a character in Sybille Bedford's narrative. James Morris, travelling in convoy with the Sultan of Oman, realised that half the royal entourage was perennially detained by fixing something vehicular, and getting 'left behind' screaming for attention was the prank *du jour*. The screaming started almost immediately for

---

[30] The past tense was also the mood of E. Lucas Bridges's *Uttermost Part of the Earth* (1948), Arthur Grimble's *A Pattern of Islands* (1952) and Gerald Brenan's *South from Granada* (1957), in which they described journeys and residencies undertaken decades ago.
[31] Eric Newby, *A Short Walk in the Hindu Kush* (London: Picador, 1974 [1958]), p. 248.
[32] Patrick Holland and Graham Huggan, *Tourists with Typewriters: Critical Reflections on Contemporary Travel Writing* (Ann Arbor, MI: University of Michigan Press, 2000), p. 36.
[33] Lewis, *A Dragon Apparent*, p. 14. Stacy Burton also notes the plane as an agent of violence in Rebecca West's Black Lamb and Grey Falcon. See Stacy Burton, *Travel Narrative and the Ends of Modernity* (Cambridge University Press, 2014), pp. 136f.

Eric Newby, whose overland journey from Turkey to the Hindu Kush got off to a bumpy start when his companion ran over an Armenian nomad and only narrowly avoided arrest. The modern traveller's desire for relentless speed and motion often caused consternation.

Speed and motion needed fuel. All travellers to the Middle East from the 1930s onwards realised that oil prospecting and Arab nationalism would change the region for ever. Yet, as Billie Melman states, this inevitable and rapid change was rarely read as an opportunity for self-determination, prosperity, urbanisation and development that Arab governments were capable of managing.[34] Instead, accounts of the Middle East in particular are tinged with what Renato Rosaldo has called the paradox of 'imperialist nostalgia', a wistful reminiscing about an authentic mode of life now corrupted by contact with the West, a process for which the European (writer) took no responsibility.[35] Jan Morris is perhaps the best example for this attitude and a notable historian of the British Empire and its hegemonic heydays of Pax Britannica (the relatively peaceful imperial century 1815 to 1914). Loyal to her own imperialist instincts, she endorsed British colonial practices as 'knavery beneficial'.[36] Thesiger was much more sceptical of British influence in the Middle East, and his romanticism has to be read as a fierce anti-modernity in which he elevated the doomed Bedu to a noble victim. Setting out for the Rub' al Kali in 1945 with a 'belief in [his] own racial superiority', he soon felt 'like an uncouth, inarticulate barbarian, an intruder from a shoddy and materialistic world'. He returned humbled from his desert journeys: 'Among no other people have I ever felt the same sense of personal inferiority.'[37] Thesiger's journeys form an existential quest for ascetic, homosocial companionship and some quintessential experience of freedom. His are not erudite Arabist volumes, but empirical books: sympathetic encounters not with artefacts, ruins, libraries and scholars, but primarily with a unique landscape and a vanishing people. Compare his remarks to how Morris concludes *Sultan in Oman* (1957): 'in all honesty I did not think of [Muscat's Gwadaris] as quite the same species as the administrator or myself ... some deep-rooted imperial instinct within me kept me rigidly apart and divided from them'.[38]

---

[34] Billie Melman, 'The Middle East/Arabia: "The Cradle of Islam"' in Peter Hulme and Tim Youngs (eds), *The Cambridge Companion to Travel Writing* (Cambridge University Press, 2002), p. 118.
[35] Renato Rosaldo, *Culture and Truth: The Remaking of Social Analysis* (London: Routledge, 1993), p. 69.
[36] Morris, *Sultan in Oman*, p. 154.
[37] Wilfred Thesiger, *Arabian Sands* (Harmondsworth: Penguin, 1991), pp. 38, 329.
[38] Morris, *Sultan in Oman*, p. 153.

Such rigid divisions were breaking up. However Eurocentrically Ursula Bower framed the remote Zemi tribe in *Naga Path*, her protective attachment to them is abundantly clear. They, in turn, thought of her as family. Her talent, like Thesiger's and Lewis's, lay in narrative vignette and visual characterisation; all took extraordinary pictures, worked from notebooks and benefited from the editorial process of memory. Here is a tantalising chapter-opening from *Naga Path*: 'At half past ten on a bright October morning Degaland the dog-boy eloped with Dinekamba's sister.'[39] Who would not want to read on? Unsurprisingly, given her anthropological remit, she is fascinated by courtship, disease, spirituality and ritual. The reader is most curious about Namkia, her manservant throughout her stay in India, and his negotiation of her role as both white British woman and 'sister'. That the travelling companion and the local guides and helpmates are no longer written out of the narrative or lumped together as 'natives' but given a name, characterisation, a voice and a history becomes more important.[40] Not only does it acknowledge the journey as a collective effort rather than fashioning it as a singular adventure; it also underlines the subjectivity of the experience through the overt literary devices used to bring these characters into the narrative. The reader easily remembers Bin Kabina of the Rashid from *Arabian Sands*, the Nuristanis Abdul Ghiyas and Badar Khan in *A Short Walk in the Hindu Kush*, Lewis's Burmese guide U Tun Win, or the discreetly abbreviated 'E.' (Bedford's lover Ethel Murphy) from *A Sudden View*.

One would not imagine that reading about a fairly desolate landscape traversed with the most basic means – on foot and on camels – could be utterly engrossing. Yet Thesiger's *Arabian Sands* is enlivened by many authoritative albeit respectful anthropological observations about the Bedu and attentive ekphrastic passages about a surprisingly varied landscape. We learn that sand comes in a myriad of colours and 'sings'; that across a vast terrain the Bedu recognise the tracks of each camel and every tribe; how bread is 'baked' in the desert; the different taste of water in each well; how one keeps clean without washing; what the rites of circumcision are for each tribal community. The narrative form thus enacts the ponderous progress of the journey and tells us what a more 'natural' pace enables us to perceive:

---

[39] Ibid., p. 79.
[40] This is not always true for the writer's gender politics: Thesiger cites male predecessors such as T. E. Lawrence, Philby or Thomas, but completely ignores the writing of Gertrude Bell or Freya Stark, who were Arabists and had also travelled through the Hadramaut.

> ... there was time to notice things – a grasshopper under a bush, a dead swallow on the ground, the tracks of a hare, a bird's nest, the shape and colour of ripples on the sand, the bloom of tiny seedlings pushing through the soil. There was time to collect a plant or to look at a rock. The very slowness of our march diminished monotony. I thought how terribly boring it would be to rush about this country in a car.[41]

A very different pace propels Jan Morris, who in 1955 rushed about this country in a car and wrote almost immediately about it (note the fourteen years that lay between Thesiger's first journey and its publication). The distinct personalities of people and camels that animate Thesiger's narrative are dots on the horizon in Morris's book. In fact, speed makes the dust-encrusted *Sultan in Oman* 'terribly boring' for the reader interested in the people of Oman, but it propels into the foreground Morris's imperial instincts. At the end of the journey, the benefits of Pax Britannica are stripped of ideological cotton wool and its capitalist bedrock exposed: 'For the first time the British in the Middle East began to see themselves ... simply as people making money.'[42]

Elsewhere, the West's consumerism invaded. On Haiti, Leigh Fermor noticed that the 'fabric of romantic dilapidation festered into an American drugstore or a milk-bar, and everywhere, in tin and plastic and cardboard, were symptoms of the Coca-Cola plague'.[43] This is a lovely example of Rosaldo's imperialist nostalgia combined with British postwar anxiety about American cultural imperialism. Surely the metaphor of Westernisation – or Western patterns of consumption – as a disease is rather problematic in a geographical area whose British and French plantations were made profitable by transported African slaves and, later, Indian labourers. The scourge was European colonialism-cum-slavery, yet its material ruins constitute 'romantic dilapidation', whereas American commodities produce mere litter.

In a world of restricted travel, popular authors borrowed from travel books. Ian Fleming, for instance, quoted from Fermor in *Live and Let Die* (1954) and Graham Greene's *The Quiet American* (1955) was surely indebted to Norman Lewis's best-selling *A Dragon Apparent*. For Peter Hulme, Lewis's career defined mainstream postwar travel writing, but in his era he was rather exceptional in anticipating the links between decolonisation and the Cold War.[44] French planters had conscripted the ethnic

---

[41] Thesiger, *Arabian Sands*, p. 60. [42] Morris, *Sultan in Oman*, pp. 153, 72.
[43] Fermor, *The Traveller's Tree*, p. 231.
[44] Peter Hulme, 'Travelling to Write (1940–2000)' in Hulme and Youngs (eds), *Cambridge Companion to Travel Writing*, p. 88.

tribes of South Annam into virtual slave labour and the ensuing shortage of hands on their own farms caused starvation. Contact with US missionaries and French anthropologists embarking on social experiments in model villages deprived them of their religion, dress and ancient social structures. Chinese-sponsored nationalist guerrillas under the Viet Minh requisitioned what food was left both from indigenous tribes and Annamite villages. Chinese traders moved in and grew rich selling to all sides. Gradually, punitive massacres by Foreign Legionnaires against the locals drove them towards the Viet Minh. However joyless the re-education programmes, Communism simply offered a better life than exploitative colonialism. In retrospect, Lewis's book explains why this region would sink into a state of permanent warfare that would last for decades: colonial powers economically dependent on plantations in South East Asia but threatened by independence movements would convince the anti-colonialist United States that their intervention against insurgents was a legitimate anti-Communist containment strategy.[45] Small wonder that journalists reporting on the Vietnam War rated Lewis so highly. Unlike Thesiger, he did not ennoble the ethnic tribes by seeing them in isolation from their political context or turning the squalor of their living conditions into some prelapsarian freedom. In fact, he was unsentimental about all the groups he found, most notably the French settlers who regarded their plantations as the 'principal show-places the country has to offer; only slightly less spectacular, perhaps, than Mount Fuji from one of its accepted viewpoints, Niagara Falls, or the Grand Canyon'.[46] Colonialism as natural wonder; tribal life exhibited in model villages. No one is possessed of that disastrous Jamesian innocence Greene embellished in *The Quiet American*. Lewis predicted the 'phantasmatic Indochina' of the French cultural imaginary: a Kipling-esque nostalgia for a neverland of lush flora, peopled with submissive Asians in a soft-focus setting of serene affluence, spiced with languid late afternoon passions predictably played out under whirring ceiling fans.[47] His drab Saigon is far from Marguerite Duras's exoticised erotic fantasy in *The Lover* (1984). Here, he cuts through such Orientalist romance: 'Laos-ized Frenchmen are like the results of successful lobotomy operations – untroubled and mildly libidinous.'[48] Graham Greene

---

[45] See Adam Piette, *The Literary Cold War: 1945 to Vietnam* (Edinburgh University Press, 2009), p. 155f.
[46] Lewis, *A Dragon Apparent*, pp. 135–6.
[47] See Panivong Norindr, *Phantasmatic Indochina: French Colonial Ideology in Architecture, Film and Literature* (Durham, NC: Duke University Press, 1996).
[48] Lewis, *A Dragon Apparent*, p. 268.

diagnosed a similar state of affairs among the bungaloid miseries of Britain's African colonies in *The Heart of the Matter* (1948) – an unpopular book, Lewis found, with French colonials keen on projecting their own version of 'blameless monotony'.

Mid-century British travel writing, then, performed a difficult transition from the imperialist habit of the past to a more uncertain, and seemingly diminished, future. Nostalgia and anti-modernity, the symptoms of post-war exhaustion and declining empires, informed its tone. Yet, as we see with Lewis's account of Indochina above, in the rare instances when these symptoms became the genre's *objects* alongside foreign people and locales, this critical awareness paved the way for the self-irony of postmodern and postcolonial travel writing.

CHAPTER 20

The Future and the End: Imagining Catastrophe in Mid-Century British Fiction

Allan Hepburn

In 1945, the Labour Party swept to victory in Britain on the election slogan, 'Let Us Face the Future'. A pamphlet issued under the same title in April 1945 laid out principles and aspirations of the Welfare State. From the perspective of the last days of the Second World War, the future was indistinct – both an immediate temporality rife with the problems of reconstruction, and a slightly more distant prospect threatened by the possibility of nuclear catastrophe. Predictions of another world war were being made even before the Second World War had ended. Mid-century British fiction thus unfolds within the ambiguous space between imminent doom and compromised futurity. Mid-century writers imagine catastrophe in terms of extinction, measurability and time after the end of human time. Above all, atomic age fiction treats catastrophe as a set of variations wrought upon the future.

Notwithstanding notable modernist examples of futurism – Aldous Huxley's *Brave New World* (1932) or H. G. Wells's *The Shape of Things to Come* (1933) – mid-century British novelists thought longer and more darkly about the future than their predecessors. The future lasts a long time, too long for some. In *The Stranger's Hand* (1952), an unfinished film treatment by Graham Greene, one character asks, 'Is this really the inevitable, is this the shabby future for us all?'[1] In Greene's narrative, hoodlums and war criminals roam throughout Europe, and will do so for the foreseeable future. In the 1940s and 1950s, many writers and critics thought that time had accelerated because of the bomb; the shabby, inevitable future arrived faster than ever before. In 1947, Peter Quennell recorded the sense of pressure that acceleration induced. He wondered whether the postwar writer had enough time to triage impressions and absorb the lessons of history: 'the fear that our time may be running short makes the process of

---

[1] Graham Greene, *No Man's Land and The Stranger's Hand*, (ed.) James Sexton (London: Hesperus, 2005), p. 92.

literary rehabilitation more complicated and less effective, and gives an air of hurried, nervous improvisation to so much modern literature'.[2] As Quennell implies, acceleration brings about heedlessness, and heedlessness increases the likelihood of catastrophe.

Catastrophe is a precondition of mid-century dystopic fiction: Rex Warner's *The Aerodrome* (1941), Aldous Huxley's *Ape and Essence* (1948), George Orwell's *Nineteen Eighty-Four* (1949), John Wyndham's *The Day of the Triffids* (1951) and *The Chrysalids* (1955), William Golding's *Lord of the Flies* (1954) and *The Inheritors* (1955), Nevil Shute's *On the Beach* (1957), L. P. Hartley's *Facial Justice* (1960) and Anthony Burgess's *Clockwork Orange* (1962). In each of these novels, catastrophe has a shifting relation to temporality and action. In *Lord of the Flies*, an atom bomb wipes out part of the population. *Facial Justice* opens 'in the not very distant future, after the Third World War'.[3] In one of the narrative vectors of *Ape and Essence*, archaeologists from New Zealand sail to California in February 2108 to look for traces of human life; during the atomic wars a century earlier, belligerents spared New Zealand because, 'like Equatorial Africa, it was too remote to be worth anybody's while to obliterate'.[4] In *Nineteen Eighty-Four*, George Orwell imagines a state of perpetual warfare around 1984, as well as a deeper future after 2050, when linguists reconstruct Newspeak as a failed language developed under the Ingsoc regime. In *The Chrysalids*, nuclear holocaust is an inevitable outcome of Cold War brinkmanship. In all of these novels, conflict reigns between generations, species and states. In each case, futuristic fiction creates opportunities to speculate about the human race and political governance. Catastrophe creates opportunities for imagining alternate forms of statehood, whether feudal, military, socialist or global.

The Future and the Novel

As a temporal genre, the novel necessarily bears some relation to the future. In a novel, an action in the present has consequences for whatever happens subsequently. The novel therefore moves through cycles of anticipation and deferral. Actions culminate in a conclusion, which is the point where the fictional future comes to a halt, even if all plot details have not been resolved. As a genre modelled directly or indirectly on the changing world,

---

[2] Peter Quennell, 'In Search of the Postwar Writer' in *Grand Perspective* (London: Contact Publications, 1947), p. 45.
[3] L. P. Hartley, *Facial Justice* (London: Hamish Hamilton, 1960), p. 9.
[4] Aldous Huxley, *Ape and Essence* (New York: Harper, 1948), p. 39.

the novel can never exhaust its subject matter. The novel necessarily has an open and inconclusive relation to reality, be it historical, contemporary or futuristic. Distinguishing between the epic and the novel, Mikhail Bakhtin focuses on temporal distance from the subject of representation: 'The epic world is constructed in the zone of an absolute distanced image, beyond the sphere of possible contact with the developing, incomplete and therefore re-thinking and re-evaluating present.'[5] By contrast with the epic, the novel inhabits a band of time in the present, from which it conjectures the future. As Bakhtin claims, the novel 'is determined by experience, knowledge and practice (the future)'.[6] Because it is premised on experience and knowledge, the novel presumes an unfinished project of world-making. Whereas the epic is sealed off from the present, in the sense that its actions are complete and the story can be told from any point in the cycle, the novel orders temporality according to beginnings, middles and ends, in which a fictional conclusion coincides with some version of completion. Imagining catastrophe – whether fascist victory as in *The Aerodrome* or nuclear devastation as in *Ape and Essence* – closes down the possibilities for the future and diminishes expectations of narrative completion beyond the end of fictional action.

The problem of the future weighed heavily on novelists' and critics' minds at mid-century. In 'Looking Backward and Forward' (1941), an editorial in *New Writing and Daylight*, John Lehmann surveyed the problems facing wartime writers. Two years later in the same journal, Philip Toynbee pronounced on 'The Decline and Future of the English Novel', with the former receiving more consideration than the latter. Toynbee blames the falling off of the English novel on 'the overweening influence of contemporary events, and the vastly enlarged scope of the novelist's territory'.[7] After the war, *New Writing and Daylight* featured a forum on 'The Future of Fiction' (1946), with contributions by Rose Macaulay, V. S. Pritchett, Arthur Koestler, L. P. Hartley, Walter Allen and Osbert Sitwell. For these six contributors, the surplus of wartime events hampered, rather than revivified, contemporary fiction. A glut of experiences made it difficult for novelists to order them into novelistic form; as Macaulay puts it, 'discontinuity has been the mood of our brittle time'.[8] Everyone, she

---

[5] Mikhail Bakhtin, *The Dialogic Imagination: Four Essays*, trans. by Caryl Emerson and Michael Holquist (Austin, TX: University of Texas Press, 1981), p. 17.
[6] Ibid., p. 15.
[7] Philip Toynbee, 'The Decline and Future of the English Novel' *New Writing and Daylight* 4 (1943–4), p. 44.
[8] Rose Macaulay, 'The Future of Fiction' *New Writing and Daylight* 7 (1946), p. 72.

writes, experienced the war as an adventure worthy of a thriller, yet not everyone had the imagination to convert experience, however thrilling, into fiction.

Reflecting on British fiction of the Second World War, Alan Munton notes that soldiers' and civilians' apprehensiveness about the future could be projected indefinitely forward as a story that has not yet reached its conclusion: 'In a massive democratization of fear every threatened person could conceive his or her own life as a narrative, not quite completed.'[9] The possible outcomes of such wartime narratives – heroism, treachery, death – are postponed for as long as possible. The will to survive pushes personal narratives forward as stories without conclusions. In wartime, the temporal structure of a novel may be distorted or disordered by fear or other psychological effects, for instance in the non-linear and sometimes hallucinatory sequences of James Hanley's *No Directions* (1943) or the jittery chronology of Elizabeth Bowen's *The Heat of the Day* (1949). In particular, mid-century novels tend to put off the future, because it may signify personal extinction or national defeat. As Munton explains, the war had to end, 'but the moment of its ending moved ahead of all anticipation, requiring a constant adjustment to all the psychological space that still lay ahead'.[10] The long haul of the war seemed even longer because the anticipated end, whatever it might be, induced fear and dread.

Imagined cataclysm creates anxiety. In Alan Sillitoe's *Saturday Night and Sunday Morning* (1958), Arthur Seaton thinks, 'these days a war could start tomorrow'.[11] He forecasts nuclear bombardment as a sudden halt to his thoughtless carousing: 'The future meant things, both good and bad.'[12] The bathos of the statement derives from Arthur's confusing his personal future with the future of the planet. For Arthur, the future means a fortnight of military training every year and a chance that the Americans will drop an H-Bomb on Moscow at any moment. In the postwar period, characters live out their relation to an unthinkable future as a horizon that is both political and apocalyptic. The end of human life, individual or collective, may happen in a flash. In such a scenario, catastrophe coincides with the end of the human species, although it does not do so in every circumstance.

According to its Greek etymology, a 'catastrophe' is a sudden turn or an overturning. Catastrophe implies movement, thus direction, speed and

---

[9] Alan Munton, *English Fiction of the Second World War* (London: Faber & Faber, 1989), p. 25.
[10] Ibid., p. 21.
[11] Alan Sillitoe, *Saturday Night and Sunday Morning* (London: Harper, 2008), p. 27.
[12] Ibid., p. 129.

change. Some catastrophes may be small, others planetary; some catastrophes may be slow, others fast. Synonyms for 'catastrophe' are all dire: disaster, failure, extreme misfortune, utter overthrow or ruin, fiasco, debacle. Whereas a 'strophe' – literally a 'turn' – designates a stanza in poetic structures, especially odes, a 'catastrophe' refers to a downward turn in dramatic structures, especially tragedies. Catastrophe signifies decline; it means a fall or a falling away. In general terms, catastrophe refers to a reversal or *peripeteia*. As Frank Kermode notes in *The Sense of an Ending* (1965), a study symptomatic of the postwar preoccupation with endings, no reader expects a novel to proceed step by step to a predestined end without some reversal of expectations. Fyodor Dostoevsky's *The Idiot* (1869) and Albert Camus' *The Plague* (1947) 'represent in varying degrees that falsification of simple expectations as to the structure of a future which constitutes peripeteia'.[13] The future never unfolds according to plan; reversals in plot defy readers' predictions. Deferrals, delays and falsifications regularly complicate expectations about the end, whether conceived as death, war or apocalypse. By invoking novels by Dostoevsky and Camus, Kermode identifies hopelessness, which is to say a predisposition to see the future as inexorably doomed, as characteristic of novels that deliberately do not gratify readers' expectations. The future is even bleaker than had been imagined. It can end only in global catastrophe and the extinction or near-extinction of the human race, especially in mid-century iterations.

After the bombing of Hiroshima and Nagasaki in August 1945, catastrophe acquired broad cultural meaning. In *God and the Atom* (1945), Ronald Knox, detective novelist and Catholic theologian, understands the airman who dropped the atomic bomb on Hiroshima as 'the symbol of a catastrophic leap in the history of human achievement'.[14] In Knox's formulation, the leap itself entails catastrophe. Instead of a leap forward, the world jumps into a spiritual quagmire. If the movement into the atomic age is catastrophic, the alternative of keeping still, of not moving at all for fear that further turns will unleash more catastrophes, implies a posture of immobility, suspension, even cowardice. In general, Knox deplores the 'debonair attitude towards the future' taken by modern

---

[13] Frank Kermode, *The Sense of an Ending: Studies in the Theory of Fiction* (Oxford University Press, 1966), p. 23. English translations of Camus' works appeared quickly after initial publication in French: *The Stranger* (1946), *The Plague* (1948), *The Rebel* (1954) and *The Myth of Sisyphus and Other Essays* (1955). Kermode, relying on British familiarity with Camus' novels, means that some novels offer fewer reversals of expectation than other novels; such novels surprise by conforming to predictable patterns and outcomes.

[14] Ronald Knox, *God and the Atom* (London: Sheed & Ward, 1945), p. 12.

scientists.[15] He especially deplores the speed and scale of catastrophe that the atomic future holds in store. Catastrophe, as envisioned in 1945, is irreversible – not just a reversal from which recovery might be expected, but total annihilation. For Knox, the only possible hope for a future unclouded by cataclysm is a reconciliation between science and spiritual life.

Philosophers, scientists and politicians who defended nuclear war were often irrationally optimistic about the scale of nuclear catastrophe. In a pamphlet entitled 'Some Political Consequences of the Atomic Bomb' (1945), E. L. Woodward concludes, with a measure of glum cheerfulness, that bombs might destroy entire cities, but such devastation will be 'local, not universal'.[16] He does not foresee the annihilation of the human race. Woodward's opinion, however, was not universally shared. After 1945, many people imagined extinction as a possible outcome of nuclear warfare. 'The construction of the atom bomb has brought about the effect that all the people living in cities are threatened, everywhere and constantly, with sudden destruction', observes Albert Einstein in *One World or None*, a book of essays written by scientists to warn against the potential of nuclear energy.[17] Einstein argues for world governance to mitigate the warmindedness of individual nations. For Einstein as for others, the only possible resolution to the conundrum of atomic armaments was cooperation among all nations of the world. In *Common Sense and Nuclear Warfare* (1959), Bertrand Russell states that: 'A large-scale war would be an utter disaster, not only to the belligerents, but to mankind, and would achieve no result that any sane man could desire.'[18] Faced with the utter annihilation of the human race, Russell, like Einstein, advocates responsible action: 'would you rather have a world in which both friends and foes survive, or a world in which both are extinct?'[19]

In the immediate postwar, scientists, convinced that they had blamelessly advanced the store of human knowledge by discovering the principles of fission, minimised the consequences of nuclear fallout and radiation. When the US Department of Defense, in conjunction with the US Atomic

---

[15] Ibid., p. 140.
[16] E. L. Woodward, *Some Political Consequences of the Atomic Bomb* (Oxford University Press, 1945), p. 7.
[17] Albert Einstein, 'The Way Out' in Dexter Masters and Katharine Way (eds), *One World or None: A Report to the Public on the Full Meaning of the Atomic Bomb* (New York: McGraw-Hill, 1946), p. 76.
[18] Bertrand Russell, *Common Sense and Nuclear Warfare* (London: George Allen & Unwin, 1959), p. 29.
[19] Ibid., p. 65.

Energy Commission, released *The Effects of Atomic Weapons* (1950), they downplayed injuries from nuclear bombs and the consequences of radiation. The report is a masterpiece of evasion; virtually every sentence is written in the passive voice: 'the extended treatment [of radiation sickness] is not meant to imply that radiation is the most important source of casualties in an atomic explosion ... While nuclear radiation may definitely be a hazard, the extent of which will depend on the type of atomic explosion, it is by no means to be regarded as being of dominating significance'.[20] Notwithstanding their vacillation, which they imagine to be scientific objectivity, the authors of the report enumerate the visible, immediate symptoms of radiation exposure – nausea, vomiting, fever, emaciation, hair loss, diarrhoea, petechia – as well as less visible, long-term effects, such as cataracts, genetic mutations, cellular sensitivity and deformation of bone marrow cells.

For some scientists and social scientists, objectivity quashes terror. In 1961, Herman Kahn calculated that thermonuclear war would cause between 10 and 60 million casualties in the United States, among a total population at the time of 180 million. Depending on the magnitude of radiation exposure, Kahn predicts up to 10 million birth defects per year after a strike, which he thinks would be a tolerable number if it meant American victory in a nuclear conflict. He refuses to say whether Americans would have automobiles, freezers, televisions and ranch houses after a 'small attack', but he does wager that the country, properly prepared with Geiger counters and decontamination manuals, 'would recover rather rapidly and effectively'.[21] Whereas Kahn takes refuge in statistics and reasonable probabilities – 'a catastrophe can be pretty catastrophic without being total', he states reassuringly[22] – mid-century novelists assessing the likelihood of thermonuclear holocaust and the effects of radiation on the environment and the human race come up with much more dreadful imaginings.

Nuclear Fiction

Catastrophe can happen at any point in a narrative sequence, even prior to the start of the sequence. Nuclear catastrophe has occurred before *On the Beach* begins on the morning of 27 December 1962. A year or so earlier –

---

[20] *The Effects of Atomic Weapons* (Washington, DC: US Government Printing Office, 1950), pp. 339–40.
[21] Herman Kahn, *On Thermonuclear War*, 2nd edn (Princeton University Press, 1961), pp. 30, 74, 47.
[22] Ibid., p. 41.

the dates are murky – nations in the northern hemisphere launched nuclear weapons at each other in a 'short, bewildering war'.[23] As a result of nuclear bombardment, radioactive particles drift slowly but surely towards Australia, where Lieutenant-Commander Peter Holmes of the Royal Australian Navy, his wife Mary and their daughter Jennifer measure out the days, perhaps months, before they will die. Inevitability regulates the plot, as it does in many plots written under the shadow of mushroom clouds. Showing the first symptoms of radiation sickness, Mary swallows government-issued pills to kill herself. Peter euthanises his daughter with an injection, then kills himself. *On the Beach* epitomises postwar catastrophe narratives by positioning human struggle against certain extinction. No single person or community of people can prevent annihilation. The novel predicts catastrophe in the near future as a consequence of the unrelenting hostility that exists among nation-states.[24]

Despite being a catastrophe with global consequences, the war in *On the Beach* leaves no historical traces. It is 'the war of which no history had been written or ever would be written now, that had flared all round the northern hemisphere and had died away with the last seismic record of explosion on the thirty-seventh day'.[25] Survivors have no one to whom they can leave a historical record. Everyone in the northern hemisphere is already dead; everyone in the southern hemisphere is scheduled to die sooner or later. Peter wonders, 'Is anybody writing any kind of history about these times?'[26] The war is full of 'too many gaps – the things we just don't know'.[27] As when workers stoke ovens with library books in *Ape and Essence*, catastrophe erases written history altogether. With the loss of books, knowledge of all sorts vanishes: botany, engineering, history. By obliterating antecedents and consequences, catastrophe levels human achievements. In *On the Beach*, some industrious survivors, vainly hoping that there will be some form of life after the extinction of human life, want to etch a history of the war on sheets of thick glass to be sealed into a concrete bunker atop Mount Kosciuszko, the highest mountain in Australia. Yet there is no end to the complications of imagining life beyond catastrophe. One woman wonders how those who come after will be able

---

[23] Nevil Shute, *On the Beach* (London: Random House, 2009), p. 3.
[24] The film version of *On the Beach* (1959) may have influenced nuclear disarmament campaigns. Members of the Campaign for Nuclear Disarmament (CND) appeared outside the cinema on the evening in 1959 when David Cornwall (aka John le Carré) and his wife Ann saw the film. Ann joined CND on the spot. See Adam Sisman, *John le Carré: The Biography* (Toronto: Knopf, 2015), p. 207.
[25] Shute, *On the Beach*, pp. 3–4. [26] Ibid., p. 81. [27] Ibid.

to read the history etched in glass. Should anyone happen to find the plates in centuries to come, they may not be able to decipher English, let alone understand the points of reference in the history of annihilation. What is 'the Cold War'? What is 'radioactivity'? In this regard, catastrophe is an absolute event that turns away from the past and inaugurates a desolate, blank, unimaginable future.

On the Beach is a novel about suspension. The action takes place in an interstice between nuclear war, which establishes a planetary fate, and death from radiation, which is an individual fate. Speaking of apocalypse, Kermode notes that there is a transitional period between the end of time and the last end: 'Before the End there is a period which does not properly belong either to the End or to the *saeculum* preceding it. It has its own characteristics.'[28] In that suspended temporality, actions occur, but they all have an over-determined relation to the final end. In the case of *On the Beach*, suspension is tinged equally by expectation and dread. Characters cannot predict the exact moment of the end that happens after the end, which is to say their own death. The temporal duration between end and final end is hard to gauge for everyone. A farmer tells Peter, 'there's not so long to go'.[29] The phrase, first heard on the radio, circulates among characters as a locution for bewilderment. Peter repeats it to himself as a mantra while considering a submarine assignment: 'On shore he could look after Mary and the baby as he had been doing, and there was now not so long to go'.[30] This sentence is grammatically suspended among several temporalities. On the one hand, from the perspective of 'now', Peter measures the unpredictable duration of human life, which is 'not so long to go'. On the other hand, he will keep up the routines of domesticity, 'as he had been doing', in the pluperfect tense. Suspended between past and future, Peter must go on – he has no choice but to go on – while hoping that temporality will be prolonged, but not by too much. He accepts a mission in a submarine because work might distract him from the inevitability of his last end. In conversation with the admiral who posts him to sea, Peter vaguely alludes to the time before radioactive fallout: 'Things aren't too easy now, compared with what they used to be, and it's a bit difficult at home. And anyway, there's not so long to go.'[31]

Catastrophe distorts or obliterates temporality. In *On the Beach*, characters try not to speak about the time prior to the war. Moira wants to prevent her lover, Dwight, from remembering his dead wife: 'She mustn't

---

[28] Kermode, *Sense of an Ending*, p. 12.   [29] Shute, *On the Beach*, p. 6.   [30] Ibid., p. 8.
[31] Ibid., p. 13.

let him think about the past.'[32] Defeatism mingles with survival tactics in a race against time. Moira, who has devoted her time to romance and flings, thinks that 'there wouldn't be time' to start a family.[33] By the same line of reasoning, 'there was now too little time to spend it in quarrelling'.[34] Moira refuses to take a typing course because 'there's no time to finish it, or use it afterwards'.[35] In the interval between nuclear war and personal death, the characters in *On the Beach* conduct their lives according to routines or fill their time with cocktails, flirtation and frivolous romances. These activities all occur within the temporality of a suspended conclusion that is bound to turn into a definite end.

Even though there is a predisposition to dismiss time in the face of nuclear devastation, spasms of counting, measuring and numbering recur throughout *On the Beach*. An obsession with temporal accuracy is commonplace in mid-century narratives. According to Ronald Knox, one British newspaper in 1945 started dating its issues by the fifth, sixth or whatever day 'of the Atomic Age' in recognition that a new era had dawned.[36] While such numbers might extend into an endless calendar, heedless of seasons and years, they could also break off at any point were there to be a nuclear war. In *On the Beach*, temporal markers have a similar effect. Characters notice the time with dreadful frequency: even Moira, as she takes pills to kill herself, looks at her wristwatch and notes that 'it showed one minute past ten'.[37] Time saturates thinking to an unusual degree in the novel. A navy captain recounts his experience of the nuclear war through adverbial temporal clauses: 'Next night he made contact with Dutch Harbor ... On the next night he failed to raise Dutch Harbor ... On the seventh day of the war he was in Manila Bay', and so on.[38] Characters wonder how long a submarine can remain submerged, or how long it takes someone to die from vomiting after radiation exposure: 'Three days? A week?'[39] Although such counting may appear to be a prolongation of time or a psychological attempt to postpone death, these temporal markers are also a countdown to disaster. By fixating on the end of human life and the end of the world, characters in *On the Beach* recognise the pointlessness of marking time.

In *Hiroshima* (1946), a report from the epicentre of nuclear catastrophe, John Hersey also measures time and distance with documentary exactness. His report, first published in a single issue of *The New Yorker*

---

[32] Ibid., p. 30.   [33] Ibid., p. 42.   [34] Ibid., p. 49.   [35] Ibid., p. 69.
[36] Knox, *God and the Atom*, p. 16.   [37] Shute, *On the Beach*, p. 312.   [38] Ibid., p. 10.
[39] Ibid., p. 187.

The Future and the End

in August 1946, starts with a precise record of time and place: 'At exactly fifteen minutes past eight in the morning, on August 6th, 1945, Japanese time, at the moment when the atomic bomb flashed above Hiroshima, Miss Toshiko Sasaki, a clerk in the personnel department at the East Asia Tin Works, had just sat down at her place in the plant office.'[40] Hersey returns to the moment of the bomb-blast from other points of view. 'The Reverend Mr. Tanimoto got up at five o'clock that morning', while a 'siren jarred [Mrs. Nakamura] awake at about seven'.[41] Dr Masakazu wakes up at 6 am on 6 August to see a guest off on a train. Hersey documents what six survivors did in the hours, then days, weeks and months after the blast. They are the creatures of time, their destinies written into the narrative of catastrophe. Although his report breaks off in 1946, Hersey implies that the consequences of radiation sickness and fallout from the bomb will continue for years to come.

Mid-century fiction might be said to dwell in a transitional slot between the end of the Second World War and the beginning of a third. Asynchrony, dead time, deferral, time loops and warped chronology proliferate in literary representations during the 1940s and 1950s. Time accelerates or decelerates, as in *The Aerodrome*. Time stands still or jerks suddenly forward, as in *The Inheritors*. Atomic weapons alter the tempo of living. Ronald Knox notes, with some despair, that 'the current of human affairs seems swifter and more ungovernable than ever'.[42] If the atom bomb demarcates a new era, as Knox feels it does, that period is characterised by the inhuman speed of technological advances. In 1945, atom bombs make 'the old, primitive days of the rocket-bomb', which is to say 1944, look quaint.[43] D. R. Davies, assessing the theological consequences of the atomic bomb in 1947, remarks on humankind's new relations to past and future: 'Man's greatest creative achievement – for the release of atomic energy can surely claim to be that – reveals the essential character of man's existence in time. It is a process of tragic self-frustration.'[44] Scientific discovery leads to weapons, and weapons lead to self-destruction. In this sense, man defeats his own best interests. 'History ends in a catastrophic climax', claims Davies, 'not in an easy ascent into Utopian fulfilment and rational harmony'.[45] While he might conclude that the bomb ushers in the end of time, Davies, with cautious optimism, concludes that 'the future lies in deepest shadow'.[46] He makes no

---

[40] John Hersey, *Hiroshima* (Harmondsworth: Penguin, 1946), p. 13. [41] Ibid., pp. 14, 20.
[42] Knox, *God and the Atom*, p. 47.   [43] Ibid., p. 58.
[44] D. R. Davies, *Theology and the Atomic Age* (London: Latimer House, 1947), p. 27.
[45] Ibid., p. 69.   [46] Ibid., p. 51.

suggestion about how one crosses the present wasteland to reach the shadowy future.

In many mid-century novels, narrators take refuge in an inaccessible and undated temporal place. The appendix to *Nineteen Eighty-Four*, which outlines 'The Principles of Newspeak', is narrated some time after 2050. In effect, the narrator speaks to the present from some unspecified future moment. Speaking back to the past, like speaking forward to the future, is a survival tactic. In the Hollywood film, *The Beginning or the End* (1947), an actor playing Robert J. Oppenheimer speaks directly to an audience in 2446, the year in which the film reels, buried in a time capsule beneath a redwood tree in California, are dug up and, presumably, screened. Oppenheimer explains that atomic energy might destroy all human life in the twentieth century: 'We know the beginning. Only you of tomorrow, if there is a tomorrow, can know the end.'[47] The film runs the risk of never being seen by its twenty-fifth-century audience because everyone has died. In this regard, Oppenheimer makes his speech into a void where the future ought to be.

Human Futures

Catastrophe novels speculate on the nature of 'the human' as a biological and ethical category. Lewis Mumford begins *The Condition of Man* (1944) with a series of questions: 'What is man? What meaning has his life? What is his origin, his condition, his destiny?'[48] For Mumford, progress governs human destiny, despite occasional lapses into barbarism. Man is designed to prevail over obstacles and perfect himself. Not everyone agrees with this triumphalist narrative of human history: George Orwell's original title for *Nineteen Eighty-Four* was *The Last Man*. 'If you are a man', O'Brien tells Winston Smith, 'you are the last man. Your kind is extinct'.[49] Winston represents the end of European humanism, and his belief in human solidarity sabotages him. He thinks a flash of mutual understanding passes between him and O'Brien when they pass each other in an office corridor. Despite his belief in human decency, even Winston succumbs, under

---

[47] *The Beginning or the End*, dir. Norman Taurog (Metro-Goldwyn-Mayer, 1947), 4:00. The title of the film alludes to a speech that Franklin D. Roosevelt was to have delivered on Jefferson Day in April 1945: 'We see peace – enduring peace. More than an end to war, we want an end to the beginnings of all wars.' Roosevelt's speech and Taurog's film both echo Winston Churchill's 'Bright Gleam of Victory' speech on 10 November 1942: 'Now this is not the end. It is not even the beginning of the end. But it is, perhaps, the end of the beginning.'
[48] Lewis Mumford, *The Condition of the Man* (New York: Harcourt, Brace, 1944), p. 3.
[49] George Orwell, *Nineteen Eighty-Four* (London: Penguin, 1987), pp. 282–3.

torture, to the exigencies of the state. For many, the threat to man, as individual, came not from the state, but from science. In *Between Past and Future* (1961), Hannah Arendt rails against the scientific definition of man as 'an observer of the universe in its manifold manifestations'.[50] For Arendt, science compromises the capacity of man to reflect on responsibilities both to himself and to the human species. The physicists' rush to split the atom, despite their knowledge of its destructive potential, 'demonstrates that the scientist *qua* scientist does not even care about the survival of the human race on earth or, for that matter, about the survival of the planet itself'.[51] In a bid for a reinvigorated humanism, Arendt wants to turn away from science and return to normal language, commonsense and empirical reality.

Mid-century dystopian fiction explores the nature of the human species in its traditional and evolutionary variants. In *The Inheritors*, white-skinned *homo sapiens* raid the camp of red-skinned Neanderthals. In *The Day of the Triffids*, the sighted and the blind mobilise against each other, while carnivorous humanoid plants mobilise against all members of the human tribe. In these novels, the passage of time brings regression rather than advance. *Ape and Essence* portrays the 'squalid disintegration of the very substance of the [human] species'.[52] Those who do not die of starvation are subject to hideous, laboratory-made diseases. 'Do you like the human race?' runs a ditty in *Ape and Essence*, to which the reply comes not unexpectedly, 'No, not much'.[53]

Dystopian fiction satirises the human appetite for violence. For the most part, the novel is generically and genetically programmed to represent human beings overcoming adversity. Protagonists face obstacles; they grow from experience. Yet the protagonist's will to power may come at a cost to human feeling and compassion. In *The Aerodrome*, Roy, the first-person narrator, willingly joins the crypto-fascist aviators who take over his English village. Although some villagers cherish hopes 'that at some future time the conditions of the past might be re-established', the aerodrome people repudiate 'the stupidity, the ugliness, and the servility of historical tradition'.[54] What the aerodrome people cannot change, they destroy. They assume that their form of governance, brutally efficient, is superior to traditional ways of life. For his part, Roy displays 'the precise qualities of the new race of men' designed by the aerodrome regime.[55] As the

---

[50] Hannah Arendt, *Between Past and Future* (New York: Penguin, 2006), p. 261.   [51] Ibid., p. 270.
[52] Huxley, *Ape and Essence*, p. 101.   [53] Ibid., p. 19.
[54] Rex Warner, *The Aerodrome* (London: Vintage, 2007), pp. 139, 178.   [55] Ibid., p. 249.

representative man of the future, Roy lacks human sympathy: 'We constituted no revolutionary party actuated by humanitarian ideals, but seemed to be an organization manifestly entitled by its own discipline, efficiency, and will to assume supreme power.'[56] *The Aerodrome* is dystopian insofar as it imagines a future where characters have been perfected out of all semblance of humanity. Reckless and ruthless, they aspire to rid themselves of all attachment to time, whether past or future. Yet the human characters, involved in an intricate plot of recrimination, revenge and incest, never do quite let go of time. Sentiment compromises the possibility of human perfectibility. The novel offers a glimpse of an alternative future, in which pilotless planes take over the duties of surveillance and warfare; in this vision of the future, human beings are rendered redundant and therefore obsolete.

In spite of such dire predictions, the novel remains a refuge for the human, even when the human is defamiliarised by being moved to strange locales and futures. Anthony Burgess comments that the postwar novel is characterised by its acceptance of 'imperfect man'.[57] Catastrophe fiction, by imagining conflicts between various kinds of government – such as the planners led by Ralph and the warmongers led by Jack in *Lord of the Flies* – holds onto a hope for humanity, in all its imperfection. V. S. Pritchett wonders, '*Are* human beings in fact so isolated, so free of responsibility, so passive before fate? Is their environment merely the dwindling ground they stand on?'[58] For Pritchett, the answer is an emphatic no. The novel in this period constantly renews its faith in the future by dramatising situations in which human beings assert their humanity.

In *The Chrysalids*, for example, a religious community in Labrador tries to preserve its ties to 'the Old People' who inhabited the world prior to nuclear war. The novel takes place in the indefinite future: 'There was no telling how many generations of people had passed their lives like savages between the coming of Tribulation and the start of recorded history.'[59] Tribulation, with its Biblical resonances of Apocalypse and Last Judgement, refers to nuclear holocaust. In the zones exposed to the worst bombardments centuries earlier, 'the ground has been fused into black

---

[56] Ibid., p. 226.   [57] Anthony Burgess, *The Novel Now* (London: Faber & Faber, 1967), p. 39.
[58] V. S. Pritchett, 'The Future of English Fiction' *Partisan Review* 15.10 (1948), 1067 (emphasis in the original). This essay is a reprint of Pritchett's contribution to the forum on the future of fiction in *New Writing and Daylight*.
[59] John Wyndham, *The Chrysalids* (New York: NYRB, 2008), p. 39.

glass'.[60] Radiation remains at such high levels that explorers sicken and die when they approach desolate zones called the Badlands. Plants and animals that show any sign of deviation are sacrificed. The same principle is imposed on people. Children born with defects caused by radiation cannot be granted Normalcy Certificates and are put to death. The local inspector explains to David that deviation cannot be human: 'Only God produces perfection, so although deviations may look like us in many ways, they cannot be really human.'[61] The community wants to prevent mutants from breeding, for fear that deviation will permanently alter human genetics. Anyone classified as non-human cannot be 'entitled to any of the rights or protections of human society'.[62] A girl with six toes has to flee to the Fringes, where outlawed mutants gather. David, who shares telepathic powers with a few other young people, is a deviant, according to the definitions laid down in Labrador. He is part of a new, perhaps superior, variant of the human species. Nonetheless, he is pursued by his own community because he exceeds narrow ideas about what comprises the human.

The Chrysalids argues for a flexible definition of the human that is not based on physical attributes. As Axel explains to David, 'what makes man man is mind; it's not a thing, it's a quality, and minds aren't all the same value; they're better or worse, and the better they are the more they mean'.[63] Axel does not evaluate people on their mental abilities; rather, he recognises that people have a wide variety of qualities, good and bad, that contribute to the spectrum of human beings. When a rescue party arrives by aircraft from Sealand to save David, Petra and Rosalind, they promise a better future: 'We are the New People – your kind of people. The people who can think-together. We're the people who are going to build a new kind of world – different from the Old People's world, and from the savages.'[64] The New People explain that the Old People are an inadequate, threatened species that clings to the past out of an instinct for self-preservation. In *The Chrysalids*, countries join together out of enlightened self-interest. When the New People cross the planet to save a few telepathic youths, they enact a limited form of global cooperation of the type advocated by Einstein and Russell. The New People do not predict an end to warfare and violence, although they do their best to mitigate situations in which conflict causes death. They represent one kind of future government, although it is government guided by principles of benevolent despotism and self-preservation.

[60] Ibid., p. 39. [61] Ibid., p. 55. [62] Ibid., p. 131. [63] Ibid., pp. 79–80. [64] Ibid., p. 156.

Although David expects to be captured, tortured and killed because of his telepathic deviance, *The Chrysalids* ends with renewed possibilities: David, Petra and Rosalind depart for a new country and a new life. Dystopian novels often end with a rescue, as when Alfie and Loola in *Ape and Essence* head to Fresno, where a community of lovers has gathered. A British naval officer arrives just in the nick of time to save Ralph from certain death in *Lord of the Flies*. In *The Day of the Triffids*, a colony of survivors decamps to the Isle of Wight to escape from the warriors who impose military rule over southern England. By holding out the possibility of rescue, dystopian novels confirm their contract with and expectations for the future. They turn to outlying locations such as Labrador or Mount Kosciuszko as a way to imagine global cooperation and interdependence. Mid-century catastrophe novels position Britain not as an isolated nation-state, but as one country among many allied in a battle against extinction.

In 1956, J. B. Priestley grumbled that 'behind our criticism of what is virtually a new society is still the same concern about the future'.[65] As a literary convention, global catastrophe causes a reassessment of the everyday and the familiar, as against the exceptional and unfamiliar forms of life that lie ahead. For many mid-century novelists, facing the future meant prophesying catastrophe. Faced with the spectre of nuclear annihilation, they endorse a mode of narration that might be called 'prophetic realism', in which predictions and facing the facts play equal parts. Mid-century novelists aim at truth telling, regardless of the brutality of the truths they have to tell. Paradoxically, novelists and narrators face the future in order to imagine an end, except when they face catastrophe in order to imagine the future.

---

[65] J. B. Priestley, *The Writer in a Changing Society* (Aldington: Hand & Flower Press, 1956), p. 2.

CHAPTER 21

Exhausted Literature: The Postwar Novel in Repose

Kate McLoughlin

The category of 'the literature of exhausted possibility' or, more succinctly, 'the literature of exhaustion' was famously posited by John Barth in 1967, writing, as he said later, as 'Mace and peppergas wafted through the academic groves'.[1] By 'exhaustion', Barth clarified, he did not mean 'anything so tired' as 'the subject of physical, moral, or intellectual decadence', but only 'the used-upness of certain forms'.[2] He gave by way of cultural example the Baroque, citing Jorge Luis Borges's definition: 'that style which deliberately exhausts (or tries to exhaust) its possibilities and borders upon its own caricature'.[3] Scrolls, crests, tendrils, trompes l'œil, valances, finials, scallops, baldachins, putti, curlicues: in this understanding, the whole riotous profusion is not so much a sign of luxurious abundance as the ironic visualisation of the running out of ideas.

For Barth, the Borgesian image of exhaustion *par excellence* is the labyrinth: 'a place in which, ideally, all the possibilities of choice (of direction in this case) are embodied, and ... must be exhausted'.[4] In the case of the three post-Second World War novels I propose to examine in this chapter – Elizabeth Taylor's *A Wreath of Roses* (1949), Angus Wilson's *The Middle Age of Mrs Eliot* (1958) and Iris Murdoch's *An Unofficial Rose* (1962) – the figure conveying artistic exhaustion is every bit as intricate as the labyrinth: the flower, most often the rose.[5] After exploring this figure across the three texts, in the final section of the chapter I address a more

---

[1] John Barth, 'The Literature of Exhaustion' [1967] in *The Friday Book: Essays and Other Non-Fiction* (London: Johns Hopkins University Press, 1984), pp. 62–67, 63, 64.
[2] Ibid., p. 64. [3] Quoted in ibid., p. 63; no reference for the Borges quotation is given.
[4] Ibid., p. 75.
[5] The three novels share more than a horticultural preoccupation. All of them feature at least one protagonist who is a war veteran: Richard Elton (who impersonates a veteran) and Morland Beddoes in *A Wreath of Roses*; Bill Eliot and David Parker (a conscientious objector who drove ambulances) in *The Middle Age of Mrs Eliot*; and Felix Meecham in *An Unofficial Rose*. The veteran functions as a figure for the spent or used-up. Two of them – *The Middle Age of Mrs Eliot* is the exception – feature hair in the same way as roses, indeed, often entwining roses and hair. There is not space to develop the

complex question: if these works *depict* artistic exhaustion, are *they themselves* also examples of exhausted literature? My response to that question involves adding nuance to Barth's definition with the help of Gilles Deleuze, a counter-illustration from Henry Green's 1946 novel *Back* and the positing of a category of literary *tiredness*.

Faded Garlands: Elizabeth Taylor's *A Wreath of Roses*

A Wreath of Roses takes as its epigraph a quotation from Virginia Woolf's *The Waves* (1931): 'I covered the whole street, Oxford Street, Piccadilly Circus, with the blaze and ripple of my mind, with vine leaves and rose leaves.'[6] Here, rose leaves are a means of distancing the self from the world: in the full original remark, Woolf's character, Rhoda, confesses immediately before the words quoted in the epigraph, 'So terrible was life that I held up shade after shade. Look at life through this, look at life through that; let there be rose leaves, let there be vine leaves.'[7] There is nothing Baroque about this proliferating foliage: the creative imagination has the energy to be fierily transformative. Taylor's novel, by contrast, portrays that imagination's limits. The dubious veteran Richard Elton is characterised by the excessiveness of his tales. In their first extended encounter, he tells Camilla that he is going to Abingford to write a book:

> 'What kind of book?' she enquired.
> 'About the war.'
> 'Oh, I see.' ('The war and his experience in it,' she thought. 'Unreadable.')[8]

'Unreadable' suggests a literary production incapable of fulfilling its own *raison d'être*. This is confirmed when Camilla enquires further. '"What experiences did you have?" she felt obliged to ask. "What were you? What did you do?"'[9] Given that Elton has, in truth, had no combat experience, his answers are both insubstantial and extravagant: 'Dropped by moonlight half-way across France', 'Sat between Gestapo men in trains'.[10] This time, the extravagance resembles Barth's and Borges's Baroque: it is the stuff of

---

point here, but the whitening or thinning of hair seems to function as another barometer of cultural exhaustion.

[6] Elizabeth Taylor, *A Wreath of Roses* (London: Virago, 2011 [1949]), p. vi.

[7] Virginia Woolf, *The Waves* (London: Grafton, 1977 [1931]), p. 138. Notably, Woolf uses roses as a gauge of imagination – critical imagination in this case – in her 1931 essay 'All About Books'. Acknowledging that '[n]o more respectable army has ever issued from the portals of the two great Universities', she questions the ability of the latest generation of critics to attend to 'the sound of the sea and the red of the rose' (Leonard Woolf (ed.), *Virginia Woolf: The Collected Essays* (London: The Hogarth Press, 1966–7), vol. 2/4, pp. 266, 267).

[8] Ibid., p. 5.   [9] Ibid., p. 6.   [10] Ibid.

boys' adventure stories, of 'passwords, disguises, swallowing bits of paper, hiding others in currant buns',[11] empty decoration rather than significant literary output. The conversation develops as follows:

> 'You must have great nerve,' she suggested, trying in this to find an excuse, a reason for the emptiness in his eyes.
> 'Not now,' he replied. 'The end of the war came at the right time for me. The last time I was briefed, a feeling of staleness came over me, a sort of tired horror ...'
> 'Tired horror!' she repeated, surprised. When he used those words, she could understand it all.[12]

This is a *faux*-exhaustion, expressed by a character who has not undergone what he claims has drained him, but Elton's performance here is also a real literary exhaustion, a weary trotting out of clichéd forms. The same is true of the fantasies about his home and family that he spins to Frances later in the novel. His final story – about his strangulation of the girl – has energy for once: it is told succinctly, and with power. But now the exhaustion is transferred to his way of life, which comprises one hotel room after another as he remains on the run from the police. Camilla suddenly realises that '[h]e is like this empty, cobwebbed house ... Room after room of echoes, there's nothing there'.[13] The image is of the labyrinth. His future consisting of only further circulation within the maze, Elton kills himself. That he is depicted doing so in exactly the same way as the suicide in the opening chapter means that his death, too, is merely repetitive. Elton is a Baroque figure or, in Taylor's preferred word, empty.

If Elton is a writer-*manqué* (he has not started his book), the character Frances is a frustrated painter. In her youth, she was praised for her work, but was herself dissatisfied with it until she 'willed herself into what she had painted'.[14] Her teachers criticised her – 'the apples, the dusters ... seemed ... not so much like apples and dusters as formerly' – but 'their verdict did not matter': '[t]he apple, the rose, were still the same, but violence swung about them'.[15] This account suggests a vigorous beginning, full of possibility (here characterised as 'violence'). But, in later years, the energy dissipated, as Taylor reveals in an extended description of the now-elderly Frances's state of mind:

> Frances awoke to her moss-roses. Each morning they annoyed her more, so endlessly repeated on a thick black trellis over the wall-paper, peeling away near the ceiling in places, leaving a powdery-looking but still flowered pattern exposed beneath. Violets, the one before last, Frances decided.

---

[11] Ibid. [12] Ibid. [13] Ibid., p. 204. [14] Ibid., p. 92. [15] Ibid., p. 92.

Unless periwinkles. She thought about wall-papers, closing her eyes. She had painted many in her time, the great blown roses in the bedrooms of small French hotels: they had come into her pictures of littered chimney-pieces, rooms reflected in mirrors, the crumpled, tumbled beds, the naked girl holding her silk stocking to the light, her skin cream and apricot against the brilliant, the shocking crimsons, pinks, vermilions of the wall ... She closed her eyes and bunches of roses were printed for an instant startlingly white upon the darkness, then faded, as the darkness itself paled, the sun from the window coming brilliantly through her lids.[16]

Vigour has stagnated into repetition: roses — and they are the second-hand artificial roses of wallpaper, at that — have colonised and cluttered Frances's paintings. These ubiquitous roses are 'great blown roses', roses past their prime, both huge (excessive) and beginning to decay. They are repeated not only in the paintings, but now, 'endlessly', on Frances's own bedroom wallpaper, annoying her and revealing the ghosts of other layers of flowers beneath them. Now, when Frances closes her eyes, she sees the after-images of roses — roses blanched of colour — spectral roses that lack even the substantiality of long-covered-over wallpaper roses. For a moment, there are roses on roses on roses, calling to mind Gertrude Stein's line 'Rose is a rose is a rose is a rose'.[17] In Stein's phrase, signification becomes circular (like the labyrinth) and therefore empty: a rose can give no more information than that it is a rose. The palimpsestic wallpaper roses in Frances's bedroom make the same point in stratified form; then, insubstantial, they disappear, annihilated by nothing more than the sunlight. In the terms of this chapter, these roses are exhausted: literally over-loaded (pasted on top of each other), they have lost their signifying effectiveness and become mere irritants.

And to Frances's mind comes the thought that her work has been only 'sentimentality'[18] — a condition in which feeling exceeds substance. 'For was I not guilty of making ugliness charming?' she asks herself.[19] Aiming at 'tenderness and intimacy', she has instead laid an 'English sadness like a veil over all [she] painted' until it became 'ladylike and nostalgic'.[20] This muted description is another account of exhausted art, an art that has been unable to substantiate the 'violence, with flames wheeling, turmoil, pain, chaos' that lies at the heart of things.[21] Of late, Frances has tried to produce

---

[16] Ibid., p. 34.
[17] The line, which Stein modified through a number of works, appeared originally in the 1913 poem 'Sacred Emily'. Gertrude Stein, *Geography and Plays* (Madison, WI: University of Wisconsin Press, 1993), pp. 178–88, 187.
[18] Woolf, *The Waves*, p. 34.   [19] Ibid.   [20] Ibid.   [21] Ibid.

a different kind of painting, to work 'from an inner darkness, groping and undisciplined',[22] but her most recent canvases are 'four utter failures to express her new feelings, her rejection of prettiness, her tearing-down of the veils of sadness, of charm'.[23] Towards the end of the novel, Frances contemplates her final work, a 'creamy-pink and yellow picture, half a mirror with reflected hands lifting a wreath of roses, a flash of golden hair'.[24] The palette is anodyne, the 'wreath' has funereal overtones, the mirror (long a figure of representative art) is fractured, the reflections suggest Baroque infinite repetition. Viewing it, Frances feels 'a great weariness'.[25] She has 'no way to turn':[26]

> There is no past for an artist. What is done is cast away, good only for the time of its creation. Work is the present and the immediate future; but her immediate future was a blank.[27]

The lack of a future vision marks the atrophying of possibilities. The next moment, Frances picks up the 'wreath of roses' lying on the work-bench and fingers the petals, 'soft and dead', that now comprise a 'faded garland'.[28] The roses are serviceable now neither as floral crown nor as funeral wreath. Frances makes a final statement of artistic exhaustion: 'I shan't paint again.'[29]

'Vegetable Ease': Angus Wilson's *The Middle Age of Mrs Eliot*

Horticulture was foundational to Angus Wilson's creative imagination, as he describes in detail in his memoir, *The Wild Garden, or, Speaking of Writing* (1963). At the 'very root' of his 'symbolic view of life' was the 'wild garden' and 'the clearing (or garden) in the wild',[30] the former deriving from his father's childhood garden in Scotland, the latter from his mother's in South Africa, the one apparently rejecting progress (in the form of cultivation), the other apparently welcoming it. Gardening informs Wilson's entire fictional oeuvre, but changes over time. In *The Middle Age of Mrs Eliot*, it is used to demonstrate what Wilson calls 'a final abnegation of life'.[31] Exhaustion is evident from the novel's start. In an

---

[22] Ibid., p. 92.
[23] Ibid., p. 35. Cf. Anthony Blanche warning Charles Ryder in *Brideshead Revisited* (1945) that 'charm' – 'the great English blight' – 'spots and kills anything it touches ... kills love ... kills art'. Evelyn Waugh, *Brideshead Revisited* (Harmondsworth: Penguin, 1982), pp. 311–12.
[24] Ibid., p. 194.   [25] Ibid., p. 193.   [26] Ibid.   [27] Ibid.   [28] Ibid., p. 194.   [29] Ibid.
[30] Angus Wilson, *The Wild Garden, or, Speaking of Writing* (Berkeley, CA: University of California Press, 1963), p. 61.
[31] Ibid., p. 58.

early passage, Meg Eliot reflects upon the 'odious obverses' that occur throughout attempts to make 'some account of life'.[32] In her husband, Bill, the 'offhand, easy indolence' with which he has 'smoothed out the tearing, breaking grind of the hard work that had given him his success' shows at such times as 'a drink-flushed, petulant, sensual coarseness, signalling red for thrombosis'.[33] In Meg herself, a 'constant, hard-working eagerness to fill life with use and pleasure, to banish the spectre of her sex, class, and age' reveals an underside of 'hungry, lean exhaustion', signalling 'red for nervous headaches, breakdown – all the boring paraphernalia of the sort of unfilled life she had so successfully avoided'.[34] In Barth's terms, the Eliots are exhausted, their time filled with Baroque activities that are simply performed for their own sake. Bill's secret gambling exhausts their money supply for no return and Meg's purchasing of antique ceramics merely circulates existing pieces. Their childlessness – and this is a theme that also appears in the other novels – completes a picture of non-productivity.[35]

In her recuperative stay at her brother, David's, nursery garden, Andredaswood, Meg encounters further cultural exhaustion. Quietist David, a conscientious objector who drove for the Friends' Ambulance Unit in Libya during the war, had previously been elected to an Oxford fellowship.[36] But on his return from the war, he 'gave it all up' for the nursery in Sussex.[37] To herself, Meg frames David's choice as one of 'isolation and hard manual work',[38] a way of life that might seem physically tiring, if mentally reinvigorating. A customer of the nursery comments in similar vein:

> 'I suppose the fascination of gardening lies a lot in the way one can plan for the future. Especially in such an insecure world. I open my morning paper and read of some fresh new horror the scientists have devised and then I plan some change in the garden that won't be fully realized for at least five or six years. It's illogical, of course, but it's some comfort.'[39]

In these remarks, gardening is the opposite of exhaustion: possibilities are planned for and enjoyed in their (literal) flowering. But David's internal reaction to the customer's comments realigns them:

---

[32] Angus Wilson, *The Middle Age of Mrs Eliot* (Harmondsworth: Penguin, 1969), p. 32.   [33] Ibid.
[34] Ibid.
[35] In *A Wreath of Roses*, Liz's son Harry makes apparent Camilla's and Frances's childlessness; in *An Unofficial Rose*, Steve, the son of Randall and Ann Peronett, is dead.
[36] David is described as espousing 'quietism' by Wilson (*The Wild Garden*, p. 58). Margaret Drabble, *Angus Wilson: A Biography* (London: Secker & Warburg, 1995), p. 248 and Marina MacKay, 'Mr. Wilson and Mrs. Woolf', *Journal of Modern Literature* (1999) 23(1) pp. 95–109, 98 pick up the word.
[37] Wilson, *The Middle Age of Mrs Eliot*, p. 53.   [38] Ibid., p. 54.   [39] Ibid., p. 164.

[T]he idiotic sentimentality about 'gardening and the future' was right in its general line. Over the years he had built up a life encompassed by simple immediate duties and recreations – an ordered present; but an ordered present demanded at least the fiction of an immediate future with simple duties and recreations to be planned. Only such a life, he had come to believe, could allow one to cross the shapeless tract of human existence with grace and with gentleness; if the path was a meaningless progress to the grave, then the more necessary to take each step as a deliberate progress to the next; he could see no other way of preserving the fiction of civilization, and nothing to recommend the indulgence of exposing it.[40]

Gardening as a statement of future possibility is a 'sentimentality' (the same word used by Taylor of Frances's exhausted paintings), a 'fiction'. Although the nursery has obliged him to go through the motions of planning, it has nevertheless been at base a 'meaningless progress'. In this view, gardening is Baroque, a form which has no significance beyond itself. 'The nursery is exactly what it is', thinks David, 'a well run commercial garden, supplying its customers with value for their money, paying its workers good wages'.[41] In this last description, the nursery is not particularly profitable – it does not *create* anything, that is – and it also fails to discharge any signifying duty: a nursery garden is a nursery garden is a nursery garden.

Although Meg has come to the nursery to be restored (and this is not the place to deal with the psychoanalytical implications of this figurative regression to childhood),[42] Andredaswood is itself exhausted. So, too, is David. His partner, Gordon, is dying in the house. In October, the nursery is full of dahlias and Michaelmas daisies, 'gaily garish with that commercial colourfulness', 'hardly beautiful', an 'obvious show';[43] Baroque flowers, in other words. Tim Rattray decides upon 'a complete reorganization of the rose culture': a redistribution of the status quo, that is, rather than a new venture.[44] David, 'anxious to produce nothing that could add to all the personal voices that were leading mankind to boiling point',[45] feels the book series that he and Gordon have been working on, *Garden Flowers in Their Homes*, has the merit of 'insipidity' since it pretends 'to nothing':[46] this is repetitive, second-hand, exhausted work. In a similar vein, Frederica Grant-Pritchard's 'sentimentalism' (the word, with all its significance,

---

[40] Ibid., p. 165. [41] Ibid., p. 119. [42] Wilson acknowledges the 'pun' in *The Wild Garden*, p. 58.
[43] Wilson, *The Middle Age of Mrs Eliot*, p. 317. [44] Ibid., p. 340.
[45] It is notable that, at the time he was writing *The Middle Age of Mrs Eliot*, Wilson himself felt paralyzed by the weight of literary expectation: 'that *so much is expected* of one all the time makes me utterly miserable', he wrote to Richard Wollheim (quoted in Drabble, *Angus Wilson*, p. 240).
[46] Wilson, *The Middle Age of Mrs Eliot*, p. 331.

appears again) appeals to him, and he likes her plan for a 'complete restoration of the garden of 1905 with no "improvements", no later species or varieties, only renewal':[47] an example of artistic endeavour that has run out of ideas. He takes up Meg's suggestion of revising his thesis, and the two of them start to read eighteenth- and nineteenth-century novels together, with Meg preparing 'an ever-extending bibliography'.[48] The activity is repetitious, taking them both back to the past and to past forms; the bibliography, like the garden reconstruction and the coffee-table books, exemplifies what Gilles Deleuze calls the 'combinatorial', the principle of 'combin[ing] the set of variables of a situation' until all possibilities have been exhausted.[49] In a remark on Hardy, David reveals that he recognises the phenomenon. 'Hardy could only fall back on melodrama when his immediate vision failed him', he tells Meg.[50] Melodrama, like sentimentality, like the Baroque, is a mode of excess, 'hyperbolic' in its gestures, repetitive in its ideas, bordering on exhaustion – it is deployed in the absence of fresh inspiration.[51] Although melodrama and quietism are ostensible opposites, what they have in common is an inability to add anything to the world. This trait – or lack of trait – is described by Wilson in *The Wild Garden*, in an extended account of how he intended the character of David to function:

> David's involvement with gardening on a commercial basis is chosen by him very deliberately as a practical background to a contemplative quietist life; the botanical books that he and Gordon write are again deliberately a commercial venture. After the death of Gordon, who for all his faults of egotism and dominance, is committed to living, David's commercially chosen pursuit assumes a more and more routine dead form. If David, as I intended, stands for surrender to sloth, despair of humanity, deliberate destruction of the human will, all under a high-minded self-deception, then his perfunctory use of gardening becomes a characteristic abuse.[52]

'Surrender to sloth, despair of humanity, deliberate destruction of the human will': these comprise what I have been characterising as exhaustion. Here, it is inflected as a kind of lack of artistic integrity, a commercialisation

---

[47] Ibid., p. 334. [48] Ibid., p. 340.
[49] Gilles Deleuze, 'The Exhausted' ['L'Épuisé' (1992)], trans. by Anthony Uhlmann, *SubStance* (1995) 24(3) pp. 3–28, 3.
[50] Wilson, *The Middle Age of Mrs Eliot*, p. 280.
[51] Peter Brooks, *The Melodramatic Imagination: Balzac, Henry James, Melodrama and the Mode of Excess* (New York: Columbia University Press, 1985), p. 3. Brooks's remark that melodrama represents 'the impossibility of conceiving sacralisation other than in personal terms' (p. 16) reinforces the idea that melodrama is exhausted tragedy: tragedy that has become merely personal, that is.
[52] Wilson, *The Wild Garden*, p. 59.

that produces only 'dead form'. David, who has succumbed to a Marvellian 'vegetable ease', is 'utterly exhausted'.[53]

Complex Roses: Iris Murdoch's *An Unofficial Rose*

A nursery garden is also the main setting in Iris Murdoch's *An Unofficial Rose*. Grayhallock rose nursery is Randall Peronett's 'creation',[54] and his rose cultivars are, it is underlined,[55] the means by which his name will be perpetuated. But Randall – mercurial, egotistical, unfaithful – who has been in his youth a 'remarkable horticulturalist',[56] is growing exhausted. In an early scene, having secluded himself from his family in his room, he is visited by his father, Hugh. There are 'three bowls of roses' on the table and the room smells of 'alcohol and roses': roses here are part of a larger evocation of decay, a sense that 'the great days of the nursery were over'.[57] Murdoch writes:

> Hugh absently picked one of the roses out of the nearest bowl. Randall preferred the Moss roses and the old roses of Provence to the metallic pink of his own creations. Hugh looked at the rose. The petals, fading through shades of soft lilac, and bending back at the edges so that the rose was almost spherical, were closely packed in a series of spirals about a central green eye.[58]

It is noteworthy that Randall prefers the older roses to his own, more lurid creations: the suggestion is that the art of breeding roses is becoming exhausted in parallel with the breeder. In the absence of robust new varieties, there is nowhere to turn but to the past. Hugh, uniquely among the characters in the three novels under discussion, actually stops to look at a single rose. It is an old rose, complex, a structure of intricate spirals and variegated colours, and it anticipates the moment when Lindsay Rimmer, Randall's mistress, is described as 'a complex rose'.[59] Randall's wife, Ann, by contrast, is, in Randall's view, 'as messy and flabby and open as a bloody dogrose', 'deadeningly structureless', and so 'destroys all [his] imagination'.[60] While Hugh 'twirl[s]' the rose he has picked from the bowl – an absent-minded gesture, but one that would reveal the flower's full splendour – Randall takes it from his father's hand and sinks back into

---

[53] Wilson, *The Middle Age of Mrs Eliot*, pp. 345, 241. In 'To His Coy Mistress', the speaker claims that, in a world of ease outside time, his 'vegetable love' would 'grow / Vaster than empires and more slow', a proto-image of Baroque profusion notable for its botanic vehicle. Andrew Marvell, *The Complete Poems*, (ed.) Elizabeth Story Donno (London: Penguin, 1972), p. 51.
[54] Iris Murdoch, *An Unofficial Rose* (Harmondsworth: Penguin, 1964), p. 11.   [55] Ibid., pp. 20, 24.
[56] Ibid., p. 24.   [57] Ibid., pp. 28, 24.   [58] Ibid., p. 31.   [59] Ibid., p. 63.
[60] Ibid., pp. 32, 64, 32.

his chair 'looking blank and limp, the rose pendant from one hand'.[61] 'Christ, how I fade!' he exclaims.[62] The rose marks both Hugh's current driftlessness and Randall's waning creative vigour.

In a later scene, Randall, who is agonising about leaving Grayhallock, goes to 'take a last look at the roses':

> He felt like a sorcerer who has created a vast palace and adorned it with gold and peopled it with negroes and dwarfs and dancing girls and peacocks and marmosets, and then with a snap of his fingers makes it all vanish into nothing... Here was the slope where he had first planted his roses... Here he had created Randall Peronett and Ann Peronett, names to keep company with Ena Harkness and Sam McGredy, and also his darling the white rose Miranda. They would live on, these purer distillations of his being, when their namesakes were only so much manure. He wondered, will I ever do all this, somewhere else, again, making roses with different names? Will I live through this whole cycle of creation again? And as some ambiguous voice in his heart answered no, and that he would now never breed a blue rose, or win the Gold Medal at the Paris Concours, or send Lindsay's name round the world in a catalogue, he told himself that he was tired of it all anyway: tired of the endless feverish race to market new floribundas and new hybrid teas, the endless tormenting of nature to produce new forms and colours far inferior to the old and having to recommend them only the brief charm of novelty. What was it all for, the expulsion of the red, the expulsion of the blue, the pursuit of the lurid, the metallic, the startling and the new? It was after all a vulgar pursuit. The true rose, the miracle of nature, owed nothing to the hand of man.[63]

Imagine that this internal monologue is about writing novels rather than breeding roses. It is a classic account of creative exhaustion (and it is an important point that Randall is also an unsuccessful playwright). The palace adorned with gold and peopled with negroes, dwarfs, dancing girls, peacocks and marmosets is pure Baroque: ornamentation for its own sake that simply repeats and increases what is already there. The latter part of the description rehearses Deleuze's combinatorial principle, the using-up of possibilities which leads to ever more fantastic art (the blue rose). The monologue resonates with the novel's epigraph, lines from Rupert Brooke's poem 'The Old Vicarage: Grantchester' (1912): 'Unkempt about those hedges blows / An English unofficial rose'.[64] As Peter Conradi notes, Brooke, writing in Berlin, was drawing a distinction between the 'orderly flowers' of Germany and the 'sweetly undisciplined' flowers of England.[65]

---

[61] Ibid., pp. 31, 32. [62] Ibid., p. 32. [63] Ibid., pp. 182–3. [64] Ibid., preliminary pages.
[65] Peter J. Conradi, *The Saint and the Artist: A Study of the Fiction of Iris Murdoch* (London: HarperCollins, 2001 [1986]), p. 74.

The distinction roughly parallels Wilson's 'garden in the wild' and 'wild garden'. There is something contrived, artificial about the orderly flowers, just as there is about the 'lurid', 'metallic' and 'startling' cultivars. (Wilson, who criticised *An Unofficial Rose* for its snobbery about 'old roses',[66] confessed elsewhere to a 'horror' of such 'deliberate and perverse exploitation of nature'.)[67] In their different ways, both Brooke's neat Teutonic flower-beds and Randall's exotic varieties are instances of artistic impoverishment: the former because they indicate imaginative limitations, the latter because they are showy only.[68] Overall, the monologue explains Randall's sense of feeling 'weary of Ann, weary of himself, and yet not able to conceive of any other life', his inability to 'see himself starting again to build up, somewhere else in England, another rose nursery'.[69] Although he does leave with Lindsay, financed by the sale of his father's Tintoretto (a work of art which, contrasting with the gaudy roses, glows with energy throughout the novel), Randall does not find new creative possibilities, but a life of indulgence – exhaustion – in Italy, the land of ruins and Old Masters.

Not Exhausted, Only Tired

The three novels under discussion, then, each depict instances of the exhaustion of the artistic imagination, whether this is literary, painterly or horticultural. These depictions are expressions of cultural anxiety: an artefact that portrays the exhaustion of art is inherently self-doubting. But to what extent are *A Wreath of Roses*, *The Middle Age of Mrs Eliot* and *An Unofficial Rose* themselves instances of exhausted literature? To answer this question requires returning to Barth's remarks on the subject, and adding to them observations made by Gilles Deleuze. In an essay written twelve years after 'The Literature of Exhaustion', Barth emphasised that his diagnosis had not meant that literature was 'kaput'.[70] Rather, he argued in 'The Literature of Replenishment' (1980), used-up artistic conventions could be 'subverted, transcended, or even deployed against themselves' to

---

[66] Angus Wilson, 'Who Cares', *The Guardian* (8 June 1962), p. 6.
[67] Wilson, *The Wild Garden*, p. 59.
[68] Cf. the Kroesigs' garden in Nancy Mitford's *The Pursuit of Love* (1945), which, despite the profusion of 'huge and hideous flowers, each individual bloom appearing twice as large, three times as brilliant as it ought to have been', is described as 'a riot of sterility'. Nancy Mitford, *Love in a Cold Climate and Other Novels* (London: Penguin, 2000), p. 74.
[69] Murdoch, *An Unofficial Rose*, pp. 60, 63.
[70] John Barth, 'The Literature of Replenishment' [1980], *The Friday Book*, pp. 193–206, 205.

generate 'new and lively work'.[71] A re-invigorated literature, that is – and what Barth had in mind was postmodern fiction – would take these exhausted possibilities, and exhaustion itself, as theme and form.[72] It would, in other words, not simply re-use old plots, themes, imagery and devices in traditional manner, but redeploy them self-reflexively, ironically and playfully – and make the redeployment itself its subject. A further twelve years after this, Deleuze, in an essay on Beckett, suggested a distinction between exhaustion and tiredness:

> The tired no longer prepares for any possibility (subjective): he therefore cannot realize the smallest possibility (objective). But possibility remains, because you never realize all of the possible, you even bring it into being as you realize some of it. The tired has only exhausted realization, while the exhausted exhausts all of the possible. The tired can no longer realize, but the exhausted can no longer possibilitate.[73]

Deleuze adds eschatological overtones to Barth's definition: exhaustion is a state not only in which all possibilities have been used up, but also in which no further or future possibilities can be imagined. Drawing on Barth and Deleuze, I would posit not a literature of exhaustion, nor yet a literature of replenishment, but a literature of tiredness, or, less grandiosely, a literary tiredness. This is a tiredness that can envisage or hypothesise possibilities (which is what I think Deleuze meant by 'possibilitate'),[74] but is not able or inclined to realise them. I suggest that *A Wreath of Roses*, *The Middle Age of Mrs Eliot* and *An Unofficial Rose* all display this condition.

The possibility which the three novels can see, but not realise, is what Barth characterises as replenishment: the rending of artistic exhaustion

---

[71] Ibid.
[72] This view of postmodernism has been challenged. Steven Connor, for example, casts repetition (exhaustion) in a more positive light, arguing that postwar fiction 'established an important link between history and novelistic narrative [by] the practice of rewriting earlier works of fiction' (Steven Connor, *The English Novel in History: 1950 to the Present* (London: Routledge, 1996), p. 166), while Mark Currie doubts Barth's very premise: 'It was always one of the least credible tenets of postmodern literary and cultural theory that we should think about the contemporary as a condition of blocked futurity, in which novelty is reduced to the simulation, repetition and recycling of past forms' Mark Currie (*The Unexpected: Narrative Temporality and the Philosophy of Surprise* (Edinburgh University Press, 2013), p. 6).
[73] Gilles Deleuze, 'The Exhausted', p. 3.
[74] The original line is 'Le fatigué ne peut plus réaliser, mais l'épuisé ne peut plus possibiliser' (Gilles Deleuze, 'L'Épuisé' in Samuel Beckett, *Quad et Trio du Fantôme ... que nuages ... Nacht und Träume* (Paris: Éditions de Minuit, 1992), pp. 57–106, 57). My understanding of this is that the tired can no longer realise possibilities, although it can see them, while the exhausted is beyond the point of being able to see possibilities, let alone realise them. The French 'possibiliser' and the English 'possibilitate' both mean 'to render possible', which seems confusingly synonymous with 'realise', posited by Deleuze as their antonym.

into form, as well as theme. But there *does* exist a novel in which such rendering occurs, using the figure of the rose, and that novel is Henry Green's *Back* (1946). *Back* features a veteran and former prisoner-of-war, Charley Summers, who has returned, postwar, to his native village. Like many veterans, Charley is hard-pressed to make sense of the civilian world he has come back to. Green concentrates this sense of disconnect in Charley's refusal to believe that his former lover, Rose, has died while he has been away, and in his belief that another woman, Nancy (actually Rose's half-sister) is in fact Rose. Miscommunications and misunderstandings abound – between Charley and Nancy, between Charley and Rose's parents, between Charley and his new secretary Dot Miller. But Green does more than describe and dramatise the failure of signification: he *realises* it. He does this by repeating the word 'rose' literally hundreds of times. It occurs as the name of the flower, as the female name 'Rose', as the past tense of 'to rise'. When flowers are denoted, they are never differentiated by variety and, overwhelmingly, their colour is red. These myriad roses blur into one another, that is to say. An idea of the effect is gained from the following description of a rose garden (itself a literary topos of long standing)[75] which has been blasted by a bomb:

> [T]hen they had before them, the outlines edged in red, stunted, seemingly withered, rose trees which had survived the blast as though it had never happened, and, for a screen at the back, a single line of dwarf cypresses, five feet high with brown trailing leafless briars looped from one to the other, from one black green foliage to its twin as green and black, briars that had borne gay rose, after rose, after wild rose.[76]

There are a number of repetitions in this passage, but the most notable – and it is typical of Green's prose throughout the novel – is 'gay rose, after rose, after wild rose', a particularly concentrated reiteration. Not for the first time in the work, Green calls to mind Gertrude Stein's phrase already mentioned above: 'Rose is a rose is a rose is a rose.' As noted earlier, in Stein's line, signification becomes circular. In Green's novel, the effect becomes what Rod Mengham describes as 'a form of surplusage'.[77] Used to

---

[75] Ten years before the publication of *Back*, in Eliot's 'Burnt Norton' (1936), the rose garden was at the height of its signifying potential, a topos in which, through the catalysing work of poetry, mutual exclusives (past, present and future; what might have been and what has been; dryness and water) could be all at once fully available. Far from exhausted, Eliot's rose garden brims with possibility to the point of saturation: 'human kind / Cannot bear very much reality'. T. S. Eliot, *The Complete Poems and Plays* (London: Faber & Faber, 1969), p. 172.
[76] Henry Green, *Back* (London: Harvill Press, 1998), p. 174.
[77] Rod Mengham, *The Idiom of the Time: The Writings of Henry Green* (Cambridge University Press, 1982), p. 172.

excess, that is, the rose is evacuated of meaning. Individually or *en masse*, Green's roses buckle under a weight of expectation, simply unable to discharge the signifying function that such reiteration and variation would seem to require. But the important point is that this emptiness of signification becomes the reader's experience – a personally lived and felt experience, rather than a subject to read about.

Back is an instance of the literature of replenishment. But the three novels I have been concentrating on, while they perceive and depict the phenomenon of artistic exhaustion, do not realise it. In this sense, they fit Deleuze's definition of tiredness: the ability to perceive, but not realise possibilities (exhaustion, it will be remembered, neither perceives nor realises). Something of this tiredness seems to have conveyed itself to critics. A reviewer in *The Times* thought the characters in *A Wreath of Roses* 'strangely dimmed'.[78] Rubin Rabinovitz considered *The Middle Age of Mrs Eliot* 'boring'.[79] A. S. Byatt found 'something perfunctory, something lifeless' about *An Unofficial Rose*, sensing that Murdoch was 'wearily covering old ground, not living anything new'.[80] These critical reactions make a further point: as yawning is contagious, so the literature of tiredness tires the reader, whose experience becomes that of witnessing unfulfilled potential.

Conclusion: Literary Tiredness

The three novels under discussion were the product of a time – postwar – when Britain was still recovering from a six-year, global armed conflict, was still (until 1954) subject to rationing and other austerity measures, was enduring strikes and cold winters and was feeling, in the words of a *Times* correspondent, 'the natural weariness of a people who have sustained great burdens for many years'.[81] Small wonder, then, that each of the works features instances of artistic exhaustion, instances that point to general anxiety about the future of creative endeavour. That this anxiety takes the nebulous form of a sense of malaise, rather than being fully formally realised, qualifies the three texts for the category of the literature of

---

[78] Anne Barnes, 'Fiction', *The Times* [London, England] (13 October 1984), p. 17. *The Times Digital Archive*, accessed 9 April 2015.
[79] Rubin Rabinovitz, *The Reaction against Experiment in the British Novel 1950–1960* (New York: Columbia University Press, 1967), p. 96.
[80] A. S. Byatt, *Degrees of Freedom: The Early Novels of Iris Murdoch* (London: Vintage, 1994 [1965]), p. 141.
[81] A Correspondent, 'Boredom and Fatigue', *The Times* [London, England] (18 October 1947), p. 6. *The Times Digital Archive*, accessed 7 April 2015.

tiredness, a category that rises above the Baroque self-indulgence of the literature of exhaustion, but does not reach the vivifying substantiality of the literature of replenishment. That instances of cultural exhaustion are presented by means of that antique literary symbol, the rose, it should be said, is not in itself indicative of fatigue. As these novels by Taylor, Wilson and Murdoch, not to mention Green's, prove, the rose, as figure, remains lushly proliferative, glowingly complex and resultantly powerful. But flowers and power are a subject for the 1960s and 1970s, and the next volume in this series.

Index

1066 and All That, 22

Abbey, Edward
   The Monkey Wrench Gang, 255
abjection, 261, 264
abortion, 9, 80, 297, 321
Achebe, Chinua, 20
   Things Fall Apart, 10
Adam, Ruth, 339
Admass, 7, 139, 201, 202
adventure fiction, 18, 34, 213, 214, 269, 355, 387
affluence, 37, 47, 116, 192, 193, 195, 247, 285, 290, 316, 324, 367
African American literature, 122
African literature, 28
Agate, James, 70
Agnew, John, 178
aircraft, 122, 125, 131, 171, 257, 363, 383
   anti-aircraft regiments, 129
   de Havilland Comet, 8
   flight, experience of, 258
   jet age, the, 112
   Luftwaffe, 99, 129
   Wellington bomber, 257
Aistrop, Jack, 153
   Backstage with Joe, 154, 155
   Bugle Blast, 153
   The Lights Are Low, 155
   Pretend I am a Stranger, 153, 154
Alain-Fournier
   Le Grand Meaulnes, 272
Aldermaston Marches, 204
Aldridge, John W., 160
alienation, 22, 34, 62, 75, 77, 89, 132, 140, 156, 193, 202, 245
Allen, Agnes
   The Story of Your Home, 217
Allen, Walter, 282, 371
Allied Control Commission, 170, 175
Allingham, Margery, 102
   The Tiger in the Smoke, 108

Allsop, Kenneth, 245, 255, 266
   Adventure Lit Their Star, 251, 255–8, 261
   The Sun Himself Must Die, 257–8
Almeida Theatre, London, 329
Ambler, Eric, 103
   The Dark Frontier, 252
   Journey into Fear, 103
American cultural hegemony, 7, 12, 18, 78, 366
American studio system, 12
Amis, Kingsley, 192
Anand, Mulk Raj, 10, 118
   Untouchable, 118
Anderson, Benedict, 129
Anderson, Lindsay, 152
Angelou, Maya, 329
angry young men, 2, 21, 26, 34, 53, 68, 77, 78, 82, 192, 194, 198, 285
angry young women, 314
Anthology of West Indian Poetry, 189
Antigua, 135
Antiquity, 197
anti-Semitism, 9, 168, 294
anxiety, 29, 170, 226, 245, *See also* Auden, *The Age of Anxiety*
   affluence, and, 316
   anxiety of influence, 15
   class, and, 12, 273
   Cold War, and, 19, 113, 164
   cultural anxiety, 17, 111, 139, 140, 395
   Dasein, and, 167
   death of others, and, 172
   decline of deference, and, 11, 72
   demobilisation, and, 6, 101, 250, 268
   domestic disorder, and, 289
   emptiness, and, 170
   futurity, and, 140
   impact of war, and, 140
   literature of, 334
   maternal, 115
   modernity, and, 33
   poetics of, 140

postwar 'remasculinisation', and, 101
sexuality, and, 10, 297, 358
social change, and, 84
transition, and, 29
war on crime, and, 107, 110, 269
writing process, and, 245, 246, 335, 398
Apartheid, South Africa, 326
Apocalypse, the, 22, 382
Apocalyptic poets, 33
Arden, John, 247, 323, 324, 325
  Live Like Pigs, 324
  Serjeant Musgrove's Dance, 324–5
  The Waters of Babylon, 323, 324
Arendt, Hannah, 168, 381
Armstrong, Richard
  Sea Change, 224
Army Bureau of Current Affairs (ABCA), Play Unit, 69, 74
Arts Council, 7, 26, 69, 73, 225, 228, 229, 235
atom bomb. *See* nuclear
Auden, W. H., 19, 33, 54, 55, 56, 57, 61, 67, 90, 139, 161, 162, 163, 164, 165, 168, 170, 171, 172, 173, 175, 177, 179, 190, 359
  '1 September 1939', 157
  The Age of Anxiety, 164, 165–70
  'Elegy for W. B. Yeats', 56
  'The Fall of Rome', 182
  'Memorial for the City', 162, 163, 164
  Paid on Both Sides, 163
Auschwitz, 59
austerity, 8, 9, 26, 37, 42, 43, 44, 46, 54, 102, 116, 144, 176, 178, 181, 183, 195, 290, 334, 342, 355, 398
  anti-austerity fantasy, 112
  austerity novel, 8, 33, 37–51
    verbal excess, and, 33, 37, 38, 39, 40, 43, 47, 48
  class intersections, and, 43, 44
  clothing shortage, 48, 49, 50
  food shortage, 9, 38, 39, 41, 44, 45, 48, 49, 147
  paper shortage, 4, 39, 182
Austria
  Austrian refugees, 71

Bacon, Francis, 183, 236, 237, 238
Bagnold, Enid
  The Chalk Garden, 78, 79
Bakhtin, Mikhail, 371
Balchin, Nigel
  Mine Own Executioner, 154
Balfour, Arthur, 159
Ballard, J. G., 23, 261
Banbury, Frith, 327, 329
Bandung Conference, 187
Barbados, 119, 135, 362

barbed wire trope, 162, 163, 164, 203, 353, 360
Barker, George, 62
Barker, Keith, 212
Barne, Kitty
  Visitors from London, 215
Barnett, Anthony, 144
Barnhisel, Greg, 184, 186, 226
Baron, Alexander, 356
Baroque, 165, 334, 385, 386, 387, 389, 390, 391, 392, 394, 399
Barth, John, 385, 386, 395, 396
Bartie, Angela, 73
Bates, H. E., 356
  'Something in the Air', 128
Baxter, Beverley, 69
Baxter, Walter
  The Image and the Search, 298
  Look Down in Mercy, 304, 305–6
Bayley, John
  In Another Country, 155
Beckett, Samuel, 68, 71, 75, 76, 78, 84, 319, 396
  All That Fall, 26
  Endgame, 320, 322
  Waiting for Godot, 65, 71
Bedford, Sybille, 355, 360, 363
  The Faces of Justice, 358
  The Sudden View, 363, 365
  The Beginning or the End, 380
Behan, Brendon
  The Quare Fellow, 322
Belgrade Theatre, Coventry, 314, 316
Bell, The, 93
Benjamin, Walter, 238
Bennett, Louise, 127, 130
  'The Victory Parade', 127
Bennett, Tony, 111, 114, 115
Bentley, Phyllis, 339
Bergen-Belsen, 359
Berger, John, 140, 237, 238, 239, 240
  G, 240
  A Painter of Our Time, 238–40, 241
Bergonzi, Bernard, 283
Betjeman, John, 339
Bevan, Aneurin, 339
Bevin, Ernest, 149
Beyond the Fringe, 320
Bildungsroman, 17, 99, 120, 246, 269, 272, 285–9
Billy Liar (film adaptation), 292, 293
birth control, 297
Black British literature, 23, 117, *See also under* theatre
black market, 44, 104, 156, 279
blackout, 4, 68, 69, 123, 129, 144, 178

Blair, Eileen, 341
Blair, Tony, 150
Blake, William, 123, 171, 206, 229, 230
Blanton, C. D., 63, 64
Blast, 153, 155
Blitz, the, 29, 47, 57, 122, 128–9, 151, 171, 172, 178, 284, 286, 293, 360
blitzkrieg, 123
Blue Lamp, The, 107, 108
Boer War, 17, 122
Boland, Bridget, 70
   Cockpit, 72, 74
bombing, 4, 55, 57, 68, 75, 87, 96, 99, 119, 120, 122, 123, 129, 161, 162, 166, 171, 172, 252, 253, 255, 257, 271, 277, 282, 284, 287, 323, 357, 363
   Coventry, bombardment of (1940), 60, 129, 286, 296
bombsites, 139, 166, 250, 251, 258, 259, 260, 261, 263, 265, 268, 284, 290, 293, 296, 359, 397
Bond, Edward, 318
Bond, James (fictional character), 34, 103, 110–16, 338
Borges, Jorge Luis, 385, 386
Borneo
   Japanese occupation of, 144
Bowen, Elizabeth, 3, 4, 15, 16, 179, 182, 247, 339, 361
   The Heat of the Day, 41–2, 155, 156, 159–60, 372
   'Summer Night', 151
Bowlby, John, 278
Bradbury, Malcolm, 283
Brane, John, 246
   Room at the Top, 284, 285, 289–92, 293, 294
Braithwaite, R. B. R.
   'The Backslider', 128
Bratby, John, 230, 236, 237
Brathwaite, Kamau, 328
Brearton, Fran
   magic numbers, 21, 35, 335
Brecht, Bertolt, 34, 68, 71, 75, 76, 78, 84, 325
   Mother Courage and Her Children, 75
Brewer, Mary F., 74
Brewster, Yvonne, 327
Bridge, L. A. M.
   'Jamaican Interlude', 128
Bridie, James, 69
bright young things, the, 42
Bristol Old Vic, The, 69
Bristol Repertory Company, 70
Bristol Theatre School, 70
Bristol University Drama Department, 70, 84
British Broadcasting Corporation (BBC), 5, 7, 13, 26, 35, 108, 117, 118, 119, 121, 122, 125, 132, 134, 161, 181, 190, 317, 341, 342, 344
   Broadcasting House, 252
   Eastern European Service, 186
   Eastern Service, 118, 340–1
   Home Service, 26, 121, 195
   Overseas Service, 117
   West Indian Service, 118
British Council, 7, 85, 161, 173, 341
British Medical Journal, 152
British Nationality Act (1948), 9, 35, 325
Brittain, Vera
   England's Hour, 16
broadcasting. *See* radio *and* television
Brooke, Jocelyn, 157, 158
   The Image of a Drawn Sword, 157
   'Something about a war', 157
Brooke, Rupert, 394
Buffet, Bernard, 237
Bull, John, 315
Bunting, Basil, 64
Burgess, Anthony, 19, 252, 382
   A Clockwork Orange, 158, 193, 370
   Malayan Trilogy, 19–20
Burkett, Jodi, 204
Burlingham, Dorothy, 268
Burt, Stephen, 66–7
Butts, Dennis, 210
Byatt, A. S., 398

Calder-Marshall, Arthur, 125, 339
Calling the West Indies, 118, 121, 122, 126, 134
Calling West Africa, 122
calypso, 120
Cambridge University of. *See* undergraduate
Campaign for Nuclear Disarmament (CND), 7, 198, 202, 204, 322
   launch of, 204
Camus, Albert, 33, 65
   The Stranger, 65–6
Canada, 96, 130
canon formation, 3, 23, 24, 25, 47, 70, 210, 211, 212, 218, 313, 316, 317, 318, 323, 326, 327
capital punishment, 9, 66, 98, 322
capitalism, 79, 112, 189, 194, 195, 198, 202, 239, 253, 263, 264, 366
   welfare capitalism, 53
Capote, Truman, 183
Carberry, H. D.
   'Oh Europe, Europe', 125–6
Caribbean literature, 10, 27, 28, 247
Caribbean Voices programme, 118, 120, 125, 127, 128
Caribbean, the, 118, 124, 189, 190, 328, 329
   as wartime space, 119
   immigration, and, 325
Carnegie Medal. *See under* prizes, literary

Carroll, David, 234
Cary, Joyce, 140, 227, 236, 240
  Art and Reality, 231
  The Horse's Mouth, 226–31, 241
Caseg Press, 88, 89
catastrophe fiction, 7, 334, 369–84
Celtic, 33, 55, 62, 63, 87, 88, 94, 222
censorship, 72, 79, 80, 164, 246, 320, 321, 339, 341
Central Office of Information, 87
Cervantes, Miguel de, 206
Chamberlain, Brenda, 88, 89, 98, 100
  'Dead Ponies', 88, 89
Chamberlain, Neville, 147
Chapman, Henry
  You Won't Always Be on Top, 321
Chiang Kai-shek, 148
children, 20, 60, 75, 94, 99, 119, 141, 150, 246, 267–81
  as dangerous, 211, 245, 246, 268–9, 275–9, 280, 281
  as 'the future', 211
  child molestation, 297
  child-centred literary text, and the, 267, 268, 269
  childlessness, 390
  death, and, 57, 58, 77, 109, 324, 328
  evacuated children, 215, 268
  impact of war upon, 12, 44, 123, 140, 246, 268–9, 278
  orphan-figure, the (adult fiction), 270, 278, 280, 292
  schoolboy reading, 17
  work, and, 223
children's literature, 209–24, 269, See also prizes, literary
  camping and tramping fiction, 213, 214
  children and work in, 223, 224
    career novel, 224
  first golden age, 224
  orphan-figure, the, 222, 269
  second golden age, 209
China, 148, 351
Christie, Agatha, 3, 101, 102, 108, 246, 280
  Crooked House, 268, 276–7
  N or M?, 114
  Taken at the Flood, 102, 103
Churchill, Winston, 47, 119, 122, 149, 152, 156, 158, 159, 321, 329, 341
  The Second World War, 139, 158, 159
  wins Nobel prize for literature (1953), 139, 158
  The World Crisis, 159
cinema, 5, 9, 12, 17, 27, 77, 104, 108, 151, 156, 158, 250, 292, 356
  decline of, 13, 317
  displacement of the literary, and the, 156

citizenship, 9, 28, 35, 269
City Reborn, A, 61
civil rights movement, 207
civilians, 49, 50, 57, 104, 155, 165, 166, 250, 254, 304, 358, 397
  bombing and morale, 151
  celebration of virtues of, 102
  citizen in uniform, 106, 107
  civilian trauma, 103
  civilian/combatant boundary, 6
Clark, Kenneth, 227
Clarke, Peter, 316
class, 27, 40, 49, 246, 247, 390
  aristocracy, 43, 47, 102
  Education Act (1944), and, 221
  in children's literature, 224
  lower classes, 17
    austerity, and, 42
  middle classes, 43, 194, 289, 291, 294
    austerity, and, 44
    decline of deference, and, 72
    dramatic arts, and, 77
    masculinity, and, 60, 66
    material deprivation, and, 37
    nostalgia, and, 8
    postwar 'remasculinisation', 101
    responses to cinema, 12
    upper middle classes, 37
    changing class structure, and, 78, 79
    travel, and, 355, 357
    wartime shortages, and, 42
    white-collar occupations, 54
  social mobility, 22, 43, 51, 245, 285–92
  upper classes, 41, 42, 258
    atrophy of, 43, 49
    austerity, and, 42, 44, 46
    children of the, 268
    sangfroid, 51
    sexual desire, and, 297
    wartime shortages, and, 41
  working classes, 11, 41, 43, 151, 235, 285, 307, 308
    dramatic arts, and, 70, 73, 74, 76, 84, 314, 316, 322
    in children's literature, 214
    kitchen sink drama, and, 77
    lack of opportunity for women, 83
    living conditions, improvement of, 41
    radio, and, 26
    Socialist Realism, and, 239
    travel, and, 357
    voices in literature of, 284
class structure, 43, 77, 223, 225, 247, 260, 270, 273, 285, 307, 358
  erosion of, 71, 72, 84, 237, 315
  resiliance of, 11, 51

classlessness, 112
Clayton, Jack, 292
Clough, Arthur Hugh, 122
Cold War, 18, 19, 75, 84, 113, 140, 145, 149, 156, 158, 161, 162, 163, 164, 173, 174, 175, 176, 177, 178, 184, 191, 203, 204, 205, 207, 226, 240, 322, 333, 337, 341, 343, 349, 351, 370, 377
  Cold War modernism, 184
  cultural Cold War, 170, 174, 175, 176, 178
  decolonisation, and, 366
  shaping literary practice, 19
Coleridge-Taylor, Samuel, 122
Collingham, Lizzie, 41
Collins, Canon, 204
Collins, Diana, 197, 198
Colonial Office, 342
colonialism, 9, 19, 34, 64, 117, 127, 182, 188, 189, 190, 294, 355, 361, 362, 366, 367, 368
  anti-colonialism, 92, 144, 145, 188, 340, 367
  colonial appropriation, consequences of, 325, 328, 329
  colonial voices in literature, 284
  in children's literature, 214
colonisation, 222
Comfort, Alex, 139, 152, 153, 156
  The Novel and Our Time, 156
comic novel, 1, 8, 17, 19, 42, 44, 46, 47, 49, 51, 99, 199, 309, 349
Committee for the Encouragement of Music and the Arts (CEMA). *See* Arts Council
Commonwealth, 9, 19, 117, 121, 135, 325
  Commonwealth soldiers, 127
Communism, 7, 87, 148, 174, 186, 187, 188, 189, 195, 230, 238, 295, 315, 321, 343, 367
  anti-Communism, 149, 174, 341, 367
  Comintern, The, 187
  Communist Party, The, 187, 234
Compton-Burnett, Ivy, 344
concentration camps, 1, 59, 147, 162, 163, 170, 323, 359
Congress for Cultural Freedom (CCF), 173, 174, 177, 184, 186, 187, 188, 190
  CIA-funding, and, 184–5
  severs ties with the CIA, 191
Connolly, Cyril, 2, 5, 140, 176, 177, 178, 179, 180, 181, 182–3, 185, 190, 191
  The Ivory Shelter, 178, 179, 180
Connor, Edric, 126
  'Bus ride in Paris – Cattle Truck to Calais', 127
Conquest, Robert, 22
  New Lines, 22, 52, 53, 54
Conradi, Peter, 394
conscientious objectors, 88, 128, 390
conscription, 4, 107, 113, 147, 156, 157, 158, 322, 357
Conservative Party, The, 43, 149, 316

general election victory (1959), 315, 316
consumer culture, 54, 60, 89, 112, 254, 289, 290, 292, 316, 363, 366, 392
  commodification of sex, 309
Cooke, Rachel, 199
Cooper, Susan, 39
Costello, John, 303
Council for the Preservation of Rural England, 198
countryside, 213, 214, 218, 219, 249
Coward, Noel, 2
Creasey, John, 103, 108, 109, 110, 111
  Gideon's Day, 107, 109
  Gideon's Staff, 109–10
Cregan, David, 318
creole, 122
crime, 98, 104, 107, 108, 109, 110, 250, 269, 280, 322, 324
  war crime, 147, 167, 172, 369
    Belsen trials, 152
    British War Crimes Act (1991), 148
crime fiction, 34, 106, 108, 345
  demob-thriller, the, 104
  detective hero, 108–10, 111, 116
    amateur detectives, 108, 113, 307
    post-WWI 'feminisation' of, 101
  golden age, 102, 108, 109, 276, 277
  hard boiled, 108, 109
  impact of WWII upon, 101–10
  police procedural, the, 102, 103, 106–10
  thriller, the, 102
Criterion, 178
Cronin, A. J., 339
Crosland, Anthony, 316
Crossman, Richard, 173, 174
Crozier, Andrew, 52
Cuba, 349, 350, 351
  Cuban missile crisis, 205
Cunard, Nancy, 339
Curtius, Ernst Robert, 170
Cyprus, 324, 362
  enosis (1953–1956), 361, 362

Dachau, 168
Dalton, Hugh (Chancellor of the Exchequer, 1945–1947), 148
Darlington, W. A., 72
Darwin, John, 19
David, Elizabeth, 356, 362
Davie, Donald, 22, 56
Davies, Andrew, 69
Davies, D. R., 379
Day-Lewis, Cecil, 90, 185, 196, 339
D-Day, 148, 263, 346, 350
DDR. *See* Germany

Index

De Jongh, Nicholas, 71
De Neufville, Lawrence, 184
De Paiva, Lennox
  'The Spy and the Informers', 128
Deakin, Roger, 249
Deardon, Basil
  The Captive Heart, 154
death, 37, 43, 58, 93, 94, 122, 372, 378, 391
  anonymous death, 57, 59
  city-destructive death, 164
  dying Europe, 88, 125, 126
  extinction, 369, 372, 373, 374, 376, 378, 379, 384
  fear of, 15
  Heideggerian philosophy, and, 168
  mass death, 57
  natural world, and, 88, 257
  warrior death cult, 175
  yearning for, 14
decolonisation, 13, 19, 21, 53, 63, 64, 65, 84, 85, 87, 176, 178, 183, 184, 187, 189, 193, 203, 204, 207, 222, 223, 247, 283, 354, 361, 362, 368
  British national identity, and, 325
  Cold War, and, 366
Deer, Patrick, 2
Deighton, Len
  Ipcress File, 158
De-la-Mare, Walter
  Collected Stories, 218
Delaney, Shelagh, 2, 317
  A Taste of Honey, 76, 83, 317, 319
Deleuze, Gilles, 163, 386, 392, 394, 396, 398
Delmer, Sefton, 173, 344, 347, 348
demobilisation, 6, 49, 50, 101, 103, 107, 108, 132, 147, 150, 154, 160, 195, 246, 249–66, 292, 397
  demobilisation suit, 49, 50
  demob-thriller, the, 104
  demob-zeitgeist, 262
  heteronormativity, and, 102, 103
  nostalgia for the war, 258
  uneasy homecoming syndrome, 251
Denton Welch, Maurice, 299
  In Youth Is Pleasure, 301–2
Departmental Committee on Homosexual Offences and Prostitution. *See* Wolfenden Report (1957)
Depression, the, 86, 195
desire, 6, 11, 13, 34, 66, 81, 103, 114, 115, 116, 158, 245, 246, 274, 288, 297–312, 367
  State regulation of, 309–12
Devine, George, 76, 314, 317, 318, 320, 323
devolution, 27, 33, 63, 64
Dexter, John, 314
Diary for Timothy, A, 150
Dickens, Monica, 18

difference, politics of, 24, 66, 72, 87, 223, 247
disability, 20, 43, 48–9, 99, 111, 112, 288, 315, 320, 375, 383
displaced persons, 74, 167, 170, 353, 360
  children as, 267, 268, 269–75
Dixon of Dock Green, 13, 108
documentary genre, 5, 12, 16, 24, 74, 85, 86, 87, 148, 154, 284, 292, 293
Dostoevsky, Fyodor, 193
Douglas, Keith, 15
Douglas, Norman, 356
draft dodging, 52
Dresbach, Glen
  'Requiem', 127
Du Maurier, Daphne
  The Years Between, 81
Dublin Magazine, 93
Dudley Edwards, Owen, 212, 223
Dunbar, Paul Laurence, 122
Duncan, Ronald, 76
Dunne, J. W., 207
Duras, Marguerite
  The Lover, 367
Durrell, Lawrence, 355, 356, 362
  Bitter Lemons of Cyprus, 361–2
dystopia, 7, 150, 334, 338, 370, 381, 382, 384

eco-activism, 255
education, 22, 223, 228, 229, 269, 329, 356
  BBC, and the, 26
  Education Act (1944), 70, 221
  educational film, 196
  Ministry of Education, 196
  neglect of scientific teaching in Britain, 197
  school-setting (fiction), 270, 271–2, 300–1, 302, 309–11
  sex education, 297, 301, 302
  the public schools, 8
  theatre-in-education (TIE), 70, 84
Egypt
  Cairo, 356
Einstein, Albert, 374, 383
ekphrasis, 140, 229, 232, 233, 234, 241, 359, 365
  definition of, 226
elegy, 33, 47, 56, 57, 58, 59, 60, 63, 89, 92, 100, 122, 296, 355, 362
  Blitz elegy, 57
  modern elegy, 57
Eleven Men Dead at Hola Camp, 326
Eliot, T. S., 2, 25, 33, 54, 55, 56, 57, 61, 118, 158, 164, 165, 178, 185
  'Burnt Norton', 287, 397
  Four Quartets, 55–6
  The Waste Land, 165, 259, 260, 282
Elizabeth II, coronation of (1953), 8

Ellison, Ralph
  Invisible Man, 183
emigration, 9, 97, 239
empire, 8, 9, 17, 18, 19, 21, 27, 28, 35, 53, 63, 64, 84, 121, 122, 127, 182, 212, 223, 284, 325, 362
  call for new empire, 182
Empire Windrush, 9, 35, 54, 117
  history of the, 134, 135
  Windrush generation, the, 10, 35, 119
Empson, William, 118
Encore, 318
Encounter, 19, 140, 176, 177, 178, 180, 181, 184–8, 189, 190, 191, 225, 227, 236, 282
  CIA-funding, and, 176, 177, 184–5, 186, 190
English Stage Company (ESC), 76, 314, 317, 318
English, James, 211
Enright, D. J., 192
Entertainer, The (film adaptation), 317
Epstein, Jacob, 226, 227, 228
escapism, 6, 124, 155, 179, 180, 181, 264, 353, 355
eschatology, 58, 396
espionage, 278, 337, 345
  Double Cross operations, 348–52
  spies, 34, 102, 111, 163, 348
Esslin, Martin, 75
Esty, Jed, 120, 133, 283
Europe, 18, 34, 59, 73, 74, 100, 124, 132, 139, 147, 155, 156, 161, 168, 173, 187, 278, 295, 344, 355, 359, 380, *See also under* theatre
  at war, 74, 124, 125, 128, 356, 358
  bomb damage, and, 162, 170, 360
  Cold War, and, 162, 163, 177
  ideological reconstruction, and, 139, 161
  loss of global power, and, 53, 59, 134
  nuclear threat, and, 164
  occupied Europe, 170, 261
  postwar immigration, and, 134
  postwar reconciliation, and, 279
evacuation, 4, 215, 268, 280, 286
Everest, conquest of, 8
Everett, Hugh, 207
exhaustion/tiredness distinction, 396
exile, 34, 71, 94, 97, 100, 133, 272, 306–7, 308
existentialism, 33, 64, 65, 66, 67

Faber and Faber, 54, 285
Fabian of the Yard, 108
Fabian Society, 188
Fagge, Roger, 193
family, 17, 38, 78, 82, 87, 103, 107, 219, 220, 222, 246, 271, 273, 276, 277, 278, 280, 285, 287, 289–92, 293, 294, 295, 313, 315, 322, 378, 387, 393

family breakdown, 80, 81, 82, 83, 87, 259, 269, 275, 276, 278, 324
family separation, 268
Oedipal drama, 291
parental responsibility, and, 278
fantasy, 15, 24, 112, 113, 143, 148, 158, 164, 216, 251, 259, 268, 270, 271, 276, 277, 289, 291, 293, 294, 329, 387
Farjeon, Eleanor
  The Little Bookroom, 218
fascism, 56, 140, 150, 155, 157, 163, 167, 168, 170, 172, 174, 175, 227, 234, 238, 371, 381
  anti-fascism, 163
  British Union of Fascists, 315
    Cable Street, 315
  pacific-fascism, 155
  post-fascism, 163
fatherhood, 82, 278–80
Faulkner, William, 182, 190
femininity
  childhood security, and, 274
  feminine other, 11
  in the *Bond* novels, 115, 116
  male fantasy, and, 286, 288, 289, 295
  muse-figure, and, 62, 92
  postwar gender roles, and, 276
  post-WWI 'feminisation' of middle class cultures, 101
feminism, second wave, 81, 83, 84, 100
Ferrebe, Alice, 24, 278, 280
Festival of Britain (1951), 7–8, 78, 86, 87, 197, 199, 230
film, 19, 195, 198, 293, 360, 380
  Bond franchise, the, 103
  British New Wave, 13, 292, 317
  British noir, 250, 349
  comedy, 13, 17
  crime, 13, 107, 108
  documentary, 85, 86, 87, 148, 151
  educational, 196
  propaganda, 340
  social problem narratives, 13
  spiv-cycle, 104, 250, 251
  spy, 132
  war, 13, 17, 27, 148, 154
First World War, 101, 163, 288
  British West India Regiment, and the, 124
  economic cost to Britain of, 8
  Gallipoli, 165
  home-front privations, and, 38
  memory of, 15, 17, 18, 162
First World War literature, 15, 16, 127, 155, 251
  battle of the memoirs, 159
Fisher, Roy, 64
Fitzrovian writers, 27, 52

Fleming, Ian, 3, 34, 103, 110, 111, 338
  Casino Royale, 111, 114, 338
  Goldfinger, 116
  Live and Let Die, 111, 114, 366
  Moonraker, 111, 112–16
Fleming, Peter, 354, 362
floral, the, 200, 257, 260
  rosebay willowherb, 250, 259, 260, 265
  roses, 385, 386, 387, 388, 389, 391, 393–9
  triffids, 261, 265, 370, 381, 384
food, 41, 50, 131, 182, 342, 356, 358, 363
  insufficiency of, 38, 39, 41, 44, 45, 48, 49, 367
  surfeit of, 47, 48
  upper class dining, and, 41
Food Office, 46
Foreman Went to France, The, 27
Forster, E. M., 118, 185
France, 153
  Maquis, the, 153
  Resistance, the, 153, 278
Fraser, G. S.
  The White Horseman, 62
French, Peter, 39
Freud, Anna, 268
Freud, Lucian, 183, 236, 237
Freud, Sigmund, 62
Fuel Office, 46
Fussell, Paul, 47, 353
futurism, 369
futurity, 5, 16, 78, 97, 121, 125, 126, 140, 147, 209, 211, 224, 239, 271, 279, 368, 369–84, 389

Galbraith, J. K., 316
Gallie, Menna, 98
Galtung, Johan, 143
Garland, Rodney, 11
  The Heart in Exile, 306–7, 308
Garnett, David, 344
Garnett, Eve
  The Family from One End Street, 214
Garton Ash, Timothy, 343
Gaskill, William, 319, 320, 326
gender, 24, 65, 71, 78, 82, 83, 84, 111, 198, 247, 303, 333, 357, 390
genocide, 57, 59
geopolitical, 140, 157, 163, 164, 174, 176, 177, 178, 191, 337, 354
George VI, and the clothing allowance, 49
Germany, 49, 171, 173, 174, 175, 394
  Allied bombardment of, 151, 161, 162, 171, 175
  Berlin Wall, the, 156
  Bundeswehr, 149
  Cold War, and, 163, 172
  Darmstadt, 171
  Double Cross operations, and the, 348, 350, 351
  German Democratic Republic (*DDR*), 147
  German refugees, 71
  Hitler Youth, 278
  Holocaust, and the, 59
  Nuremberg, post-WWII, 359, 360
  post-WWII Allied occupation, 151, 152, 155
  Reichswehr, 155
  reunification of (1994), 147
  stereotyping of, 40, 114, 152, 358, 395
  surrender of, 147
  US bombing survey, and the, 166, 168, 170, 171, 360
  war guilt, and, 151, 172
  Wehrmacht soldiers, 167, 170
  West Germany
    Wirtschaftwunder, 143
  West Germany, restoration of sovereignty of (1952), 147
Gestapo, 167, 171, 386
Ghana, 187
Giacommetti, Alberto, 237
Gide, André, 179
Gielgud, Sir John, 80
Gindin, James, 285
globalisation, 27, 334, 363
Gododdin, the, 93
Goebbels, Joseph, 174, 175
  Michael, 174
Golding, William
  The Inheritors, 370, 379, 381
  Lord of the Flies, 147, 246, 280, 370, 382, 384
  Pincher Martin, 147
Good Companions, The (film adaptation), 198
Goodby, John, 52, 57
Goon Show, The, 26, 320
Gopinath, Praseeda, 115
Gorki, Maxim
  The Lower Depths, 73
Gouge, Elizabeth
  The Little White Horse, 216
Gowland Hopkins, Sir Frederick, 196
Graham Bower, Ursula, 357
  Naga Path, 357, 358, 365
Graham, Eleanor, 214
  The Children Who Lived in a Barn, 214
Graham, W. S., 54
Graves, Robert, 62
  The White Goddess, 62
Gray, Thomas, 122
Greaves, Derrick, 236
Green, G. F.
  First View, 270
  In the Making, 269, 271, 272, 275, 278

Green, Henry, 42, 43, 47
  Back, 48–9, 154, 251, 386, 397–8, 399
  Caught, 47, 284, 299, 303–4
  Concluding, 299, 309–11
  Loving, 284
  Nothing, 42, 43, 49
Greene, Graham, 3, 19, 139, 156, 158, 285, 334, 337, 339, 349, 351
  The Heart of the Matter, 349, 368
  The Human Factor, 349
  The Ministry of Fear, 349
  No Man's Land, 156–7
  Our Man in Havana, 339, 349–52
  The Quiet American, 349, 366, 367
  The Stranger's Hand, 156, 369
  The Third Man, 156–7
grief, 6, 12, 14, 17, 18, 38, 39, 100, 127, 251, 291
Grigson, Geoffrey, 177, 178
Guattari, Felix, 163
guilt, 14, 18, 59, 95, 169, 273, 289
  war guilt, 155
Gunn, Thom, 2, 22, 54, 66, 67
  Fighting Terms, 66–7
  The Sense of Movement, 66–7
Guomindang, the, 148
Gurdjieff, George, 206
Guyana, 135, 189
Gwenallt Jones, D., 92, 100
  'Rhydcymerau', 91, 92

Hall, Radclyffe, 11
Hamilton, Patrick, 2, 5, 39
  Hangover Square, 252
  Slaves of Solitude, 5, 39–41, 155
Hammond, Andrew, 205, 337
Hancock's Half Hour, 26
Hanley, James, 29, 339
  No Directions, 29, 372
Hardy, Thomas, 63
Harlem Renaissance, 122
Harris, Richard, 321
Harrisson, Tom, 144
Hartley, L. P., 246, 282, 371
  Facial Justice, 370
  The Go-Between, 268, 273–5, 278, 280
Harwood, Elain, 231
Haw Haw, Lord, 119
Hawkes Priestley, Jaquetta, 7, 140, 192–208
  'Art in the Crystalline Society', 197
  The Beginning of History, 196
  Figures in a Landscape, 196
  A Land, 140, 197, 199–200
  Man and the Sun, 204–5
  Man on Earth, 201, 205
  'The Proper Study of Mankind', 197

A Quest of Love, 198
Hawkes, Christopher, 196
Hazell, Vivian, 120
  'After the Raid', 120
Heaney, Seamus, 94
Hearne, John
  Voices under the Window, 119
Heffernan, James A. W., 234
Heidegger, Martin, 167, 170
  Dasein, 167, 168
Heinemann, 252
Hemingway, Ernest, 182
Hennessy, Peter, 230
Henriques, Fernando
  'Earthquakes and Bombs', 128–9
Hepworth, Barbara, 196, 200
Heriot, Charles, 320
heritage, 93, 209, 210, 216, 218, 219, 220, 223, 224
heroism, literary constructions of, 34, 66, 101, 102, 109, 111, 285, 355, 372
  criminal hero, the, 104, 112
  'damaged' male heroes, 103
  gendering of the hero-figure, 102
  policeman as hero of modernity, 107
  postwar masculine norms, and, 109
  temperate hero, the, 113
Hersey, John
  Hiroshima, 7, 378, 379
heteronormativity, 34, 104, 105, 111, 115, 116, 146, 297, 298, 312
  erosion of, 84
heterosexism, 308
  postwar family, and the, 6
heterosexuality, 55, 62, 299, 303, 308, 311, 355
Hewins, Nancy, 70
Hewison, Robert, 21
Hewitt, John, 93, 95, 96, 100
  'The Colony', 94, 95
highbrow, 26, 76, 184, 185, 196
Hill, Geoffrey
  For the Unfallen, 58–9
Hillary, Edmund, 8, 355
Hinden, Rita, 187, 188, 189, 190
Hiroshima, 7, 23, 174, 359, 373, 379
Hitler, Adolf, 120, 121, 131, 152, 153, 157, 175, 227
Ho Chi Minh, 148
Hoggart, Richard, 12, 289, 291
Holden, Inez, 5
Holdsworth, Nadine, 321
Hollar, Constance, 124
Holocaust, the, 23, 59, 75, 84, 127, 139, 168, 169, 170, 295
home, 26, 46, 217
  country house, the, 72, 219, 220, 221, 273
  displacement from, 294

domesticity, and, 34, 38, 40, 44, 71, 77, 102, 107, 111, 155, 209, 237, 267, 289, 290, 311
home-centredness, 13
homelessness, 353
housing policy, 46, 148, 316, 326
ideological concept of, 9, 18, 81, 83, 210, 212, 217, 223, 267–81, 353, 357, 387
rejection of, 106
unheimlich, as, 287, 293
home front, 5, 6, 38, 42, 144, 154, 155, 304
homophobia, 10, 11
homosexuality, 9, 10, 11, 47, 66, 67, 79, 83, 99, 270, 272, 297, 298, 299, 304, 305, 306–7, 308, 309, 311
law reform, and, 198, 245
prosecution of, 80, 298, 309, 321
theatre censorship, and, 80–1
homosociality, 34, 81, 104, 105, 106, 113, 254, 255, 270, 272, 274, 301, 302, 304, 305, 306, 364
criminal fraternity, the, 107
male homosocial continuum, 304
Honduras, British, 135
Horizon, 5, 33, 65, 140, 176–9, 180, 181, 182–3, 185, 191
birth-date of, 179
post-1945, 182, 183
Horner, Ruth
'The Hour', 126
Hosain, Attia, 10
Phoenix Fled and Other Stories, 10
Howe, Irving, 48
Howkins, Alun, 213, 216
Hughes, Ted, 54, 64
Hawk in the Rain, 54
Lupercal, 54
Hugo, Victor, 249
Huk, Romana, 61
Hulme, Peter, 366
Humphreys, Emyr, 99
A Toy Epic
Hungary, 239
Hungarian Revolution (1956), 21, 187, 230, 234, 239, 315
Soviet invasion of (1956), 53
Hunt, Peter, 218
Husserl, Edmund, 168
Hutchison, David, 74
Huxley, Aldus, 150, 384
Ape and Essence, 370, 371, 376, 381
Brave New World, 369
hydrogen bomb. *See under* nuclear
Hyman, James, 226, 237

imagined community, 64
imagism, 56
immigration, 10, 11, 54, 117, 134, 176, 222, 284, 323, 329
cultural dislocation, and, 328
imperialism, 27, 63, 64, 65, 145, 148, 149, 182, 217, 355, 357, 362, 363
anti-imperialism, 25, 119, 187, 189, 207
BBC, and, 122
British regions, and, 33
facilitator of travel, as, 354
imperial decline, 183
imperialist nostalgia, 364, 366
post-imperial world, 29
post-imperialism, 295, 334
post-WWI English anti-imperialism, 101
incest, 79, 99
Independent Television (ITV), 13, 317
India, 18, 325
Indian independence, 9, 148
Indian literature, 10, 28
industrial unrest, 9
Information Research Department (IRD), 161, 174, 343
Innes, Hammond, 103, 104, 106
Air Bridge, 105
Campbell's Kingdom, 105–6
The Killer Mine, 104, 105
The Lonely Skier, 104
Institute of Contemporary Arts (ICA), 178
International Africa Institute, 45
internationalism, 34, 97, 189, 190
Ionesco, Eugène, 68, 75, 319
Ireland, 42, 56, 93, 339
Easter Rising (1916), 90
Irish diaspora, 97
Irish Free State, establishment of (1921), 63
Irish literature, 62, 94
Iron Curtain, 156, 162, 353
Isherwood, Christopher, 177, 179
Isles, Norman, 285
Italy, 153
It's That Man Again (*ITMA*), 26, 319

Jackson, Ada, 128
Behold the Jew, 128
Jamaica, 119, 124, 128, 133, 135, 328
emigration, and, 35
Montego Bay, 130
Port Royal Earthquake (1692), 128–9
Jameson, Fredric, 53, 65
Jameson, Storm, 359
Jamie, Kathleen, 249

Japan
  occupation of Borneo, and the, 144
  restoration of sovereignty of (1952), 147
Jefferies, Richard
  After London: or, Wild England, 259, 261
Jellicoe, Ann, 318
  The Sport of My Mad Mother, 82–3
Jenkins, Elizabeth, 339
Jennings, Elizabeth, 22, 54
Jennings, Humphrey, 86, 91, 139, 150, 151, 152
  A Defeated People, 151
  Family Portrait, 86–7
  Fires Were Started, 151
  The Silent Village, 87
Jews, 43, 59, 128, 149, 168, 169, 172, 294, 315, 323, 356
John, Errol, 247, 328, 329
  Moon on a Rainbow Shawl, 326–329
Johnson, James Weldon, 122
Johnson, Ken 'Snake Hips', 122
Jones, David, 54, 61, 62, 89, 155
  The Anathemata, 61–2
Josselson, Michael, 184, 185, 186, 187, 188, 189, 190
Joyce, James, 100, 179
  Ulysses, 133
Judt, Tony, 8
Jung, Carl, 62, 140, 164, 165, 198, 201, 204, 206, 207
Jünger, Ernst, 174, 175
  Feuer und Blut, 174
juvenile delinquency, 9, 80, 107, 192, 269, 277, 281
  Borstal, 280

Kafka, Franz, 157, 193
  The Trial, 157
Kahn, Herman, 375
Kai-shek, Chiang, 148
Kalliney, Peter J.
  Commonwealth of Letters, 25, 26
Keery, James, 52
Kennedy, A. L.
  Day, 154
Kenya, 18, 20
  Mau Mau rebellion, 20, 326, 354
Kermode, Frank, 373, 377
Kersh, Gerald
  'A Soldier–His Prayer', 127
Keynes, John Maynard, 228
  Keynesian economic policy, 53, 229
Kidd, Kenneth, 210, 211, 212
Kinder Scout, mass trespass of (1931), 223
King, Francis, 268
  Never Again, 269–273, 275, 278
Kinsey Report, The (1948), 80

Kinsey, Alfred
  Sexual Behaviour in the Human Male, 298, *See also under* science
Kipling, Rudyard, 122
Kirwan, Celia, 343
Knowles, Ronald, 75
Knox, Ronald, 379
  God and the Atom, 373, 374, 378, 379
Koestler, Arthur, 177, 190, 230, 282, 344, 355, 371
Korea, 18
Krips, Valerie, 219, 220
Kristol, Irving, 177, 185, 186, 187, 188
Künstlerroman, 241, 272
Kynaston, David, 9, 13, 26, 37, 46, 54, 283

Laban, Rudolf, 76
Labour Party, The, 43, 188, 195, 198, 316
  Attlee administration, 18, 43, 147, 181, 182, 229
  Common Wealth, and, 255
  Festival of Britain (1951), and the, 199
  general election victory (1945), 7, 69, 81, 149, 158, 369
labyrinth, 385, 387, 388
Lacey, Stephen, 324, 329
Lady Chatterley Trial (1960), 80
Lambert, Calvin
  'A Requiem for the West', 125
  'War Planes', 125
Lamming, George, 118, 119, 190
  The Emigrants, 10
  In the Castle of My Skin, 119
Lamont Stewart, Ena, 70
  Starched Aprons, 73
Larkin, Philip, 22, 51, 52, 54, 55, 60, 140, 192, 208, 246, 284, 285
  'Continuing to Live', 51
  A Girl in Winter, 51
  'I Remember, I Remember', 60
  Jill, 51, 284–9, 290, 291, 293, 294, 295
  The Less Deceived, 60
  The North Ship, 54–5, 63
Laski, Marghanita, 139, 149, 150, 246
  Little Boy Lost, 268, 278–80
  Love on the Super-tax, 149
  To Bed with Grand Music, 150
  Tory Heaven, 149, 150
Lasky, Mel, 177, 184
Last Grain Race, The, 362
Last, Nella, 38
Lawrence, D. H., 56, 88, 193
Lawrence, T. E.
  The Mint, 154
Le Carré, John, 352
Leavis, Q. D., 12
Lee, Laurie, 339

Lees-Milne, James, 47
Lehmann, John, 178, 282
  New Writing and Daylight, 282, 371
Leigh Fermor, Patrick, 355, 357, 362, 366
Lessing, Doris, 293–5
  Each His Own Wilderness, 82
  The Golden Notebook, 193, 295
  In Pursuit of the English, 246, 284, 293–5
  Martha Quest, 295
Lévi-Strauss, Claude, 201
Lewis, Alun, 89
Lewis, C. S., 269
Lewis, Norman, 355, 357, 359, 360, 362, 363, 365, 367, 368
  A Dragon Apparent, 366, 367
  Naples '44, 358
Lewis, Wyndham, 153, 155
Library Association, 210
Lidice massacre (1942), 87
Life and Death of Colonel Blimp, 17
Light Programme, The, 26
Light, Alison, 101
Littlewood, Joan, 70, 71, 75, 76, 316, 317, 318, 321
  Theatre Workshop, 76, 318, 321
Liverpool Old Vic, 73
Lloyd Wright, Frank, 200
Lockwood, Margaret, 6
Lodge, David, 291
Lodwick, John, 245, 252
  Peal of Ordnance, 251–5, 261, 262
  Raiders from the Sea, 252
London Magazine, 282
London Old Vic, 76
  wartime removal to Lancashire, 72
London Philharmonic Advisory Council, 196
London Playhouse, 74
London, UK, 4, 26, 27, 41, 42, 57, 58, 72, 82, 85, 90, 110, 118, 127, 130, 133, 146, 251, 252, 254, 258, 259, 260, 294, 299, 302, 304, 307, 309, 315, 318, 323, 349
  bomb damage, and, 55, 75, 151, 171, 282
  literary scene, 10, 27, 90, 119
  nature around, 255, 256, 259, 261, 265
  Olympic games (1948), 7
  theatre scene, 65, 69, 71, 72, 73, 74, 76, 84
Longfellow, Henry Wadsworth, 122
Longley, Michael, 94
Look Back in Anger (film adaptation), 317
Lopez, Tony, 52
Lost World of the Kalahari, The, 362
Low, Gail, 9
Lukács, Georg, 187, 190, 225

Mabey, Richard
  The Unofficial Countryside, 265

  Weeds, 265
Macaulay, Rose, 245, 258, 260, 282, 361, 371
  The World My Wilderness, 44, 251, 258–61, 265, 282
MacColl, Ewan, 70, 71, 76
  The Travellers, 72
MacDiarmid, Hugh, 85, 90, 91, 92, 97, 99, 100
  'The Gaelic Muse', 92
  'Glasgow', 90
  'The Kind of Scot I Want', 92
  Lucky Poet, 90, 92
  'On Reading Professor Ifor Williams's "Canu Aneurin" in Difficult Days', 93
MacDonald, Dwight, 177, 190
MacFarlane, Basil
  'The Heroes', 132–3
MacFarlane, Clare, 123
  'Daphne', 124
Macfarlane, Robert, 249, 263
MacInnes, Colin, 139
  To the Victors the Spoils, 155
MacKay, Marina, 2, 284, 345
Mackenzie, Compton
  Water on the Brain, 351
Mackenzie, Norman, 225
Maclaren-Ross, Julian
  Of Love and Hunger, 351
MacLean, Sorley, 91, 92, 100
  'Hallaig', 91
Macmillan, Harold, 315, 316, 339
MacNeice, Louis, 95, 117, 118, 177
  Autumn Journal, 95
  'Life of Lord Leverhulme', 264
  'Neutrality', 254
  'Northern Ireland and her People', 95
  'Western Landscape', 95
Madge, Charles, 144
Mahon, Derek, 94
Mailer, Norman
  The Naked and the Dead, 160
Mais, Roger, 118, 119
  'Now We Know', 119
Malaya, 19
  Malayan Emergency, 354
Manning, Olivia, 177, 356
Mansfield, John
  'Celebration', 130–1
Markandaya, Kamala, 10
  Nectar in a Sieve, 10
marriage, 33, 38, 44, 47, 66, 81, 82, 115, 116, 128, 166, 222, 234, 235, 276, 277, 279, 297, 300
  adultery, 297, 302, 305, 311
  divorce, 297
  rejection of, 79, 81, 222

Marshall Islands
    United States' nuclear tests (1952), and the, 205
Marson, Una, 118, 121, 122, 123, 124, 125, 127, 128, 190
    'The Dolls', 122, 123
    'In the Darkness', 122
    'The Poet', 122, 123
    Towards the Stars, 128
    'The Warning', 122
    'Wishing', 123
Martienssen, Anthony, 107
Martin, Kingsley, 204
Marwick, Arthur, 229
Marxism, 75, 187, 204, 324
    anti-marxism, 187
    dialectical materialism, 240
masculinity, 11, 62, 65, 101, 111, 116
    austerity, and, 102
    cadet masculinities, 103, 107, 110, 113
    'damaged' masculinity, 102, 103, 105, 245
    effeminacy, and, 55
    emasculation, and, 17, 103, 133
    hegemonic masculinity, 109
    heterosexuality, and, 55
    in crisis, 82
    male dominance, and, 111
    masculine authority, 110
    middle class, 60
    peacetime masculinity, forging of, 107
    phallic symbolism, and, 116, 202
    rise of 'temperate' masculinity, and the, 101
    work, and, 102, 103, 104, 105, 107, 108, 109, 111, 112, 113, 114, 116
    wounded masculinity, 254, 255
Mason, James, 6
Mass Observation, 7, 38, 144
    Little Kinsey (1949), 298, 300, 301
    wartime Coalition government, and the, 144
Matisse, Henri, 7
Matthews, Susan, 230
Maugham, Somerset, 252
Maxwell Fyfe, Sir David, 80
Maxwell, Gavin, 245, 261, 262
    Harpoon at a Venture, 251, 261–5
    Ring of Bright Water, 263
Mayne, William
    A Grass Rope, 216, 218
McKay, Claude, 122
McLeish, Robert, 70
McLellan, Robert
    The Laird o' Torwatletie, 73
McLeod, John, 295
McLoughlin, Kate, 14
McNeill, Janet, 96, 98
    Tea at Four O'Clock, 96, 97
McQuillan, Martin, 345
Mead, Stella
    'Normandy', 128
Mellor, Leo, 2, 25, 296
Mellor, Roger, 198
Melman, Billie, 364
Melville, Herman
    Moby Dick, 263
memorialisation, 16, 127
memory, 17, 40, 48, 60, 96, 128, 130, 132, 146, 148, 164, 170, 220, 257, 285, 365
    artist as 'rememberer', 89
    cultural memory, 26, 91, 210, 217
men
    emasculation, and, 81, 103
    fear of the mother, and the, 82
    flight from women, and, 66
    homosexuality, and, 66
    in crisis, 82
    male dominance, and, 111
    male privilege, and, 45, 71
    postwar gender roles, and, 82
    travel, and, 355
    war-'damaged' men, 34, 81, 103, 130
    warrior masculinity, and, 18
    work, and, 329
    working-class culture, and, 12
Mengham, Rod, 397
meritocracy, 103, 109, 113, 149, 150
Methuen, 323
metropole/periphery, 10, 26, 27, 41, 63, 69, 72, 73, 91, 124, 130, 131, 135, 246
metropolis, 28, 69, 72, 73, 164, 168, 259, 319, 320, 354
    colonial migration, and, 117
metropolitan, 26, 27, 42, 53, 119, 121, 299, 314
Meyer, Elizabeth, 168
MI5, 161, 174, 348
MI6, 344, 348, 349, 350, 351
middlebrow, 24, 28, 71, 234, 237
Miller, Arthur
    The Crucible, 77
Millions Like Us, 27
Mills, John, 148
    In Which We Serve, 148
    Land of Promise, 148
    Waterloo Road, 148
    The Way to the Stars, 148
Milosz, Czeslaw, 185
Ministry of Information (MOI), 333, 338, 339, 340, 341, 342, 343, 356, *See also* espionage *and* propaganda
    Basic English, 341
    Cultural Relations Department, 161
    Senate House, 341

misogyny, 66, 82, 131
  colonialism, and, 328
Mitchell, W. J. T., 233
Mitford, Nancy, 1, 47, 177, 297
  The Blessing, 297
  Don't Tell Alfred, 297
  Love in a Cold Climate, 47, 297, 300
  Pigeon Pie, 1, 2, 16
  The Pursuit of Love, 17, 47, 297
Mitric, Ana, 180
Mittelholzer, Edgar, 119
Moberly, Sir Walter, 143
modernism, 21, 23, 24, 25, 27, 29, 42, 56, 61, 133, 147, 182, 225, 239, 240, 241, 284, 288, 353, 369
  aesthetics of, 232
  anti-modernism, 78, 238
  child subject, and, 271
  Cold War modernism, 184, 226
  fascism, and, 227
  in documentary film, 86
  late modernism, 236, 287
  literary magazines, and, 177, 179, 184
  militarist modernism, 153
  modernist interiority, 16
  modernist realism, 237
  modernist solipsism, 238
  periodisation, and, 53
  totalitarianism, and, 56, 227
  transition to postmodernism, and, 23, 140, 145
  vs. realism, 225, 226, 232, 236, 237, 238
  working-class dramatic arts, and, 71
Monat, Der, 184
monomania, 263
Montagu Case, 298
Montagu, Edward Douglas Scott, Lord, 10, 11
Montague, John, 94, 95, 96, 100
  'Like Dolmens Round My Childhood, the Old People', 94
Montaigne, Michel de, 206
Monty Python's Flying Circus, 320
Moore, Brian, 95, 96, 100
  The Lonely Passion of Judith Hearne, 95–99
Moore, Harry, 283
Moore, Henry, 200
Moorehead, Alan, 355, 356
Moretti, Franco, 145
Morris, James, 355, 363, 364, 366
  Sultan in Oman, 364, 366
Morrison, Blake, 60
Mosley, Oswald, 315
motherhood, 58, 66, 80, 81, 82–3, 123, 128, 147, 166, 222, 275, 276, 277–8, 328
  Bildungsroman, in the, 271
  childbirth, 297
  de-idealisation of, 294
  maternal deprivation, 278, 280, 281
  rejection of, 79, 81, 83
Motion, Andrew, 286
Mountbatten, Louis, 1st Earl Mountbatten, 148
mourning. *See also* grief
  refusal of, 57
Movement poets, 23, 26, 52, 53, 55, 60, 64, 192, 285
Muir, Edwin
  One Foot in Eden, 63–4
multiculturalism, 19
Mumford, Lewis
  The Condition of Man, 380
Munton, Alan, 372
murder, 20, 21, 65, 66, 98, 108, 109, 131, 223, 241, 251, 276, 277, 295, 346, 350, 387
Murdoch, Iris, 204, 335
  An Unofficial Rose, 385, 393–5, 396, 398, 399
Murphy, Ethel, 365
music, 12, 13, 26, 76, 82, 121, 130, 132, 196, 258, 313, 322

Nabokov, Nicholas, 173
Nagasaki, 174, 373
Nagy, Imre, 187
Naipaul, V. S., 119
  Miguel Street, 119
  The Mystic Masseur, 10
National Health Service, 315
national identity, 111, 223, 247
  British, 8, 27, 28, 34, 85, 86, 87, 90, 99, 119, 199, 219, 222, 224
  British regional identity, 34, 63, 64, 85, 87, 88, 213
  Cornish, 93
  English, 62, 102, 114, 115, 158, 200, 218, 362, 394
  in children's literature, 209–213, 216, 217, 218, 221–224
  migration, and, 118
  nation language, and, 327, 328
  Northern Irish, 85, 93, 94
  Scottish, 92
  stereotyping, and, 358
  Welsh, 63, 90
  West Indian, 124
  women, and, 222
national security, 111–116
National Service, 12, 147, 322
  National Service Act (1949), 147
National Theatre Company, 318
nationalism, 63, 64
  Arab, 356, 364
  Black nationalism, 187
  English, 64, 217
  Irish, 63

nationalism (cont.)
  Jamaican, 119, 125
  Scottish, 64, 92
  Welsh, 64, 90
  West Indian, 120, 121
Nazism, 42, 71, 87, 112, 113, 123, 128, 132, 144, 147, 148, 163, 167, 168, 169, 170, 171, 172, 175, 181, 261, 323, 360
  denazification, 152, 172
Nelson, Michael
  A Room in Chelsea Square, 299, 309
neoliberalism, 145, 150
neo-romanticism, 250
Netz, Reviel, 163
New Apocalypse, 52, 61, 62
New Criticism, 56
New Humanism, 206
new nature writing, 245, 249, 250, 251, 259, 266
  amateur naturalism, 255–8
  naturalism, 261, 265
New Romantic, 22, 52, 53, 61, 62
New Romantic Anthology, The, 62
New Statesman, 156, 179, 188, 192, 193, 196, 197, 204, 236, 237, 282
New Verse, 178
Newby, Eric, 355, 364
  A Short Walk in the Hindu Kush, 363, 365
Newby, P. H., 267
Nicholson, Norman, 64
Nicholson, Steve, 320
Nietzsche, Friedrich, 193
Nineteen Eighty-Four (broadcast adaptation), 13
Nkrumah, Kwame, 187
Norgay, Tenzing, 8
Norman, Frank
  Fings Ain't Wot They Used T'Be, 318
normativity, 34, 155
North, Joseph, 145
Northern Ireland, 27, 34, 85, 93, 94, 95, 96, 98, 99, 100
  partition of, 85, 93, 99
  position of women in, 96
  Troubles, the, 95
Northern Irish literature, 93, 94, 95, 96, 97, 99
  Northern Renascence, 94, 97
  Ulster poets, 85, 93
Norton, Mary
  The Borrowers, 219, 220–1
nostalgia, 2, 8, 16, 17, 35, 78, 79, 112, 113, 114, 116, 124–5, 209, 219, 221, 222, 224, 225, 247, 258, 267, 269, 275, 281, 284, 353, 362, 367, 368, 388
nuclear

annihilation, 7, 113, 205, 370, 374, 375, 376, 378, 382, 384
atomic age, the, 113, 334, 369, 373, 378
  post-atomic world, 29
atomic weapons, 7, 114, 116, 127, 139, 143, 144, 147, 164, 203, 206, 322, 333, 369, 372, 373, 374, 379
  disarmament, 140, *See also* Campaign for Nuclear Disarmament (CND)
fallout, 374, 377
first nuclear testing (1952), 205
nuclear deterrent, 112
nuclear energy, 374, 379, 380
Nuclear Test Ban Treaty (1963), 205
nuclear threat, 84, 164, 194, 198, 205, 369, 372
nuclear war, 65, 322, 370, 374, 378, 382
radiation, 374, 375, 376, 377, 378, 383

O'Casey, Sean, 70
O'Connor, William Van, 283
O'Malley, Andrew, 221
O'Neill, Eugene, 73
Observer, 282
occupation, 144, 146, 147, 148, 151, 152, 155, 156, 157, 158, 160, 170, 261, 278, 359
Old Bill and Son, 17
Olivier, Laurence, 198, 339
Olympic games (1948), 7
Oppenheimer, J. Robert, 380
Orwell, George, 13, 48, 118, 121, 143, 334, 337, 340, 341, 343, 351, 359
  Animal Farm, 341
  The English People, 341
  Nineteen Eighty-Four, 47, 48, 278, 280, 311, 339, 341–3, 370, 380
  'On a Ruined Farm near the His Master's Voice Gramophone Factory', 257
  'Politics and the English Language', 183
Osborne, John, 22, 77, 78, 192, 317, 319
  The Entertainer, 198, 319, 322
  Look Back in Anger, 21, 53, 68, 72, 77, 78, 82, 192, 193, 194, 314, 317, 319, 322
Osmond, Edward
  A Valley Grows Up, 217
Our Time, 225
Ouspensky, P. D., 206, 207
Overy, Richard, 151
Owen, Wilfred, 155
Oxford, University of. *See* undergraduate

Padmore, George, 187, 188, 189, 190
Pakistan, 325
  creation of (1947), 9, 63
Palestine, 18
Pan-Africanism, 187, 189

Pan-African Congress (1945), 187, 189
paranoia, 17, 19, 157, 255, 346
Paris, Michael, 17
Partition, India and Pakistan (1947), 9, 63, 148
   immigration, and, 325
pastoral, the, 16, 53, 58, 59, 62, 63, 92, 114, 124, 155, 355
patriotism, 16, 42, 86, 119, 121, 124, 127, 133
peace, 6, 7, 14, 21, 48, 75, 81, 102, 107, 126, 127, 139, 143, 144, 145, 146, 147, 148, 150, 153, 154, 157, 158, 163, 207, 250, 253, 254, 255, 262, 322
   as instrument of propaganda, 143
   as performance, 145, 151
   enforcement of, 139
   'outbreak' of, 146
   pacifism, 70, 152, 179, 325
      pacific fascism, 155
   post-WWII occupation of Germany, and the, 152
Pearce, Philippa
   Tom's Midnight Garden, 219, 220, 222
Pearsall, Cornelia, 162
Penguin, 323
Penguin New Writing, 5, 178, 197
periodisation, 35, 53–6, 145, 146
peripeteia, 373
Petts, John, 88, 89
phantasy. See fantasy
Philby, Kim, 349, 352
phoney war, 1, 297, 304
picaresque, 252, 283, 355, 363
Picasso, Pablo, 7
Picture Post, 5
Piette, Adam, 4, 40, 60, 157
Pimpernel Smith, 132
Pinter, Harold, 75, 84
   The Birthday Party, 75, 82
   The Caretaker, 75
   A Slight Ache, 75
   wins Nobel Prize for Literature (2005), 75
Pirandello, Luigi, 75
Piscator, Erwin, 68
Plain, Gill, 279, 303
Plowright, Joan, 314
Poetry London, 5, 178
police, 34, 103, 106, 107, 108, 109, 110, 254, 276, 278, 280, 340, 387
   military police, 358
   police state, 10
   policing of sexuality, 298, 299, 307
   theatre censorship, and, 321
Political Warfare Executive (PWE), 173, 344, 345, 346, 347–8
postcolonialism, 212, 245, 329

postcolonial aesthetic, 9
postcolonial literature, 19–21, 25, 28
   canonical, 9
postmodernism, 23, 24, 284, 295
   literary exhaustion, and, 396
   reimagination of travel literature, and the, 334
   transition from modernism, 23, 140, 145
Pound, Ezra, 54, 55, 56
Powell, Anthony
   A Dance to the Music of Time, 50-1
Powell, Michael, 17
pre-Raphaelites, 226
Presley, Elvis, 67
Pressburger, Emeric, 17
Priestley, J. B., 7, 8, 70, 71, 79, 117, 140, 192–208, 384
   (and Jaquetta Hawkes Priestley) *Journey Down a Rainbow*, 201, 202
   An Inspector Calls, 79
   Bright Day, 195
   'Britain of the Unicorn', 207
   Desert Highway, 71
   English Journey, 195
   Festival at Farbridge, 199
   The Good Companions, 194, 199
   I Have Been Here Before, 199
   Johnson Over Jordon, 199, 205–6
   'Lay Sermon to Nomadmass', 203
   'Letter to a Returning Serviceman', 195
   Literature and the Western Man, 206
   Man and Time, 207
   Out of the People, 195
   Postscripts, 193, 195
   They Came to a City, 71
   'Thoughts in the Wilderness', 192
   Three Men in New Suits, 49, 195, 254
   Time and the Conways, 199
prisons, 11, 79, 131, 294, 322, 324
prison camps, 49, 154
prisoners of war (POWs), 6, 120, 154, 163, 256, 345, 397
Pritchett, V. S., 282, 371, 382
prizes, literary, 75, 94, 139, 158, 209–24
   canon-formation, and, 210, 211, 218
   Carnegie Medal, 140, 209, 210, 211, 212, 213, 214, 215, 217, 218, 219, 221, 223, 224, 246
   Newbery Medal, 210, 211, 212
propaganda, 4, 17, 39, 40, 85, 119, 143, 150, 156, 172, 173, 174, 175, 237, 333, 337, 338, 339, 340, 341, 342, 343, 347, 348, 352
   black propaganda, 173, 338, 339, 344, 345, 348
      black operations, 19, 346
   disinformation, 344, 346, 350
   informational warfare, 338
   travel writers, and, 356

prostitution, 79, 80, 323
Pryce-Jones, David, 46
psychoanalysis, 82, 268, 298, 302, 309, 391
psychogeography, 249
Pudney, John
    'When Bullets Prove', 128
Puffin Picture Books, 215
Pujol Garcia, Juan (GARBO), 349, 350, 351
Pym, Barbara, 8, 44, 45, 46, 49
    Excellent Women, 44–5, 49–50
    Jane and Prudence, 45, 50
    Less than Angels, 44
Pynchon, Thomas, 23

Quatermass Experiment, The, 13
Quennell, Peter, 369

Rabelais, François, 206
Rabinovitz, Rubin, 398
race, 247
racial policy, 20
racism, 41, 169, 171, 294
    dramatic arts, in the, 326
    'race riots', 10, 326
    racial barriers, 25
    racial discrimination, 10, 130, 294, 326, 328, 355, 362
    racial tension, 13
radio, 5, 26, 27, 28, 34, 87, 108, 117–35, 140, 164, 173, 187, 193, 195, 229, 255, 319, 341, 377
    black broadcasts (propaganda), 344, 347, 348
    radio comedy, 26
Ragg, T. M., 214
Raine, Kathleen, 61
Ramazani, Jahan, 57
Rann, 93
Ransome, Arthur, 213, 223, 269
    Pigeon Post, 209, 212, 213, 214, 218
rape, 96, 147
rationing, 4, 8, 33, 37, 38, 39, 41, 42, 49, 50, 54, 144, 147, 181, 285, 339, 342, 398
Rattigan, Terence, 77, 78
    The Deep Blue Sea, 72, 77, 82
Rawlinson, Mark, 2, 280
Rayman, Sylvia, 80
realism, 24, 78, 84, 133, 216, 225, 226, 229, 232, 233, 235, 236, 237, 238, 239, 240, 241, 280
    aesthetics of, 24, 232
    battle for, 140, 226, 236
    class consciousness, and, 236
    documentary realism, 12, 44
    Epic theatre, and, 75
    in the police procedural, 109
    kitchen sink realism, 68, 70, 77, 238
    modernist realism, 237

prophetic realism, 384
social realism, 236, 283, 314, 317, 324
social realism *vs.* Socialist Realism, 239
Socialist Realism, 226, 239
stage realism, 74
working-class realism, 76
Rebellato, Dan, 316, 323
Reckord, Barry, 247, 327, 328
    Flesh to a Tiger, 326, 327, 328
    For the Reckord, 327
reconstruction, 3, 6, 8, 81, 87, 104, 139, 143, 149, 154, 161, 178, 224, 225, 229, 240, 246, 278, 292, 296, 369, 392
    Ministry of Post-War Reconstruction, 196
    rebuilding of Coventry Cathedral (1951), 230–1
Redcam, Tom
    'O Little Green Island Far Over the Sea', 124
Redgrave, Michael, 154
Reed, Carol, 156, 349
Rees, Goronwy, 180, 181
Reeve, N. H., 251
refugees, 51, 71, 74, 148, 170, 297, 353, 357, 360
regions, the, 26, 27, 41, 53, 63, 64, 69, 72, 85–100, 213, 317
rehabilitation, 106, 111, 152, 250, 254, 260, 334, 370
Reid, V. S.
    The Leopard, 20–1
Reisz, Karel, 292
religion, 59, 60, 70, 95, 96, 99, 164, 200, 205, 231, 367, 379, 382
    atheism, 100
    Christianity, 56, 57, 58, 61, 62, 87, 123, 230
        Catholicism, 96, 373
        decline of, 60, 72
        Protestantism, 93, 96
    diabolism, 99
    religious turn, the, 33, 61, 62
    sacred, the, 53, 57, 58, 61, 62, 231
Remarque, Erich Maria
    All Quiet on the Western Front, 160
Renault, Mary, 11, 299
    The Charioteer, 298, 304, 305, 306
    The Friendly Young Ladies, 301, 302–3
returning soldiers. *See* demobilisation
Reynolds, Kimberley, 210
Rhys, Jean, 96
Richardson, Tony, 76, 317, 326
Ridley, John, 70
Roberts, Lynette, 147
    Gods with Stainless Ears
Room at the Top (film adaptation), 292
Roosevelt, Franklin, 122
Roper, Hugh Trevor
    The Last Days of Hitler, 153

Rosaldo, Renato, 364, 366
Rose, Jacqueline, 209, 216
Rose, Sonya, 27
Rosenberg, Isaac, 15
Rotha, Paul, 148
Routledge and Keegan, 214
Royal Academy, 226, 227
Royal College of Art, 235, 236
Royal Court Theatre, 75, 76, 77, 198, 314, 315, 317, 318, 319, 320, 323, 326, 327
Royal Shakespeare Company (RSC), 318
Ruinenlust, 361
rural, 27, 33, 88, 91, 92, 124, 150, 208, 209, 213, 214, 215, 216, 218, 219, 223, 239, 313, 315, 316
Russell Taylor, John, 317, 319, 320, 326
Russell, Bertrand, 204, 383
   Common Sense and Nuclear Warfare, 374
Russell, Ray, 232, 234

Saint-Amour, Paul, 24
Salton-Cox, Glynn, 25
Saltzman, Harry, 317
Sandby, Paul, 227
Sartre, Jean-Paul, 33, 64, 65, 68
   'Engaged Literature', 183
   Huis Clos, 183
Sassoon, Siegfried, 155
   'The Colonel's Cup', 128
   'Fox Hunting Man', 128
Sayers, Dorothy L., 102
Schlesinger, John, 292, 293
Schwartz, Bill, 354
science, 114, 184, 196, 198, 200, 201, 205, 390
   moral responsibility, and, 381
   national self-celebration, and, 7, 86
   nuclear war, and, 374, 375, 379
   scientific ambition, 7, 205, 381
   sexology, 298, 309
   social science, 144
   two cultures debate, and the, 197, 200, 208
science fiction, 24, 333, 338
Scotland, 27, 28, 34, 63, 64, 73, 85, 87, 88, 90, 91, 92, 93, 97, 99, 100, 260, 261, 262, 265
   conscription of Scottish women, 27
   Edinburgh Fringe Festival, 7, 74
   Edinburgh International Festival, 7
   Glasgow Citizens' Theatre, 69
   Glasgow Unity Theatre, 69, 73
   postwar position of women in, 98
Scottish literature, 62, 64, 90, 91, 92, 93, 94, 97, 98, 99
   Gaelic poetry, 85
   Gaelic-language literature, 91, 92, 99
   Scots literature, 85, 91, 99
   Scottish women writers, 98

Seabrook, Jeremy, 149
Second World War, 24, 27, 85, 101, 164, 267, 304, 334
   Allied victories in North Africa (1942), 5
   as impetus for social change, 78
   Battle of Britain, 81
   collapse of grand narratives, and the, 65
   colonial and indigenous wartime service, and, 357
   crime fiction, and, 101–10
   cultural co-existence with WWI, 15, 16, 17, 18, 124, 139, 283
   decline of deference, and the, 71
   economic cost to Britain of, 8
   in the West Indian literary imagination, 119, 127, 128
   intelligence operations, and, 337
   Jervis Bay, sinking of the, 286
   literary periodisation, and, 55
   long Second World War, the, 14
   memory of, 15
   modern art, and, 227
   outbreak of, 4, 5, 88, 117
   rise of the 'temperate' hero, and the, 101
   Second World War culture, 172
   West Indian war service, and, 119, 120, 121, 124, 130, 328
Second World War literature, 2, 14–15, 16, 18, 40, 50, 127, 251, 372
   effects of modern warfare, and the, 57, 58
   postmodernism, and, 23
secrecy, 333, 334, 337, 338, 339, 343, 345, 349
   Official Secrets Act, 351
secret state, 173, 339, 352
Sedgwick, Eve, 304
Selvon, Sam, 20, 41, 119, 129
   A Brighter Sun, 119, 129
   The Lonely Londoners, 10, 22, 41
   'We Also Served', 129–30
sexual assault, 115
sexual exploitation, 99
sexuality, 10, 11, 34, 57, 58, 77, 97, 99, 150, 289, 297–312, 358
   Bildungsroman, in the, 269, 272, 273, 274
   masturbation, 302
   sexual cultures, 298
   sexual identity, 246
   sexual repression, 99
Seymour, A. J., 189, 190
Shakespeare, William, 70, 73, 206, 252, 318
Shapira, Michael, 268
Shaw, George Bernard, 73
Sheeky Bird, Hazel, 213, 223
Shelden, Michael, 179, 183

418 Index

Shelley, Elsa
  Pick-Up Girl, 79–80
Shepherd, Nan, 91
Sherry, Norman, 351
Shipton, Diana, 362
  The Antique Land, 362
short fiction, 5, 16, 43–4, 151, 257–8, 270, 286
Shute, Nevil, 334, 356
  On the Beach, 370, 375–8
Sickert, Walter, 235, 238
Sillitoe, Alan
  'The Loneliness of the Long Distance Runner', 280–1
  Saturday Night and Sunday Morning, 372
Simpson, N. F. (Wally), 319, 320
  One Way Pendulum, 319
  A Resounding Tinkle, 319
Sinclair, Iain, 265
Sinfield, Alan, 10, 53, 193, 194, 308
Sissons, Michael
Sitwell, Edith, 47, 185
Sitwell, Osbert, 47, 282, 371
Six Five Special, 13
Slater, Montagu, 339
slavery, 169, 328, 366, 367
  anti-slavery, 122
Smith, Jack, 236, 237
Smith, James, 161, 173
Smith, M. G.
  '1945', 130
Smith, Stevie, 14, 54
  The Holiday, 14
Snow, C. P., 225, 229
  The Two Cultures and the Scientific Revolution, 197
socialism, 69, 70, 79, 140, 150, 181, 182, 183, 186, 188, 189, 195, 239, 240, 297, 313, 315, 316, 339, 370
  democratic socialism, 187
Society of Theatre Research, 84
South Asian literature, 10, 117
Soyinka, Wole, 318, 326
  The Invention, 326
Spanish Civil War, 1, 82, 297, 315
Spark, Muriel, 19, 37, 38, 44, 50, 98, 99, 100, 173, 334, 337, 343–5
  The Comforters, 98, 99
  Curriculum Vitae, 346
  A Far Cry from Kensington, 38
  The Girls of Slender Means, 37, 49, 50
  The Hothouse by the East River, 345
  Loitering with Intent, 38, 50
  Memento Mori, 339, 345–8
  The Prime of Miss Jean Brodie, 99, 345
Spectator, 196

Speer, Albert, 360
Spence, Basil, 230, 231
Spender, Stephen, 3, 4, 19, 90, 139, 161, 170, 171, 172, 173, 174, 175, 176, 177, 178, 185, 186, 187, 189, 190, 191, 226, 344, 359, 360
  European Witness, 170, 171, 172
  'Responsibility'
  September Journal, 4
spiv, 308
spy fiction, 42, 103, 110–16, 128, 334, 337, 345, 348–52
Stalin, Joseph, 175
Stanislavski, Constantin, 76
Stark, Freya, 356, 357, 362, 363
Stein, Gertrude, 388, 397
Stern, James, 161, 167, 170, 359, 360
  The Hidden Damage, 161, 162, 166
Stewart, Susan, 287
Steyn, Juliet, 236
Stone, E. Laurie
  'Nostalgia', 124–5
Stonebridge, Lyndsey, 2, 284
Stonor Saunders, Frances, 176, 184
Strachey, Dorothy
  Olivia, 300–1
Strachey, John, 190
Strand Films, 85
Streatfield, Noel
  The Circus Is Coming, 214, 223–4
Stuart, Francis, 252
Sturm und Drang, 253
subjectivity, 6, 62, 101, 115, 167, 170, 232, 238, 245, 246, 247, 251, 269, 271, 278, 287, 290, 334, 365, 396
sublime, the, 261, 262
Suez crisis, 3, 21, 53, 203, 322
suicide, 9, 77, 79, 81, 154, 235, 241, 275, 277, 307, 321, 376, 378, 387
Sunday Night at the London Palladium, 13
surrealism, 53, 62, 86, 319
surveillance, 19, 161, 173, 255, 309, 311, 333, 337, 341, 382
Sutcliff, Rosemary
  The Lantern Bearers, 217, 222
Sutherland, Graham, 200, 237
Sutton, Jim, 284
Swanzy, Henry, 118
Sylvester, David, 140, 236, 237, 238
Symonds-Roberts, Michael, 249

Talawa Theatre Company, 327
Tambimuttu, M. J., 10, 178
A Taste of Honey (film adaptation), 317
Taylor, Donald, 86
Taylor, Elizabeth, 140, 232, 234, 237, 240, 246, 335

Index

Angel, 234–6, 237, 241
At Mrs Lippincote's, 38
A Game of Hide and Seek, 275–6, 298
A View of the Harbour, 232–3, 235, 241
A Wreath of Roses, 44, 251, 385, 386–9, 391, 395, 396, 398, 399
technocracy, 89, 103, 113, 116, 308
teenager, 80, 280, 297
   emergence of, 13
television, 13, 108, 157, 207, 311, 316, 317, 333
   wartime shut down of, 13
temporality, 3, 16, 203, 207, 219, 220, 268, 270, 271, 334, 360, 361, 369, 370, 371, 372, 377, 378–80, 382
   asynchrony, 379
Tennyson, Alfred Lord, 122
theatre, 2, 4, 21, 22, 26, 34, 53, 65, 68–84, 140, 155, 198, 199, 205, 206, 245, 246, 247, 313–30
   Black British theatre, 326–9
   British New Wave, 77, 314, 317
   British Theatre Conference, 196
   comic theatre, 76
   community theatre, 70
   Epic theatre, 75, 315
      Verfremsdungseffekt, 75
   European, 34, 68, 71, 74, 84, 183, 318, 319
   fringe theatre, 70, 73, 76
   Living Newspapers, 74
   mobile audiences, 68
   regional theatre, 26, 69, 70, 72, 73, 74, 84, 314, 316, 319, 320, 327
   Site-Specific, 74
   staging, and, 34, 68, 71, 72, 74, 76, 77, 82, 246, 316
   state funding, and, 69
   touring companies, 68, 69, 70, 73
   vital theatre, 318, 321, 329
   wartime closure, 4
Theatre of the Absurd, 75, 76, 84
   British Absurdist movement, 319, 320
Thesiger, Wilfred, 355, 357, 362, 364, 365, 367
   Arabian Sands, 353, 365, 366
Third Man, The, 349
Third Programme, The, 26, 181
Thirkell, Angela, 8, 46
   Love Among the Ruins, 46–7
Thomas, Dylan, 47, 52, 53, 55, 61, 62, 85, 86, 89, 90, 95, 99, 100, 117, 118, 177, 183, 339
   Deaths and Entrances, 57–8
   'The Festival Exhibition', 87
   Our Country, 85, 86, 91
   Under Milk Wood, 26, 118
   Wales–Green Mountain, Black Mountain, 85, 86
Thomas, Edward

The South Country, 259, 261
Thomas, Gwyn, 99
   The Dark Philosophers, 99
Thomas, R. S., 88, 89, 90, 92, 99, 100
   An Achre of Land, 63
   Cymru or Wales?, 90
   'Cynddylan on a Tractor', 89
   Song at the Year's Turning, 63
   The Stones of the Field, 63
   'Welsh Landscape', 90
Thompson, Francis, 121
Times Literary Supplement, 282
Tolkien, J. R. R.
   The Hobbit, 214
   Lord of the Rings, 208
total war, 3, 4, 12, 15, 57, 143, 157, 247, 398
totalitarianism, 56, 107, 158, 163, 170, 174, 175, 181, 207, 278, 341, 360
Toynbee, Philip, 371
trauma, 12, 23, 44, 102, 129, 146, 153, 154, 161, 168, 170, 172, 246, 251, 273, 274, 290
   amnesia, 112, 251, 261
      amnesiac thriller, 252
   civilians, and, 103
   cultural, 247
   legacy of war, and the, 168, 245
   not being at war, of, 158, 245, 250, 263, 266
   post traumatic stress disorder, 262
   post-traumatic symptoms, 6, 29, 102
   prewar trauma, 304
   shell shock, 49
   traumatised cityscape, the, 161
travel, 19, 103, 353
   impact of war upon, 353, 356, 357
   package tourism, 334
   tourist/traveller distinction, 353
travel literature, 19, 86, 88, 201–4, 249, 334, 353–68
   British intelligence (espionage), and, 356, 357, 358
treachery, 42, 352, 372
Treece, Henry, 62
Trinidad, 128, 135, 327, 328, 329
   American military occupation of, 119, 128
   immigration, and, 41
Tristes Tropiques, 362
Trocchi, Alexander, 97, 100
   Young Adam, 98
Trumbo, Dalton
   Johnny Got His Gun, 254
Trumpner, Katie, 269
Turing, Alan, 80
Turnbull, Olivia, 73
Turner, J. M. W., 227
Turner, Walter, 196

Tutuola, Amos
  The Palm Wine Drinkard, 10, 118
Tynan, Kenneth, 68, 77, 327

undergraduate, 8, 43, 51, 285–9
unemployment, 7, 85, 86, 104, 316
UNESCO, 173, 196
unheimlich, 287
Union of Soviet Socialist Republics (USSR), 113, 164, 176, 177, 181, 186, 234, 239
  global ascendancy of, 53, 170
  Hungarian Revolution (1956), and the, 53, 187, 230, 315
  Khruschev and Bulganin visit London (1956), 323
  Komsomol, The, 278
  nuclear testing, and, 205
  Soviet ideology, 18
United Nations, 127
United States of America (USA), 176, 195, *See also* under prizes, literary
  Central Intelligence Agency (CIA), 140, 176, 349
    establishment of *Encounter*, and the, 184–5
  global ascendancy of, 53, 170, 177, 203
  nuclear testing in the Marshall Islands (1952), 205
  Pueblo Indians, 201, 202
  South-West, Priestleys' tour of the, 201–4
  US Atomic Energy Commission
    Effects of Atomic Weapons, 375
  US bombing survey, 161, 166, 167, 168, 174, 175
Upward, Edward
  'Mortmere', 157
urban, 119, 124, 129, 155, 201, 202, 214, 219, 235, 236, 250, 259, 260, 261, 266, 364
urban/rural, 27, 88, 89, 215, 216, 219
utopia, 11, 149, 178, 194, 315, 379

Valentine, Alan
  The Age of Conformity, 202
Van der Post, Laurens, 355
Van Gogh, Vincent, 193
VE Day (Victory in Europe), 127, 130, 131, 144, 146, 250, 252, 265, 342
venereal disease, 80, 346
Verdenal, Jean, 165
veterans, 34, 49, 102, 104, 111, 125, 154, 254, 285, 288, 293, 397
Vietnam
  evacuation of Saigon, 145
  Vietnam war, 148, 367
Vine, Steve, 57
violence, 192, 259, 360, 361
  aeroplanes as agents of, 363
  against women, 154
  as expression of male suffering, 103
  as impetus for change, 4
  as reparation of identity, 103
  barbed wire trope, and the, 163
  children, and, 268
  class struggle, and, 223
  gender crisis, and, 82
  hardboiled crime fiction, and, 109
  homophobic violence, 11
  misogynistic violence, 131
  modernist text, in the, 16
  racist violence, 10
  rejection of, 104
  representation of, and the, 58
  traumatised desire for, 251, 252, 253, 254, 261, 262
  ultraviolence, 263
Vipont Foulds, Elfrida
  The Lark on the Wing, 224
Virtue, Vivian, 123, 124
visual arts, the, 88, 140, 200, 225–41, 387, 388, 389, 391, 395
  literary practice, and, 226, 232
  totalitarianism, and, 227
VJ Day (Victory in Japan), 144, 147, 342
Vorticism, 153

Wain, John, 22, 192
Walcott, Derek, 118, 190
Wales, 27, 28, 34, 63, 64, 73, 74, 85, 87, 88, 89, 90, 91, 93, 98, 99, 100
  conscription of Welsh women, 27
  Royal Welch Fusiliers, 180
warfare state, 18, 149, 176
Warner, Rex
  The Aerodrome, 158, 370, 371, 379, 381–2
Wasson, Sara, 2
Waterhouse, Keith
  Billy Liar, 292
Waters, Chris, 11, 245
Watkins-Pitchford, D. J. (B. B.)
  The Little Grey Men, 215, 216, 218, 223
Watson, Peter, 178, 179
Watts, George Frederick, 234
Waugh, Alec
  The Sugar Islands, 363
Waugh, Evelyn, 16, 17, 42, 252, 353, 356, 360
  Brideshead Revisited, 16, 17, 47, 48
  Sword of Honour trilogy, 16, 17, 48
  When the Going Was Good, 363
Way, Brian, 70
Weeks, Jeffrey, 298, 299
Welch, Ronald

Knight Crusader, 217, 223
welfare, 121, 228, 229, 240
welfare capitalism, 60
welfare state, 41, 145, 148, 149, 176, 198, 208, 284, 307, 369
Weller, F. D.
　'There Is a Tavern in the Town', 132
Wells, H. G.
　The Shape of Things to Come, 369
Welsh literature, 62, 64, 89, 90, 92, 93, 97, 99, 118
　Second Flowering, 97
　Welsh-language literature, 85, 91, 92, 99
Welsh Review, The, 5
Wesker, Arnold, 247, 314, 318
　Chicken Soup with Barley, 82, 314, 315, 320
　Chips with Everything, 322
　I'm Talking about Jerusalem, 314, 315, 316
　The Kitchen, 314
　Roots, 313, 314, 315–16, 319, 322, 327
West African literature, 10, 117
West Indian literature, 5, 20–1, 35, 117–35
West Indies, 124, 190
　British radio-broadcasting, and, 119, 121
　emigration, and, 9
　immigration, and, 41, 117
　migration, and, 118
West, Rebecca, 117
　Black Lamb and Grey Falcon, 353
　Greenhouse with Cyclamens, 358
　The Return of the Soldier, 251
Whitman, Walt, 122
Wiener, Norbert, 202
wild writing, 250
Wildeblood, Peter, 11, 298, 299
　Against the Law, 10, 11, 299
Wiles, John
　Never Had It So Good, 316
Wilford, Hugh, 184, 188
Williams, Emlyn, 28
Williams, Ian
　'Cassie', 128
Williams, Raymond, 53, 194
Williamson, Henry, 155
Wilson Steer, Philip, 228
Wilson, Angus, 11, 43, 335, 395
　Collected Stories, 43–4
　Hemlock and After, 307–8
　The Middle Age of Mrs Eliot, 385, 389–93, 395, 396, 398, 399
　The Mulberry Bush, 77
　The Wild Garden, 389, 392
　'The Wrong Set', 43
Wilson, Colin, 206
　The Outsider, 22, 65, 193, 206
Wilson, Rev. Douglas, 127

wireless. *See* radio
Wisner, Frank, 184
witnesses, 171, 172, 174
Wolfenden Report (1957), 11, 80–1, 299, 311
Wolfenden, Sir John, 11
women, 227
　all-female Shakespeare productions, 70
　conscription of, 27
　de-idealisation of women's lives, 294
　demobilisation, and, 6, 102, 103, 105
　Education Act (1944), and the, 221
　employment, and, 18, 111, 114, 115, 306
　fallen woman, the, 81–2
　female body, the, 83
　female wartime agency, 116
　gender identity, and, 18, 44
　in patriarchal society, 44, 98, 111, 202
　in the *Bond* novels, 116
　Indian women writers, 10
　male fantasy, and, 288, 289
　mother/whore archetype, 82, 83
　national identity, and, 222
　nuclear disarmament, and, 204
　Other, as, 66
　postwar gender roles, and, 34, 71, 81, 82, 83, 96, 111, 277
　pregnancy outside marriage, and, 79, 321
　sexual double standard, and the, 79
　spinsterhood, 102
　travel, and, 355, 357
　war-'damaged' men, and, 34
　West Indian women and futurity, 121
　working class women and lack of opportunity, 83
Woodfall Films, 317
Woodhouse, Monty, 184
Woods, Gregory, 308
Woodward, E. L., 374
Woolf, Leonard, 177, 188
Woolf, Virginia, 177, 179, 237, 286
　Between the Acts, 16
　Mrs Dalloway, 251
　To the Lighthouse, 232, 233, 234, 235
　'Walter Sickert', 235
　The Waves, 239, 386
Woollacott, Janet, 111, 114, 115
Wordsworth, William, 63, 122
Worsley, T. C., 282
Wyllie, Andrew, 71
Wyndham, John, 261, 334
　The Chrysalids, 370, 382–4
　The Day of the Triffids, 370, 381, 384
　The Kraken Wakes, 333

Xavier, Sister Mary, 121

Yacowar, Maurice, 235
Yeats, W. B., 22, 55, 56, 66
Yelin, Louise, 294
Young, Michael
  Rise of the Meritocracy, 150
youth, 58, 280, 308, 310
  conservatism of, 227
  fear of, 11
  television programming for, 13
  youth culture, 54, 176

Zarhy-Levo, Yael, 317
Zedong, Mao, 148
Zionism, 356